This book is to be returned on or before
the last date stamped below

-6. FEB. 1990

-6. NOV. 1986          CANCELLED          **17 DEC 2002**

26. NOV. 1986          22. APR. 1993

16. JAN. 1987          CANCELLED          **13 APR 2004**

                       10. MAR. 1995

CANCELLED

# CORPORATE FINANCE LAW

AUSTRALIA AND NEW ZEALAND
The Law Book Company Ltd.
Sydney : Melbourne : Perth

CANADA AND U.S.A.
The Carswell Company Ltd.
Agincourt, Ontario

INDIA
N.M. Tripathi Private Ltd.
Bombay
*and*
Eastern Law House Private Ltd.
Calcutta and Delhi
M.P.P. House
Bangalore

ISRAEL
Steimatzky's Agency Ltd.
Jerusalem : Tel-Aviv : Haifa

MALAYSIA : SINGAPORE : BRUNEI
Malayan Law Journal (Pte.) Ltd.
Singapore

PAKISTAN
Pakistan Law House
Karachi

# CORPORATE FINANCE LAW

By

**Robert Burgess**, LL.B. (Lond.), Ph.D. (Edin.)

*Reader in Law, University of East Anglia*

LONDON
SWEET & MAXWELL
1985

Published in 1985 by
Sweet & Maxwell Limited of
11, New Fetter Lane, London.
Computerset by Promenade Graphics Limited, Cheltenham.
Printed by Robert Hartnoll (1985) Limited,
Bodmin, Cornwall.

**British Library Cataloguing in Publication Data**

Burgess, Robert
    Corporate finance law.
    1. Corporations—Finance—Law and legislation
    —Great Britain
    I. Title
    344.106'66      KD2094

    ISBN 0–421–31120–7 ✓

# Preface

Corporate Finance is the term used to describe the processes through which companies and nationalised industries raise the funds required to meet their perceived capital needs. The role of the law in this, as in other areas of economic and financial activity is to provide the instruments by which and to regulate the transactions through which these processes operate. In particular this book seeks to describe within their legal context the principal transactions involved and the procedures observed in their implementation. Insofar as it reflects any particular bias it is towards the part played by the institutions, and more especially the banks, as sources of finance. It does, however, devote considerable time and space to the increasing role of government and government agencies in this field.

Many people and bodies have provided generous assistance to me in the course of the preparation of this book and it would take many pages to list all those involved. Special thanks, however, must go to the University of East Anglia, Norwich, and to the University of Otago, Dunedin, New Zealand, for providing me with the time and many of the facilities which allowed me to undertake this venture. To friends in the banking community in East Anglia, London and overseas (and most especially to John Russell in Norwich and Mike Walker in London) I owe much and in particular the benefits of their wide experience. To Butterworth & Co. (Publishers) Ltd., to the Council of the Stock Exchange and to Granville & Co. go my thanks for permission to use and reproduce copyright material. The manuscript, frequently revised to cater for the many significant changes that have occurred since the summer of 1982 when I began work on it, was translated with patience, care and no little humour into a manageable typescript principally by Carolyn Bassett in Norwich and Shirley Hughes in Dunedin. Carolyn Bassett and Elizabeth Edser also assisted with the preparation of the Tables.

The law is stated as at the end of January 1985 but with amendments to take account of the companies consolidation legislation.

The shortcomings, inevitably, remain my own.

Bungay,                                          Robert Burgess
Suffolk,
September 1985

# Contents

CONTENTS

# Table of Cases

*[References in this table are to paragraph numbers.]*

# Table of Statutes

*[References in this table are to paragraph numbers.]*

# Table of Statutory Instruments

*[References in this table are to paragraph numbers.]*

# 1. Financing Corporate Enterprise

Corporate finance is the term applied to that collection of processes through which a company obtains and deploys the resources available to it to meet the requirements of its business. The function of the law in this, as in other areas of economic activity, is to provide a suitable framework within which these processes can operate. More specifically, that function can be seen as the provision of instruments by which, and the regulation of transactions through which, a company may meet its capital needs.

**1.01**

*Corporate Finance*

## CAPITAL REQUIREMENTS

Companies require finance on many and varied occasions according to their differing circumstances and needs. An analysis[1] of corporate capital-raising according to the nature of the financial need identifies three broad categories of capital need, namely:

**1.02**

*Capital Needs*

(1) capital required to start up new businesses—"Start-up Capital";
(2) capital required to develop, expand or preserve existing businesses—"Development Capital"; and
(3) capital for new technology/high risk ventures—"Venture Capital."

### Start-up capital

It is perhaps inevitable that raising capital in order to set up a new business should present greater difficulty than acquiring further capital for an existing business. Apart from the obvious fact that the business will have no retained profits to capitalise (and as such have no internal resources to look to), it will have no record of trading to provide an inducement to outsiders to invest in it. Estimates as to the future profitability of the company and the degree of risk attaching to any investment made in it would have to be made on the basis of the nature of the company's intended business, the likely market for its products and the reputations of its proprietors,[2] matters which may or may not be sufficient to attract external funding.

**1.03**

*Factors in Financing New Businesses*

---

[1] The analysis and terminology adopted here are those of the Wilson Committee in their *Interim Report on the Financing of Small Firms* (1979) Cmnd. 7503.

[2] In relation to the types of individual setting up new businesses for the first time the Wilson Committee found (*op. cit*, p.4) that they fell into 3 broad categories. "First, there are those starting completely from scratch, with the proprietors having no experience in, or connection with, existing enterprises. Secondly, there are ex-employees of existing firms starting up in similar or related areas. Finally there are those who take over existing businesses with the intention of developing them along different lines. Each of these groups brings rather different experiences to their task and the financial problems they face may also differ  . . . not least because of the difference in the degree of risk they present to potential bankers."

Because of this the principal source of initial capital for a business tends to be the proprietor himself, sometimes in conjunction with members of his family. Normally a proprietorial stake is in the form of equity[3] although the more sophisticated may try to hedge their bets by taking a share/loan mix. A proprietor's own capital may be supplemented by loan finance, usually provided by one of the clearing banks by way of an overdraft or possibly a term loan.[4]

*Sources of Funds for New Businesses (1) Proprietors*

**1.04** Start-up capital is sometimes available from a number of specialised institutions, mainly in the public sector. None of these, however, exists specifically to help new businesses and for the most part the funds available from these sources fo 'business starts' is limited, such provision being made on a small scale and regarded as ancillary to their main activities.

*(2) Institutions*

Local authorities, acting under the Local Government Act 1972 and a variety of private Acts may be able to provide assistance in a number of ways, including loans for land and buildings. In only a few instances, however, usually on the basis of private Acts, are local authorities able to advance equity.[5]

*(3) Local Authorities*

**1.05** Some proprietors with established connections may be able to obtain indirect finance in the form of generous trade credit from suppliers with an interest in fostering the development of their business. Other forms of indirect financing include leasing, hire purchase and factoring. Leasing[6] is an especially useful form of finance for companies not anticipating incurring immediate tax liabilities and thereby being unable to obtain the maximum benefits[7] from the tax allowances available in respect of capital expenditure. Hire purchase is an alternative but does not possess the tax and, more especially, the balance sheet advantages of leasing. Nevertheless, it can reduce a company's immediate financing requirements and in so doing release funds which would otherwise be tied up for other uses.

*(4) Forms of Indirect Financing*

Factoring may be used to improve a company's cash flow and, additionally, can be combined with other services of value, especially to small firms, such as the collection of accounts.[8]

**Development capital**

**1.06** A company may wish to raise additional capital for any number of reasons. In a period of expansion it may need funds to finance new investment in premises or equipment to meet a growth in demand or an anticipated market opportunity; it may wish to expand its existing stock or finance increased work in progress; it may wish to take over another business that competes with or is complementary to its existing operations. Even if not expanding currently a company may wish

*Occasions for Raising New Capital*

---

[3] For a consideration of equity and loan financing see further at Chapter 2, below.
[4] Such loan facilities, however, frequently involve the giving of a personal guarantee or some other form of collateral security by the proprietor.
[5] See further at Chapter 8, below.
[6] See further at Chapter 3, below.
[7] Albeit reduced since the Finance Act 1984. See further at § 5.21 below.
[8] See further at Chapter 4, below.

to build up a cash reserve to provide a cushion against anticipated adverse trading conditions in the future or to enable it to take advantage of fortuitous circumstances should they occur. Funds may be required to finance the provision of credit to customers, or perhaps to maintain operations at existing levels. In adverse trading conditions additional capital may be required to overcome temporary cash-flow problems.

Evidence submitted to the Wilson Committee[9] suggested that methods of financing differ considerably among the various sectors of industry and commerce. "Industrial and commercial enterprises in both private and public sectors rely to a considerable extent on internal resources—depreciation provisions and retained profits.[10] The public corporations[11] obtain the balance of their funds from the National Loans Fund, with temporary use being made of bank facilities and funds also being drawn from the international markets in some circumstances. Private industry and commerce rely much more on the banks, on long-term loans when conditions permit, and on issues of new equity capital."

In all sectors, however, funds generated internally by the retention of profits constitute the single most important source of additional capital. Over the three decades from 1952—1982 only very rarely did the proportion of new capital raised by industrial and commercial companies from internal sources fall below 50 per cent. of the total capital raised by such companies.[12] But apart from its quantitative significance internally generated finance is important because it provides additional equity. The point is that established businesses may require additional injections of equity not only for expansion but simply to maintain their current position. During the latter part of the 1970s and through to 1982 the high levels of inflation greatly increased the amount of working capital required for continued operation even where the real volume of business was unchanged. Furthermore, the high and volatile interest rates prevalent throughout this period raised the cost of borrowing and made many businesses and their bankers ever more conscious of the prudential limits on gearing, thereby increasing the demand for additional equity.[13] Given the comparatively low price levels for equities during the 1970s the incentive was for additional equity to be internally financed, if possible.

**1.07**

*Importance of Internally Generated Funds*

Nevertheless, internal funds alone will often not be adequate to meet a company's requirements for additional capital, especially given the low level of real profitability achieved by businesses over the last decade and a half. Nominal profits may at times have been high but much of this "profit" has frequently been needed merely to maintain assets intact and to "withstand the ravages of high nominal interest rates on working capital."[14]

**1.08**

*External Funds*

[9] *Committee to Review the Functioning of Financial Institutions* (Main Report) 1980 Cmnd. 7937 at para. 453.
[10] See further at Chapter 5, below.
[11] See further at §§ 2.112 *et seq.*
[12] Wilson Committee (Main Report), para. 456 and Table 34, supplemented from *Financial Statistics* 1980–82.
[13] See further at § 2.07 below.
[14] Wilson Committee (Small Firms) at p.10.

*(1) Bank Advances*

*(2) Stock Exchange Issues*

The bulk of external capital provided over the last 15 years has been in the form of bank finance, some of which has contained a foreign currency element.[15] One of the features of corporate capital-raising over this period has been the small proportion[16] that capital raised via Stock Exchange issues bears to the total capital raised from all sources, and this in spite of the substantial sums raised from the privatisation issues since 1980.[17] The principal reason for this must be that small and medium-sized companies do not have a Stock Exchange listing for their securities and as such lack this particular means of access to the London capital market.[18] Indeed the evidence suggests[19] that few such companies have sought a Stock Exchange listing during this period.[20] One explanation may be that the costs and obligations associated with the obtaining of a full Stock Exchange listing[21] have increased. Another may lie in the level of equity prices (especially during the 1970s) which may have deterred companies from disposing of part of their equity at prices which the owners might have considered unreasonably low.[22] A third influence may have been the fact that unlisted securities possess certain capital transfer tax advantages over listed securities. At the other end of the scale, funds for the public corporations have not been raised via the Stock Exchange since 1956.[23]

Of the capital raised by means of Stock Exchange issues of company securities (whether through the listed market or the unlisted securities market) over the past 15 years the overwhelming proportion has been in the form of equity with only a negligible amount taking other forms.[24]

**1.09**

*(3) Government and Government Agencies*

Finance may be available from government sources, either from central government itself by way of assistance from the Department of Trade and Industry or through one of the government agencies. DTI financing may take the form of grants for plant, equipment and buildings, low interest or interest free loans, loan guarantees, interest-relief grants or removal grants. Finance from a government agency, and especially from one of the Development Agencies, may be in the form of loan or a participation in the equity of an undertaking.

**1.10**

*(4) Indirect Financing*

Forms of "indirect" financing are important to established businesses as an alternative to the direct raising of additional capital: some facilities, such as the receipt of trade credit and leasing arrangements, are encountered across the whole spectrum of business activity regardless of the size of the business involved. Others, such as hire purchase and credit factoring, tend to be used more by small and medium-sized companies.

---

[15] Wilson Committee (Main Report) at paras. 455/456 and Table 34; also *Financial Statistics* 1980–82.

[16] Only in 1975 was it in excess of 10 per cent. of the total; Wilson Committee (Main Report) at Table 34.

[17] The recent exception being 1984 with the privatisation of British Telecom.

[18] See below at §§ 1.15 *et seq.*

[19] Wilson Committee (Small Firms) at p.14.

[20] But many smaller and medium-sized companies have "gone public" via the Unlisted Securities Market and the Over-the-Counter markets.

[21] See below at Chapter 6.

[22] Wilson Committee (Small Firms) at p.14.

[23] Since the Finance Act 1956, s.42 changed the method of financing.

[24] Wilson Committee (Main Report) at para. 456 and *Financial Statistics* 1980–82.

The use of bills of exchange as a means of financing is long established in overseas trade. During the 1970s there was an increase in their use in domestic trading as well, although such use has tended to be restricted to larger companies
possessing the necessary financial standing.

**1.11**

*(5) Bills of
Exchange*

## Venture capital

The financing of high risk projects presents problems that go beyond those
encountered in start-up or development capital-raising. High risks inevitably
mean that fewer sources of external capital will be available which in turn means
that the cost of such funds as are available will be correspondingly high. Those
prepared to invest in such ventures understandably seek to minimise the risk
involved and in so doing demand both the means of capitalising on the success of
the venture (which in practice usually means taking a stake in the equity) and
obtaining the best possible safeguards in case the venture turns out badly.

**1.12**

Large companies are inevitably in a better position than smaller concerns to
obtain finance for high-risk ventures. Where the amounts involved are comparatively small in relation to the company's total resources that finance may be
capable of being supplied from internal sources. In cases where external funding
is required this can often be obtained through the banking system or other normal sources. Even where the project is large and the amount of finance required
is substantial in relation to the company's balance sheet it is not uncommon for
investment packages to be constructed to provide the necessary funds.[25] Ultimately, what finance is available and the form that it takes will depend on the
calculus of the degree of risk and the prospect of future profits. It follows therefore that even large companies may find that normal sources of finance are not
available to them where a combination of the size of the project and a very high
level of risk make the provision of funds unjustifiable on ordinary commercial
grounds.

For smaller companies this calculus of risk and prospect of future profit results
in many more ventures being regarded as unjustifiable on ordinary commercial
grounds. The very fact of a company's small size increases the risk factor in projects where substantial amounts of capital are required. Often the only source of
capital is the private fortune of the proprietor.[26]

---

[25] *e.g.* in the financing of the North Sea exploitation. See further Wilson Committee (Main Report)
at para. 533.

[26] Evidence to the Bolton Committee (Report 1971, Cmnd. 4811: *Committee of Inquiry on Small
Firms*) indicated that the provision of venture capital is definitely a field for expertise. One U.S.
company with over 20 years experience in this field apparently backed, over this period, an equal
number of winners and losers. Since, however, the gains proved to be very large and because the
company managed to extricate itself fairly quickly from losing situations the overall outweighed
the losses.—Report, para. 12.65.
There are a number of institutions specialising in the provision or procurement of venture capital.
In the public sector there are the National Research Development Corporation (part of the British
Technology Group) which concentrates on financing the research and development efforts of
small companies, and Technical Development Capital (part of Investors in Industry), which concentrates on providing finance for production and marketing of products that have passed the pro-
totype or development stage. In addition there are a number of private venture capital companies
which are mostly subsidiaries of merchant banks, investment trusts and insurance companies;
these provide finance mainly for production and marketing.

# THE CAPITAL MARKET

**1.13**

*The Capital Market*

External funds are made available to companies primarily through "the capital market." Traditionally this term has been used to refer to the stock market and in particular the market in new issues. In the context of modern corporate financing, however, "the capital market" has come to be understood in a wider sense as embracing the whole complex of institutions and arrangements through which capital may be raised.[27]

In general economic terms the function of a capital market can be said to be to enable the flow of funds generated within the economy to be made available to those who need them on terms acceptable to the supplier. To be able to discharge this function such a market requires[28]:

(1) A range of financial instruments capable of accommodating the needs both of those supplying and of those seeking to raise funds; and

(2) A mechanism whereby the price of funds can be set in a fair and consistent manner.

**The range of financial instruments**

**1.14**      Thus far we have considered the forms in which capital may be raised in terms of the broad distinction between equity and loan capital. In many cases, and especially in relation to small businesses, a more sophisticated analysis is unnecessary. Nevertheless British company law permits companies to issue various types of security and to enter into contracts (within the scope of their objects) enabling funds to be introduced in a number of different ways. Ideally, the instruments available should enable a company to acquire the finance it requires in the form best suited to the needs of its business; and, equally, the range of instruments should be capable of producing an arrangement of combination of arrangements allowing suppliers of funds to secure their interests appropriately.

**Debt forms**

**1.15**      The raising of funds through the issue of debt has a number of features which make it potentially attractive both for the investor and for the company. Since the debt principal is a liability of the company and the interest a charge against its income and a liability until paid, from an investor's standpoint debt has the attraction that it tends to be more secure, both as to income and repayment of capital, than equity. The interest is payable whether or not the company has made profits and loan creditors rank for repayment before shareholders.

From the standpoint of the company debt has the attractions of interest being deductible from profits before taxation and of repayment terms being fixed irrespective of any depreciation in money values.

The issue of debt may take a number of forms.

[27] Including public sector agencies. See below at Chapter 8.
[28] Wilson Committee (Main Report) at paras. 641–643.

### (i) Debentures and Loan Stocks

The Companies Act 1985[29] defines debenture as including debenture stock, bonds or other securities of a company. The most common form of debenture involves a liability to pay a fixed rate of interest on specified dates and to repay the principal on the dates or dates stipulated. Not all debentures however, contain this liability to repay. Prior to 1914 it was not uncommon for companies to create "perpetual" or "irredeemable" debentures, the only liability to repay under such instruments arising on a default or on the liquidation of the company. *Debentures*

*Perpetual Debentures*

It is not necessary under the terms of the statutory definition for the debt to be secured by a charge or mortgage over assets of the company. The modern fashion, however, is to use the term "debenture" in connection with loans raised on some security; where no security is given the issue tends to be of "unsecured loan stock." *Unsecured Loan Stock*

Where security is given it is normally constituted by a floating charge over the company's entire undertaking. Sometimes debentures are secured by a fixed charge over specified property in which even they are commonly termed "mortgage debentures." Sometimes loan stocks are secured by an outside guarantee, an arrangement often found in cases of loans being raised by subsidiary companies, the guarantee being provided by the parent. *Mortgage Debentures*

*Guaranteed Debentures*

### (ii) Notes

These have traditionally comprised short of medium-term loan agreements which are usually unsecured. They amount to mere promises to pay, the holders ranking with ordinary creditors in a winding up. However, during 1985 the clearing banks have raised large sums through the issue of perpetual floating-rate notes, the holders ranking with equity shareholders in a winding up.

### (iii) Convertible loan stocks

A convertible loan stock is a borrowing agreement under which the lender has the option, within a specified future period, of converting part or all of the loan into equity share capital on stipulated terms. If the lender does not exercise the option the stock runs through to maturity and repayment falls due in the ordinary way. The rate of interest carried by a convertible stock is usually higher than the dividend yield on the equity but, because of the potential equity participation, not as high as would otherwise be appropriate for a loan stock.[30]

Convertible loan stocks have often been used as part of the consideration in a take-over since they defer dilution of the equity capital of the acquiring company until some future date when it is anticipated that the benefits of the take-over will have been established.

---

[29] C.A. 1985, s. 744.
[30] That is, where the loan stock does not carry conversion rights.

**Shares**

1.16    Share capital is the risk-bearing capital of the company. It represents, together with reserves, the shareholders' participation in the business, whether or not on terms which afford a preference as to the payment of dividend or, in the event of a liquidation, as to the return of capital. Dividends on shares may only be paid out of profits (whether earned in the current year or brought forward from previous years) and on the recommendation of the directors.

Share capital may be either:

(i) preference capital; or
(ii) equity (ordinary share) capital.

1.17
*Preference
Shares*

Preference shares may confer preferential rights as to the payment of a dividend or as to the return of capital in a liquidation or both as against ordinary shareholders. In return for these preferential rights holders of such shares normally have no vote at shareholders' meetings except in relation to proposals for the variation of their rights.[31]

The dividend is payable as a fixed percentage after tax.

Preference shares may be of the following types:

(*a*) *Cumulative preference shares.* These carry the right to payment of accumulated arrears of dividend as soon as the company has sufficient profits to make such a payment.

(*b*) *Redeemable preference shares.* These carry the right to be redeemed on a specified date. In some cases the redemption price incorporates a premium over the nominal value of the shares.

(*c*) *Participating preference shares.* These carry the right to a fixed dividend before payment is made to ordinary shareholders but, in addition, confer a further participation in the company's profits, often related to the dividend payments on ordinary shares.

(*d*) *Convertible preference shares.* These carry rights of conversion into ordinary shares on secified dates and at specified prices.

1.18
*Ordinary
Shares*

Ordinary shares constitute the true equity of the company, bearing the risks of failure and carrying the rewards of success to a greater extent than other forms of capital. They provide no guarantee or security as to dividend or capital but confer on shareholders certain proprietorial rights including the right to the company's assets in a liquidation once the creditors[32] have been paid in full. Ordinary shareholders possess the right to vote at company meetings, to appoint and dismiss directors, and to reject or reduce (but not to increase) the dividend recommended by the directors. Subject to this last power, an ordinary shareholder's income entitlement is to such dividends as the directors may declare.

Forms of ordinary share capital may be created which do not carry the full rights otherwise attached to ordinary shares. These are:

[31] Additionally, preference shareholders sometimes have a vote when their dividend is in arrears.
[32] Including for this purpose holders of loan stock and preference shares.

(*a*) Non-voting, or restricted-voting shares[33]

(*b*) *Deferred shares.* These normally confer full rights as to voting and to the return of capital in a liquidation, but have their eligibility for a dividend deferred until a stipulated date or until the company's profits have attained a specified level.

(*c*) *"B" shares.* This is the most common designation for shares issued by some companies (often investment trust companies) which have their dividend in the form of fully paid shares rather than cash.

(*d*) *Redeemable ordinary shares.* These may carry full ordinary share rights or rights which are restricted in any of the ways outlined in this paragraphs, but which carry the right, exercisable at the option of the shareholder or the company, according to the terms of issue, to be redeemed on specified conditions.[34]

## Warrants

Companies sometimes, either as an alternative to issuing convertible loan stock or as an inducement to subscribe for loan stock, issue "warrants" to subscribers in proportion to the amount of stock subscribed for. Such warrants are essentially contracts entered into by the company to issue securities (usually ordinary shares) to warrant holders at a stipulated price on specified dates. Warrants are normally assignable separately from the stock with which they were issued. **1.19**

Warrants carry no entitlement or eligibility in respect of income.

## The price-setting mechanism and information flow

In a market possessing the benefit of an adequate[35] range of available financial instruments potential suppliers of funds should be able to make a choice as between a variety of risks. The price-setting mechanism should be capable of producing a situation where the cost of funds represents "an unbiassed reflection[36] . . . of future returns taking into account the risk of the investment involved. The cost of capital facing users of finance, as seen in the prices of the securities which they issue will then be at a minimum in the circumstances and different users of finance will then be confronted by a cost of capital which consistently (that is without bias) reflects the difference in prospects and risk between different securities as perceived in the market."[37] **1.20**

*Operation of the Price-Setting Mechanism*

Given the existence of appropriate financial instruments the key to this efficient operation of the market is the availability of information about the companies

---

[33] These securities used to be designated "A" shares but now must be specifically designated as non-voting, at least if a Stock Exchange Listing is to be obtained for them.
[34] C.A. 1985, ss. 159 *et seq.*
[35] The Wilson Committee (Main Report at para. 644) found the current range of financial instruments to be generally adequate.
[36] That is the best guess possible at the time.
[37] Wilson Committee (Main Report) at para. 644.

whose securities are on offer. Indeed, modern capital market theorists have developed the concept of an "efficient" market as being one in which[38]:

*Efficient*
*Markets*

(a) prices quickly reflect all currently available information as to the future returns expected from each security; and

(b) expected future returns are reflected in security prices in the light of their relative degrees of riskiness (since investors generally require to be compensated for accepting risk).[39]

However, while an efficient market will react appropriately to the information it receives, the prices resulting from that reaction will represent a truer reflection of the risks attaching to a particular security the better the information it has to deal with. It is therefore of the utmost importance to those operating in the market that they have available to them information that is adequate in terms of both quantity and of quality. For companies seeking to raise funds in the market the inevitable consequences of such an imperative is that prospective suppliers of funds will seek disclosure of all relevant information about the state of its business and management and the uses to which it intends to put the funds raised.

**1.21**

*Disclosure—*
*General*
*Obligations*

A company's particular obligations as to disclosure and the legal framework within which those obligations operate differ according to whether the finance required is to be raised privately (in practice almost always from financial institutions) or whether it is to be raised through the securities markets. In the former case the basic approach of the law is to allow the parties a general freedom to contract[40] and to leave with the prospective supplier of funds the onus of obtaining the information necessary to satisfy himself that the company is a suitable one in which to invest. Ideally therefore, a potential investor should undertake an investigation into the company's affairs in order to satisfy himself that the degree of risk is acceptable and that the required level of return can be obtained.

Capital-raising through the securities markets assumes an involvement by the public at some stage, whether directly in the subscription for a new issue, or subsequently when securities placed with institutions are unloaded. This prospect of public involvement has led the law to depart from its basic approach and to lay down specified requirements as to the matters to be disclosed when a public issue of securities is made.[41] These specifications are regarded as minimum requirements which may be expanded either at the option of the company making the issue (an unlikely event) or to comply with the terms of admission to a particular

[38] "An efficient market is defined as a market where there are large numbers of profit maximisers actively competing with each other, trying to predict the future market values of individual securities. Relevant current information is available on equal terms to all participants in such a market. Competition among the many participants leads to a situation where, at any point in time, actual prices of individual securities reflect information concerning events that have already occurred and also of events which the market expects to take place in the future. Thus, in an efficient market, at any point in time, the actual price of a security will be a good estimate of the present value of the payments which its holders expect to receive." Wilson Committee (Main Report) at para. 671.

[39] Wilson Committee (Main Report) at para. 648.

[40] Subject to any restraints imposed on such freedom by the general law (*e.g.* as to unfair contract terms, restraint of trade, etc.).

[41] See below at Chapter 6.

market.[42] Furthermore, admission agreements between individual companies and the authorities or other persons responsible for the running of a particular market will as a matter of course, provide for the publication of results and other price-sensitive information by the company after the issue has been made and so long as the securities continue to be quoted on that market.

### Disclosure—the problem of quality of information

Whether funds are sought privately through negotiation with a financial institution or publicly through an issue on a securities market the obtaining of a sufficient quantity of information to enable an informed investment decision to be made presents no insuperable problem. In the case of a public issue access to the market is made conditional upon its provision; in the case of a privately negotiated funding facility a prospective supplier of funds will simply refuse to proceed if required information is not made available. However, it is another matter to ensure that the information supplied is adequate in terms of quality. The framework of law within which capital-raising operations are conducted seeks to deter the provision of defective information by the imposition of criminal liability on the company and/or the officers concerned and by making available a variety of civil remedies to those who have been induced to provide funds on the basis of such information. Nevertheless, what the law provides is only a framework. The best safeguard against shortfalls in quality is the diligence of the supplier of funds in checking the details of the information given and forecasts made. In the case of a public issue of securities the name and reputation of the issuing house and/or brokers managing the issues are often felt to be a better guarantee than legal sanctions, although where the issue is to be made on one of the markets under the jurisdiction of the Council of the Stock Exchange, the documents containing the relevant information are subject to scrutiny by the Stock Exchange authorities.

**1.22**

## LEGAL SANCTIONS

### (1) Criminal liability

Criminal liability in respect of the provision of defective information derives from section 19 of the Theft Act 1968 and section 13(1) of the Prevention of Fraud (Investments) Act 1958.

Section 19 of the Theft Act provides[43]:

**1.23**

*Theft Act 1968, s.19*

> "An officer or person purporting to act as an officer of a body corporate or unincorporated association who, with intent to deceive its members or creditors about its affairs, publishes, or concurs in publishing, a written

---

[42] Whether statutory (as in the case of admission to the Stock Exchange Official List—Stock Exchange (Listing) Regulations 1984 (S.I. 1984 No. 716) or contractual (as in the case of admission to the Stock Exchange Official List or Unlisted Securities Market).

[43] See further below at § 6.21.

document or account which, to his knowledge, is or may be misleading, false or deceptive in a material particular is guilty of an offence."

To achieve a conviction under section 19 fraudulent intent must be shown; it is not sufficient to show that the accused was merely negligent.

Other limitations should be noted, namely that section 19 extends only to written statements and accounts: it does not, seemingly, cover oral statements or forecasts, or promises, whether oral or in writing.

The Theft Act 1968 has no application in Scotland.

Section 13(1) of the Prevention of Fraud (Investments) Act 1958[44] provides:

*Prevention of Fraud (Inv.) Act 1958, s.13(1)*

"Any person who by any statement, promise or forecast which he knows to be misleading, false or deceptive, or by any dishonest concealment of material facts, or by the reckless making (dishonestly or otherwise) of any statement, promise or forecast which is misleading, false or deceptive, or attempts to induce another person

    (a) to enter into or offer to enter into—

        (i) any agreement for, or with a view to, acquiring, disposing or, subscribing for or underwriting securities . . . "

[shall be guilty of an offence]

Section 13(1) is wider than section 19 of the Theft Act in a number of respects. In the first place it is not limited to proof of fraudulent intent, its being sufficient to show recklessness. In *R.* v. *Grunwald*[45] it was held that a statement is reckless if it is a rash statement to make and without a real basis of facts to support it. Like section 19, however, it is not sufficient to show that the accused was merely negligent.

Section 13(1) is not restricted to written statements; liability may ensue whatever the form of the "statement, promise or forecast" and whatever the medium via which it is transmitted.

Section 13(1), unlike section 19 of the Theft Act, does extend to Scotland.

## (2) Civil liability: misrepresentation

**1.24**

*Meaning of Misrepresentation*

It is a general principle of law that contracts may be repudiated if induced by misrepresentation[46] whether that misrepresentation was fraudulent or innocent. In accordance with this principle agreements with a company for the provision of funds may be set aside by the provider of those funds if it can be shown:

    (a) that a misstatement was made by or on behalf of the company;

    (b) that the misstatement was as to some material fact;

    (c) that it was relied on by the provider of funds in deciding whether or not to make the funds available; and

    (d) that the provider of funds acted promptly after learning of the true facts.

[44] As amended by the Protection of Depositors Act 1963 (now Banking Act 1979, Sched. 6).

[45] [1963] 1 Q.B. 935.

[46] *Smith* v. *Chadwick* (1882) 20 Ch.D. 27; *Anderson's Case* (1881) 17 Ch.D. 373; *Re Scottish Petroleum Co.* (1883) 23 Ch. D. 413 CA; *Ex p. Wainwright* (1890) 62 L.T. 30; *Blakiston* v. *London & Scottish Banking and Discount Corp.* (1894) 21 R. 417; *Re Kent County Gas Co.* (1906) 95 L.T. 756.

For there to be a misrepresentation there must be "some active misstatement **1.25**
of fact, or, at all events, such a partial and fragmentary statement of fact as that
the withholding of that which is not stated makes that which is stated absolutely
false."[47]

In many cases the misstatement will be quite easy to demonstrate, as, for
example, in *Reese River Silver Mining Co.* v. *Smith*[48] where the statement that a
particular mine was in full operation and making large daily returns was shown
to be false, or in *Greenwood* v. *Leather Shod Wheel Co.*[49] where statements that
patented articles had been developed beyond the experimental stage and were a
commercial success were demonstrably untrue.

More difficult are cases where the statements made were true insofar as they
went but were defective in that they failed to disclose material facts. One line of
decisions seem to be based on the rule that "mere silence as regards a material *Omissions*
fact which the one party is not under an obligation to disclose to the other cannot
be a ground for rescission"[50] while other cases observe the principle that the
statements at issue are to be taken as a whole and in context: "half a truth is
better than a downright falsehood."[51] Certainly "if by a number of statements
you intentionally give a false impression and induce a person to act upon it, it is
not the less false although if one takes each statement by itself there may be difficulty in showing that any specific statement is untrue."[52] In *R.* v. *Kyslant*[53] it was
held that a prospectus in which all statements were literally true but which failed
to disclose information about the source of dividend payments was false in a
material particular. Even where the omission is innocent, if it relates to a
material fact so as to render the statement as a whole misleading, it seems that
the privider of funds may rescind. In *Coles* v. *White City (Manchester) Grey-
hound Association*[54] a description of land purchased by the company as being
"eminently suitable" for its operations omitted, albeit innocently, to state that
the land had been scheduled for town planning purposes and that the company
would not be entitled to compensation was held sufficient to enable a subscriber
for shares in the company to rescind.

Where a statement was true at the time it was made but events have occurred
which render it false the company is under an obligation to make known the new

---

[47] *Peek* v. *Gurney* (1873) L.R. 6 H.L. 377, *per* Lord Cairns at p.403.
[48] (1869) L.R. 4 H.L. 64.
[49] [1900] 1 Ch. 421; see also *Stirling* v. *Passburg Grains Ltd.* (1891) 8 T.L.R. 71.
[50] *Per* Chitty J. in *Turner* v. *Green* [1895] 2 Ch.205, at p.209 quoting *Fry on Specific Performance*;
    see also *per* Fry J. in *Davies* v. *London and Provincial Co.* (1878) 8 Ch.D. 469 at p.474; and *per*
    Cockburn C.J. in *Twycross* v. *Grant* (1877) 2 C.P.D. 469, at p. 532, C.A.
[51] *Per* Lord MacNaghten in *Gluckstein* v. *Barnes* [1900] A.C. 240 H.L. at pp.260, 261.
[52] *Per* Lord Halsbury L.C. in *Aaron's Reefs* v. *Twiss* [1896] A.C. 273, P.C. at p. 281; see also *per*
    Lord Blackburn in *Brownlie* v. *Campbell* (1880) 5 App. Cas. 925, H.L., at p.950; and in *Smith* v.
    *Chadwick* (1884) 9 App. Cas. 187 H.L. at p. 201.
[53] [1932] 1 K.B. 442.
[54] (1928) 45 T.L.R. 230; see also *Ross Estates Investment Co.* (1868) L.R. 3 Ch. 682; *McKeown* v.
    *Boudard Peveril Gear Co.* [1896] W.N. 36, C.A.; *New Brunswick and Canada Rail and Land Co.*
    v. *Coneybeare* (1862) 9 H.L.C. 711; *Peek* v. *Gurney* (1874) L.R. 3 Ch. 682.

*Change of*
*Circumstances*

position.[55] Failure to do so constitutes an omission amounting to a *suggestio falsi*. Equally where an untrue statement had been made unintentionally a failure to disclose the true facts is regarded as a misleading omission.[56]

*Facts,*
*Opinions, Pro-*
*mises and*
*Forecasts*

For the misrepresentation to give rise to a right of action it must relate to an existing fact, a requirement that may create difficulties where the statement at issue is a forecast or statement of intent or future policy. The rule seems to be that while "anticipation of future results is not a statement of fact"[57] the form of words used may be sufficient to constitute a representation of fact. "If you are looking to the language as the language of hope, expectation and confident belief that is one thing; but you may use language in such a way as, although in the form of hope and expectation, it may become a representation of existing facts."[58] On this basis statements as the how funds raised are to be deployed, what cash and credit control practices are to be adopted, whether or not a sinking fund is to be established to fund capital repayments would amount to representations of existing fact. By the same token assertions that a particular happening or result is expected when in reality it is not expected would constitute a misrepresentation.[59]

**1.26**

For a misstatement to give rise to a right to rescind it must be as to some material fact. Misstatements or omissions which are innocent and concern merely trivial matters do not give rise to such a right.[60]

*Misrepresen-*
*tation as to*
*Material Facts*

Whether or not a misrepresentation is material will depend on the context in which it is made. The following (by no means an exhaustive list[61]) have been held in their respective contexts to be material:

(1) a statement as to the persons who are, or are to be, directors[62];

(2) a statement as to the company's market share[63];

(3) a statement as to the value of the company's surplus assets[64];

(4) a statement as to the stage of development of the company's products or processes[65]; or

(5) a statement as to the company's rights under substantial business contracts.[66]

---

[55] *Davies* v. *London and Provincial Co.* (1878) 8 C.D. 469. Likewise if a statement is untrue when made but subsequent events cause it to become true it is nonetheless regarded as a misrepresentation. In *McConnel* v. *Wright* [1903] 1 Ch. 546, C.A., a statement to the effect that specified property had been acquired when in fact the acquisition did not take place until some time later was held to be a misrepresentation.

[56] *Ibid.*; see also *per* Lord Blackburn in *Brownlie* v. *Campbell* (1880) 5 App. Cas. 925, H.L. (Sc.), at p.950; and *Arnison* v. *Smith* (1889) 41 Ch.D. 341.

[57] *Per* Lord Esher M.R. in *Bentley* v. *Black* (1893) 9 T.L.R. 580, C.A.

[58] *Per* Lord Halsbury L.C. in *Aaron's Reefs* v. *Twiss* [1896] A.C. 273, H.L. at p.284.

[59] *Edgington* v. *Fitzmaurice* (1885) 29 Ch.D. 459, CA; *Karberg's Case* [1892] 3 Ch.1, C.A. at p.11.

[60] *City of Edinburgh Brewery* v. *Gibson's Trustees* (1869) 7 M. 886 (Ct. of Sess.).

[61] See Palmer, *Company Law* (23rd ed., 1982) at paras. 21.30–21.32 for a full list.

[62] *Re Scottish Petroleum Co.* (1883) 23 Ch.D. 413; and see cases cited at n.46 above.

[63] *Hyde* v. *New Asbestos Co.* (1891) 8 T.L.R. 121.

[64] *Re London and Staffordshire Fire Insurance Co.* (1883) 24 Ch.D. 149.

[65] *Stirling* v. *Passburg Grains Co.* (1891) 8 T.L.R. 71; *Greenwood* v. *Leather Shod Wheel Co.* [1900] 1 Ch.421.

[66] See *Palmer* cited above at n.61.

For a supplier of funds to succeed in rescinding the funding or subscription agreement[67] it must be shown that the misrepresentation was made by the company or on its behalf. Questions often arise as to how far the company is or should be responsible for statements made. In *Lynde* v. *Anglo-Italian Hemp Co.*[68] the effect of the authorities was summarised as being that to establish the company's responsibility it has to be shown that the representations were either:

**1.27**

*Responsibility for Misstatements*

(1)  made by the directors or general agents of the company; or
(2)  made by a special agent of the company acting within the scope of his authority[69]; or
(3)  known to the directors to have been made at some time before the funding/subscription agreement was made; or
(4)  known by the directors to form the basis of the contract.

From this it will be apparent that representations made prior to the formation of the company may become a ground for rescission, as may statements made by persons who are strangers to the company by virtue of the subsequent knowledge of the directors. Thus in *Karberg's Case*[70] an application for shares made on the faith of a prospectus prepared by the promoter and subsequently accepted was held by the Court of Appeal to have been properly set aside on the grounds that statements in the prospectus amounted to misrepresentations and that the prospectus, although prepared by the promoter, had been adopted by the company.

Before an investor can set aside a funding or subscription agreement he must show that the statement constituting the misrepresentation was relied on by him and was an inducement to provide funds.[71] It is not necessary to show that the misrepresentation was the sole cause of the investor's entering into the agreement but it must be shown to have been a substantial reason for doing so. In *Edgington* v. *Fitzmaurice*[72] the plaintiff was induced to subscribe for shares partly as a result of his own misreading of the company's prospectus but largely by reason of a misrepresentation contained therein. It was held that the agreement could be rescinded despite the part played by the plaintiff's misreading of the document.

**1.28**

*Reliance on Mis-statement*

The approach of the courts in ascertaining whether an investor has been induced to provide funds by a particular statement or statements is said to be an objective one. What this means is that where the statement appears to the court to be likely to induce investment the court will permit rescission unless the plaintiff admits that he did not act on the strength of the statement[73] or the court

---

[67] See further at Chapter 2, below for a consideration of funding and subscription agreements.
[68] [1896] 1 Ch. 178.
[69] This includes a person whose acts are subsequently ratified. Thus in *Hilo Manufacturing Co.* v. *Williamson* (1911) 28 T.L.R. 164, where directors knew that one of their number was obtaining subscriptions for shares, the company was held responsible for representations made by him.
[70] [1892] 3 Ch. 1, C.A.; see also *Tamplin's Case* [1892] W.N. 146.
[71] Note that the plaintiff must be prepared to specify the statement that provided the inducement; see *Re Christineville Rubber Estates* [1911] W.N. 216.
[72] (1885) 25 Ch.D. 459.
[73] *Per* Lord Halsbury in *Arnison* v. *Smith* (1889) 41 Ch.D. 348, C.A., at p.369.

reaches the conclusion that, irrespective of the representation, the investor would still have provided the funds. In this latter case the investor will not have been prejudiced and so will not be allowed to withdraw from his contract.[74]

**1.29**

*Need to Act Promptly*

An investor will only be permitted to withdraw from his contract if he seeks relief within a reasonable time after discovering the true state of affairs. What is reasonable will depend on the circumstances of each case. It has been said that where "a person has contracted to take shares in a company and his name has been placed on the register, it has always been held that he must exercise his right of repudiation with extreme promptness after his discovery of the fraud or misrepresentation."[75] Certainly the party seeking to rescind should act while the company is still a going concern. Once a company has gone into liquidation it is generally too late for the right to rescind to be exercised.[76]

The right to rescind may also be lost as a result of the actions or behaviour of the plaintiff. If the plaintiff, being aware of his entitlement to rescind, does anything to affirm the contract, that affirmation will cause the right to be lost.[77] The following have been held to amount to affirmation:

(1) attendance at meetings of the company[78];
(2) acceptance of interest or dividend payments[79];
(3) attempts to assign rights or interests under the contract[80];

in the absence of proceedings having been commenced.[81]

**(3) Civil liability: misrepresentation and actions for damages**

**1.30**

If the right to repudiate the contract is unavailable or inappropriate an action for damages may lie against the person or persons responsible for the misrepresentation where it can be shown that the misrepresentation was either:

(1) fraudulent; or
(2) within the ambit of the Misrepresentation Act 1967; or
(3) negligent.

---

[74] *Smith* v. *Chadwick* (1884) 9 App. Cas. 187.

[75] *Per* Lord Davey in *Aaron's Reefs* v. *Twiss* [1896] A.C. 273, H.L., at p.294. See also *per* Baggallay L.J. in *Re Scottish Petroleum Co.* (1883) 23 Ch.D. 413, C.A., at p.434: "The delay of a fortnight in repudiating the shares makes it to my mind doubtful whether the repudiation in the case of a going concern would have been in time. No doubt where investigation is necessary some time must be allowed, as in *Central Railway Co. of Venezuela* v. *Kisch* (1867) L.R. 2 H.L. 99 where a period of two months was allowed. But when, as in the present case, the shareholder is at once fully informed of the circumstances he ought to lose no time in repudiating." See also *Re Christineville Rubber Estates* [1911] W.N. 216 (four months).

[76] The point is that the right to repudiate can only be exercised while no other rights or interests intervene. The occurrence of a winding-up brings in such other rights (namely those of creditors and contributories). See further *Tennant* v. *City of Glasgow Bank* (1879) 4 App. Cas. 615 H.L. (Sc.); *Burgess's Case* (1880) 15 Ch.D. 507.

[77] *Clough* v. *London and North Western Railway* (1872) L.R. 7 Ex. 26.

[78] *Sharpley* v. *Louth and East Coast Railway* (1876) 2 Ch.D. 663.

[79] *Scholey* v. *Central Railway of Venezuela* (1869) L.R. 9 Eq. 266n.

[80] *Ex p. Briggs* (1866) L.R. 1 Eq. 483 (attempt to sell shares).

[81] *Tomlin's Case* [1898] 1 Ch. 104.

It is to be noted that where the misrepresentation appears in a prospectus or in listing particulars published in connection with a proposed public issue of securities for which admission is sought either to the Stock Exchange Official List or Unlisted Securities Market such prospectus or listing particulars must contain a statement that the directors of the company issuing the securities accept responsibility for the accuracy of the contents thereof.[82]

To establish fraud it must be shown "that the false representation has been made:

    (1) knowingly, or

    (2) without belief in its truth; or

    (3) recklessly, careless or whether it be true or false.

**1.31**

*Meaning of Fraud*

To prevent a false statement being fraudulent, there must . . . always be an honest belief in its truth. And this probably covers the whole ground for one who knowingly alleges that which is false has obviously no such honest belief."[83]

In addition to establishing that the misrepresentation was fraudulent "it is the duty of the plaintiff to establish . . . that this fraud was the inducing cause to the contract, for which purpose it must be material, and it must have produced in his mind an erroneous belief influencing his conduct."[84] One might add, since damages are a compensatory remedy, that the plaintiff must demonstrate that he has suffered loss as a result.[85]

Damages are most commonly sought against directors or promoters of a company, although in appropriate cases the action may be brought against the company itself on the basis that the company is vicariously liable for the acts of its agents or of its servants in the course of their employment.[86] In cases where damages are sought from the company itself the plaintiff will be required to show, in addition to the matters mentioned above, that those purporting to act on behalf of the company were so authorised to act.

The right to sue the company (as opposed to the directors or other persons responsible for the fraudulent statement) is restricted by the ruling of the House of Lords in *Houldsworth* v. *City of Glasgow Bank*[87] that damages may not be recovered in an action for fraudulent misrepresentation against a company unless the contract itself is capable of being rescinded by reason of the misrepresentation. It follows from this that once winding-up proceedings have been commenced an action for damages can no longer be sustained since the commencement of winding-up proceedings will put an end to the right to rescind.

An action against the company seeking rescission of the contract and against the company or the directors or promoters claiming damages for fraud or deceit[88] may be combined in one writ.[89]

---

[82] See further below at Chapter 6.

[83] *Per* Lord Herschell in *Derry* v. *Peek* (1889) 14 App.Cas. 337 H.L., at p.374.

[84] *Per* Lord Selbourne in *Smith* v. *Chadwick* (1884) 9 App. Cas. 187 H.L., at p.190.

[85] *Smith* v. *Chadwick, ibid.* at p.195; see also *Pasley* v. *Freeman* (1789) 3 T.R. 51.

[86] See generally *Palmer, Company Law* at paras. 9.37 *et seq.; Gore-Browne* at Chapter 5.

[87] (1880) 5 App. Cas. 317 H.L.(Sc.).

[88] In England the action will be for the tort of deceit and in Scotland for fraud.

[89] *Frankenburg* v. *Great Horseless Carriage Co.* [1900] 1 Q.B. 504, C.A.

*Measure of Damages*

The quantum of damages will be measured by reference to the amount of the loss incurred. In the case of a subscription contract[90] providing for a participation in the equity of the company the measure of damages will be the difference between the actual value[91] of the shares at the time of allotment and the amount paid for them.[92] In the case of a loan agreement the measure will be the amount advanced.[93]

**1.32**

*Misrepresentation Act 1967 s.2(1)*

In England and Wales (but not in Scotland) an action derived from the action for damages in tort for fraudulent representation may be available in cases where fraud cannot be established. Section 2(1) of the Misrepresentation Act 1967 provides:

> "Where a person has entered into a contract after a misrepresentation has been made to him by another party and as a result thereof he has suffered loss, then, if the person making the representation would be liable in damages in respect thereof had the misrepresentation been made fraudulently, that person shall be so liable notwithstanding that the representation was not made fraudulently, unless he proves that he had a reasonable ground to believe, and did believe up to the time the contract was made, that the facts represented were true."

To sustain an action under section 2(1) therefore a plaintiff still has to show that the representation induced the plaintiff to provide the funds to which the contract relates and that it was defective in a material respect.[94] Furthermore, if anything should supervene which would have rendered an action for damages for fraudulent misrepresentation incompetent that same event would seemingly render an action under section 2(1) similarly incompetent. On this basis it is thought that the decision of the House of Lords in *Houldsworth* v. *City of Glasgow Bank*[95] to the effect that no action for damages can be sustained unless the plaintiff is in a position to have the contract rescinded for misrepresentation will apply equally to actions for damages under section 2(1) with the consequence that the commencement of winding-up proceedings will prevent the bringing of an action under the Act against the company.[96]

Once the elements of liability under section 2(1) have been established, judgment for the plaintiff must follow unless the defendant can prove that he believed the representation to be true and that such belief was reasonable.

---

[90] See below at Chapter 2.

[91] In arriving at a figure for "actual value" all circumstances are to be taken into account including the subsequent failure of the company unless it can be shown that that failure was due to causes not present at the time of allotment. If the company was inherently unsound the shares may have an actual value of nothing. In this event the measure of damages would be the price paid for the shares.

[92] *Peek* v. *Derry* (1888) 37 Ch.D. 541; *Arnison* v. *Smith* (1889) 41 Ch.D. 348 at p. 363; *McConnel* v. *Wright* [1903] 1 Ch. 546 at pp.554, 555 *per* Collins M.R.

[93] Plus a sum representing consequential loss (if any such is suffered), *Doyle* v. *Olby* (*Ironmongers*) *Ltd.* [1969] 2 W.L.R. 673, C.A.

[94] And, of course that loss resulted. See above at § 1.31.

[95] (1880) 5 App. Cas. 317, H.L.

[96] Provided that such commencement preceded the commencement of proceedings under section 2(1).

Section 2(2) of the Misrepresentation Act 1967 permits the court to award damages in lieu of rescission in the case of an innocent misrepresentation where it is in the interests of justice to do so. It should be emphasised that the power of the court under section 2(2) is entirely discretionary; there is no compulsion (as there is in a case brought under section 2(1)) for the court to award damages in lieu of rescission.[97]

**1.33**

*Misrepresentation Act 1967, s.2.(2)*

Where the provision of funds was induced by a defective statement negligently made, it may be possible for the provider of the funds to recover damages in tort in respect of any loss suffered. The basis of the action is that those soliciting funds owe a duty of care to those who might be persuaded to invest in the company[98] to ensure that the information provided about the company and its management and business is accurate. If what is provided amounts to "unsound advice or misleading information or . . . an erroneous opinion"[99] as a result of which the plaintiff is induced to invest in the company those responsible will be liable in negligence.[1] In *Esso Petroleum Co.* v. *Mardon*[2] a businessman was induced to invest in a petrol filling-station on the basis of statements made to him by servants of the petroleum company as to the throughput of petrol that could be expected. In the event these forecasts proved to be inaccurate to a material extent and in consequence the value of the plaintiff's investment declined. The company was held liable.

**1.34**

*Damages for Negligent Mis-statements*

Actions for damages for loss induced by negligent misstatements lie against those responsible for the misstatements. Accordingly a party suffering loss may proceed against the directors or agents of the company as being the persons who actually made the statements, or against the company itself where it can be shown that the statements were made within the scope of the authority of those making them. If it is desired to proceed against the company, however, the restriction arising from the rule in *Houldsworth* v. *City of Glasgow Bank*[3] that an action will not lie unless the contract itself is capable of being rescinded because of the misrepresentation would appear to apply here also.[4]

It has been argued[5] that in the context of corporate finance the action for damages for negligent misstatement is of only secondary importance in view of the alternative remedy available under section 2(1) of the Misrepresentation Act 1967. More particularly, it is said that in an action based on negligence it is necessary to show that the person making or the company responsible for the defective statement owed a duty of care to the person in receipt of it,[6] that the

**1.35**

*Utility of Actions for Negligent Mis-statements*

---

[97] Section 2(3) operates to prevent the possibility of a "double damages" award resulting from the successful pursuit of claims under both ss.2(1) and 2(2).

[98] *Esso Petroleum Co.* v. *Mardon* [1976] Q.B. 801, C.A. See also *Mutual Life and Citizens Assurance Co.* v. *Evatt* [1971] A.C. 793, P.C.; *Box* v. *Midland Bank Ltd.* [1979] 2 Lloyds Rep. 391; *J.E.B. Fasteners* v. *Marks* [1983] 1 All E.R. 583, C.A.

[99] *Per* Lord Denning M.R. in *Esso Petroleum Co.* v. *Mardon* [1976] Q.B. 801 at p. 820.

[1] Under the principle in *Hedley Byrne & Co. Heller & Parnters* [1964] A.C. 465, H.L.

[2] [1976] Q.B. 801, C.A.

[3] (1880) 5 App. Cas. 317, H.L. (Sc.).

[4] See above at §§ 1.31 and 1.32.

[5] *Gore-Browne on Companies* (43rd ed. 1981) at para. 11.14.

[6] In most cases in the context of corporate financing activities such a duty will exist.

defective statement amounted to a breach of that duty and that loss to the plaintiff resulted. In contrast, in an action under the Misrepresentation Act the burden is on the defendant who must prove belief in the accuracy of his statement and the reasonableness of that belief.

Nevertheless, an action for damages for negligent misstatement would appear to have the advantage of wider application in that:

(a) an action under the Misrepresentation Act will lie only between the parties to the agreement, that is between the investor providing the funds and the company receiving them, whereas under the *Hedley Byrne/Mardon* principle the directors or other persons who made the statements made also be sued; and

(b) The Misrepresentation Act does not apply to Scotland[7] and under Scots law no contractual action for damages in respect of a misstatement is possible unless fraud can be established.[8] On the other hand a delictual action based on negligence is perfectly competent.

### (4) Contractual terms

**1.36**    Where funding is provided pursuant to a contract privately negotiated by the company and those providing the funds, the terms of the contract will frequently seek to provide for the possibility that submissions made or other information supplied might prove to be defective.

### (a) Loan Agreements

Where the funding is by way of a loan the provisions of the loan agreement will normally confer on the lender the right to terminate the agreement and demand immediate repayment of the funds advanced should it transpire that any statement or representation of fact or intention made by or on behalf of the borrower proves to be inaccurate in any material respect.[9]

It will be noted that the terms of such provisions are drafted so as to confer a power to terminate rather than causing a termination *per se*. The point is that in certain cases it may be considered best to continue with the investment (especially where the defect arises from a statement of intent not being carried out for reasons acceptable to the lender or where the defect comprises a misstatement of fact innocently made in circumstances which cast no adverse reflection on the integrity of the borrower company's management) and such a power permits the lender to adopt that course.[10]

### (b) Share subscription agreements[11]

Prior to the coming into force of the Companies Act 1981 it was difficult to achieve the same right to withdraw from a company where the funding was given

---

[7] See Walker, *The Law of Contracts and Related Obligations in Scotland*, (1979) at para. 14.90.

[8] The significance lies in the way damages are assessed. Damages in delict are measured by reference to the actual loss suffered whereas damages in contract damages may be awarded in respect of loss of an anticipated bargain.

[9] Or indeed in any respect whatsoever.

[10] Additionally, clauses drafted in this way avoid problems of definition as to exactly when the agreement terminates.

[11] See further at Chapter 2, below.

in return for an equity stake or a holding of preference shares. The problem was that company law made no provision for shareholders to be able to demand that companies "buy back" shares issued by them. Accordingly, while an investor might have a remedy (either in damages or by way of a rescission of the contract of allotment) it was not possible contractually to require a company to redeem share capital. One way to avoid this, however, was to extract a collateral covenant from the directors and/or proprietors of the company requiring them to purchase the shares at the issue (or some other stipulated) price.

Since the passing of the 1981 Act this curse is no longer strictly necessary in that it is now possible for companies to issue shares (whether ordinary or preference) that are redeemable at the option of the shareholder or the company.[12] Institutions providing equity funding therefore can now secure through the terms of issue the right to withdraw from a company although it may still be thought desirable to extract a covenant from the directors and/or proprietors of the company as an additional safeguard.

### Public issues: scrutiny of offer documents

It has long been the case that companies seeking admission for their securities to the Stock Exchange Official List or, more recently, the Unlisted Securities Market are required to submit in draft form the relevant prospectuses or listing particulars to the Quotations Department of the Stock Exchange for scrutiny to ensure that all the information demanded by the term of admission has been disclosed.[13] **1.37**

The Stock Exchange (Listing) Regulations 1984[14] have designated the Council of the Stock Exchange as the "competent authority" for the purposes of three EEC Council Directives[15] relating to the admission of securities to the Official List thereby giving it a statutory role and conferring on it statutory obligations. It is provided, however, that the Council shall not be liable in damages by reason only of non-compliance with or contravention of any of the obligations which emanate from the Directives and are imposed by the Regulations, nor shall it be so liable in respect of anything done or omitted to be done by it in connection with its functions as competent authority unless the act or omission complained of was done or omitted to be done in bad faith.[16] The single exception to this exclusion of liability provision is the obligation to ensure that listing particulars contain the required information[17] being such information as "is necessary to enable investors and their investment advisers to make an informed assessment of the assets and liabilities, financial position, profits and losses, and prospects of the issuer of the securities and of the rights attaching to such securities."[18]

*Role of the Stock Exchange*

---

[12] C.A. 1981, ss. 45 *et seq.* Now C.A. 1985, ss. 159 *et seq.*

[13] See further at Chapter 6, below.

[14] S.I. 1984 No. 716.

[15] Council Directives Nos. 79/279/EEC (The Admission Directive); 80/390/EEC (The Listing Particulars Directive); and 82/121/EEC (The Interim Reports Directive).

[16] S.I. 1984, No.716, Reg. 8(1).

[17] Listing Particulars Directive, Art. 5. See further at Chapter 6, below.

[18] *Ibid.* Art. 4(1).

While no such statutory obligation exists[19] in respect of prospectuses or listing particulars published in respect of securities for which a quotation on the Unlisted Securities Market is sought it is suggested that an action for damages would lie to any aggrieved investor should the Quotations Department negligently fail to ensure that its own prospectus requirements are met. It would seem to be beyond argument that the Council of the Stock Exchange owes a duty of care to those who subscribe for securities which are to be traded on its markets.[20]

The nature and limits of the obligation on the Stock Exchange authorities should perhaps be emphasised. It is an obligation to ensure that requirements as to the quantum of information to be disclosed are met; it does not extend to the quality of the information that is disclosed. The fact of listing or quotation does not imply a warranty by the Stock Exchange that the information contained in a prospectus is accurate and not misleading or that the securities in question have any particular value.[21] The ultimate safeguard for the investor[22] remains the sanctions and remedies available under the general law.

## CAPITAL MARKET REGULATION

### The nature of capital market regulation

**1.38**

*Statutory and Non-Statutory Regulation*

The traditional approach to market regulation in the United Kingdom has been to devise methods which operate as informally as possible with less emphasis on statute and more on non-statutory forms of regulation, especially self-regulation.[23] Indeed, the impression is sometimes given that, within the United Kingdom context, statutory and non-statutory forms of regulation are mutually inconsistent. The reality, however is that all financial institutions and markets are regulated by a mixture of statutory and non-statutory rules. Over the capital market as a whole there is a great diversity of regulatory arrangements in operation, some of which are predominantly statute-based allowing those within their jurisdiction relatively little discretion, whereas others, though operating within a statutory framework, are to a large extent self-regulatory. However, even those sectors of the capital market subject to a high degree of statutory regulation invariably utilise non-statutory contributions in one form or another.[24]

[19] At present. If and when the Prospectus Directive is adopted and implemented such a statutory obligation will exist.

[20] Indeed it acknowledges such a responsibility, at least in relation to the listed market, *Admission of Securities to Listing,* para. 1.

[21] It should also be noted that the Registrar of Companies has no duty to check the accuracy of prospectuses filed wih his office. He is concerned to ensure only that the documents comply with the statutory requirements.

[22] Such as it is. See the comments in the Gower Report (1984 Cmnd. 9125) at para. 9.21.

[23] Self-regulation is claimed to have produced advantages in terms of the range and cost of financial services available in Britain and of the competitive edge shown by British institutions overseas. The attitude of the regulatory authorities is often quoted as one of the main attractions of London as a centre for international business.—Wilson Committee (Main Report) at para. 1072.

[24] The Wilson Committee concluded (Main Report) at para. 1100 that the issue was not "whether statutory methods of supervision are preferable in some absolute sense, but whether the existing balance between the two, and equally if not more importantly the type of each presently used" for the different groups and markets were appropriate to their particular circumstances.

For many years the main thrust of the regulatory system had been directed towards the achievement of an adequate level of disclosure by those soliciting funds from the public. Increasingly however the Bank of England and the Department of Trade and Industry, as the bodies responsible for ensuring that the overall arrangements for he regulation of the capital market (and indeed of the financial system as a whole) are both adequate and appropriate to the needs of suppliers and consumers of finance and financial services, came to appreciate the importance of protecting the interests of consumers of financial services and to consider the ways in which this protection could best be achieved.[25]

While the rules governing disclosure remain, within the system of regulation they have been accompanied by the establishment of supervisory bodies to oversee various sectors of the market. Some of these had been in existence for many years. An obvious example is the Council of the Stock Exchange which has exercised self-regulatory functions in connection with the securities markets (or more precisely, the principal securities market) but which has now had a significant part of its functions put on a statutory basis.[26] Likewise, the Bank of England has exercised various functions in relation to the supervision of the banking system; since the passing of the Banking Act 1979 the rather loose and semi-formal system of banking regulation has been replaced with a much more formal statute-based structure.

*Forms of
Regulation*

One of the functions of establishing regulatory bodies and of formalising the structure within which they operate has been to impose greater restrictions on market entry through the use of authorisation requirements. The Banking Act 1979, for example, requires institutions to be designated as banks by the Bank of England before they are permitted to carry on the business of banking[27]; similarly the Insurance Companies Act 1974 laid down a strict set of criteria for insurers to satisfy before they are granted authorisation by the Department of Trade and Industry. An important aspect of the authorisation procedures for both banks and insurance companies is the requirement that those who control or manage them should be regarded as "fit and proper persons" to undertake those responsibilities. There are requirements to the same effect in the legislation[28] governing the licensing of dealers in securities; furthermore the Stock Exchange operates a comparable, albeit non-statutory, set of requirements in respect of those who are or would be directors of companies with a Stock Exchange listing or Unlisted Securities Market quotation for their securities.

Companies seeking to raise capital are affected by the regulatory system in two ways. If seeking funds from an institution that institution will have been subject to authorisation procedures of some kind to enable it to operate in the market at all. As a consumer of finance the company is therefore in a position to reap the benefits of the system in terms of stability and security of supply. However, a company seeking to raise funds by public issue[29] is itself seeking access to

---

[25] Wilson Committee (Main Report) at para. 1074.
[26] Stock Exchange (Listing) Regulations 1984 (S.I. 1984 No. 716).
[27] Also, anyone wishing to take deposits has to be authorised by the Bank or exempted under the Act.
[28] Licensed Dealers (Conduct of Business) Rules 1983 (S.I. 1983 No. 585).
[29] See below at Chapter 6.

a sector of the market and as such can be expected to have to comply with whatever authorisation and admission requirements are imposed by the market authorities.

### Regulation of the securities markets

**1.40**      The primary objective in providing for the regulation of the securities markets has been described[30] as "the maintenance of a fair and orderly market in which all investors can deal on equal terms with equal and adequate information and opportunity."

*Regulatory Bodies*

The statutory aspects of regulation prior to 1984 were administered by the Department of Trade and Industry, with day-to-day responsibility being left largely to non-statutory bodies. The most important of these were (and still are) the Council for the Securities Industry, the Council of the Stock Exchange, and the City Panel on Take-overs and Mergers. Oversight of the system as a whole rested with the Bank of England/Department of Trade and Industry Joint Review Body.

In 1984 the statutory/non-statutory balance altered slightly in that the Council of the Stock Exchange was given certain statutory functions in relation to the market in listed securities.

### Composition of the securities markets

**1.41**      The importance of the securities markets as a source of external funding lies in the fact that they provide a means whereby companies can raise funds from the public through new issues. For a new issue market to be effective, however, there must exist an active trading market in securities since this provides future marketability and gives an indication of the terms on which new capital can be raised.

*Primary and Secondary Markets*

In the United Kingdom the principal trading market in securities is the Stock Exchange which provides new issue (or primary) markets in which new capital can be raised and secondary markets in which existing securities can be traded. The Stock Exchange provides markets for three categories of security, namely:

(a) listed securities;
(b) unlisted securities; and
(c) eurobonds.

Since 1972 the markets provided by the Stock Exchange have been supplemented by "over-the-counter" markets operated by various licensed dealers in securities.

Alternative (and competing) facilities to those provided by the Stock Exchange have since 1974 been available to those institutional investors subscribing to ARIEL.[31]

---

[30] Wilson Committee (Main Report) at para. 1121.
[31] ARIEL is the acronym for Automated Real-Time Investments Exchange Ltd.

## SECURITIES MARKETS

### (1) The market in listed securities

The Stock Exchange market in listed securities is the market in which are **1.42**
traded:

(1) securities issued by the British government;
(2) securities issued by other United Kingdom public sector bodies;
(3) United Kingdom company securities;
(4) securities issued by overseas companies; and
(5) securities issued by overseas governments, public authorities and institutions.

For a company to obtain access for its securities to this market it must be prepared to meet detailed disclosure requirements imposed by the Stock Exchange authorities[32] and to enter into a contract with the Stock Exchange committing it, its directors and officers, to observe certain standards in relation to the release of regular financial and trading information, the preparation of interim and annual reports and accounts and the adequate disclosure of price-sensitive information and significant share dealings.[33]

### (2) ARIEL

ARIEL was set up by the Accepting Houses Committee to provide institu- **1.43**
tional subscribers with an alternative and potentially cheaper facility than that available through the Stock Exchange for the transaction of dealings in securities. Under the ARIEL system the participating institutions deal directly, albeit anonymously, with each other using computer terminals.

Having begun operations in 1974 the ARIEL system now covers the equity securities of more than 1,000 United Kingdom registered companies together with the largest debenture and convertible stocks and the more important local authority securities.

### (3) The unlisted securities market

In its present form[34] the Unlisted Securities Market (USM) dates from **1.44**
November 1980 when he market was launched with the primary object of pro-

---

[32] The Quotations Committee, consisting of 12 members of the Council of the Stock Exchange and assisted by the Quotations Department, is responsible for the regulation of listed companies by means of disclosure and for the processing of the documents to be published and announcements to be made.

[33] See further below at Chapter 6.

[34] Originally dealings in unlisted securities took place under Rule 163(2) of the Rules of the Stock Exchange which permitted brokers to find matching orders for the securities either from among their own clients or through a jobber dealing in the securities. The facility provided a convenient instrument for companies unable or unwilling to comply with the requirements for a listing in relation to matters such as disclosure: all that was required by way of disclosure was an annual balance sheet and accounts. The drawback associated with Rule 163(2) was that every transaction within it required the permission of the Council of the Stock Exchange. While in practice this seldom led to

viding a formal regulated market designed to meet the needs of those smaller, less mature companies unlikely to apply for a full listing. Companies seeking a quotation for their securities on this market have to comply with disclosure requirements similar to but less stringent than those demanded for a full listing. Such companies are also required to give a "General Undertaking" (serving the same function as and based on the Listing Agreement formerly applicable where a full listing was sought) as to corporate conduct and the release of regular specified types of financial and trading information.

### (4) The "over-the-counter" markets

**1.45**     The first "over-the-counter" market facility in Britain was established in 1972 by M.J.H. Nightingale and Co. (now Granville and Co.) to manage issues for and a secondary market in the shares of a number of companies without a Stock Exchange listing. Since 1972 other licensed dealers have established their own such markets.

The operating practices of those responsible for "over-the-counter" (OTC) markets differ widely with some operators acting almost exclusively as agents, matching buyers and sellers, and acting as principals on their own behalf only when a matching party cannot be found or arising from their positions as option or warrant holders.[35] Others, in contrast, take up positions on their own behalf as normal business practice.

Each licensed dealer operating an OTC market lays down its own rules governing disclosure and the release of financial and trading information, with the company being required to comply with these as a condition of market entry.

The attractiveness of OTC markets was increased significantly by the provisions of the Finance Act of 1983 and 1984 giving effect to the government's "Business Expansion Scheme."[36] Under the terms of this scheme the tax allowances given to investors in qualifying unquoted companies are withdrawn if the company acquires a Stock Exchange listing or USM quotation within three years of the investment being made.[37] In contrast dealings in a company's shares on an OTC market will not cause the allowance to be withdrawn.

much delay and was designed to afford some measure of protection for the interests of investors it nevertheless constituted an inhibition on the evelopment of a formal market.

The first expansion of facilities came wth the promulgation of Rule 163(3). This was designed to facilitate the raising of risk capital for a number of unproven ventures such as those being undertaken by North Sea oil exploration companies. Prior permission was not needed for individual transactions. The essence of the matter was disclosure with Rule 163(3) companies being required to submit to disclosure requirements (see further at Chapter 6, below) similar to those required for a full listing.

In 1979 the Stock Exchange published a consultative document setting out proposals for formalising the market in unlisted securities. This involved the replacement of Rule 163(2) dealings while the arrangements under Rule 163(3) would continue unchanged. In the event while the establishment of a formal market did cover many transactions which would otherwise have been carried out under Rule 163(2) that facility remains.

[35] See further at Chapter 6 below.
[36] See further at Chapter 8, below.
[37] F.A. 1983, s.26 and Sched. 5 as amended by F.A. 1984, s.37.

### (5) The eurobond market

The eurobond[38] market is an international over-the-counter market con-  **1.46**
ducted mainly by telex or telephone between the market-makers, notably British
merchant banks and banking institutions from the United States, Europe and
Japan. Because of the existence of exchange controls in some countries, the
terms of which make it impractical to invest in securities not listed on a recognised stock exchange, most issues are listed on the Stock Exchange, London, or
on the Luxembourg bourse, although few actual dealings take place there.

The eurobond market is both a primary market, with governments, public
agencies and industrial and commercial companies using its facilities to raise
medium/long-term funds, often in foreign currency, and a secondary market.
London is by far the largest centre of its operations both in relation to new issues
and dealings in the secondary market. There are two systems[39] through which 95
per cent. of deals are cleared.[40]

## REGULATORY AGENCIES

### (1) The Council of the Stock Exchange

Because of its predominant position in the United Kingdom securities markets  **1.47**
much of the burden of regulation of those markets has inevitably fallen on the
Stock Exchange. In relation to both the listed market and the USM the jurisdic-  *Basis of Auth-*
tion of the Stock Exchange authorities has traditionally been based on contract,  *ority of Coun-*
whether that contract is:  *cil of Stock*
*Exchange*

(a) the mutual contract between member firms which gives the Stock
Exchange its existence and which imposes obligations on member firms to
conduct their business in accordance with the Rules and Regulations of  *(1) Contract*
the Stock Exchange and with a formal Code of Dealing which is supplemented from time to time[41];

(b) the former Listing Agreement or USM General Undertaking which, in
regulates the behaviour of companies with a full Stock Exchange listing or
USM quotation[42]; or

(c) an agreement by investors using the Stock Exchange to abide by "the

---

[38] A "eurobond" is a negotiable debt security denominated in external currency, almost invariably
issued in bearer form. See further at Chapter 2, below.

[39] Euro-Clear Clearance Systems Ltd. (owned by Morgan Guaranty) and Cedel S.A. (owned by a
consortium of a large number of banks).

[40] See generally the Gower Report 1984, cmnd. 9125 at paras. 6.09 *et seq.*

[41] Regulation of Member Firms is undertaken through the Council's Committees on Membership,
on Commissions and Dealings and on Firms' Accounts, and on the staff of the Membership
Department. The Quotations Committee and Quotations Department are also involved in investigations into suspected irregular or abnormal dealings.

[42] See above at §§ 1.42 and 1.44 and below at §§ 6.67 and 6.89. Note that although there is no longer
a formal Listing Agreement as such, obligations derived from it are still imposed on companies as
conditions of admission to listing. See The Yellow Book—(Admission of Securities to Listing)
Section 5.

rules, regulations and usages of the Stock Exchange" through the terms of brokers' contract notes.[43]

**1.48**

*(2) Statute*

Responsibility for discharging the regulatory functions in relation to the Stock Exchange's markets and for exercising jurisdiction in connection therewith rests with the Council of the Stock Exchange. In addition to the authority and powers given to it by the Rules and Regulations of the Stock Exchange the Council has been designated the "competent authority" for the purposes of the EEC Council Directives on Admission to Official Listing,[44] Listing Particulars,[45] and on the publication and content of Interim Reports.[46] In its capacity as competent authority the Council has acquired a number of statutory powers and functions.[47] These are as follows.

*In relation to the admission of securities to official listing*

(1) To decide on the admission of securities to official listing[48];

(2) To reject an application for official listing[49] if, in its opinion, the issuer's position is such that admission would be detrimental to investors' interests[50];

(3) Solely in the interests of protecting investors, to make admission of a security to official listing subject to any special condition[51] which it considers appropriate and of which it has expressly informed the applicant[52];

(4) To refuse to admit to official listing a security already officially listed in another EEC state where the issuer fails to comply with the obligations resulting from admission in that state[53];

(5) To make public the fact that an issuer is failing to comply with the obligations resulting from official listing[54];

(6) To require an issuer whose securities have been admitted to official listing to provide it, as competent authority, with all the information which it considers appropriate in order to protect investors and ensure the smooth operation of the market[55];

(7) Where the protection of investors or the smooth operation of the market so requires, to require an issuer to publish such information in such form

---

[43] See further Wilson Committee (Main Report) at paras. 1143 *et seq.*
[44] Council Directive No. 79/279/EEC (The Admission Directive).
[45] *Ibid.* No. 80/390/EEC (The Listing Particulars Directive).
[46] *Ibid.* No. 82/121/EEC (The Interim Reports Directive).
[47] Stock Exchange (Listing) Regulations 1984, reg. 4(1). The Council is empowered (by Reg. 4(2)) to arrange for the discharge of its functions as competent authority by any committee, sub-committee, officer or employee of the Council.
[48] Admission Directive Art. 9(1).
[49] *Ibid.* Art. 15(1) requires that decisions of competent authorities refusing admission to listing or suspending a listing shall be subject to a right to apply to the courts.
[50] *Ibid.* Art. 9(3).
[51] That is over and above the general conditions imposed by the Directive. See further at Chapter 6, below.
[52] Admission Directive Art. 10.
[53] *Ibid.* Art. 11.
[54] *Ibid.* Art. 12.
[55] *Ibid.* Art. 13.1.

and within such time limits as it (*i.e.* the competent authority) considers appropriate[56];

(8) To suspend the listing of a security where the smooth operation of the market is, or may be, temporarily jeopardised or where the protection of investors so requires[57]; and

(9) To discontinue the listing of a security.[58]

*In relation to the scrutiny and publication of listing particulars*[59]

(1) To scrutinise and, where appropriate, approve the publication of listing particulars as complying with the requirements as to form and content laid down by the Listing Particulars Directive[60]; and

(2) In an appropriate case (and in any event only after an examination of the case on its merits) to call for an additional report from the company's official auditor.[61]

*In relation to the information to be published on a regular basis by Companies whose Shares have been Admitted to Official Stock Exchange Listing.*[62]

(1) To receive copies of half-yearly reports from listed companies and to ensure that their form and content comply with the requirements of the Interim Reports Directive[63]; and

(2) In cases where the particular requirements of the Interim Reports Directive are unsuited to a company's activities or circumstances, to ensure that suitable adaptations are made to such requirements.[64]

## (2) The Panel on Take-overs and Mergers

The Panel was set up in 1968 as a result of an initiative by the governor of the **1.49** Bank of England following widespread criticism of some of the practices adopted in a period of intense take-over activity during the 1960s.[65] Its function

---

[56] *Ibid.* Art. 13.2. Should the issuer fail to comply with such requirement the Stock Exchange may itself publish such information after having heard the issuer.

[57] *Ibid.* Art. 14. 1.

[58] *Ibid.* Art. 14.2.

[59] See further at Chapter 6, below.

[60] Listing Particulars Directive Art. 18.

[61] *Ibid.* Art. 19.

[62] See further at Chapter 6, below.

[63] Interim Reports Directive, Art. 9.2.

[64] *Ibid.* Art. 9.3.

[65] The Panel includes representatives from bodies on the City Working Party (see further at n.66 below) together with an independent chairman and deputy chairman appointed by the Governor of the Bank of England, the chairman of the Council for the Securities Industry (see further at § 1.50 below) and the President of the Institute of Chartered Accountants in England and Wales. Much of the Panel's day-to-day work is delegated to a small executive consisting of a Director-General, two deputies, a secretary and other executive staff. The Director-General, the secretary and the other executives normally serve on secondment from private firms or from the Bank of England so as to secure a balance of merchant banking, stockbroking, accounting and legal backgrounds. The deputies are permanent employees so as to achieve an element of continuity.

is to administer and interpret the City Code, a body of principles and rules drawn up originally by the City Working Party[66] and revised from time to time to take account of changes in take-over practices.

The present Code applies to offers for all public companies, whether listed on the Stock Exchange, quoted on the USM or not, but not to offers for private companies.[67] Its principal objective is to ensure that take-over bids for those companies within its jurisdiction are fairly conducted. In pursuing this objective the Code seeks to secure[68]:

(a) equity as between all shareholders of a company involved in a take-over bid[69];

(b) the provision of adequate information and sufficient time to make a judgment on the merits of the offer; and

(c) the position of shareholders in relation to the actions of the directors in connection with the offer: in particular, directors of a company for which an offer has been made should not do anything to frustrate the offer by the exercise of their powers of management before shareholders have had an adequate opportunity to consider it[70];

The Code is not concerned with the merits of a particular bid.

Day-to-day supervision of the Code is undertaken by the Panel executive, who work closely with the Quotations Department of the Stock Exchange on whom they rely for detailed monitoring of the documentation issued. While the Panel do not approve take-over bids in advance[71] they do expect to be consulted in cases of doubt about the application of the Code and to be supplied with copies of all relevant documents.

Neither the Code nor the Panel have statutory backing or jurisdiction. Their authority rests on the acceptance of the Panel and executive rulings by the general financial community and by the associations which make up its membership.[72]

### (3) The Council for the Securities Industry[73]

**1.50**     The Council for the Securities Industry (CSI) is a non-statutory body which was set up in 1978 and whose objectives were described by the Bank of England at the time as being:

---

[66] The City Working Party consists of representatives of the main institutional investors, the clearing banks, the merchant banks, the Stock Exchange and the C.B.I.

[67] See below at §§ 7.61 *et seq.*

[68] See generally Wilson Committee (Main Report) at paras. 1147 *et seq.*

[69] In particular, where control of a company has a value in itself the control premium should be shared by all shareholders. Control should not therefore be acquired by discriminatory purchases. This means that all shareholders in a company subject to a take-over bid should have the opportunity of receiving the same price.

[70] The directors should take independent advice on the offer.

[71] Unlike the Council of the Stock Exchange in relation to the public issue of securities for which admission to the Official List or USM is sought.

[72] The main sanction available is that of public censure. In serious cases the Panel can draw its findings to the attention of the Stock Exchange or any association to which the individual or concern belongs for such sanctions as they may have at their disposal.

[73] See generally Wilson Committee (Main Report) at paras. 1155 *et seq.*

(a) to maintain the highest ethical standards in the conduct of business within the securities industry;

(b) to keep under constant review the evolution of the securities industry, market practice and related codes of conduct and to scrutinise the effectiveness of existing forms of regulation and te machinery for their administration;

(c) to maintain arrangements for the investigation of cases of alleged misconduct within the securities industry and breaches of codes of conduct or practice and to keep these arrangements under review;

(d) to initiate new policies and codes as necessary concerning activities in the securities industry other than those properly within the domestic province of each individual constituent member.[74]

(e) to resolve differences on matters of principle between constituent parts of the securities industry;

(f) to consider the need for changes in legislation affecting the activities of the securities industry and to examine any proposals for such legislation; and

(g) to ensure liaison with the European Commission on securities industry matters and the implementation of the European Community Capital Markets Code of Conduct.

Most of the detailed work of the CSI is done through its committees of which the most important is the Markets Committee. This committee has assumed the role formerly performed by the City Working Party and in addition has the general function of formulating and amending any codes of conduct which may be considered necessary, considering proposed United Kingdom and European Community legislation, and acting as the consultative body about changes in the Stock Exchange requirements for admission to its markets.[75]

---

[74] The CSI has a chairman and deputy chairman, both of whom are appointed by the Governor of the Bank of England. The membership is made up of the chairmen of:
The Accepting Houses Committee
The Association of Investment Trust Companies
The British Insurance Association
The Consultative Committee of Accountancy Bodies
The Committee of London Clearing Bankers
The Confederation of British Industry
The Issuing Houses Association
The Panel on Take-overs and Mergers
The National Association of Pension Funds
The Council of the Stock Exchange
The Unit Trust Association
The Assoction of Licensed Dealers in Securities
and representatives of overseas banks and overseas brokers in London. The Bank of England is also represented and the chairman of the Quotations Committee of the Stock Exchange is a member *ex officio*. Additionally, there are three lay members nominated by the Governor to represent individual investors and the wider public interest.

[75] The CSI's main activities since its establishment have included the drawing-up of draft codes of conduct for dealings in securities and for issuing houses in respect of new issues.

### (4) The Joint Review Body[76]

**1.51**      The Joint Review Body was set up in February 1977 and is charged with the general oversight of all aspects of the supervision including the identification of any potential gaps in the arrangements. Representation is confined to the Bank of England and the Department of Trade and Industry at official level.[77]

It has been observed[78] that in its present form the Joint Review Body is little more than a formalisation of discussions which would have taken place anyway. It has no statutory foundation and, even within the non-statutory framework of regulation, does not have an obvious place in the hierarchy of regulatory agencies, with the CSI not regarding itself as being in any way accountable to it and the Joint Review Body itself not reporting formally to Parliament. Its activities[79] however do have an influence on general policy formulation within the Bank and the Department.

### (5) The Department of Trade and Industry

**1.52**      In addition to fulfilling the general governmental role of ensuring that the regulatory agencies, whether statutory or otherwise, operate and develop in such a way as to be appropriate to meet the needs of market users[80] the Department of Trade and Industry has specific statutory functions under the Prevention of Fraud (Investments) Act 1958 in relation to the licensing of dealers in securities[81] and the distribution of circulars relating to investment in securities.[82]

# FINANCIAL INSTITUTIONS AND MARKETS

**Banks, Banking and the Money Markets**

**1.53**      According to the Wilson Committee[83] bank finance constitutes the single most important source of external funding for companies in the United Kingdom. The

*Banks*      commercial banks, which provide most of this funding, range from vast multi-branch organisations to specialised institutions with a single office. They include those whose orientation is mainly towards domestic business, such as the major

---

[76] See generally the Wilson Committee (Main Report) at paras. 1161 *et seq*. Note also its recommendations (as yet not implemented) at paras. 1111–1119 for the establishment of a similar body with more wide-ranging powers to oversee both the securities and financial markets.

[77] The DTI is represented by the deputy secretary responsible for the securities markets and other City matters, assisted by the under secretary in charge of the Companies Division and by an assistant secretary. The Bank is represented by the Deputy Governor, assisted by the head of department responsible for te securities markets and an adviser.

[78] Wilson Committee (Main Report) at para. 1162.

[79] *i.e.* the discussions.

[80] See above at § 1.39.

[81] Prevention of Fraud (Investments) Act 1958, ss.1–9.

[82] *Ibid*. s.14.

[83] Wilson Committee (Main Report) at paras. 455, 456.

clearing banks,[84] subsidiaries of major international banks with a heavy involvement in the eurocurrency market and which also engage in corporate lending and deposit business in this country, consortium banks,[85] and branches of overseas banks[86] whose presence is designed mainly to provide their parents with access to the London financial markets.

An important role in the financing of corporate enterprise in the United Kingdom is played by the merchant banks and accepting houses.[87] Although substantial lenders in their own right the primary function of these institutions is that of procuring finance through the organisation and underwriting of public issues in the securities markets and (the more especially in the case of accepting houses) through the granting of acceptances,[88] the arranging of eurobond issues,[89] and the management of syndicated credits.[90]

Also involved in the provision of banking services to industry[91] are the finance houses. These institutions have traditionally been primarily involved in the provision of medium-term instalment credit facilities to industry and to private consumers. As the volume of their business has expanded so its nature has become more diverse with some houses offering a range of banking facilities[92] and with many providing leasing[93] and factoring[94] services.

---

[84] The London clearing banks are the dominant force in retail deposit banking in England and Wales. They also play a very substantial part in sterling wholesale deposit and lending business and are also active in international banking. Through their subsidiaries they control most of the retail banking business in Northern Ireland and have substantial shareholdings in the Scottish clearing banks. All the London clearers have merchant and wholesale banking subsidiaries which engage a significant proportion of their business. Several also participate in consortium banks. All are involved through subsidiary or associated companies in instalment credit and leasing business.

[85] Consortium banks are institutions created by international consortia of banks to carry out specialised activities which are international in character. The consortium banks' predominant activity is the provision of foreign currency loans to corporate and public borrowers mostly, though not exclusively, overseas. Consortium banks are active in loan syndications and in the managament or under-writing of international bond issues.

[86] There are currently in excess of 200 overseas banks and their subsidiaries operating in London. While, as a group their business is largely wholesale, some banks whose presence is long-established play an important part in the financing of trade and in domestic banking business. Their facilities available to British companies usually take the form of foreign-currency loans. Overseas banks also compete with accepting houses in the provision of acceptance credit.

[87] All the accepting houses are merchant banks, but not all merchant banks are accepting houses.

[88] See below at §§ 2.60 *et seq.*

[89] See below at §§ 2.47 *et seq.*

[90] See below at §§ 2.53 *et seq.*

[91] The banking activities of some finance houses are such that they have been recognised as banks by the Bank of England and included in the banking statistics.

[92] The Banking Act 1979, Sched. 2, para. 2 provides that an institution may be recognised (by the Bank of England) as a bank if it provides a wide range of banking services (or a highly specialised banking service) covering:
   (a) current and deposit account facilities or the acceptance of funds in the wholesale money markets;
   (b) finance in the form of overdraft or loan facilities or the lending of funds in the wholesale money markets;
   (c) foreign exchange services;
   (d) finance through the medium of bills of exchange and promissory notes together with finance for foreign trade; and
   (e) financial advice or investment management services and facilities for arranging the purchase and sale of securities.

[93] See below at Chapter 3.

[94] See below at Chapter 4.

**1.54**

*Banking Business*

In very general terms the business of banks may be classified according to whether it is retail or wholesale business.

Retail business on the deposit side is primarily concerned with cash withdrawal and money transmission, operations requiring a network of branches and therefore in practice being largely the province of the clearing banks. Retail loan facilities tend to be provided on relatively standard terms (although obviously varying according to the status, nature and creditworthiness of the borrower).

Wholesale business includes the taking of large deposits (at higher rates than are paid on ordinary retail deposits), the making of large loans and the deployment of funds in money market instruments.

While virtually all of the commercial banks engage in some wholesale activities, some (in particular the merchant banks and overseas banks) centre their business on them.[95] However the single most important group of institutions participating in the wholesale money markets are the discount houses.

**1.55**

*The Money Markets*

The "money markets" are the mechanisms through which wholesale (and mainly short-term) funds are channelled from lenders to borrowers. There is no physical market place with transactions being conducted by telephone or telex.

The London money markets are made up of a series of highly integrated groups of financial institutions which facilitate the lending and borrowing of wholesale funds through short-term deposits and negotiable paper. The markets themselves are divided into the discount and parallel markets, the latter being further divided into sterling and eurocurrency markets.[96]

*The discount market*

*Operation of the Discount Market*

The most important activity in the discount market is the weekly Treasury Bill tender[97] which is always underwritten by the discount houses. The market is always prepared to exchange Treasury Bills for cash and cash for Treasury Bills with the commercial banks. In return the banks lend a proportion of their surplus funds to the market at call. If one bank is short of money it calls for funds from the market knowing that the market can probably recoup this outflow from another bank which is in surplus. If there is no surplus cash available the dis-

---

[95] The scale of an individual bank's wholesale business will depend on its capital base and the extent to which it is willing to hold assets of a longer maturity than its liabilities, as well as on its ability to obtain a profitable lending business. The market for wholesale deposits is extremely price-sensitive and minor differentials can lead to substantial flows of funds between institutions.

[96] The discount houses account for most of the business on the discount market and a substantial proportion of parallel market business. Besides the discount houses the other participants in the London money markets are two discount brokers and the money trading departments of a number of banks.

[97] The Treasury Bill tender is the means by which the government borrows short-term funds from the money markets. At the weekly tender the discount houses undertake to apply collectively for all the Bills on offer, thereby enabling the Treasury at all times to meet the expected financial requirements of the following week. Under the arrangement each discount house is obliged to subscribe for an agreed minimum quota. A house may, however, tender for any additional amounts it thinks fit and to decide at what price it will tender.

The non-clearing banks also bid for Treasury Bills but the clearing banks generally buy them in the secondary market where they can also be purchased by institutional, corporate and private investors.

count houses, not keeping large reserves, can go to the Bank of England as lender of last resort to make good this shortage. In such a case the Bank may act neutrally either by "buying out the shortage," normally through the purchase of Treasury or local authority bills or by lending money overnight against the security of Treasury, local authority or eligible commercial bills or short-dated government securities. As an alternative, the Bank sometimes offers indirect help by purchasing Treasury Bills from the clearing banks, thereby putting them in funds which they will generally pass on to the discount houses.

Besides the market in Treasury Bills the discount market undertakes the discounting of commercial bills, that is the purchasing of a bill at its face value less the "discount." The level of the discount in any particular case is dependent on the level of interest rates, the state of the money markets, the standing of the acceptors, the length of time the bill has to run before it falls due and the demand for and supply of such bills.[98]

A third component of the discount market is the "call-money" market. Call money comprises funds which are both secured (its being an essential feature of transactions in the discount market that the sums involved are secured) and either immediately callable or placed overnight.

*The parallel market*

Since the early 1960s a second money market has developed in unsecured monetary instruments, notably inter-bank unsecured deposits[99] and certificates of deposit,[1] but also finance house deposits,[2] inter-company loans,[3] and various

---

[98] See further below at §§ 2.60 *et seq.*

[99] The inter-bank market is the largest of the sterling parallel markets. Deposits are not negotiable or transferable. Sums may be lent on an overnight basis, at call or for a fixed term, the majority of transactions being for periods of under 3 months.

On the short-term eurocurrency markets, banks borrow on an unsecured basis from each other for periods ranging from overnight to as long as five years. Most borrowing is for periods of six months or less.

[1] A Certificate of Deposit (CD) is a negotiable instrument issued by a bank certifying that a specified sum of money has been deposited with it at a fixed or floating rate of interest and that at a stated maturity date the deposit will be repaid with interest by the receiving bank; CDs are issued at par on an interest-to-maturity rather than a discount basis.

The first CDs were in eurocurrency, denominated in U.S. dollars and issued by London banks in 1966. Since then this market has expanded rapidly, both in terms of the value of the funds placed and the currencies in which they are denominated. However the Bank of England will not permit CDs to be denominated in currencies (*e.g.* Deutschmarks and Swiss Francs) the responsible monetary authorities for which are known to be anxious to discourage the use of their currencies in this way.

The first sterling CDs were introduced in 1968 and it has been estimated (Wilson Committee, Appendix III at para. 3.350) that over 100 banks currently issue them in the primary market.

Despite the certification on the document sterling CDs are unsecured paper and not eligible as security for loans or for rediscounting at the Bank of England. Other banks, however, do accept CDs as security for call money.

[2] Deposits are made with finance houses on an overnight basis and for periods of from 3–6 months.

[3] The inter-company market developed in the late 1960s to get around restrictions on bank lending. Rather than depositing with a bank a company with surplus funds was able to lend these directly to another company, often with a bank acting as agent.

local authority instruments.[4] These instruments may be denominated in sterling or in eurocurrency.

The principals in this market are the discount market institutions, the commercial banks and other financial institutions, and commercial and industrial companies. In the main, however, funds are placed through brokers.

### Institutions collecting longer-term funds

**1.56**    A characteristic of institutions engaged in banking or banking-related activities is that their business involves the taking of deposits which are usually highly liquid an using them to make loans or acquire other assets with longer average maturities. In contrast, the institutions in this group have as their most important characteristic the circumstance that funds placed with them are for the most part long-term. Some of these funds are received pursuant to long-term contractual arrangements (as in the case of pension funds and life assurance companies) with the consequence that their flow to the institutions concerned is relatively steady and predictable.

All of the institutions within this group invest in company securities[5] so that individually and as a group they constitute an important source of funds for companies seeking to raise external capital.

### Pension funds and insurance companies

**1.57**    Pension funds are institutions whose function is to secure an accumulation of financial resources to meet future pension liabilities.[6] Funds are built up from contributions paid by employers and, usually, by employees together with income arising from investment of the investment of the assets out of which, ultimately, pensions and other benefits will be paid.

The business of insurance companies is broadly divisible into two classes, namely:

(1)  long-term business, which is predominently life assurance; and
(2)  general business, comprising fire, accident, motor and marine assurance.

Both the operation of pension schemes and conduct of life business involve the accumulation of funds by way of contributions or premiums. Eventually an outflow of funds in the event of a retirement, a death or maturity of a policy will

---

[4] These include short-term local authority loans at call, overnight, at 2 or 7 days notice or for fixed periods of up to 364 days plus 7 days notice.

Local authority bills may be issued for periods of up to 12 months and are generally discountable at the Bank. However, local authority negotiable bonds (for periods of from 1–5 years) do not rank as eligible security at the Bank for loans to the discount market nor as reserve assets for the banking system.

[5] Among others, notably government an other public sector securities.

[6] Funded occupational pension schemes fall into 2 categories, namely:

(1)  self-administered schemes, where the funds are directly invested in various markets; and
(2)  insured schemes, where the funds are invested by, and the risk borne by a life insurance company.

The fund management of self-administered schemes is often sub-contracted to life offices or other fund management specialists.

occur. However, provided that sufficient new business is taken on, the contributions and premiums being received will largely cover current payments and claims with any excess of payments generally being met out of income received on assets held. It follows, therefore, that a pension fund or life office will normally retain its existing assets effectively in perpetuity and is likely to be adding to them regularly. In principle, therefore, it can lend out or otherwise invest its fund on a long-term basis. In consequence it is unsurprising that the pattern of investment by pension funds and life offices shows[7] a heavy preponderance of company securities, over half in he case of pension funds (of which more than 90 per cent. are equities).

General insurance business differs from life business both as to the nature of the contract involved and in the consequencies for the flow of funds to the insurers concerned. Inevitably these differences have implications for the pattern of investment undertaken.

Unlike life policies contracts taken out within the field of general insurance are essentially short-term (usually of a year's duration) with liability to the insurer resulting from insured events occurring within that period. The investment consequence of this is that, of necessity, a substantial proportion of an insurer's technical reserves have to be in a very liquid form.[8] Unsurprisingly, therefore, a much greater proportion of general insurance companies' assets are held in cash or short-term investments.

Nevertheless, general insurance business does involve the payment of premiums on a regular basis with the consequence that some of this income will be available to meet claims so that not all of an insurer's technical reserves need be held in liquid form. Moreover, if new business is continually taken on, many claims can be met out of the new premiums being received so that general insurance companies may retain a fund of assets more or less permanently. As such, general insurance companies are also substantial holders of long-term assets, although the Wilson Committee found that public sector securities were more prominent in their portfolios than was the case with life offices or pension funds. Of the company securities held by general insurance companies almost 85 per cent. were in equities.[9]

**Unit trusts**

Unit trusts are trusts in the legal sense, investors receiving units in proportion to their contributions and thereby acquiring a fractional interest in the assets of the trust and in the income earned by those assets. Unit trusts are "open-ended" in that individual trusts may increase their capital by issuing new units and likewise decrease their capital when investors wish to redeem their investment. Additional securities are purchased to match incoming subscriptions and assets sold to match withdrawals. Investment in a unit trust may be made in a lump sum or under regular payment schemes.[10]

**1.58**

[7] Wilson Committee, Appendix III, Tables 3.44–3.51.
[8] *Ibid.*
[9] Wilson Committee (Main Report) at para. 166.
[10] Regular subscription schemes were introduced in the 1950s and in 1961 life insurance schemes were introduced involving regular subscription to unit trusts.

The investment practices of unit trusts are restricted by two factors, namely:

(1) the stated policy and objective of the fund, whether it is intended to maximise income or capital growth and whether it is intended to concentrate
investment in specific sectors; and

(2) the requirement of the Prevention of Fraud (Investments) Act 1958[11] that
authorised unit trusts limit the scope of their investments to quoted
shares, debentures and government securities.[12]

Most unit trust portfolios consist very largely of equities.

**Investment trust companies**

**1.59**   Unlike unit trusts, investment trust companies are not trusts in the legal sense
but are joint stock companies incorporated under the Companies Acts; many of
them possess a Stock Exchange listing. It follows from this that acquisition of
investment trust company shares does not give an investor a direct interest in the
underlying assets held by the trust and that investment trust company share
prices do not necessarily reflect the value of those underlying assets.

Being joint stock companies funds for investment derive from what has been
subscribed as share and loan capital.

The legislative restrictions imposed on unit trusts with regard to investment
portfolios have no application to investment trust companies; in consequence,
their investment practice is governed almost entirely by the trust's general policy
objectives. Most investment trusts are "general" funds although some concentrate on particular industries or geographical areas. Some seek to maximise long-
term capital growth while others seek to produce a high income; some ("split
level") trusts have a capital structure permitting one class of ordinary shareholder to be entitled to all the income produced with a second class obtaining the
benefit of any capital appreciation.[13]

The bulk of investment trust funds are invested in company securities, mostly
in equities although with some loan stock and preference shares. However a substantial proportion of total investment trust company assets are in overseas
securities.

**Specialised financing agencies**

**1.60**   This group of financial institutions is composed of special agencies set up to
meet the requirements of specific categories of borrower not adequately catered
for elsewhere. These institutions are to be found in both public and private sectors and the proliferation of public sector agencies since 1970 has made them an
important element of the capital market.[14]

---

[11] s.17.
[12] And cash. Prior to the removal of Exchange Controls in 1979 it was common practice for unit
trusts to have substantial foreign currency borrowings under "back-to-back" loans matched with
sterling deposits.
[13] See above at § 1.18.
[14] See below at Chapter 8 for a consideration of the position and role of government agencies as
sources of corporate finance.

The private sector agencies, known statistically as "special finance agencies,"[15] were set up with official support but were financed by banks and other financial institutions or by issuing securiies on the market. Their subsequent funding derives from the same sources with the consequence that the terms on which they make funds available to companies reflects the cost to them of obtaining the funds.

The specialised agencies provide a wide range of financial facilities for business, their common feature being that they are generally prepared to supply finance in situations where the risks may be higher, or the period before a return is obtained longer, than would generally be acceptable to other sources of finance. Many of these agencies supply both equity and loan funding although some were set up to provide loan finance only.

In addition to the agencies prepared to back ventures across the broad spectrum of industrial and commercial activity there are others specialising in particular sectors and types of project. These include the development capital companies which make available venture and development capital to growing unlisted/unquoted companies.[16]

# STIMULATING INVESTMENT IN CORPORATE ENTERPRISE: TAX INCENTIVES

At one time it was not uncommon for local businessmen and others within a **1.61** community to invest in local enterprises whose proprietors were known to them, such investments being made for family, personal or community reasons as well as for purely commercial ones. With time the extent of such participation has declined and as a consequence ceased to represent a source of external finance of any significance. The Wilson Committee[17] suggested that attempts might be made through the medium of the tax system to make such participations more attractive. Accordingly, during the period 1980–1984, a number of tax incentives were introduced in an attempt to stimulate investment in smaller companies.

### Investment reliefs under the general law

While provisions specifically designed to stimulate such investment were noti- **1.62** ceably absent from the tax code the general law of income and capital gains tax did include a small number of provisions affording a small measure of relief to investors which were available in respect of such participations. These were:

---

[15] The more important of these include Investors in Industry and its subsidiaries, the Industrial and Commercial Finnce Corporation, Finance Corporation for Industry, Finance for Shipping; Technical Development Capital; Equity Capital for Industry; the Commonwealth Development Finance Company; the Agricultural Mortgage Corporation and the Scottish Agricultural Securities Corporation.

[16] Some of these have been established for many years. More recently, many more have been set up, often involving joint ventures between banks, insurance companies, pension funds and, in a number of cases, the British Technology Group (formerly the National Enterprise Board) and the Development Agencies.

[17] Wilson Committee (Small Firms) at paras. 43–44.

(a) the standard capital gains tax loss relief;
(b) a relief from capital gains tax in respect of losses incurred on loans made to trading companies; and
(c) relief from income tax in respect of certain interest payments.

### CGT loss relief

**1.63** Under the general law the main relief available in respect of investment losses was (and continues to be) the standard capital gains tax loss relief.[18] This permits realised allowable losses to be set against chargeable gains realised in the same year of assessment and for any such losses unrelieved in this way to be carried forward and set against the chargeable gains of succeeding years.[19] However the relief is not available in respect of all investment losses and in particular is not available in respect of losses incurred on loans except where the loan was made in consideration of the issue by the company of debt securities or, more precisely and in the language of the Capital Gains Tax Act 1979, constitutes a "debt on a security."[20]

On the other hand the relief is available where the investment in a company is in the form of shares, whether acquired by way of subscription or purchase,[21] or in the form of loan stock,[22] again irrespective of the method of acquisition.

### CGT special loss relief[23]

**1.64** The general rule for capital gains tax purposes is that no chargeable gain or allowable loss may result to the original creditor[24] in respect of a disposal of a debt other than a debt on a security.[25] Section 136 of the Capital Gains Tax Act 1979 creates an exception to this rule by providing for a relief to be given in respect of losses incurred on loans made to trading companies.

The qualifications for the granting of the relief are[26]:

(1) that the money lent is used by the borrower wholly for the purposes of a trade carried on by him, not being a trade which consists of or includes the lending of money;
(2) that the borrower is resident in the United Kingdom; and
(3) that the debt created is not a debt on a security.

The relief may be claimed where the outstanding amount of the principal has

---

[18] Capital Gains Tax Act 1979 (hereafter C.G.T.A. 1979) s.4.
[19] Unless the taxpayer was a dealer in securities in which event any loss would almost inevitably be treated as a trading loss.
[20] C.G.T.A. 1979, s.82. See further at §§2.56 *et seq.* for a consideration of what amounts to a debt on a security and related matters.
[21] Or, indeed, by gift.
[22] Loan stock being a "debt on a security."
[23] See further at § s.2.58, below.
[24] Relief is available, however, where the creditor is an assignee of the original debt.
[25] C.G.T.A. 1979, s.134(1).
[26] *Ibid.* s.136(1).

become irrecoverable and where the claimant (the original lender) has not assigned his right to recover that amount.[27]

The benefit of the relief is also available to guarantors in respect of losses incurred through the enforcement of the guarantee.[28]

**Interest relief**

While payments of interest by companies are generally allowable as deduc- **1.65** tions for corporation tax purposes[29] (whether as a business expense or as a change on income) payments of interest by individuals are only allowable as a deduction for income tax purposes if the loan on which the interest is payable was incurred for a qualifying purpose.[30] One such qualifying purpose is the acquisition of an interest in a "close company,"[31] whether that acquisition is by way of subscription for shares or stock or as a result of a purchase from an existing shareholder or stockholder.[32]

More specifically, interest on a loan to an individual is allowable if the loan is applied[33]:

(a) in acquiring any part of the ordinary share capital of a close company; or
(b) in lending money to such a close company which is used wholly and exclusively for the purposes of the company's business[34]; or
(c) in paying off another loan, interest on which would have been allowable had it not been paid off, where the first loan was used for (a) or (b) above.

For the relief to be apply two conditions must be satisfied, namely that:

(1) in the period from the application of the proceeds of the loan to the payment of the interest the borrower has not received any capital from the company; and
(2) when the interest is paid the company continues to be a close company.

Where the borrower has a "material interest"[35] in the company a further condition is imposed, namely that if the company is an investment company no property held by the company is used as a residence by the borrower, save that this further condition does not apply where the borrower has worked for the greater part of his time in the actual management or conduct of the business of the company.[36]

---

[27] *Ibid.* s.136(3). Further, the claimant and the borrower must not have been spouses, or companies within the same group at the time the loan was made or any any subsequent time.
[28] *Ibid.* s.136(4).
[29] See further at §§ 5.25–5.27, below.
[30] F.A. 1972, s.75; F.A. 1974, Sched. 1 paras. 9, 10.
[31] Essentially, an unlisted company resident in the United Kingdom under the control of 5 or fewer participators or any number of participators who are directors—I.C.T.A. 1970, s.282(1). See further at § 5.50, below and notes thereto.
[32] Although obviously only an acquisition by way of subscription will contribute to the company's funds.
[33] F.A. 1974, Sched. 1, para. 9(1).
[34] Or the business of an associated company which is also a close company.
[35] An interest of 5 per cent. or more.
[36] F.A. 1974, Sched. 1, para. 10(1).

Where the borrower does not have a material interest but does possess a shareholding in the company it is required that he shall have worked for the greater part of his time in the actual management or conduct of the business of the company before the interest payable is eligible for relief.[37]

### Investment reliefs under Finance Acts 1980–83

**1.66** Under the general law the only expenditure that was allowable against an individual's income was interest paid on a loan incurred for a qualifying purpose. The most important feature of the reliefs introduced since 1980 are that they permit the sum involved to be relieved against the taxpayer's income.

Since 1980 three separate reliefs have been introduced, albeit that at the present time one of them has been superseded. The reliefs are:

(a) Relief for Losses incurred in respect of Investment in Unquoted Shares;
(b) Relief under the "Business Start-up Scheme"; and
(c) Relief under the "Business Expansion Scheme."

### The loss relief

**1.67** This relief was introduced by section 37 of the Finance Act 1980 to permit a taxpayer to offset losses incurred in respect of certain investments made in companies whose shares do not have a Stock Exchange listing or USM quotation.

The relief is available where the investment in question is disposed of and the disposal gives rise to an allowable loss for capital gains tax purposes. It follows therefore that if no such loss accrues there can be no scope for the operation of this relief. The terms of the relief are framed so that the taxpayer can choose whether to have the loss relieved against his income or chargeable gains. The loss cannot, however, be relieved twice; if section 37 is relied on the right to deduct the amount of the loss from the taxpayer's chargeable gains ceases. In most cases, of course, it will be advantageous to set the loss against income. Nevertheless, investors with little taxable income in a year of assessment may find it advantageous for the loss to be dealt with as capital.[38]

Not all losses that are allowable for captal gains purposes, however, attract the relief. The requirements laid down relate to the nature of the investment giving rise to the loss, the mode of its acquisition and the circumstances of its disposal. More specifically:

---

[37] *Ibid.* para. 10(2).
[38] Note in this respect the provisions of F.A. 1980, 137(2). Where any excess relief accrues this may be carried forward and claimed as a deduction in priority to any loss claim made in that succeeding year, but any loss then remaining unrelieved becomes a capital loss usable only within the capital gains tax framework.

The relief may be claimed against the income of the individual, excluding that of his spouse, if so desired. The relief is given first against earned income, then investment income, then the spouse's earned income and the spouse's investment income.

Relief under F.A. 1980 is given before relief for trading losses set against other income under the provisions of I.C.T.A. 1970, s.168 or F.A. 1978, s.30.

(1) the investment must comprise shares in the company;
(2) the company must be a "qualifying trading company";
(3) the shares must have been subscribed for; and
(4) the disposal must have been by bargain at arms length or other specified transaction.

The relief applies only where the investment is in "shares" in the company. It **1.68** follows therefore that losses incurred in respect of debentures or other loan stock holdings will only be relieved, if at all, under the ordinary capital gains tax rules.

The definition of shares for the purposes of section 37 limits the application of the relief further by stipulating[39] that the shares must consist of "ordinary share capital," a term which excludes preference shares conferring only a fixed-rate dividend without any further entitlement to participate in the profits of the company.

The company in which the investment is made must be a "qualifying trading **1.69** company." To come within this description a company must satisfy two primary conditions, namely:

(1) that none of its shares have been quoted since its incorporation or, if later, during the twelve months prior to subscription of the shares disposed of; and
(2) that it has been resident in the United Kingdom since incorporation.

Additionally the company must possess two other qualifications, namely that—either

(3a) it was a trading company[40] on the date of the disposal of the shares; or
(3b) that it had ceased to be a trading company within three years of the date of disposal and had not within this period been an excluded company, defined[41] as an investment company, a holding company of a non-trading group, or a company carrying on a trade of dealing in shares, securities, land, trades or commodity futures or some other trade carried on other than on a commercial basis with a view to profit;

---

[39] F.A. 1980, s.37(12) and F.A. 1981, s.36(6) both incorporating I.C.T.A. 1970, s.526(5).
[40] F.A. 1980, s.37(2) defines a trading company as a company other than an excluded company (see n.80, below) which is:
    (a) a trading company within the meaning of F.A. 1972, Sched. 16, para. 11; or
    (b) the holding company of a trading group.
"Trading group" means a group the business of whose members, taken together, consists wholly or mainly in the carrying on of a trade or trades. However for the purpose of this definition any trade carried on by a subsidiary which is:
    (i) an excluded company; or
    (ii) not resident in the United Kingdom
is treated as not constituting a trade.
F.A. 1972, Sched. 16, para. 11(1) defines trading company as "any company which exists wholly or mainly for the purpose of carrying on a trade and any other company whose income does not consist wholly or mainly of investment income."
[41] By F.A. 1980, s.37(12).

and either

    (4a)  had been a trading company for a continuous period of six years up to the date of disposal; or

    (4b)  had been a trading company for a shorter continuous period up to that date and had not before the beginning of that period been an excluded company.[42]

**1.70**      For the relief to be available the taxpayer must have "subscribed for" the shares in question, the shares having been issued in consideration of money or money's worth.[43]

It follows from this that:

    (a)  shares received as a result of a bonus issue will not be eligible for relief, although shares received pursuant to a rights issue would seem to qualify; and that

    (b)  shares acquired from another shareholder through a sale and purchase or other transaction will not qualify.[44]

Where the capital of the company has been the subject of a scheme of reconstruction undertaken for bona fide commercial reasons[45] so that the holding subscribed for is now represented by other shares or securities, the relief is preserved so as to be available in respect of any loss arising on a disposal of the new securities.[46]

The disposal giving rise to the loss must be of a specific type to come within the scope of the relief. To qualify the disposal must be either[47]:

    (1)  By way of a bargain at arm's length for full consideration; or

    (2)  By way of a distribution in the course of dissolving or winding up the company; or

    (3)  A deemed disposal[48] on the shares becoming of negligible value.

**1.71**      As originally enacted in the Finance Act 1980 the relief was available only to individuals. However, in the following year it was extended[49] to investment companies satisfying certain conditions. These conditions are that "the company disposing of the shares[50]:

---

[42] F.A. 1980, s.37(5).

[43] *Ibid.* s.37(3).

[44] However, where one spouse has acquired shares by subscription in consideration of money or money's worth and has transferred them to the other spouse (who made the disposal giving rise to the loss) by a transaction *inter vivos* the relief is preserved: F.A. 1980, s.37(4).

[45] The reconstruction must be bona fide. If it is not s.37(8) excludes the relief. See *I.R.C.* v. *Brebner* [1967] 2 A.C. 18, H.L. for a consideration of what constitutes bona fide commercial reasons.

[46] F.A. 1980, s.37(7). Note also that where an investor has built up a holding of shares in the company some of which have been subscribed for (and so qualify for relief) and others which have been acquired otherwise than by subscription and disposes of some shares, the question of whether the shares disposed of form part of the qualifying shares is to be decided on a last-in, first-out basis: F.A. 1980, s.37(9).

[47] *Ibid.* s.37(6).

[48] Under C.G.T.A. 1979, s.22(2).

[49] By F.A. 1981, s.36.

[50] *Ibid.* s.36(1).

(a) is an investment company on the date of the disposal and either:
    (i) has been an investment company for a continuous period of six years ending on that date; or
    (ii) has been an investment company for a shorter continuous period ending on that date and has not before the beginning of that period been a trading company or an excluded company; and
(b) was not associated with, or a member of the same group as, the qualifying trading company at any time in the period beginning with the date when it subscribed for the shares and ending with the date of disposal."[51]

A qualifying investment company may claim for the loss to be offset against either:

(1) income of the accounting period in which the loss was incurred, or one ending within the twelve month period up to the beginning of that accounting period[52];

or

(2) surplus franked investment income[53] in accordance with the provisions of section 524 of the Income and Corporation Taxes Act 1970.[54]

### Relief under the "business start-up scheme"

The Finance Act 1981 contained provisions[55] designed to encourage invest- **1.72** ment by individuals in new businesses by permitting investors to claim relief against income for sums invested in qualifying companies. Under the original terms of the scheme[56] the relief applied to shares issued in the 1981–82, 1982–83 or 1983–84 years of assessment. In 1983 however the scheme was effectively superseded by the somewhat wider "Business Expansion Scheme" and the relief in respect of shares issued in the 1983–84 year of assessment withdrawn.[57]

### Relief under the "business expansion scheme"

The provisions of section 26 of and Schedule 5 to the Finance Act 1983[58] gov- **1.73** ern the investment relief made available to individuals who, directly or via an

---

[51] The effect of para. (b) is to make it impossible for a parent company to set losses on shares subscribed for in its subsidiaries against its income for corporation tax purposes.

[52] Relief is given after relief for an earlier loss but before any deduction for charges on income or expenses of management. The relief is given against income of a later accounting period before that of an earlier accounting period. Where the loss is carried back to the previous twelve months the income arising for that accounting period for which the relief is available is subject to an apportionment and only that apportioned to the period after that time may be used to absorb the relief: F.A. 1981, s.36(3) and (4).

[53] See further at §§ 5.35 and 5.36 and notes thereto.

[54] Should the company elect to do this it must do so within 2 years from the end of the accounting period in which the loss was incurred: F.A. 1981, s.37.

[55] F.A. 1981, ss.52–67 and Scheds. 11 and 12, as amended by F.A. 1982, ss.51–52.

[56] F.A. 1981, s.52(9).

[57] F.A. 1983, s.26(2).

[58] As amended by F.A. 1984, s.37.

approved investment fund, subscribe for shares in qualifying companies in the period of the operation of the scheme.

Under the terms of the scheme a qualifying individual may claim as a deduction from his total income the amount subscribed for eligible shares in the year of assessment in which the investment was made. The maximum investment is £40,000 per year[59] with a minimum investment of £500 per year.[60]

The scheme applies to shares in qualifying companies issued between April 6, 1983 and April 5, 1987.[61]

The availability of the relief is subject to a number of conditions as to:

    (a) the eligibility of claimants;
    (b) the size and nature of the investment;
    (c) the companies in which investment may be made;
    (d) the business carried on by such companies.

**(1) Eligible claimants**

**1.74**    The relief is available to individuals (but not to companies) who satisfy the following conditions, namely:

    (1) That the individual is resident and ordinarily resident in the United Kingdom at the time when the shares are issued;
    (2) That he acquires his holding by subscription[62] on his own behalf; and
    (3) That he is not "connected with" the company during "the relevant period."[63]

An individual is connected with the company if he, or an associate of his,[64] is:

    (1) an employee of the company or of a partner of the company; or
    (2) a partner of the company; or

---

[59] F.A. 1983, Sched. 5, para. 3.
[60] Unless made via an approved (by the Revenue) investment fund.
[61] F.A. 1983, s.26(1).
[62] The relief only applies to shares obtained as a result of a subscription to the issue. Shares acquired from another shareholder through a sale and purchase or other transaction will not attract relief: F.A. 1983, Sched. 5, para. 4(1).
    Special rules apply to husband and wife to the effect that in general disposals can take place *inter se* while they are living together without the relief being lost. Where however there is a subsequent disposal by the transferee spouse to a third party the relief may be wthdrawn. Furthermore if there is a subsequent divorce or the parties cease living together the investment is deemed to have been disposed of by the transferor at market value or, if greater, for the actual consideration received, resulting in a possible reduction or withdrawal of the relief: F.A. 1983 Sched. 5, para. 12.
[63] The "relevant period" means the period beginning with the incorporation of the company (or, if the company was incorporated more than two years before the date on which the shares were issued, beginning two years before that date) and ending five years after the issue of the shares: F.A. 1983, Sched. 5, para. 2(7)(*a*).
[64] *Ibid.* para. 4(2), incorporating F.A. 1981, s.54(2). Associate is defined as including husband, wife, parent and grandparent, child or grandchild (but not brother or sister) F.A. 1981, s.67(1) and I.C.T.A. 1970, s.303(3).

(3) a director[65] of the company or of another company which is a partner of the company; or

(4) directly or indirectly in possession of or entitled to acquire more than 30 per cent. of:

    (A) the issued ordinary share capital of the company; or

    (B) the loan capital[66] and issued share capital of the company; or

    (C) the voting power of the company[67];

    (D) the assets of the company in a winding up[68] or

(5) in control[69] of the company.

Additionally, an individual is also treated as connected with a company with which he would not otherwise be connected if he subscribes for shares as part of an arrangement under which another person subscribes for shares in a different company with which any party to the arrangement is connected.[70]

## (2) Size and nature of the investment

The relief is available in respect of subscriptions for "eligible shares" in a **1.75** qualifying company issued by the company for the purpose of raising money for a qualifying trade which is being carried on by it or which it intends to carry on.[71]

---

[65] This however does not include a director who neither receives nor is entitled to any payment from the company during the five years beginning with the date on which the shares were issued. For this purpose "payment" does not include (F.A. 1981, s.54(3)):

    (a) any payment or reimbursement of travelling or other expenses wholly, exclusively and necessarily incurred by him or his associate for the performance of his duties as a director of the company;

    (b) any interest which represents no more than a reasonable commercial return on money lent to the company;

    (c) any dividend or other distribtion which does not exceed a normal return on the investment;

    (d) any payment for the supply of goods which does not exceed their market value; and

    (e) any reasonable and necessary remuneration which:

        (i) is paid for services rendered to the company in the course of a trade or profession (not being secretarial or managerial services or services of a kind provided by the company itself); and

        (ii) is taken into account in computing the profits or gains of the trade or profession [of the recipient].

[66] For the purposes of this provision "loan capital" includes any debt incurred by the company.

    (a) for any money borrowed or capital assets acquired by the company; or

    (b) the loan capital and issued share capital of the company; or

    (c) the consideration the value of which to the company was (at the time the debt was incurred substantially less than the amount of the debt (including any premium thereon) F.A. 1981, s.54(5).

However, no debt incurred by the company in overdrawing an account with a person carrying on a business of banking is to be treated as loan capital of the company if the debt arose in the ordinary course of that business. F.A. 1983, Sched. 5, para. 4(3).

[67] F.A. 1981, s.54(4).

[68] *Ibid.* s.54(6).

[69] "Control, in relation to a body corporate, means the power of a person to secure:

    (a) by means of the holding of shares or the possession of voting power in or in relation to that or any other body corporate; or

    (b) by virtue of any powers conferred by the articles of association or other document regulating that or any other body corporate,

that the affairs of the first-mentioned body corporate are conducted in accordance with the wishes of that person" I.C.T.A. 1970, s.534.

[70] F.A. 1983, Sched. 5, para.4(4).

[71] *Ibid.* para. 2(1).

"Eligible shares" are defined as new ordinary shares which, throughout the period of five years beginning with the date on which they are issued, carry no present or future preferential right to dividends or to a company's assets on its winding-up and no present or future preferential right to be redeemed.[72]

The minimum investment attracting the relief is £500 in any year of assessment; relief continues to be attracted to the extent to which investment in any year of assessment does not exceed £40,000.[73] The investment may be made directly or through the medium of an approved[74] investment fund. A number of such funds ha ve been set up by merchant banks and others to channel Business Expansion Scheme investment into appropriate companies.

### (3) "Qualifying companies"

**1.76**   To qualify for relief the investment must be in a company that is a "qualifying company." A company is a qualifying company if it is incorporated in the United Kingdom and complies with the following requirements[75]:

   (a) It must, throughout the relevant period,[76] be an unquoted company which is resident in the United Kingdom and not resident elsewhere.[77] Companies whose shares have a quotation on the Unlisted Securities Market are not regarded as unquoted for the purposes of these provisions and so are not qualifying companies for the purposes of the relief. In contrast, companies whose shares are traded on an "Over-the-Counter" market are regarded as unquoted and so may be qualifying companies.

and

   (b) It must exist wholly, or substantially wholly, for the purpose of carrying on wholly or mainly in the United Kingdom one or more qualifying trades[78]; or

   (c) It must be a company whose business consists wholly of[79]:
      (i) the holding of shares or securities of, or the making of loans to, one or more qualifying subsidiaries of the company; or

---

[72] *Ibid.* para. 2(2).

[73] *Ibid.* para. 3.

[74] See para. 19 for the provisions governing subscriptions made via nominees and approved funds.

[75] *Ibid.* para. 5(1).

[76] The "relevant period" in this context means (*ibid.* para. 2(7)(*b*)) the period beginning with the date on which the shares were issued and ending either three years after that date or, where the company was not at that date carrying on a qualifying trade, three years after the date on which it subsequently began to carry on such a trade.

[77] *Ibid.* para. 5(2).

[78] *Ibid.* para. 5(2)(*a*). Note that a qualifying trade may be carried on through one or more "qualifying subsidiaries." Para. 17 requires that such subsidiaries
   (1) have been incorporated in the United Kingdom;
   (2) satisfy the requirements of para. 5(2)(*a*);
   (3) satisfy the requirements of F.A. 1981, s.65(2)—that the subsidiary be under the total and sole control of the qualifying company which must hold all the issued shares and possess all the voting rights.
There must not be in existence any arrangements which could cause this conditions to cease to be satisfied.

[79] *Ibid.* para. 5(2)(*b*).

(ii) both the holding of such shares or securities, or the making of such loans and the carrying on wholly or mainly in the United Kingdom of one or more such qualifying trades.[80]

and

(d) Its share capital does not include at any time during the relevant period[81] any issued shares that are not fully paid up.[82]

If a company is wound up or dissolved within the relevant period[83] it automatically ceases to be a qualifying company.[84] However, if it is shown that that winding up or dissolution is for bona fide commercial reasons and is not part of a tax avoidance scheme,[85] and the company's net assets, if any, are distributed to its members or dealt with as bona vacantia before the end of the relevant period or, in the case of a winding up, the end (if later) of three years from the commencement of the winding up,[86] the company will not be regarded as having ceased to be a qualifying company.

A company is disqualified from being a qualifying company if:

(1) it controls (or together with another person connected with it[87] controls) another company or is under the control of another company (or of another company and any person connected wih that other company)[88]; or

(2) it is a 51 per cent. subsidiary of another company or itself has a 51 per cent. subsidiary[89]; or

(3) its trade is connected with the trade of another person in the manner specified in paragraph 5(8) of Schedule 5 to the Finance Act 1983.[90]

## (4) Qualifying trades

For a business of the company to constitute a "qualifying trade" it must, during the relevant period, be conducted on a commercial basis and with a view to  **1.77**

---

[80] See above at note 78.
[81] See above at note 76.
[82] F.A. 1983, Sched. 5, para. 5(6).
[83] Se above at note 76.
[84] F.A. 1983, Sched. 5, para.5(4).
[85] *Ibid.* para. 5(5)(*a*).
[86] *Ibid.* para. 5(5)(*b*).
[87] See above at § 1.74 and notes thereto.
[88] F.A. 1983, Sched. 5, para.5(7)(*a*).
[89] *Ibid.* para. 5(7)(*b*). Note that the disqualifications mentioned in para.5(7)(*a*) and (*b*) do not apply to qualifying subsidiaries.
[90] This occurs where, after April 5, 1983, an individual acquires a controlling interest in the company's trade and
    (1) at any time in the period beginning two years before and ending three years after the date on which the shares were issued or, if later, the date on which the company began to carry on the trade (F.A. 1983, Sched. 5, para. 10) that individual has, or has had, a controlling interest in another trade; and
    (2) the trade carried on by the company, or a substantial part of it,—
        (i) is concerned with the same or similar types of property or parts thereof or provides the same or similar services or facilities as the other trade; or
        (ii) serves substantially the same or similar outlets or markets as the other trade.

the realisation of profits[91] and must not at any time during the relevant period[92] consist to any substantial extent of[93]:

(1) dealing in commodities, shares, securities, land or futures; or

(2) dealing in goods otherwise than in the course of an ordinary trade or wholesale or retail distribution[94]; or

(3) banking, insurance, money-lending, debt-factoring, high-purchase financing or other financial activities; or

(4) leasing (including letting ships on charter or other assets on hire) or receiving royalties or licence fees[95]; or

(5) providing legal or accountancy services; or

(6) providing services for any trade carried on by another person which consists to any substantial extent of activities within paras. 1–5 above and in which a controlling interest is held by a person who has a controlling interest in the company[96];

Farming was specifically excluded from the list of qualifying trades by the Finance Act 1984.[97] The 1985 Finance Act contains provisions intended to extend this list to include companies engaged in research and development. Such inclusion is intended to apply to shares issued by such companies after April 5, 1985. In contrast the 1985 Act also contains provisions to exclude property development from the activities qualifying for relief under the Scheme.

**Withdrawal or reduction of relief**

1.78    No relief is given until the company has carried on the qualifying trade for four months. If the company has not begun trading when the shares are issued it must begin to carry on the trade within two years after the date of such issue.[98]

   If the conditions for the granting of the relief cease to be satisfied within the

---

[91] F.A. 1983, Sched. 5, para. 6(3).

[92] See above at § 1.76 n.76.

[93] F.A. 1983, Sched. 5, para. 6(2), incorporating F.A. 1981, s.56(2).

[94] See F.A. 1981, Sched. 11 for details of what are regarded as indications that the trade is such an ordinary trade, and Sched. 12 for details of what are regarded as indications to the contrary.

[95] This does not apply to royalties and licence fees in respect of films received by companies engaged throughout the relevant period in the production of films—F.A. 1984, s.37 (applicable in respect of issues post March 13, 1984).

[96] For the purposes of the qualifications a person is treated as having a controlling interest in a trade:

   (a) in the case of a trade carried on by a company if:

      (i) he controls the company; or

      (ii) the company is a close company and he or an associate of his is a director of the company and the beneficial owner of, or able directly or through the medium of other companies or by any other indirect means to control, more than 30 per cent. of the ordinary share capital of the company; or

      (iii) not less than half of the trade could be regarded (see I.C.T.A., s. 253(2)) as belonging to him;

   (b) in any other case, if he is entitled to not less than half of the assets used for, or the income arising from, the trade: F.A. 1981, s.56(8).

   In deciding whether a person has a controlling interest the rights and powers of an associate are treated as being attributed to the person.

[97] F.A. 1983, Sched. 5, para. 6(2).

[98] *Ibid.* para. 2(4).

relevant period[99] the relief is withdrawn.[1] Equally, if the investor disposes of his holding in whole or in part otherwise than by bargain at arms' length the relief is withdrawn entirely in respect of the shares allocated.[2]

Where relief has been given in respect of an investment that relief may be reduced (rather than withdrawn) in three circumstances. These are:

(a) where shares or stock from the holding have been disposed of by way of a bargain at arms' length. In such a case the relief is reduced by the amount or value of the consideration received.[3]

(b) where the investor has received "value" from the company within the relevant period the relief is reduced by the amount of that value.[4]

*Reduction of the Relief (i) Sale of Shares at Arms' Length (ii) Receipts of "Value"*

An investor is treated as receiving value from the company where the company—

(A) repays, redeems or repurchases any of its share capital or securities belonging to the investor or makes any payment to him for giving up his right to any of the company's share capital or any security on its cancellation or extinguishment;

(B) repays any debt owed to the investor other than a debt which was incurred by the company:

(1) on or after the date on which he subscribed for the shares in respect of which the relief is claimed; and

(2) otherwise than in consideration of the existinguishment of a debt incurred before that date;

(C) makes to the investor any payment for giving up his right to any debt other than an ordinary trade debt[5] on its extinguishment.[6]

In these cases the value received by the investor for the purpose of the reduction in the relief is the amount receivable by him or, if greater, the market value of the shares securities or debt in question.[7]

An investor is likewise treated as receiving value from the company where the company:

(D) releases or waives any liability of the investor to the company or discharges, or undertakes to discharge, any liability of his to a third per-

---

[99] See above at note 63.

[1] F.A. 1983, Sched. 5, para. 2(6).

[2] Where part only of the holding is alienated and the holding comprises shares acquired at different times the disposals are matched against acquisitions on a First-in, First-Out basis (*ibid.* para. 7(2A). Where an investor's holding comprises shares some of which have attracted relief and others which have not and a part disposal is made that disposal is to be regarded as relating to the shares which attracted the relief before those which did not. *Ibid.* para. 7(2).

[3] *Ibid.* para. 7(1)(*b*).

[4] *Ibid.* para. 8 incorporating F.A. 1981, s.58.

[5] Defined as "any debt for goods supplied in the ordinary course of a trade or business where the credit given does not exceed six months and is not longer than that normally given to customers of the person carrying on the trade or business: F.A. 1981, s.58(8).

[6] Besides ordinary trade debts also included within this category are debts by way of payments due in respect of items mentioned in s.54(3)(*a*) (reimbursement for expenses, etc.) or (*e*) (remuneration, etc.)

[7] F.A. 1981, s.58(4)(*a*).

son[8]; in such a case the amount of the value received is the amount of the liability[9];

(E) makes a loan or an advance to the investor[10]: in such a case the amount of the value received is the amount of the loan or advance[11];

(F) provides a benefit or facility for the investor[12] in such a case the amount of the value received is the cost to the company or providing the benefit or facility less any consideration given for it by the investor[13];

(G) transfer an asset to the investor for no consideration or for consideration less than its market value or acquires an asset from him for consideration exceeding its market value[14]: in such a case the amount of the value received is the difference between the market value of the asset and the consideration, if any, given for it[15];

(H) makes to him any other payment[16] except a payment of a kind mentioned in paras. (A)–(E) above or a payment in discharge of an ordinary trade debt[17]: in such a case the amount of value received is the amount of the payment[18];

(I) is wound up or dissolved and the investor receives in respect of ordinary shares held by him any payment or asset[19]; in such a case the amount of value received is the amount of the payment or, as the case may be, the value of the asset.[20]

(c) where, within the relevant period, the company[21]:

*(iii) Repayment, Redemption or Repurchase of Shares*

(A) repays, redeems or repurchases any of its share capital belonging to any member other than the investor or any other individual whose relief is thereby reduced; or

(B) makes to such member any payment for giving up his rights to any of the company's share capital or its cancellation or extinguishment.

In such cases the amount of relief to which the investor is entitled is reduced by the amount receivable or by the nominal value of the share capital, if greater.

**1.79**    Where the relief has not been withdrawn special rules apply to cover the pos-

---

[8] *Ibid.* s.58(2)(*d*).
[9] *Ibid.* s.58(4)(*b*).
[10] *Ibid.* s.58(2)(*e*).
[11] *Ibid.* s.58(4)(*c*).
[12] *Ibid.* s.58(2)(*f*).
[13] *Ibid.* s.58(4)(*d*).
[14] *Ibid.* s.58(2)(*g*).
[15] *Ibid.* s.58(4)(*e*).
[16] Payment or transfer are defined for the purpose of thes provisions as including payments or transfers made indirectly to an individual or for his benefit: s.58(9)(*a*). Individual includes an associate: s.58(9)(*b*).
[17] *Ibid.* s.58(2)(*h*).
[18] *Ibid.* s.58(4)(*f*).
[19] *Ibid.* s.58(3).
[20] *Ibid.* s.58(4)(*g*).
[21] *Ibid.* s.59(2).

ition arising on a subsequent disposal of the shares by the investor. Paragraph 16 of Schedule 5 to the Finance Act 1983 provides that in making the computation as to profit or loss the sums allowable as deductions from the consideration received for the shares are to be determined without regard to the relief save that where the amount of such deductions exceeds the consideration (so that an allowable loss would result) they are to be reduced by an amount equal to the amount of the relief or the excess whichever is the lesser.[22]

---

[22] Para.16(1). Note that this rule does not apply to disposals as between husband and wife. Where an individual's holding of shares contains some which carry relief and others which do not if a reorganisation of the company's capital should occur the shares qualifying for relief are preserved as a separate holding for capital gains purposes through the reorganisation: *ibid.* para. 16(3).

# 2. Borrowing

In the context of corporate finance the term "borrowing" is used to refer to two sets of obligations entered into by a company. First, and more precisely, a company's borrowing means its debt obligations incurred as a result of loans taken out, negotiable instruments issued or debt securities outstanding. Used in this sense "borrowing" serves to distinguish these obligations from those attaching to the company's equity or preference capital.

"Borrowing" however is also raised in a wider sense to comprehend not only funds raised through the creation of debt but also capital-raising through the issue of equity and preference securities. In this wider sense "borrowing" is a composite term denoting a company's obligations on capital account.

**2.01**

*Meaning of Borrowing*

The form a company's borrowing takes should, in principle at least, relate to the purpose for which the funds are being obtained. So long-term funds would normally be associated with the financing of long-term investments such as premises or plant and equipment whereas short-term funds would be used to finance the carrying of stocks or perhaps to acquire financial assets. In practice, however, long-term funds are commonly used in relation to the continuous circulation of short-term assets, while companies with very high rates of growth might utilise short-term funds in part to finance long-term assets.[1] Certainly over the past 10 to 15 years the high cost of long-term funds[2] has had the effect of encouraging companies to borrow from the banks at short or medium-term even though this has involved the mismatching of the periods of maturity of assets and liabilities. Many larger companies have adopted systems of "overall financial programming" whereby neither particular forms of finance nor specific capital-raising operations were directly related to a specific end use.[3]

**2.02**

*Matching Borrowing and Investment*

Short-term finance is almost always in the form of debt and is provided mostly by way of bank advances under overdraft arrangements. Such facilities permit a considerable degree of flexibility, "allowing unforeseen shortfalls in internal cash flow to be offset, the timing of raising more permanent outside funds to be adjusted to suit the convenience of the borrower and to take advantage of changing market conditions, and a proportion of short-term assets—particularly working capital requirements—to be financed."[4] Bank overdrafts are also frequently used as a source of finance of last resort when other forms of finance are temporarily unavailable or too expensive.

**2.03**

*Short-term Funding*

---

[1] See generally Thomas *The Financing of British Industry* 1918–76 (1978) at p.16.
[2] High cost being represented by high long-term interest rates and low equity prices. See Wilson Committee (Main Report) at para. 509.
[3] Wilson Committee (Main Report) at para. 509.
[4] *Ibid.* at para. 530.

**2.04**    It is sometimes possible to obtain special short-term facilities tailor-made to suit the particular needs of individual companies. Among these has been the provision of "cocktails" of a variety of foreign-currency loans bearing different maturity dates. Over the past few years, however, the raising of loans in foreign countries has been regarded as something to be undertaken with some caution because of exchange-rate fluctuation uncertainties.[5]

**2.05**    Debt is also the form in which medium-term finance is raised, sometimes by way of a "hard core" element in overdraft finance to fund "permanent" working
*Medium-term* capital, but increasingly, since the mid-1970s, through medium-term variable—
*Funding* rate loans, sometimes linked to the funding of specific projects.[6] The increasing use of this form of finance results from a modification of policy by the banks seeking to replace the "hard core" element in overdrafts by loan arrangements providing a greater degree of permanence and a higher rate of interest.

**2.06**    Long-term funds may be procured either by the issue of debt or of equity securities, what is appropriate or available being determined by the state and
*Long-term* character of the company. "In order to borrow funds by the issue of debt and
*Funding* have a reasonable hope of a full subscription a company would need to be of a certain size, maturity and have an acceptable record of past performance, with some assurance that future earnings would be adequate to maintain interest payments. Debt, therefore, is suitable for companies with stable earnings patterns and which also have assets by way of security for such debenture borrowing. Equity issues on the other hand are not so demanding in terms of prerequisites. A company can seek equity capital without possessing an equivalent base of assets or security, or a history of past dividend payments; the main asset that is being offered is that of future profit-earning capacity. It is thus a suitable means of financing small quantities of fixed assets and particularly where profit performance is variable so that dividends can be passed over without threat of bankruptcy proceedings."[7]

**2.07**    Almost inevitably the primary factor[8] in making a decision as between equity or debt funding is that of cost: more specifically, which form is, in real terms,
*Equity or Debt* cheaper. The process of calculating the real cost involves taking into account the
*Cost* effects of taxation and inflation on interest and dividend yields.
    In principle the cost of equity is the dividend yield at any given time plus an allowance for expected future dividend growth, a factor which may be expected
*(1) Direct Cost* to result in a rising share price. As dividend levels are likely to vary with performance the nominal cost cannot be calculated in advance with much precision. Debt at fixed rates of interest is, in contrast, capable of a precise calculation in nominal terms. Loans carrying variable interest rates of course involve uncertainties of a comparable kind to equities.

---

[5] Additionally, commercial bills enjoyed a considerable popularity during the 1960s and 1970s, especially when other forms of borrowing were restricted during periodic credit squeezes.
[6] Wilson Committee (Main Report) at para. 529.
[7] Thomas, *op. cit.* at p.4.
[8] Wilson Committee (Main Report) at para. 508, 509.

The broad effect of the tax structure is to favour financing through the issue of debt securities rather than equity, loan interest being an allowable deduction against corporate profits[9] whereas the payment of dividends attracts liability to advance corporation tax.[10] Moreover, in periods of inflation this relief on interest has the further effect of becoming, in part, a relief on the repayment of capital, the point being that during such periods interest rates tend to be higher than at other times[11] so as to make some allowance for the loss of value of capital through inflation. *(2) Taxation*

Indeed, it is essential to bring the inflation factor into any cost calculation for its own sake as well as for its effect on the true tax burden. Where a company is in a position of being able to make a choice as to the form of its funding on the basis of cost, inflation will have the dual effect of reducing the time cost but of increasing the nominal cost through the higher interest rates referred to above. While, on the one hand, this has the effect that in real terms the debt is being repaid from the very first year, on the other, the consequentially higher rates of interest impose a severe burden on a company's cash flow position.[12] Bringing these factors together the cost calculation in respect of debt financing involves estimates as to the level of inflation and its consequential effects, as to the real value of the debt when it falls due for repayment and, where appropriate, on the levels of floating rates of interest. *(3) Inflation*

A second factor affecting the form in which long-term finance is obtained is that of the company's gearing ratio, that is the relationship between its indebtedness and its equity capital ("capital gearing") and the relationship between interest charges and available earnings ("income gearing" or "interest cover"). In practice lenders generally determine the limits of a company's borrowing capacity by reference to this relationship. According to the Wilson Committee[13] most companies adopt self-imposed target ratios that are much tighter than those applied by lenders, apparently for three main reasons: **2.08**

*Gearing Ratio*

### (a) Provision of a margin

By adopting a stricter ratio a company effectively provides itself with a margin, so permitting the possibility of an extension of borrowing[14] should this be necessary. This in turn provides companies with a degree of flexibility in that unexpected temporary cash flows can be absorbed without risking damage to the business itself.

---

[9] I.C.T.A. 1970, s.248(3).
[10] F.A. 1972, s.84.
[11] Although the current comparatively low rates of inflation in Britain have not resulted in much of a fall in rates in real terms.
[12] Evidence to the Wilson Committee (Main Report) at para. 508, indicated that over the decade 1970–1980 many companies found that the level of long-term fixed interest rates had become prohibitively expensive.
[13] Wilson Committee (Main Report) at paras. 519, 520.
[14] Used here in the narrower sense. See above, at § 2.01.

### (b) Independence and security

Low gearing (that is, where a company has only a small proportion of its financing in the form of external loans) ensures a degree of independence and security for a company. If profits, and with them interest cover, fall, the effect may be to bring into operation a loan covenant rendering the loan subject to immediate repayment. Such a situation would, at best, compel the company to renegotiate with its lender; at worst the company could be faced with having to find a buyer for its business or with going into liquidation.

### (c) Credit rating

A company's gearing affects its credit rating which in turn has a direct effect on the cost of loan finance available to it and some indirect effect on its share price. Companies wishing to maintain the highest possible credit rating in international markets require interest cover of at least four times, or even more for loans raised in the United States capital market.

**2.09**

*Risk*

A third factor affecting the form in which long-term finance may be obtained is that of risk. A company whose assets are readily realisable will need only a low proportion of its capital as equity, in contrast to a company operating in a specialised sector and having as its principal assets, say, special-purpose machinery to make a new product which would become virtually worthless should the product fail. In general it can be said that the more specialised the investment, the longer its terms and the higher the risk of loss, the greater will be the need for equity.

The risk factor militates in favour of equity funding in this way: if interest cover is ample, the company being relatively lowly geared, lenders tend to accept more readily the company's judgment of risks, whereas if interest cover is thin lenders become more obviously concerned about the negative aspects of their position, in that if the firm fails they will stand to lose their investment while if it does exceptionally well their return will be limited to the payments of interest stipulated for. An equity participation, on the other hand, does at least hold out the prospect of rich pickings if the venture succeeds.[15]

# LOANS

### Loans and borrowing

**2.10**

*Loans*

A loan is a contract under which one party advances or otherwise makes available to another a sum of money in consideration of a promise, express or implied, to repay the sum involved, whether or not at a premium and with or without interest.[16]

While the making of a loan agreement necessarily gives rise to a debtor/credi-

---

[15] Wilson Committee (Main Report) at para. 517.
[16] *Chitty on Contracts* (25th ed., 1983) at para. 3157.

tor relationship as between the parties not all forms of indebtedness constitute loans or borrowing. The provision of customer credit is one such example. Where a company buys goods or services on account for settlement at a given date it has been held that such an arrangement does not amount to borrowing money from the seller[17] while the account is unpaid. In *Re H.P.C. Productions Ltd.*[18] Plowman J. cited as an example of this the case of a stockbroker buying securities for a client's account, the cost of the transaction causing the account to become overdrawn. An in *Potts* v. *I.R.C.*[19] the issue concerned an account between the taxpayer and a company he controlled. At the relevant time the account was in debit, the question being whether this state of affairs amounted to a loan. It was held by the House of Lords that although the relationship between the taxpayer and the company was one of debtor and creditor it was not also one of borrower and lender.

*Accounts in Debit*

In such cases the courts were seeking to give effect to what they conceived to be the intention of the parties. While trading relationships give rise to debts those debts will not amount to loans unless the business of the parties involves the granting of loans. Thus, for example, when a company's bank account is overdrawn, given the nature of banking, the debt created is legally a loan[20] and the relationship between the company and its bankers one of borrower and lender.

*Overdrafts*

Even where the business of the parties involves the granting of loans however, it does not follow that credit facilities extended amount to loans. So, for example, an ordinary hire-purchase transaction does not amount to a loan of money. The important elements in credit transactions are their legal nature and form. In most cases[21] the two will go together, the form of the transaction demonstrating its legal nature. Economic effect is not generally relevant.[22] Thus while a hire-purchase transaction and a credit-sale have similar economic affects their legal natures are very different, with the latter transaction only being to a loan.

*Purchases on Credit*

The importance of form can be illustrated by contrasting the cases of *I.R.C.* v. *Port of London Authority*[23] and *Spargo's Case.*[24] In the former case the taxpayer issued loan stock as consideration for the acquisition of certain property. It was held by the House of Lords that although the issue of the stock constituted the Authority debtors of the vendors the transaction was not one of borrowing but

---

[17] *Chow Yoong Hong* v. *Choong Fah Rubber Manufactory* [1962] A.C. 209 at p.216, P.C.

[18] [1962] 1 Ch. 466 at p.472.

[19] [1951] A.C. 443, H.L.

[20] *Brooks & Co.* v. *Blackburn Benefit Building Society* (1884) 9 App. Cas. 857 H.L.; (affirming *Blackburn Building Society* v. *Cunliffe, Brooks & Co.* (1882) 22 Ch. D. 61, C.A.); *Chambers* v. *Manchester and Milford Rly. Co.* (1864) 5 B. & S. 588; *Looker* v. *Wrigley* (1882) 9 Q.B.D. 397; *Blackburn & District Benefit Building Society* v. *Cunliffe, Brooks & Co.* (1885) 29 Ch. D. 902, C.A.

[21] Except where it is shown that the form of the transaction is a front, intended to hide the real nature of the transaction.

[22] *British Rly. Traffic and Electric Co.* v. *Kahn* [1921] W.N. 52; *Automobile & General Finance Corpn.* v. *Morris* (1920) 73 S.J. 451; *Olds Discount Co.* v. *Cohen* [1938] 3 All E.R. 281n; *Trade Promotion Trust* v. *Young* (1940) 84 S.J. 640; *Premior Ltd.* v. *Shaw Bros* [1964] 1 W.L.R. 978. See also *Alec Lobb (Garages) Ltd.* v. *Total Oil G.B. Ltd.* [1985] 1 All E.R. 303.

[23] [1923] A.C. 507, H.L.

[24] (1873) L.R. 8 Ch. 407.

of sale and purchase. In *Spargo's Case,* however, it was held that where the parties made a contract indicating an intention that the purchaser company should acquire property at a stipulated price, and that the company should then borrow the sum required from the vendor, the borrowing being secured by an issue of debentures, the arrangements constituted a loan to the company.

*Sale and Leaseback/ purchase*

In *Yorkshire Railway Wagon Co.* v. *Maclure*[25] the question arose as to whether a sale and lease-purchase transaction amounted to a loan. In this case the company, having exhausted its borrowing powers, entered into a transaction whereby it sold part of its equipment but entered into a collateral agreement with the purchaser allowing it to resume possession of the said equipment on hire at a rental fixed at a level sufficient to repay the purchase money plus interest. The agreement contained a provision for repurchase for a nominal consideration at the end of the term. The arrangements were held not to amount to a loan.[26]

*Repayments*

An essential characteristic of a loan is that the sum borrowed must at some time be repaid. In most cases the loan agreement will specify a repayment date or lay down a schedule by reference to which repayments are to be made. Where, however, money is lent without any stipulation as to the time for repayment the position would seem to be that a present debt is created which is generally repayable at once without any prior demand.[27] An exception is made in respect of overdrawn bank accounts where a prior demand must be made.[28] The requirement for repayment has given rise to problems where the transaction is not bilateral but tripartite. Can it "properly be said that, if A, out of his own money, pays a sum to B for and at the request of C, A has paid the sum by way of loan, and by way of loan to C?"[29] In *Re H.P.C. Productions Ltd.*[30] the case concerned a claim to offset certain moneys owed by a Swiss company to X's estate against obligations under certain transactions whereby payments in foreign currency were made by the company at X's request to third parties outside the United Kingdom in respect of deals made for X's benefit. Plowman J. held that the arrangements in question did not give rise to a lender/borrower relationship between the parties and so did not amount to a loan. An important factor in arriving at his conclusion was the lack of accountability of the parties. It would seem that had the recipient of the funds been legally accountable for them to the person at whose request payment was made the transaction would have amounted to a loan.

**2.11**   The question of whether a transaction amounts to or involves a loan is of importance in relation to a company's legal capacity to raise finance. The prin-

---

[25] (1882) 21 Ch. D. 309, C.A.; *cf. Manchester, Sheffield and Lincolnshire Rly. Co.* v. *North Central Wagon Co.* (1888) 13 App. Cas. 554 H.L. and *Alec Lobb (Garages) Ltd.* v. *Total Oil G.B. Ltd., supra.*

[26] But see *Coveney* v. *Persse Ltd.* [1910] 1 I.R. 194, C.A. where it was held that there was a borrowing where the transaction comprised a sale with a collateral agreement providing for redemption by the vendor of goods comprised in the sale.

[27] *Norton* v. *Ellam* (1837) 2 M. & W. 461; *Re George* (1890) 4 Ch. D. 627. See further *Chitty On Contracts* at paras. 3165 *et seq.*

[28] *Joachimson* v. *Swiss Banking Corp.* [1921] 3 K.B. 110, C.A.

[29] *Potts* v. *I.R.C.* [1951] A.C. 443, at p.464 *per* Lord MacDermott.

[30] [1962] 1 Ch. 466.

ciple is that companies governed by the provisions of the Companies Acts have no inherent borrowing powers.[31] Power to borrow must generally be expressly written into a company's constitution and the almost invariable practice is to provide for such an express power in the company's memorandum of association.

An exception to this rule applies in the case of trading or commercial[32] companies which are regarded as having implied powers to borrow up to a reasonable amount, on either a secured or unsecured basis,[33] for the purposes of their businesses.[34] While apparently useful this implied power is in practice too indefinite to be relied on given the problems not infrequently encountered of deciding whether a company is or is not a trading company, whether the borrowing is required for the purposes of the company's business and what is a reasonable amount.

Just as a company's constitution will normally confer the power to borrow so also it will often impose a limit on that power. If a company's memorandum expressly or impliedly limits its borrowing powers any borrowing beyond that limit is *ultra vires* and therefore void,[35] and any security given in respect of the excess is also void.[36] It is possible to amend the memorandum by special resolution to increase or remove the limits unless the memorandum itself specifically prohibits such an alteration.[37] Where the memorandum imposes no limit on the power to borrow but a limitation is imposed by the articles it has been held in an Irish case[38] that a general meeting of the company cannot sanction any borrowing in excess of that limit. However, there would appear to be nothing to prevent the limits being amended or reviewed by special resolution.[39]

---

[31] On borrowing powers of companies see generally *Palmer* at Chapter 42.

[32] *Re Hamilton's Windsor Steelworks Co., ex parte Pitman and Edwards* (1879) 12 Ch.D. 707; *Bank of Australasia* v. *Breillat* (1847) 6 Moo. P.C.C. 152 (banking co.); *Australian Auxiliary Steam Clipper Co.* v. *Mounsey* (1858) 4 D. & J. 733 (shipping co.); *Bryan* v. *Metropolitan Saloon Omnibus Co.* (1858) 3 de G. & J. 123 (bus co.); *Re Patent File Co., ex parte Birmingham Banking Co.* (1870) 6 Ch. App. 83 at pp.86, 88. (file-making co.); *Gibbs and Weims Case* (1870) L.R. 10 Eq. 312 (insurance co.); *General Auction Estate and Monetary Co.* v. *Smith* [1891] 3 Ch. 432 (auction co. whose objects included the discounting of commercial bills).

[33] Provided such borrowing or giving security is not expressly prohibited.

[34] No power of borrowing is implied when the company is not a trading or commercial undertaking Re *Badger, Mansell* v. *Viscount Cobham* [1905] 1 Ch. 568.

[35] And cannot be subsequently ratified, even if the borrowing limits are increased. See *Ashbury Railway Carriage and Iron Co.* v. *Riche* (1875) L.R. 7 H.L. 653; *Fountaine* v. *Carmarthen Rly. Co.* (1848) L.R. 5 Eq. 314 (security void also). See also *Re Companies Acts, ex parte Watson* (1888) 21 Q.B.D. 301. Note that the Companies Acts do not impose any limits on the amounts which companies may borrow. Where the memorandum or articles of association restrict the borrowing powers of directors and the directors purport to borrow in excess of their powers but not in excess of the companies borrowing powers (*e.g.* where articles prevent directors borrowing in excess of a secified sum except with the sanction of the shareholders) the borrowing may be ratified by the company in general meeting, an ordinary resolution being sufficient for the purpose. See *Grant* v. *United Kingdom Switchback Railways Co.* (1888) 40 Ch.D. 135, C.A.

[36] *Fountaine* v. *Carmarthen Rly. Co. supra.*

[37] Companies Act 1985 s. 17.

[38] *Re Bansha Woollen Mills Co.* (1887) 21 L.R. Ir. 181. It is probable that the company could in any event sanction the excess borrowing in such a case. See *Grant* v. *United Kingdom Switchback Railways Co.* (1888) 40 Ch.D. 135.

[39] *Grant* v. *United Kingdom Switchback Railways Co., supra; cf; Re Olderfleet Shipbuilding and Engineering Co.* [1922] 1 I.R. 26.

If a company borrows in circumstances which render the borrowing *ultra vires* the principle is that no debt arises either at law or in equity. This has the consequence that the lender cannot recover the money lent in any personal action.

*Ultra Vires Borrowing*

Lending institutions therefore, as a matter of course, almost always insist on sight of a company's memorandum and articles of association before committing themselves to granting loan facilities.[40] The inability to recover in an action *in personam*[41] does not however mean that a lender is totally without remedies in relation to an *ultra vires* borrowing. He may be entitled to a tracing order, or in the case of a mixed fund, to a declaration of charge if the money lent can be traced to any property held by the company or by a third party having no better equity.[42] If, and to the extent that, the funds cannot be specifically traced but have contributed to an increase in the company's total assets, the whole available fund will be treated as belonging to the lenders and to the company *pari passu* according to the amounts respectively provided by them.[43]

*Lenders' Remedies*

Quite separately from the right to trace, a lender may also recover in that he is entitled to be subrogated to those creditors of the company who have been paid out of the loan and to recover the amounts so paid against the company.[44]

## Loan facilities

**2.12**     Loan facilities will be available primarily from the commercial banks, but also from finance houses and insurance companies. These may take a number of forms:

### (a) Overdrafts

An overdraft facility is essentially a line of credit made available by a bank to its customer through the normal use of the customer's current account. Such a facility may come into being as a result of an agreement expressly entered into or arising by implication[45] from the circumstances. Such an agreement must be supported by consideration although it has been held that an implied term as to the

*Nature of an Overdraft*

---

[40] In spite of the Companies Act 1985, s. 35 which puts a lender or other person dealing with a company in good faith in the position of not being bound to inquire about the company's capacity to contract with him. The point is that if a lender suspects or is aware of information which might cause him to suspect that the company's borrowing may be *ultra vires* the element of good faith will not be present.

[41] *Re National Permanent Benefit Building Society, ex parte Williamson* (1869) 5 Ch. App. 309; *Blackburn Building Society* v. *Cunliffe, Brooks & Co.* (1882) 22 Ch.D. 61, C.A. (affd. *sub. nom. Brooks & Co.* v. *Blackburn Benefit Building Society* (1884) 9 App. Cas. 857, H.L.); *Baroness Wenlock* v. *River Dee Co.* (1885) 10 App. Cas. 354, H.L.: *Baroness Wenlock* v. *River Dee Co.* (1887) 19 Q.B.D. 155, C.A.; *Sinclair* v. *Brougham* [1914] AC 398 HL.

[42] *Sinclair* v. *Brougham, supra.*; *Re Diplock* [1948] Ch. 465 C.A., at p.532 (affd. on other grounds *sub nom. Ministry of Health* v. *Simpson* [1951] A.C. 251, H.L.

[43] *Sinclair* v. *Brougham, supra; Re Diplock, supra* at pp. 526–532.

[44] *Att.-Gen* v. *De Winton* [1906] Ch. 106; *Baroness Wenlock* v. *River Dee Co.* (1887) 19 Q.B.D. 155 at p.165; *Sinclair* v. *Brougham, supra.* Note that this right is not be confined to debts existing at the time of the loan/overdraft. The test is whether the company's liabilities are increased by the loan, *Baroness Wenlock Case, supra.*

[45] *Armfield* v. *London and Westminster Bank* (1883) Cab. & El. 170; *Ritchie* v. *Clydesdale Bank* (1886) 13 R. 866.

payment of interest would be sufficient consideration.[46] In practice a company's overdraft will have been expressly negotiated with agreed limits as to time and amount.

From a borrower's point of view the use of an overdraft as a means of financing has many advantages. It is informal, the documentation often comprising no more than a letter from the bank confirming previously agreed terms; it is flexible in that within the agreed limits the company is able to draw on the account as and when it requires to do so, thereby giving the company rather than the bank control over how much is drawn down; and it is relatively cheap, interest being charged only on the daily outstanding balance.

It is, however, an inherent feature of overdraft facilities that overdrawn balances are repayable on demand.[47] While it is not the practice of the banks to exercise this right where the company is conducting its business in a proper and *Disadvantages* businesslike manner its existence, nevertheless, does involve the company in a degree of vulnerability. Where, for example, government monetary policy imposes restrictions on bank lending, overdrafts are an obvious primary target.

Interest is charged on the overdrawn balances at a rate normally expressed as a margin over the bank's base rate. This margin, and therefore the actual rate charged, will differ according to the nature and size of the company's business, according to whether and if so what, security is available and according to what terms, if any, have been agreed as to repayment.

### (b) Short-term loans

A short-term loan is one taken out for a specified period of up to three years on terms requiring repayment at or by the end of the period, usually in practice according to an agreed repayment schedule. While monthly scheduled repayments tend to be most commonly encountered (especially in short-term loans from the clearing banks) it is the practice to frame repayment schedules to suit company cash-flow patterns where this is more convenient.

Short term loans are less flexible than overdrafts in that they are normally made subject to express conditions as to the use to which the funds advanced may be put and as to drawings. For example, it is not uncommon for drawings on *Short-term* loan accounts to be permitted only on production of specified documentary evi- *Loans and* dence (as in the case of stage payments made during a construction project).[48] *Overdrafts* On the other hand, short-term loans do not possess the inherent characteristic of overdrafts that the outstanding balance is repayable on demand. However, it is common practice for the loan agreement to contain a condition to the effect that should terms of the said agreement be infringed, notice may be given requiring immediate repayment.[49]

This form of financing is thought by the banks to be appropriate to fund

---

[46] *Fleming* v. *Bank of New Zealand* [1900] A.C. 577, P.C.
[47] Unless an express term as to a period of notice has been agreed.
[48] Thus a loan to finance a building project prior to the receipt of long-term funds will often necessitate the production of architects' certificates supporting the stage payments to be made.
[49] In some doubtful cases banks have extended this so as to be able to require repayment on demand should the circumstances appear to them to warrant it.

investment by companies which appear to have resources available for the progressive reduction of the loan during a two-to-three year period or alternatively to provide bridging finance for a period between the purchase of an asset and a corresponding sale.[50]

Security, where available, will normally be required although the nature of the security (whether for example, by way of a charge over company property or in the form of guarantee from the directors, or both) will depend on the circumstances of the case.

As with overdrafts the rates of interest charged differ according to the purpose of the loan and the status of the customer and are geared to the bank's base rate. As with overdrafts an arrangement fee is often required in addition to interest.

### (c) Medium-term loans

The use of medium-term loan finance has increased markedly during the last decade, largely because of two factors:

*Growth in Medium-term Loan Finance*

(1) the policy of the banks to convert the "hard core" element of overdrafts that is permanently taken up into the fixed term contractual loans; and
(2) the creation of special facilities to assist with financing the development of small businesses.

*Overdraft Conversion*

Conversion of overdrafts has advantages for the banks in that it has enabled them to charge the higher interest rates that are appropriate to term lending and it had provided them, through the fixed repayment schedules, with greater certainty. An additional factor has been the difficulties which arise from time to time in relation to compliance with monetary control requirements caused by uncertainty about the extent to which agreed but unutilised overdraft facilities would be drawn upon. It was felt that the fixed repayment schedules of term lending made it easier to reduce the aggregate level of lending wihout the ill-will generated by a general calling-in of overdrafts or reduction in overdraft limits.[51]

*Medium-term Project Loans*

Standard medium-term loans are available in sterling or foreign currencies on a variable-rate basis. Interest rates are normally limited to the London Inter-Bank Offered Rate,[52] interest being charged on the outstanding balance. As with short-term loans repayment schedules can be tailored to individual circumstances and so, for example may be arranged to match the cash flow from a particular project. Similar flexibility can be shown wih regard to security, which, if taken, may also be limited to a particular project rather than to the business as a whole. While the medium-term loans may be offered on an unsecured basis the existence and extent of any security will be reflected in the interest rate charged.

Most medium-term loan agreements contain covenants designed to protect the lender's interests by requiring periodic information as to the company's trading position and providing for repayment if forecasts are not met and if repayments or interest payments are not made. Business development loans for small companies are offered by all of the clearing banks and many finance houses

---

[50] As for example where the new premises are purchased prior to the sale of the existing ones.
[51] Wilson Committee (Main Report) at para. 799.
[52] Sometimes one finds fixed-rate medium term loans.

under one label or another. They provide up to £100,000 over a period of from one to five years (and in some cases up to ten years) for working capital, the acquisition of plant, machinery or vehicles, the acquisition or extension of business premises or for the purchase of a business itself. The interest rate charged in respect of such loans is generally fixed at the outset with the total interest for the borrowing calculated for the whole period and added to the principal. Repayment of the resulting sum is then made by periodic (usually monthly) equal instalments over the period of the loan.

### (d) Long-term loans

By the early 1980s the raising of long-term loan capital from the institutions had become comparatively rare. The Wilson Committee[53] recorded that from 1963 to 1972 companies obtained 15 per cent. of their total external funds by means of industrial debentures and unsecured loan stocks, generally with terms of at least 20 years, while since 1974 the market had virtually dried up with net redemptions in several years.[54] In 1983 there was something of a revival with large public issues of unsecured loan stock by some of the London clearing banks but there has been little since to indicate a genuine revival.[54a] It remains to be seen what, if any, effect the "deep discount" bond provisions of the Finance Act 1984 will have on this situation.

*Deficiencies in the Supply of Long-term Loan Finance*

At the root of the problem has been the period of high inflation and volatile interest rates experienced over the 1970s and early 1980s. However, other factors seem to have been involved as well.

In the first place the very nature of the commitment involved makes long-term lending *per se* unattractive to the banks. Every financial institution faces the task of prudential balance sheet management—the maintenance, relative to the nature of its liabilities, of an appropriate mix between long-term assets (which generally carry a higher return) and short-term, more liquid assets. The problem for the banks and other deposit-taking institutions is that their deposits are generally short-term.[55] While their non-overdraft finance is generally provided for longer periods, clearly the longer the period the greater the element of risk. Nevertheless, while the banks may not be in the market for the provision of such finance they are potentially capable (especially the merchant banks) of procuring it, the obvious sources being the longer-term savings institutions such as the insurance companies or pension funds. The problem here is the matching of the length of commitment with the nature of the investment. For commitments extending beyond 10 to 12 years many institutions are looking more for an equity investment, especially if the company involved is small or medium-sized. It may be that, ultimately the only source of long-term funding is the securities markets.

Perhaps the principal difficulty has been that there is no longer much of an

---

[53] Wilson Committee (Main Report) at para. 809.

[54] This covers the whole spectrum of long term lending including both institutional and securities market loans.

[54a] But note the issue of perpetual floating rate notes made by the London clearing banks in early 1985.

[55] Wilson Committee (Main Report) at para. 150.

area where the needs of long-term borrowers can be satisfied on terms acceptable to would-be long-term lenders. The Wilson Committee recognised the dormancy of the long-term fixed interest market but was pessimistic about any possibility of improvement,[56] the main problem being "uncertainty about what the real interest rate will turn out to be. Potential borrowers do not want to be exposed to excessive interest rates in relation to the world about them because of an unexpected fall in the rate of inflation. Lenders with liabilities in real terms do not wish to lend at what turns out to be a negative real rate and therefore have to hedge against an unexpected rise. Risk aversion on both sides prevents agreement being reached on an appropriate nominal rate, even though the chances are that the real rate which lenders would be prepared to accept would be lower than that which companies are prepared to pay."[57]

One answer might be in extending the use of floating rate obligations from short and medium-term "notes"[58] to long-term debt since this would diminish the risk of capital loss attaching to fixed rate securities. Whether, however, companies would be prepared to submit to the long-term restrictions and conditions attaching to a security whose cost might escalate to unacceptable levels is doubtful.

For the smaller company the prospect of long-term loan finance from the institutions seems remote and from the securities markets, out of the question. For the medium-sized company likewise, except possibly as part of a package designed to prepare for flotation at a future date, although in such an event the debt element of the package is likely to be convertible into equity at some stage, or else only medium-term. The best prospects for long-term loan finance lie with the larger companies, although in such cases the securities markets rather than the institutions are likely to be the suppliers.

### Loan agreements

**2.13**

*Contents of Loan Agreements*

Loan agreements may be constituted with varying degrees of formality according to the nature, size and length of the facility being provided. An overdraft, for example, will often be agreed orally and evidenced simply by a letter from the company's bankers confirming the limit permitted. Fixed-term loans however are almost invariably made by reference to a formal document setting out in detail the conditions under which the funds are being advanced and the obligations of the borrower in connection therewith. Some types of loan are made on basically standard terms[59] so that the loan agreement is contained in a (more-or-less) standard form document, while others are individually constructed to take account of the circumstances of the particular companies concerned, with the loan agreement being specially drawn up on that basis. In considering the contents of loan agreements it is convenient to divide the subject matter as follows:

[56] The banks, it should be emphasised, state that they are always prepared to listen to any reasonable proposition; and indeed in relation to the financing of the North Sea explotation have been prepared to make long-term investments of that nature. Wilson Committee (Main Report) para. 152.
[57] Wilson Committee (Main Report) para. 810.
[58] As indeed has happened. See above at n.54a.
[59] See above at § 2.12.

(a) Extent of the loan facility;
(b) Purpose;
(c) Interest;
(d) Repayment;
(e) Security;
(f) Creditor-protection covenants;
(g) Borrowing limits.

Special considerations apply to international loan agreements.

### Extent of the loan facility

If the loan facility is provided in the form of an overdraft the extent of the facility will simply be the agreed overdraft limit. Within that limit it is generally the case that a company will be able to draw funds at the times and in the amounts of its choosing. Indeed this flexibility (along with comparative cheapness) is the principal attraction of overdrafts. Where, however, a company is in difficulties it is often the case that restrictions will be placed on the use that can be made of the facility. A typical restriction is that drawings above a specified level require the prior approval of the bank: in extreme cases such approval may be required for any drawing.

*2.14*

*Overdrafts*

Where the facility is in the form of a term loan the amount advanced will obviously be the amount agreed. Sometimes, and especially in the case of loans to larger companies or where the size of the loan is not large judged against the size of the company's business, this sum is made available in its entirety: sometimes it is made available in tranches over a period of months (or perhaps years). In cases where the purpose of the loan is to provide finance for a specified project it is normal practice for the full amount of the facility to be made available in tranches subject to the condition that the next tranche will be advanced only on submission and approval of appropriate documentary evidence.

*Term Loans*

Loan facilities for general business development are sometimes made available subject to satisfaction of conditions as to profit growth. For example, an initial facility of £100,000 may be granted (either in one payment or in tranches) in the first year with an undertaking to make available a further £150,000 in the following year if profit targets for the first year are attained.

### Purpose

The loan agreement will normally specify the purpose for which funds are being advanced. That purpose may be of a general nature such as the financing of working capital, stocks, plant and machinery for its existing business. Or it may be more specific such as the acquisition of an additional business or new premises. Where the money is lent for a specific purpose and that purpose fails the lender may have remedies *in personam* and *in rem*.

*2.15*

The normal remedy for failure to meet the obligation to repay the loan in accordance with the terms of the agreement is a personal action against the borrower for the money. However, failure of a specified purpose for which the money was lent may entitle the lender to bring an action *in rem* for the recovery

*Actions in Rem*

of the money itself.[60] Such a remedy will be of especial importance where the debtor company has failed with heavy liabilities, since, in the absence of security, an action *in personam* would be unlikely to procure repayment in full. In *Quistclose Investments Ltd.* v. *Rolls Razor Ltd.*[61] it was held that for such a right *in rem* to arise and be enforceable in an insolvency it was sufficient to show that the funds advanced had been lent on condition that they should be applied for a specific purpose. If the funds had not been so applied so that the purpose failed and a resulting trust arose in favour of the lender.

## Interest

**2.16**

*General Rules on the Charging of Interest*

It is a general rule of English law that, except in special cases,[62] interest is not payable on a debt or loan in the absence of an express term[63] in the loan agreement or a course of dealing between the parties or custom to that effect.[64] In most cases concerned with corporate finance express provision will have been made but in the exceptional case where such provision has been omitted the lender will have to show that it has been the common practice between the parties for interest to be charged, as for example in *Re Anglesey*[65] where it shown that in the past the debtor had paid interest on similar accounts without objection, or that payment of interest arises out of a custom or usage of a particular trade or business of whih the transaction in question formed a part.[66] The customs and usages of banking have been held sufficient to permit the charging of interest at a reasonable rate on overdrafts[67] without the necessity for express agreement.

Where interest is chargeable the charge is made, in the absence of an express term or custom to the contrary,[68] on the basis of simple rather than compound

---

[60] *Re Nanwa Gold Mines Ltd.* [1955] 1 W.L.R. 1080.

[61] [1968] Ch. 540 C.A., affd. [1970] A.C. 567, H.L.

[62] The general rule is a principle of common law. The special cases are equitable exceptions which provide for interest to be payable:

    (i) on a mortgage debt even though the deed is silent as to interest; *Mendl* v. *Smith* (1943) 112 L.J. Ch. 279; *Petre* v. *Duncombe* (1851) 20 L.J. B. 242; *Re Fox, Walker & Co.* (1880) 15 Ch. D. 40.

    (ii) in respect of a guarantor who has paid the creditor (to be indemnified by the debtor): *Re Fox, Walker & Co.* (1880) 15 Ch.D. 400.

    (iii) in relation to a sale or other disposition of land which is specifically enforceable: *Birch* v. *Joy* (1852) 3 H.L.C. 565; *International Rly.* v. *Niagara Parks Commission* [1941] A.C. 328, P.C.; *Re Priestley's Contract* [1947] Ch. 769; *Inglewood Pulp Co.* v. *New Brunswick Electric Power Commission* [1928] A.C. 492 (statutory expropriation).

[63] *Carlton* v. *Bragg* (1812) 15 East 419; *Chalis* v. *Duke of York* (1806) 6 Esp. 45.

[64] *Re Gosman* (1881) 17 Ch. D. 771; *London Chatham and Dover Railway* v. *South Eastern Railway* [1893] A.C. 429, H.L.

[65] [1901] 2 Ch. 548; See also *Great Western Insurance Co.* v. *Cunliffe* (1874) L.R. 9 Ch. 525; *Re Duncan & Co.* [1905] 1 Ch. 307.

[66] *Ikin* v. *Bradley* (1818) 8 Taunt. 250.

[67] *Crosskill* v. *Bower, Bower* v. *Turner* (1863) 32 L.J. Ch. 540 at p.544; *Gwyn* v. *Godby* (1812) 4 Taunt. 346.

[68] *Fergusson* v. *Fyffe* (1841) 8 Cl. & F. 121 at p.140; *Williamson* v. *Williamson* (1869) L.R. 7 Eq. 542.

interest. However, it has been held that banking practice is sufficient to justify the periodic addition of interest to the amount advanced, thereby in effect obtaining compound interest.[69]

The loan agreement will specify the rate at which interest is to be charged and the time when the interest charged is due to be paid. Where the lender is a person or body other than the company's bankers (and in some instances,[70] even in the case of advances by them) the agreement may stipulate the method of payment.[71]

*Rate of interest*

Since the Usury Laws Repeal Act 1954 there has been no statutory control[72] over the rate of interest that may be agreed by the parties.[73] As a matter of practice it would appear that small companies tend to be charged higher rates[74] than larger ones and that unsecured loans command higher rates than when security is provided to compensate for the greater degree of risk. Insofar as rates differ as between lenders those charged by finance houses tend to be higher than those charged by the banks.

A loan agreement may provide for the rate of interest charged to be fixed at the time of the facility being taken up or variable throughout the period of its use. Overdrafts have traditionally been on a variable-rate basis and inceasingly the practice is for short-term and medium-term loans to be made on this basis also, the actual rate charged being geared to the clearing banks' or finance houses base rates or the London Inter-Bank Rate.[75] Long-term loans have traditionally been arranged on a fixed rate basis although there is currently a movement towards floating rates in this category also.

*Payment of interest*

The amount of interest payable for a loan facility, and in some instances the true rate of interest, are closely bound up with the rules and practices governing payment.

Banking practice in respect of overdraft interest provides for a "constructive" rather than an actual payment, the borrower's current account being debited at regular intervals, traditionally half-yearly (but occasionally, and increasingly,

---

[69] *I.R.C.* v. *Holder* [1931] 2 K.B. 81, C.A. (affd. on other grounds *sub. nom. Holder* v. *I.R.C.* [1932] A.C. 624, H.L.); *Paton* v. *I.R.C.* [1938] A.C. 341 H.L. The right to charge compound interest is based on acquiescence. However, it has been suggested (Paget, *Law of Banking* 8th ed. p.133) that the practice is now so well settled that it could probably be supported without proof of acquiescence.

[70] Where, for example, the debtor company has several accounts with its bankers.

[71] *e.g.* by bankers' draft at a specified office by a specified date.

[72] Not even under the Counter Inflation Acts of the 1970s.

[73] But interest in excess of 5 per cent. is on liquidation of the debtor company deferred until all other debts have been paid in full, *Re Theo Garvin Ltd.* [1969] 1 Ch. 624.

[74] Wilson Committee (Small Companies) at p.23 suggests a margin of up to 2 per cent. over rates charged to larger companies.

[75] LIBOR.

quarterly) with the amount of interest due.[76] The amount debited is the gross amount of interest due without deduction of tax, the debtor company paying the interest being entitled to tax relief on the amount paid.[77] In *Paton* v. *I.R.C.*[78] the House of Lords held that where the interest charge is added to existing indebtedness the interest is not "paid" as such. The point is that in such a case or in a case where, as a result of the interest debit, the current account becomes overdrawn the effect is to add the interest to the principal and in consequence cause it to lose its quality of interest and to become capital.[79]

Traditionally the practice in respect of term loans has been for the agreement to provide for interest to be paid half-yearly in arrears on fixed dates. In the case of long-term and some medium-term loans where the principal is repayable on maturity this still tends to be the case. Increasingly, however, medium-term and short-term loans are granted subject to conditions requiring repayment of the principal by instalments over the period of the agreement. In such cases the periodic (quarterly and often monthly) "repayments" are calculated so as to include an element of interest.[80] That interest element, more especially if the loan is at a variable-rate, is often calculated on a reducing-balance basis. In some cases, however, interest under fixed-rate loan agreements is charged throughout the entire period of the agreement on the full amount advanced without making allowance for the repayments of principal made during that period in accordance with the agreed repayments schedule. The effect of such provisions is to increase the true rate of interest charged to a level in excess of the nominal rate provided for in the agreement.[81]

Interest under term loan agreements is paid gross without deduction of tax, the company paying the interest being entitled to tax relief in respect of such payments.

**Repayment**

**2.18**

*Overdrafts*

It has already been mentioned[82] that under the general law money lent without stipulation as to the time for repayment causes a present debt to be created which is generally repayable at once and wihout any prior demand.[83] An exception to this principle however applies to debts embodied in bank accounts and has the effect that such debts only become repayable on demand.[84] Bank overdrafts therefore, in the absence of a stipulation to be contrary in the conditions governing the provision of the facility, are repayable on demand.

Term loans, by their very nature, will have some provision for repayment

---

[76] *I.R.C.* v. *Holder* [1931] 2 K.B. 81, C.A.
[77] For tax deductibility of interest see below at §§ 5.07 *et seq.*
[78] [1938] A.C. 341, H.L.
[79] *I.R.C.* v. *Holder, supra.*
[80] Some packages provide for "interest holidays" during the first two years of the agreement.
[81] The provisions of the Consumer Credit Act 1974 requiring publication of Actual Percentage Rates (APR) in respect of finance for personal consumers have no application to corporate finance.
[82] At § 2.10, above.
[83] *Norton* v. *Ellam* (1837) 2 M. & W. 461; *Atterbury* v. *Jarvie* (1887) 2 H. & N. 114 at p.120; *Re George* (1890) 44 Ch. D. 627.
[84] *Joachimson* v. *Swiss Bank Corporation* [1921] 3 K.B. 110 C.A.

since in the absence of stipulations to the contrary repayment will fall due on
maturity, that is at the end of the term. The normal practice is for term-loan     *Term Loans*
agreements to contain specific sets of provisions as to repayments. These provisions:

(1) specify the repayment date as being at the end of the term or, alterna-
    tively, set out a schedule by reference to which the repayments are to be
    made;
(2) set out the circumstances in which the date or dates for repayments can be
    brought forward at the instance of the lender; and, in certain cases,
(3) permit accelerated repayment at the instance of the borrower.

Stipulations providing for the acceleration of repayments at the instance of the
lender are either default provisions, considered at § 2.35, below or provisions
otherwise designed to protect the lender's interest. These are considered at
§ 2.36, below. With the increased use of variable-rate term loans provisions permitting accelerated repayment at the instance of the borrower have become
comparatively rare. Borrowers in a sufficiently strong bargaining position have
sought to include such provisions in fixed-rate agreements with a view to taking
advantage of periods of lower interest rates, should these occur during the currency of the loan, to refinance the borrowing on more favourable terms.

Occasionally a loan agreement will stipulate for the amount borrowed to be     **2.19**
repaid with the addition of a premium, generally where the lender is a private
individual rather than an institution or other undertaking in the business of providing finance. The object[85] of such an exercise is to obtain a part of the return
on the loan in capital rather than income form, thereby providing a means of
reducing the amount of income tax that would otherwise be payable. In *Lomax
v. Peter Dixon and Sons Ltd.*[86] the Court of Appeal held that a premium would
be treated for tax purposes as interest if the loan agreement failed to provide for
the payment of interest at all, or, if it did, failed to provide for the payment of
interest at a commercial rate.

As far as the company is concerned premiums present few problems except
possibly in connection with borrowing limits imposed by the memorandum or
articles, any borrowing being measured against the limits by reference to the
amount of the principal plus premiums[87] rather than the amount of the principal
alone.

## Security

Most, indeed probably all, of a company's indebtedness to banks and other     **2.20**
financial institutions is likely to be secured, especially if such borrowing has or is

---

[85] Premiums are sometimes encountered in connection with default clauses, lenders stipulating for an
   additional payment if a default occurs. Such a clause has been consistently held to be a penal
   nature and therefore void, *Protector Endowment Loan and Annuity Co. Ltd.* v. *Grice* (1880) 5
   Q.B.D. 592.
[86] [1943] K.B. 671, C.A.
[87] *Rowell & Son* v. *C.I.R.* [1897] Q.B. 194.

likely to have any degree of permanence. Equally, any private investor (or the proprietor) introducing loan capital into a company is almost certain to insist on some measure of security. Certainly in respect of companies seeking loan finance the existence and quality of available security are important factors in decisions whether to lend and, if so, how much and at what rate of interest.

**2.21**

*Guarantees*

It is often the case that in addition to formal security lenders will require the obligations under a loan agreement to be backed by the guarantee of some third party. For example loans for small companies are frequently required to be guaranteed by the directors and/or proprietors. Likewise parents or groups of companies frequently guarantee the loans of their subsidiaries.[88] In cases where guarantees are required by lenders the credit of the guarantor will sometimes be the basis for the whole loan transaction.

**2.22**  The object of taking a guarantee is to provide for a second source of repayment should the principal debtor prove to be unable to meet its obligations. It is unsurprising therefore that documents of guarantee usually:

(a) seek to put the guarantor under the same obligations as the principal debtor[89]: and

(b) seek to provide immediate recourse to the guarantor in the event of a default.

Guarantees are normally given at the time the loan agreement is signed. Sometimes however they are given subsequently in which event it is important to ensure that the consideration for the guarantee is good.[90] While the consideration given does not of necessity have to be expressly stated in the guarantee document the normal practice[91] is for it to be so stated. Where it is so stated fulfilment of the consideration is regarded as a condition precedent to the incurring of liability by the guarantor.

**2.23**  Guarantees are frequently expressed to be "continuing." This description is normally inserted to avoid the consequence of the rule in *Clayton's Case*[92] whereby the liability of a guarantor may be reduced by payments in by the prin-

---

[88] Thus, for example, loans raised through the local subsidiary of a multinational group in the country in which it (*i.e.* the subsidiary) is resident will normally require to be backed by a guarantee from the parent. See generally in relation to international guarantees Wood, *The Law and Practice of International Finance* (1980) at Chapter 13.

[89] With the consequences that guarantee documents frequently contain provisions that would have been found in a loan agreement with a guarantor had the guarantor been the direct borrower. These include:

    (i) Covenants (*e.g.* negative pledge clauses; *pari passu* clauses; supply of information clauses, etc.)

    (ii) Representations and warranties;

    (iii) Grossing-up clauses;

    (iv) Provision for payments to be made free of tax, etc.

[90] If a guarantee is given subsequent to the agreement of the lender to waive a default of the borrower, to extend the time for payments in return for a guarantee or to treat a condition precedent as satisfied, such can constitute good consideration. See further Wood *op. cit.* at para. 13.3(2).

[91] Wood, *op. cit.* at para. 13.3(2).

[92] (1810) 1 Mer.572.

cipal debtor leaving subsequent drawings on the loan facility unprotected, as for example in the case of a guarantee given in respect of an overdraft which, if not stated to be a continuing guarantee, would be extinguished by repayments of the overdraft leaving further advances up to the overdraft limit without guarantee cover.

Where a guarantee is enforced the guarantors become liable to make the payments due under the guarantee. In such a case the guarantors become entitled by subrogation the rights of the lender and may in consequence obtain the benefit (if any remains) of any formal security given by the company.[93]  **2.24**

If a company has the power to borrow it will have have the power, subject to any limitations specified in its memorandum of articles, to secure any borrowing it might make.[94] Subject to any such limitations that security may comprise present and future assets[95] of whatever nature, present and future income and any uncalled share capital.[96] In *Re Pyle*,[97] however, Cotton L.J. suggested that a mortgage to a shareholder of the calls on his own shares would not be valid as being in reality a set-off.  **2.25**

It is not necessary for the security to be given at the time the loan is made.[98] Indeed, when a company's borrowing requirements increase beyond the limits of its original overdraft facility it is usually for the security taken to cover the amount already borrowed by this means.

When a company has borrowing powers and the exercise of these powers by the directors are not restrained by its memorandum or articles the directors, acting under their general power to conduct the business of the company, can borrow and give security without any further authority from the company.[99] As a result a company may borrow and incur debts in any manner in which an individual may do so.  **2.26**

*Methods of Giving Security (1) Any means Open to Individuals*

---

[93] *In Re International Life Assurance Society* (1870) 10 Eq. 312.

[94] *Re Patent File Co.* (1870) L.R. 6 Ch. App. 83; *Australian Auxiliary Steam Clipper Co.* v. *Mounsey* (1858) 4 K. & T. 733; *Bryon* v. *Metropolitan Saloon Omnibus Co.* (1850) 3 de G. & J. 123.

[95] Including book debts not yet due, *Illingworth* v. *Houldsworth* [1904] A.C. 353, H.L. *Bloomer* v. *Union Coal Co.* (1873) 16 Eq. 383.

[96] The power does not however extend to:
   (i) capital which can only be called up in the event of a winding up under C.A. 1985, s.120: *Bartlett* v. *Mayfair Property Co.* [1898] 2 Ch. 28, C.A.
   (ii) the amount payable under the guarantee in the case of a company limited by guarantee: *Re Pyle Works* (No. 1) (1890) 44 Ch.D. 534 at pp.574, 584.
   However it does extend to capital which can only be called up with the sanction of a special resolution: *Newton* v. *Anglo-Australian Investment Co.* [1895] A.C. 244, P.C.

[97] (1890) 44 Ch. D. 534, C.A.

[98] See *Re Patent File Co.* (1870) L.R. 6 Ch. App. 83; *Australian Auxiliary Steam Clipper Co.* v. *Mounsey* (1888) 4 K. & J. 733; *Landowners West of England and South Wales Land Drainage and Inclosure Co.* v. *Ashford* (1880) 16 Ch. D. 411; *Seligman* v. *Prince & Co.* [1895] 2 Ch. 617, C.A.

[99] The Companies (Alteration to Table A etc.) Regs. 1984 (SI 1984 No. 1717) Table A, art. 70 provides that the directors may exercise all the company's powers including therefore the powers to borrow money, mortgage or charge the company's undertakings, etc.

*(2) Debentures Fixed and Floating Charges*

The most usual form of secured borrowing by a company is on debentures,[1] the security being provided by way of either a fixed or a floating charge or a combination of the two.[2] Which type of charge is employed in any given case will depend to a large extent on the nature of the assets available as security, the requirements of the lender and the nature and requirements of the company's business. In general a fixed charge, being "one that without more fastens on ascertained and definite property or property capable of being ascertained and defined"[3] tends to be used in respect of freehold or leasehold property (and fixtures) and occasionally in respect of stocks and shares owned by the company but little else.

Such a charge provides lenders with a specific security[4] and ensures that the poperty burdened cannot be dealt with except subject to the lender's interests. A floating charge on the other hand allows the company much more flexibility in dealing with its assets. Such a charge provides lenders with an immediate equitable security "subject to a right to the company in the ordinary course and for the purposes of the business of the company, but not otherwise, to dispose of the assets as though the charge had not existed . . . "[5] "It is a general charge upon the undertaking as a whole, not attracted to specific assets, and the company is at liberty, so long as the undertaking is continued, to deal with all the assets not specifically charged in the ordinary course of its business."[6] Accordingly, when borrowings are secured by floating charge the security given comprises the undertaking, property and assets of the company, both present and future, and including (where the memorandum and articles permit) uncalled capital. A floating charge will crystalise[7] and thereby become specific in the event of the

---

[1] Debentures are somewhat imprecisely defined by the Companies Act 1985, s.744 as including debenture stock, bonds and other securities of a company whether constituting a charge on the assets of the company or not. Although this definition encompasses unsecured debentures the term is usually encountered in relation to secured borrowing (see *Knightsbridge Estates Trust Ltd.* v. *Byrne* [1940] A.C. 613, H.L. at p.625). Thus, according to Bowen L.J. in *English and Scottish Mercantile Investment Co.* v. *Brunton* [1892] 2 Q.B. 700, C.A. at p.712, debentures normally take one of three forms:

> "The first is a simple acknowledgement, under seal, of the debt; the second, an instrument acknowledging the debt and charging the property of the company with repayment;
> and the third, an instrument acknowledging the debt, charging the company with repayment and, further restricting the company from giving any prior charge."

[2] On debentures and security generally see *Palmer Company Law* (23rd ed., 1982) Chapters 43–48; *Gore-Browne Companies* (43rd ed., 1977) Chapters 17–19 and especially Gough, *Company Charges* (1978).
[3] *Illingworth* v. *Houldsworth* [1904] A.C. 355, H.L. at p.358 *per* Lord Macnaghton.
[4] See Gough *op. cit.* at pp.67–71.
[5] *Per* Cozens-Hardy J. in *Wallace* v. *Evershed* [1899] 1 Ch. 891 at p.894.
[6] *Per* Cozens-Hardy J. in *Re H.H. Vivian & Co. Ltd. Metropolitan Bank of England and Wales Ltd.* v. *H.H. Vivian & Co. Ltd.* [1900] 2 Ch. 654 at pp.657–8.
[7] According to Gough (*op. cit.* at pp.85–88) all the grounds for crystallisation, as they emerge from the cases, postulate the stoppage of the company as a going concern and the consequential cessation by the company of trading in the ordinary course (at least as regards the assets subject to the floating security). He suggests that a floating security crystallises in the following circumstances, namely:
>   (i) if the company goes into winding-up;
>  (ii) if the company itself stops trading in fact without as yet being in a winding up;
> (iii) if the company disposes of the whole of its undertaking or trading assets with a view to the cessation of trading;

company ceasing to be a going concern or of a creditor obtaining or exercising some remedy with a view to the protection or enforcement of his security.[8]

It is the practice for loan agreements to make specific provision for the priority of charges created to secure the company's borrowings. Such provision, especially if different lenders are involved, should seek to define the relationship of charges as between particular loans.

*2.27*

*Priority*

Under the general law the rules governing priority as between charges are essentially the same as those governing priority between legal and equitable interests generally. Accordingly, charges will put in order of creation save that creditors secured by a legal mortgage or charge will rank before an earlier equitable mortgage or charge if they have no notice, actual or constructive, of the earlier equitable interest. Subject to this, however, a floating charge will be postponed to any subsequently created fixed charge (legal or equitable) since, by its nature, a floating charge permits a company to deal with its assets and such powers to deal with assets includes the power to mortgage them.[9] There is no such implied authority, though, to create subsequent floating charges ranking first. A second floating charge will only obtain priority if either:

*The General Law*

*Fixed and Floating Charges*

(a) the instrument creating the first floating charge contained an express provision permitting the creation of later floating charges ranking first[10]; or

(b) the second floating charge is "more specific" in that it relates only to a part of the company's assets while the first is in general terms covering the entire undertaking.[11] Even so the second charge must be so restricted that it does not affect substantially the whole of the company's assets.[12]

*First and Subsequent Floating Charges*

In order to preserve the position of creditors under first-created floating charges it is common to include in the deed a provision expressly prohibiting the future creation of fixed charges to rank in priority to, or *pari passu* with, the floating charge. Such a prohibition will, in the absence of some fraud, misrepresentation or negligence,[13] be sufficient to bring a subsequent equitable fixed charge even without notice.[14] It will not however be sufficient to protect the priority of the chargee against a subsequent legal charge where there is no notice since the latter chargee would rank as a bona fide purchaser.[15]

---

(iv) if a creditor takes possession of assets of the company subject to the security through seizure under power or licence;

(v) if a creditor has a receiver appointed over assets of the company subject to the security;

(vi) if a creditor obtains or exercises some other remedy with a view to the protection or enforcement of the security.

[8] For a discussion of the covenants relating to such protection and enforcement, see below at § 2.35.

[9] *Wheatley* v. *Silkstone and High Moor Coal Co.* (1885) 29 Ch. D. 175.

[10] *Re Benjamin Cope & Sons Ltd.* [1914] 1 Ch. 800.

[11] *Re Automatic Bottlemakers Ltd.* [1926] Ch. 412.

[12] *Ibid.* at p. 423.

[13] *Re Castell & Brown Ltd.* [1898] 1 Ch. 315, where title deeds had been left with the company thereby giving its ostensible authority to create the second mortgage.

[14] *Re Castell & Brown Ltd. supra.*

[15] And see below as to the effect of registration.

**2.28**    The general law of priority of charges is affected by sections 395–398 of the Companies Act 1985[16] which requires particulars of certain mortgages and charges created by companies registered in England and Wales[17] to be delivered to the Registrar of Companies within 21 days after the date of their creation. The mortgages and charges currently requiring registration under this provision are:

(a) a charge for the purpose of securing any issue of debentures[18];

(b) a charge on uncalled share capital of the company;

(c) a charge created or evidenced by an instrument which, if executed by an individual would require registration as a bill of sale[19];

(d) a charge on any land wherever situated or any interest therein but not including a charge for any rent or other periodical sum issuing out of land;

(e) a charge on book debts of the company;

(f) a floating charge on the undertaking or property of the company;

(g) a charge on calls made but not paid;

(h) a charge on a ship or any share in a ship;

(i) a charge on goodwill, on a patent or a licence under a patent, on a trade mark or on a copyright or a licence under a copyright.

While failure to comply with the registration requirement does not affect the personal right of the creditor under the charge[20] to bring an action for the money due or to prove in liquidation (as an unsecured creditor) such failure does, "so far as any security on the company's property or undertaking is conferred thereby," have the effect of rendering that security or undertaking void as against the liquidator or any creditor of the company.[21] The consequences of this on the rules as to priorities are twofold. First, a charge which is not duly[22] regis-

---

[16] Companies Act 1985, s.407, requires every limited company to keep a register of charges and to enter therein particulars of all charges specifically affecting property of the company and of all floating charges on the undertaking or property of the company. The priority of charges however is not affected by the omission from or defect in the register kept by the company.

[17] See below at § 2.29 for registration of charges in respect of companies registered in Scotland.

[18] It is thought that this category relates to the *public* issue of debentures; otherwise, it would render all subsequent categories otiose.

[19] The Bills of Sale Act 1878, s.4, defines a bill of sale as a mortgage or charge on "personal chattels" which in turn are defined as goods or other artices capable of complete transfer by delivery. The definition also includes fixtures and growing crops when separately assigned or charged but excludes shares and other securities in companies as well as other choses in action. The courts hae extended this exclusion to cover certain transactions and tangible moveable property, namely:

   (i) pledges: *Dublin City Distillery* v. *Doherty* [1914] A.C. 823, H.L.

   (ii) hire-purchase transactions: *Stoneleigh Finance Ltd.* v. *Phillips* [1965] 2 Q.B. 537, C.A.

The Bills of Sale Act also specifically exclude:

   (a) a charge on goods situated outside England and Wales (s.4).

   (b) transfers of goods in the ordinary way of business (s.4).

   (c) transfers of documents used in the ordinary course of business as proof of the possession or control of goods (s.4).

   (d) letters of hypothecation or lien on imported goods where they are warehouses, purchased, stored or reshipped or delivered by a purchaser (s.1).

[20] The effect of ss.395–398 of the Companies Act 1985 is that anything within classes 1–9 which creates a charge at law or in equity requires registration. See *Gorringe* v. *Irwell India Rubber Works* (1886) 34 Ch.D. 128 at p.134 *per* Cotton L.J.; and *National Provincial and Union Bank of England* v. *Charnley* [1924] 1 K.B. 431, C.A. at pp. 449, 450 *per* Atkin L.J.

[21] Companies Act 1985, s.395.

[22] The act provides machinery for rectification of a defect in the register. This however will not be permitted to allow a charge to regain priority.

tered within the registration period is void and will lose whatever priority it might otherwise have had[23], and secondly, registration affects the operation of the doctrine of notice in that an entry on the register constitutes actual notice to those who search the register and constructive notice to those who do not.[24] In *Wilson* v. *Kelland*[25], however, it was held that while registration gave notice of the existence of a charge it did not constitute notice of the terms of the instrument creating it beyond those appearing on the face of the register. Accordingly, while registration would be sufficient to preserve priority for an equitable prior charge as against a subsequent legal mortgage or charge it would not give protection to those entitled under a floating charge containing an express prohibition on the creation of subsequent fixed charges ranking in priority to it since a subsequent legal chargee could still claim to be a bona fide purchaser for value wthout notice in relation to the prohibition.[26] In an attempt to guard against this happening and thereby to afford greater protection to floating charges the practice has developed of including the prohibition among the particulars of the charge to be registered. The Registrar has accepted this practice and the assumption is that registration of particulars including a prohibition will give constructive notice of the prohibition. It must be said, however, that this assumption has not yet been tested in the courts.

The law governing the priority and registration of charges in respect of companies registered in Scotland effectively dates from the passing of the Companies (Floating Charges) (Scotland) Act 1961 which made it competent for Scottish-registered companies to secure borrowings by means of a floatiung charge,[27] laid down rules as to priority and added new provisions in the Companies Act 1948[28] concerning registration. The relevant provisions are now contained in sections 409–424 of the Companies Act 1985.

**2.29**

*Companies Registered in Scotland*

Section 410(4) of the 1985 Act provides that the charges which must be registered by a company registered in Scotland are:

*Registration of Charges*

  (a)  a charge on land wherever situated, or any interest therein;
  (b)  a security over the uncalled share capital of the company;
  (c)  a security of incorporated moveable property of any of the following categories:
      (i)   the book debts of the company,[29]
      (ii)  calls made but not paid,
      (iii) goodwill,
      (iv)  a patent or licence under a patent,
      (v)   a trademark,
      (vi)  a copyright or licence,

---

[23] *Re Monolithic Building Co.* [1915] 1 Ch. 643.
[24] *Wilson* v. *Kelland* [1910] 2 Ch. 306; *Re Standard Rotary Machine Co.* (1906) 95 L.T. 829.
[25] [1910] 2 Ch. 306.
[26] *Re Valletort Laundry Co.* [1903] 2 Ch. 654; *Re Standard Rotary Machine Co., supra.*
[27] Prior to 1961 the law of floating charges derived from the ruling of the Court of Session in *Carse* v. *Coppen* 1951 S.C. 233 which declared their characteristics imcompatible with the rules for the constitution of a security under Scots law. See, in particular *per* Lord Cooper P. at p. 239.
[28] Pt. IIIA.
[29] By s.412 the deposit of a negotiable instrument to secure payment of book debts for the purpose of securing an advance for the company is not registrable under s.410.

(d) a security over a ship or any share in a ship; or

(e) a floating charge.

As in England registrable charges must be registered within 21 days of creation, failure to do so rendering a charge void as against the liquidator and any creditors. When a charge becomes void under the provision[30] the sum secured becomes immediately repayable. Failure to register does not adversely affect a creditors personal right to sue under the contract of loan.

*Priority*

The rules as to priority of charges derive from section 5(2) of the 1961 Act. This provides that fixed securities will in general have priority over floating securities, subject to the qualification that a floating charge which was registered before a fixed charge was created will have priority where the instrument creating the floating charge contains a clause prohibiting the creation of securities ranking before or *pari passu* with the charge.[31]

As between charges of the same type, whether fixed or floating, priority will in general be governed by the order of registration.[32] Where, however, instruments creating the first charge expressly provide that subsequent charges will rank *pari passu* with it then effect is given to that provision.[33]

Floating charges, as in England, are deferred to the claims of preferred creditors in a liquidation.[34]

**2.30**

*Certificate of Registration*

Upon registration the Registrar is required to furnish a certificate in relation to the charge, stating the amount thereby secured. In *National Provincial and Union Bank of England Ltd.* v. *Charnley*[35] it was held that this requirement as to the amount secured would be sufficiently completed with by the words "all sums now due or to become due."

*Conclusive Evidence that Registration Requirements Complied with*

The Registrar's certificate is conclusive evidence that the requirements of the Act as to registration have been complied with[36] and the courts will not go behind the certificate to enquire as to whether there has been any irregularity.[37] Thus in *Re Eric Holmes (Property) Ltd.*[38] the particulars submitted for registration gave a false date as that of the creation of the charge, the true date being outside the 21 days period. Having been registered, and a certificate issued on the basis of the false date the charge was nonetheless held to be valid and the certificate conclusive evidence that the registration requirements had been complied with. Likewise in *Re C.L. Nye Ltd.*[39] the Court of Appeal held that notwithstanding that the date of the charge had been incorrectly stated in the particulars, once the certificate had been granted, it became conclusive evidence that all the requirements of the Act as to registration had been complied with so

---

[30] s.409(1).
[31] C.A. 1985, s.413.
[32] Companies (Floating Charges) (Scotland) Act, 1961, s.5(3).
[33] *Ibid.*
[34] *Ibid.* s.5(5).
[35] [1924] 1 K.B. 431, C.A.; See also *Re Mechanisations (Eaglescliffe) Ltd.* [1966] Ch. 20.
[36] C.A. 1985, s.401(2) (English-registered companies) and s.417(2) (Scottish-registered companies).
[37] *National Provincial and Union Bank of England* v. *Charnley* [1924] 1 K.B. 431, C.A.; *Re Mechanisations (Eaglescliffe) Ltd., supra.*
[38] [1965] Ch. 1052.
[39] [1971] 1 Ch. 443, C.A.

that, in effect, the requirement that particulars be delivered within 21 days was not a condition precedent to the Registrar's jurisdiction to register a charge or issue a certificate.

Given the possibility of defects in the register, albeit that rectification may be possible,[40] it follows that a prospective lender cannot rely exclusively on the information available to him from the course, and should supplement it with further enquiries. This precaution is reinforced by the possibility that statements in the certificate, while technically accurate, may be incomplete or out of date. For example, the statement of the total amount of secured debt in the annual return relates only to the date to which the return is made up. And a statement that the amount secured consists of "all sums now due or to become due" does not provide details as to how much the company actually owns on the security.

*Limitation of the Registration/Certificate System*

Loan agreements will normally seek to define the relationship of a company's bank overdraft with its other borrowing, especially if that other borrowing is in whole or in part from other lenders. Two separate points need to be taken into account.

**2.31**

*Overdrafts*

### The initial ranking

The problem of initial ranking is whether, at the time security is first given, the overdraft is to rank *pari passu* with the term-loan finance provided and, if so, to what extent. The problem arises from the fact that the debenture securing the borrowing, whether by fixed or floating charge, will be for a finite amount. In arriving at this figure a decision will have to be taken between the lenders as to the extent to which this figure is to include amounts already advanced or to be advanced on overdraft. The fixing of such a limit would have the consequence that any subsequent advances in excess of it would have to be secured by a second charge. In the absence of a provision in the first debenture permitting subsequent charges to rank equally with it such a second charge would necessarily be postponed to the first debenture. The extent of the bank's wilingness to accept such a situation would obviously depend on the company's financial situation.

### Further advances

If the overdraft is secured by a first charge and a second charge is created over the same property, registration of that second charge will constitute notice to the bank. Any further advances, therefore, made after the registration of the second debenture would be made with notice of it and would therefore be postponed to it. If, therefore, the account is continued payments made by the debtor company into it will, under the principle in *Clayton's case*,[41] operate to reduce and ulti-

---

[40] C.A. 1985, s.404; but see *Archibald Campbell, Hope & King Ltd, Petitioners* 1967 S.C. 21 where a debenture trust deed included a power to issue further debenture stock, and this was later done by supplemental trust deed, but the registration of the earlier deed was held to be incapable of rectification to show that the security subjects were security for the second debenture stock issue as well as the first.

[41] (1816) 1 Mer. 572.

mately pay off the amount of the debt outstanding at the time of the later debenture. At this point the bank will become postponed to the later lender since all subsequent advances will rank after the amount lent under the second debenture.[42] To meet this danger banking practice is to rule off and close the account of learning of the second debenture thereby retaining its charge for the balance then due on the overdrawn account.[43]

**2.31A**

*Subordination*

A change in the ranking of securities will be an integral part of a subordination agreement entered into as part of a refinancing programme in circumstances where the company needs an injection of substantial additional capital which cannot be obtained within the existing hierarchy of priorities. Subordination is in substance a transaction whereby an existing creditor agrees to the deferment of payment of sums owing to him until another creditor has been paid in full.[43a]

**2.32**

*Trust Deeds*

Where a debenture is created in favour of two or more lenders the practice is for this to be effected through a trust deed. This matter is discussed below in relation to the issue of debt securities.[44]

**2.33**

*Subsidiaries*

In cases where the debtor company has one or more subsidiary companies the security provisions of the loan agreement will normally seek to bring the assets of the subsidiaries within the scope of the charge. If such assets are not directly charged the debenture holders will only have recourse to them indirectly via the parent company's shareholding. Such indirect recourse is generally considered unsatisfactory since, in relation to the subsidiary's assets, the debenture holders will rank after all creditors (secured or unsecured) and any preference shareholders if, as if often the case, the parent company holds only ordinary shares. To overcome this problem some groups adopt a policy that all group properties are to be owned by the parent company thereby ensuring that important assets are available directly to the parent for use as security.

*Collateral Charges*

Another method of using the assets of subsidiary companies for security is to have the subsidiary participate directly in giving security for the group's borrowing. Where the subsidiary is wholly owned the normal course will be for it to give a guarantee[45] to the parent and execute a collateral charge (usually a floating charge) to underpin the guarantee. This collateral charge will subsist until the principal monies and any interest outstanding are paid off.

If the subsidiary company is not wholly-owned problems may arise in connec-

---

[42] *Deeley* v. *Lloyds Bank* [1912] A.C. 756, H.L.; *Hopkinson* v. *Rolt* (1861) 9 H.L.C. 514; *London and County Bank* v. *Ratcliffe* (1881) 6 Ap. Cas. 722, HL; *Bradford Banking Co.* v. *Henry Briggs & Co.* (1886) 12 App. Cas. 29, H.L.

[43] Sometimes overdrafts are granted on terms whereby the security is given to secure the sums already advanced and such other advances as have been agreed up to a stated limit. In such a case, where the bank is contractually bound to make the futher advances should it be called up it can effectively tack its further advances onto its earlier ones irrespective of the question of notice. However to ensure this result the particulars of the charge sent for registration should make clear that the obligation to make further advances exists.

[43a] See generally Wood, *op. cit.* at Chapter 17 and authorities cited there.

[44] See below at §§ 2.61 *et seq.*

[45] If more than one subsidiary is involved the subsidiaries will jointly and severally guarantee the obligation.

tion with the position of minority shareholders.[46] To overcome any such problems it will usually be prudent to obtain the assent of such minority shareholders before the assets are charged; certainly if the subsidiary has a Stock Exchange listing minority shareholder assent will have to be obtained.[47]

Non-resident subsidiaries, being outside the jurisdiction of the English and Scottish courts are usually excluded from such direct charging arrangements.

Where the assets of a group of companies have been collectively charged to secure the group's borrowing it is not uncommon for arrangements to be made for the provision of an overall overdraft for the group with facilities being made available to subsidiaries and the individual debit and credit balance being offset one against the other. *Group Overdraft Facilities*

The loan agreement will provide for the debenture security to become enforceable immediately against the debtor company or charging group if in the case of the company or any of its subsidiaries: **2.34** *Enforcement of Security*

(a) A notice is issued or an order made for:
   (i) a winding up; or
   (ii) the appointment of a receiver, save, in the case of a company within a group, where the order is made in favour of another member of the group;
(b) A judgment is made against the company for an amount in excess of £x, or if an execution or a distress warrant is levied, and payment is not made within two to four days;
(c) Any stoppage of payment[48] is made or any threat to cease to carry on the company's business;
(d) Any change occurs in the nature of the company's business without the permission of the debenture holder;
(e) Any other mortgage or charge purporting to rank equal with, or in priority to, the existing debenture is created without the permission of the existing debenture holder;
(f) The company's bank overdraft exceeds the level stipulated in the debenture without the permission of the existing debenture holder;
(g) The company fails to make on the due date any payment of interest or repayment of principal;
(h) The company or its directors are in breach of any covenant or undertaking contained in the debenture;
(i) (In the case of a private company) if X does or is unable to carry out his duties as chairman/managing director or is in breach, for whatever reason, of his service agreement.[49]

---

[46] See further below, at Chapter 7.
[47] See further below, at Chapter 6.
[48] C.A. 1985, s.518(1).
[49] This provision is normally inserted in agreements for loans to private companies where one man (or a small number of individuals) is vital to the success of the company's business. It is possible for the company to take out an insurance policy on such a person's life to act as, or as part of, the security for the debenture. The policy will be assigned to the debenture holder and, on maturity, any balance remaining after repayment of the debt will revert to the company. Such a course of action is quite common in the early years of a business especially if the asset cover within the company is insufficient to repay the debenture or where such repayment would involve liquidating the company.

### Creditor-protection covenants

**2.35**

*Individual Covenants*

Most loan agreements contain a number of covenants imposing obligations on the debtor company for the purpose of safeguarding the interests of the lender. These covenants attempt to provide for the particular circumstances of individual businesses. Thus, for example, if in the case of a private company one or two individuals are considered to be vital to the success of the enterprise it is common for the company to covenant to take out and keep up an insurance policy on the lives and continual good health of the individuals concerned.

*Standard Covenants*

In addition to covenants geared to the particular nature and circumstances of the company's business a number of obligations have become more or less standard to all loan agreements whatever the character of the business concerned. The obligations concerned are:

*(1) Positive Covenants*

  (a) to conduct the business of the company in a proper and efficient manner; to keep proper books of account, and to allow these to be inspected by the debenture holders; to make true and proper entries of all dealings and transactions of the company;

  (b) to pay all rent, rates and other outgoings promptly and to observe all covenants affecting the company's property;

  (c) to file all particulars and returns concerning the registration of mortgages and charges in accordance with the Companies Acts;

  (d) to keep all buildings, plant and machinery in a good state of repair[50] and not to destroy or dismantle any such buildings, plant and machinery except for the purpose of replacing obsolete plant and equipment;

  (e) to allow debenture holders to inspect the company's buildings;

  (f) to inform the debenture holders of any notice or proceedings affecting the property and of any notices or proceedings affecting any properties subsequently acquired;

  (g) to keep fully insured[50] through a recognised insurance company all property and plant and to pay promptly all premiums on insurance policies taken out in pursuance of this covenant; to provide, when and where required, a certificate to the effect that all assets are fully insured.

  (h) to keep the debenture holders informed of the company's business, and to furnish them with information as required; to provide them with annual accounts within a period of four months from the end of the company's financial year;

  (i) to make any payments due under any agreements made by or judgments awarded against the company.

**2.36**

*(2) Negative Covenants*

In addition the company covenants that neither it nor its subsidiaries, except with the approval of the debenture holders, will:

  (a) make any change in the financial year of the company from that operating at the date of the debenture;

---

[50] In the event of the company defaulting on its obligation to keep the poperty in a proper state of repair or in keeping the property fully insured, the lender can undertake the repairs or insurance itself and recover the amount from the company.

(b) acquire any shares or assets in any other company or business, give guarantees or credit (other than normal trade credit), or to make loans or advances except to its charging subsidiaries;

(c) enter into any hire-purchase agreements without the unanimous approval of the board;

(d) transfer, sell or otherwise dispose of the whole or any substantial part of the company's business, undertaking, shareholding in any subsidiary, freehold or leasehold property or any assets except for the purpose of replacing such assets or purchasing new assets in the ordinary course of business[51];

(e) make any increase in the emoluments or pensions payable to directors or past directors beyond those provided for in their service agreements with the company, or previously disclosed in writing;

(f) [in the case of a private company] make any dividend payment, repayment of capital to shareholders except as permitted in the articles or required to be made in order to avoid a shortfall determination under Schedule 16 of the Finance Act 1972.

## Borrowing limits

A further negative covenant is on occasion inserted in loan agreements **2.37** between institutional lenders and private companies imposing an overall borrowing limit on the company, the object of such a covenant being to guard against the possibility of the company's overburdening itself with debt.

While such limits can be expressed in terms of a fixed sum it is more usual for them to be calculated by reference to the company's net asset cover and interest cover and expressed as a factor of its adjusted capital and reserves.[52]

## International loan agreements[53]

Loans raised internationally involve many of the same considerations as those **2.38** raised domestically with the consequence that the terms of the relevant loan documents bear many similarities to those considered above. Nevertheless the additional external hazards that attach to international lending and the increased

---

[51] And excepting transfers, etc, to charging subsidiaries.

[52] A company's adjusted capital and reserves are obtained by adding to the issued and paid-up share capital (ordinary and preference) its consolidated capital and revenue reserves (including amounts to be revised from a revaluation of properties and the consolidated revenue reserves of the group) and deducting from the figure to ascertain:
   (i) minority shareholders' interests in charging subsidiaries;
   (ii) reserves and sums set aside for;
   (iii) goodwill items and intangible assets;
   (iv) capitalised research and development;
   (v) any distribution or proposed distribution from profits earned prior to the last accounts (except to another group member) which exceeds the amount provided for it in the last audited balance sheet;
   (vi) any debit balance on the revenue reserves of the subsidiaries.
   (vii) any other adjustments felt appropriate by the company's auditors (*e.g.* deduction of excess depreciation above that covered by the relevant capital allowance)

[53] See generally Wood, at pp. 233 *et seq.*

difficulties of monitoring the actual use of funds lent overseas have brought about the inclusion in international loan documents of clauses purporting to provide compensating protection by:

(a) stringently defining the borrowing company's right to receive the funds loaned;

(b) particularising the procedures for drawing the funds loaned, for repaying them and restrictively prescribing pre-payments rights; and

(c) expanding the warranties required of borrowers.

**2.39**     Most international loan agreements are drafted so as to remain inoperative until the satisfaction of certain conditions precedent. These conditions fall into

*"Right to Bor-*   two groups, namely:
*row" Con-*
*ditions*      (a) those to be fulfilled before the borrower's right to borrow arises; and

(b) those which have to be fulfilled separately prior to each borrowing.

*(a) Conditions to be fulfilled before the borrower's right to borrow arises*

The purpose of this set of conditions is to suspend the obligation of the lenders until the security for the loan is in place and all the legalities in connection therewith are in order. The documentary requirements in relation to these conditions will include receipt of:

(1) guarantees and other security documents;

(2) copies of all necessary authorisations (for example board resolutions, shareholder approvals, government decrees, requisite approvals of local authorities);

(3) copies of all necessary governmental and exchange control consents;

(4) copies of all relevant constitutional documents of the borrower (*e.g.* memorandum and articles of association);

(5) legal opinions, where appropriate; and

(6) for joint project financing,[54] evidence that other loan agreements which provide additional finance for the project have been entered into.

*(b) Conditions to be fulfilled separately prior to each borrowing*

Most international loan agreements contain drawdown provisions stipulating the period or periods during which borrowings may be made. These are usually drafted by reference to periods of notice designed, *inter alia*, to ensure that it remains "safe" for the lender to meet his obligations under the loan agreement. Among the conditions of this type most commonly encountered are:

(1) that the representations and warranties made and given at the date of the loan remain true (with the loan being suspended under the financial and contractual position of the borrower are the same as that warranted as at the date of the starting of the agreement);

[54] Joint project financing is normally carried out through the medium of a locally created company, often with the participation of local interests. See further Wood, *op. cit.* at Chapter. 14.

(2) that no event of default has occurred and is continuing[55];

(3) that duly executed notes evidencing the obligations of the borrower have been received;

(4) that evidence of expenditure qualifying under the terms[56] of the loan agreement has been received; and

(5) where appropriate, that further opinions and documents have been received (for the purpose of satisfying the lender that there have been no changes in the law that might invalidate the obligations).

The loan agreement will stipulate: **2.40**

*Drawdown Provisions*

(a) a fixed period during which the borrower may draw upon the loan, such period being usually drafted by reference to periods of notice to enable the lender, *inter alia*,[57] to process the instruction, and

(b) the place where the funds loaned are to be made available.[58]

In agreements relating to joint project financing clauses governing the application of the funds advanced are often encountered.

The normal practice, reflecting the preferred policy of lenders, is for the agreement to contain provisions stipulating that the loan be repayable by instalments over a given period (rather than by a single lump sum at the end of the term).[59] **2.41**

*Repayment Provisions*

It is usual for lenders to seek to restrict a borrower's right of pre-payment in order to safeguard the life of their investment. In some cases this restriction takes the form of a disincentive to pre-pay in that a premium becomes payable. An exception to this general practice occurs in relation to project loans, the relevant agreements frequently incorporating recapture clauses requiring pre-payments if the profits from the project exceed a given level. **2.42**

*Prepayment Provisions*

In cases where pre-payment is permitted and where the loan is repayable by instalments it is usual[60] for partial pre-payments to be applied against the outstanding instalments in their inverse order so as to shorten the life of the loan.

As in domestic loan agreements the scope of the representations and warranties required by a lender will depend on the creditstanding, circumstances and nature of the borrower. However certain requirements are encountered so frequently as to have become almost standard form conditions. Essentially these fall into two groups, namely: **2.43**

*Warranties and Representations*[61]

---

[55] This condition is designed to reduce the risk of the borrower's drawing down a loan in order to buy time or pay off another defaulted obligation at a time when a default has occurred but has not matured into a full event of default because a grace period or remedy notice has not expired.

[56] In cases (*e.g.* joint projects) where the application of the loan proceeds is monitored.

[57] See above at § 2.39.

[58] In practice transfers to bank accounts in a third country are not favoured since they subject the lender to the risk of currency restrictions being introduced by the relevant states.

[59] The reason for this is that a single (or "bullet") repayment might strain the resources of the borrower, especially if it had been imprudent enough to fail to set aside reserves year by year or where the borrower lacks the credit strength to refinance the loan on maturity.

[60] In accordance with normal banking practice.

[61] See further Wood, *op. cit.* at pp.240 *et seq.*

  (a) legal warranties; and

  (b) warranties as to the borrower's financial condition.

### (a) Legal Warranties

These take the form of statements by the borrower warranting that various legal requirements have been met. The matters on which warranties are usually demanded are as follows.

(1) *Status.* The borrower has been duty incorporated, is validly existing and in good standing, that it is legally capable of and qualified to transact business in every jurisdiction where such capacity and qualification are necessary.

(2) *Power, authority etc.* The borrower has the necessary constitutional rights and power to enter into and duly perform the loan agreement; the loan agreement has been authorised by the appropriate constitutional procedures; and the loan agreement has been duly executed by the borrower.

(3) *Conflict of Laws etc.* The making and performance of the loan agreement does not and will not contravene any law, regulation or court order or the constitutional documents of the borrower or any contract or mortgage binding on the borrower or affecting the assets.

(4) *Binding nature and enforceability of agreement.* The loan agreement is the valid and legally binding obligation of the borrower enforceable in accordance with its terms.

(5) *Official consents.* All necessary governmental and official consents for the making and performance of the loan agreement by the borrower have been obtained, including (where appropriate) any consents necessary to enable the borrower to acquire foreign currency and transmit it abroad.

(6) *Filings.* No filings, recordings or registrations with any public or official body or agency are necessary or desirable in relation to the making, performance, validity or enforceability of the loan agreement.

### (b) Warranties as to the borrower's financial condition

These take the form of statements by the borrower warranting various matters likely to affect its financial condition or prospects. Many of these (for example, warrants as to litigation, defaults on loans or claims under contracts) are encountered in domestic loan agreements in substantially the same form. Likewise the general warranty as to financial fitness[62] is similar to its domestic counterpart.

---

[62] Such a warranty would normally state:
    (i) That the most recent audited financial statements of the borrower show a true and fair view of the borrower's financial condition as at their date and of the results of the operations of the borrower for the financial period ending on that date;
    (ii) that the borrower has the material liabilities not disclosed in those accounts; and
    (iii) that there has been no adverse change in the financial condition of the borrower since that date.

It is often the case that an international loan agreement is accompanied by a **2.44** promissory note. In some cases the function of the note is merely to act as evidence of the agreement, the loan contract containing all of the obligations of the *Notes* parties with the note duplicating the more important of them.

In other cases the obligations under the agreement are embodied in the terms of the note itself with the loan contract performing the function of a subscription agreement.[63]

### Eurocurrency floating rate loans

Eurocurrency loan agreements are increasingly made on a floating rate basis **2.45** and in addition to the standard conditions and warranties discussed above usually contains provisions dealing with:

(a) the calculation of interest payments;
(b) "unwinding" costs;
(c) market disturbances; and
(d) increased costs.

Interest payments are calculated by reference to the London Inter-Bank **2.46** Offered Rates[64] and the loan agreement will contain provisions for a stipulated percentage above that rate. Such interest payments are calculated and made in *Calculation of* respect of a specified interest period and fixed at the beginning of that period. It *Interest Rates* follows therefore that loans enduring for a time in excess of one interest period will bear a rate that will "float," that is vary from period to period.[65]

Eurocurrency loan agreements usually contain provisions designed to ensure **2.47** that scheduled repayments and any voluntary pre-payments are matched with the maturity of underlying deposits.[66] The function of such provision is to avert *Unwinding* any loss to the lender which might otherwise occur as a result of the changing *Costs* requirements of the borrower. The mechanism for achieving this is the inclusion of a clause providing for the payment of an indemnity in the case of a non-borrowing or a compulsory payment otherwise than on the maturity of an interest period.[67]

---

[63] See further Wood, *op cit.* at pp.244 *et seq.*

[64] The idea underlying eurocurrency loans is that the bank making the loan borrows matching funds from other banks in the market for on-lending. These funding deposits are taken for short fixed terms (*e.g.* 3, 6 or 12 months). At the end of each period the bank repays the deposit (plus interest) and immediately reborrows another deposit for a further period. The interest rate payable by the ultimate borrower is a percentage above the rate at which the bank borrows the underlying deposits from other banks in the London inter-bank market. In practice many banks fund loans out of their own pool of funds without going to the market. These arrangements nevertheless involve a calculation on the notional rate that would have been charged by the bank had it gone into the market.
It follows from this that the cost of the loan to the ultimate borrower will depend (actually or constructively) on the credit of the lending bank. In the case of syndicated loans or credits the LIBOR of selected reference banks are averaged out for the purposes of interest determination.

[65] Some loans are theoretically repayable at the end of each interest period. The practice however is to avoid situations where the borrower is placed in a position where it is required to repay and reborrow.

[66] See above at n. 64.

[67] See further Wood, *op. cit.* at para. 10.8(3).

**2.48**

*Market Disturbance Clauses*

Market disturbance clauses are intended to provide for the situation where market conditions are such that the lender is unable to obtain a funding deposit in the designated market.[68] Standard form clauses provide that in the event of such a disturbance the parties must negotiate in good faith for a specified period (often 30 days) with a view to agreeing an alternative basis for the continuance of the loan.

In one form of clause if the agreement is reached[69] the borrower must prepay. An alternative form of clause provides that in the absence of agreement the lender must certify an alternative basis upon which it will continue the loan, giving the borrower the right to accept or reject it. In the event of the borrower's rejecting it then prepayment must follow.

**2.49**

*Provisions re Increased Costs*

It is common for a eurocurrency loan agreement to incorporate provisions designed to insulate the lender against increases in costs or other erosions of the margin constituting its gross profits.

The provisions encountered in such agreements tend to be of two kinds, namely:

(a) those seeking to protect the lender against the effects of withholding taxes; and

(b) those designed to afford protection against regulatory impositions on the bank which increase its direct costs in funding the loan but which are not reflected in the cost of deposits in the market.

The standard practice[70] is to include clauses providing that if any change in the law or in its application increase the cost to the banks of making or maintaining or funding a loan the borrower will compensate the bank for the amount of such increase.

**Optional currencies**

**2.50**

*Currency Conversion Clauses*

Where banks have access to numerous currencies in the market a borrower can be provided with the flexibility of converting the loan into other currencies during its continuance. The mechanics of the operation involve a repayment of the old currency and a re-advance by the bank in the new currency. After conversion interest and principal are then denominated in the new currency.

In practice the banks are not prepared to allow optional currencies to become out of line with the original base currency and loan agreements incorporating optional currency facilities provide for an adjustment to be made at the beginning of each interest period by reference to the then prevailing rate of exchange.

---

[68] In such cases in the absence of express provision questions would then arise as to the moment of fixing the interest rate, whether any interest is payable at all and indeed whether the entire loan agreement is frustrated by supervening circumstances.

[69] Note that the lender is under no obligation to reach agreement.

[70] See Wood, *op. cit.* at para. 10.8(5).

**Loan syndication**

The size of some loans (especially international loans) is so large that no single financial institution possesses the resources or inclination to lend the entire sum on its own. In such cases the loan is raised through a syndicate of banks, each bank contributing a portion of the sum advanced. **2.51**

The normal procedure where a company needs loan finance of such a magnitude that syndication becomes necessary is for a single bank to be authorised to arrange the loan. This bank (the managing bank) will thereupon: **2.52**

  (a) settle in outline with the company the financial and other terms on the basis of which the loan is to be promoted;
  (b) approach other[71] prospective lenders in the market and provide them with details of the proposed loan and information about the borrower in order to enable them to decide whether or not to participate;
  (c) negotiate the details of the loan agreement with the company.

The information provided by the managing bank serves the same function as a set of Listing Particulars issued in respect of a Stock Exchange issue. However, while such information will as a matter of course be prepared with a corresponding degree of care,[72] it is thought that the relevant document will not fall within the prospectus requirements of the Companies Act since the narrowness and closed nature of a syndicate represent the antithesis of an offer to the public.[73]

In practice there are two basic methods of syndication, namely: **2.53**

  (a) where all members of the syndicate participate directly and are parties to the loan agreement; and
  (b) where only one bank is a party to the loan agreement[74] and the participation of other syndicate members is undertaken pursuant to a collateral agreement.

It is an underlying principle of loan syndication that each participant should be entitled to receive payment from the borrower and that the borrower should not be entitled to discriminate as between the common lenders. Nevertheless the practicalities of syndication arrangements render it convenient for matters relating to the drawing down of the loan, the receipt of payments from the borrower and other functions in connection with the management of the loan to be undertaken by one of the members acting on behalf of the syndicate as a whole rather than for each bank to deal with the borrower on an individual basis. Accordingly the loan agreement will contain a provision appointing one of the syndicate **2.54**

---

[71] It would be most unusual for the managing bank (usually the company's own merchant bankers) not to participate in the loan.
[72] As to the preparation of a prospectus for the purpose of a Stock Exchange flotation, see below at §§6.30 *et seq.*
[73] For the definition of a prospectus see C.A. 1985, s.744; and see below at §§6.09 *et seq.*
[74] In this type of arrangement the fact of the loan having been syndicated is not normally disclosed to the borrower.

banks as agent for the syndicate to carry out certain functions on behalf of all the participants in the loan.

The loan agreement will normally contain provisions dealing with the following matters.[75]

*Drawdown of the loan*

Instead of each of the syndicate banks making a separate payment or payments to the borrower in respect of its obligations under the loan the agreement will provide for the agent to act as a conduit pipe for such payments. The banks will be required to make their payments into a designated account in the name of the agent. The agent will then transfer the whole amount due to the borrower.

It should be noted however that the agency provisions are mere administrative arrangements rather than fundamental conditions of the loan. In the unlikely event of a default by one of the syndicate in relation to the drawdown provisions the borrower should therefore proceed directly against the defaulting bank[76] rather than against the agent.

*Payments by the borrower*

By the same token the loan agreement will provide that all payments by the borrower under the terms of the loan shall be made into a designated account in the name of the agent for distribution among the participant banks *pro rata* according to their respective entitlements.

It is clear that under the terms of such a provision the borrower has no right to appropriate payments to a particular lender. Should the borrower make such a direct payment in breach of this condition so as to give the lender more than its *pro rata* share the lender would probably hold the moneys so received on constructive trust for the other participants and so be bound to hand back the preferential payment to the agent for redistribution.

*Management functions*

Among the functions delegated[77] to the agent are those of ensuring that any conditions precedent to the drawing down of the loan have been satisfied before any payment is made to the borrower. The agent is usually required so to certify.

In addition the agent is normally charged with monitoring the borrower's financial condition and alerting the syndicate members to the possibility (or actuality) of a default.

Given the onerous nature of these functions it is usual for the loan agreement to contain exculpation clauses to give some measure of protection.

---

[75] See generally Wood, *op. cit.* at Chapter 11.
[76] Or against the managing bank for breach of the finance supply agreement.
[77] For a specimen agency delegation clause see Wood, *op. cit.* at p.264.

*Indemnity*

The loan agreement will normally contain provisions whereby the agent may claim an indemnity in respect of costs incurred in the performance of its duties. Often the burden of this indemnity is made to fall on the borrower. Certainly the agreement will provide the agent with a right of clawback in respect of any costs arising from the agent's having to use its own funds to cover shortfalls caused by time lags in payments.

**2.55**

*Indirect Participation Agreement*

Whereas in cases of loan agreements to which all the participant lenders are parties the borrower will be required to deal with one or them as agent, where the syndication arrangements are contained in a separate agreement the borrower will deal with the lead bank as principal. In such cases any rights of recourse by syndicate members will be against the lead bank rather than directly against the borrower.

Under the terms of the separate synidcation agreement the lead bank grants a participation to each syndicate member of a specified percentage of the total loan. For its part the participant undertakes to provide funds to the lead bank for use by the lead bank in order to cover that proportion of the loan. In consideration of this and in pursuance of the participation granted the lead bank covenants to distribute to each syndicate member its *pro rata* share of receipts from the borrower.

**Loans and losses**

**2.56**

*Tax Relief on Losses*

While the creditor-protection covenants of a loan agreement are designed to enable a lender to take steps to enforce his security and thereby preserve the substance of his investment it nevertheless happens from time to time that these steps are not or cannot be taken, that the company fails and that the loan cannot be wholly recovered, if at all. Where loss occurs in this way it is sometimes possible that its effects on the lender can be reduced through the medium of the tax system.

*(1) As a Business Expense— Bad Debts*

In the case of loans from financial institutions whose business involves the making of loans the position is relatively straightforward. Such amounts as cannot be recovered are included in the institution's bad debts provision and are deductible as a business expense of the relevant accounting period. Where the level of such bad debts exceeds the institution's income and a trading loss results that loss can be used as all trading losses can, either as a charge against current (non-business) income, or against the profits of future years, or in the case of a terminal loss, against the profits of previous years.

*(2) As a Capital Loss*

If the loan has been provided by non-institutional sources and cannot be deducted as a bad debt (for example, it had been obtained from family or other private sources) the loss may in certain circumstances be deductible for capital gains tax purposes. These circumstances are where the loan is:

    (a) a "debt on a security,"[78] or
    (b) a "qualifying loan."[79]

[78] C.G.T.A. 1979, s.82.
[79] *Ibid.* s.136.

**2.57**

*Debt on a Security*

For a loan to qualify as a debt on a security it would appear that it must be manifested in the form of loan stock or similar company security and that what at first sight might appear to be the substance of the matter, namely, whether the debt created by the loan is charged on any property, is irrelevant, section 82 of the Capital Gains Tax Act 1979 defining "security" as including loan stock or similar security of any company whether secured or unsecured. Indeed the Revenue have ventured the opinion that while unsecured loan stock would fall within the statutory definition, a mortgage or debenture issued by a company to secure a single debt would not.

In *Aberdeen Construction Group Ltd.* v. *I.R.C.*[80] substantial advances were made by a company to its wholly-owned subsidiary on inter-company loan account. On the question of whether these loans amounted to a debt on a security the courts sought to distinguish between a debt and a debt on a security, the fomer being a pure unsecured debt as between the original borrower and lender while the latter referred to a debt (which might be unsecured) which is in the form of a marketable security, possessing a nature and character which would remain constant in all transmissions or which, if not marketable, has at least such characteristics as would enable it to be dealt with and, if necessary, converted into shares or other company securities.[81] The sums advanced were held to be more in the nature of pure unsecured debts than marketable securities.[82]

By way of contrast in *W. T. Ramsay Ltd.* v. *I.R.C.*[83] the case concerned an artificial tax avoidance scheme which involved the artificial creation of a gain on a debt which was not a debt on a security and matching it with a loss on shares in the company which incurred the debt. The Court held that the debt in question was in reality a debt on a security since it was similar to loan stock in that it had all the characteristics of loan stock and was evidenced by a document[84] which was similar to a loan certificate and fulfilled the functions of such a certificate.

Inevitably, while these somewhat imprecise criteria may be adequate to produce a clarification at the extremes of the spectrum of corporate debt borrowing, until they are further refined by the courts it must be a matter of doubt as to whether any given loan will qualify as a debt on a security. Nevertheless, it would seem to be possible to signpost a few of the land-marks.

*Loan Accounts*

Certainly, after the *Aberdeen Construction Group* case inter-company loan accounts in relation to companies within the same group and probably generally do not qualify as debts on a security, lacking the qualities of "loan-stock marketability." It is possible for the terms on which such facilities are set up to be contained in or evidenced in documentary form but there is unlikely to be anything comparable to a stock certificate issued to loan stock holders.

---

[80] [1978] A.C. 885, H.L.
[81] *Ibid.* at p.895 *per* Lord Wilberforce.
[82] In *Cleveley's Investment Trust* v. *C.I.R.* (1971) 47 T.C. 300, the Court of Session held that loan stock issued in respect of a loan amounted to a debt on a security.
[83] [1982] A.C.300, H.L.
[84] In this case a statutory declaration made by a director.

*Term Loan*

Equally, it would seem that a term loan from a single lender, whether or not granted against the security of company assets, would not qualify as a debt on a security. Such a loan would almost invariably be constituted or evidenced in writing and the rights of the lender would be capable of assignment but these rights would nevertheless not compare in terms of marketability or the capacity to be dealt in with a loan stock.

By the same token a single loan provided by a number of lenders jointly would not qualify if it took the form of an ordinary debenture. It is suggested, however, that if the company created debenture stock and constituted the loan by way of a debenture stock trust with the trust deed setting out the rights of the lenders, the terms and units of transferability, made provision for the issue of stock certificates to each of the contributors in respect of their contributions for the loan such a loan would qualify as a debt on a security. On the same principle, and on the authority of *Cleveleys Investment Trust* v. *C.I.R.*,[85] such arrangements made in respect of an advance by a single lender, with that lender being the sole stockholder would appear also to qualify.

*Short or medium-term "notes"*

It is not uncommon for loans to be raised through the issue of "Notes," that is against a promise to pay on a specified date. Public issues, especially in the eurocurrency markets are made by this means as are many of the syndicated loans raised internationally. A note, or more accurately, a promissory note, has the characteristic of negotiability, and as such is inherently marketable and easily dealt in. It is suggested that such an instrument would come within the term "similar company security" in the statutory definition of security.[86] If this is correct then it would follow that a loan raised by this means, whether from a group of borrowers or, by analogy with the single loan-stock holder of the *Cleveley's Investment Trust* case, from a single borrower would qualify as a debt on a security.

*Loan or debenture stock*

It is clear both from the terms of the definition in section 82 and from the decisions of the Court of Session in *Cleveleys Investment Trust* v. *C.I.R.* and *Aberdeen Construction Group Ltd.* v. *I.R.C.*[87] that loans raised through the issue of loan stock, even to a single stockholder, do qualify as debts on a security.

A loss incurred on a loan may also be deductible for capital gains tax purposes **2.58** if it is a "qualifying loan" within the terms of section 136 of the Capital Gains Tax Act 1979. A loan to a company will be a qualifying loan if:

*Qualifying Loans*

[85] (1971) 47 T.C. 300.
[86] C.G.T.A. 1979, s.82.
[87] [1977] S.T.C. 302 affd on this point [1978] A.C. 885, H.L.

(1) the company is resident in the United Kingdom;

(2) the company uses the money loaned wholly for the purposes of its trade or lends it to another company within the same group for use in its trade[88];

(3) the loan is not a debt on a security;

(4) the loan has become irrecoverable but has become so otherwise than as a result of the terms of the loan or of any arrangements of which the loan is a part or as a result of any act or omission of the lender;

(5) the lender has not assigned his right to recover the loan; and

(6) the loss is not taken into account in calculating the lender's income or corporation tax profit.

The relief under section 136 also extends[89] to payments of interest or capital made by a person under a guarantee of a loan which is a qualifying loan or would

*Guarantees* be a qualifying loan but for being a debt on a security.

The relief operates by allowing the amount of the loan that has become irrecoverable (or part) under the guarantee to be treated as an allowable loss accruing when the claim for relief is made.[90]

Section 136(2) however provides that the relief is not available where the borrower and lender are companies within the same group[91] either when the loan is made or at any subsequent time or, in the case of a loan guarantee, additionally where the guarantor and the lender were companies within the same group when the guarantee was given or at any subsequent time.[92] It follows therefore that in cases where the restriction applies indebtedness should take the form of a debt on a security.

# BILLS OF EXCHANGE[93]

## Borrowing via bills of exchange

**2.59** "A bill of exchange is an unconditional order in writing, addressed by one person to another, signed by the person giving it, requiring the person to whom it is

*Bill of* addressed to pay on demand or at a fixed or determinable future time a sum cer-
*Exchange* tain in money to or to the order of a specified person, or to bearer."[94]

For a bill of exchange to be a means of raising funds it must be "accepted" by the person on whom it is drawn. Acceptance is acknowledgement by the drawee

*Acceptance* of his assent to the order of the drawer[95] imposing on him an obligation to make payment according to the tenor of his acceptance.[96] An acceptance may be

---

[88] The trade, however, must not be a money lending trade.

[89] C.G.T.A. 1979, s.136(4).

[90] *Ibid.* s.136(3).

[91] Group for this purpose consists of a resident company and its resident 75 per cent. subsidiaries: C.G.T.A. 1979, s.136(10)(*c*).

[92] *Ibid.* s.136(4)(*d*).

[93] See generally Byles, *The Law of Bills of Exchange* 25th ed., 1983).

[94] Bills of Exchange Act 1882, s.3(1).

[95] *Ibid.* s.17(1).

[96] *Ibid.* s.54(1).

general, as where the drawee's assent is without qualification,[97] or it may be qualified, as for example by designating a place for payment.[98]

Acceptance confers on a bill the character of negotiability. As a negotiable instrument the bill may be transferred by delivery, if made out to bearer, or by delivery and indorsement, if made out to order.[99]

*Negotiability*

Bills of exchange may be either "trade bills," drawn by one trader on another in respect of individual transactions[1] or sets of transactions between them, or "finance" or "bank bills" drawn in pursuance of an acceptance credit facility made available by a bank or accepting house.

**2.60**

An acceptance credit facility is a line of credit granted for the purpose of financing trading assets. The minimum size of such a facility is currently £100,000–£150,000. The principles upon which the facility is made available are as follows.

*Acceptance Credit Facilities*

(1) *There must be an underlying transaction or series of transactions.* A common situation where an acceptance credit facility is granted is when an importer has completed a contract for an overseas customer for settlement at a stipulated date in the future or at a future date in accordance with the customs and usages of the particular trade.[2] Again, an importer of raw materials may wish to finance the purchase of these materials prior to their sale as finished goods.[3] Or, it may be that a British company merely wishes to finance stocks pending their resale.[4]

*Principles of Acceptance Credit*

(2) *That transaction or transactions must be self-liquidating.* The purpose of an acceptance credit facility is primarily to bridge a gap between a large financial outlay and the time when the company receives a return from it.[5] However, since the source of funds for the provision of such a facilitiy is the wholesale money market and in particular the discount market[6] the institution granting the facility will wish to be certain that it will be in funds to meet its commitment on the acceptance. Accordingly, therefore, facilities are seldom granted in respect

---

[97] *Ibid.* s.19(1) and (2).

[98] *Ibid.* s.19(2). Where a particular place of payment is specified the place is not regarded as the exclusive place of payment (s.19(2)(c)) and the acceptor can be sued for payment at another place. Where, however, it is expressly stipulated that the bill is to be paid at a particular place only and not elsewhere the acceptor can only be sued at that place. In the event of the acceptor adding on exclusive place of payment to his acceptance the holder of the bill is entitled to treat the acceptance as qualified and the bill as dishonoured (s.44). He cannot claim this right if the payment is not made exclusive: see *Bank Polski* v. *K.J. Mulder & Co.* [1942] 1 K.B. 497.

Where an acceptance is qualified in this way the drawer, if he regards the acceptance as unsatisfactory, can make the bill unsaleable.

[99] *Ibid.* s.31.

[1] For example, a purchaser of goods or services rather than remitting the purchase price on open account may allow the vendor to draw a bill of exchange on him payable in, say, 90 days. Such an arrangement holds the advantage for the purchaser that it permits him a certain period of credit and for the vendor that he obtains a negotiable asset which he can use to raise funds to cover this interval. Note that trade bills are naturally found in the export trade.

[2] As a condition of granting such a facility the exporter will normally be required to take out credit insurance, usually under an E.C.G.D. policy.

[3] Notably those using commodities, *e.g.* tobacco, tea, wool, timber etc.

[4] See Schmitthoff, *The Export Trade* (7th ed. 1980) Chapter 21.

[5] Acceptance credit facilities are often employed by firms with a seasonal or cyclical pattern to their financing needs.

[6] See above at §1.55.

of individual transactions where the proceeds of the transactions financed will not have been received to repay the amount made available. Where a general, rather than an individual, facility is granted this problem can be overcome by the drawing of further bills.

(3) *Security.* The provision of an acceptance credit facility will, in the ordinary course only be made against some form of security, although borrowers of high standing such as large listed companies or public corporations may obtain unsecured facilities. Where the facility relates to an individual transaction the security normally takes the form of a charge or lien over the assets that are the subject of the transaction.[7] In cases where the facility is made available on a longer term basis further security may be required in the form of a fixed charge over specified assets of the company.

(4) *Extended facilities.* Extended facilities are available permitting the borrower to draw bills as required up to an agreed limit. In some cases the facilities are made available "until further notice" in which event it is reviewed periodically.

**2.61**

*Financing via Bills of Exchange*

An accepted bill may be used as a means of raising finance, either by using it as security for a loan or by having it discounted.

*Security for a loan*

Where a bill is given as security for a loan[8] the position of the lender is that of pledgee, having a lien over the bill for the amount advanced. As such the lender acquires an independent title and right to sue and may hold the bill against the true owner until his debt is satisfied.[9] He may not however in the ordinary course negotiate it, in the absence of a provision to the contrary in the loan agreement. Where the loan remains unpaid on the contractual repayment date the proper course[10] is for the lender to continue to hold the bill until maturity, to present it for payment, and use the proceeds to repay the amount of he advance together with any costs[11]; any balance remaining should be returned to the borrower or held as trustee for him.[12] If the bill is payable on a fixed date and, for whatever reason, the lender neglects to present it for payment he will have to bear any loss incurred by the omission.[13]

---

[7] Where the underlying transaction is the import of goods the security often takes the form of the relevant shipping documents.

[8] A bill deposited with a banker as security for an advance or overdraft does not, in contrast to a bill given for a debt, suspend the remedy for the debt. There is nothing in law to prevent a banker from suing for an overdraft during the currency of a bill at a fixed date which he has taken as security: see *Peacock* v. *Pursell* (1843) 14 C.B.N.S. 728.

[9] Se Paget, *Law of Banking* (9th ed., 1982) at pp.415 *et seq.*

[10] Paget, *op. cit.*

[11] *Barclays Bank Ltd.* v. *Aschaffenburger Zellstoffwerke A.G.* [1967] 1 Lloyds Rep. 387, C.A.

[12] *Barclays Bank Ltd.* v. *Aschaffenburger Zellstoffwereke A.G.*, *supra.* Note that in respect of indebtedness to a banker, the banker could retain such surplus to meet further indebtedness of the customer: see *Jones* v. *Peppercorne* (1858) Johns 430; *Inman* v. *Clare* (1858) John 769; *Re London and Globe Financing Corpn. Ltd.* [1902] 2 Ch. 416; Re *Bower, Earl of Strathmore* v. *Vane* (1886) 33 Ch. D. 586.

[13] *Peacock* v. *Pursell, supra.*

*Discounting*

To discount a bill of exchange is to purchase it for an amount being the face value of the bill less a sum representing interest for the period for which the bill has to run. While, given the nature of the bill, discounting is a means of lending, it differs from taking as security in that the bank or discount house making the purchase takes the bill as transferee for value. To discount a bill is to negotiate it with the consequence that the discounter is free to deal with the bill as he pleases. As holder of the bill the discounter can claim performance of the obligations stipulated in it and has the normal right to sue on a bill if it is dishonoured. If the bill is complete and *ex facie* regular and the discounter took it in good faith and for value and without notice of any defect in the title of the person negotiating it to him and before it was overdue and without notice that it was dishonoured then the discounter, as "holder in due course," will hold the bill free from any defect of title of prior parties as well as from mere personal defences available to prior parties amongst themselves, and may enforce payment against all parties named on the bill.

## DEBT SECURITIES

Debt financing which does not take the form of privately negotiated loans[14] **2.62** will invariably be obtained by a company via the issue of debt securities. Sometimes funds will be raised by means of a rights issue with loan stock being offered to existing shareholders: often an issue will be made to the public generally. Given that such an issue is seeking funds from a potentially large number of investors this form of financing is generally speaking open only to those companies of sufficient size and standing to have access to the securities markets.[15]

### Constitution of debt securities

Debt securities will take the form of an issue of debentures or debenture/loan **2.63** stock. Unless those providing the finance are a very small number of bodies or individuals (and even then) it is generally more convenient to effect the issue through the medium of a trust with the lenders becoming entitled to a beneficial interest in equity in the rights under the contract of loan to which the company and the trustees are the parties. This beneficial interest is represented by a holding of stock in respect of which a certificate is issued.

Debenture securities are very occasionally issued by British companies[16] in

---

[14] See above at §§2.10–2.55.

[15] Although not exclusively so. It is always open to institutional lenders and others to make their investments in return for an issue of stock. We have seen (*supra* at § 2.57) that there may be the advantages for private lenders in such a course since the loan would rank as a debt on a security.

[16] The power to issue debentures to bearer in Scotland derives from C.A. 1985, s.197. Insofar as companies in England are concerned the power to issue such securities derives from the law merchant, creating an exception to the rule of general application that a debt cannot be assigned merely by delivery of the document that creates or evidences it. Additionally, a company may be estopped from denying its liability to pay a debenture if it has invited persons to accept a transfer by delivery, and has held out or represented that the debentures so transferred give the bearer a right to be paid: see *Re Agra and Masterman's Bank* (1867) 2 Ch. App. 391; *Re Blakely Ordnance Co.* (1867) 3 Ch. App. 154; *Re Natal Investment Co.* (1868) 3 Ch. App. 355; *Re Imperial Land Co.* (1871) 11 Eq. 478 at p. 487; *Goodwin* v. *Roberts* (1876) 1 App. Cas 476; *Eaglesfield* v. *Londonderry* (1877) 4 Ch. D. 702, C.A.; *Re Romford Canal Co.* (1883) 24 Ch. D. 85.

the form of bearer bonds. Such bonds are negotiable instruments transferable by transfer of the certificates which set out the terms of issue or refers to the place where such terms can be inspected. Bearer bonds are issued with coupons attached, the presentation of which to the company's paying agent at the appropriate time will alone ensure payment of interest to the holder.

The issue of bearer securities by British companies and public corporations is made subject to Treasury consent by section 10 of The Exchange Control Act 1947. Prior to 1979 this requirement was deemed to have been satisfied where the securities had been deposited with a bank or other authorised depository.[17] With the dismantling of exchange controls in 1979 these requirements ceased to operate even though the Exchange Control Act 1947 was not repealed.

### Loan stock trust

**2.64**   The deed of trust executed in respect of an issue of debenture or loan stock will normally deal with the following matters.

*Parties*

The parties to the trust deed will be the borrower company and the trustee, usually a trust corporation since one of the requirements[18] for admission to listing by the Stock Exchange is that the sole trustee or one of the trustees must be a trust corporation having no conflicting interest.

The parties clause would read:

> THIS TRUST DEED is made the  . . . day of  . . . BETWEEN [*borrower company*] having its registered office as [*address*] (hereinafter called the company) of the one part and [*trust corporation*] having its registered office at [*address*] of the other part.

*Recitals*

This clause refers to the resolution by which the stock was created and gives the designation of the stock in question, (*i.e.* whether it is debenture stock, unsecured loan stock, convertible loan stock, *etc.*) It should be noted that one of the requirements[19] for admission to listing on the Stock Exchange is that the designation of securities is not to include the word "mortgage" unless the securities are to a substantial extent secured by a specific mortgage or charge.

> WHEREAS the company on the  . . . day of  . . . by a resolution of its board of directors created  . . . . . . percent. [First Mortgage] [Convertible] Debenture Stock 19 . . . and determined to constitute and secure the same in manner hereinafter appearing.

---

[17] E.C. Notice 10.
[18] Stock Exchange—Admission of Securities to Listing, Section 9 Chapter 2.
[19] *Ibid.* at para. 6.2.

*Issue clauses*

These clauses provide for the issue of stock and for the provision of certificates to stock holders. They also normally provide for the stock's transferability stating the minimum amount of stock (usually 1p) that may be transferred

"1. The stock may be issued to such persons at such times and on such terms and either on par or on a premium or on a discount as the company may think fit. The stock shall be transferable in units of 1p."

"2. Every stockholder shall be entitled to receive one certificate for the amount of the stock held by him but joint holders shall be entitled to only one certificate for the stock held jointly by them which certificate shall be delivered to that one of the joint holders whose name first appears in the register and the company shall not be bound to register more than [four] persons as the joint holders of any of the stock. The certificates for stock shall be under the seal of the company affixed with the authority of the directors and in the manner provided by the articles of association for the time being of the company. The certificates for the stock shall be in the form or substantially in the form shown in the first schedule hereto and have indorsed thereon conditions in the form or substantially in the form also shown in that schedule. The company shall comply with the provisions of the stock certificates and perform the several conditions indorsed thereon respectively and the stock shall be held subject in all respects to such conditions which shall be deemed to be incorporated herein and shall be binding upon the company and the stockholders and all persons claiming through or under them respectively. The deed will also provide for the company to open and maintain a register of stockholders."

*Amount of stock*

These clauses set out the amount of stock to be issued and provide for all the stock so issued to rank pari passu in all respects and without discrimination or preference. If it is intended or desired to make provision for the issue of additional stock at some future time this should be dealt with here.

"3. The Principal amount of the [original] stock is limited to . . . The whole of the [original] stock shall rank pari passu in all respects and without discrimination or preference.

Power is reserved to the company at any time and from time to time to create and issue additional debenture stock either so as to rank pari passu in all respects and to form a single issue with the original stock or upon such terms and conditions as to rate of interest redemption and otherwise as the directors may determine but to rank pari passu in point of security with the original stock subject to the following conditions and provisions, namely:

(1) The aggregate principal amount of such additional stock so created shall not exceed . . . ;

(2) No additional stock shall be issued credited as fully or partly paid up by capitalisation of profits or reserves;

(3) No additional stock not being identical in all respects with the original stock shall be redeemed (other than on enforcement) so long as any of the original stock is outstanding;

(4) Any additional stock shall be constituted and secured by a deed or deeds in favour of the trustees expressed to be supplemental to this deed in such form as the trustees shall approve, and shall not be or become a charge upon any part of the mortgaged premises unless and until the company shall deliver to the trustees a properly stamped and executed deed constituting the same, and in no case shall this deed apart from such supplemental deed or deeds be deemed to constitute a security for debenture stock in excess of the original stock."

*Payment of principal and interest*

While section 193 of the Companies Act 1985 empowers a company to issue perpetual[20] debentures or loan stock, whether secured or otherwise, modern debt securities issued by companies normally provide for a redemption date, or sometimes for a period of (usually five or ten) years during which the company may exercise its right to redeem all outstanding stock on giving requisite notice in writing to the stockholders.

The standard repayment clause reads:

*Repayment/*
*Redemption*
*Clause*

"4. The company will on the . . . day of . . . or on such earlier date as the security hereby constituted becomes enforceable and the trustees determine or become bound to enforce the same pay to the trustees at the registered office or such other place as the trustees shall approve in writing the principal amount of the stock."

A trust deed will sometimes provide for the setting up of a sinking fund out of which stock can be redeemed from time to time or purchased in the market. The terms of the deed governing its operation will naturally set out the position with regard to interest on unredeemed stock and specifically whether this is to be used to augment the fund.[21]

(1) The stock shall be redeemed by the operation of a sinking fund under the provisions following:

---

[20] See generally Palmer *Company Law,* at paras. 43.04–43.06. Note that "one-way option" securities *i.e.* those redeemable at the option of the company (see *Edinburgh Corporation* v. *British Linen Bank* [1913] A.C. 33 H.L) are essentially in the same category, not being repayable at the demand of the holder.

[21] Such a provision will not be inferred: see *Morrison* v. *Chicago and North West Granaries Co.* [1898] 1 Ch.263. Note that if the sinking fund is to be applied in the redemption of loan stock by purchase, as is usually the case, the trustees are under a duty to use it to the best advantage of all concerned, including the company. In *National Trust Co.* v. *Wicher* [1912] A.C. 377, D.C. trustees were held not bound to accept the lowest tender where, by accepting an offer for a larger block for sale, they could effect a more beneficial redemption.

(a) The company shall in each year while any of the stock remains outstanding on or before the . . . day of . . . set aside [and pay to the trustees] as a sinking fund the sum of £ . . . , and a further sum equal to the interest (without deduction of income tax) which would have been payable during the then current year on all stock previously redeemed out of the sinking fund if such stock had remained outstanding.

*Sinking Fund Provision*

(b) The company shall forthwith upon such setting aside endeavour to purchase in the open market at the lowest price not exceeding . . . per £100[22] of stock at which it is possible to purchase it so much of the stock as the sum set aside shall suffice to purchase.

(c) On or before the last day of the month next succeeding such setting aside as aforesaid the company shall cause a drawing to be made in such manner as is hereinafter provided of so much of the stock as the year's sinking fund payment less any amount expended in the purchase of the stock in the open market shall be sufficient to redeem (without taking into account any interest accrued or to accrue thereon) and shall apply the said sinking fund payment to the redemption of the stock so drawn.

*(2) Drawings*

(2) Where any part of the stock is to be selected for redemption by drawings the drawings shall be made by one of the officers of the company at the registered office of the company or at some other place approved by the trustees in the presence of a notary public or a solicitor of the Supreme Court. Notice in writing of the date time and place of every such drawing shall be given by the company to the trustees and the trustees or any person appointed by them shall be entitled to be present at every such drawing. Every such drawing shall be [in sums] of [£100] of stock [and] made in such manner as the company (subject to the reasonable approval of the trustees) shall determine as convenient for selecting the amount of stock required to be drawn. The company shall give notice to the holders of the stock drawn that such stock has been drawn.

*(3) Selection of Stock to be Redeemed by Drawings*

(3)(a) Every stockholder any of whose stock is due to be redeemed under condition . . . hereof [or any of the provisions hereof] shall not later than the due date for such redemption deliver up his stock certificate to the company and if any certificate so delivered up includes any stock not then due to be redeemed the company may enface such certificate with a memorandum of the date and amount redeemed and return the same or may cancel such certificate and issue to such stockholder a new certificate for the balance of the stock held by him and not so due to be redeemed and return the same or may cancel such certificate and issue to such stockholder a new certificate for the balance of the stock held by him and not so due to be redeemed.

*(4) Delivery up of Stock Certificates*

(b) If any stockholder any of whose stock is due to be redeemed under condition . . . hereof [or any of the provisions hereof] shall fail or

---

[22] If the stock is to be quoted on the Stock Exchange, the lots into which the stock is to be divided for the purpose of a drawing must not be more than £100, or £1,000 if the outstanding stock subject to redemption is not less than £2,000,000.

*(5) Holding of Redemption Monies by Trustees*

refuse to deliver up the stock certificate held by him at the time and place fixed for the redemption of the stock to which such certificate relates or shall fail or refuse to accept payment of the redemption monies payable in respect thereof the monies payable to such stockholder shall be set aside and paid to the trustees and shall be held by them in trust for such stockholder and such setting aside shall be deemed for all the purposes of this deed to be a payment to such stockholder and interest on such stock shall cease to accrue as from the date fixed for redemption thereof and the company shall thereby be discharged from all obligations in connection with such stock. If the trustees shall place the monies so paid to them on deposit at a bank the trustees shall not be responsible for the safe custody of such monies or for interest thereon except such interest (if any) as the said monies may earn whilst on deposit less any expenses incurred by the trustees.

The clause providing for repayment of the pincipal of the debt is often coupled with a covenant to pay interest thereon. The necessity for such a covenant is the common law rule that interest is not payable on a debt except by agreement.[23] The standard form in which such a covenant is cast is as follows:

"The company will until the whole of the stock has been paid off or redeemed pay to the trustees at the registered office of the company or at such other place as aforesaid[24] interest on such principal amount for the time being out-standing at the rate of . . . per cent per annum half yearly on the . . . day of . . . and the . . . day of . . . in every year the first of such payments to be made and calculated in accordance with the terms of issue of the stock. Provided that every payment to any stockholder on account of principal or interest shall be a satisfactory of the covenant of the company in this clause contained."

*Covenants by the company*

As in a loan agreement[25] with a private individual or institution a company will enter into positive and negative covenants relating to the conduct of its business, the preservation of its assets and to provide accounts and information where appropriate. The form of such covenants contained in a trust deed is as follows:

6. The company hereby covenants with the trustees that at all times during the continuance of this security:

*Covenants (1) To Maintain and Repair*

(1) it will maintain and keep in proper order repair and condition such parts of the [specifically] mortgaged premises as are of a repairable nature and the trus-

---

[23] *Higgins* v. *Sargant* (1823) 2 B. & C. 348; *Page* v. *Newman* (1829) 9 B. & C. 378. And see at § 2.16 *supra*.

[24] *i.e.* such other place as the trustees shall approve in writing in relation to the repayment of the principal of the debt. If no place is named for repayment of the principal it is the duty of the company as debtor to find and pay the debenture stock holder: see *Thorn* v. *City Rice Mills* (1889) 40 Ch. D. 357.

[25] See above, at §§2.35, 2.36.

tees shall have power in the event of any such part of the [specifically mortgaged premises being or becoming out of proper order repair or condition themselves to repair or to put and maintain the same in proper order and condition and any expenses incurred by the trustees and their costs and charges therein shall be a debt due from the company payable on demand and while unpaid shall be a charge on the mortgaged premises ranking in priority to this security;

(2) it will insure and keep insured to the satisfaction of the trustees and to the full [replacement] value thereof all such parts of the mortgaged premises as are of an insurable nature against loss or damage by fire explosion lightning storm tempest flood (where appropriate) aircraft and things dropped therefrom and such other risks as in accordance with sound commercial practice are normally insured against by companies carrying on a similar business in one or more insurance offices to be approved by the trustees or with Lloyd's underwriters [and will insure and keep insured as aforesaid against consequential loss for [two] years following the happening of any risk so insured against] and will procure that the interest of the trustees as mortgagees is duly noted on the policies of insurance and will produce the policies of such insurance to the trustees if required and duly pay or cause to be paid the premiums and other sums of money payable in respect of such insurance and if required produce to the trustees the receipt for the same within [seven] days of the same becoming due. All monies received by virtue of any such insurance shall so far as they are in respect of part of the specifically mortgaged premises be deemed part of the specifically mortgaged premises and shall be paid the trustees and shall be applied in making good the loss or damage in respect of which the monies were received or in such other manner as the trustees shall approve; *(2) To Insure Premises*

(3) it will not remove or destroy or suffer to be removed or destroyed any part of the specifically mortgaged premises except for the purpose of renewing or replacing the same and will in such case forthwith renew or replace the same accordingly; *(3) Not to Remove Property*

(4) it will duly and punctually pay perform and observe all rents rates taxes stamp duties covenants and other obligations whatsoever which ought to be paid or to be observed or performed by the company in respect of any part of the mortgaged premises; *(4) To Pay Rent, Rates and Taxes*

(5) it will permit the trustees or any person or persons authorised by them at any time and from time to time during the usual times of business so long as any money shall remain due upon the security of this deed to inspect and examine any part of the specifically mortgaged premises and will afford the trustees and their agent access to the specifically mortgaged premises and render them or him such assistance as may be required for any of the purposes aforesaid; *(5) To Allow Inspection of Mortgaged Premises*

(6) it will keep proper books of account which shall at all reasonable times be open to inspection by the trustees or any receiver appointed by them and any person appointed by the trustees or any such receiver for that purpose and will furnish to the trustees or any such receiver or agent all such information relating to the business or affairs of the company as they or he shall require [and will deliver to the trustees at least [twenty-one] days before the annual general meeting of the company each year a copy [*or* . . . copies] of the balance sheet and profit and loss account of the company certified by the auditors of the company *(6) To Provide Accounts and Other Information*

and copies of the auditors' and directors' reports thereon together with copies of any other documents required by law to be attached thereto[26];

(7) it will carry on and conduct its business in a proper and efficient manner;

*(7) To Carry on Business Properly*

(8) it will permit the trustees to hold the title deeds of the specifically mortgages premises;

*(8) Custody of Title Deeds*

(9) it will forthwith on receipt of the same deliver to the trustees all orders directions notices and any other thing whatsoever affecting or likely to affect the specifically mortgaged premises but the company shall be entitled at its own expense to take a copy thereof;

*(9) Transmission of Notices*

(10) it will duly register this mortgage and charge so as to comply with the provisions of sections 395–398 of the Companies Act 1985;

*(10) Registration of Charges*

[(11) it will not without the written consent of the trustees register, under the Land Registration Acts 1925 and 1936 or any statutory modification or re-enactment thereof, its title to the specifically mortgaged premises or any part thereof and the costs of registering a caution against such registration shall be deemed to be costs properly incurred by the trustees hereunder;]

*(11) Not to Register Premises under L.R.A. without Permission*

(12) it will comply with the requirements of the Town and Country Planning Acts (that is to say the Town and Country Planning Act 1971 so far as such requirements relate to the specifically mortgaged premises or any part thereof and will promptly produce to the trustees any notice order direction requisition premission or other document served on it in connection with such Acts which affects or is likely to affect the specificaly mortgaged premises or any part thereof;

*(12) To comply with T. & C.P. Acts*

[(13 Within [two] months of [the conversion of any of the stock into ordinary shares of the company whether effected voluntarily or compulsorily pursuant to the conditions indorsed on the certificates therefor and of] any purchase of the stock made by the company in accordance with the conditions indorsed on the certificate therefor [or such conditions] it will furnish to the trustees particulars of the same].

*(13) To give Particulars of Conversion and Purchase*

### Obligations and liability of trustees

The primary function of the trustees of a debenture/loan stock trust is to watch over the affairs of the company on behalf of the stockholders taking such action as may appear to them to be necessary to safeguard the interests of their beneficiaries. In practice however the trustees appear to regard their role rather differently, as being to discharge a custodial rather than an interventionist function, with their responsibilities being to secure the documents relating to the issue, in some cases to maintain the register of stockholders (although the trust deed normally requires the company to do this) and to attend to the half-yearly issue of warrants for the payments of interest (although, again, in most cases the trustee will not be actively concerned with this, leaving it to the company's registrars). Furthermore the modern trust deed reinforces this view by including a clause

---

[26] C.A. 1985, s.240 imposes a statutory obligation to send accounts to debenture and debenture stock holders.

providing that the trustees shall not be bound to enforce the covenants entered into by the company.

Such a clause is frequently in the following form:

> 7.[(1)] The trustees may but shall not be bound unless [(subject to the provisions of sub-clause (2) of clause [8] hereof)] requested to do so in writing by the registered holders of not less than [one-fifth] part of the stock for the time being outstanding or by an extraordinary resolution to enforce or take any step to enforce the covenants in clause [6] hereof contained, and (subject to any such request as aforesaid) may waive on such terms and conditions as they shall deem expedient any of the covenants and provisions hereinbefore contained and on the part of the company to be performed and observed.

In addition the trust deed often contains a similar clause in relation to the management of the company. Thus:

> [(2)]. [until this security shall have become enforceable and the trustees shall have determined or become bound to enforce the same] the trustees shall not be in any manner bound or concerned to interfere with the management of the company or its business or affairs or the custody care preservation or repair of the mortgaged premises or any part thereof unless [(subject to the provisions of sub-clause (2) of clause [8] hereof)] requested to do so by an extraordinary resolution.

If a stockholder wishes to take steps himself to enforce the security he may, in England at least, proceed directly[27] by joining the trustees as co-plaintiffs or, if they refuse to be so joined, as co-defendants.[28] In Scotland it is doubtful whether the rules or procedure permit this course. Some trust deeds make specific provision for a stockholder to pursue his rights directly without the consent of the trustees but require a period of notice (usually one week) to be given to the trustees.

Nevertheless the trustees as trustees will be subject to the obligations imposed on them by the general law of trusts and will be entitled to the powers, reliefs and indemnities conferred on them by that law. Most trust deeds seek to enlarge upon this with express clauses seeking to define or exclude situations which might give rise to liability. Such a clause commonly take the following form:

> 8. [(1)] Without prejudice to the powers and reliefs conferred on trustees by the general law, by this deed or by the Trustee Act 1925 [or Trusts (Scotland) Acts 1921 and 1961] or any statutory modification or re-enactment thereof, the trustees shall have the following powers:
>
> (a) To employ and pay at the cost of the company in discharge of their duties under this deed any servant or agent to do any thing or transaction any business to be done or transacted hereunder, without being under any liability for any default of such servant or agent;

---

[27] Note that where the security is by debenture (as opposed to debenture stock) there is no problem in either England or Scotland about going to court for the appointment of a receiver.
[28] See *Franklin* v. *Franklin* [1915] W.N. 342.

(b) To rely on the advice of any lawyer, broker, surveyor, valuer or accountant or other professional person without incurring any liability for so relying notwithstanding that such professional person may have been employed by the company or may otherwise not be dis-interested and without incurring liability for any error in the transmission of any such advice or by reason of the same not being authentic;

(c) To delegate any of their discretions under this deed to any officer or servant of the trustees believed by them to be competent and responsible and to delegate any of their powers and duties under this deed to such persons (including any such officer or servant as aforesaid) as they shall think fit, and to confer power to sub-delegate, without incurring any liability for the default of any person to whom such discretions powers or duties are delegated or sub-delegated;

(d) To act upon the directions of an extraordinary resolution without incurring any liability in case it is subsequently shown that the meeting at which the resolution was passed was irregular or the resolution was otherwise invalid;

(e) To deposit any of the documents of title relating to the mortgaged premises with any banker or firm of solicitors or accountants or in any safe or other place where securities are commonly kept without being further responsible for their safe keeping;

(f) To accept such title as the company has to any of the mortgaged premises without being liable for accepting a defective title;

(g) To allow any of the stockholders' money to be paid direct to the company without being concerned to see to the application thereof;

And generally none of the trustees shall be liable for any error of judgment committed in good faith unless it shall be proved that he was negligent in ascertaining the pertinent facts and the trustees their officers servants and agents and any receiver appointed by the trustees shall be entitled to be indemnified out of the mortgaged premises so far as may be lawful in respect of all liabilities incurred in the execution of the trusts of this deed.

At one time it was usual to conclude this clause with a blanket exemption covering everything except fraud. Now, however, section 192 of the Companies Act 1985 cuts down the effectiveness of such a term rendering it void insofar as it would have the effect of exempting a trustee from or indemnifying him against liability for breach of trust where he fails to show the degree of care and diligence required of him, having regard to the provisions of the trust deed conferring on him any powers, authorities or discretions. The application of this provision is restricted, though, so that it is not to operate to deprive a trustee of any exemption or right to be indemnified in respect of anything done or omitted to be done while such a term was in force.[29] More specifically it will not invalidate:

(a) any release otherwise validly given in respect of anything done or omitted to be done by a trustee before the giving of the release; or

---

[29] C.A. 1985, s.192(3).

(b) any provision enabling such a release to be given;

     (i) on the agreement of a majority of not less than three-fourths in value of the stockholders present and voting at a metting summoned for the purpose; and

     (ii) either with respect to specific acts or omissions as on the trustees dying or ceasing to act.[30]

*Remuneration of trustees*

The trust deed will normally contain a covenant by the company to pay the trustees remuneration as a specified level. The terms of the deed will normally seek to define with some precision the consequences for the payment of such remuneration of the appointment of a receiver.[31] Furthermore trustees commonly insist upon a declaration that this remuneration is to be paid out of the property charged (where the loan is secured) in priority to the principal debt, thereby seeking to ensure payment even in the event of the property being sold.

The trustees remuneration clause is commonly in the following form:

9. The company shall during the continuance of this security pay to the trustees in respect of their services as trustees remuneration at the rate of . . . per annum such remuneration to accrue from day to day from the date of the first allotment of any of the stock [and to be increased whenever any additional stock shall be issued by a sum equal to £ . . . per annum for each complete £ . . . of additional stock so issued such increase to be effective in every case from the date of issue of the additional stock in question] [PROVIDED that if this security shall become enforceable the said remuneration and increased remuneration (if any) shall thereupon be doubled]. All such remuneration shall be payable in arrear on the . . . day of . . . and the . . . day of . . . in each year. The company shall in addition pay all travelling and other costs charges and expenses which the trustees shall incur in connection with the execution of the trusts hereof and the exercise of the powers and discretions hereby vested in them together with interest thereon as hereinafter provided. The said remuneration and increased remuneration (if any) shall continue notwithstanding that a receiver shall have been appointed or that the trusts hereof shall be in course of administration by or under the direction of the court. All remuneration costs charges and expenses due to the trustees or to any receiver appointed by them shall be payable upon demand and pending payment shall carry interest at the rate of . . . per cent per annum.

10. The trustees may retain and pay to themselves out of any monies or the proceeds of any investments in their hands upon the trusts of this deed all sums owing to them or any receiver appointed by them in respect of remuneration costs charges expenses or interest or by virtue of any indem-

---

[30] C.A. 1985, s.192(2).
[31] See *Re Piccadilly Hotel* [1911] 2 Ch. 534; *Re Angloe-Canadian Lands* [1918] 2 Ch. 287; *Re British Consolidated Oil Corp.* [1919] 2 Ch. 81; *Re Locke and Smith* [1914] 1 Ch. 687, C.A.

nity from the company to which they are entitled hereunder or by law or by virtue of any release or indemnity granted pursuant to the provisions set out in the [third] schedule hereto and all such sums as aforesaid shall be an additional charge upon the mortgaged premises and shall rank in priority to the claims of the stockholders.

## Types of debt securities

**2.65**    The various categories of debt securities and the characteristics of each have been mentioned in general terms in Chapter 1 above.[32] Since the mid-1970s the amount of capital raised through the securities market by British companies through the medium of debt securities has been very small. While eurobond issues,[33] often with share warrants attached, have been fairly common during the last five years the raising of loan capital on the domestic markets is still at a low level.

Of the types of debt securities issued through the markets since the war easily the most common has been unsecured loan stock. During the late 1960s and early 1970s convertible loan stocks were fairly extensively employed in take-over and merger situations. In addition, apart from secured debenture stock, companies have from time to time raised funds through the issue of short or medium term and, most recently, perpetual "notes."

## Unsecured loan stock

**2.66**    For a company to be able to raise funds through an issue of unsecured loan stock it ought to have a record of success over past years and sound prospects of future success, at least until the redemption period arrives, the point being that an investment in such stock is secured, not by any legal guarantee but by the company's continued successful performance. Nevertheless a measure of legal protection is afforded by the inclusion in the trust deed covenants by the company on behalf of itself and its subsidiaries seeking to ensure that in the event of a liquidation the assets of the company or group will not be consumed in the payment of secured creditors. These covenants fall into four groups.

### Restrictions on the right of the company to issue further stock

*Stockholder Protection Covenants*    In most cases the company will make a single issue of a particular stock with no intention of increasing or extending it in the futre. Nevertheless many trust deeds[34] contain provisions reserving power to the company to issue additional stock and in order to prevent the absorbtion of the company's income in debt interests to a degree which might put its future stability or development in jeopardy it is usual to include a covenant restricting the company's right to do this in circumstances where the amount of outstanding stock is below specified levels. Such a covenant would take the following form:

[32] At §1.15 *et seq.*
[33] See above at §§2.38 *et seq.* and below at §§2.76 *et seq.*
[34] See above at §2.64.

[11. Subject to the restrictions on borrowings contained in clause 3 hereof the company shall have the right to create and issue additional unsecured loan stock carrying such rights as to interest premium redemption conversion and otherwise as the company may determine (hereinafter called additional stock)

PROVIDED that

(1) No additional stock shall be issued unless the gross amount of one year's interest on the aggregate amounts of the stock and any additional stock which would be outstanding immediately after such issue shall be certified in writing by the auditors to the trustees to be less than [one-third] in amount of the annual average of the combined profits less losses (if any) of the company and of its subsidiaries (so far as they are attributable to the company) for the least number of financial periods immediately preceding the date of the auditors' certificate in respect of which audited accounts have been made up covering a period of at least [thirty-five] months but less than [forty-eight] months.

The combined profits are to be arrived at for the foregoing purpose

(a) after adjustment to take account of any interest in any subsidiary acquired or disposed of during the financial periods concerned or thereafter or to be acquired or disposed or contemporaneously with or in connection with the proposed issue;

(b) after charging all interest except on the stock and any additional stock, interest on borrowings previously repaid out of the proceeds of or replaced by the issue of shares or of any stock or additional stock and interest on borrowing proposed to be so repaid or replaced within . . . months from the date of the proposed issue;

(c) after charging overseas taxation but before charging United Kingdom taxation;

(d) after charging all other expenses (including depreciation and directors' emoluments); and

(e) after making any other adjustments that the auditors may consider appropriate.

(2) No additional stock shall be issued or paid up in whole or in part by way of capitalisation of reserves or undivided profits.

(3) Unless it forms one class with the stock no additional stock shall be issued having a final maturity date before [*date of redemption*] or be redeemed at the option of the company whilst any of the stock remains outstanding nor shall the additional stock have a sinking fund which during the life of the stock would operate if applied by drawings to redeem such additional stock at a faster rate than that at which the stock is being redeemed.

(4) In the event of any additional stock being issued on terms that it shall form a single issue with the stock the sinking fund referred to in condition [ . . . ] of the form of certificate set out in the first schedule hereto will be increased as provided in that condition.]

*Restrictions on borrowings and charges*

Clearly the greatest single threat to unsecured loan stockholders is the subsequent creation of secured debenture stock which by its nature would rank in priority to any unsecured borrowing. Equally, borrowing otherwise than by the issue of stock (for example by way of bank overdraft) if secured would also obtain priority and if unsecured would rank alongside the stock. In order therefore to minimise the risk to the stockholders while at the same time avoiding unduly fettering the company in relation to future fund-raising operations the trust deed will contain a covenant restricting the company's right to create charges and to borrow outside specified limits.

12.(1) The company hereby covenants with the trustees that except with the previous sanction of an extraordinary resolution and so long as any part of the stock remains outstanding it will procure that:

(A) the aggregate principal amount outstanding of all group borrowings (as hereinafter defined) will not at any time exceed an amount equal to . . . times the group capital and reserves (as hereinafter defined); and the aggregate principal amount (including any fixed premium payable on final repayment) outstanding of all preferred group borrowings (as hereinafter defined) will not at any time exceed . . . times the group capital and reserves;

(B) neither the company nor any subsidiary will create any mortgage or charge over any part of its undertaking or assets except as follows, but subject always to the limitations contained in paragraph (A) of this sub-clause:

(i) specific mortgages or charges on any freehold or leasehold property acquired after . . . for the purpose of meeting the cost of acquiring such property to secure a principal amount which when added to the principal amount secured by any subsisting mortgage or charge thereon does not exceed . . . per cent of the purchase price plus any expenses incurred in the acquisition and for this purpose where the property is acquired subject to any such subsisting mortgage or charge the purchase price shall be treated as the amount paid plus the principal amount secured by the subsisting mortgage or charge;

(ii) specific mortgages or charges on freehold or leasehold property already owned by it on . . . or subsequently acquired for the purpose of meeting the cost of erecting buildings or installing plant and machinery to secure a principal amount not exceeding . . . per cent of that cost or at the option of the company of the additional value of the property by reason of the erections or installations made as determined by a valuation made on a basis approved by the trustees by a professional valuer approved by the trustees;

(iii) any specific mortgage or charge in substitution for or replacement of any mortgage or charge created under sub-paragraph

(i) or (ii) of this paragraph or permitted to subsist under paragraph (C) of this sub-clause to secure an amount not exceeding the maximum amount at any time owing on such security whether still outstanding or not at the time of the subsitution or replacement PROVIDED that where assets are substituted they shall not without the consent of the trustees be of substantially greater value than the assets for which they are substituted;

(C) neither the company nor any subsidiary will permit to subsist any mortgage or charge over any part of its undertaking or assets except as follows but subject always to the limitations contained in paragraph (A) of this sub-clause:

    (i) any specific mortgages or charges existing on their respective freehold or leasehold properties on . . . ;

    (ii) any specific mortgages or charges on freehold or leasehold properties acquired subject to such mortgages or charges after . . . ;

    (iii) any mortgages or charges on the freehold or leasehold property of an after-acquired subsidiary existing at the time when it becomes a subsidiary;

    (iv) any mortgages or charges by the company or a subsidiary in favour of a subsidiary or the company so long as the benefit of the mortgage or charge is retained by the company or the subsidiary as the case may be:

(D) PROVIDED ALWAYS that notwithstanding the foregoing provisions of this clause if immediately after and as a result only of the acquisition by the company or a subsidiary of a freehold or leaschold property subject to a mortgage or charge or of an after-acquired subsidiary having preferred borrowings outstanding the aggregate principal amount of all group borrowings then outstanding exceeds the limit imposed by paragraph (A) of this sub-clause it shall not be deemed to be a breach of the provisions of such paragraph but the company shall within six months of such acquisition procure the aggregate principal amount of all group borrowings to be reduced by the amount of such excess and pending such reduction no further indebtedness for borrowings shall be incurred by the company or any subsidiary.

(2) For the purposes of this clause:

"group borrowings" means to the extent that they are not otherwise taken into account:

*Definitions (1) Group Borrowings*

    (a) monies borrowed by the company or by any subsidiary, excepting amounts owing by the company to a subsidiary or by a subsidiary to the company or another subsidiary and excepting any amounts expressly excepted or excluded in paragraphs (b), (c), (d) and (e) of this definition;

    (b) the principal amount (including any premium which may be or become payable on repayment) of any debentures of the company or any subsidiary (whether the same may be or have been issued for cash or wholly or partly for a consideration other than cash) excepting any such debentures which are for the time being owned by the company or any subsidiary;

(c) the principal amount raised by acceptance by the company or any subsidiary or by any bank or accepting house under any acceptance credit opened on behalf of the company or any subsidiary;

(d) the nominal amount of any issued and paid-up share capital (other than equity share capital) of any subsidiary excepting any such share capital which is for the time being owned by the company or any other subsidiary;

(e) the nominal amount of any issued share capital and the amount of any monies borrowed by the company or any subsidiary (not being share capital beneficially owned by or borrowed monies the benefit of indebtedness in respect of which is owned by the company or any subsidiary) the repayment whereof or the payment of interest or dividends whereon is guaranteed or secured in while or in part by the company or any subsidiary.

PROVIDED that monies borrowed by the company or any subsidiary for the purpose of repaying within . . . months in whole or in part any group borrowings shall not pending their application for such purpose be deemed to be group borrowings and references to the borrowing of money or to borrowings shall be construed accordingly;

"preferred group borrowings" means the aggregate principal amount outstanding of all group borrowings excluding:

*(2) Preferred Group Borrowings*

(a) borrowings of the company which are not secured; and

(b) borrowings of any after-acquired subsidiary owing at the date of its becoming a subsidiary other than monies borrowed from bankers or others in the ordinary course of business.

and references to preferred borrowings shall be construed accordingly;

"group capital and reserves" means at any material time the amount standing to the credit of the share capital account of the company plus the aggregate amount standing to the credit of the consolidated capital and revenue reserves of the company and the subsidiaries (including any share premium account or capital redemption reserve fund of the company) plus or minus the amount standing to the credit or debit (as the case may be) of the consolidated profit and loss account of the company and the subsidiaries based on the latest published consolidated accounts of the company

*(3) Group Capital and Reserves*

PROVIDED that:

(A) there shall be excluded from the calculation aforesaid

(i) any sums set aside for future taxation; and

*Borrowing Limit Calculation*

(ii) any amounts attributable to minority interests in subsidiaries;

(B) there shall be deducted from the amount arrived at by the calculation aforesaid

(i) any amount attributable to goodwill or any other intangible asset;

(ii) any amount by which the book value of the quoted investments shown in the consolidated balance sheet incorporated
in such accounts exceeds the market value of those investments; and

(iii) a sum equal to the amount by which the book values of any
assets (not being current assets) of the company or of any subsidiary are written up after . . . or in the case of an after-
acquired subsidiary after the date of its becoming a subsidiary, but so that

    (a) no deduction shall be made under this head in respect
of the writing up of fixed assets to the extent that there
is at the same time written off an amount of goodwill or
other intangible asset representing part of the cost of
acquisition of shares or other property;

    (b) no deduction shall be made under this head in respect
of any writing up of the book values of any freehold or
easehold property having an unexpired term of more
than . . . years of the company or any subsidiary if the
following conditions be satisfied, namely:

        (i) the writing-up shall result from a revaluation
carried out for the purposes of sub-paragraph
(ii) of sub-clause (1)(B) of this clause or a revaluation of the whole or substantially the whole
of such freehold and leasehold properties of the
company and the subsidiaries other than
properties which have been revalued during the
preceding . . . years for the purposes of sub-
paragraph (ii) of sub-clause (1)(B) of this
clause;

        (ii) the revaluation shall have been made on a basis
approved by the trustees (who shall for this purpose be entited to require such revaluation to be
made by a professional valuer approved by the
trustees);

        (iii) in arriving at the amount of such writing up due
provision shall have been made for any taxation
which would or might arise on or as a consequence of the realisation of the properties the
book values of which are so written up on such
basis as the auditors may consider appropriate;
and

        (iv) unless the revaluation is made pursuant to sub-
paragraph (ii) of sub-clause (1)(B) of this clause
the date of any such revaluation of any property
shall be at least . . . years after the date of the
last previous such revaluation and so that any
increase in the book value of any assets result-

ing from their transfer by the company to a subsidiary or by a subsidiary to the company or to
another subsidiary shall be deemed to result
from a writing up of the book value of such
assets;

(C) there shall be added to the amount arrived at by the calculation
aforesaid any amount by which the market values of the listed investments shown in such balance sheet exceeds the book value of those
investments;

(D) such adjustments shall be made to the amount arrived at by the
calculation aforesaid as shall be necessary and appropriate to take
account of any subsdiary not consolidated in such accounts as aforesaid and any increase in or reduction of the issued and paid up share
capital of the company or the share premium account or capital
redemption reserve fund of the company and of the subsidiaries since
the date to which the consolidated balance sheet incorporated in
such accounts shall have been made up and the amount by which any
distribution out of profits earned before the date of such balance
sheet recommended, declared or made since that date exceeds the
amount povided therefor in such balance sheet shall be deducted;

(E) such other adjustments shall be made to the amount arrived at by the
calculation aforesaid as to the auditors shall seem necessary or
appropriate;

(F) The certificate of the auditors as to the amount of the group capital
and reserves at any time shall be conclusive and binding for all purposes.

*Asset preservation covenants*

As in the case of a secured debenture stock so an unsecured loan stock trust
deed will include covenants aimed at preserving the companys assets either from
distribution through improper transactions or from the consequences of damage
or destruction.

13. The company shall not and shall procure that no subsidiary will except
with the consent of the trustees sell transfer lend or otherwise dispose of the
whole or part (being in the aggregate substantial in relation to the company
and all the subsidiaries as a whole) of their respective undertakings or assets
(except in the ordinary course of trading operations or to a subsidiary or the
company if such assets will not thereby become subject to a mortgage or
charge) whether by means of a single transaction or a number of transactions related or not. For this purpose none of the following shall be
deemed to be a sale, transfer, loan or disposal:

(i) The exchange of assets for other assets of a similar nature and
approximately equal value;

(ii) The sale of freehold or leasehold or other property for cash and the
application of the proceeds of the sale in the acquisition of the property whether freehold or leasehold;

(iii) The application of the proceeds of an issue of share or loan capital for the purposes for which it was expressly intended.

Additionally the trust deed wil contain covenants requiring the maintenance and insurance (where appropriate) of the company's assets.[35]

*Stock Enforcement*

Although there is no security to enforce nevertheless trust deeds for unsecured loan stock include provisions setting out procedures whereby the stock may become repayable prior to the redemption date in the event of a breach of covenant. Essentially this procedure involves the calling of a stock-holders' meeting and the passing of a resolution declaring the stock to be immediately repayable.

The occasions on which such action may be taken correspond to those in a secured debenture stock deed.[36] In addition provision is made for the enforcement machinery to be brought into play in the event of a security on another loan being enforced against the company and in the event of contravention of the borrowing limits imposed on the company by the trust deed.

14. (1) The trustees may at their discretion and shall upon the request in writing of the registered holders of at least [$\frac{1}{5}$] in nominal amount of the stock or upon being so directed by an extraordinary resolution by notice in writing to the company declare the stock to have become immediately payable:

(a)–(i) [See below, clause 23, paras. (1)–(9), *substituting* the property of the company *for* the mortgaged premises in *paras.* (3) *and* (6) *and substituting* to the stockholders *for* this security *in para.* (6)];

*Default in Payment of Interest etc.*

(j) if the security constituted by any mortgage or charge upon the whole or any part of the undertaking or assets of the company [or of any subsidiary] shall become enforceable and steps are taken to enforce the same and the taking of such steps shall be certified in writing by the trustees to be in their opinion prejudicial to the stockholders;

*Security Becoming Enforceable*

(k) if any borrowings excluded for the purpose of paragraph (A) or (B) of sub-clause (1) of clause 3 hereof pursuant to the proviso to the definition of group borrowings in sub-clause (2) of clause 3 hereof are not applied in the repayment of other monies borrowed within four months of the relevant transaction which caused the provisions of such proviso to apply and but for such exclusion either of the limits imposed by paragraph (A) or (B) of sub-clause (1) of clause 3 hereof would then be exceeded.

*Contravention of Borrowing Limit*

(2) Upon any such declaration being made as aforesaid the said principal monies shall be deemed to have become immediately payable at the time of the event which shall have happened as aforesaid.

---

[35] See above at §2.64.
[36] *Ibid.*

### Secured loan/debenture stock

**2.67** Where the loan is secured the trust deed will contain the mortgage or charge in favour of the trustees as a result of which the trustees will be placed in the position of mortgagees of the property charged so that, subject to any provision in the deed, they become entitled to exercise all the powers of mortgagees including those relating to the enforcement of the security.

The terms of the clauses relating to the security given will provide for the ranking of the charge and will seek to define the position of any subsidiaries of the company since the security afforded by the trust deed might possibly be impaired if the subsidiaries were free to take unlimited sums of money by borrowings or through the issue of preference shares.

> 15. [(1)] The company as beneficial owner hereby charges by way of first legal mortgage with the payment of the [original] stock [premiums (if any)] and interest thereon and all other monies intended to be hereby secured all the freehold property described in the first part of the second schedule hereto and all the leasehold property described in the second part of that schedule together in each case with all buildings and structures now or hereafter erected thereon and all plant machinery and fixtures now or hereafter affixed thereto.
>
> [(2) If and whenever the company shall acquire [after the date of this deed] any freehold or leasehold property the company shall forthwith inform the trustees in writing of the acquisition and as soon as may be practicable shall deliver to the trustees the deeds and documents in its possession relating to the property so acquired. Subject to any lessors' or other consents that may be required (which consents the company shall use its best endeavours to obtain) the company shall thereupon at its own expense execute sign and do all things which shall be necessary to grant to the trustees a valid first legal mortgage of such property in such form as the trustees shall require as further security for the stock and interest thereon and all other monies intended to be hereby secured.] [Any mortgage or charge created under this proviion shall be postponed and rank subsequently to any mortgage or charge granted pursuant to clause 17(1)(d) below.]
>
> [(3) Not later than the 31st January in each year the company shall deliver to the trustees a certificate in writing signed by [one] of the directors giving particulars of all freehold and leasehold properties acquired by it during the preceding calendar year or stating, if this be the case, that no freehold or leasehold properties were acquired by the company during such year].
>
> 16. The Company hereby charges in favour of the trustees its undertaking and all its assets both present and future including any uncalled capital with the payment of stock and interest thereon and all other monies intended to be hereby secured and such charge shall (except as regards the specifically mortgaged premises) be a first floating charge and shall accordingly in no way hinder or prevent the company (until the security hereby constituted shall have become enforceable and the trustees shall have determined or become bound to enforce the same) from selling alienating leasing paying dividends out of the profits of or otherwise disposing of or dealing with in

the ordinary course of its business the mortgaged premises other than the specifically mortgaged premises.

17. (1) The company shall be entitled to

[(a)  create and issue additional stock in manner hereinbefore provided ranking pari passu in all respects or in point of security with the charges hereby created or agreed to be created;]

(b)  create floating charges [over its book debts, stock-in trade and work in progress *or as the case may be*] ranking [in priority to or] *pari passu* with the floating charge hereby created to secure borrowing in the ordinary course of its business from bankers not exceeding . . . in the aggregate at any one time outstanding;

(c)  create mortgages or charges whether fixed or floating ranking pari passu in point of security with the charges hereby created or agreed to be created to secure sums borrowed or raised by the company to be applied in repaying redeeming or purchasing the whole but not a part of the stock for the time being outstanding PROVIDED that any such mortgage or charge shall only be created at the time of or immediately preceding the repayment redemption or purchase for the purpose of which the said sum is being borrowed or raised;

[(d)  create specific mortgages or charges ranking in priority to the floating charge hereby created upon any freehold or leasehold property including all buildings and structures from time to time erected thereon and all plant machinery and fixtures from time to time affixed thereto acquired by it after the date hereof [otherwise than from a subsidiary]

PROVIDED that

(i)  the mortgage or charge in question is created at the time of the acquisition of the property thereby mortgaged or charged or within the period of [two months] next following such time;

(ii)  the principal amount secured by the mortgage or charge in question does not exceed a sum equal to [two-thirds] of the purchase price paid for such property or if such property was acquired for a consideration other than cash a sum equal to [two-thirds] of the amount which shall be shown to the satisfaction of the trustees to be the then market value of such property; and

(iii)  such property is not purchased wholly or partly out of the proceeds of issue of any of the stock.]

(2)  Save as hereinbefore provided in this clause the company shall not be at liberty to create any mortgage or charge upon the undertaking uncalled capital or assets of the company present or future or any part thereof ranking in priority to or *pari passu* with the floating charge hereby created.

[18.[37](1) The company shall procure that save with the written consent of the

---

[37] If the company has no subsidiaries and is unlikely to have any it may be prepared to accept a complete prohibition on subsidiaries in which case this clause would be unnecessary.

*Subsidiaries*

trustees [*or* with the authority of an extraordinary resolution] no subsidiary of the company will

   [(a)  create any mortgage or charge upon its undertaking or assets or any part thereof otherwise than in favour of the company or another subsidiary of the company;]

    (b)  borrow any monies otherwise than from

        (i)  the company; or

       (ii)  another subsidiary of the company; [or

      (iii)  its bankers in the ordinary course of business];

    (c)  give any guarantee or accept any bill (other than a bill relating to payment for goods purchased in the ordinary course of business);

    (d)  issue any share capital (except ordinary share capital) otherwise than to the company or another subsidiary of the company or as part of a transaction whereby such subsidiary ceases to be a subsidiary of the company.

[(2) The company shall not and shall procure that no subsidiary of the company will save with such written consent [*or* authority] as aforesaid sell or otherwise dispose of any beneficial interest in any share capital (except ordinary share capital) of or any mortgage or charge created by or any indebtedness of any subsidiary of the company PROVIDED that the foregoing provision of this sub-clause shall not apply to any sale or disposal made in connection with a transaction whereby the subsidiary in question will cease to be a subsidiary of the company.]

*Trusts of Mort-gaged Premises*

19. The trustees shall permit the company until the security hereby constituted shall have become enforceable and the trustees shall have determined or become bound to enforce the same to hold and enjoy the mortgaged premises and to receive and apply as it thinks fit all rents and income arising therefrom and (subject to the provisions of this deed) to carry on thereon and therewith any of the businesses authorised by its memorandum of association for the time being. Upon the security hereby constituted becoming enforceable the trustees may (subject to the provisions hereinafter contained as to notice where such provisions are applicable) in their discretion and shall upon the request in writing of the registered holders of not less than [one-fifth] part of the stock for the time being outstanding or upon the request of an extraordinary resolution enter upon and take possession of the mortgaged premises or any part thereof and may as aforesaid in their discretion and shall upon the like request sell call in collect and convert into money the same or any part thereof with all such powers as to the manner in which such sale calling in collection and conversion shall be made as are contained in section 101 of the Law of Property Act 1925 concerning the powers incident to the estate and interests of mortgagees as if the same were fully set out and incorporated herein and by way of extension thereof such sale calling in collection and conversion may be made for such consideration as the trustees shall deem sufficient whether the same shall consist of cash or shares or debentures in some other company or companies or other property of whatsoever nature or partly of one and partly of some other species of consideration and whether such consideration shall be presently payable

or by instalments or at some future date and whether such deferred or future payments shall be secured or not and in all other respects and manner and for any other consideration as the trustees shall think fit and without being liable to account for any loss of or deficiency in such consideration and PROVIDED that the trustees shall not have been negligent in ascertaining the pertinent facts; and for the purposes aforesaid or any of them may execute and do all such assurances and things as they shall think fit. PROVIDED ALWAYS that section 103 of the Law of Property Act 1925 shall not apply to this deed or to the trust or power of sale calling in collection or conversion hereinbefore contained.

20. At any time or times before the security hereby constituted shall have become enforceable and the trustees shall have determined or become bound to enforce the same trustees may at the cost and request of the company and without any consent by the stockholders but without due regard to the interests of the stockholders do or concur with the company in doing all or any of the things which the company might have done with or in respect of the specifically mortgaged premises had not this security been created and particularly but not by way of limitation may sell let exchange surrender develop deal with or exercise any rights in respect of all or any of the specifically mortgaged premises upon such terms or for such consideration or in any such manner as is hereinbefore in clause [19] mentioned and having due regard to the interests of the stockholders as they shall think fit PROVIDED that all property of any description and all net capital monies arising from or receivable upon any such dealing as aforesaid and remaining after payment thereout of the costs and expenses of and incidental to such dealing shall be and become part of the specifically mortgaged premises and shall be assured or paid to the trustees by the company or shall be dealt with by the company as the trustees shall direct or approve.

*Power of Trustees to Concur with the Company in dealing with Specifically Mortgaged Premises*

21. (1) At any such time or times as aforesaid the trustees may at the cost and request of the company and without any consent of the stockholders but with due regard to the interests of the stockholders utilise or apply any monies or the proceeds of any investments for the time being forming part if the specifically mortgaged premises for any of the following purposes:

*Application of Monies Forming Part of Specifically Mortgaged Premises*

  (a) the payment off of any charges on the specifically mortgaged premises ranking in priority to or pari passu with the charges created by or pursuant to this deed;

  (b) the improvement or protection of the specifically mortgaged premises or any part thereof or the addition thereto of any buildings structures fixed plan or machinery or other fixtures;

  (c) the purchase or acquisition of any buildings land easements or other rights relating to land;

  (d) the recoupment of the company in respect of any improvements made to the specifically mortgaged premises or the addition thereto of any buildings structures fixed plant or machinery or other fixtures.

(2) Unless utilised or applied as aforesaid such monies shall be invested by the trustees in one or more of the investments hereinafter authorised.

119

*Withdrawal of*
*Specifically*
*Mortgaged*
*Property on*
*Substitution of*
*other Property*

22. At any such time or times as aforesaid the company shall at its own cost [and with the consent of the trustees] be at liberty to withdraw any of the specifically mortgaged premises from such of the trusts hereof as exclusively relate to the specifically mortgaged premises upon substituting other property whether of the same or a different tenure or kind but of a value equal to or greater than the value of the property proposed to be withdrawn; but in such event the company must prove to the satisfaction of the trustees (who shall be entitled to make at the cost of the company such investigations as to the property proposed to be substituted as they think fit) that the property proposed to be substituted for the same is of a value equal to or greater than the property proposed to be withdrawn and that such property is suitable for the purposes of the company.

23. Subject as hereinafter provided the stock and all unpaid interest which has accrued thereon shall become immediately payable and this security enforceable upon the happening of any of the following events:

(1) If the company makes default for [one month] in the payment of any interest owing on the stock;

(2) If the company makes default in the payment of any principal monies owing in respect of the stock;

(3) If a distress or execution or other process is levied or enforced upon or sued out against any part of the mortgaged premises [or any part of the property of any subsidiary of the company] and is not paid out, withdrawn or discharged within [seven] days;

(4) If the company [or any subsidiary of the company] stops or threatens to stop payment of its debts or ceases or threatens to cease to carry on its business;

(5) If the company [or any subsidiary of the company] is unable to pay its debts within the meaning of section 518(1) of the Companies Act 1985 or any statutory modification or re-enactment thereof;

(6) If an incumbrancer takes possession or a receiver is appointed of the whole or any part of the mortgaged premises [or of the whole or any part of the property of any subsidiary of the company] and such possession or appointment is certified by the trustees to be prejudicial in their opinion to this security;

(7) If an order is made or an effective resolution is passed for winding up of the company [or any subsidiary of the company], except for the purpose of a reconstruction or amalgamation on the terms of which have been approved in writing by the trustees;

(8) If the company without the written consent of the trustees sells or otherwise disposes of the whole or any substantial part of its undertaking or assets;

(9) If the company commits or threatens to commit a breach of any of the covenants or provisions herein contained and on its part to be observed and performed (other than any covenant for the payment of interests [or] principal monies [or premiums] owing in respect of the stock).

PROVIDED that on the happening of any event specified in sub-clauses (1)

(3) or (9) the stock shall nevertheless not become immediately payable and this security shall not become enforceable unless and until

    (i) the trustees shall have first served on the company a preliminary notice requiring the company as the case may be to pay the interest in arrear or to remove discharge or pay out to the satisfaction of the trustees such distress execution or process or to perform and observe the covenant or provisions the breach whereof has been committed or threatened and the company shall have failed or neglected for a period of [fourteen] days to comply with such notice; or

    (ii) the trustees being of opinion that delay might prejudice the stock-holders shall by notice to the company declare this security to be enforceable.

24. Without prejudice to the generality of the provisions of clause [5] hereof at any time or times after the security hereby constituted shall have become enforceable and the trustees shall have determined or become bound to enforce the same the trustees shall have power to do all or any of the following things:

    (1) Carry on the business or any part of the business of the company as agents of the company;

    (2) Employ and dismiss such agents managers clerks accountants servants workmen and others upon such terms as they shall think proper;

    (3) Repair and keep in repair the buildings [factories works machinery plant] and other property of a repairable nature comprised in the [specifically] mortgaged premises and for this purpose the trustees shall have power in so far as the same may be necessary to apply in the name of the company for any licence permission or consent required under any statute order regulation or byelaw made by any competent authority;

    (4) Provide all such machinery materials and things as they may consider necessary;

    (5) Insure all or any of the mortgaged premises which are of an insurable nature against loss or damage by fire and other risks in such sums as they shall think fit;

    (6) Settle arrange compromise and submit to arbitration any accounts claims questions or disputes whatsoever which may arise in connection with the said business or the mortgaged premises or in any way relating to this security and execute releases or other discharges in relation thereto;

    (7) Bring take defend compromise submit to arbitration and discontinue any actions suits or proceedings whatsoever civil or criminal in relation to the mortgaged premises;

    (8) Allow time for payment of any debts either with or without security;

    (9) Execute and do all such acts deeds and things as to the trustees as may appear necessary or proper for or in relation to any of the purposes aforesaid;

    (10) Demise the specifically mortgaged premises or any part or parts

thereof for such terms at such rents and generally in such manner and upon such conditions and stipulations as the trustes shall think fit;

(11) Raise and borrow money on the security of the mortgaged premises or any part thereof in priority to this deed or otherwise upon such terms as they shall think fit;

(12) Generally do and cause to be done such acts and things as the company might have done in the ordinary conduct of its business as well for the protection as for the improvement of the mortgaged premises.

25. (1) At the request of the company or at any time after this security shall become enforceable [or at any time when in the opinion of the trustees this security is likely to become enforceable] or this security or any part thereof is in the opinion of the trustees in jeopardy the trustees may, and shall upon the request in writing of the registered holders of not less than [one-fifth] part of the stock for the time being outstanding or upon the request of an extraordinary resolution, appoint by writing a receiver of all or any part of the mortgaged premises upon such terms as to remuneration and otherwise as the trustees shall think fit and the trustees may from time to time remove any receiver so appointed and appoint another in his stead. A receiver so appointed shall be the agent of the company[38] and the company shall be responsible for such receiver's acts and defaults to the exclusion of liability on the part of the trustees and the stockholders. Nothing herein contained shall render the trustees or any of the stockholders liable to any such receiver for his remuneration costs charges or expenses or otherwise.

(2) If in the opinion of the trustees [this security is no longer likely to become enforceable or if in their opinion] no part of this security is any longer in jeopardy the trustees may discharge any receiver so apppointed but the trustees shall be entitled before exercising such power to demand from the company such indemnities agreements and covenants (including an agreement or covenant to execute at the request of the trustees a further assurance of the floating charge hereby created) as the trustees shall deem fit.

26. A receiver so appointed shall be entitled to exercise all powers conferred on a receiver by the Law of Property Act 1925 (save that section 103 of that Act shall not apply) and by way of addition to and without limiting those powers any such receiver shall have all the powers given to the trustees hereunder of entering upon and taking possession of calling in collecting converting into money and carrying on concurring in carrying on and selling leasing and dealing with the undertaking business and assets of the company or any part thereof and shall be entitled to the same protection and to exercise the same discretions as are given to the trustees hereunder in relation to those powers or any of them and shall also have such other of the powers and discretions given to the trustees hereunder as the trustees may

*Appointment and Removal of Receiver*

---

[38] A clause in this form was held sufficient to enable a receiver to bring an action in the name of the company: *M Wheeler & Co. Ltd.* v. *Warren* [1928] Ch. 840, C.A.

from time to time confer on him PROVIDED that such receiver shall comply with all directions from time to time given to him in writing by the trustees with regard to the exercise of all or any powers and discretions vested in him or with regard to the payment to the trustees upon the trusts hereof of all or any monies for the time being in his hands.

27. All monies arising from any sale calling in collection or conversion hereunder and all monies received by the trustees or any receiver appointed by them hereunder at any time after this security shall have become enforceable shall be held by the trustees or by the receiver receiving the same (subject to any prior ranking claims thereon) upon trust to apply the same for the following purposes and in the followng order of priority in payment of: *Trust of Proceeds of any Realisation*

    (a) all costs charges expenses and liabilities incurred and payments made in or about the exercise of the trust for conversion or otherwise in relation to this deed by the trustees or any receiver appointed by them hereunder including all remuneration payable to the trustees and any such receiver with interest thereon as hereinafter provided;

    (b) the interest owing upon the stock pari passu and without any preference or priority;

    (c) the principal monies owing upon the stock pari passu and without any preference or priority;

and the surplus (if any) shall be paid to the company. PROVIDED that if the trustees shall be of opinion that the security may prove deficient payments may be made on account of principal monies and before the interest or the whole of the interest on the stock has been paid but such alteration in the order of payment of principal monies and interest shall not prejudice the right of the stockholders to receive the full amount to which they would have ben entitled if the primary order of payment had been observed or any less amount which the sum ultimately realised from the security may be sufficient to pay.

28. The trustees shall give to stockholders at least [seven] days' notice of every distribution made by them to stockholders and the trustees shall be entitled at their discretion to withhold payment of any monies due to be distributed to any person or persons registered or entitled to be registered as the holders of any of the stock pending production or delivery to the trustees of the certificate or certificates for the stock in order that a note of the distribution may be indorsed thereon. Any monies the payment whereof is for the time being withheld by the trustees pursuant to this clause shall be placed by them at the risk of the person or persons entitled thereto in a deposit account with a bank and so much of any stock as equals the amount of any principal monies for the time being withheld from the person or persons registered or entitled to be registered as the holders of that stock shall not carry interest while such monies are being withheld (save any interest allowed on the deposit account in which such monies are placed). The receipt of the registered holder of any of the stock or of the first-named of joint holders for any monies paid by the trustees in respect of that stock shall be a good discharge to the trustees for those monies. *Distribution*

**Short or medium term notes**

**2.68**    While unsecured loan stocks tend to be issued in respect of longer term borrowing companies have employed "notes" as a means of raising unsecured funds from the public over a short or medium term. Notes are in essence merely promises to pay conferring no priority over other unsecured creditors. Indeed it sometimes occurs that notes provide that their holders are to rank after other creditors, albeit before shareholders in a winding up.[38a]

Unsecured notes usually take a short and simple form of which the following is an example:

"

. . . . . . . LIMITED
(Incorporated under the Companies Act 1948)

Issue of . . . [rate of interest] unsecured notes of x each under the authority of clause . . . of the memorandum of association and regulation . . . of the articles of association and pursuant to a resolution of the directors dated . . . Interest at the rate of . . . per cent per annum is payable half yearly on the . . . day of . . . and the . . . day of . . . in each year.

*Covenant*         No . . .                          NOTE                          [100]

*(1) Principal*   1. . . . P.L.C. (hereinafter called the company) will on the . . . day of . . . or on such earlier date as the principal monies hereby covenanted to be paid shall become payable in accordance with the conditions endorsed hereon pay to [name] or [address] or the other registered holder or holders hereof the principal sum of [100].

*(2) Interest*    2. The company will until the whole issue of notes has been paid off or reduced pay to the trustees at the registered office of the company interest on the principal sum at the rate of . . . per cent per annum half yearly on the . . . day of . . . and the . . . day of . . . in every year the first of such payments to be made on [date].

3. This note is issued subject to the conditions indorsed hereon. Given under the Common Seal of the company this . . . day of . . . 198                          "

The conditions indorsed on the note correspond to those found in an issue of unsecured loan stock as to:

*Conditions*       (a) the events on the occurrence of which the notes will become immediately repayable;
(b) the obligations on the company to insure or otherwise take steps to preserve its assets.

In addition most issued of notes provide that the principal sum may be paid off by the company together with unpaid interest to the date of payment at any time

[38a] In certain recent issues the terms have ranked holders with ordinary shareholders in a winding up.

prior to the stipulated redemption date on giving not less than 30 days notice in writing.

The 1985 Budget contained proposals to enable companies with a Stock Exchange listing or USM quotation to raise finance through regular issues of short-dated notes of less than five years maturity. The problem has been that regular issues of such securities have been regarded as taking deposits and as such required the issuer to be licensed or a deposit-taker under the provisions of the Banking Act 1979. An amendment in the Banking Act to dispense with this requirement under certain conditions is contained in the Banking Act (Exempt Transactions) (Amendment) Regulations 1985.[38b] The conditions are:

    (i) The issuer must have its shares listed on the Stock Exchange or traded on the USM;

    (ii) The issue may carry either a fixed or floating rate of interest;

    (iii) The notes will have to be issued with a prospectus or limiting particulars;

    (iv) The notes may be issued or traded only in denominations of £100,000 or more;

    (v) The notes must have a minimum maturity of one year; and

    (vi) Permission must be obtained from the Bank of England on the size and timing of issues.

### Convertible loan stock

Convertible loan stock is conventional unsecured loan or secured debenture stock with the addition of an option permitting the holder to convert all or part of his holding into equity share capital on stipulated terms within a specified period. Traditionally convertibles had been employed in situations where other forms of debt security funding were unavailable and the issue of equity impractical or inappropriate. In such circumstances convertibles had the attraction of allowing investors to "have it both ways" offering on the one hand the security of a charge[39] over the company's assets to fall back on in the event of the company's failing and an increasing return through a direct stake in the earnings of the company should it succeed. Thus convertible loan stocks were considered an appropriate instrument for the raising of finance by companies entering into risky or speculative ventures but with the prospect of high rewards. Equally, they were a convenient vehicle for use by institutions in financing growing companies not yet in a position to raise capital through the securities markets.[40]

From 1957 onwards, however, the potentialities of convertible loan stock came to be more widely recognised following a large public issue of such stock by I.C.I.; thereafter, convertibles came to be seen as means of issuing and of acquiring a deferred equity stake in a company. Two important developments reinforced this changed perception:

**2.69**

*Nature of Convertible Loan Stocks*

*'Hedging Finance'*

---

[38b] S.I. 1985 No. 564.

[39] Assuming the stock was issued on a secured basis.

[40] For institutions convertibles also carried the advantages of providing a prospect of an ultimate stake in the equity along with a high current income.

(a) The change in the structure of corporate taxation in 1967 with the introduction of corporation tax created a situation where interest on corporate debt was tax-deductible, either as a business expense brought into account in computing profits or as a charge on income deductible from profits. Companies therefore were provided with an incentive to defer the issue of equity and the issue of a convertible stock allowed companies to raise equity capital on a deferred basis and obtain a tax advantage during the period of deferral.

(b) The take-over and merger boom of the late 1960s produced an appreciation of the convertible loan stock as a useful form of consideration. By comparison with cash (which became increasingly scarce during successive credit squeezes), ordinary shares (which were expensive to service and also involved the dilution of existing shareholders' interests) and conventional debt (which had inflationary drawbacks) convertible loan stocks were seen as having distinct advantages. Thus for "the shareholder whose shares are being bid for, there is a guaranteed income at an attractively high rate; there is an option to convert into equity as a hedge against inflation; there is deferment of capital gains tax liability (which applies to cash payments); and there is the longstop of a fixed date for repayment at par if things go wrong. For the company making the bid there is a lower interest rate than there would be with a striaghtforward loan stock; there is tax relief on the servicing cost; there is breathing space before conversion in which to achieve and consolidate the benefits of the merger . . . and there is the enormous advantage of making the bid in a form attractive to recipients."[41]

**2.70**

The terms of issue of early British convertibles provided for a conversion period of five years duration falling between the third and seventh year from the date of issue. However, from the later 1960s onwards conversion periods have tended to become longer with periods of up to (and in some cases in excess of) ten years being quite usual. Furthermore the practice has been for the actual period elapsing before conversion takes place also to increase.

In *Moseley* v. *Koffeefontein Mines*[42] it was held that the price of issue of convertible loan stock must not be such as to enable conversion to have the effect that fully-paid shares will be issued at a discount.[43] The modern practice has in fact been to the opposite effect with conversion prices having been set at a premium, that is with the price at which the first conversion into equity could be made being in excess of the price of the company's equity (and therefore almost invariably in excess of its par value) on the day of issue of the stock. During the 1960s the tendency was for this conversion premium to rise with the general trend of share prices.[44] Since then, however, the growing practice has been to use a constant conversion premium of 10–15 per cent. over the market price at issue.

A feature of convertible issues by British companies has been for the terms of issue to provide for the conversion price to rise during the conversion period, the

---

[41] See Thomas at pp. 156–7.
[42] [1904] 2 Ch. 108, C.A.
[43] In this case the loan stock was issued at a discount and was immediately convertible into fully paid shares of equal face value to the stock.
[44] See Thomas, *supra.*

object being to provide an incentive to convert at the earliest opportunity, thereby reducing the amount of borrowing and giving the capital structure greater certainty.[45]

Most convertible loan stocks issued through the securities market carry a term of 25 years to redemption.

While conversion rights remain unexercised convertible loan stocks retain the character of debt securities with stockholders having the benefit of the protection afforded by the covenants[46] (and, where appropriate, security) contained in the trust deed. Thus if the conversion period is allowed to pass the stock will run through to maturity and redemption will take place in the ordinary way. Where conversion rights are exercised the conversion operates to redeem and cancel the stock to which the rights relate so that from the date of conversion the company's covenants and other obligations under the trust deed in respect of that holding cease.

**2.71·**

*Effect of Conversion*

### Debt securities with warrants attached

One advantage accruing to a company raising capital through an issue of convertible loan stock was the consequence that the presence of conversion rights operated to reduce the coupon which the stock would otherwise have been obliged to carry, albeit at the cost of the loss of a degree of certainty and control[47] over the company's capital structure. An alternative device for raising deferred equity has been the issue of conventional unsecured loan stock or notes (or secured debentures) with warrants attached entitling the holder to subscribe for ordinary shares at a specified price during a specified period. In most cases the warrants are transferable independently, although not in every case. Such an issue will preserve the "edge" in terms of interest rates enjoyed by a company issuing convertible securities while at the same time avoiding the uncertainties associated with conversion issues. Furthermore, unlike a conventional convertible issue, an issue of loan stock with warrants attached provides for the receipt of further capital as and when the subscription warrants are taken up.

**2.72**

Where this form of capital-raising is adopted the exercise of the subscription option does not operate to affect the loan stock or income with which the warrants were issued. Accordingly the covenants entered into by the company in the trust deed will remain operative until redemption.

---

[45] The main disadvantages of convertibles would appear to be that they reduce a company's control over its own capital structure, the point being that since it is the stockholder rather than the company who decides whether and when the option is to be exercised, if the stockholder decides not to convert the company may be left with a weight of debts to service for a considerable time. Because of this many companies have been prepared to pay more for a conventional loan stock issue rather than place themselves in an equivocal position with a conversion issue.

[46] See above at §§2.64–2.67.

[47] See above at §2.70 and n. 45.

### The issue of debt securities

**2.73**

*What Amounts to an "Issue"*

Under the general law debt securities are issued by a company when the trust deed or other document of constitution[48] is sealed with the common seal of the company and delivered to the trustees.[49] It has been held that debentures (and therefore presumably trust deeds through which an issue of debenture/loan stock is constituted) which have been sealed but not delivered are not issued,[50] although it is not clear what significance this rule has (apart from its effect on the company's liability to loan capital duty) since an agreement to issue debt securities is specifically enforceable if made for valuable consideration[51] and the securities agreed to be issued will be treated in equity as having been issued.[52] So in *Day* v. *Rubber and Mercantile Corp.*[53] it was held that a person entitled to specific performance of an agreement to issue debentures was to be regarded as having the rights of a debenture holder and, specifically in this case, the right to vote.

It is often the case that a company's articles of association will prescribe particular formalities for the execution and issue of such securities. These formalities must be complied with since any irregularity on the face of the securities will render then invalid. On the other hand securities apparently in order will not require their holders to make enquiries as to whether all the necessary formalities have been complied with.[54] A provision in a company's articles that irregularities would not affect debentures was held to be sufficient to protect a bona fide holder of a debenture issued under circumstances that the holder might have discovered the irregularity.[55] However holders with notice have been held not to be so protected.[56]

*Agreement to Issue Debt Securities*

Section 195 of the Companies Act 1985 created an exception to the general rule of English and Scots Law that a contract for the loan of money is not capable of specific enforcement. It provides for a contract with a company to take up and pay for debentures to be enforceable by an order for specific performance or implement. Since the Companies Act definition of debenture[57] includes debenture stock, bonds and other securities of a company, whether constituting a charge on the assets of the company or not it is clear that all forms of debt securities issued by a company come within the ambit of the section.

Certainly where a loan has been made specific performance of the agreement to give security will be ordered,[58] even though the company might have lost

---

[48] *e.g.* a mortgage or charge.

[49] Or mortgages or charges where the allotment is made to specific allottees.

[50] *Mowatt* v. *Castle Steel and Iron Works* (1887) 37 Ch.D. 260; *Derby Canal Co.* v. *Wilmot* (1808) 9 East 360; *Levy* v. *Abercorris Slate and Slab Co.* (1887) 37 Ch. D. 260.

[51] C.A. 1985, s.195.

[52] *Re Perth Electric Tramways* [1906] 2 Ch. 216 at pp. 219–220 citing *Levy* v. *Abercorris Slate and Slab Co., supra.*

[53] [1923] 2 Ch. 528.

[54] *County of Gloucester Bank* v. *Rudry Merthyr Co.* [1895] 1 Ch. 629; C.A.; *Re Romford Canal Co.* (1883) 24 Ch.D. 85. But see *Ruben* v. *Great Fingall Consolidated Co.* [1904] 2 K.B. 712, C.A.; [1906] A.C. 439, H.L. (no liability on forged debenture).

[55] *Davies* v. *Bolton & Co.* [1894] 3 Ch. 678.

[56] *Re Worcester Corn Exchange Co.* (1804) 3 de G. M. & G. 480; *Davis' Case* (1871) 12 Eq. 516.

[57] C.A. 1985, s.744.

[58] *Hermann* v. *Hodges* (1873) 16 Eq. 18.

other power to give security at the time the agreement was made.[59] Most of the cases however have concerned the position where the amount of the loan has not been paid in full, as for example where the terms of issue provide for the amounts subscribed to be paid in instalments and a subscriber defaults on an instalment. In *Bass* v. *Clively*[60] it was held that a subscriber who defaults on an instalment loses his right to compel performance on the ground that since he is unwilling or unable to perform his part of the bargain he cannot compel the company to perform its part. He cannot therefore compel the company to give security (where this is appropriate) or to pay him interest. It has been held[61] however that debenture holders who were in default as regards payment of instalments were entitled on a distribution to be paid rateably according to the amounts they had subscribed without first having to pay the amounts owed by them.

*Payment in Instalments*

An issue of debt securities will take place on receipt by the company of the full amount of the loan. Where payment of the loan is made in instalments it is usual for scrip certificates to be issued in respect of the amount paid. In the case of secured loan (debentures) these certificates evidence part performance of the agreement to issue the debentures which operates to create a charge over the relevant assets of the company even though the debentures have not actually been issued.[62] As such the charge should be registered to secure priority. The certificates will normally contain a statement to the effect that a formal bond will be issued to the holder on payment of the full amount due.

*Scrip Certificates*

In *Seligman* v. *Prince*[63] the Court of Appeal held that debentures might properly be issued in respect of an existing debt.

The issue of debt securities attracts loan capital duty at the rate of 50p per £100 (or fraction of £100).[64]

Where debt securities are issued to the public through the securities markets the requirements for admission to listing or quotation on these markets must be complied with. These are considered in Chapter 6 below, in conjunction with the requirements of the Companies Act concerning the public issue of securities. At this juncture, however, mention should be made of the requirements of the Control of Borrowing Order 1958[65] which makes the timing of issues of securities by companies raising not less than £1,000,000 subject to approval by the Bank of England on behalf of the Treasury.[66]

**2.74**

*Public Issues*

---

[59] *Re Bagnalstown and Wexford Railway* (1870) 4 Ir. R. Eq. 505.

[50] (1829) Tamlyn 80. See also *Kuala Pahi Estates* v. *Mowbray* (1914) 111 L.T. 1072, C.A. where the conditions of allotment expressly gave the company the right to forfeit debentures for non-payment of an instalment.

[51] *Seaver* v. *Smelting Corp.* [1915] 1 Ch. 472. Note that *Bass* v. *Clivley, supra* was not cited in this case.

[52] *Re Strand Music Hall* (1865) 3 de G. J. & S. 147; *Pegg* v. *Neath Tramways* [1898] 1 Ch. 183; *Re Queensland Land and Coal Co.* [1894] 3 Ch. 181; *Simultaneous Printing Syndicates* v. *Fowerater* [1901] 1 K.B. 771; *Re Perth Electric Tramways* [1906] 2 Ch. 216.

[53] [1895] 2 Ch. 617, C.A.; See also *Howard* v. *Patent Ivory Co.* (1888) 35 Ch.D. 156 at p.169.

[54] F.A. 1899, s.8, as amended by F.A. 1967, ss.28–29.

[55] S.I. 1958 No. 1208 as amended by S.I. 1959 No. 455 and S.I. 1970 No. 708 (revoking S.I. 1967 No. 69) made under the Borrowing (Control and Guarantees) Act 1946.

[66] Under the Control of Borrowing Order 1958, art.8(1) and (2) Treasury consent is required for a company to borrow more than £50,000 in 12 months. However, Arts. 8A(1) and (2) now contain a general exemption from obtaining such consent for money raised by the issue of shares or deben-

**2.75**    Debt securities may be issued at par, at a premium (or at par subject to repayment with a premium or at a discount. In relation to issues at a discount, however, special rules apply to convertible loan stocks and to "deep discount" bonds.

*Convertible loan stocks*

While convertibles, like other loan stocks, may be issued at a discount the level of that discount must not be such as to infringe the rule against issuing shares at a discount. In *Moseley* v. *Koffeefontein Mines*[67] debentures were issued entitling the holder to call for the allotment of fully-paid shares of the same nominal amount in satisfaction thereof. Since the debentures were immediately convertible the issue was held to be a patent attempt to engineer the issue of shares at a discount. While the question of whether conversion options not exercisable until the expiration of a period after the issue of debentures would also infringe the rule was expressly left open, it was thought that the matter should be judged by reference to the amounts involved rather than the proximity of conversion dates to the time of issue.

*Deep discount bonds*

The Finance Act 1984 provides for a special tax regime to apply to debt securities issued at a "deep discount"[68] the essence of which is to treat the discount as containing an element of income taxable in the hands of the bondholder when the bond is redeemed or disposed of. Insofar as the company is concerned the difference is treated as a loss which is claimable when the bonds are redeemed.

---

tures. The general exemption does not apply however where the transaction is effected by or on behalf of a person resident outside the United Kingdom and is not a transaction consisting of or including the purchase of non-sterling securiies (*i.e.* securities on which capital monies, dividends and interest are payable solely in a currency other than sterling) art. 8A(3).

[67] [1904] 2 Ch. 108, C.A.

[68] F.A. 1984, s.36 and Sched. 9. A "deep discount security" is defined (by s.36(2)) as "any redeemable security which has been issued by a company at a deep discount, other than:

(a) a share in the company;

(b) a security in respect of which the amount payable on redemption is determined by reference to the movement of the retail prices index . . . or any similar general index of prices which is published by, or by an agent of, the government of any territory outside the United Kingdom; or

(c) a security, the whole or part of which falls . . . within the meaning of "distribution" in the Corporation Tax Acts.

A "discount" means any amount by which the issue price of a redeemable security is less than the amount payable on redemption of that security.

A "deep discount," in relation to any redeemable security, means a discount which:

(a) represents more than 15 per cent., of the amount payable on redemption of that security; or

(b) is 15 per cent. or less, but exceeds half Y per cent. of the amount so payable (where Y is the number of complete years between the date of issue of the security and the redemption date.

The amount payable on redemption does not include any amount payable by way of interest.

The redemption date in relation to any redeemable security means the earliest date on which, under the terms on which the security is issued, the holder of the security will be entitled to require it to be redeemed by the company which issued it.

However, under the 1984 provisions the company may deduct the income element for any income period ending in its accounting period from its total profits for that period.[69] Any incidental costs of issuing the securities, if not deductible under section 36 or under the general law, may be deducted under section 38 of the Finance Act 1980.

Deep discount securities offer advantages to companies seeking to raise funds in that:

(a) they allow the company to have the immediate use of the funds raised and to use the money which would otherwise go in interest payments in the business itself; and

(b) the income element can, at the option of the company, be set against its total profits (as a charge on income) during the period to redemption.

From the point of view of investors they permit the income element to be taxable either during the redemption period or allow to amount of the discount to fall to

---

[69] *Ibid.* Sched. 9, paras. 2–8.

The length of an *income period* depends on the terms on which the security has been issued: if interest is payable every 6 months (the normal case for interest-bearing securities) the income period will be the 6 months ending with the date of payment; in the case of a zero-coupon security the income period is a year ending immediately before the anniversary of the issue date, or a period of less than a year, beginning on an anniversary and ending on the redemption date (para. 2(7)).

The *income element* for any income period is found by applying the formula:

$$X \times (m{-}P) \times \frac{I}{P}$$

where $I$ = the company's income

$P$ = profits as defined for the purposes of the relief; and

$X$ = fraction fixed annually by statute

F.A. 1984, s. 20(2) fixes the fraction for the financial years 1983–1986 as follows:

| Financial Year | Marginal Relief Fraction |
| --- | --- |
| 1983 | $\frac{1}{20}$ th |
| 1984 | $\frac{3}{80}$ ths |
| 1985 | $\frac{1}{40}$ th |
| 1986 | $\frac{1}{80}$ th |

where A is the "adjusted issue price" (*i.e.* the aggregate of the issue price of the security and the income elements from all previous income periods); B is the yield to maturity; and C is the amount of interest attributable to that income period (para. 2(3)). Where it is necessary to determine the income element for a period falling within an income period (*e.g.* in the case of a disposal within an income period), the income element is treated as accruing evenly over the income period (para. 2(4)).

The right to make a deduction prior to redemption is available to a company provided that:

(a) the cost of paying the discount is borne by the company;

(b) the income element would not otherwise be deductible in computing the company's taxable profits; and

(c) at least one of the following conditions are met (para. 3(3)); namely

(1) that the company exists wholly or mainly for the purpose of carrying on a trade;

(2) that the deep discount security was issued wholly and exclusively to raise money for purposes of a trade carried on by the company;

(3) the company is an investment company (para. 3(4)).

The right to deduct under Sched. 9 does not apply if the bonds are held beneficially by an associated company (para. 4) or is issued by a close company and is beneficially owned by a participator or associate or company controlled by a participator (para. 5).

The facility under Sched. 9 is not available if the bonds have been issued with the sole or main purpose of retaining a reduction of tax liability by the operation of the relief.

be taxed in the year the bond is redeemed or disposed of, thereby (as in the period 1984–87) providing an investor with an opportunity to take advantage of any designated fall in the tax rate.

Deep discount securities are issued either at a nil rate of interest (in which event the discount represents an investors total income return—the normal case) or carrying a low coupon with the discount representing the difference between the nominal rate and the true rate with which the loan has been burdened.

### Eurobonds

**2.76**    Eurobonds are merely debt securities denominated in a foreign currency and therefore exhibit the characteristics of debt securities denominated in sterling. However, because they are a means of raising funds internationally, a eurobond issue contains elements not always present in a domestic bond issue.

**2.77**    The arrangements for a eurobond issue involve the establishment of three separate but linked groups. Primary responsibility rests with the managers to the issue, normally a small group of merchant banks and sometimes including a stockbroker. The second group comprises the underwriters, a larger group of financial institutions who agree to underwrite the issue while the third group, the "selling group" usually comprises several hundred professional dealers in securities whose function it is to place the bonds with outside investors.[70] The managers and underwriters are also usually members of the selling group.

**2.78**    The managers solicit expressions of interest in the bonds from dealers usually dispatching to the latter a preliminary (that is, subject to amendment and expressly stated as being such) prospectus.[71] Having ascertained the likely response the managers then:

(1) fix the final coupon[72] and issue price with the issuer;
(2) confirm the commitment of the underwriters;
(3) enter into a subscription agreement with the issuers;
(4) allot bonds to selling group members to whom selling agreements have been sent;
(5) obtain a listing for the bonds;
(6) procure the execution of the necessary documentation; and
(7) make available to the issuer the proceeds of the issue against delivery of the bonds.

**2.79**    The principal documents for a eurobond issue are:

(a) *The prospectus.* This gives information about the issue and must comply with the requirements of the Companies Acts and the Stock Exchange.[73]

---

[70] A selling group is necessary in order to obtain the benefit of the "sophisticated investor" exemption from prospectus legislation.

[71] Referred to as the "red herring."

[72] Often and increasingly eurobonds carry a zero coupon.

[73] The requirements of the Stock Exchange are a modified version of the general prospectus requirements. See below at §§6.35 *et seq.*

(*b*) *The subscription agreement.* This sets out the terms upon which the managers agree to purchase or procure purchasers for the bonds on a specified date, subject to the fulfilment of certain conditions precedent.[74] The subscription agreement also contains representations and warranties by the issuer on the lines of those found in term loan agreements and indemnities by the issuer to cover the managers should they be sued for misrepresentation in the prospectus.

(*c*) *The underwriting agreement.* This is entered into by the managers as agents for the issuer and the underwriters setting out the terms upon which the underwriters agree to underwrite the issue.

(*d*) *Selling agreements.* These are entered into between the managers and selling group members and set out the terms upon which the members of the selling group agree to deal in the bonds. Selling agreements normally contain a number of restrictions:

(1) prohibiting the distribution of the bonds and offering material in contravention of the securities laws;
(2) prohibiting representations other than those contained in the prospectus[75];
(3) (sometimes) prohibiting sales below the agreed price for the period of the primary distribution.[76]

(*e*) *Managers' agreement.* This is an agreement between the managers delegating the organisation of the issue to the lead manager or managers and providing for the division of management commission.

(*f*) *Trust deed.* This corresponds with and fulfils the same function as a trust deed in a domestic bond issue.

(*g*) *The bonds.* These will be issued in bearer form by the issuer and will contain the terms on which the loan has been subscribed. One of the realities of obtaining finance through eurobond issues is that these terms must provide for interest to be paid gross and with no formality, certification of residence or treaty claim.

The requirement that interest be paid gross (that is free of withholding tax) created problems for British companies in that section 54 of the Income and Corporation Taxes Act 1970 provided that interest paid by companies (or indeed by any person) to persons or bodies resident outside the United Kingdom must be paid under deduction of tax. To overcome this problem the practice developed of making the issue through a finance subsidiary in a territory that imposed no withholding tax on interest. Most commonly that territory has been the Netherlands, the funds raised being lent to the parent company and the interest on that loan being paid gross by reason of the double taxation agreement with the Netherlands.

Since the passing of the Finance Act 1984 however that practice may become

---

[74] For example, the furnishing of all necessary authorities.
[75] The purpose of this prohibition is to guard against the possibility that such statements may contravene local securities laws or be traceable back to the managers and issuer and fix them with liability.
[76] In order to maintain the price.

unnecessary for many eurobond issues, section 35 providing that interest on quoted eurobonds[77] shall be outside the scope of section 54 and so may be paid gross by the issuing company.[78] The limitation of the privilege to *quoted* eurobonds, however, has the consequence that British companies wishing to have access to private placements available in certain financial centres will continue to require an overseas finance subsidiary.

(*h*) *Fiscal agency agreement (or, where there is a trustee, a paying agency agreement)*. This is entered into between the issuer and a bank whereby the issuer appoints a bank as fiscal or paying agent and sub-paying agents in various international centres for the purpose of making payments to bond-holders. If a company wishes to take advantage of the provisions of section 35 of the Finance Act 1984 to pay interest gross, ideally payment should be made with a paying agent overseas.[79]

# THE ISSUE OF EQUITY AND EQUITY-TYPE SECURITIES

**2.80**      Equity capital represents a direct stake in the fortunes of a company and provides share cover for its debt borrowing.[80] For companies with a Stock Exchange listing or other securities market quotation the raising of equity capital will normally take the form of a rights issue in compliance with the terms of the continuing obligations imposed as a condition of admission.[81] The issue of equity by unquoted companies however will normally be an important element in an institution-provided funding package where the company's level of debt borrowing is high so that its capital gearing ratio[82] makes it desirable that additional share capital be provided to ensure an acceptable degree of balance of risk and return for the institution and for the company a more balanced capital structure. Furthermore some institutions seek to derive part (or indeed most) of their profits from such a venture in the form of a capital gain to be realised on the disposal of its holding either on a subsequent flotation of the company[83] or agreed take-over or merger.[84] The practicalities of such an exercise require an equity participation conferring a direct stake in the growth of the company's assets and business.

---

[77] "Quoted Eurobond" is defined as a security which:

   "(a) is issued by a company;
      (b) is quoted on a recognised stock exchange;
      (c) is in bearer form; and
      (d) carries a right to interest" (F.A. 1984, s.35(7)).

[78] F.A. 1984, s.35(1) and (2).

[79] However the benefits of s.35 will still be available where the payment of interest is made by or through a person in the United Kingdom where the person who is the beneficial owner of the quoted eurobond and is entitled to the interest is not resident in the United Kingdom; or where the quoted eurobond is held in a recognised clearing system. F.A. 1984, s.35(2). "Recognised clearing system" is defined (by s.35(7)) as "any system for clearing quoted eurobonds which is for the time being designated . . . as a recognised clearing system."

[80] "Equity is the key to resource . . . . [it] gives a firm independence . . . [and] allows firms to take the long view," Wilson Committee (Main Report) at paras. 511, 512 and 514.

[81] See below at §§6.67 and 6.90.

[82] See above at § 2.08.

[83] See further at Chapter 6 below.

[84] See further at Chapter 7 below.

**Equity securities**

Equity securities are basically of two kinds:  **2.81**

(a) Ordinary shares, being equity capital in its purest sense; and
(b) Preference shares which, while not equity in the true sense, are frequently used by institutions in funding arrangements for private companies as "equity-substitutes."

**Ordinary shares**

Except insofar as the memorandum or articles of assocition of the company or terms of issue of the securities so provide ordinary shares confer on their holder an entitlement "to receive dividends when declared (subject to any priority as to dividend enjoyed by preference shareholders), to have his appropriate proportion of the company's assets after payment of creditors paid or transferred to him on a winding up (subject again to any priority enjoyed by preference shareholders) and to exercise and vote for each share that he holds at the general meetings of the company."[85]

Given these characteristics it follows that capital-raising through an issue of ordinary share simpliciter has two consequences. First, it dilutes the stakes of existing shareholders in the company, since the newly issued shares will rank equally with existing shares in respect of their claims on profits (for distribution as dividend) and on assets. If the issue is by way of rights, however, existing shareholders have the opportunity to maintain the proportion of their stake in the company, and thereby the proportion of their existing claims on profits and assets. For this reason, *inter alia,* quoted companies raising additional equity capital are required, in the absence of exceptional circumstances, to do so by way of rights. Secondly, it reduces the degree of control enjoyed by existing shareholders since the new shares will carry votes that may be used in the same way and to the same effect as those attaching to existing shares. Again the raising of the additional capital by means of a rights issue avoids this result.

In cases where a rights issue is undesired or inappropriate, where for example control of a company rests with a family or other small grouping whose members are unable or unwilling to subscribe for new shares, a special class of ordinary shares may be creating the terms of issue conceding equality of ranking with existing shares in respect of dividends and rights on a winding-up but conferring no voting rights at all. Such issues have commonly been made by quoted companies, subject to observance of adequate standards of publicity and disclosure required by the Stock Exchange authorities. They have only infrequently been made to institutions however since, especially in the case of private companies, the voting power that goes with their shareholding (often of the order of 20 or 25 per cent.) is an important instrument for influencing policy should the need arise to take steps to preserve their investments.

---

[85] Gore-Browne, Companies (43rd ed., 1977) at para. 14.3.

## Preference shares

**2.82**     Preference shares are prima facie irredeemable fixed interest securities carrying with them membership of the company,[86] an entitlement to the payment of dividends in priority to ordinary shareholders and/or, if the memorandum, articles or terms of issue so provide, to the return of capital. In the last resort the rights of a preference shareholder depend on the construction of the relevant parts of such memorandum, articles or terms of issue.

**2.83**     As with ordinary shares dividends on preference shares may only be paid out of profits available for the purpose with the right to payment accruing when such dividend is declared.[87] It follows therefore that a shareholder's right to dividend is subject to the power of the directors, acting in good faith,[88] to carry sums to reserve. Accordingly, where finance is being provided from an institutional source, it is not unusual for the terms of issue to commit the company to pay dividends where profits have been earned to cover the amount of the dividend. The point is that a stable dividend flow is important to institutions since they will require to cover the cost to them of the funds they have provided.

*Preference Dividends*

Because preference dividends may not be paid in the absence of available profits the terms of issue will normally seek to ensure that dividend rights are cumulative[89] so that arrears in one year may be made up of profits in subsequent years. The terms of issue will also seek to define the position of any arrears in the event of a winding-up supervening. The general rule of company law is that in the absence of an express provision to the contrary arrears are prima facie not payable.[90] A common provision to ensure payment is that in a winding-up arrears of dividend "whether earned or declared or not" should be paid down to

---

[86] In practice however the ordinary incidents of membership with regard to voting at company meetings apply to preference shareholders only in a restricted form. Although the general rule requires that in the absence of company provision preference shareholders should have the same voting rights at general meetings as other shareholders, there is in practice almost always such a provision. Often it is provided that holders of preference shares are not entitled to receive notice of or to attend or vote at general meetings in respect of their shares except in respect of resolutions involving a variation of their rights or a reduction of capital or a winding up. Cumulative preference shareholders are usually given voting rights while their dividend is in arrears for longer than a specified period. However in *Coulson* v. *Austin Motor Co.* (1927) 43 T.L.R. 493 it was held that in the case of a non-cumulative preference shareholder, where dividends had not been paid for some years owing to the adverse trading position of the company, they should not be regarded as being in arrear, so that shareholders were not entitled to attend and vote at the company meeting.

[87] Unlike the position with debt securities. In *Heslop* v. *Paraguay Central Co.* (1910) 54 S.J. 234 debentures were issued with interest payable only out of profits. It was held that the whole of the profits so far as necessary were to be applied for the purpose of payment.

[88] *Bond* v. *Barrow Haemalite Steel Co. Ltd.* [1902] 1 Ch. 358. However the directors must act fairly in th interests of all classes of shareholders: *Henry* v. *Great Northern Railway Co.* (1887) 1 de G. & J. 606 at p.638.

[89] Although in the absence of any provision (or inference from other provisions) to the contrary the shares will be presumed to be cumulative: *Henry* v. *Great Northern Railway Co.* (1857) 1 de G. & J. 606; *Webb* v. *Earle* (1875) L.R. 20 Eq. 556; *Foster* v. *Coles and N.B. Foster & Sons Ltd.* [1906] W.N. 107.

[90] *Re Crichton's Oil Co.* [1902] 2 Ch. 86, C.A.; *Re W. Foster & Son Ltd.* [1942] 1 All E.R. 314; *Re Ward Skinner & Co. Ltd.* [1944] Ch. 323; *Re Catalinas Warehouse & Mole Co. Ltd.* [1947] 1 All E.R. 51. Note however that the presumption is easily rebutted. Thus in *Re Bridgewater Navigation Co. Ltd.* [1891] 2 Ch. 317 C.A. arrears were held to be payable where the articles declared that profits available for dividend belonged to the preference shareholders to the extent of their stipulated rate of dividend. In *Bishop* v. *Smyna and Cassaba Railway* (No. 1) [1895] 2 Ch. 285 the

the commencement of the winding up as the date of payment, as the case may be, is priority to capital.

The level of dividends on preference shares is specified as a percentage of the par value of the shares. Traditionally this percentage is fixed although there is nothing in principle to prevent the terms of issue stipulating for the coupon rate to float, subject only to the requirements that the formula for calculating the rate and amount of any given payment be defined with sufficient certainty. Any participation over and above this stipulated percentage must be expressly provided for. In *Will* v. *United Lankat Plantations Co.*[91] the terms of issue provided for shares to carry a preferential dividend of 10 per cent. with the articles providing that subject to any priorities that might be given or the issue of any new shares the profits of the company were to be distributed by way of dividend "among the members in accordance with the amounts paid on the shares held by them." The House of Lords held that the preference shareholders were not entitled to share rateably in any residual profits on the basis that the terms of issue, making specific provision for dividend rights, were to be construed as exhaustively defining the shareholders' entitlements.[92]

*Participation in Profits*

In the absence of provision to the contrary preference shareholders rank alongside ordinary shareholders in winding up, repayment of capital or other reconstruction.[93] In *Scottish Insurance Corporation Ltd.* v. *Wilsons and Clyde Coal Co.*[94] the House of Lords held that this equal ranking did not extend to participation in surplus assets. Where such participation is desired therefore the terms of issue must so provide. One way of achieving this end is to make the issue of "preferred ordinary" shares, in effect a hybrid of preference and ordinary shares conferring rights to dividend corresponding to those of cumulative preference shares[95] with rights of ordinary shareholders in respect of capital. Alternatively the securities can be issued as preference shares but with an option to convert into ordinary shares during a specified period.

**2.84**

*Participation in Capital*

In modern conditions preference shares are mainly used in the provision of development capital to private companies by institutions being appropriate in that they produce, like loan stock, a stable income flow without having an adverse effect on capital gearing ratios or involving problems concerning control of the company and dilution of its equity. The single most important reason however for their attractiveness to institutions is the tax treatment of preference divi-

**2.85**

*Use of Preference Shares— (1) Private Companies*

same result was held to apply where the dividend was payable irrespective of its being declared. In some cases the articles have conferred "a preferential right to dividend" while the terms of issue sought to give "priority as to dividend and capital." The use of this combination was held to confer a right to payment of arrears on th basis that priorities as to dividend while the company was carrying on business were conferred by the first phrase that the second must be taken as dealing with te position on a winding-up. See *Re Walter Symons Ltd.* [1934] Ch. 308; *Re F. de Jong & Co. Ltd.* [1946] Ch. 211; *Re F. W. Savory Ltd.* [1951] 2 All E.R. 1036; *Re Wharfedale Brewery Co. Ltd.* [1952] Ch. 913.

[91] [1914] A.C. 11, H.L.; See also *Steel Co. of Canada* v. *Ramsay* [1931] A.C. 270, p.c., at p.274.

[92] *Ibid.* at p.17 *per* Lord Haldane L.C.

[93] *Griffith* v. *Paget* (1877) 6 Ch. D. 511; *Birch* v. *Cropper* (1889) 14 App. Cas. 525, H.L.

[94] [1949] A.C. 462, H.L.

[95] In *J.I. Thornycroft & Co. Ltd.* v. *Thornycroft* (1927) 44 T.L.R. 9 it was held that the preference share rules applied to preferred ordinary shares in relation to dividends so that in the absence of a specific provision to rebut it the presumption that the dividend is cumulative applies.

dends. These rank as qualifying distributions and as such constitute franked investment income[96] in their hands. As franked investment income dividends received are not subject to corporation tax as profits and can be passed on by the recipient institution to its own shareholders without incurring liability to advance corporation tax.[97]

For the company the principal advantages of preference capital over loan capital are:

(1) that, unlike debt interest which is payable irrespective of the company's position, dividends are only payable if there are profits available for the purpose, with the right of the shareholder to payment accruing only when a dividend is declared.[98] Preference capital therefore permits a company a degree of latitude in the application of its income not possible with loans. The point however should not be overstated since where profits are available, although in theory the right of the directors to transfer them to reserve exists, in practice this right may not be exercisable, either because of a specific provision in the terms of issue to that effect[99] or because the preference shares were issued as part of a larger funding package and non-payment could give rise to a right on the part of the institution to enforce loans that constitute other parts of the package.

(2) that an issue of preference shares will not infringe existing borrowing limits; and

(3) that an issue of preference share will not adversely affect the company's capital gearing ratio.[1]

*(2) Public Companies*

On the oher hand the use of preference shares by quoted companies has declined to the extent that prior to the setting up of the Unlisted Securities Market preference borrowing had virtually lapsed into disuse.[2] The most important single element in this decline[3] was the change in the rules of company taxation

---

[96] F.A. 1972, s.88.

[97] *Ibid.* s.89.

[98] *Bond* v. *Barrow Haematite Steel Co. Ltd.* [1902] 1 Ch. 358.

[99] As in *Bishop* v. *Smyrna and Cassaba Railway (No. 1)* [1895] 2 Ch. 285.

[1] Note that after the 1965 tax reforms many companies declined to convert existing preference capital into loan stock for this reason holding that there was a greater risk of insolvency where debentures replaced preference shares. See Thomas at p.160.

[2] Except in the case of a few industries such as water supply. Since the establishment of the U.S.M. a number of companies have obtained quotations in respect of their convertible preference shares. It is doubtful, however, whether this amounts to a reversal of the trend since these issues will have been made prior to quotation as part of a package for the financing of what would still have been a private company, the quotation being obtained in part to impove the marketability of the shares.

[3] Between the wars and in the early post-war period preference shares were extensively used by limited companies as ameans of raising long-term capital with the amount raised in this way rivalling those raised by loan stocks in the immediate post-war years. Apart from the changes in the structure of corporate taxation other factors in the decline were:

(1) The decision of the House of Lords in *Scottish Insurance Corp. Ltd.* v. *Wilsons and Clyde Coal Co. Ltd.* [1949] A.C. 462 which reduced the appeal of preference shares to investors by holding that in the absence of a specific provision to the contrary in the company's articles of association preference shareholders were not entitled to a share in the company's surplus assets after a return of paid-up capital on a winding-up.

(2) The rise in interest rates from 1951 onwards which tended to restrain the use by companies of fixed-interest securities generally. Furthermore this disincentive to issue preference share was accompanied by a growing demand for equities on the part of investors which effectively allowed companies little scope for choice.

brought about by the introduction of corporation tax in 1965. Specifically the comprehensive allowance of interest on debt as a deduction in the computation of a company's taxable profit made it in general more advantageous for the company to issue debt securities rather than other forms of capital. Preference dividends not only lacked the quality of being so deductible but also attracted liability to advance corporaion tax.[4]

The change in the tax system resulted not only in the drying-up of preference share issues on the securities market but also in concerted moves by many companies to rid themselves of the tax disadvantage to them arising from their existing preference capital. Accordingly, schemes of arrangement were entered into whereby holders of preference shares were induced to agree to their cancellation and replacement by issues of unsecured loan stock by the offers of a slightly higher interest yield and the greater degree of security enjoyed by creditors of a company as against shareholders.

**Redeemable equity**

Section 58 of the Companies Act 1948 permitted a company to issue redeemable preference shares provided that certain conditions were complied with. This provision was repealed by the Companies Act 1981 and replaced by more general provisions permitting companies to issue redeemable shares, whether preference or ordinary. **2.86**

The power of a company to issue redeemable shares is now contained in sections 159–161 of the Companies Act 1985 which provide that a company limited by shares or limited by guarantee and having a share capital may, if authorised to do so by its articles, issue shares which are to be redeemed or are liable to be redeemed at the option of the company or the shareholder. This power differs from that under the 1948 Act in that the option to redeem may now be granted to the investor rather than being confined to the company. In principle therefore it would seem possible to incorporate additional protection to equity investment by including in the terms of issue covenants by the company corresponding to those inserted in a loan stock trust deed[5] and by stipulating for the right to redeem to become exercisable[6] (in advance of any contractual redemption date) on the occurrence of a breach of covenant. The subscription agreement containing the terms of issue will need to provide for the procurement of a change in the company's articles authorising redemption in such circumstances.[7] *Power to Issue Redeemable Shares*

No redeemable shares may be issued at any time when there are no issued shares of the company which are not redeemable.[8]

---

[4] Which accounted for their attraction to institutional investors. While private companies were subject to the same tax rules they were in many cases constrained by the terms on which institutional finance was available to them.

[5] See above at §§2.64–2.66.

[6] On service of notice to the company.

[7] C.A. 1985, s.160(7). Further the terms of redemption must provide for payment on redemption: *Ibid.* s.159(3).

[8] *Ibid.* s.159(2).

**2.87**          Redeemable shares may only be redeemed under section 160 out of the com-
*Redemption*     pany's distributable profits or out of the proceeds of a fresh issue of shares made
*Payments*       for the purpose of the redemption. The attractiveness of this latter course would
                 be reduced by the provisions of section 47 of the Finance Act 1973 rendering
                 such a replacement issue a chargeable transaction for the purposes of liability to
                 stamp duty. This consequence is alleviated to some extent by section 161(1) and
                 (2) of the Companies Act 1985 which provides that such a replacement[9] issue
                 will constitute a chargeable transaction if and only if the actual value of the
                 shares so issued exceeds the value of the shares redeemed at the date of their
                 redemption. Furthermore, where the issue of shares does constitute a charge-
                 able transaction the amount on which stamp duty will be chargeable is to be the
                 difference between the amount on which duty would have been chargeable had
                 the shares not been issued as replacements for the redeemed share capital and
                 the value of the shares redeemed at the date of redemption.

Where the terms of issue provide for a premium to be payable on redemption
that premium, must be paid out of the distributable profits of the company.[10] In
cases where the redeemable shares were issued at a premium however any premium payable on their redemption may be paid out of the proceeds of a fresh
issue of shares made for the purpose of redemption. The amount which may be
so payable is whichever is the less of:

(1) the aggregate of the premiums received by the company on the issue of
    the shares redeemed; or
(2) the current amount of the company's share premium account including
    any sum transferred to that account in respect of premiums on the new
    shares).

Payments made in respect of such premiums operate to reduce the amount of the
company's share premium account by the amount so paid.[11]

Shares redeemed under these provisions are treated as cancelled on redemption, with the amount of the company's issued share capital being reduced by the
nominal value of the shares redeemed.[12]

**2.88**          Sections 159–161 apply to public and private companies alike. Private com-
                 panies, however, possess an additional power to redeem by virtue of sections 171
                 and 172. These provide that a private company may, if authorised to do so by its
                 articles, make a payment in respect of the redemption of its own shares out of

---

[9] *Ibid.* s.161(3) provides that shares issued by a company:
   (a) up to the nominal amount of any shares which the company has redeemed under section
       159; or
   (b) before the redemption of shares which the company is about to redeem shall be regarded as
       issued in place of the shares redeemed or (as the case may be) about to be redeemed under
       this section.
Shares about to be issued for the purpose of funding a redemption are not to be treated as issued
for that purpose unless the shares to be redeemed are actually redeemed within one month from
the issue of the new shares: *ibid.* s.161(4).
[10] *Ibid.* s.160(1)(*b*).
[11] *Ibid.* s.160(2).
[12] *Ibid.* s.160(4). However a redemption is not to be taken as reducing a company's authorised share
capital.

capital.[13] Such capital payments, however, may only be made to the extent that there are insufficient funds available for the purpose under sections 159–161.[14] Furthermore before a permissible capital payment can be made complex procedures must be gone through involving the passing of a special resolution approving the redemption, the making of a statutory declaration by the directors and the taking of steps to ensure the required publicity.[15]

The timetable in respect of a redemption out of capital runs from the date of the statutory declaration. This must be made by the directors in the prescribed form[16] specifying the amount of the pemissible capital payment for the shares in question and stating that, having made full inquiry into the affairs and prospects of the company, they have formed the opinion[17]:

**2.89**

*Redemption Procedure*

(a) as regards the initial situation immediately following the dates on which the payment out of capital is proposed to be made, that there will be no ground on which the company could then be found to be unable to pay its debts; and

(b) as regards its prospects for the year immediately following the redemption, that, having regard to their intentions with respect to the management of the company's business during that year and to the amount and character of the financial reserves which will in their view be available to the company during that year, the company will be able to carry on business as a going concern (and will accordingly be able to pay its debts as they fall due) throughout that year.[18]

To the statutory declaration must be annexed an auditors' report addressed to the directors stating that the auditors have inquired into the company's state of affairs, that the amount specified in the statutory declaration as the permissible capital payment has been properly calculated, and that they are not aware of anything to indicate that the opinion expressed by the disclosure[19] in the declaration as to the matters required to be mentioned there is unreasonable in all the circumstances.[20]

The payment of capital for the purpose of redeeming shares must be approved by a special resolution[21] of the company. This resolution must be passed on, or within the week immediately following, the date of the statutory declaration.[22] The resolution will not be effective, however, for the purpose of complying with

**2.90**

*Special Resolution*

---

[13] *Ibid.* s.171(1).
[14] *Ibid.* s.171(3).
[15] *Ibid.* s.173(1).
[16] *Ibid.* s.173(5).
[17] In forming their opinion with regard to the company's initial situation the directors are required by *ibid.* s.173(4) to take into account both the contingent and prospective liabilities of the company.
[18] *Ibid.* s.173(3).
[19] Note that any director who makes a declaration under s.173 without having reasonable grounds for the opinion expressed there shall be liable (s.173(6)).
    (a) on conviction on indictment to imprisonment for a term not exceeding two years or a fine or both; and
    (b) on summary conviction, to imprisonment for a term not exceeding six months, or a fine not exceeding the statutory maximum, or both.
[20] *Ibid.* s.173(1).
[21] *Ibid.* s.173(2).
[22] *Ibid.* s.174(1).

the statutory redemption procedure, unless the statutory declaration and auditors' report are available for inspection by members of the company at the meeting at which the resolution is passed.[23]

Special rules govern the voting on the resolution. Essentially these operate to prevent the votes in respect of shares that are to be redeemed being decisive in favour of the resolution. It is provided that[24] the holder of the shares in question will make the resolution ineffective for the purposes of making the permissible capital payment if he votes in favour of the resolution and the resolution would not have been passed had he not so voted. Any votes cast by a shareholder in respect of other shares (*i.e.* shares not affected by the resolution) will not affect the validity of the resolution provided they are cast on a poll (rather than a show of hands).

**2.91**

*Publicity*

Since a payment out of capital affects both shareholders and creditors of the company the procedure for making permissible capital payments requires that steps be taken to publicise the proposed payments. If objection to a payment is then taken the creditors or members of the company, as the case may be, can petition the court for the cancellation of the resolution.[25]

The publicity rules provide that within the week immediately following the date of the resolution for payment out of capital the company must cause to be published in the Gazette[26] a notice:

(a) stating that the company has approved a payment out of capital for the purpose of acquiring its own shares by redemption;

(b) specifying the amount of the permissible capital payment for the shares in question and the date of the resolution for payment out of capital;

(c) stating that the statutory declaration of the directors and the auditors' report are available for inspection at the company's registered office; and

(d) stating that any creditor of the company may at any time within the five weeks immediately following the date of the resolution for payment out of capital apply to the court under section 176 of the Companies Act 1985 for an order prohibiting the payment.

In addition, within that same week the company must either[27]:

---

[23] *Ibid.* s.174(4).
[24] *Ibid.* s.174(2),(3).
[25] *Ibid.* s.176(1). The right of challenge is available to any creditor of the company and any member of the company other than one who has consented to or voted in favour of the resolution. To be valid the challenge must be made within 5 weeks of the date on which the resolution was passed. If an application is made to the court the company is required (s.176(3)):
    (a) forthwith to give notice of that fact to the Registrar of Companies (the notice must be in the prescribed form); and
    (b) within 15 days from the making of any order of the court or such longer period as the court may by order direct, deliver an office copy of the order to the Registrar.
A company failing to comply with these requirements and an officer who is in default is liable on summary conviction to a fine not exceeding $\frac{1}{5}$ of the statutory maximum or, on conviction after continual contravention, a default fine not exceeding $\frac{1}{50}$ of the statutory maximum (s.176(4)).
[26] *Ibid.* s.175(1).
[27] *Ibid.* s.175(2),(3).

(1) cause a notice to the same effect to be published in an appropriate national newspaper[28]; or

(2) give notice in writing to that effect to each of its creditors.

The statutory declaration and auditors' report are required to be kept at the company's registered office during a statutory period and are to be kept open for inspection by any member or creditor of the company without charge.[29] The statutory period is a period beginning on the "first notice date"[30] ad ending five weeks after the date of the resolution for payment out of capital.[31] The right of inspection may be exercised during business hours[32] and can be enforced, in the event of refusal by the company, by court order.[33]

Not later than the first notice date the company must deliver to the Registrar of Companies a copy of the statutory declaration of the directors and auditors' report.[34]

If no challenge is made to the resolution payment out of capital must be made not earlier than five, nor more than seven weeks after the date of the resolution.[35]

**2.92**

*Payment*

The amount of any permissible capital payment depends upon the extent to which the company has available profits and for the proceeds of any fresh issue of shares made for the purpose of redemption. With regard to the latter the company is not obliged to make such an issue but if it does the issue proceeds must be used for the purpose of paying monies due on the shares on redemption.

What profits are "available profits" to be used to fund the redemption in priority to payments out of capital falls to be determined according to the rules contained in sections 171 and 172 of the Act of 1985, adapting for the purpose the rules as to distributable profits contained in Part III of the Companies Act 1980. Essentially available profits are the company's distributable profits as shown by its relevant accounts less any distributions lawfully made after the date of the relevant accounts and before the date of the statutory declaration.[36]

*Available Profits*

---

[28] An appropriate national newspaper means, in the case of a company registered in England and Wales, a newspaper circulating throughout England and Wales, and, in the case of a company registered in Scotland, a newspaper circulating throughout Scotland.

[29] *Ibid.* s.175(6).

[30] The first notice date is the date on which the company first publishes:
  (i) the notice in the Gazette; or
  (ii) the notice in an appropriate national newspaper (or alternatively gives written notice to its creditors);
  whichever is the earlier, *ibid.* s.175(4).

[31] *Ibid.* s.175(6).

[32] *Ibid.*

[33] *Ibid.* s.175(8). If inspection is refused the company and every officer of the company who is in default will be liable on summary convictions to a fine not exceeding $\frac{1}{5}$ of the statutory maximum or, on conviction after continual contravention, to a default fine not exceeding 1/50 statutory maximum: s.175(7).

[34] *Ibid.* s.175(5).

[35] *Ibid.* s.174(1).

[36] *Ibid.* s.172(4),(5).

*(1) Relevant accounts*

A company's relevant accounts for the purpose of calculating any permissible capital payment it may wish to make are those which relate to any date within the period of three months immediately preceding the date of the statutory declaration[37] and are such as are necessary to enable a reasonable judgment to be made as to the relevant items[38] mentioned therein, namely profits, losses, assets, liabilities, provisions, share capital and reserves.

*(2) Distributable income*

Distributable profits are a company's accumulated, realised profits, so far as not previously utilised by distribution or capitalisation, less its accumulated, realised losses so far as not previously written off in a reduction or reorganisation of capital duly made.[39]

*(3) Distributions lawfull made*

Section 172(4) provides that the following items are to be included within the meaning of the expression "distributions lawfully made," namely:

(a) financial assistance lawfully given by a private company out of its distributable profits in any case where assistance is required to be so given by section 270(3)[40];

(b) any payment made by the company in respect of a purchase by it of any of its own shares,[41] excepting any payment lawfully made otherwise than out of distributable profits; and

(c) any payment falling within section 168.[42]

**2.93**    When a company redeems share capital provision has to be made in the company's balance sheet for the cancellation of the shares redeemed. This is done by reference to a fund known as the "capital redemption reserve."[43]

*Capital Redemption Reserve*    Where the redemption is funded entirely from distributable profits an amount equal to the nominal amount of the shares cancelled must be transferred to the capital redemption reserve[44] to balance the accounts. Where the redemption is

---

[37] *Ibid.* s.172(6).

[38] *Ibid.* s.270(2).

[39] *Ibid.* s.263(3).

[40] *Ibid.* s.270(3),(4) authorises a company to give financial assistance only if the company has net assets which are not thereby reduced, or to the extent that these assets are thereby reduced, if the assistance is provided out of distributable profits.

[41] See further below at §2.94.

[42] *i.e.* payments made in consideration of acquiring an option to purchase its own shares under a contingent purchase contract (*ibid.* s.320), any variation of an off-market purchase contract (*ibid.* s.319) or contingent purchase contract (s.320) or release from any of the obligations with respect to authorised purchase (ss.319–322) being payments from distributable income.

[43] *Ibid.* s.170. The reserve is a capital fund and subject to the rules relating to share capital with provision for full capitalisation by an issue of bonus shares: s.170(4).

[44] *Ibid.* s.170(1).

funded partly out of profits and partly out of the proceeds of an issue of shares only the amount of profits used are to be transferred to the reserve.[45] Equally, where the redemption is funded partly out of profits and partly from a permissible capital payment the amount of distributable profits used must be transferred to the capital redemption reserve.[46]

In cases where the redemption is funded wholly (there being no available distributable profits) or partly out of capital and the amount of the permissible capital payment in respect of the shares redeemed is greater than their nominal value then the amount of the excess may be deducted from the amount of the capital redemption reserve (if any), share premium account or fully paid share capital[47] and form any amount representing unrealised profits of the company standing to the credit of the company's revaluation reserve.[48] If the deduction is made against this latter fund it must be on the basis that in the opinion of the directors the amount involved is no longer necessary for the purpose of the accounting policies adopted by the company.[49] Where the funding for the redemption is provided partly from the proceeds of a fresh issue of shares such proceeds are treated as part of the permissible capital payment for this purpose.[50]

The legislative provisions permitting companies to issue redeemable equity securities were part of a larger package which included the conferring of power on companies to purchase their own shares. In the context of corporate finance such a power is relevant only in respect of unquoted companies and then only to the extent that it serves to counter the disincentive to invest in such companies arising from the lack of a market in which such securities are traded and the probable lack of resources of other (and usually majority) shareholders which might otherwise make possible a "buy-out".[51] Nevertheless, to the extent that the company rather than its proprietors possesses the necessary resources to effect such a buy-out, the powers of repurchase constitute a potentially valuable instument whereby smaller companies may be enabled to raise equity finance that would otherwise be denied to them.

**2.94**

*Purchase by a Company of its own Shares*

The procedures and rules governing the purchase by a private company of its own shares out of capital are the same as those governing the redemption of equity securities out of capital. Acordingly therefore §§ 2.68–2.93 above apply equally to purchases as to redemptions. Equally, the provisions of sections 159–161 are applied[52] to purchases out of distributable profits as the proceeds of

---

[45] *Ibid.* s.170(2).
[46] *Ibid.* Sched. 6, para. 3.
[47] *Ibid.* Sched. 6, para. 4(*a*).
[48] *Ibid.* Sched. 6, para. 4(*b*).
[49] *Ibid.* Sched. 4, para. 34(4).
[50] *Ibid.* Sched. 6, para. 7.
[51] The "buy-back" provisions were enacted in response to a recommendation of the Wilson Committee (Small Firms) at pp.11, 12 made with a view to increasing the flow of equity finance to small businesses. "Outside investors could then be given some stake in the future prosperity of the company in return for the risk they take in helping to finance it until the point is reached where funds generated in the business can be utilised by the company to pay them off. This would enable the proprietor to maintain voting conrol and provide a means for backers to realise their investment (para. 15).
[52] By C.A. 1985, s.162(2). The general power to purchase is contained in s.162(1).

a fresh issue of shares in the same way as it applies to the redemption of redeemable shares.[53] As with redemptions, a company may not purchase any of its shares if as a result of the purchase there would no longer be any member of the company holding shares other than redeemable shares.[54]

**2.95**

*Contracts for the Purchase of its own Shares*

An unquoted company[55] (which in practice will almost invariably be a private company) will effect the purchase of its own shares by private agreement rather than through the securities markets. The contract embodying this agreement may be a straightforward contract of purchase[56] or it may be a "contingent purchase contract" being a contract:

(a) which does not amount to a contract to purchase the relevant shares; but
(b) under which the company may (subject to any conditions) become entitled or obliged to purchase those shares.[57]

Such a contingent purchase contract could prove extremely useful in attracting external equity investment in that it could be incorporated into the terms of issue of securities whereby the entitlement or obligation to re-purchase becomes operative on the occurrence of specified events. There, for example, a greater degree of security than was hitherto possible could be afforded to investors by the insertion of covenants and warranties corresponding to those found in a loan stock trust deed, breach of which would, on service of written notice to the company, oblige it to purchase the shares in question.[58] Equally, if the investor proved agreeable, the terms of issue might contain provisions entitling the company to effect a purchase on attaining a specified level of turnover or profit. In such a case, of course, the terms of issue would have to provide a formula for calculating the value of the shares to be purchased.

The rights acquired by a company under a contract of purchase are not capable of being assigned.[59] Such rights may however be released in pursuance of an agreement provided that approval is obtained in advance by special resolution.[60]

Any payment made by a company in consideration of[61]:

(a) acquiring any right with respect to the purchase of any of its own shares in pursuance of a contract of purchase;
(b) the variation of any contract; or
(c) the release of any of the company's obligations with respect to the purchase of any of its own shares must be made out of the distributable profits of the company.

---

[53] Save that the terms and manner of purchase need not be determined by the articles as required by *ibid.* s.160(3).
[54] *Ibid.* s.162(2).
[55] Given that the share purchase facility is scarcely a means of procuring finance for public and quoted companies the provisions of the "buy-back" legislation in relation to such companies are outside the scope of this book.
[56] C.A. 1985, s.164(1).
[57] *Ibid.* s.165(1).
[58] See above at §§2.64–2.66. See also §2.86 in relation to issues of redeemable shares.
[59] C.A. 1985, s.167(1).
[60] *Ibid.* s.167(2).
[61] *Ibid.* s.168(1).

If this requirement is not satisfied the consequent purchase (if the payment was made to acquire an option to purchase or a variation of a right to purchase) or release (if the payment was made to obtain that) is rendered void.[62]

The terms of a proposed contract of purchase must be authorised by a special resolution of the company before the contract is entered into,[63] albeit that the authority conferred by any such resolution may be varied, revoked or from time to time renewed by further special resolutions.[64] Companies are empowered to agree to variations of existing contracts but only if the variation is authorised by a special resolution of the company before the company agrees to it.[65]

**2.96**

*Authorisation by Special Resolution*

A special resolution of the company concerning the authority for a proposed contract of purchase will not be effective to confer, vary, revoke, or renew such authority (as the case may be) unless certain requirements as to inspection are complied with. These are[66] that a copy of the contract (if it is in writing) or a written memorandum of its terms (if it is not) must be available for inspection by members of the company both:

(a) at the registered office of the company for not less than the period of 15 days ending with the date of the meeting at which the resolution is proposed; and

(b) at the meeting itself.

Any memorandum of the terms of a contract of purchase must include the names of any members holding shares to which the contract relates, and any copy of the contract made available for this purpose must have annexed to it a written memorandum specifying any such names which do not appear in the contract itself.[67] The object of these latter rules is to make operable special rules governing the voting on the resolution. These, as in the case of a special resolution authorising the redemption of shares out of capital, seek to prevent the votes in respect of shares that are to be purchased in pursuance of the contract from being decisive in favour of the resolution,[68] and by the same means. Thus the holder of the shares in question will make the resolution ineffective for the purpose of authorising the contract of purchase if he votes in favour of the resolution and the resolution would not have been passed had he not so voted. Any votes cast by the shareholder in respect of other shares (*i.e.* shares not affected by the resolution) will not affect the validity of the resolution provided they are cast on a poll rather than a show of hands.

Where the purpose of the special resolution is to authorise a variation of the terms of an existing contract of purchase the documents that must be made available for inspection are[69]:

---

[62] *Ibid.* s.168(2).
[63] *Ibid.* ss.164(2) and 165(2).
[64] *Ibid.* s.164(3).
[65] *Ibid.* s.164(7).
[66] *Ibid.* s.164(6).
[67] *Ibid.*
[68] *Ibid.* s.164(5).
[69] *Ibid.* s.164(7).

(a) a copy or memorandum (as the case may require) of the original contract;
(b) a copy of any variations previously made; and
(c) details of the variation for which authority is sought.

**2.97** Companies are required to register particulars of shares purchased under the authority of section 162 of the Act of 1985 with the Registrar of Companies and *Disclosure of* to keep a copy of any contracts of purchase at their registered offices. *Particulars* The registration rules require that within a period of 28 days beginning with the date on which the shares purchased are delivered to the company the company must deliver to the Registrar for registration a return in the prescribed form stating with respect to shares of each class purchased:

(a) the number and nominal value of those shares; and
(b) the date on which they were delivered to the company.[70]

Particulars of shares delivered to the company on different dates and under different contracts may be included in a single return.[71]

Copies of written contracts for purchase (and memoranda of the terms of unwritten ones) must be kept available for inspection without charge to a member of the company at the company's registered office for a period of 10 years beginning with the date on which the contract was completed or, in the case of a contingent purchase contract, the date on which the contract otherwise determines (by the expiry of the option/obligation to purchase).[72] The right of inspection may be exercised during business hours subject to such reasonable restrictions or the company made in general meeting impose, provided that not less than two hours in each day are allowed for inspection,[73] and may be specifically enforced by court order.[74]

**2.98** Where a company under an obligation to purchase or redeem shares fails to meet that obligation the remedies available to persons thereby prejudiced are restricted by section 178 of the Companies Act 1985. This provides that prior to a liquidation such a person cannot sue for damages,[75] nor can he sue for specific performance of the terms of redemption or purchase if the company is able to show that it cannot meet the cost of redeeming or purchasing the shares out of distributable profits.[76]

---

[70] *Ibid.* s.169(1). If default is made in delivering to the Registrar any return by s.169 every officer of the company who is in default shall be liable:
    (a) on conviction on indictment to a fine;
    (b) on summary conviction to a fine not exceeding the statutory maximum or, on conviction after continued contravention to a default fine not exceeding one tenth of the statutory maximum.
[71] *Ibid.* s.169(3).
[72] *Ibid.* s.169(4). If default is made in complying with this requirement or if an inspection is refused the company and every officer of the company who is in default shall be liable on summary conviction to a fine not exceeding $\frac{1}{5}$ of the statutory maximum or, on conviction after continued contravention, for a default fine not exceeding $\frac{1}{50}$ of the statutory maximum.
[73] *Ibid.* s.169(5).
[74] *Ibid.* s.169(8).
[75] *Ibid.* s.178(2). In point of fact is seems doubtful whether an action would have been available in any event: see *Houldsworth* v. *City of Glasgow Bank* (1880) 5 App. Cas. 317, H.L. See also *Re Addlestone Linoleum Ltd.* (1887) 37 Ch. D. 191, C.A.
[76] *Ibid.* s.178(3).

Where the company has been wound up and the contractual redemption or purchase date has passed the terms of redemption or purchase may be enforced in a liquidation,[77] but only if in the perid between the contractual date for redemption or purchase and the transaction the company would have been able to meet its obligation out of distributable profits.[78] Furthermore, the amount claimed in the liquidation is postponed to the other debts[79] and liabilities of the company (other than any due to members in their character as such)[80] and to any rights attaching to preference shares[81] but is payable in priority to other amounts payable to the members of the company.[82]

Where a company effects a purchase of its own shares any profit accruing to the shareholder would, under the general law, be treated as a qualifying distribution by the company[83] and as such chargeable to advance corporation tax on the part of the company and taxed as income in the hands of the shareholder at the highest rate applicable to him for the year of assessment in question. However the Finance Act 1982 contains provisions[84] enabling such a profit to be treated for the purposes as a capital gain in the hands of the shareholder thereby attracting only a potential liability to capital gains tax.

**2.99**

*Tax Treatment of Profits Accruing to Shareholders on Purchase of Shares*

To obtain the benefit of these provisions the company must not be listed on the Stock Exchange or quoted on the Unlisted Securities Market[85] and must be a trading company or a holding company of a trading group.[86] The shareholder must be a United Kingdom resident[87] and must have been the owner of the shares for five years before the purchase[88] or three years in the case of a purchase affected on the death of a shareholder).[89]

If the shareholder disposes of his entire shareholding in the company as a result of the sale and purchase the benefit of the provisions will be lost if it can be shown that the only or main purpose of the transaction was to procure a tax advantage.

Where the shareholder does not dispose of his entire shareholding in the company as a result of the sale and purchase then for him to obtain the benefit of the provision:

(a) his interest in the company must be substantially reduced, that is his interest after the purchase by the company, expressed as a percentage of the issued share capital before repurchase[90];

---

[77] *Ibid.* ss.178(4) and (5).
[78] *Ibid.* s.178(5).
[79] *Ibid.* s.178(6)(*a*).
[80] *Ibid.*
[81] *Ibid.* s.178(6)(*b*).
[82] *Ibid.* s.178(7).
[83] F.A. 1972, s.84(4) and I.C.T.A. 1970, s.233(2).
[84] F.A. 1982, s.53(1) and Sched. 9.
[85] *Ibid.* s.53(1)(*a*).
[86] *Ibid.*
[87] *Ibid.* Sched. 9, para. 1.
[88] *Ibid.* s.53(1)(*b*).
[89] *Ibid.* Sched. 9, para. 2.
[90] *Ibid.* Sched. 9, para. 3(2).

(b) immediately after the share purchase by the company the vendor must not own more than a 30 per cent. interest in the company; and

(c) the only or main purpose of the transaction must not have been to enable the shareholder to participate in the company's profit without receiving a dividend or otherwise for the avoidance of tax.[91]

The Revenue operate a clearance procedure whereby a proposed purchase can be cleared as being eligible for the exemption from advance corporation tax and income tax.[92] Transactions failing to obtain clearance will be treated as involving a distribution and the parties taxed on that basis.

### Rights issues

**2.100** Companies may raise additional equity capital through a rights issue to existing shareholders. In principle this method of raising capital is available to any

*Stock Exchange Requirements* company, public or private, although the practicalities are such, especially where the sums required are substantial, that rights issues will normally only be of use to companies with a broad shareholder base, usually acquired as a result of a securities market quotation. It has long been the case that companies with a Stock Exchange listing making a new issue for cash of equity securities or securities having an element of equity must offer these securities in the first place to its equity shareholders[93] unless these shareholders have agreed in general meeting to other specific proposals.[94] The substance of this requirement was made of general application to British-registered companies, public or private, by the Companies Act 1980 which conferred on existing shareholders a right of preemption in respect of new equity securities[95] issued for cash.[96] The relevant provisions, now section 89(1) of the Companies Act 1985, enact that:

" . . . a company proposing to allot any equity securities:

*Right of Pre-emption* (a) shall not allot any of these securities on any terms to any person unless it has made an offer to each person who holds relevant shares[97] . . . to allot to him on the same or more favourable terms a proportion of these securities which is as nearly as is practicable

---

[91] *Ibid.* s.53(1)(*b*).

[92] *Ibid.* Sched. 9, para. 10.

[93] *Meaning here shareholders other than preference shareholders.*

[94] Admission of Securities to Listing, Section 5, Chapter 2, para. 38.

[95] "Equity security" is defined by s.94(2) as meaning "a relevant share in the company (other than a share shown in the memorandum to have been taken by a subscriber thereto as a bonus share) or a right to subscribe for, or to convert any securities into, relevant shares in the company. Reference to the allotment of equity securities or of equity securities consisting of relevant shares of a particular class shall include references to the grant of a right to subscribe for, or to convert any securities into, relevant shares in the company or, as the case may be, relevant shares of a particular class, but shall not include references to the allotment of any relevant shares pursuant to such a right; "Relevant shares," in relation to a company, means shares in the company other than:
(a) shares which as respects dividends and capital carry a right to participate only up to a specified amount in a distribution; and
(b) shares which are held by a person who acquired them in pursuance of an employees' share scheme or, in the case of shares which have not been allotted, are to be allotted in pursuance of such a scheme (s.94(3),(5)).

[96] C.A. 1985, s.89(4).

[97] See above at note 95.

> equal to the proportion in nominal value held by him of . . . relevant shares . . . [98]; and
>
> (b) shall not allot any of these securities to any person under the period during which any such offer may be accepted has expired or the company has received notice of the acceptance or refusal of every offer so made."

The conferment of the right of pre-emption under section 89(1) is particularised where a company's capital structure contains different clauses of equity securities, for example voting and non-voting ordinary shares, and the company's memorandum or articles of association contain provisions giving pre-emption rights to holders of securities of a particular class in respect of new issues of securities of that class.[99] In such a case the general pre-emption right conferred by section 89(1) is qualified to the extent that when new shares of a particular class are issued the rights of pre-emption of shareholders of other classes may be exercised only after the exercise of that right by the shareholders of the class in which the new shares are being issued.[1] Accordingly if such an issue is fully subscribed by shareholders of he particular class in which the new shares are being issued the section 89(1) pre-emption rights of other classes of shareholders would have nothing to operate on.

*Different Classes of Shares*

Although the pre-emption rights conferred by section 89 are of general application provision is made for these rights to be excluded or modified if specified steps are taken.

**2.101**

In the case of a private company section 91 provides that the statutory pre-emption rights are not to apply if excluded by a provision contained in the company's memorandum or articles. If no such provision exists and it is desired to exclude the statutory rights the articles can be altered by special resolution.

*Exclusion and Modification of Pre-emption Rights*

In the case of a private or public company section 95 provides that the statutory pre-emption rights may be excluded altogether or applied subject to such modifications as the directors may determine where the directors are given such power by the articles of the company or by special resolution to that effect.[2] Equally the company may by special resolution resolve[3] that the statutory pre-emption right shall not apply to a specified allotment or that if it is to apply such application is to be subject to any modification that may be specified in the resolution. The validity of such a special resolution (or of a special resolution to renew such a resolution) is made subject to certain formal requirements.[4] These

---

[98] C.A. 1985, s.89(1)(*a*) applies in "relevant shares" and "relevant employee shares," the latter being defined (s.94(4)) as shares of the company which would be relevant shares but for the fact that they are held under an employees' share scheme." Accordingly when calculating the proportion of new securities to which an existing shareholder is entitled to have a right of pre-emption, his shareholding is to be measured against the aggregate of relevant shares and relevant employee shares.

[99] *Ibid.* s.89(2).

[1] *Ibid.* s.89(3).

[2] *Ibid.* s.95(1). This section aplies where the directors of a company are presently authorised either by the articles or by the company in general meeting to exercise powers of the company to allot securities: s.80.

[3] *Ibid.* s.95(2).

[4] *Ibid.* s.95(5).

are that the resolution must have the recommendation of the directors, and that there has been circulated, with the notice of the meeting at which the resolution is proposed, to the members entitled to have that notice a written statement by the directors setting out:

(a) their reasons for making the recommendation;

(b) the amount to be paid to the company in respect of the equity securities to be allotted; and

(c) the directors' justification of that amount[5];

A power to disapply the statutory pre-emption right whether conferred by the company's articles or by a special resolution ceases to have effect when the authority to which it relates expires without being renewed or is revoked. By virtue of section 80(8) that authority may be given, vested, revoked or renewed by ordinary resolution notwithstanding that it alters the articles of the company. If the authority is renewed the power, or as the case may be the secial resolution, may also be renewed (by special resolution) for a period not longer than that for which the authority is renewed.[6]

A copy of a special resolution passed to exclude or modify the statutory pre-emption rights must be published by the Registrar in the London Gazette.[7]

**2.102**

*Procedure on Rights Issues*

The normal procedure adopted by a company making a rights issue requires the circularising of members of the company announcing the issue and the purpose for which the funds are to be raised and setting out the terms of the issue. The circular letter to shareholders will be accompanied by a provisional allotment letter in respect of the shares for which each shareholder is entitled to apply. In making an allotment the directors resolve that the shares be allotted to the parties named in the provisional allotment letters or to their nominees on condition that the allotment is accepted on or before a given date. Both statute[8] and Stock Exchange Regulations[9] require the offer to remain open for at least 21 days.

The terms of issue will also set out what is to happen in respect of (a) fractional entitlements and (b) entitlements not being taken up.

(*a*) *Fractional entitlements.* These will, in the ordinary course be disregarded altogether, considerations of convenience dictating a policy of rounding-down to the nearest whole share. Formerly it used to be quite common for the terms of issue to provide that fractions would be sold and the proceeds remitted to those entitled, although rising postal charges have rendered this an expensive course

---

[5] A person who knowingly or recklessly authorises or permits the inclusion in a statement circulated under *ibid.* s.95(5) of any matter which is misleading, false or deceptive in a material particular is liable:
  (a) on conviction on indictment to a fine or a term of imprisonment not exceeding two years, or both; and
  (b) on summary conviction to imprisonment for a term not exceeding six months, or a fine or both: s.95(6).

[6] *Ibid.* s.95(3).

[7] *Ibid.* s.711.

[8] *Ibid.* s.90(6).

[9] Admission of Securities to Listing Section 3, Chapter 2, Part 2, para. 2.23.

of action, the more especially when the amounts involved are usually quite small. Occasionally the terms will provide for fractions to be aggregated together and sold in the market for the benefit of the company.

Some companies have adopted policies of permitting a rounding-up of the fraction, providing a mechanism whereby a shareholder can purchase the outstanding fraction.

(*b*) *Entitlements not being taken up.* Occasionally rights are not taken up and thereby allowed to lapse as a result of oversight. More usally rights will have been allowed to lapse where their market value was such as to prevent their sale at a profit.[10] Where the possibility of an undersubscription is foreseen the company will often dispatch with the provisional allotment letter an excess share application form providing a facility for these shareholders who wish to take up excess shares.[11]

*Lapsed Rights*

Listed companies are bound by the terms of admission to the Stock Exchange Official List[12] which require that shares not taken up should, unless arrangements to the contrary have been specifically approved by shareholders, be dealt with either by way of such an offer to existing shareholders to take up excess shares or by way of sale for the benefit either of the company (the most frequently adopted course) or of the shareholder involved.

In practice however rights issues by quoted companies will normally be underwritten, in which event such provisions become superfluous.

## Subscription agreements

For most unquoted companies the narrowness of their shareholder base will render the making of a rights issue impractical. Where this is the case the most usual source of external equity capital will be a financial institution, either acting alone or in concert with other institutions as members of a syndicate. The instrument through which funding is made available is a subscription agreement, the substance of which is that the institution(s) will subscribe in cash[13] for a stipu-

**2.103**

---

[10] Provisional allotment letters being negotiable, shareholders not wishing or unable to take up their entitlements will seek to sell their rights in the market for what they will fetch.

[11] The advantage to investors being the avoidance of dealing costs that otherwise be associated with the acquisition of additional shares.

[12] See above at n. 9.

[13] In cases where shares are issued for a consideration that does not comprise cash the rules differ as between private and public companies.
(a) In so far as *private companies* are concerned the general rules of company law apply rendering any form of consideration prima facie valid so long as it satisfies the ordinary contractual requirements as to the validity of consderation. (For example in *Re Eddystone Marine Insurance Co.* [1893] 3 Ch. 9, C.A. past consideration was held not to be valid consideration). Indeed a court will not enquire as to the adequacy of the onsideration is whether it was really of a value equal to the par value of the shares issued, unless the consideration was illusory or had an obvious money value showing that a discount had been allowed (See *Re* Theatrical Trust Ltd. Chapman's Case [1895] 1 Ch. 771; *Re Almada & Tirito Co.* (1888) 38 Ch. D. 415, 423 C.A. *Re Wragg Ltd.* [1897] 1 Ch. 796, C.A.; *Ooregum Gold Mining Co. of India* v. *Roper* [1892] A.C. 125, H.L.; *Re White Star Line* [1938] Ch. 458, C.A.).
(b) The acceptance of non-cash consideration by *public companies* is however much more circumscribed, the Companies Act 1985 providing detailed regulation of the matter.
The regulations fall into 3 groups.

(i) Prohibited consideration

lated number of shares of a specified class at a stated price. That price will be at or above the par value of the shares, section 100 of the Companies Act 1985 preventing the allotment of shares at a discount.[14] Where the shares are issued at a premium section 130 of the Companies Act 1985 requires the company to transfer a sum equal to the aggregate amount of the premium to a share pre-

Two forms of non-cash consideration are prohibited namely:
   (1) consideration which consists of an undertaking to do work or provide service whether in respect of payment of the nominal value of the shares or any premiums payable on them: s.99(2).
   (2) consideration which is or includes an undertaking which is to be or may be performed more than five years after the allotment: s.102.

Where an allotment is made in contravention of either of these two prohibitions the allottee becomes liable to pay the amounts or value of the consideration in cash (*i.e.* the nominal value of the shares and any premium, or if the consideration was only partly the undertaking the proposition of that amount represented by the undertaking) together with interest at the appropriate rate: ss.99(3) and 102(2). Subsequent allottees are jointly and severally liable with the allottee where the latter has incurred liability under either of these provisions unless he is a bona fide purchaser for value without notice of the actual contravention at the time of purchase, or unless he derived title to the shares from such a purchaser: s.112.

The company and any officer in default are liable to a fine: s.114.

(ii) Permitted consideration

   In other cases non-cash consideration is permitted. Where an allotment is made in return for such consideration s.103 provides that an expert valuation of the consideration must be obtained with the repor having been made to the company during a six month period preceding the allotment and a copy of the report sent to the allottee: s.103(1).

There are two exceptional cases where such reports are not necessary; namely (s.103(5)):
   (1) allotments by a company in connection with a takeover offer by it for all the shares or all the shares of a particular class of another company; and
   (2) allotments in connection with a proposed merger of the company with another company.

Liability provisions corresponding to these mentioned in relation to the Prohibited Consideration rules apply also to contravention of these rules.

(iii) Assets acquired from subscribers

   A public company is prohibited by s.104 from agreeing with a subscriber to its memorandum for the transfer from him to the company or another person of one or more non-cash assets in return for a consideration equal at the time to one-tenth or more of the nominal value of the company's then issued share capital within the "initial period" *i.e.* 2 years from either:
      (1) the issue of a certificate under s.117 in relation to the company's formation as a public company;
      (2) the date of registration in relation to a joint stock company registered under s.685; or
      (3) the date of registration in relation to a public company constituted from a private company.

Such agreements, however, may be validated if certain conditions are met. These are:
   (A) that the consideration to be received by the company and any consideration other than that to be given by the company are valued and a report on them made to the company within the six months preceding the agreement;
   (B) that the terms of the agreement have been approved by an ordinary resolution of the company; and
   (C) that copies of that resolution and of the report have been circulated to members of the company entitled to receive notice of the meeting not later than the giving of the notice of the meeting at which the resolution is proposed.

See generally Gore-Browne, *Companies* para. 18.3.

[14] s.100(2) provides that where shares are issued at a discount the shares are to be treated as paid up save for the discount and the allottee is to be liable to pay to the company the amount of that discount plus interest thereon at the appropriate rate.

mium account.[15] The amount of the share premium account must appear in the balance sheet.[16]

It is usual for the subscription agreement to provide that the amount subscribed is to be payable "forthwith." Where, however, the terms of the agreement provide for payment to be made in instalments section 10(1) of the Act of 1985 requires a minimum initial subscription payment of at least one quarter at the time of the allotment.

Sometimes the subscription is made conditional upon changes in the composition of the board of directors, although a more usual policy is for institutions to reserve the right to board representation should they deem it necessary.

The subscription clauses of the agreement will commonly take a form corresponding to the following:

THIS AGREEMENT is made the . . . day of . . .

BETWEEN

A B of [address] C D of [address] and E F G [address] (hereinafter called the directors) the directors of . . . Limited (hereinafter called the company) of the one part

AND

. . . Limited/P.L.C. having its registered office at [address] (hereinafter called the subscribers) of the other part.

WHEREAS

(1) The company is a private company limited by shares incorporated in England/Scotland under the provisions of the Companies Acts 1948–81 and has an authorised share capital of . . . divided into . . . shares of . . . each of which . . . and no more have been issued and are fully paid up.

(2) A.B., C.D. and E.F. are all the present directors of the company

(3) The subscribers have agreed to subscribe for . . . shares of . . . each in the company for the consideration and upon and subject to the terms and conditions hereinafter contained.

NOW IT IS HEREBY AGREED as follows:

(1) The subscribers shall forthwith subscribe in cash at par for . . . ordinary shares of . . . each in the company (hereinafter clled the said shares) ranking for dividends and in all other respects *pari passu* with all existing issued ordinary shares of the company and the direc-

*Agreement to Subscribe*

---

[15] The share premium account is to some extent assimilated to the share capital itself. The rules as to reduction of capital apply to it as if it were paid up share capital except that it may be applied, *ibid*.s.130:

    (i) in paying up unissued shares of the company to be issued or fully paid bonus shares;

    (ii) in writing off preliminary expenses or the expenses of or commission part or any discount allowed on any shares or debentures; or

    (iii) in providing for the premium payable in redemption of any redeemable preference shares or debentures.

Distribution of a company's share premium account is equivalent to an actual return of paid up capital. See *Re Hodder & Tolley Ltd.* [1975] N.Z.L.R. 395.

[16] C.A. 1985, Sched. 4, para. 8.

tors shall procure the company to allot and issue the said shares to the subscribers.

(3) Completion of the said subscription shall take place at [address] when:

*Completion*

(a) The subscribers shall deliver to the company a form of application for the said shares and shall pay to the company the sum of . . . in cash therefor; and

(b) The directors shall procure the allotment and issue by the company to he subscribers of the said shares and shall deliver to the subscribers the certificate for the said shares; and

[(c) The directors and the subscribers shall procure:

(i) The appointment as additional directors of the company of such three persons as the subscribers may require

(ii) The resignation of A.B., as a director of the company and of C.D., as secretary of the company in each case wthout any claim for compensation or otherwise

(iii) The adoption by the company of new articles of association in the form of the draft annexed hereto and marked "A" . . . ]

**2.104** Subscription agreements will include covenants and warranties by the company and its directors designed to ensure that the company's business is carried on in a satisfactory manner and generally to preserve the substance of the investment made. Unlike the covenants in a loan stock trust deed there is no question conditions operating to trigger enforcement procedures although it is at least arguable that such provisions are now possible in principle since the enactment of redemption and repurchase provisions by the Companies Act 1981. The usual practice is to insert indemnity covenants for the benefit of subscribers in the event of the occurrence of specified liabilities accruing through the company to the subscribers themselves.

1. The directors hereby warrant to and covenant with the subscribers as follows:

*Covenants and Warranties*

*(1) Capital*

(a) That at the date hereof the authorised and issued share capital of the company is as recited above; that no loan capital has been issued by the company and remains outstanding; that no share or loan capital of the company is under option; and that pending completion of the issue of the said shares to be subscribed as aforesaid no share or loan capital will be created or issued and no options will be granted by the company which could result in the issue of any share or loan capital;

*(2) Balance Sheet*

(b) That the audited balance sheet of the company as at [*date*] a copy of which is annexed hereto and signed for identification on behalf of the directors and subscribers (hereinafter called the said balance sheet) gives a true and accurate statement of the financial position of the company as at the date thereof; that save as mentioned herein there have been no material alterations or variations in the financial position of the company since the date of the said balance sheet; and that the book value of the net assets of the company will at completion be not less than it was at the said [*date*];

(c) That save as has been disclosed to the subscribers in writing or save in the ordinary course of business or save as mentioned herein since the said [*date*] the company has not disposed of any of its assets otherwise than in the ordinary course of business and pending completion will not do so; *(3) Non-disposal of Assets*

(d) That since the said [*date*] the business of the company has been carried on in the ordinary and usual course and save as has prior hereto been disclosed to the subscribers in writing no contracts other than normal contracts necessitated by day-to-day business have been entered into by the company and that pending completion the said business will be so carried on and that without the written consent of the subscribers no unusual or abnormal contracts will be entered into; *(4) Carrying on of Business*

(e) That the company has not knowingly done or omitted to do any act or thing in contravention or breach of any of the provisions of the Companies Act 1985 the Business Names Act 1985 the Exchange Control Act 1947 the Borrowing (Control and Guarantees) Act 1946 or the Banking Act 1979 (or any Acts which replace) or any regulations made thereunder and that the company will not pending completion do any act or thing in contravention or breach of such Acts or regulations as aforesaid or any of them; *(5) Compliance with Acts and Regulations*

(f) That all the returns particulars resolutions and other documents required to be filed with or delivered on behalf of the company to the Registrar of Companies pursuant to the provisions of the Companies Acts 1985 have been correctly and properly made up and filed or delivered; *(6) Returns, etc.*

(g) That at the date hereof there is not outstanding any insurance service or other business contract between the company and any other person which cannot be determined upon not more than twelve months' notice without payment of compensation or damages and that pending completion no such contract wil be entered into by the company; *(7) Outstanding Contracts*

(h) That at the date hereof the company is not in the course of acquiring has not acquired and pending completion will not acquire or agree to acquire any assets on hire purchase credit sale or deferred payment terms; *(8) Hire Purchase Transactions*

(i) That since the said [*date*] the company has not save as has been disclosed to the subscribers in writing incurred any commitments for capital expenditure such as would fall to be disclosed in its accounts to be made up at the end of its current financial year; *(9) Capital Expenditure Commitments*

(j) That at the date hereof the company has not given any guarantees which are outstanding that it is not under any liability to give any guarantees and that pending completion no guarantee will be given by the company; *(10) Guarantees*

(k) That at the date hereof there are no mortgages charges or other incumbrances on or over the whole or any part of the assets of the

*(11) Mort-gages, etc.*

company and that pending completion no such mortgages charges or other incumbrances will be created given or granted;

(l) That since the said [*date*] no dividend bonus or other distribution has been declared paid or made on any share in the capital of the company and that pending the completion no such dividend bonus or distribution will be so declared paid or made;

*(12) Dividends*

(m) That save for normal debt collection the company is not engaged in any litigation or arbitration and that the directors are not aware of any facts likely to give rise to any litigation or arbitration;

*(13) Litigation*

(n) That there are no existing service agreements or contracts between the company and any of its officers and employees which are not determinable without compensation by [one month's] notice or less and that pending completion the company will not enter into any service agreement or contract which is not so determinable;

*(14) Service Agreement*

(o) That since the said [*date*] the persons who are the directors of the company within the meaning of the provisions of the Finance Act 1972 relating to close companies have not been paid and pending completion will not be paid or become entitled to any remuneration other than directors' fees payable under article . . . of . . . per annum cash [the sums of money disclosed in a letter dated the . . . from the company to the subscribers];

*(15) Directors' Remuneration*

(p) That the company is not under any legal liability to pay pensions superannuation allowances or the like to any of its past or present directors officers or employees or their dependants and that there are no pension schemes or arrangements for payment of pensions or death benefits or similar arrangements in operation in relation to the company;

*(16) Super-annuation*

(q) That the returns made by the company for taxation purposes are correct and on a proper basis and are not the subject matter of any dispute with or claim by the appropriate revenue authorities and that the directors are not aware of any dispute or claim and that full provision has been made in the said balance sheet for all taxation which has been or may be assessed in respect of or calculated by reference to profits inome or gains of the company earned or accrued up to and including the said [*date*];

*(17) Taxation*

(r) That the company has not made or given or agreed to make or give since the said [*date*] and pending completion will not make or give any such loan or advance as is mentioned in section 75 of the Finance Act 1965 or any distribution (save only for the dividend herinbefore mentioned) within the meaning of that Act (as amended by the Finance Act 1966);

*(18) Loans*

(s) That the directors have disclosed to the subscribers all material facts known to them relating to the business and finances of the company.

*(19) Disclosure*

2. The directors hereby covenant with the subscribers that the directors will at all times indemnify the subscribers from and against any depletion of the assets of the company by reason of:

*Indemnity*

(a) Any income tax which may pursuant to sections to of the Finance Act 1972 be assessed in the name of the company on the directors or any other person or persons who may have been members of the company and become payable by the company in respect of any income or profits accrued up to the completion date hereinbefore referred to by virtue of his or their interest therein;

(b) Any sum assessed on the company under the provisions of section 77 of the Finance Act 1965 in respect of any accounting period of the company which has already ended or will end prior to the completion date;

(c) The recovery of any tax from the company on the counter-action of any tax advantage obtained or obtainable by the company pursuant to sections 21 to 28 of the Finance Act 1960 (as amended by Schedule 15 to the Finance Act 1965 and section 39 of the Finance Act 1966) provded that the act or the whole of the acts giving rise to or requiring such recovery or counter-action shall have occurred prior to the completion date;

(d) Any claim for capital transfer tax payable by the company upon or by reason of the death of any person or persons living or dead who may have been members of the company by virtue of the provisions of the Finance Act 1975 or any amendment or statutory re-enactment thereof;

(e) Any claim by the revenue authorities for corporation tax income tax development land tax or capital gains tax on profits income or gains of the company earned or accrued up to and including the [*date*] in excess of that already paid or for which provision has not been made in the said balance sheet;

(f) Any claim by the Customs and Excise authorities for value added tax due in respect of the period up to and including the [*date*] in excess of that already paid or for which provision has not been made in the said balance sheet;

(g) Any costs incurred by the company in contesting or settling any such claim assessment recovery or counter-action (whether threatened or made) as is mentioned in this clause.

3. All covenants warranties representations indemnities and other obligations of whatsoever kind given made or undertaken by the directors under this agreement shall (except for any obligations fully performed on completion) continue in full force and effect notwithstanding the completion of the subscription hereby agreed to be made.

*Continuance*

## BORROWING BY PUBLIC SECTOR ENTERPRISES

Capital raising is not, of course, the sole concern of enterprises in the private sector. The nationalised industries have substantial capital requirements, inevitably so given their dominant position in the provision of energy, public transport and formerly of communications, and in the production of iron and steel. These undertakings are vested in statute-created public corporations whose

**2.105**

*Corporate Finance and the Nationalised Industries*

sources of finance, capital structure and methods of financing differ significantly from what is encountered in corporate enterprise in the private sector.

**2.106**

*Financial Powers and Obligations of Public Corporations*

Public corporations, being creatures of statute, have their financial powers and obligations determined by the provisions of the Acts creating them. The pattern of obligations was set by the nationalisation legislation of 1946–9.[17] In general terms the corporations were expected to pay their way: more specifically, the minimum required was that a corporation's revenues should "on an average of good and bad years (or some similar phrase) be not less than sufficient to meet all items properly chargeable to revenue, including interest, depreciation, the redemption of capital and the provision of revenue."[18] This obligation to earn sufficient revenue to meet costs "taking one year with another" was made more precise following the 1961 White Paper *"The Financial and Economic Obligations of the Nationalised Industries."*[19] Thenceforth deficits were expected to be matched by surpluses over a five year period. The setting of financial targets was intended to bring about a situation where income would exceed outgoings and that larger savings would accrue to enable current asets to be replaced and capital developments financed.

A further review was undertaken in 1967 which advised that investments should be directed to those activities where the anticipated returns were highest. With greater freedom to adjust prices and in pricing policy it was hoped that efficient investment would yield larger surpluses for financing.[20]

**2.107**

*Self-financing*

*Limits of Internal Funding*

Whether, and to what extent, public corporations should be self-financing has been a matter of controversy for decades. Certainly it is clear that the corporations have the capacity to be self-financing. Many of them are statutory monopolies and most have an effective monopoly strong enough to generate sufficient finance to meet their capital needs by raising their prices to a level necessary to produce the required amount of savings. But the fact that self-financing almost invariably involves raising prices means that it also has a directly inflationary effect on the economy as a whole. The consequence has been that in spite of the greater freedom enjoyed by the corporations as to pricing policy and levels following the 1967 White Paper,[21] governmental counter-inflation policies have frequently operated to restrict their freedom and so to limit the extent in which he self-financing of capital requirements could be achieved. The general pattern for private industry has been that about three quarters of the finance needed for capital expenditure has come from funds generated internally.[22] As a group the nationalised industries have not been able to rely so greatly on a high self-financing ratio with the consequence that their need for external finance has been that much greater.

---

[17] Bank of England Act 1946, Coal and Industry Nationalisation Act 1946, Transport Act 1947, Gas Act 1948, Iron and Steel Act 1949.
[18] White Paper: *"The Financial and Economic Obligations of the Nationalised Industries"* 1961 Cmnd. 1337, para. 5.
[19] Cmnd. 1337, para. 4.
[20] Thomas at pp. 280/281.
[21] *"Nationalised Industries: A review of Economic and Financial Objects"* Cmnd. 3437, 1967.
[22] Thomas *op. cit.* at p. 280/281.

To the extent that the public corporations cannot meet their financing requirements from their own resources they rely primarily on loan finance. The original nationalisation Acts[23] set out various ways in which money could be borrowed and laid down limits on that facility. So, for each industry a statutory borrowing limit is stipulated for the finance of capital expenditure and within that limit ministerial approval is required.[24] Under the borrowing provisions of the Acts an assessment is made as to the expected requiremets of the respective industries for periods of four to seven years. These periods are then divided into two by the setting of an intermediate limit which may not be exceeded without the passing of an Affirmative Resolution of he House of Commons. As the statutory limits are approached amending legislation is passed providing new and higher limits to meet estimated future needs.[25]

All the nationalised industries possess powers to borrow temporary funds from banks and other financial institutions in order to meet short term working capital needs and day-to-day fluctuations in cash requirements. Bank lending to nationalised industries is privileged in that it has always been exempted from the "ceilings" placed from time to time on advances to the private sector. Short term loans are made at $\frac{1}{2}$ per cent. or 1 per cent. above the Syndicated Base Rate[26] and are backed up by a government guarantee as to principal and interest, the guarantee being renewed periodically up to a stated limit for each undertaking.

Loans by superannuation funds to their parent corporation are a second, albeit much less important, source of short term finance available to nationalised industies. Other sources tapped on a small scale include loans from short term money markets, for example the local authority loan market and the inter bank market.[27] Additionally, acceptance credits have ben used in respect of export transactions being in the form of 90 day bills of exchange with a Treasury guarantee attached.[28]

In the decade up to 1956 the nationalised industries' longer term borrowing requirements were met by a combination of bank advances and stock issues. The legislation creating the public corporations to which were entrusted the electricity, gas and transports undertakings conferred powers to borrow by way of stock issues.[29] The first stocks issued were for compensation purposes, but up to

**2.108**

*External Finance*

*Borrowing Powers and Procedure*

**2.109**

*Short-term Funding*

**2.110**

*Long-term Funding*

---

[23] See above at n. 17.
[24] With a few exceptions (*e.g.* National Coal Board) ministerial consent is not required for the temporary borrowing for working capital purposes.
[25] See further W.A. Robson, *"Nationalised Industry and Public Ownership,'* London (1962) and H.G. Webb—*"The Economics of the Nationalised Industries,"* London (1973).
[26] A rate agreed from time to time by the banks in the light of their base rates.
[27] Thomas, *op. cit.* at p. 301.
[28] By the British Steel Corporation. For payment of inter-industry deliveries of products bills of exchange have also been used. These bills are then discounted on the London Discount Market. In 1974 the British Gas Corporation used trade bills to finance payments to natural gas suppliers whenever favourable conditions prevailed in the money markets. In 1976 public corporations borrowed over £60 million via commercial bills. See further Thomas *op. cit.* at p.306.
[29] See above at n. 17 for the more important of the Nationalisation Acts. Note that the National Coal Board never made stock issues. It borrowed from the Exchequer from its inception.

*(1) To 1956—
Bank Ad-
vances and
Stock Issues*

1956 several issues were made to finance capital expenditure programmes. The practice was for new capital expenditure to be financed by bank overdraft facilities as and when it was incurred. These overdrafts were then cleared from the proceeds of stock issues usually in sums of around £150 million.[30]

All the relevant stocks were issued at a fixed rate of interest and with specified redemption dates and were guaranteed as to capital and interest by the Treasury. Nevertheless, the responsibility of meeting interest and capital redemption liabilities rested with the individual corporations rather than the Exchequer unless and until the guarantee should be invoked.

**2.111**

*(2) Change of
Methods of
Funding*

After the 1956 Budget issues of stock by nationalised industries ceased. The Finance Act 1956[31] conferred on the Treasury the power to make advances to the public corporations for long-term purposes. Thenceforth their needs would be met directly by the Exchequer.

In point of fact the change from financing via the capital market to financing by way of Exchequer advances was not as abrupt as might at first sight appear. Most of the issues made just prior to this had met with poor response and the stock had had to be taken up by the authorites and financed by issuing Treasury Bills to the banking system.[32] If the reality was that the public corporations were being financed by central government it was proper that the legal forms governing the corporations' financing should be brought into line.

The change also had advantages in terms of cost for while the nationalised industries' stocks were classified as gilt-edged, the terms on which they could in practice be issued were fractionally worse than those obtained by the governmet itself. "The only result of this was to make their borrowing slightly more expensive, an extra cost which consumers, or possibly taxpayers, would pay for no purpose."[33]

**2.112**

*(3) National
Loans Fund
Advnces*

Direct government finance takes the form of payments to the corporations from the National Loans Fund. Normally such payments take the form of long-term loans. The principle underlying the terms of borrowing is that the period for which an advance is made is to match the length of the expected life or lives of the assets to be financed.[34] The rate of interest is determined at the time of the advance and relates to the rate paid by the Exchequer for market funds of comparable maturity with the rate being adjusted upwards to the earest 0.125 per cent. to cover the costs of debt management.[35] The terms of a loan may provide for it to be repayable in instalments or at maturity; in the latter event it is not uncommon for there to be a requirement for the setting up of a sinking fund, in

---

[30] Thomas, *op. cit.* at p.295.

[31] s.42.

[32] See Thomas, *op. cit.* at pp. 295–298.

[33] Wilson Committee (Main Report) at para. 541. Additionally, having separate issues for individual corporations would make it more difficult for the Bank of England to manage the gilt-edged market.

[34] In the case of electricity, gas, transport and the Post Office loans are normally for 25 years which is about the average life of their assets. Loans to the NCB are more usually for periods of 15 years, except for loans related to the provision of coal stocks which are for periods of 1–5 years only. See Thomas, *op. cit.* p.298.

[35] Thomas *op. cit.* at p.299.

which case the funds so allocated are left with the industry to cover financial needs.

If a corpration fails to generate sufficient income to cover the cost of interest payments, then in the absence of a capital reconstruction or revenue subsidy additional funds have to be borrowed to meet the interest liabilities. This in turn increases the interest burden for the future and is clearly an unsatisfactory expedient where there is no realistic likelihood of generating a compensating increase in earnings. A method of avoiding this is to cease to carry forward automatically all debts on capital.[36] This involves the creation of a form of equity capital resembling that of the equity capital of a private sector company.

**2.113**

*(4) Public Dividend Capital*

Introduced in 1963 for BOAC as an experiment this Exchequer Dividend Capital, subsequently renamed Public Dividend Capital, was felt to be "suitable for those nationalised industries which are fully viable but which are especially subject to fluctuating returns as a result of their trading conditions, the nature of their assets, etc.[37] As with ordinary shares in a private sector company the dividend declared and therefore the return on such capital would depend on a corporation's revenue. The average return over a whole cycle[38] is supposed to amount to the average yield on National Loans Fund advances, so that in the long run this form of finance should be no cheaper. The advantage to a corpration, however, is an improvement in its cash flow, permitting greater flexibility in pricing at times when the market is difficult or competition intense.[39]

Public Dividend Capital is felt to be unsuitable for corporations in regular deficit. Since such capital would never produce a dividend finance in this form would be equivalent to a straight revenue subsidy; support is provided in this way instead.[40]

An alternative form of capital reconstruction is the "capital write-off," "including a reassessment and consequent write-off of part of an industry's capital liabilities to the Exchequer, a suspension of interest charges on part of a capital debt, a transfer to the Exchequer of an industry's liabilities in respect of market stocks or the write off of an accumulated deficit which has previously been covered by borrowing. In all cases the effect is to reduce interest payments . . . [and as such] is equivalent to a continuing subsidy paid by the Treasury which is equal to the interest on the capital written off."[41]

**2.114**

*(5) Write-offs/ Subsidies*

From 1968[42] the principal nationalised industries were given power to obtain long or medium term finance for their investment programmes or for the pur-

**2.115**

---

[36] *Ibid.*
[37] Select Committee on Nationalised Industries, 1967–8 "Ministerial Control of Nationalised Industries," Vol.ii (H.C. 371–2) Treasury Evidence, p.11.
[38] A cycle in the undertaking's busiess.
[39] Wilson Committee (Main Report) at para. 544.
[40] *Ibid.*
[41] Thomas *op. cit.* at p.291. Full details of the write-offs are given in the Anual Reports of the corporations affected. See also Notes to the Central Government Capital Account in the Blue Book. (*Financial Statistics*).
[42] Gas and Electricity Act 1968, Iron and Steel Act 1969; Post Office Act 1969; Coal Industry Act 1971.

*(6) Foreign Currency Borrowing*

pose of repaying their domestic debts by means of foreign currency borrowing. The currency proceeds of such loans were paid into the Exchange Equalisation Account with the equivalent amount in sterling being paid out to the corporation.

*Exchange Cover Scheme*

Coupled with this power to borrow in overseas capital markets was the Exchange Cover Scheme[43] introduced in 1969 and under which both interest and capital were guaranteed by the Treasury. The Scheme was one element in a strategy for the defence of sterling and operated by transferring to the Treasury the risks of loss which would be incurred if sterling depreciated. The effect of the guarantee was that the extra cost of repaying the borrowed currency arising from a sterling depreciation would be met by the Treasury. The operation of the Scheme including the timing and terms of any borrowing to which it is applied is under the control of the Bank of England.

Some of the foreign currency loans taken out by the public corporations have maturities of up to 25 years, although the bulk of the borrowing has been for shorter periods.[44] From the corporations' point of view the main advantage of such loans has been the lower interest cost as compared with that of National Loans Fund finance. Even after allowing for the addition of Treasury charges for exchange guarantees and underwriting substantial savings could be made.[45]

**2.116**

*Companies in Public Ownership*

In addition to the public corporations a number of industrial and commercial companies are wholly or partly in public ownership. The capital structures and sources and uses of funds of these companies are not in principle different from private sector industrial enterprises although the practice, especially in respect of the less successful, has been for the government rather than the markets to be the source of additional long-term capital.

*Privatisation*

Nevertheless, the conspicuous success of some large listed companies[46] in which the government had a substantial and direct equity stake contributed to the attractions for the idea that some public corporations would benefit from being "privatised."[47] The feeling was that exposure to market forces and access to private finance coupled with the greater flexibility afforded by a company's capital structure and a freedom from some of the social responsibilities to which public corporations are subject would lead to greater efficiency in operation, a better service for consumers and greater profits in the form of dividends for the State.

**2.117**

The idea that funds could be attracted to the corporations by the issue of some kind of equity was not new. In 1956 the Herbert Committee[48] recommended that Electricity Boards should be allowed access to the market on the basis that such access would have psychological value in justifying actions on pricing and

---

[43] See Bank of England Report and Account, February 1974 (at p.20) for details of Exchange Cover Schemes. The Scheme was withdrawn in 1972 with the floating of sterling but returned in 1973.

[44] Thomas *op. cit.* at p.303.

[45] See Thomas, *op. cit.* at pp. 303, 304 for individual details.

[46] *e.g.* British Petroleum.

[47] Usually the public stake in companies has been indirect, often via the National Enterprise Board/British Technology Group.

[48] Cmnd. 9672. See Webb, at pp. 138/9.

investment to the public. The Radcliffe Committee[49] felt differently. In its view the nationalised industries could not by their nature offer a share of the ownership of their undertakings to private investors; they could not pledge their assets and they were not free to determine their prices. It seemed unlikely that a "nationalised industry equity" with a fluctuating yield (and perhaps in some years no yield at all) and without a government guarantee would attract much money.[50]

Nevertheless, by 1968 some industries were expressing a desire to raise equity or fixed interest capital on the market arguing that it would provide greater flexibility in timing and in the terms of issue so as to meet their special requirements.[51]

While a small number of sales of state-owned businesses[52] to private investors was made during the period 1970–74 it was not until 1980 that the privatisation of public corporations began. In that year British Aerospace was reconstituted[53] as a public limited company and 51 per cent. of its shares sold to the public, a Stock Exchange quotation being obtained for the shares. In 1982[54] the exploration and production operations of the British National Oil Corporation were hived off to a newly formed company, Britoil. Fifty-one per cent. of its shares were offered by tender.[55] In 1983 a corresponding flotation was successfully effected for Associated British Ports Holdings, while in 1984 the biggest Stock Exchange flotation ever was made with the privatisation of British Telecom.[56]

Similar flotations are planned for British Airways in 1986 and for British Shipbuilders and British Gas at unspecified future dates.

---

[49] *Committee on the Working of the Monetary System, Report*, Cmnd. 827 (1959).
[50] *Ibid.* at para. 593. A view followed by the 1961 and 1967 White Papers.
[51] Select Committee on Nationalised Industries (1967–68), Minutes of Evidence.
[52] *e.g.* Thomas Cook & Son.
[53] British Aerospace Act 1980. The remaining government shareholding was sold off in 1985.
[54] Pursuant to Oil and Gas (Enterprise) Act 1982.
[55] Not entirely successfully, with more than 70 per cent of the issue being left with the underwiters.
[56] Pursuant to the Telecommunications Act 1984.

# 3. Leasing

Leasing is a means of financing the use of an asset rather than the ownership. As an instrument of finance it holds out a number of potential advantages[1] to companies in terms of:

    (a) cost;
    (b) cash flow conservation;
    (c) balance sheet;
    (d) flexibility of financing;
    (e) safeguarding against obsolescence;
    (f) certainty of outgoings.

The extent to which the factors mentioned above actually do confer advantages will obviously vary as between companies. For example, in relation to *cost* companies which are in a non-tax-paying position and expect that position to continue for some years will almost certainly find that leasing is cheaper than other methods of asset acquisition. On the other hand companies with substantial tax liabilities may find that the capital allowances available in respect of a purchase (together, possibly, with a regional development grant) make that form of acquisition cheaper. With regard to the other factors:

## (1) *Cash flow conservation*

Although frequently stated as an advantage of leasing whether leasing actually does conserve cash flow is a matter of some doubt. The point is that the cash flow effect of leasing is to transfer outflows from current to future accounting periods. While the cash flow advantages to a company embarking on a single lease transaction may be initially substantial as compared with purchase,[2] large amounts of leasing result in large outward cash flow commitments in future years which effectively restrict the amount of new expenditure which can be undertaken in those years.

## (2) *Balance sheet*

Leasing is often referred to as "off balance sheet" finance because British (unlike American) accounting standards do not require leasing commitments to be included therein. Accordingly, so the argument runs, leasing provides an additional form of finance which does not affect other borrowing. There would

---

[1] See further Hubbard, *Finance Leasing* (1980) at Chapter 4; Clark, *Leasing* (1978) at Chapter 4.
[2] See further, Hubbard, *supra*.

appear, however, to be no good reason why loan agreements should not be drafted so as to include convenants requiring the lender's consent to (at any rate large amounts of) leasing obligations entered into by the borrower.

### (3) *Flexibility*

Many companies undertake some leasing to keep their options open and to be aware of changes in the markets, even if the cost may be slightly greater than that incurred by choosing the cheapest form of purchase finance. It may be doubted however whether a large proportion of a company's financing would be by way of leasing if it were not cost effective.

### (4) *Safeguarding against obsolescence*

This is a common reason given for leasing. It is an understandable reason where the lease can be terminated at short notice without major penalty (an operating lease) but it is difficult to appreciate how, in the case of a lease where the lessee pays out the full cost of the asset (a finance lease), even on early termination, leasing provides any better safeguarding than purchasing.

### (5) *Certainty of outgoings*

Because a lease is a fixed contract its terms are known and cannot be changed so long as the lessee continues to meet his obligations in respect of rent. Unlike a loan a lease cannot be made repayable on demand. In consequence it is often argued that budgeting for leasing is easier than budgeting for purchasing.

In the case of some companies leasing may be the only means of procuring the use of assets necessary to carry on their business.

**3.02**

*Nature of Lease*

*Type of Lease*

A lease may be described[3] as a contract between the owner of an asset (the lessor) and a second party (the lessee) whereby that second party is granted exclusive use of the asset over an agreed period in return for a stipulated consideration. Leases of land have been common transactions for centuries and a sophisticated body of law of immense proportions has grown up in relation to them.[4] By way of contrast chattel leasing is a relatively modern business activity, albeit one that has grown substantially in popularity and scope in Britain over the last 20 years, an expansion that has taken place in large measure because of

---

[3] There appears to be no legally authoritative definition of "lease" that is appropriate both to leases of land and of chattels. In cases where it has been felt to be necessary to make provision for both, separate definitions are usually attempted. Thus, for example, in Capital Gains Tax Act 1979, Sched. 3, para. 10(1) provides that lease:—

    (a) in relation to land, includes an underlease, sublease or any tenancy or licence, and any agreement for a lease, underlease, sublease or tenancy or licence and, in the case of land outside the United Kingdom, any interest corresponding to a lease as so defined;

    (b) in relation to any description of property other than land, means any kind of agreement or arrangement under which payments are made for the use of, or otherwise in respect of, property.

[4] See generally Woodfall, *Landlord and Tenant* (28th ed., 1978).

the tax treatment accorded to leasing arrangements, with available capital allowances[5] providing attractions for companies with cash resources to undertake leasing business and the ability to have rental payments treated as deductible expenses in the computation of profits for corporation tax purposes[6] conferring benefits on lessees.

## LEASES OF LAND AND BUILDINGS—SALE AND LEASEBACK

A company may raise capital by selling premises owned by it and retain possession by taking a lease back from the purchaser. In some cases the transaction will take the form of an assignment of the vendor's interests while in others it will be effected by a grant of a head lease with the head lessee granting possession by means of a sub-lease. Such an assignment or grant will normally be regarded as a part-disposal for the purposes of possible corporation tax liability in respect of capital gains[7] and for the purposes of any charge to development land tax in respect of any realised development value.

It used to be the fashion (and indeed it still occasionally occurs) for the lease-back arrangement to provide for the vendor company to re-acquire its original estate or interest. The idea behind these arrangements was to regard the payments of rent under the lease (or sub-lease) back as being part payment for the re-purchase of that original interest. Provided the whole amount of the rent was accepted as being a deductible expense in the computation of profits for corporation tax purposes the effect was for the re-purchase to be subsidised by the Revenue. Inevitably the level of rent payable under such arrangements was higher than would otherwise be the case in an ordingary commercial agreement. Devices of this nature are now caught by section 491 of the Income and Corporation Taxes Act 1970 which restricts the amount of rent under a lease-back arrangement[8] allowable as a deduction to a "commercial rent."[9]

**3.03**

---

[5] See below at §§5.21 *et seq*.

[6] See below at §§5.09 *et seq*.

[7] On the basis of *Sargaison* v. *Roberts* [1969] 1 W.L.R. 951 in the case of an assignment and on general principles where the transaction takes the form of a grant of a head lease followed by a grant of a sub-lease.

[8] s.491 applies in two kinds of situation:

(1) where land or an interest in land is transferred and on, or subsequent to, the transfer, and as a result of a lease of the land, or any part of it, or any other transaction, the transferor or any person associated with him becomes liable to pay rent under the lease (defined as including any lease, underlease, sublease or any tenancy or licence; and in the case of land outside the United Kingdom or any interest corresponding to a lease or defined, *ibid*. s.491(12));

(2) where land or any "interest" in land is transferred (but there is no actual lease-back transaction) and on, or subsequent to the transfer, and as a result of any transaction affecting the land or an interest in it, the transferor or any person associated with him becomes liable to make any payment (other than rent under a lease) by way of rentcharge or other payment connected with the land for which the relief is available:

[9] Commercial rent is defined thus:

(1) in respect of payments of rent under a lease on the open-market rent of the land at the time when the actual lease was created, assuming a lease of the same duration as the actual lease and assuming the liability for maintainence and repairs as provided under the actual lease, being a lease which provides for a rent payable at uniform intervals and at a uniform rate, or if the rent payable under the actual lease is progressive and such that the rent payable for any year is not less

Where a sale and leaseback arrangement involves the assignment for a consideration of a leasehold term having not more than 50 years to run with the premises being leased back to the assignor for a term of 15 years[10] or less and the rent payable under the new lease is allowable as a deduction,[11] section 80 of the Finance Act 1972 provides for a proportion of the consideration received for the sale (or surrender) of the original lease to be treated as taxable income. The proportion of the consideration so taxable is ascertained by applying to the amount of the consideration the formula

$$\frac{16 - n}{15}$$

where n is length of the new lease.

The amount so arrived at is treated as a receipt of the company's trade for which the rent payable under the new lease is an allowable deduction.[12]

**3.04**

*Relative Advantages/ Disadvantages of Sale and Leaseback as against Borrowing*

With the removal by section 491 of the tax subsidy on repurchase it is questionable whether, as a means of raising finance, sale and leaseback has any, or any significant, advantages over borrowing. Given that rental costs tend to reflect interest rates it is unlikely that any advantages present would relate to cost.

It is apprehended that sale and leaseback might be appropriate where the company's capacity to borrow way in some was restricted as where:—

(a) further borrowing would require consent (which might not be forthcoming) under the terms of existing borrowing agreements[13];
(b) further borrowing would take the company over its agreed borrowing limits; or
(c) governmental restrictions on borrowing generally make the raising of a loan in the particular instance impracticable.

On the other hand most term loan agreements include provisions[14] restricting the right of the borrower to sell or otherwise dispose of substantial assets. It is likely that sale and leaseback arrangements effected in any of the ways mentioned in § 3.03 above would fall within the scope of such restrictions.

than that payable for any previous year, a rent progressing by steps proportionate to those provided by the actual lease, *ibid.* s.491(8);

(2) in respect of payments which are not rent but are related to rentcharges and similar payments, as the open market rent at the time of the transaction under which the payments become due which might be expected to be paid under a tenant's repairing lease being, where the payments are to be made over a period of 200 years or more, or the obligation to make the payments is perpetual, a lease of 200 years, and where the payments are to be made over a period of less than 200 years a lease of that duration, *ibid.* s.491(9).

[10] If the lessor or the lessee has the power to determine the lease early or if the lessee had the power to vary his obligations under the new lease to his benefit the term of the new lease is ascertained by reference to the earliest date at which the determination or variation could be effected.

[11] If the leaseback arrangement increases the rent paid for the premises to more than a current commercial rent that rent would be subject to partial disallowance under s.491.

[12] In a case where the company is not carrying on a trade the portion of the consideration is chargeable under Case VI of Schedule D.

[13] See above at §2.36.

[14] See above at §§2.36 and 2.66.

# EQUIPMENT LEASES

### Leases as contracts for hire

Equipment leases may be described as contracts between a lessor and lessee **3.05**
for the hire of a specific asset selected from a manufacturer or vendor of such
assets by the lessee. The lessor retains ownership of the asset. The lessee has *Nature of*
possession and use of the asset on payment of specified rentals over a period.[15] *Equipment Lease*
Juridically such contracts provide for the bailment[16] of the asset leased and as
such, in addition to those rights and obligations arising out of the contractual
relationship between them, confer and impose upon the parties the rights and
obligations of bailors and bailees.[17] In particular, the lessee, as bailee may have
recourse to remedies such as trespass or conversion for the protection of the possession conferred by the contract. The availability of such remedies provides the
lessee with the means to prevent anyone, including the lessor, from interfering
with the leased asset[18] otherwise than in accordance with the express terms of
the contract.

It is inherent in a contract for the hire of a chattel that the hirer receives both **3.06**
possession of the chattel and the right to use it[19] in return for a consideration to
be paid to the hiree.[20] More specifically, certain obligations are imposed on the *Terms Implied*
parties either by the common law, statute or both,[21] albeit that the content of *into Contracts*
those obligations can in most cases[22] be varied or excluded by the express terms *of Hire*
of the particular contract.

The Supply of Goods and Services Act 1982 provides for certain terms to be
implied into "a contract for the hire of goods."[23] These terms include[24]:

[15] Equipment Leasing Association, *Equipment Leasing* (2nd Revision, 1976) at p. 1.
[16] In Scots law an equipment leasing transaction would be classified as a contract of hire.
[17] Obligations under bailment are independent of any liability in tort, although liability under one
may overlap with liability under the other. See Chitty, *Contracts* (25th ed., 1983) para. 2342 and
authorities cited there.
[18] *Lee* v. *Atkinson and Brook* (1609) Yelv. 172; *Turner* v. *Hardcastle* (1862) 11 C.B. (N.S.) 683.
[19] See *Beecham Foods Ltd.* v. *North Supplies (Edmonton) Ltd.* [1959] 1 W.L.R. 643.
[20] *McCarthy* v. *British Oak Insurance Co. Ltd.* [1938] 3 All E.R. 1.
[21] The relevant statute, the Supply of Goods and Services Act 1982 provides (s.18(3)) that its operation shall not prejudice the operation of " . . . any rule of law whereby any condition or warranty
(other than one relating to quality or fitness) is to be implied in . . . a contract for the hire of
goods."
[22] See Unfair Contract Terms Act 1977, ss.2, 3 and especially s.7 for exceptions.
[23] Defined as a contract under which one person bails or agrees to bail goods to another by way of
hire whether or not services are provided and whatever the nature of the consideration, 1982 Act,
s.18(1). Excluded from the definition however are hire-purchase agreements, *ibid.* s.6.
[24] The 1982 Act also implies terms on hiring by description or sample. Specifically, where in a contract for the hire of goods:
  (i) the bailor bails or agrees to bail the goods by description there is an implied condition that
  the goods will correspond with the description; *ibid.* s.8;
  (ii) the bailor bails or agrees to bail the goods by reference to a sample there is an implied condition:
    (a) that the bulk will correspond with the sample in quality; and
    (b) that the bailee will have a reasonable opportunity of comparing the bulk with the
    sample; and
    (c) that the goods will be free from any defect, rendering them unmerchantable, which
    would not be apparent on reasonable examination of the sample, *ibid.* s.10(2).

(a) "an implied condition on the part of the bailor that in the case of a bailment he has the right to transfer possession of the goods by way of hire for the period of the bailment"[25];

(b) "an implied warranty that the bailee will enjoy quiet possession of the goods for the period of the bailment except so far as the possession may be disturbed by the owner or other person entitled to the benefit of any charge or encumbrance disclosed or known to the bailee before the contract is made"[26];

(c) "an implied condition that the goods supplied under the contract are of merchantable quality"[27]; except

    (i) as regards defects specifically drawn to the bailee's attention before the contract is made; or

    (ii) if the bailee examines the goods before the contract is made, as regards the defects which that examination ought to reveal[28];

(d) where the bailee, expressly or by implication, makes known to the bailor in the course of negotiations conducted by him in relation to the making of the contract,[29] any particular purpose for which the goods are being bailed, "an implied condition that the goods supplied under the contract are reasonably fit for that purpose,[30] whether or not that is a purpose for which such goods are commonly supplied,"[31] save that such condition is not implied where the circumstances show that the bailee does not rely, or that it is unreasonable for him to rely as the skill or judgment of the bailor.[32]

**3.07**    The obligations on the bailee arising out of a contract of hire are:—

(a) to pay the agreed rental or other hire charge[33];

(b) to take reasonable care of the chattel hired during the period of the hire[34];

---

[25] And further that "in the case of an agreement to bail he will have such a right at the time of the bailment," *ibid.* s.7(1).

[26] *Ibid.* s.7(2).

[27] *Ibid.* s.9(2). Note that this condition is implied only if the bailor "bails goods in the course of a business" although s.9(8) extends its application to cover a person who "in the course of a business is acting as agent for another" except where the bailee knows (or ought to know) that the principal is not bailing in the course of business. See Chitty, *op. cit.* at paras. 4160 and 4161.

[28] *Ibid.* s.9(3).

[29] Or to a credit broker who sold the goods to the bailor before they were bailed–*ibid.* s.9(4).

[30] Note that conditions (c) and (d) in the text overlap to some extent with the undertaking as to fitness implied by the common law. This is to the effect that the owner who lets out a chattel on hire must take reasonable care to see that it is in a reasonably fit condition for the purpose for which the bailee is to use it. See further Chitty, *op. cit.* at para. 2381 and authorities cited there.

[31] *Ibid.* s.9(5). See above at note 27 as to the application of this provision.

[32] Or credit-broker, *ibid.* s.9(10).

[33] *McCarthy* v. *British Oak Insurance Co. Ltd.* [1938] 3 All E.R. 1.

[34] With the consequence that the hirer will escape liability if it can be shown that any damage was not due to the negligence of the hirer, *British Crane Hire Corpn. Ltd.* v. *Ipswich Plant Hire Ltd.* [1975] Q.B. 303 esp. at pp. 311–313; *Sanderson* v. *Collins* [1904] 1 K.B. 628 (liability for employee): See Chitty, *op. cit.* at para. 23–8 for consideration of hirer's general obligations in respect of repairs and maintenance.

(c) to use the chattel[35] for the purpose for which it was let[36];

(d) to return the chattel hired on the expiration of the agreed period[37]; and

(e) to pay the costs of such return.[38]

While all equipment leases may properly be described as contracts for hire it is **3.08** not the case that all contracts for hire may properly be regarded as leases. In particular "lease-purchase" arrangements, despite their name, are in substance *Lease and* hire-purchase agreements rather than leases. Although, like leases, lease- *Lease/Hire* purchase arrangements involve periodic rental payments and confer exclusive *Purchase* use of the asset covered by the agreement for the period of the agreement the transactions are fundamentally different in that the lessee under a lease has no right or option to own the asset at any time whereas the rentals under a lease-purchase agreement are in part payment of principal towards ownership to be obtained at the end of the contract. This feature has the consequence that available capital allowances that may be claimable in respect of capital expenditure incurred in a lease purchase go to the user of the asset. In contrast under a lease such allowances go to the owner.

Leasing facilities provided by the leasing industry in the United Kingdom are of three types:

(a) *Finance leases*. These are leases for the major part of the asset's economic *Types of Lease* life, which are non-cancellable or cancellable only on payment of a major penalty and from which the lessor expects to obtain his normal profit on an asset without being involved in further activity.

(b) *Operating leases*. These are considered to be all other leases, but which in consequence have the characteristics that they are cancellable by the lessee at short notice and without major penalty, and that they are arrangements under which the lessor expects to release or sell the asset, obtaining significant portions of his total profit on the asset from each successive transaction; and

(c) *Contract hire facilities*. These combine some of the characteristics of both finance and operating leases.

### Finance leasing

According to the Equipment Leasing Association a finance lease "is a contract **3.09** involving payment over an obligatory period of specified sums sufficient in total to amortise the capital outlay of the lessor and give some profit."[39] When taken

---

[35] *Burnard* v. *Haggis* (1863) 14 C.B. (N.S.) 45; *Walley* v. *Holt* (1878) 35 L.T. 631. (Hirers held liable both in contract and tort in respect of loss caused by user of bailed chattel for purposes not contemplated by the contract of hire. See further Palmer, *Bailment* (1979) at pp. 751–756.

[36] Note however that the authority granted to the hirer to use the chattel will be construed as conferring on him (in the absence of express provision in the contract to the contrary) implied authority to do in relation to the chattel anything reasonably incidental to its reasonable use, *Burnard* v. *Haggis, supra*; *Walley* v. *Holt, supra*.

[37] *British Crane Hire Corporn. Ltd.* v. *Ipswich Plant Hire Ltd., supra* at pp. 311–312.

[38] *Ibid.* at p. 312.

[39] Equipment Leasing Association, *Equipment Leasing* (2nd Revision, 1976) at p. 2.

with the Association's general definition of lease (quoted at § 3.05, above) this definition attributes to finance leases a number of characteristics:

(a) The involvement of the lessor in the transaction is purely as financier, the leased equipment being chosen by the lessee with whom rests responsibility for its suitability and condition. As such the terms of the lease will reflect the lessor's desire for the transaction to be self-financing. The mechanism for achieving this is a prescription for an "obligatory period" during which the agreement is incapable of being cancelled by the lessee at least without major penalty, usually calculated at a level sufficient to indemnify the lessor against any loss. It is during this period that the lessor seeks to recover through the rental paid by the lessee sufficient funds to cover the costs and to realise its profit. At the end of the obligatory period, the lessor's costs having been recovered, the lessee is commonly given an option either to continue the lease at a reduced rental or to share in the profits of any sale.[40]

(b) While the lessor retains ownership of the leased asset that ownership confers no right of use or of control beyond the stipulations as to the lessee's permitted user contained in the lease. Provided that the rentals are paid and the other terms of the agreement complied with the lease provides the lessee with the exclusive right to use the equipment during the period of the agreement.

(c) Since the equipment leased is purchased by the lessor at the request of the lessee the responsibility for its suitability and condition at the outset of the agreement rests with the lessee. It follows therefore that finance leases contain provisions excluding or severely modifying the terms implied into contracts of hire by the Supply of Goods and Services Act 1982 or by the common law.[41] Similarly, during the currency of the agreement responsibility for repairs, maintenance and insurance of the equipment, obligations normally associated in other contracts with ownership itself, rests with the lessee.

(d) Just as important "obligations of ownership" are made to rest with the lessee so also are the risks of ownership. Those relating to damage or destruction can be covered by insurance. Those arising from trading conditions or technical development cannot. Accordingly it is a feature of finance leases that the risks and burdens of obsolescence of the equipment leased is made to fall primarily on the lessee.

**3.10**

*Types of Asset Leased*

Virtually any tangible asset possessing qualities of durability may be leased. Among the items frequently acquired through finance leasing arrangements are aircraft, ships, railway locomotives and rolling stock,[42] buses, cars, fork lift trucks, lorries and other commercial vehicles, drilling rigs, quarrying and hiring equipment, oil and gas production and refining plant, generators, electrical apparatus, office equipment and computers, ultrasonic instruments, X-ray and hospital equipment, nuclear rods, machine tools, printing presses, internal telephones, hotel equipment and vending machines.

---

[40] It follows from this that the residual value of the asset remaining at the end of the obligatory period is not a significant factor in the lessor's calculation of return.

[41] See above at §3.06.

[42] As in the case of British Rail.

Capital expenditure on almost all[43] of these items qualified for the 100 per cent. first-year allowance[44] on machinery and plant[45] and although this allowance was claimable only by lessors[46] its availability has had considerable significance for lessees in two respects:

(a) The decision as to the form of financing the acquisition of the asset (that is, whether to lease it or borrow the funds to purchase it) might depend on the extent to which a prospective lessee could directly obtain the maximum benefit from the allowance. In the case of lease financing benefit would be passed on to the lessee in the form of reduced rentals. In situations where the company had no, or insufficient available, profits against which to set the allowance this benefit passed on might be decisive.

(b) Leasing aagreements normally provide that the lessee is to bear the risk of a lessor's not being entitled to claim the allowance. Where such is the case the consequences of a lessor's not being entitled to claim the allowance will be an increase in the rental charged to a level necessary to maintain the lessor's rate of return on its investment.

The availability of the first-year allowance in respect of leased assets was redefined by the provisions of section 64 of the Finance Act 1980. Under these provisions a first-year allowance will only be available in respect of expenditure on **3.11**

---

[43] Special rules apply to ships (where free depreciation is available), see below at §5.21 and to motor cars. In relation to these the general rule is that expenditure on motor cars of a type commonly used as private vehicles does not qualify for the FYA, F.A. 1971, s.43. Instead a 25 per cent. writing-down allowance is given in respect of the period in which the expenditure was incurred provided that the car was brought into use before the end of that period. However such WDA's are limited to £2,000 for cars costing more than £8,000, F.A. 1971, Sched. 8 para. 10, as amended by F.A. 1976, s.43 and F. (No.2) A. 1979, s.14(5).

However F.A. 1971, s.43(1)(c) exempts from these restrictions commercial vehicles and motor cars provided wholly or mainly for hire to members of the public in the course of a trade. Accordingly cars acquired by leasing companies and leased to customers are eligible for the 100 per cent. FYA. Note however that this exemption applies only to companies who are *actually in the business of leasing cars to the public*. It follows that a subsidiary formed to acquire cars which its parent company leased would not satisfy this requirement.

Sched. 8 of F.A. 1971 contains anti–avoidance measures designed to withdraw the benefit of FYA's in any of the following circumstances:

    (i) The lessor and the seller of the equipment are "connected persons" (a company is connected with another when one is under the control of the other or when they are both under common control) other than a sale in the normal course of the trade of the vendor;

    (ii) The equipment is sold and leased back (other than before the asset is brought into use) and continued to be used by the seller as a person connected to the seller.

    (iii) The sale or main purpose of the transaction is the obtaining of a FYA.

[44] F.A. 1984, s.58(1)(b) provided for the progressive withdrawal of FYAs over the period March 13, 1984 to April 1, 1986. See further below at §§3.12 *et seq*.

[45] For definition of plant see *Yarmouth* v. *France* (1889) 19 O.B.D. 647, C.A.; *IRC* v. *Barclay Curle & Co.* (1969) 45 T.C. 221, H.L. and *Ben-Odeco Ltd.* v. *Powlson* [1978] 1 W.L.R. 1093, H.L.

Note that the expenditure on buildings does not so qualify, expenditure on alterations to existing buildings incidental to the installation of machinery and plant (including laying the necessary foundations and strengthening floors) may be treated as if it were expenditure on that machinery and plant and thereby qualify.

[46] F.A. 1971, s.45(1)(a) provides fo a taxpayer to be eligible to claim capital allowances on expenditure incurred on the acquisition of machinery and plant in a period provided that the machinery and plant belongs to him at some point during that period. Machinery and plant is treated as belonging to a person if the expenditure is incurred under a contract which provides that the person shall or may become the owner of the equipment. Hence lessors qualify to claim the allowances (as do hirers other than financiers under a hire/lease purchase contract).

the provision of machinery or plant for leasing where it appears that the machinery or plant will be used:

(a) for a qualifying purpose;

(b) in the requisite period; and

(c) will not at any time within that period be used for any other purpose.

(a) *Qualifying purpose*

Machinery or plant is used for a qualifying purpose at any time when:—

(i) it is used by a lessee who uses it for the purposes of a trade other than that of leasing, and that lessee would have been entitled to a first-year allowance had he bought the machinery or plant at that time and incurred capital expenditure in doing so; or

(ii) the person who incurred the expenditure uses the machinery or plant for short term leasing[47]; or

(iii) the machinery or plant is leased to a lessee who uses it for short term leasing, provided that the lessee is either resident in the United Kingdom or uses the machinery or plant for short term leasing for the purposes of a trade carried on by him in the United Kingdom; or

(iv) the person who incurred the expenditure uses the machinery or plant for the purposes of a trade other than that of leasing.[48]

There are special provisions in relation to ships, aircraft, and transport containers.[49]

---

[47] For these purposes, *short term leasing* means the leasing of machinery or plant so that:
    (a) the machinery or plant will not normally be leased to the same person for 30 or more consecutive days nor for more than 90 days in any period of 12 months; or
    (b) the machinery or plant will not normally be leased to the same person for more than 365 consecutive days and during the requisite period the aggregate of the periods for which it is leased otherwise than within definition (a) above will not exceed two years.

[48] F.A. 1980, s.64(2).

[49] In addition to the qualifying purposes of general application, a ship is also used for a qualifying purpose at any time when it is let on charter in the course of a trade which consists of or includes operating ships. But this applies only if the person carrying on the trade is resident in the U.K. or carries on a trade here; he must also be responsible as principal for navigating and managing the ship throughout the period of the charter and for defraying all expenses in connection with the ship throughout that period or substantially all such expenses other than those directly incidental to a particular voyage or to the employment of the ship during that period. However, this extended definition of qualifying purpose does not apply in relation to expenditure incurred after March 9, 1982, if the main object, or one of the main objects, of chartering out a ship is to obtain the first-year allowance (F.A. 1980, s.64(6A) as inserted by F.A. 1982, s.71(2)). But this rule does not apply to expenditure incurred after March 9, 1982, which is payable under a contract entered into before March 10, 1982, if the ship concerned is brought into use not later than March 31, 1984 (F.A. 1982, s.71(5)). This extended definition of qualifying purpose also applies with any necessary modifications in relation to aircraft (F.A. 1980, s.64(6)).
A transport container is also used for a qualifying purpose at any time when:
    (a) the container is leased in the course of a trade carried on by a person resident in the U.K. (or by a non-resident trading in the U.K.) if that trade consists of or includes the operation of ships or aircraft and the container is at other times used by the lessor in connection with the operation of ships or aircraft; or
    (b) the container is leased under a succession of leases to different persons most or all of whom are not connected with each other.
These specific qualifying uses for transport containers are in addition to (and not instead of) the general qualifying uses listed at (a) to (d) in the text, so the use to which a container is put is a qualifying use if it is within any one of more of the criteria (F.A. 1980, s.64(7)).

(b) *Requisite period*

The requisite period is the shorter of:

(i) the period of four years from the date of first use by the person who incurred the expenditure, or
(ii) the period from the date of first use by the person who incurred the expenditure to the date on which the machinery or plant ceases to belong to that person if it is within that period of four years.[50]

(c) *Uses for qualifying purpose*

A claim for a first-year allowance where the conditions relating to qualifying purposes are satisfied must be accompanied by a certificate which must contain statements:

(i) that the machinery or plant in question will be used for a qualifying purpose in the requisite period; and
(ii) that it will not be used for any other purpose in that period; and
(iii) that it has not been used for any other purpose in any part of the requisite period which has already elapsed; and
(iv) a description of the machinery or plant in question or, if the claim or deduction relates to more than one item of machinery or plant and those items are of different kinds, a description of the different kinds and the amount claimed or deducted for each of them.[51]

Where the conditions prescribed in section 64 cannot be met so that the full first-year allowance is not available section 65 provides for the lessor to be entitled to a 25 per cent. writing-down allowance. Furthermore, if an asset in respect of which a full first-year allowance has been granted ceases to be used for a qualifying purpose within the requisite period the writing down allowance becomes available in substitution for the first-year allowance.[52]

**3.12**

*Withdrawal of First-Year Allowance*

The extent to which the writing-down allowance will be the only allowance available will progressively increase as a direct consequence of the provisions of the Finance Act 1984[53] which lay down a timetable for the phasing out of first-year allowances on machinery and plant. According to this timetable the pre-Finance Act full allowance of 100 per cent. has been reduced to 75 per cent. in respect of expenditure incurred between March 13, 1984 and April 1, 1985, and to 50 per cent. in respect of expenditure incurred on or after April 1, 1985 and

---

[50] F.A. 1980, s.64(9). However if the provisions of F.A. 1982, s.90 as to international leasing (see below at note 63) apply to expenditure the period of time in relation to that expenditure is 10 years rather than 4, F.A. 1982, s.70(3) and (9).
[51] F.A. 1980, s.67(1).
[52] *Ibid.* s.66. In this event the whole matter is dealt with when the non-qualifying use begins.
[53] F.A. 1984, ss.58–59 and Sched. 12.

before April 1, 1986. No first-year allowance will be available in respect of expenditure incurred on or after April 1, 1986.[54]

However, capital expenditure incurred after March 13, 1984 and before April 1, 1987 consisting of payments under a contract entered into on or before March 13, 1984 will still be eligible for a full first-year allowance at the pre-Finance Act rate of 100 per cent. provided that the payments are made by the person incurring the expenditure or by the person whose contractual obligations that person has assumed with a view to entering into leasing arrangements. In this connection a lessor is to be taken to have assumed, with a view to entering into leasing arrangements, the contractual obligations of a lessee if, and only if[55]:

(i) arrangements exist under which the lessor will lease the machinery or plant to the lessee[56]; and

(ii) the obligations of the lessee under the contract have been taken over by the lessor or have been discharged on the lessor's entering into a new contract for the provision of the equipment concerned.

**Pre-lease procedures**

**3.13**    In practice most finance lease agreements take between one and three months to negotiate, the period in any particular case depending on the size and complexity of the agreement, the number of lessors approached for quotations and the nature of the asset(s) to be leased. The primary factor, however, governing the length of this period of negotiation is the "lead-in time" between order and delivery of the assets. If this period is lengthy it is common for the lessee to place an order prior to arranging appropriate finance, in part because the actual delivery time is likely to be uncertain and in part because prospective lessors will usually be unwilling to quote rates so far into the future. Where the lead-in time is short there will be greater certainty about delivery dates and a correspondingly greater willingness on the part of the lessors to provide quotations. In such cases the usual (and prudent) course is for lease finance to have been arranged prior to the placing of the order. If lease finance has not been arranged by the time for delivery leasing as a method of financing is not automatically precluded if the asset has been brought into use. The point is that lease finance may still be possible on a sale and leaseback basis although first-year allowances will only be available to a lessor if the asset had not been brought into use.[57]

---

[54] *Ibid.* Sched. 12, para. 2(1). Note that Sched. 12, paras. 5–9 contain anti-avoidance provisions applicable in respect of contracts entered into between March 14, 1984 and March 31, 1986 where the sole or main benefit which might have been expected to be gained by incurring the expenditure when it was incurred and not at some later time was the securing of either:

    (a) a FYA rather than a writing-down allowance; or

    (b) a higher rate of FYA.

The effect of the provisions is to spread the expenditure over the period between the date of the contract under which the expenditure was incurred and the date by which the contract is to be fully performed (or, if earlier, March 31, 1987).

[55] F.A. 1984, Sched. 12, para. 2(2) and (3).

[56] See further at §3.17, below.

[57] F.A. 1971, Sched. 8.

In seeking quotations for lease finance a lessee would normally be expected to **3.14** provide information as to:—

 (i) the type of equipment to be acquired;
 (ii) an estimate of its normal economic life;
 (iii) the purchase price and supplier's payment terms;
 (iv) the expected date of delivery;
 (v) the proposed location of the asset; and
 (vi) the lessee's financial position.

### (a) *The type of equipment to be acquired*

As has been mentioned[58] virtually any type of equipment may be and is made subject to a finance leasing arrangement. However, the type of equipment may have different capital allowance consequences (for example, ships or motor cars) and may, if required to be physically attached to premises, present problems as to whether the machinery and plant have become fixtures and thereby regarded as part of the premises themselves.

Where the leased equipment will or may become a fixture it will usually be necessary for the lessee to obtain an undertaking[59] from his landlord or mortgagee acknowledging the lessor's interest in the equipment and his right to *Fixtures* remove it in the circumstances stipulated for in the lease. In cases where equipment is to be affixed to premises owned by the lessee it is usual for a lessor to insist that no mortgage (or further mortgage) be created over the property without such an undertaking.

### (b) *An estimate of the normal economic life*

Information as to the normal economic life of the asset is important in arriving at the length of the "obligatory" period provided for in the lease. Given that it will be over this period that the lessor will seek to recoup his expenditure and realise most (if not all) of his profit via the rentals paid by the lessee the ascertainment of a realistic figure is obviously of importance to the lessee and as such will become an important matter for negotiation.

### (c) *Purchase price and suppliers payment terms*

Both of these matters affect the cost to the lessor of purchasing the asset and as such may have an effect on the ultimate rental payable by the lessee.

In relation to payment terms it is not uncommon for a supplier to require progress payments during the period of construction of the asset. In such a case the normal course is for the lessor to require from the lessee either reimbursement or an indemnity to provide against the possibility of non-delivery.

---

[58] Above at §3.10.
[59] See *per* Harman J. in *Stokes* v. *Costain Property Investments* [1983] 1 W.L.R. 907. However it should be noted that such an undertaking does not bind any subsequent landlord or mortgagee who takes the premises as bona fide purchaser without notice of the lessor's interest.

(d) *The expected date for delivery*

This is important in that the date for delivery of the asset will normally determine:

   (i) the date on which the supplier issues the invoice for the equipment, which, in the absence of any express provision to the contrary in the supply agreement, in turn will determine:

     (1) the period within which payment must be made; and

     (2) the period in respect of which the lessor may make his claim for first-year (or other) allowance; and

   (ii) the tax and interest rate assumptions[60] on which the lessor's profit calculation will be based and which in turn will be reflected in the rental charged to the lessee. It is normal to specify these assumptions in the lease agreement and to provide for variation at the instance of the lessor should they not be operable at the date of expenditure.

(e) *The proposed location of the asset*

Since the dismantling of the system of exchange controls in the United Kingdom the restrictions on exports and offshore leasing activities formerly applied by the Bank of England no longer operate.[61] Nor does the tax system seek to place obstacles in the path of those seeking lease finance for plant and machinery to be located overseas, capital allowances[62] being available to lessors in the same way as they would have been available had the relevant equipment been located in the United Kingdom.[63] Where, however, a leasing transaction involves payments in foreign currency the possibilities of exchange losses may have an effect on the negotiation of the leasing agreement terms.

Payments in foreign currency may arise in two situations:

*Foreign Currency Elements*

   (i) A lessor may have financed the acquisition of the machinery and plant by way of a foreign currency loan, taking advantage of cheap fixed-rate export finance made available by a foreign supplier. In such a case the usual practice is for the lessee to agree to indemnify the lessor against any exchange losses that might accrue to the lessor from any depreciation in the value of sterling. Where such indemnity provisions are agreed the lease will usually also contain a "parity

---

[60] These will normally be calculated by reference to the relevant Finance House Base Rate or LIBOR.

[61] Prior to the ending of exchange controls on October 23, 1979 permission was required to lease abroad equipment that had been manufactured abroad. Such permission was granted only on condition that any claim to FYA was limited to 25 per cent. For the transitional provisions governing expenditure incurred in the period October 23, 1979 until May 5, 1980 see F.A. 1980, Sched. 12.

[62] Where capital allowances are claimed in respect of assets purchased with foreign currency the amount of those allowances is calculated by reference to the sterling equivalent of that foreign currency expenditure as at the date on which it was incurred. Similarly any balancing charges that may arise in respect of a sale of the asset for foreign currency are based on the sterling equivalent of the sale proceeds at the time of the disposal.

[63] Subject to the operation of F.A. 1982, s.70 and Sched. 11 which seek to deal with the situation of an asset being used by a person in a trade which is outside the U.K. tax net by reducing the allowance. The 1982 provisions however do not apply where the lessee is a company resident in the U.K., F.A. 1982, s.70(1).

adjustment clause" permitting the lessee to participate in any exchange profits that might accrue from any appreciation in the value of sterling.

While any exchange loss to the lessor, being on capital account, would not qualify as a deduction in computing the trading profits of the lessor[64] it is at least arguable that payments under indemnity provisions might be deductible by the lessee as rental, and therefore revenue payments and that, by the same token, parity adjustment payments might be treated as revenue receipts. It is suggested, however, that the better view is that such items are more properly regarded as payments or receipts of capital and that their effect on the amount of rental payable does not affect their intrinsic nature.[65]

(ii) The terms of the lease may, unusually as between a British resident lessor and lessee, require the rental to be payable in foreign currency. Any exchange profit accruing to the lessor from currency fluctuations is treated as being incidental to his trade of leasing and taxable as part of the profits of that trade.[66] In view of the lessor's inability to deduct any corresponding loss on foreign currency borrowing incurred to finance the transaction it is common for lessors to seek to gross up any exchange parity adjustments by reference to the rate of tax payable in order to avoid any ultimate loss.

(f) *The lessee's financial position*

As with any other form of financing, the lessor, as provider of the finance, will require to be satisfied that the degree of risk associated with the transaction is acceptable. In the same way that a lending institution would require to be satisfied as to a prospective borrower's financial position so also a lessor will require information as to the lessee's financial position in order that an assessment of risk may be made. Indeed since from a credit-worthiness standpoint a finance lease can be compared to a medium-term loan[67] secured on the equipment the same kinds of enquiries to obtain the same kinds of information as to the credit standing of the lessee will require to be made by a lessor as would be made by a bank or other institutional lender. Thus information as to the nature of the lessee's business, the quality of its management, its financial position as shown by its latest (and in some cases earlier recent) accounts, and its future prospects, especially from the standpoint of whether the projected future cash flow can realistically meet the rentals and other expected outgoings during the period of the lease.

---

[64] *Imperial Tobacco Co.* v. *Kelly* (1943) 25 T.C. 292, C.A.; *Davies* v. *Shell Co. of China Ltd.* (1950) 32 T.C. 133.

[65] *I.R.C.* v. *Land Securities Investment Trust* [1969] 1 W.L.R. 604, H.L.

[66] *Landes Bros.* v. *Simpson* (1934) 19 T.C. 62.

[67] Although in some circumstances financial institutions may regard one form of medium-term finance as more risky than another, a finance lease, a secured loan on the equipment (for 100 per cent. of its cost) and a hire purchase facility (without an initial deposit) carry similar degrees of credit risk. Groups providing a range of financial services normally assess the creditworthiness of a prospective customer on the same basis, whatever the type of equipment finance required. Accordingly if a bank or finance house has refused to lend or provide hire purchase facilities for the purchase of equipment it is unlikely that an associated leasing company would be more willing to provide a leasing facility for the use of the same equipment. See further Clark, *Leasing* at pp. 63 and 217–220 for a consideration of the features of risk in leasing.

If, after an evaluation of the information received the transaction appears to a lessor to carry a higher level of risk than it would normally willingly accept it may seek to protect its position in the same way as other financial institutions by taking additional security and/or demanding a higher rental to be paid.

**3.15**

*Insurance*

While there is no specific statutory obligation[68] in the United Kingdom requiring the insurance of leased equipment such insurance is taken out as a matter of normal practice in finance leasing arrangements and the details of the insurance cover to be effected figure as an important item in pre-lease agreement negotiations. Both lessor[69] and lessee[70] have insurable interests in the equipment but finance leasing practice is for insurance to be effected by and/or at the expense of the lessee. Such insurance cover[71] is normally sought in respect of physical loss or damage to the equipment and in respect of possible legal liability from third party claims relating to its use.[72]

**3.16**

*Purchasing
Procedures*

It is a feature of finance leasing that it is the lessee, rather than the lessor, who selects the equipment to be leased and who negotiates the main purchase terms with the supplier. The arrangements under which the processes of ordering, purchasing and leasing take place may be of three types:

(i) those where agreement as to the terms of the leasing facility have been agreed prior to the making of the order;
(ii) those where no such agreement has been achieved prior to the placing of the order; and
(iii) those where no such agreement has been achieved prior to the date of delivery.

---

[68] However, in the case of motor vehicles s.143 of the Road Traffic Act 1972 renders it unlawful for a person to use, or permit any other person to use, a motor vehicle on the road unless the use of the vehicle is insured against liability in respect of death or personal injury to third parties. Under this provision a lessor would be criminally liable if it permitted the vehicle to be used and, possibly, also liable for damages to the extent that any uninsured lessee is unable to satisfy any claim. To overcome this problem it is common for leasing arrangements to prohibit the lessee from using the vehicle without cover satisfying the statutory requirements, thereby making any such use without permission and therefore outside s.143.

[69] As owner.

[70] The lessee has an insurable interest similar to that of a purchaser.

[71] See further below at §3.17.

[72] The principal insurable risks which both lessee and lessor would normally require to have covered are:
    (i) Physical loss or damage
        Fire
        Special perils (storm, tempest and flood, explosion, earthquake, riot and civil commotion, etc.)
        Accidental damage
        Theft (where the equipment is moveable)
    (ii) Legal liability
        Employer's liability
        Liability to persons or property of persons other than employees.

In cases where a leasing facility has been set up prior to the placing of an order for the equipment the purchase may be effected either:

(a) Directly by the lessor; or

(b) By the lessee as agent for the lessor.

(a) *Direct purchase*[73]

Under direct purchase procedures the lessor places the order for the equipment directly with the supplier and signs the purchase order. Under these arrangements there is no contractual relationship between the lessee and supplier at any stage or in any capacity. It follows that any claims against the supplier should be pursued by the lessee via the lessor.

(b) *Agency*

As in all agency matters the part properly played by the lessee as agent for the lessor depends on the terms of the arrangement under which the agency exists. Two forms of agency arrangement are commonly encountered. Under the first[74] the authority of the lessee is restricted to the placement of the order. Payment is made by the lessor to whom the invoice should be sent by the supplier. Under the second[75] the lessee places the order with the supplier and makes payment, obtaining reimbursement from the lessor.

No formality is required for the appointment of the lessee as agent for the lessor, whichever form of arrangement is employed.[76] In practice, however, such arrangements are normally evidenced in a memorandum or agreement setting out the main terms of the agency. Such a memorandum will usually seek to include:

(i) a description of the specific items or at the type(s) of goods to be covered by the agency agreement;

(ii) a limitation on the total cost of the goods to be ordered;

(iii) a requirement that the purchase orders be limited to goods to be delivered by a specified date[77];

(iv) an acknowledgement that the lessee is to accept delivery of the goods from the supplier on behalf of the lessor;

(v) a recital that all goods covered by the agency agreement are, upon their acceptance by the lessee, to become subject to the provisions of the leasing agreement; and

(vi) (if the agency arrangement covers payments to the supplier) undertakings by the lessee to pay invoices on their due dates and by the lessor to reimburse the lessee in a specified manner.

---

[73] This procedure is thought to be particularly suitable for large-value items requiring a special form of purchase agreement rather than a standard purchase order, see Clark, *op.cit.* at p.70.

[74] Agency to Order.

[75] Agency to Pay.

[76] See generally *Bowstead Agency* (15th ed., 1985) at pp. 28 *et seq.*

[77] Which will be the final availability date for the leasing facility.

**3.18**

*(2) Where Order Placed Prior to Arrangements of Leasing Facility*

Where the lessee has already placed an order for the equipment by the time the leasing facility is agreed, if the lessor is to be introduced into the purchase prior to the delivery and invoicing this may be achieved either:

   (i) by novation; or

   (ii) by assignment.

In the case of a novation the original purchase order is cancelled and replaced by a new and identical order from the lessor whereas under an assignment the rights of the lessee are transferred to the lessor. From the lessor's standpoint the former method is preferable since an assignment would still leave the supplier with a possible right of action against the lessee under the contract should the lessor default on his obligations and fail to make due payment.

**3.19**

*(3) Where Leasing Facilities not Arranged until after Delivery*

Where leasing facilities have not been agreed by the time of the delivery and invoicing of the equipment leasing finance may be arranged on a sale and lease-back basis. However, for the lessor to qualify for the 100 per cent. first-year allowance the sale to the lessor must take place before the asset is brought into use in the lessee's business.[78]

### Terms of the lease

**3.20**

While the requirements of individual lessees and the practices of individual lessors must inevitably differ according to the circumstances of each case nevertheless, although finance leases have not become standard form documents, they have over the last 15 years tended to become broadly similar along the following lines.

(a) *Definitions*

> "In this lease "the equipment" means [description] and shall include all additions and accessories thereto and all replacements and renewals thereof whether made before or after the date of this lease."

(b) *Title*

*Ownership with Lessor*

*Equipment not to be Fixture*

> "(1) The equipment is and shall remain the property of the lessor and the lessee shall have no right or interest therein otherwise than as lessee.
> (2) As between the lessor and the lessee and their respective successors in title the equipment hereby demised shall remain personal property and shall continue in the ownership of the lessor notwithstanding that the same may have been offered to any land or building."

(c) *Term*

> "The lessor hereby lets and the lessee takes on lease from the lessor upon the terms and conditions hereinafter mentioned the said equipment for a term of . . . years commencing on the . . . day of . . . ."

[78] F.A. 1972, s.68 and F.A. 1971, Sched. 8.

(d) *Rental*

(1) The lessee shall pay to the lessor during the said term of rental of . . . per [month/quarter, etc.] payable on the . . . the first rental payment to be made on the . . . day of . . . . All payments of rental however shall be paid to the lessor at [address] or at such other address as the lessor may from time to time specify. Payments made by post shall be at the risk of the lessee.

*Amount and Payment of Rental*

(2) Punctual payment of the rental shall be of the essence of this lease. If any rental or part thereof shall remain unpaid for more than 14 days after becoming due the lessee shall be in default.[79]

*Payment of the Essence*

(e) *Convenants by the lessee*

"The lessee shall throughout the said term:

(1) Punctually pay all amounts of rental payable hereunder;

(2) Pay to the lessor interest on overdue rentals at the rate of . . . per cent. per annum until payment thereof such interest to run from day to day and to accrue after as well as before any judgment;

*Punctual Payment*

*Interest on Overdue Instalments*

(3) Keep the equipment in good and serviceable repair and condition (fair wear and tear only excepted) and replace all missing damaged or broken parts with parts of equal quality and value and in default of so doing permit the lessor to take possession of the equipment for the purpose of having repairs carried out and repay to the lessor the full cost of such repairs and the lessor shall have a lien on the equipment until such repayment but exercise of such lien shall not prevent the accrual of rental hereunder;

*To Repair*

(4) Ensure that the equipment is operated in a skilful and proper manner and by persons who are competent to operate the same;

(5) Punctually pay all registration charges licence fees rent rates taxes and other outgoings payable in respect of the equipment or the use thereof or in respect of any premises in which the equipment may from time to time be placed or kept and produce to the lessor on demand the last receipts for all such payments and in the event of the lessee making default under this sub-clause the lessor shall be at liberty to make all or any of such payments and to recover the amount thereof from the lessee forthwith;

*Operation of the Equipment*

*To pay all Charges, etc. and in Default Permit Lessor to Pay and Recover*

(6) Permit the lessor and any person authorised by the lessor at all reasonable times to enter upon the premises in which the equipment is for the time being placed or kept for the purpose of inspecting and examining the condition of the equipment;

*To Permit Lessor to Enter and Inspect*

[79] Some leases continue "and shall be deemed to have repudiated this lease." It is suggested that the form given in the text provides greater flexibility permitting the agreement to remain *in esse* while the situation clarifies yet reserving the rights of the lessor to terminate by notice (see below at §3.20(I)) should this be necessary. A deemed repudiation would appear to work against the interests of both parties where the delay in payment was accidental or where the contract was otherwise such as to render it advantageous for the lease to continue.

(7) Keep the equipment at all times in the possession and control of the lessee and not remove the same [from the place where it is installed by the lessor] without the consent in writing of the lessor;

*To keep the Goods in Lessee's Possession*

(8) Notify the lessor of any change in the lessee's address and upon request by the lessor promptly inform the lessor of the whereabouts of the equipment;

*To Notify Lessor of Altered Address or Whereabouts of Equipment*

(9) Indemnify the lessor against loss of or damage to the equipment or any part thereof from whatever cause arising and whether or not such loss or damage results from the negligence of the lessee;

*To Indemnify Lessor Against Loss of or Damage to Equipment*

(10) Punctually pay for all servicing of and repairs and other work done to the equipment and for spare parts and accessories thereof and keep the equipment free from distress execution or any other legal process;

*To keep Equipment Free from Distress, etc.*

(11) Ensure that in so far as the equipment is affixed to any land or building such equipment shall be capable of being removed without material injury to the said land or building and that all such steps shall be taken as are necessary to prevent title to the equipment from passing to the owner of the said land or building. The lessee shall be responsible for any damage caused to any such land or building by the affixing of the equipment thereof or the removal of the equipment therefrom (whether such affixing or removal be effected by the lessor or the lessee/and shall indemnify the lessor against any claim made in respect of such damage.

*To Ensure that Equipment Affixed to Realty can be Removed without Material Damage*

(12) Obtain all necessary licences permits and permissions for the use of the equipment and not to use the equipment or permit the same to be used contrary to law or any regulation or bye-law for the time being in force.

*To Obtain all Consents, etc. for use of Equipment*

(f) *Damage, loss, third party claims and insurance*

(1) The lessee shall throughout the said term indemnify the lessor against all claims and demands made upon the lessor by reason of any loss injury or damage suffered by any person from the presence of the equipment or the use thereof.

*Lessor's Indemnity Re Third Party Claims*

　　(2)(a) The lessee shall immediately after the signing of this lease insure the equipment and keep the same insured throughout the term against loss or damage by accident fire theft and other risks usually covered by insurance in this type of business for which the equipment is for the time being used, the equipment to be insured to the full replacement value thereof with [name of insurance company] under a comprehensive policy of insurance free from restirction or excess in the name of the lessee[80] bearing an indorsement recording the lessor's interest and stating that repayment is to be made to the lessee under the policy until the lessor's interest has been discharged.

*Insurance (1) Obligation to Insure*

(b) Should the lessee be in default of the obligation to insure as described in clause 2(a) above the lessor may insure the equipment in accordance with the terms specified in the said clause and recover the cost thereof from the lessee forthwith.

(c) The lessee shall throughout the currency of the lease punctually pay all premiums payable under the said policy, produce the receipts for such payments to the lessor on demand, do everything necessary to maintain the said policy in full effect and not do anything whereby the said policy will or may be vitiated.

*To pay Premiums*

(3) The lessee hereby irrevocably appoints the lessor to be the agent of the lessee for the purpose of receiving all monies payable under the said policy and giving a discharge therefor.

*Lessor to be Agent for Lessee Re Receipt of Policy Monies*

(4) Where the equipment or any part thereof is lost, stolen, destroyed or damaged by the negligence or wrongful act of a third party the lessee shall immediately notify the lessor thereof shall not compromise any claim without the consent of the lessor shall allow the lessor to take over the conduct of any negotiations (except in relation to claims of the lessee for personal injuries loss of use of the equipment or loss or damage to the property of the lessee unconnected with the equipment) and shall at the expense of the lessee take such proceedings (in the sole name of the lessee or jointly with the lessor) as the lessor shall direct holding all sums recovered together with any monies received by the lessee under any policy of insurance taken out for the lessor and paying or applying as the lessor directs such part thereof as is necessary to discharge the lessee's liability to the lessor at the date of such payment and to compensate the lessor for the loss or destruction of or damage to the equipment any surplus being retainable by the lessee for the lessee's own benefit.

*Loss or Damage to Equipment*

(5) If the equipment shall be damaged during the terms of this lease and in the opinion of the insurers it is economic that such damage be made good all insurance monies payable under the said policy shall be applied in making good the said damage.

*Application of Insurance Monies*

(6) If the equipment shall be lost stolen destroyed or damaged to such an extent as to be in the opinion of the insurers incapable of economic repair the insurance monies payable under the said policy shall at the option of the lessor

---

[0] Or in the joint names of lessor and lessee.

187

(a) be applied so far as possible in replacing the equipment with equipment of similar type and quality in which event the fresh equipment shall be held by the lessee under the terms of this lease; or

(b) be paid to the lessor to the extent necessary to discharge the lessee's liability to the lessor at the date of such payment and to compensate the lessor for the loss theft or destruction of or damage to the equipment any surplus being paid to the lessee but if the insurance monies paid to the lessee are insufficient to discharge the lessee's said liability and to compensate the lessor as aforesaid the amount of the deficiency shall forthwith be paid by the lessee to the lessor and thereupon this lease shall come to an end.

(7) Save as provided by sub-clause (6)(b) of this clause the loss theft or destruction of or damage to the equipment shall not affect the continuance of this lease or the lessee's liability for payment of rental hereunder.

*Effects of Loss or Damage*

(8) The lessee shall not be liable for fair wear and tear of the equipment and the burden of depreciation resulting from such fair wear and tear shall fall upon the lessor.

*Fair Wear and Tear*

(g) *Assignment and subletting (lessee)*

The Lessee shall not

(1) sell assign sub-let pledge mortgage charge incumber or part with possession of or otherwise deal with the equipment or any interest therein nor create nor allow to be created any lien on the equipment whether for repairs or otherwise and in the event of any breach of this sub-clause by the lessee the lessor shall be entitled (but shall not be bound) to pay to any third party such sum as is necessary to procure the release of the equipment from any charge incumbrance or lien and shall be entitled to recover such sum from the lessee forthwith;

(2) sell mortgage charge demise sub-let or otherwise dispose of any land or building on or in which the equipment is kept or enter into any contract to do any of the aforesaid things without giving the lessor at least six weeks' prior notice in writing and the lessee shall in any event procure that any such sale mortgage charge demise sub-lease or other disposition as the case may be is made subject to the right of the lessor to repossess the equipment at any time (whether or not the same or any part thereof shall have become affixed to the said land or building) and for that purpose to enter upon such land or building and sever any equipment affixed thereto.

(h) *Lessor's right to assign*

The lessor shall be entitled to assign this lease or any right or rights hereunder including the right conferred on the lessor to enter upon land or buildings to inspect the equipment and to sever and repossess the same and any assignment of this lease by the lessor shall be deemed to include an assignment of the lessor's rights to enter sever and repossess.

## (i) *Default*

(1) If the lessee shall make default in payment of any of the sums payable hereunder or shall fail to observe or perform any of the other terms and conditions of this lease whether express or implied or if the lessor shall on any reasonable ground consider itself insecure the lessor may without prejudice to any pre-existing liability of the lessee to the lessor by notice in writing left at or sent by prepaid post to the above-mentioned address or at or to the registered office or any business address or the lessee or the lessee's last known business address determine this lease and upon such notice being so served sent or left this lease shall for all purposes determine and thereafter the lessee shall no longer be in possession of the equipment with the consent of the lessor and subject to the provisions hereinafter contained and any pre-existing liability of the lessee hereunder neither party shall have any rights against the other.

*Termination by Lessor by Notice*

(2) If a winding-up order shall be made against the lessee or if the lessee shall pass a resolution for voluntary winding up (otherwise than by way of amalgamation or reconstruction) or shall make any arrangement with its creditors or any assignment for the benefit of such creditors or if distress or execution shall be levied or threatened upon the equipment or upon any of the lessee's property or if any judgment against the lessee shall remain unsatisfied for more than fourteen days or if the lessee shall abandon the equipment then this lease shall automatically and without notice determine and subject to the provisions hereinafter contained and any pre-existing liability of the lessee hereunder neither party shall have any rights against the other.

*Automatic Termination of Lease in Stated Events*

(3) Where this lease is determined or comes to an end pursuant to the provisions contained in this clause and the lessor suffers loss as a result of being unable to re-let the equipment at a rental as much as that payable under this lease for the whole period between the date of such determination or coming to an end and the date on which this lease would have expired by effluxion of time if it had not been determined or come to an end as aforesaid the lessor shall be entitled to recover the amount of such loss from the lessee.[81]

*Lessor may Recover from Lessee Loss Suffered by Termination*

(4) In the event of default by the lessee hereunder the lessee shall pay to the lessor all expenses (including legal costs on a full indemnity basis)

---

[81] This formula has the advantage that it is not open to attack as a penalty as it is in terms limited to the loss actually suffered by the lessor. It has, however, the disadvantage that some considerable time may elapse before the amount of the lessor's claim can be quantified. If it is desired to fix the lessee's liability immediately on termination then some more definite formula should be adopted, *e.g.*, that the lessee shall pay as liquidated damages a sum representing a stated percentage of the rental that the lessor would have received for the unexpired period of the lease if it had not come to an end prematurely.

*To Pay all
Legal and
Other
Expenses*

incurred by or on behalf of the lessor in ascertaining the whereabouts of taking possession of preserving insuring and storing the equipment and of any legal proceedings by or on behalf of the lessor to enforce the provisions of this lease.

### (j) *Variation clauses*

The rental will have been fixed in accordance with certain assumptions as to[82]:

    (a)  the rate of corporation tax remaining stable;
    (b)  the obtaining of a first-year allowance by the lessor; and
    (c)  interest rates.[83]

Since any deviation from these assumptions will have an effect on the lessor's investment return it is usual for finance leases to include provisions designed to protect that rate of return. Examples of such provisions are:

*Corporation
Tax Changes*

    (1)  "If, for any period during the currency of this lease, the rate of corporation tax from time to time in force shall be in excess of the rate in force at the date hereof the lessee shall pay to the lessor additional sums by way of rental. The amounts of such additional sums will be determined by applying to the amounts of rental specified in clause (d) above an increase of the same proportion as the increase in the rate of corporation tax in force for that period bears for the rate of corporation tax in force at the date hereof."[84]

*Failure to
Obtain FYA*

    (2)  "If the lessor shall fail to obtain in respect of the cost of acquisition of the equipment a first-year allowance of 100 per cent. or, having obtained such an allowance in respect of such cost is required to repay it wholly or in part the lessee shall pay to the lessor such additional amount as will, taking into account the amount of any first-year allowance obtained and retained and any writing-down or other capital allowance that may be granted in lieu of a first-year allowance placed the lessor in the same position as would have appertained had the lessor obtained (or retained, as the case may be) a first-year allowance of 100 per cent."

*Interest Rate
Change*

    (3)  "If for any period during the currency of this lease the National Westminster Bank Base Rate shall exceed . . . per cent. the lessee shall pay during such periods such additional amounts by way of rentals as are equivalent to the sums by which such Base Rate exceeds . . . per cent.

---

[82] In addition, in more complex leasing agreements, variation clauses are included to take account of exchange rate variations and differences between actual progress payments and those forecast in the original leasing calculations.

[83] The sensitivity of lease payments to interest rate changes is most marked in the period until the lessor receives the first-year allowance. When the full allowance was at 100 per cent. the lessor's net investment in the lease would have declined to a minimal level after this point so that interest rate fluctuations would have had a correspondingly minimal effect on his return. However with the phasing out of first-year allowances this will no longer be the case.

[84] This assumes that the lessor is unwilling to pass on the benefits of any reduction in the rate of corporation tax.

per annum multiplied by the percentage of the total rentals still then out-standing."[85]

(k) *Termination of lease*

Upon the expiration or earlier termination of this lease the lessee shall if required by the lessor deliver up the equipment to the lessor at the address of the lessor stated in this lease or at such other address as the lessor may specify or if not so required shall hold the equipment available for collection by the lessor or its agents and the lessor or its agents may without notice retake possession of the equipment and may for that purpose enter upon any land or buildings on or in which the equipment is or is believed by the lessor or its agents to be situated and if the equipment or any part thereof is affixed to such land or buildings the lessor shall be entitled to sever the same therefrom and to remove the equipment or part thereof so severed and the lessee shall be responsible for all damage caused to the land or buildings by such removal.

*On Termination Lessee to Deliver up Equipment: Lessor may Repossess and may Sever Equipment Affixed to Realty*

(l) *Lessee's right to renew for a further term*

If the lessee having observed and performed all the covenants and con-ditions of this lease shall desire to renew this lease and shall give notice of such desire not less than . . . months prior to the expiration of the term hereby granted the lessee shall be entitled to a new lease of the equipment for the term of . . . commencing on the date of expiration of this lease at a rental of . . . a month but otherwise upon the same terms and conditions as those herein contained including [or excluding] the right of renewal as afore-said.[86]

*Lessee's Right to Renew for a Further Term*

Where the lessee chooses not to renew for a further term the lessor has the option of

(a) attempting to re-let the equipment, probably on an operating basis; or (and more probably),
(b) selling it.

In cases where this second option is contemplated at the commencement of the lease it is common for the lease to permit the lessee to take a large percentage[87] of the net proceeds of sale.[88]

---

[85] The interest rate variation clause here is geared to the clearing banks' base rate. Other and equally applicable measures at the Finance Houses Base Rates and LIBOR. See further Hubbard at Table 3.2 for examples of variation in operation.

[86] Some agreements give the lessee an option to take a fresh lease of new equipment of a similar des-cription at a rental representing the current market rental at the date of the new lease or alterna-tively at a rental to be agreed or in default of agreement determined by an arbitrator. There is, however, much to be said for leaving this to be negotiated between the parties towards the expiry of the original lease, since radical changes in the trading activities of the lessor company may have taken place by the end of the original leasing period and indeed replacement equipment may not be available.

[87] Often as high as 98 per cent.

[88] Finance leases often contain further clauses, for example, that the lessor's rights are not to be pre-judiced by the granting of time, etc.; and excluding the lessor from any liability that might other-wise be incurred in respect of any condition or warranty. See further *Encyclopaedia of Forms and Precedents* Vol. 10 at pp. 675–681.

**Operating leases**

**3.21**

*Definition of
Operating
Lease*

The Equipment Leasing Association[89] defines an operating lease as "any other [is other than a finance lease] type of lease—that is to say, where the asset is not wholly amortized during the non-cancellable period, if any, of the lease, and where the lessor does not rely for his profit on the rentals in the non-cancellable period."

The characteristics of an operating lease are generally the converse of those of a finance lease, with both risks and benefits of ownership resting with the lessor.[90] As such the lessor under an operating lease is normally the party responsible for repairs, maintenance and insurance of the equipment and who bears the risks of obsolescence. Furthermore there is nothing comparable to the "obligatory period" of a finance lease: in operating leasing the lessee generally has the right to terminate the arrangement without major penalty.

*Characteristics
of Operating
Leasing*

A fundamental difference between finance and operating leasing is that in the latter the role of the lessor is not merely as financier for the lessee in relation to the acquisition of the asset leased: operating leasing is a business which derives its profits not on a single transaction basis but from the leasing of an asset over successive transactions with each transaction contributing a significant portion of the lessor's total return. A further difference following upon this is that an operating lessor takes significant account of the residual value of an asset at the end of each transaction. Such residual value is an important element in the lessor's profit calculation which calculation inevitably takes some account of expected sale proceeds. There is no place in operating leasing for the division of ultimate sale proceeds between lessor and lessee that is a frequent occurrence in finance leasing.

**3.22**

*Types of Assets
Leased on
Operating
Leases*

As with finance leasing virtually any kind of equipment can be the subject of an operating lease and the various items listed in § 3.10 above is equally relevant in the concept of operating leasing. From the standpoint of lessees operating leasing can present an attractive alternative to other forms of asset acquisition when the relevant asset is required for a relatively short period. This is particularly so in industries where the rate of technological change is rapid, where there is consequently much uncertainty about the future economic life of equipment and where as a result there is a natural reluctance to commit capital resources to the acquisition of such equipment.

*Benefits to
Lessees of
Operating
Leases*

It has been said[91] that the operating lessor's function in assuming the obsolescence risk in these circumstances is comparable to those of an insurer. The lessor collects a premium from each lessee and the sum total of all the premiums collected is sufficient to cover the cost of the losses from the unrecovered value of the absolete machines. Lessees are content to allow the lessor's profit for this risk taking because it reduces their exposure to individual loss.

Operating leasing is generally highly specialised with lessors tending to confine their activities to particular types of assets. For items of equipment such as computors, for example, the lessor may also be the manufacturer (or at least a

---

[89] *Equipment Leasing* (2nd Rev., 1976) at p. 2.
[90] See Hubbard, *op. cit.* at pp. 11 *et seq.*
[91] Clark, *op. cit.* at p. 63.

subsidiary of the manufacturer). The advantages to lessees of this are that because lessors are so placed they are in a better position to estimate the extent of obsolescence and (especially when they are manufacturers also) may to some extent be in a position to control when it occurs. As such, taken together with their capacity as specialists to acquire large numbers of the assets in which they specialise, lessors are able to offer attractive terms by reflecting economies of scale in the rentals charged.[92]

Whereas most finance leases are individually negotiated arrangements tailor-made to meet the requirements of particular lessees most operating leases are substantially "off-the-peg" arrangements entered into on the basis of standard form Conditions of Leasing. Important items such as the length of the lease and, especially in the case of bulk leasing, the unit rental are often matters for individual negotiation but with the lessor assuming most of the responsibilities for the preservation of the asset and the continuance of its productive life many of the detailed matters for specific negotiation in relation to finance leases assume a position of little or no importance. **3.23**

It follows from what has been said that the terms of an operating lease are much less onerous to the lessee in terms of the number and extent of obligations than are the terms of a finance lease. Thus an operating lease would be unlikely to contain provisions comparable to those set out in § 3.20 above at Clauses (e)(3)(9)(10); (f)(1)–(7); (j)(1)–(4). **3.24**

*Terms of Operating Lease*

### Contract hire

Contract hire has been described as "a separate type of leasing."[93] It applies mainly to cars and commercial vehicles[94] and has been developed by finance houses and motor dealers as a means of providing motor vehicles on a fleet basis. **3.25**

*Contract Hire and Operating Leasing*

In the case of contract hire, both the user and the owner intend that the vehicle shall be returned to the owner at the end of the agreed period of hire. The period, usually between 12 and 36 months, is such that the vehicle still possesses a reasonable proportion of its useful life when it is returned. There will frequently be an undertaking from the dealer to repurchase the vehicle from the finance house on expiry of the hiring period, if required to do so, at an agreed price. In some contract hire arrangements, maintenance is provided by the owner and the cost included in rentals, but in others the user either maintains the vehicles himself or enters into a maintenance contract directly with a garage.

Contract hire differs from operating leasing in that, with the latter, although the length of the lease might be quite short it is generally capable of renewal so that the total lease period is unknown at the start of the lease: the lease period is quite certain in the case of contract hire.[95]

---

[92] These include purchase discounts, higher sale proceeds and in maintenance and reconditioning costs, see Clark, *supra*.

[93] Clark, *op. cit.* at p. 63.

[94] And construction equipment.

[95] Clark, *op. cit.* at p. 63/64.

# 4. Credit Factoring[1]

In many industries the granting and utilisation of trade credit facilities[2] has traditionally been an important element of the terms on which business has been conducted. Such facilities represent to the recipient an indirect source of finance in that their use serves to free other financial resources for use elsewhere and thereby ease that recipient's working capital requirements.

The nature and extent of particular facilities will normally[3] depend on the specific terms of the contract between the supplier and the recipient company although it is often the case that such terms are standard and are mentioned in statements appearing on supplier's invoices.

Credit facilities generally take the form of either—

(a) an extended (and specified) period during which payment may be made; or
(b) a discount for prompt payment.[4]

## PURPOSE AND NATURE OF FACTORING

If the use of credit facilities can operate to free a recipient company's resources it follows that the granting of such facilities will of necessity have the opposite effect. By the same token delays in payment, even where the terms of business do not involve the provision of credit, will likewise have the effect of tying up a proportion of the supplying company's working capital. "Accounts receivable may be 'liquid' or 'quick' assets, but until such time as they are paid they are effectively frozen."[5]

The factoring of a company's customer trade indebtedness provides a mechanism whereby a significant part of the capital thus tied up can be released. Factor-

---

[1] See generally Biscoe, *Credit Factoring* (1975).
[2] See Thomas, *op. cit.* at pp. 256–259 for the assessment of the significance of trade credit as a source of finance.
[3] Such facilities may enter into business arrangements by implication as a custom of the particular trade.
[4] The extent of the benefit obtained will obviously differ from case to case. However, it is quite common for the benefit derived from a discount for prompt payment to outweigh by a considerable margin the countervailing benefits of retaining the funds required for payment until the last possible moment. See Thomas, *supra* at note 2.
[5] Biscoe, *op. cit.* at p. 14.

ing arrangements may take a number of forms: all however involve an assignment by the company of its book debts[6] in return for a payment, either in advance or on the maturity of the debt, of a specified percentage thereof.

## Assignment of book debts

**4.03**   Under English law an assignment of a debt may be effected either:

(a)  under the provisions of section 136(1) of the Law of Property Act 1925; or
(b)  under the equitable rules governing the assignment of choses in action.

(a) *Assignment under Section 136(1) of the Law of Property Act 1925*

Section 136(1) provides:

"Any absolute assignment in writing under the hand of the assignor (not purporting to be by way of charge only) of any debt[7] or other legal thing in action, of which express notice has been given to the debtor, trustee or other person from whom the assignor would have been entitled to claim such debt or thing in action, is effected in law (subject to equities having priority over the right of the assignee) to pass and transfer from the date of such notice:

(a)  the legal right to such debt or thing in action,
(b)  all legal and other remedies for the same, and

(c)  the power to give a good discharge for the same without the concurrence of the assignor."

It is apparent from the terms of section 136(1) that for a purported transfer of a debt to amount to an effective statutory assignment thereof it must satisfy the requirements:

(a)  that it be absolute;
(b)  that it be in writing; and
(c)  as to notice.

(a) By "absolute" is meant that the transfer must not be conditional in any way and specifically that it must not purport to be by way of charge only. Never-

---

[6] In *Independent Automatic Sales Ltd.* v. *Knowles and Foster* [1962] 3 All E.R. 27, Buckley J. defined book debts (following *Shipley* v. *Marshall* (1863) 16 C.B. (N.S.) 566) in this way, (at p. 34):

"  . . . if it can be said of a debt arising in the course of a business and due or growing due to the proprietor of that business that such a debt would or could in the ordinary course of such a business be entered in well-kept books relating to that business that debt can properly be called a book debt whether it is in fact entered in the books of the business or not."

See also *Re Haigh's Estate* (1907) 15 Sol. Jo. 343. *per* Porter J. at p. 343. Note also *Paul and Frank Ltd.* v. *Discount Bank (Overseas) Ltd. and Board of Trade* [1967] Ch. 348.

[7] Debts, for the purposes of s.136(1), do not include future debts: *Tailby* v. *Official Receiver* (1883) 13 App. Cas. 523, H.L.; *Holt* v. *Heatherfield Trust Ltd.* [1942] 2 K.B. 1—or parts of debts—*Re Steel Wing Co. Ltd.* [1921] 1 Ch. 349, *Williams* v. *Atlantic Assurance Co.* [1933] 1 K.B. 81; *Walter & Sullivan Ltd.* v. *Murphy and Sons Ltd.* [1955] 2 Q.B. 584.

theless it would appear that assignments made for the purpose of providing security may be regarded as absolute if made by way of mortgage.[8] The distinction seems to be between a transfer which involves the ownership of the debt passing to the assignee (as in the case of a mortgage) and one which merely provides the other party (the factor) with rights of enforcement. An assignment will be regarded as absolute where "it is clear from the instrument as a whole that the intention was to pass all the rights of the assignor in the debt . . . to the assignee."[9]

*(1) "Absolute" Nature of Assignment*

Where an instrument of assignment employs the word "absolutely" it has been held that this demonstrates an intention, in point of form, that the assignment be absolute and that this in turn constitutes evidence that the parties intend it to be absolute in substance.[10]

(b) The requirement that the assignment be in writing will be satisfied by any written instrument; it is not necessary that the instrument be a deed.[11] However, such writing must be "under the hand of the assignor" and in the case of a company it may well be that it is felt appropriate for the instrument of assignment to be sealed with the company's seal.

*(2) Writing*

In cases where the assignment is effected by a director or other agent or representative of the company there is Commonwealth authority to the effect that the instrument must make it clear that the signatory is executing the document in a representative, rather than a personal, capacity. In a Canadian case[12] an assignment executed by a duly authorised officer of the company was held not to be "under the hand of the assignor" company where the document made no reference to the capacity in which the officer was signing.[13]

(c) The giving of notice to the debtor is an essential ingredient in the statutory assignment of a debt. If notice is not given, or is inadequately or improperly given, the assignment will be ineffective for the purposes of section 136(1).[14] The notice should state[15] the fact that the debt has been assigned and should ideally direct that payment should be made to the assignee. A common form of Notice of Assignment is a statement that:

*(3) Notice*

> "The debt due under the attached invoice has been assigned to and is payable only to our factors . . . [name] of . . . [address] whose receipt alone will be recognised as due and proper discharge."

---

[8] *Tancred* v. *Delagoa Bay, etc. Rly, Co.* (1889) 23 Q.B.D. 239; *Hughes* v. *Pump House Hotel Co. Ltd.* [1902] 2 K.B. 190.

[9] *Hughes* v. *Pump House Hotel Co. Ltd. ibid.* at p. 194.

[10] *Comfort* v. *Betts* [1891] 1 Q.B. 737, C.A. at p. 740 *per* Fry L.J.

[11] *Re Westerton, Public Trustee* v. *Gray* [1919] 2 Ch. 104.

[12] *Mahoney* v. *Traders Finance Corporation Ltd.* (1958) 17 DLR (2nd) 432.

[13] It is clear that the court would have held the assignment to be "under the hand of the assignor" if the representative capacity of the officer had been stated. However see *Wilson* v. *Wallani* (1880) 5 Ex. D. 155.

[14] However such a purported assignment may still have effect as an equitable assignment.

[15] In *Denney Gasquet & Metcalfe* v. *Conklin* [1913] 3 K.B. 177, Atkin J. held that the notice must merely bring to the debtor's attention with "reasonable certainty" the fact that the debt had been assigned. However *quaere*, even whether on that test the facts of the case could be said to have done that. See criticism in Biscoe, *Credit Factoring*, at p. 101. See also *Imperial Bank* v. *Georges* (1910) 14 W.L.R. 654.

Notice will be inadequately given if the statement made is reasonably capable of bearing an alternative meaning. It "is not enough that the notice should be capable of being understood to mean that the debt is assigned. It must be plain and unambiguous, and not reasonably capable when read by an intelligent business man, of a contrary construction."[16]

It seems also that a notice inaccurately stating the date of the assignment will be invalid since such a notice is in effect notice of a document which does not exist.[17] However there would appear to be no necessity for the notice to "give the date of the assignment so long as it makes it plain that there has in fact been an assignment so that the debtor knows to whom he has to pay the debt in the future."[18] For an inaccuracy to render a notice invalid it must be as to some material particular, such as the identity of the parties to the assignment,[19] the transaction under which the debt arose and, possibly, it would seem the amount of the debt.[20] It seems that inaccuracies in the contents of superfluous statements will not affect the adequacy of a notice and can be ignored.[21]

It would appear that notice may properly be given by either assignor or assignee (or, presumably, both) since section 136(1) is silent on the matter. The section is likewise less than explicit as the form such assignment must take although it has been held that it must be in writing and furthermore that the requirement that it be in writing is mandatory. In *Hockley and Papworth* v. *Goldstein*[22] the debtor could neither read nor write and as such was not given written notice of the assignment of his debt because it was felt that such a course would be pointless. Instead the assignment was read over to him twice and he was found to have understood the contents. It was nevertheless held that even in these circumstances oral notice was insufficient and that written notice had to be served.

Certainly it seems clear that a copy of the actual instrument of assignment sent to the debtor could constitute sufficient[23] and express notice for the purpose of section 136(1) although, as has been commented elsewhere,[24] in the context of factoring this would be an impractical and, one might add, irrelevant course without a useful function. As a matter of practice the principal method used in factoring to give notice of assignment is by printing, typing, stamping or sticking it on the invoice. Sometimes, as an additional precaution a notice may also be contained on statements of account sent to the customer by the factor. As

---

[16] *James Talcott Ltd.* v. *John Lewis & Co. Ltd.* [1940] 3 All E.R. 592, C.A. at p. 599 *per* du Parcq L.J.

[17] *Stanley* v. *English Fibres Industries Ltd.* (1899) 68 L.J.Q.B. 839; approved in *W.F. Harrison & Co. Ltd.* v. *Burke* [1956] 1 W.L.R. 419, C.A. Note that such a mistake does not apparently affect an equitable assignment: *Whittingstall* v. *King* (1882) 46 L.T. 520.

[18] *Van Lynn Developments Ltd.* v. *Pelias Construction Co. Ltd.* [1969] 1 Q.B. 607, 613, C.A. *per* Lord Denning M.R.

[19] But see *Denney Gasquet & Metcalfe* v. *Conklin, supra* at note 15 where Atkin J. upheld as sufficient a notice which failed to identify the assignees by name (they were referred to, correctly, as trustees) or as assignees.

[20] *W.F. Harrison & Co. Ltd.* v. *Burke, supra.*

[21] *Van Lynn Developments Ltd.* v. *Pelias Construction Co. Ltd., supra per* Lord Denning M.R. at p. 613.

[22] (1921) 90 L.J.K.B. 111.

[23] *Van Lynn Developments Ltd.* v. *Pelias Construction Ltd, supra* at p. 615 *per* Widgery L.J.

[24] Biscoe, *Credit Factoring* at p. 101.

regards debts already invoiced and on the sales ledger and assigned to the factor at the commencement of factoring, notice is normally given in a letter from either the company or the factor to the debtor.

Notice is regarded as having been given when it is received by the debtor.[25] In cases where the debtor is a company it is sufficient for the notice to be sent to the address of a branch or factory of the company. It is unnecessary to address it to a particular individual within the company,[26] the company's internal arrangements relating to the officers responsible for making the payment being considered to be of no concern to the assignor or to the factor.

There are no statutory time limits within which the notice must be given[27] although it has been held[28] that notice served after the commencement of an action will be ineffectual.

### (b) *Equitable assignments*

Purported assignments failing to meet the requirements of section 136(1) may still have effect as equitable assignments.[29] Thus in *Whittingstall* v. *King*[30] it was held that a mistake in the notice as to the date of assignment which rendered it ineffective as a statutory assignment did not prevent it taking effect in equity.

The formal requirements of an equitable assignment are far from strict with no particular form of words being necessary provided the language employed makes it clear that the assignor intends the assignee to have the benefit of the debt. "It may be couched in the language of command. It may be a courteous request. It may assume the form of mere permission. The language is immaterial if the meaning is plain. All that is necessary is that the debtor should be given to understand that the debt has been made over by the creditor to some third person. If the debtor ignores such a notice he does so at his peril."[31] The assignment will normally be in writing although this is not strictly necessary[32] in relation to existing debts.

---

[25] *Holt* v. *Heatherfield Trust Ltd.* [1942] 2 K.B. 1.

[26] *Wm. Brandt's Sons & Co. Ltd.* v. *Dunlop Rubber Co.* [1905] A.C. 454 at pp. 459, 465 H.L. *per* Lord MacNaghton.

[27] *Bateman* v. *Hunt* [1904] 2 K.B. 530, C.A.

[28] *Compagnia Colombiana de Seguros* v. *Pacific Steam Navigation Co.* [1965] 1 Q.B. 101, 129 *per* Roskill J.

[29] *Wm. Brandt's Sons & Co.* v. *Dunlop Rubber Co.* [1905] A.C. 454, H.L. at p. 461 *per* Lord MacNaghton.

[30] (1882) 46 L.T. 520.

[31] *Wm. Brandt's Sons & Co.* v. *Dunlop Rubber Co.*, *supra* at p. 462 *per* Lord MacNaghton. Followed in *German* v. *Yates* (1915) 32 T.L.R. 52 at p. 53 per Lush J.; *Letts* v. *I.R.C.* [1957] 1 W.L.R. 201 at p. 214 *per* Upjohn J.

[32] *Tibbets* v. *George* (1836) 5 Ad. & El. 107; *Brown Shipley & Co.* v. *Kough* (1885) 29 Ch. D. 848 at p. 854 *per* Chitty J.; *G B Peacock Land Co. Ltd.* v. *Hamilton Milk Producers Co. Ltd.* [1963] N.Z.L.R. 576 at p. 585 *per* McCarthy J. However, where writing is required by some particular rule of law then the assignment must be in that form. Thus in *Re Whitting, Ex p. Hall* (1879) 10 Ch. D. 415, C.A. the assignment was for future rents which, being interests in realty required to be at least evidenced in writing by s.4 of the Statute of Frauds. Biscoe, *Credit Factoring* at p. 104 suggests that "an equitable assignment of an existing debt must be in writing signed by the client, or by his agent duly authorised in writing because 'a disposition of an equitable interest or trust subsisting at the time of the disposition, must be in writing signed by the person disposing of the

Nevertheless, there must be an actual assignment: a mere mandate or authority is insufficient.[33] And the assignment must identify the debt concerned[34] and be communicated to the assignee.[35] Technically, notice of the assignment need not be given to the debtor, lack of notice not having the effect of impairing the validity of the assignment in any way. However in practice notice will almost invariably be given in order:

(i) to prevent the debtor paying the amount of the assigned debt to the company and obtaining good discharge therefor;

(ii) to obtain priority, so far as possible, over other competing interests; and

(iii) to prevent the debtor setting up further equities against the assignee factor.

Where the equitable rules are relied on to give effect to the purported assignment it is necessary in any action for the assignor to be joined as a party whereas as between assignee and debtor, section 136(1) permits an assignee to proceed without this being necessary.[36]

**4.04**    In Scots law a debt may be assigned by an instrument of assignation followed or accompanied by intimation (notice) to the debtor.

*Assignation of Debts—Scotland*

(a) *Instrument of assignation*

Since the passing of the Transmission of Moveable Property (Scotland) Act 1862 instruments of assignation tend in practice to conform to or be modelled on the statutory form contained in Schedule A to that Act.[37] However section 3 of the Act expressly preserved the validity of "the forms at present in use." At that time two forms were in common use. In the first the assignor made separate assignations of the debt and the instrument constituting it whereas in the second the assignor constituted to the assignee both the amount of the debt and the instrument and surrogated or substituted the assignee in place of the assignor. In relation to these forms no particular form or language was required; it was sufficient that the language used clearly indicated a transfer.[38]

same or by his agent there only lawfully authorised or by will L.P.A. 1925, s.53(1)(c)." It is submitted that this view is incorrect in that it confuses the equitable transfer with the legal nature of the right transferred (*i.e.* the existing debt). Where, however the assignment covers future debts (as will be the case in relation to most factoring agreements) such debts being equitable choses in action will require to be in writing to comply with section 53(1)(c).

[33] *Re Williams, Williams* v. *Ball* [1917] 1 Ch. 1 at pp. 6–8 *per* Lord Cozens-Hardy M.R.

[34] *Percival* v. *Dunn* (1885) 29 Ch. D. 128; *Palmer* v. *Carey* [1926] A.C. 703, H.L.; *Brice* v. *Bannister* (1878) 3 Q.B.D. 569.

[35] *Re Hamilton, Fitzgeorge* v. *Fitzgeorge* (1921) 124 L.T. 737, at p. 739 *per* Lord Sterndale M.R.

[36] *Durham Bros.* v. *Robertson* [1898] 1 Q.B. 765 at p. 774 *per* Chitty L.J.

[37] Schedule A provides:

I *A.B.*, in consideration of, &c. [*or otherwise, as the Case may be*], do hereby assign to *C.D.* and his Heirs or Assignees [*or otherwise, as the Case may be.* the Bond [*or other Deed, describing it,*] granted by *E.F.*, dated, &c. by which [*here specify the Nature of the Deed, and specify also any connecting Title, and any Circumstances requiring to be stated in regard to the Nature and Extent of the Right required*]. In witness where, &c.
[*Insert Testing Clause in usual Form.*]

[38] *Carter* v. *McIntosh* (1862) 24 D. 925; *Caledonian Insurance Co.* v. *Beattie* (1898) 5 S.L.T. 349; *Brownlee* v. *Robb* 1907 S.C. 1302; *cf. McCutcheon* v. *McWilliam* (1876) 3 R. 565.

(b) *Intimation*

While the assignation of the debt will be sufficient to entitle the assignee to the benefit thereof notice of the assignation must be given to the debtor to complete the assignee's right and make it effective against all parties.[39]

At common law it was competent to make intimation by producing the instrument of assignation to the debtor, delivering a copy of it to him, and obtaining an attested or holograph acknowledgment.[40] This mode of intimation is still valid. However section 2 of the Act of 1862 provides for two alternative modes, namely:

(i) by a notary public delivering a certified copy of the assignation to the debtor and certifying intimation in the statutory form set out in Schedule C to the Act[41]; or

(ii) by the assignee or his agent transmitting a certified copy of the assignation by post and obtaining the debtor's written acknowledgment of receipt by him of the copy.

In either case the copy need contain only such part of the instrument of assignation as relates to the debt.

Traditionally[42] assignments of book debts to factors in Britain have been by way of purchase, partly because in some forms of factoring this was obviously    **4.05**

---

[39] Stair III. 1.6.; Ersk. III 5.3.; Bell *Commentaries* II.16; *Liquidator of Union Club* v. *Edinburgh Life Assurance Co.* (1906) 8 F. 1143.

[40] Bell, *Lectures in Conveyancing* I.312.

[41] Schedule C provides the following form of intimation:

> I(A.)        of the City of        Notary Public, do ·hereby attest and declare, That upon the        Day of        and between the hours of        and        I duly intimated to B. [*here describe the Party*] the within-written Assignation [*or otherwise, as the Case may be*], *or* by Assignation granted by [*here describe it*], and that by delivering to the said *A.* personally [*or otherwis*] by leaving for the said *A.* within his Dwelling House at E., in the Hands of [*here describe the Party*], a full Copy thereof, [*or if a partial copy here quote the Portion of the Deed which has been delivered,*] to be given to him; all of which was done in presence of *C.* and *D.* [*here name and describe the Two Witnesses*], who subscribe this Attestation along with me. In witness whereof:
> [*Insert Testing Clause in usual Form, to be subscribed by the Party and the Two Witnesses.*]

[42] Biscoe, *Credit Factoring*, at p. 89 writes:

"The legal method of conducting factoring in England has been for the factor to take assignment, by way of purchase, of client's book debts which

(a) are enforceable against the client;

(b) are enforceable against the customers;

(c) have priority, as far as possible, over competing interests third parties;

(d) avoid payment of *ad valorem* stamp duty;

(e) avoid the restrictive provisions of the Moneylenders Acts 1900–1927, which, however, are about to be repealed; [and have since been repealed];

(f) avoid public registration of assignments on the reasoning (which not everyone shares) that such registration would deter some businesses from factoring. The point is related to the priorities question above, because the two statutory provisions requiring public filing of assignments of book debts affect priorities as between the factor and, (i) in the case of general assignments, the trustee in bankruptcy of a client who is a sole trader or partnership (section 43 of the Bankruptcy Act 1914); and, (ii) in the case of charges or assignments by way of mortgage, the general creditors of a corporate client in liquidation (Companies Act 1948, s.95)."

the most appropriate legal form but also because assignments by way of purchase avoided (it was believed) the restrictive provisions of the Moneylenders Acts 1900–1927 which applied to the business of moneylending but not to the business of purchasing debts.[43] Since the repeal of these Acts by the Consumer Credit Act 1974 became effective on January 27, 1980[44] the most pressing need to employ this form in those factoring arrangements providing for recourse to the company in the event of a debtor default has disappeared. Practices are slow to change however and in many cases the old form continues to be employed in these arrangements even though, given the nature of the transaction, an assignment by way of mortgage would be more appropriate.

## Factoring arrangements

**4.06**

*Classification of Factoring Arrangements*

All factoring arrangements seek to provide a financial facility for the companies entering into them.[45] In many cases this facility is provided as part of a larger package which includes the factor's taking over the company's sales ledger administration, credit control function (including collection of debts) and, where the arrangement is "without recourse,"[46] credit protection.

Factoring arrangements admit of two basic classifications, namely:

(a) according to who bears the credit risk; and
(b) according to the time when payments are to be made by the factor.

## Credit risk

**4.07**

*Recourse and Non-Recourse Factoring*

In the factoring context "credit risk" means the risk that the debtor will be financially unable to pay the debt due.[47] Where the factoring arrangement is "without recourse"[48] the factor assumes the credit risk of such debts so that if the debtor fails to make payment the cost is borne by the factor rather than the company. It should be noted however that even in "non-recourse" factoring arrangements if the customer fails to pay for any reason other than financial inability the factor has recourse to the company.

Where the arrangement provides for the factor to have recourse the position is that, although the debt is assigned to the factor, the credit risk remains with the company, to whom the factor has recourse if the debtor fails to pay for any reason.

---

[43] "There are many ways of raising cash besides borrowing. One is by selling book debts. . . . " *per* Lord Devlin in *Chow Yoong Hong* v. *Choong Fah Rubber Manufactory* [1962] A.C. 209, 216, P.C.

[44] Consumer Credit Act 1974 (Commencement No 5) Order 1979 (S.I. 1979 No. 1685).

[45] Those providing only such facilities (almost invariably on a recourse basis) are known as "Invoice Discounting" facilities.

[46] See below at §4.07.

[47] Biscoe, *Credit Factoring*, at p. 6.

[48] Also known as "old-time" factoring.

**Payments by the factor**

Both recourse and non-recourse arrangements may provide for payment to be made by the factor "at maturity" or "in advance."   **4.08**

(a) *Maturity factoring*

Maturing factoring is designed for companies with substantial equity capital who have the strength to satisfy their financing requirements on an unsecured basis from banks or other financial institutions but require the additional non-financial services that are provided as part of many factoring packages.[49]

Most maturity factoring arrangements are conducted on a non-recourse basis. Such arrangements provide for the purchase price of the debts assigned to be paid by reference to the debt's "maturity date" or on collection.[50] By "maturity date" is meant the estimated actual collection date of the debt which in most industries will be later than the due date. Often for administrative reasons the maturity dates of all debts purchased in a period (usually a month) are arranged with the resultant date being referred to as the "average maturity date."

In recourse maturity factoring arrangements[51] the purchase price is paid on collection.

(b) *Advance factoring*

Under advance factoring arrangements, whether on a recourse or non-recourse basis, the factor pays for debts in advance of their average maturity date or collection, as required by the company. Frequently the agreement provides for the payments to be made on assignment. The amount of such advance payments will depend upon the terms of the agreement but the practice is for such agreements either to specify an upper percentage limit (often 80 per cent. of the value of the debts) or else formally to reserve to the factor an absolute discretion as to amount while informally working out an arrangement with the company for the advance of an appropriate amount to satisfy its needs from time to time. The balance of the purchase price is known as the "client's equity" or "factor's reserve" and provides the factor with a margin to be used as security against any claims or defences which debtors may raise against the company in respect of approved debts and for any risk of non-payment in respect of unapproved debts.

Some agreements fail to make provision for the balance of the purchase price of a particular debt to be paid but instead stipulate for the purchase consideration to be credited to the company's current account and for the factor to make advance payments against the credit balance in the account subject to the specified upper percentage limit as absolute discretion, as the case may be. The object of such provisions is to accommodate an accounting practice allowing advance

---

[49] Biscoe, *op. cit.* at p. 8.
[50] Or, sometimes, on the earlier insolvency of the debtor.
[51] Recourse maturity factoring arrangements are rarely encountered in practice.

payments to be viewed globally against total debts purchased and outstanding less outstanding debts.[52]

### Bank participation

**4.09**     Factoring arrangements sometimes involve the participation of the company's bankers.[53] In such cases the object of the exercise is to create a situation whereby the company's bankers become prepared to extend loan financing facilities to the company beyond what would otherwise be appropriate on the basis of the company's balance sheet and profits. The willingness of a bank to increase its lending to the company is based on:

(i) the circumstance that the factor in policing the company's debts through its sales ledger administration and credit control; and
(ii) the factor's credit strength.[54]

It goes without saying that bank participation is only encountered in non-recourse factoring arrangements.[55]

The mechanics of factoring arrangements involving bank participation require the granting of a security, invariably by way of floating charge, over the amounts due to the company from the factor under the factoring agreement: it is against this amount that the bank lends. Coupled with this is an undertaking by the factor (with the company's agreement) to pay all sums into the company's bank account and to inform the bank periodically[56] of the current state of affairs regarding the said amounts due.

---

[52] Biscoe argues (*op. cit.* at p. 8) that such a practice is objectionable conceptually in that "it seems to detract from the purchase concept and hints of a revolving loan against the security of an assignment of debts." Since the repeal of the Moneylenders Acts however it is no longer necessary for assignments to be by way of purchase rather than mortgage.

[53] Biscoe writes (*op. cit.* at p. 9):
"The attractions of bank participation factoring (a) for the bank are that it enables the bank to increase its lending business and to forge a closer relationship with small and medium businesses which may well grow into important banking customers; (b) for the factor are that it enables him to eliminate or reduce the risk of loss inherent in advance factoring and to increase his overall return on funds employed, while having little effect on net income since factoring profits are derived largely from the factoring charge which is not directly related to financing; (c) for the client are that the security of the arrangement may enable the bank to lend to it at a higher level and possibly at a cheaper interest rate than it would otherwise command and/or that the factor's discount equivalent under advance factoring, and the arrangement enables it to continue its banking relationship on a closer basis which may stand it in good stead in the future."

[54] Essentially the varying credit status of a number of debtors are replaced by that of the factor who will be an institution of undoubted credit standing.

[55] Factoring with bank participation is operated on a maturity basis where the bank is to provide all the financing. Where the arrangement provides for the financing to be shared by the factor, factoring is on an advance basis to the extent of the factor's financing obligation. For example the arrangement may provide for the factor to make advance purchase payments of 50 per cent. of the value of purchased debts with the bank lending against the security of the company's 50 per cent. equity (*i.e.* the balance). In either event the amount of the bank's loan is normally expressed as a specified amount rather than as a percentage of the equity in the debts. See Biscoe, *op. cit.* at p. 9.

[56] Often daily.

**International factoring**

The problems of financing, credit control and such like that in domestic trad- **4.10**
ing make factoring an attractive option for companies[57] tend to be magnified in

[57] Biscoe, *op. cit.* at pp. 11–18 examines the advantages of factoring. These are stated as being

(i) *Credit security*
This of course is only applicable in non-recourse factoring.

(ii) *Improved efficiency*
This takes on a number of aspects including more management time for producing, sales and planning. It is suggested however that probably the greatest benefit is in terms of accelerated cash flow.

(iii) *Higher credit standing*
This is stated as assuring "a more reliable flow of merchandise from suppliers," facilitating bank and other financing and lowering interest rates on borrowed funds.

(iv) *Avoidance of increased Debt (or, by the same token a dilution of equity)*
Biscoe argues (*op. cit.* at p. 16):
Unsecured loans equivalent in amount to 80 per cent. of debts outstanding, the typical factoring advance payment, are usually unavailable to a client from other sources on the basis of the balance sheet and profit criteria on which such loans are normally made. Even if loans of comparable levels and at comparable rates are available, they have three inherent deficiencies compared to factoring finance:

they weaken the client's balance sheet whereas factoring finance, being consideration for the sale of an asset, and not a loan, has the opposite effect . . . despite the fact that the debtors asset on the balance sheet is reduced. However, in the case of recourse factoring a contingent liability should be noted in the balance-sheet footnotes;
repayment schedules must be planned for and met whereas factoring finance is self-liquidating;
long-term debt agreements, in particular, usually contain inconvenient and restrictive covenants, such as maintenance of liquidity ratios at certain levels, and commitment fees on available funds regardless of usage. Clauses such as these are not found in factoring agreements currently in use.

(v) *Increased return on capital*
Biscoe argues (*op. cit.* at pp. 17–18):
If a client offers credit terms of net 30 days and his customers pay on average 30 days slow, his trade debts are turning over six times per year. In other words, every pound of working capital tied up in debts is available for re-use through conversion to cash only six times per year. With factoring finance on the basis of 80 per cent. of the value of the debts 80 per cent. of the debts therefore take no days to turn over and are equivalent to sales for cash. Taking into account the 20 per cent. which is not paid over immediately, the debts on average take only 12 days to turn over, *i.e.* they turn over more than 30 times per year. This results in improved profitability through a better return on capital either because of a greater volume of business on the same amount of capital, or the same amount of business on a small amount of capital.

Flexibility
Factoring provides flexibility in two ways. In the first place, availability is directly geared to sales, normally up to about 80 per cent. thereof, without any ceiling as to amounts, so that as sales increase so does availability without the inconvenience and delay of negotiating new limits, as with most other types of financing. Indeed, by this formula, the amount of funds available can be well in excess of net worth whereas bank lending is invariably limited to a conservative percentage of net worth. Secondly, the extent to which the availability is utilised is entirely up to the client. Unlike bank facilities there is no commitment fee on unused available funds.
This flexibility is particularly useful to meet occasional but healthy problems such as financing extra machinery, storage facilities, or stock to meet a big order, for the client need not draw down any funds, ordinarily he knows that the funds are always available to meet these special situations.

international operations. For example, credit is typically for longer periods than in domestic selling and it has been estimated that perhaps twice or three times as much working capital is frozen in international book debts as in domestic book debts. Factoring companies have developed a mechanism for overcoming these problems by enlisting the assistance of factors overseas or by utilising the services of overseas branches of locally resident factors.

This mechanism involved the following steps:

(1) The exporting company's factor ("the export factor") arranges with a factor or branch overseas ("the import factor") for the latter to assume responsibility for credit control and protection. In cases where the export factor and import factors are separate corporate entities such arrangements will necessitate two separate but linked agreements, the first between the exporting company and the export factor and the second between the export factor and the import factor. Under these agreements the export factor assumes specified responsibilities to the exporting company while the import factor assumes similar responsibilities to the export factor. There is thus no direct obligation owed by the import factor to the exporting company.

(2) The export factor approves whatever orders the import factor is prepared to approve.

(3) The exporting company assigns the relevant debts to the export factor without notice of assignment.

(4) The export factor reassigns those debts to the import factor with notice of assignment endorsed on the invoices. This has the effect of enabling the import factor to collect the debts. It also provides the debtor with a local payment facility which, in countries with operative exchange controls, obviates the necessity of obtaining control bank permission to remit payments abroad.

## THE FACTORING AGREEMENT

### Pre-agreement procedures

**4.11**     Factoring facilities represent a means of providing companies with short-term finance coupled with, in the case of non-recourse arrangements, a credit guarantee. As with other forms of finance before the facility will be made available those responsible for its provision will require to be satisfied as to the levels of risk and prospective profitability attached to their investment. Accordingly, just as a lending institution would undertake an investigation of the company and its business so also a factor will require to be satisfied as to the suitability of the company. The law as to negligent and fraudulent misrepresentations applies to statements made by or on behalf of the company in relation to the factor's investigation just as it would apply to statements made in connection with the provision of other forms of institutional finance.[58]

More specifically a factor will require information on the following matters.

---

[58] See above at §§1.22 *et seq.*

(a) *The company*. Information will be required as to its proprietors and management, its history, the industry in which it operates and its methods of operation, its turnover, its financial position and future prospects.

(b) *Business costs*. Especially insofar as they relate to the prospective provision of a factoring facility, information will be required on business costs. Thus the company will be required to furnish information as to the number of its customers, the number of invoices it issues, any unusual debt collection problems and what provision is made for bad debts.

(c) *Customers*. Information required will include an assessment as to their quality, location and exposures.

(d) *Debts*. Specific information is required as to credit terms, turnover rate, dilutions (*e.g.* by discount).

### Form of the agreement

The form of factoring agreements has been influenced to some extent by a desire on the part of the factor[59] to avoid the stamp duty that would otherwise be payable on the assignment. Essentially an instrument of assignment of book debts by way of purchase is regarded for stamp duty purposes as a conveyance on sale[60] and any contract of agreement for the sale of any equitable interest in debts is chargeable with the same *ad valorem* duty as a conveyance on sale.[61]

**4.12**

*Stamp Duty*

Instruments which are or are treated as being conveyances on sale are subject to *ad valorem* duty at the rate of 1 per cent. of the consideration paid[62] subject to an exemption in cases where the amount or value of the consideration is less than £30,000 and is certified as so being and not being part of a larger transaction or series of transactions in respect of which amount or value of the consideration exceeds £30,000.[63]

However for duty to be chargeable at all there must be some instrument on which it can be charged: if there is no instrument there is no charge to duty. The form of agreement most commonly used seeks to achieve an equitable assignment without the necessity of executing an instrument of assignment. It operates in this way:

(a) The terms on which the factoring facility is being provided are set out in a "master agreement" normally contained in a letter from the factor to the company concerned. The company is required to signify acceptance of those terms by affixing its seal to a copy of the letter and returning it to the factor.

*Master Agreements—Agreements to Agree*

---

[59] This desire is based on cost. The factoring charge is usually between $\frac{1}{2}$ per cent. and $2\frac{1}{2}$ per cent. of turnover. Payment of 1 per cent. *ad valorem* duty would make factoring unprofitable for the factor if the duty had to be met out of the factoring charge. If passed on to the company it would make factoring too expensive by comparison with other forms of financing.

[60] Stamp Act 1891, s.54.

[61] *Ibid.* s.59.

[62] *Ibid.* First Schedule.

[63] Finance Act 1984, s.109. There is also provision for duty at a reduced rate to be charged in respect of transactions in respect of which the amount or value of the consideration exceeds £30,000 but is not more than £50,000 and the instrument so certifies.

(b) The terms effectively constitute an agreement to agree to factor debts owed to the company. Essentially the master agreement binds the company to offer specific existing debts for sale to the factor as they arise, such sale to be on the terms set out in the agreement.

(c) In pursuance of this written offer to assign such debts is made by the company as and when they arise. This written offer is then accepted by the factor in some form that does not include writing.

(d) Under the ordinary law of contract the acceptance of an offer supported by consideration constitutes a binding contract or agreement to assign. In *Tailby* v. *Official Receiver*[64] an agreement made in writing was held to effect an equitable assignment. Such an assignment would of course render the transaction dutiable. However in *Carlill* v. *Carbolic Smoke Ball Co.*[65] it was held that a written offer to assign which is accepted otherwise than in writing does not bring a stampable document into existence.

(e) The terms of the master agreement will specify the form in which the acceptance is to be made. The simplest form is inaction by the factor, acceptance being deemed to have been made after the expiration of, say, 48 hours after the receipt of the offer unless non-acceptance or a counter-offer is communicated to the company. The problem with this mode of acceptance is that it hinges on the time of receipt by the factor being readily ascertainable. To overcome difficulties that might arise in this connection some agreements provide for acceptance to be by conduct, normally the payment of the purchase price.

**4.13**

*Statutory Assignments*

The master agreement will normally contain, as a back-up provision, a convenant for further assurance requiring the company to execute a statutory assignment if requested by the factor. Clearly in the event of such a provision being implemented the resulting instrument of assignment would prima facie be stampable unless the amount or value of the debts assigned were within the exemption limits. In such a case however it is doubtful whether the necessary certification that the assignment did not form part of a larger transaction or series of transactions exceeding the exemption limits could properly be made.

**4.14**

By way of contrast some factoring agreements are in the form of contracts for the purchase of present and future debts. The problems of liability to stamp duty on assignments are sought to be overcome either by reference to method discussed in § 4.13 above, or, alternatively, by "notification" to the factor as and when the debts arise, the idea underlying this practice being that "notification" does not operate as an assignment. However such a belief would seem to be questionable and furthermore, even if it were to have foundation, it is suggested that the absence of an assignment would prejudice the rights of the factor in relation to the debtor. It may be wondered how, in the absence of an assignment, collection or enforcement could properly be made or indeed whether any notice served on the debtor would have any validity or effect.

---

[64] (1888) 13 App. Cas. 523, H.L.
[65] [1892] 2 Q.B. 484, affd. [1893] 1 Q.B. 256, C.A.

**Contents of the agreement**

Factoring agreements normally contain provisions covering the following **4.15**
matters:

(i) The agreement to sell and purchase or to offer to sell the company's book
debts, etc.;
(ii) Recourse/non-recourse;
(iii) Convenants and warranties by the company;
(iv) Notice of assignment;
(v) Flow of documents;
(vi) Termination.

Other provisions will vary according to the nature of the agreement.

**Agreement to sell/agreement to offer to sell**

Where the agreement takes the form of a contract for the sale and purchase of **4.16**
present and future debts the operative part will usually be on the following lines:

> The Company agrees to sell and the Factor agrees to purchase free from all
> liens and other encumbrances and upon and subject to the terms and con-
> ditions contained herein all of the book debts, invoice debts, accounts,
> notes, bills, acceptances and/or other forms of obligation (hereinafter col-
> lectively referred to as "receivables") owned by or owing to the Company
> which are in existence at the date of the commencement of this Agreement
> or which come into existence during the term of this Agreement in respect
> of transactions entered into by the Company for the sale of goods to cus-
> tomers in the United Kingdom, and/or the provision of services for cus-
> tomers in the United Kingdom, in the ordinary course of the Company's
> business, not being customers who are a subsidiary, co-subsidiary, parent or
> associated company of the Company or under the same director or share-
> holder control as the Company.

Where the agreement takes the form of an agreement to offer for sale such
debts as may from time to time become due separate provisions relating to the
offer by the company and its acceptance by the factor will appear.

1. *Offers*

(a) The Company agree to offer to sell to the Factor upon the terms and conditions of this agreement all debts from time to time owing to them by their customers and to complete and deliver to the Factor at least once during each week
(or during such other period as the parties may from time to time together agree)
an offer in such form as the Factor may from time to time require.
(b) Every offer will:

> (i) offer to sell to the Factor every debt not previously offered to
> them;

    (ii)  be accompanied by the original and one copy of each invoice relating to each debt the subject of the offer, together with such evidence as we may require of the delivery of the goods, the carrying out of the work or the performance of the services in respect of which each debt has been incurred;

  (iii)  be on the terms and conditions of this agreement.

2. *Acceptances*

(a) Acceptance of any debt offered to the Factor will be constituted either by their despatching a payment on account of the Purchase Price to the Company or to its authorised representative or by the Factor not despatching to the Company a notice of non purchase in relation to the debt within four working days from the first working day after the Factor's receipt of the Company's offer, which ever occurs first.

(b) Upon the Factor's acceptance of any offer all the Company's interest in the purchased debts and all remedies for enforcing the same including without limitation of the foregoing any right of lien, stoppage in transitu or other rights arising in the Company's favour as unpaid seller in relation to any goods in respect of which the purchased debts have been contracted shall vest in the Factor.

**Recourse/non recourse**

**4.17**    Clearly the terms of the agreement will require to spell out whether the factor is to assume the credit risk and if so in relation to which debts. Generally the mechanism for defining which debts a non-recourse factor will assume the risk for is on the following lines:

3. *Approved and unapproved debts*

*Non-Recourse Provisions*

(a)  THE FACTOR WILL HAVE NO RIGHT OF RECOURSE TO THE COMPANY in respect of an approved debt or part of a debt if failure of the customer to pay is due to its financial inability, but the Factor will have a right of recourse to the Company in respect of an unapproved debt or part of a debt if for any reason it is unpaid by its due date of payment or if there is a breach of any other warranty or covenant in paragraph 9(b) relating to that debt.

(b)  A debt purchased by the Factor is an approved debt if:

    (i)  at the time of the Factor's acceptance a credit line for the customer owing the debt has been established by the Factor and notified to the Company in writing, and the debt or part of it comes within such credit line, to the extent that it comes within it; or

  (ii)  The Factor give the Company written notice that we approve the debt or part of it to the extent of the amount approved.

Provided that an approved debt will become an unapproved debt if:

    (i)  The Company is in breach of any warranty or covenant in paragraph 9a relating to the debt;

    (ii)  The customer disputes payment of the debt or any part of it for any reason and the Company do not promptly issue a credit for the amount in dispute;

    (iii)  The Factor withdraws its approval of the debt, which the Factor may do at any time before delivery of the goods or performance of the services to which it relates.

  (c)  If the Factor has not notified the Company of a credit line for a customer at the time that the Company receives an order from that customer, the Company will promptly request the Factor in writing to establish a credit line, or, if it is sufficiently urgent, the Company may make its request by telephone.

Where the factoring arrangement is on a recourse basis[66] the right of recourse is normally exercised by requiring the company to repurchase debts in respect of which the right is exercised. The provisions governing the exercise of this right *Recourse* are normally drafted by reference to the covenants and warranties given by the company and are set out in § 4.21 below.


## Purchase price

In the case of non-recourse arrangement payment of the purchase price is nor- **4.18** mally made by the factor by reference to the Average Maturity Date of the relevant debts,[67] as follows:

4. *Purchase price of debts*

  (a)  The Factor shall pay the Company the Purchase Price of every purchased debt on the Average Maturity Date, except that if the Company require it the Factor may at its discretion pay the Company any portion of the Pur- *Non-Recourse* chase Price, normally to a maximum of 80 per cent. thereof, before the Average Maturity Date.

  (b)  "Average Maturity Date" means a date which the Company will notify to the Factor from time to time calculated by averaging the dates upon which payment is to be received in respect of all debts purchased by the Factor in a particular calendar month based on prior ledger experience.

Recourse arrangements are normally on an Advance basis with the payment of the purchase price being provided for on the following basis:

5. The Factor shall pay the Company the *purchase price* of every purchased *debt* by paying the Company the relevant *purchase instalment* and *collection instalment*

---

[66] Note that Invoice Discounting (*i.e.* Factoring where only financial facilities are provided) is always on a recourse basis.
[67] See above at §4.08.

*Recourse*

(a) The *purchase instalment* will be paid to the Company on the next *remittance day* after your offer provided that it is the subject of an *offer* received not later than 10.00 am on the previous working day, otherwise on the following *remittance day*; in a case where notice of non-purchase is despatched to the Company and the Factor decides subsequently to purchase the *debt*, on the next *remittance day* after the Company's decision to purchase.

(b) *Collection instalments* will be paid to the Company on the next *remittance day* after their receipt by the Factor, provided they are received not later than 10.00 am on the previous working day, otherwise on the following *remittance day*.

**4.19   Notice of Assignment**[68]

6. The Company agrees to endorse on the original and every copy of each invoice relating to a purchased debt a notice

"The debt arising under this invoice has been assigned to and is payable to [*name of Factor*] of [*address*], whose receipt is the only valid discharge of the debt. If this invoice is not found to be correct in all respects [*name of Factor*] must be notified immediately."

**Collection of debts**

**4.20**   The agreement will seek to define the rights of the factor and the obligations of the company in relation to the collection of debts during the period of the agreement.

7. (a) The Factor and the Company's assigns will have the sole and exclusive right of collecting and enforcing payment of every *debt* offered to the Factor by the Company and the Company will not, except at the Factor's request, be concerned in or attempt the collection of any such *debt*.

(b) The Company agrees, if so requested by the Factor, to co-operate to procure such collection and enforcement, and agrees that for such purpose the Factor and/or its assigns may institute and conduct legal proceedings in the Company's name and that the Factor shall have full control of such proceedings.

(c) The Company will not at any time deliver any original or copy invoice, credit note or receipt in relation to any *debt* offered to the Factor direct to any debtor but the Company will deliver all such invoices, credit notes and receipts to the Factor.

(d) The Company will immediately deliver to the Factor any payment,

---

[68] In Invoice Discounting arrangements Notice of Assignment is not given to customers although the factor normally reserves the right to give such notice at its discretion, the object being to protect his security.

whether in cash or by cheque or other negotiable instrument, which the Company receives from a *customer* in or towards payment of any *debt* offered to the Factor and the Company will not deal with, mark, endorse or otherwise interfere with any such negotiable instrument. Until so delivered the Company will hold in trust for the Factor any such payment received in respect of a purchased *debt*.

(e) If a *customer* makes either to the Factor or to the Company a general payment on account of his or its indebtedness, whether or not arising under this letter, to either or both the Factor and the Company and makes no appropriation of such payment it will be appropriated first towards such indebtedness in respect of purchased *debts*, secondly towards the discharge of financial liability (if any) on the Company's part arising from obligations incurred by the Company under this agreement, and the balance (if any) will be appropriated in such manner as the Company may determine. Any such general payment will immediately be delivered to the Factor, and if it exceeds the amount so appropriated by the Factor the Factor will immediately pay the Company the amount of such excess.

(f) The Company will not, without obtaining the Factor's prior written consent, waive or modify any of the terms of a contract with a *customer* giving rise to a purchased *debt* and in particular, but without in any way detracting from the generality of the foregoing, the Company will not extend the time for payment or give credits or customer discounts. Upon giving the Factor's written consent to a credit or customer discount in respect of a purchased *debt* on which the *purchase instalment* has been paid to the Factor, the Company will reimburse the Factor with . . . per cent. of the amount of such credit or customer discount.

In Invoice Discounting arrangements the company collects the debts as agent of the factor and remits such collections *in specie*.

In cases where the factoring arrangement does not cover all the debts accruing to the company so that some debts remain unpurchased it is not uncommon for the agreement to provide for such debts to be collected by the factor and the proceeds remitted to the company as specified terms as follows:

8. (a) In consideration of the Factor agreeing to collect payments due from *customers* in respect of unpurchased *debts* the Company will pay the Factor (i) the *factoring charge* in respect of all such *debts*; (ii) such *refactoring charge* (if any) as would be payable under paragraph 10(b) if the . . . had been a purchased . . .

(b) The Factor will remit to the Company on *remittance days* the net proceeds received by the Factor of any unpurchased *debt* after deduction of the *factoring charge* and any *refactoring charge* payable in respect thereof

(c) The *factoring charges* in respect of unpurchased *debts* will become due to the Factor from the Company on despatch of the Factor's notice of non-purchase.

### Covenants and Warranties

**4.21**    Essentially the convenants and warranties given by the company are designed to provide the factor with a guarantee that the debts purchased are valid and enforceable and that they will not involve disputes. In relation to non-recourse arrangements the covenants and warranties differ as between approved and unapproved debts.

9.  (a) The Company warrants and covenants with respect to each debt purchased by the Factor:

*Non-Recourse*

(i) that the contract between the Company and the Company's customer under which the debt arises is valid binding and enforceable according to its terms;

(ii) that the Company has fully performed its obligations under the agreement giving rise to the debt and that the debt has not been disputed by the customer and is a bona fide obligation of the customer and arises in the ordinary course of the Company's business;

(iii) that the customer has not repudiated, rescinded or claimed damages in respect of the contract under which it arises or made a counterclaim or claimed a right of set-off;

(iv) that the Factor shall obtain and at all times continue to possess a good unencumbered title to the debt with priority over any interest or claim of any other party in or to the debt;

(v) that all information, reports and other papers and data furnished to the Factor (including details of every offer submitted by the Company under paragraph 1) are accurate and correct in all material respects and complete;

(vi) that the Company shall not without obtaining the Factor's prior written consent waive or modify any terms of the contract which gives rise to the debt except as provided by paragraph 7(f).

(b) The Company also warrant and covenant with respect to each unapproved debt purchased by the Factor and with respect to the unapproved part of each approved debt purchased by the Factor:

(i) that it will be paid in full by its due date;

(ii) that the customer will at all times be able to pay the debt; and

(iii) that the customer will not commit an act of bankruptcy, commence to be wound up whether voluntarily or otherwise, cease to carry on business, draw a cheque which is dishonoured, call a meeting of or make an arrangement or composition with creditors, or permit a judgment to remain unsatisfied for seven days;

(iv) that no receiver of the assets of the customer shall be appointed nor shall any distress or execution be levied on threatened upon such customer's goods or premises.

Where the arrangement is with recourse the agreement will normally provide that any breach of warranty or covenant will bring the right of recourse into *Recourse*   operation. Thus:

If there be any breach of any of the above warranties in relation to any purchased *debt* the Company will reimburse the Factor with the excess of any *purchase instalment* and *collection instalment* paid to the Company in relation to such *debt* plus the *factoring charge* over the amount paid to the Factor by the *customer*.

Furthermore:
10. (a) If:
    (i) any *customer* shall dispute the validity of or the amount payable in respect of a purchased *debt*; or
    (ii) any *customer* shall institute proceedings to rescind or claim damages for the breach of any contract under which a purchased *debt* arises; or
    (iii) any *customer* shall not pay the full amount payable in respect of a purchased *debt* by the *due date*; or
    (iv) any *customer* makes a counter-claim or set-off in answer to a claim for a purchased *debt*; or
    (v) without obtaining the Factor's prior written consent the Company waive or modify any terms of the contract with the *customer* which gives rise to a purchased *debt*; or
    (vi) the Company commits a breach of any term of the contract with a *customer* under which a purchased *debt* arises; or
    (vii) the Company commits a breach of any term of this agreement or of any contract arising from acceptance of an *offer*; or
    (viii) any *customer* who has not fully paid all his *debts* sold to the Factor, enters into liquidation whether compulsory or not, commits any act of bankruptcy, ceases to carry on business, draws a cheque which is dishonoured, calls a metting of creditors, makes an arrangement or composition with creditors or permits a judgment to remain unsatisfied for seven days; or
    (ix) a receiver of any such *customer's* assets shall be appointed; or
    (x) any distress or execution is levied or threatened upon any goods or premises of any such *customer*;

the Factor may in its discretion at any time after such event without limitation of other rights available to the Factor hereunder give the Company written notice requiring the Company to repurchase the Factor's interest in any *debt* owed to the Factor by such *customer* which the Factor have purchased from the Company and upon receipt of such notice the Company will be bound to purchase that interest from the Factor and in consideration therefor shall forthwith pay to the Factor the excess of the *purchase instalment* (and *collection instalments* of any) paid to the Company in relation to such *debt* plus the *factoring charge* over the total amount received by the Factor in or towards settlement of the *debt* together with all other charges due to the Factor under this agreement in respect thereof and upon such payment being made, and upon receipt of the Company's written request, the Factor shall at the Company's expense reassign the *debt* to the Company.

(b) Where any *customer* has not paid to the Factor the book value of a purchased *debt* . . . calendar months after the *due date* the Factor may, in lieu of exercising its rights under paragraph 10(a) and without prejudice to those rights, make a *refactoring charge* in respect of that *debt* or any part thereof until paid. So long as the Factor does not exercise such rights the Company agrees to pay the Factor such *refactoring charge* which will become payable on the first day of each month which next follows the month end in respect of which it is calculated.

## 4.22 Accounts

11. (a) The Factor will maintain such accounts as it may consider appropriate and convenient to record these transactions.
    (b) The Factor may at any time set off any amount due to it from the Company against any amount due from the Factor to the Company.
    (c) Within 15 days after the last day of each month the Factor will send the Company a statement of account. Unless within a period of 10 days from receipt of any such statement the Company notifies the Factor in writing that the Company question all or any part of it, that statement will be deemed to be accurate.
    (d) If any account delivered to the Company under this paragraph shows a balance due from the Company to the Factor the Company will immediately pay that amount to the Company.

### Records, information and disclosure

4.23 In order to protect their position, factors will normally require to be kept fully informed as to the company's financial position and as to any information coming into the hands of the company that might relate to the debts factored or the customers of the company whose debts are or may be covered by the factoring facility.

12. (a) The Company will keep books of acount, will permit the Factor or its authorised representative at all reasonable times to inspect such books and any other documents in the Company's possession, custody or control relating to any debt and will deliver to the Factor free of charge all or any of such documents, or copies thereof and copies of all relevant entries in such books when requested to do so by the Factor.
    (b) Not later than three months after the end of each of the Company's financial years the Company will cause a proper audit to be completed of its books of account and those of related companies in relation to that financial year and a copy of the audited accounts, the auditors' and directors' report to shareholders, as required by law, to be forthwith delivered to the Factor.
    (c) The Company agrees to supply the Factor with monthly, quarterly or interim financial statements relating to its business and the business of

any parent subsidiary co-subsidiary or other related business in such form and at such times as the Factor may reasonably require.

(d) The Company will at all times, whether before or after the sale of a debt, disclose to the Factor all matters of fact and opinion known to or held by the Company or its servants or agents concerning the credit worthiness of customers and the validity of the debt and will assist us in every way to safeguard the Factor's interest.

(e) The Company will notify the Factor in writing immediately and, where possible, in advance:

　　(i) of any change in the terms upon which the Company usually contracts or have contracted for the supply of goods, the carrying out of work or the performance of services; and

　　(ii) of the happening of any event referred to in paragraph 9 or tending to affect any warranty or covenant in that paragraph.

(f) The Company will immediately upon learning thereof report to the Factor reclaimed, repossessed or returned merchandise, customers' claims and disputes and any other matter affecting debts.

(g) The Company will give the Factor prior written notice of any financial obligation, conditional or otherwise, which the Company enters into with anyone other than trade creditor.

(h) There is no existing charge or other encumbrance on the Company's assets other than whatever the Company has notified to the Factor in writing, and the Company will not charge or otherwise encumber its assets in the future without giving the Factor at least one week's prior written notice.

## Assignments　　　　　　　　　　　　　　　　　　　　　　　　　**4.24**

13. The Company will whenever requested by the Factor in writing so to do forthwith at the Company's own cost execute, stamp and deliver to the Factor a deed in a form approved by the Factor assigning to the Factor any purchased debt, together with the benefit of all guarantees or other securities for or in respect of the same and will, if requested by the Factor, forthwith give notice in writing of any such assignment to any customer whose debt is thereby assigned.

## Power of attorney　　　　　　　　　　　　　　　　　　　　　　**4.25**

14. In consideration of 5p the Company hereby irrevocably appoints the Factor as its attorney both during and after the termination of this agreement in the Company's name and on the Company's behalf to execute and do all documents and things required in order to give effect to the provisions of this agreement including (but without limiting the generality of the foregoing) the endorsement on the Company's behalf of any negotiable instrument and the execution of a legal assignment or legal assignments of all or any debts which may from time to time be sold by the Company to the Factor in pursuance of this agreement. The Factor is hereby empowered to appoint and remove at pleasure any substitute or agent for itself in respect of all or any of the matters aforesaid.

## 4.26 Termination

15. (a) This agreement will continue in force unless and until determined by either the Factor or the Company giving to the other not less than three months' written notice to expire at, on or after the expiration of fifteen months from the date hereof.

    (b) If the Company commits a breach of any term of this agreement the Factor may terminate this agreement forthwith upon giving the Company written notice.

    (c) Termination of this agreement will not affect any rights or obligations of either the Factor or the Company in relation to any debt purchased prior to such termination and the provisions of this agreement will continue to bind both the Factor and the Company so far and so long as may be necessary to give effect to such rights and obligations.

    (d) Any notice of termination given by either the Factor or the Company to the other must either be delivered by hand to the party concerned or its authorised agent or sent by registered post or recorded delivery to such party at its principal place of business or its registered office.

    (e) If this agreement is terminated by either party hereto under paragraph (b) above the Factor may retain any amount received by it in respect of any debt as security for the satisfaction of any financial liability on the Company's part (whether accrued or not) arising under this agreement or under any contract for the purchase of debts by the Factor.

## 4.27 Other matters

16. (a) The Factor has the sole and exclusive right to factor the Company's debts and while this agreement continues the Company will not without the Factor's prior written consent sell, encumber, assign or transfer any debt to any other person.

    (b) No forbearance or indulgence granted by the Factor to the Company or to any customer will in any way discharge the Company from the Company's liabilities to the Factor under this agreement or establish a precedent.

    (c) The Company agrees to indemnify and keep tthe Factor indemnified against any claim of whatsoever nature by a customer against the Company.

    (d) All costs paid or payable by the Factor in respect of any claims or proceedings against any customer in respect of any such claim or proceedings the Company will render the Factor every assistance.

## 4.28 Charges

17. (a) If in any period of twelve months expiring on the anniversary of the date of this agreement, the total of all factoring charges paid in such period is less than the Minimum Factoring Charge the Company will pay the Factor a sum equal to the deficiency.

    (b) If upon termination of this agreement before the expiry of any such twelve month period for any reason other than the Factor's default, the total of all factoring charges paid in such period is less than the Minimum Factoring Charge the Company will pay the Factor a sum equal to the deficiency.

## Definitions

18. (a) "Collection instalment" means . . . per cent. of each payment received by the Factor from a *customer* in or towards settlement of a purchased *debt*.

   (b) "Customer" means any person to whom the Company supplies goods or for whom the Company carried out work or performs services.

   (c) "Debt" means an amount (whether or not presently payable) which is due to the Company at the time of the Company's *offer* for goods supplied, work done or services performed, and in calculating the book value of a *debt* any reduction agreed between the Company and its *customer* and any discount which the Company's *customer* is entitled to deduct upon prompt payment are excluded.

   (d) "Due date" means the last day of the month following the month in which a *debt* is incurred (or such other day the Factor and the Company may together agree).

   (e) "Factoring charge" means . . . per cent. of the book value of a *debt*.

   (f) "Minimum factoring charge" means £ . . .

   (g) "Factor's discount" means the sum calculated from day to day at whichever is for the time being the greater of . . . per cent. per anum above XYZ Bank Base Rate and . . . per cent. per annum upon the excess for the time being of:

the total of the *purchase instalment* and every *collection instalment* paid to the Company by the Factor in respect of a purchased *debt* plus the *factoring charge*:

over the total amount received by the Factor in or towards settlement of the *debt*.

(See also note below.)

   (h) "Offer" means an offer of *debts* made by the Company to the Factor in accordance with paragraph 1.

   (i) "Purchase instalment" means . . . per cent. of the book value of a purchased *debt* less the *factoring charge*.

   (j) "Purchase price" in relation to a *debt* means the book value of the *debt* less the total of the *factoring charge* and the *factor's discount* in respect of the

   (k) "Refactoring charge" means a sum calculated from month to month at the rate of . . . per cent. per month on that part of a *debt* which is unpaid . . . months after the *due date*.

   (l) "Remittance day" means the day or days in each week as agreed between us from time to time; or, in any week in which that day is not a business day, the next folowing business day.

# 5. Financing from Internal Resources

As a source of capital a company's internal resources have traditionally been **5.01** regarded as being of the highest importance. According to the Wilson Committee external finance was regarded by companies as "essentially a means of making good any shortage of internal funds whether arising, on the one hand, from periodical and foreseen peak demands or, on the other, from occasional and unanticipated shortfalls in internal cash flow."[1]

Internal funds derive from savings made by a company in the form of retentions of revenue received from its trading and other operations. Such savings comprise two main elements, namely:

   (a) provision for depreciation; and
   (b) undistributed profits.

While it has long been the rule that companies,[2] unlike public corporations,[3] **5.02** are under no legal oblgation to make provision out of revenue to cover depreciation of their fixed or wasting assets[4] it is nevertheless accepted[5] that it is commercially prudent to do so. For more than a century the tax system has sought to give varying degrees of encouragement for this practice by providing relief from or allowances[6] against taxes on income for specified categories of capital expenditure.[7]

---

[1] *Committee to Review the Functioning of Financial Institutions,* (Main Report) 1980 Cmnd. 7937 at para. 506.

[2] *Re Kingston Cotton Mill Co.* (No. 2) [1896] 1 Ch. 331 (affd.) [1896] 2 Ch. 279, C.A.); *Bolton* v. *Natal Land and Colonisation Co.* [1892] 2 Ch. 124 (fixed assets); *Lee* v. *Neuchatel Asphalt Co.* (1889) 41 Ch.D. 1; *Wilmer* v. *McNamara & Co.* [1895] 2 Ch. 245.

[3] The statutory obligations contained in the creating Acts stipulated for a minimum financial performance for public corporations on the basis that the income of individual corporations should "be not less than sufficient to meet all items properly chargeable to revenue including interest, depreciation. . . . " (*The Financial and Economic Obligations of the Nationalised Industries,* 1961 Cmbd. 1337 at para. 5).

[4] They must, however, make such provision in respect of circulating capital: see *Verner* v. *General and Commercial Investment Trust* [1894] 2 Ch. 239 at p. 266 *per* Lindley L.J.

[5] The Jenkins Committee recommended (1955 Cmnd. 1749, paras. 349, 350(i) and 397(a)) that such a legal obligation be created.

[6] Originally (*i.e.* under the Income Tax Act 1842) no provision whatever was made for depreciation, probably because at the time income tax was regarded as a temporary expedient that could be dispensed with in due course. As income tax came to be accepted as having the characteristic of permanence those involved in its administration began to take account of the practices of making provision for depreciation. "There is evidence . . . that certain bodies of local Commissioners were making general allowances for wear and tear of machinery. From the first, too, a liberal construction had been placed upon the rule allowing repairs or alterations of implements and this enabled taxpayers to claim amounts expended on renewals or replacements." (*Royal Commission on the Taxation of Profits and Income,* 1955 Cmnd. 9474, para. 309). These practices varied from area

**5.03**    A company's undistributed profits are what remains after allocations have been made to meet debenture and other fixed interest payments, what is to be written off as depreciation, what is due in taxes and what is to be distributed by way of dividend. In considering the internal resources of a company as a source of funding therefore what is available to the company will depend on:

(a)  the company's gross profit;
(b)  the charges to be set against that profit;
(c)  the amount that may be distributed as dividend;
(d)  the factors affecting what is distributed and what is retained.

## THE COMPANY'S GROSS PROFIT

**5.04**    While companies are required to produce accounts giving a "true and fair view" of their profits and losses for each financial year and to comply with detailed rules governing the form and content of those accounts the Companies Acts do not actually define profit. Traditionally the computation of profit has been regarded as an accounting exercise rather than a legal procedure and although there are two areas[8] where the composition of a company's profit is a matter of legal, as distinct from merely commercial, concern the legal principles involved

---

to area and from industry to industry, but in manufacturing districts the Revenue came to accept "the scale allowed by the manufacturers themselves sitting as Commissioners" (Cmnd. 9474, para. 313).

Formal sanction was given to the practice of allowing depreciation by the Customs and Inland Revenue Act 1878, s.12 which provided for a statutory allowance as "representing the diminished value by reason of wear and tear during the year" of plant and machinery used for the purposes of the taxpayer's trade. The principle of giving an allowance for wear and tear was extended to buildings by the Income Tax Act 1918 which introduced a special allowance for mills, factories and other similar premises on the ground that vibrations from the machinery might weaken the fabric of the buildings.

Wear and tear allowances, however, did not cover obsolescence, that is the loss in value resulting from the need to instal new or improved machinery and plant to replace that which, although not worn out, had become out of date. In 1897 the Revenue, by administrative concession, began to permit an allowance for obsolescence, "the deduction being so much of the cost of replacement as was equivalent to the written-down value of the old plant and machinery less any sum realised by its sale" (Cmnd. 9474, para. 311). This practice received statutory recognition in the Income Tax Act 1918.

[7] For a consideration of the modern statutory provisions governing the tax treatment of depreciation see below at §§ 5.20 and 5.21.

[8] These are (i) The corporation tax legislation, which is concerned with company profits as a tax base; and (ii) the distribution rules which are concerned wit company profits as a fund from which dividends can be paid. Note the comment of *Gore-Browne on Companies* (42nd ed., 1972) at p. 618: "Company law, revenue law and the principles of accountancy are interrelated groups of principles, each paramount in its own sphere. It is for the accountant to determine what is profit, for the company lawyer to state what can be distributed out of that profit and for the revenue lawyer to state how that distribution should be taxed. Fundamentally, though revenue law has introduced many exceptions the basic equilibrium between the three groups of principles remains." It might perhaps be observed that the impact of taxation is not confined to being a charge on distributions (see below at § 5.49).

rely upon accountancy practice[9] as the source from which the rules of measurement derive.[10]

" 'Profits' implies a comparison between the state of a business at two specific dates usually separated by an interval of a year. The fundamental meaning is the amount of gain made by the business during the year. This can only be ascertained by a comparison of the assets of the business at the two dates . . . We start therefore with this fundamental definition of profits, namely, if the total assets of the business at the two dates be compared, the increase which they show at the later date as compared with the earlier date . . . represents in strictness the profits of the business during the period in question."[11]

**5.05**

*Definition of Profits*

More specifically, a company's gross profit[12] contains two elements, namely:
(i) *Its current earnings.* These comprise the company's trading surplus, a sum arrived at by deducting from the receipts of the company's business the expenditure laid out to earn those receipts.
(ii) *Its capital profits.* These comprise surpluses obtained on the sale of the company's fixed assets for more than their cost price.

*Components of Gross Profit*

Additionally, a company may have income and/or capital gains from investments which will need to be brought into account.

## CURRENT EARNINGS

### (1) Receipts

The receipts to be brought into account for the purpose of calculating a company's trading surplus comprise those sums received by the company in respect of goods or material supplied or services rendered in the course of its business during the relevant accounting period.

**5.06**

The principal category of such receipts will of course comprise the proceeds of

---

[9] "The concern of this court in this connection is to ascertain the true profit of the taxpayer. That and nothing else, apart from express statutory adjustments, is the subject of taxation in respect of a trade. In so ascertaining the true profit of a trade the court applies the correct principles of the prevailing system of commercial accountancy. I use the word 'correct' deliberately. In order to ascertain what are the correct principles it has recourse to the evidence of accountants." *Per* Pennycuick V-C. in *Odeon Associated Theatres Ltd.* v. *Jones* (1971) 48 T.C. 257, 273, affd. CA [1973] Ch. 288. See further Burgess [1972] B.T.R. 308.

[10] So also the rules governing public corporations where the legislation defining their financial obligations requires individual corporations to generate revenues that should be "not less than sufficient to meet all items properly chargeable to revenue, including interest, depreciation, the redemption of capital and the provision of reserves" (1961 White Paper Cmnd. 1337 para. 4). Note that this is more stringent than the ordinary accountancy conception of profit.

[11] *Per* Fletcher Moulton L.J. in *Re Spanish Prospecting Co. Ltd.* [1911] 1 Ch. 92 at 98, 99, C.A.

[12] Note the comments of Ferguson J. in *Brandte* v. *W.G. Tatham Pty. Ltd.* [1965] N.S.W.R. 126, 127: "In my view net profit is the only true profit. The term 'gross profit' is a manufactured term which does not mean profit at all, but merely money received, part of which may or may not be a profit. Indeed the term may be applied to receipts in transactions which show a loss. In ordinary parlance profit means financial gain, that is to say money received over and above the money expended."

*Sales Proceeds*

*Subsidies*

*Compensation Payments*

*Incidental Receipts*

the sales of the trading stock[13] or the charges made for its services. Additionally, however, sums received in lieu of such receipts or in lieu of profits that might otherwise have been earned should also be included. Under this head would come payments in the nature of a subsidy from public funds to assist in the carrying on of the company's business.[14] Equally payments made by a parent company to a subsidiary as a supplement to its trading revenue and in order to preserve its trading stability should be included.[15] It seems also that sums received in respect of trading stock whether by way of compensation on compulsory acquisition[16] or damages for breach of contract[17] or for tort[18] should be treated in like manner.

Sums arising incidentally in the course of the company's business may also require to be included as receipts. An example of such sums would be payments received by a company (often in the nature of a royalty) in return for permitting the use of patents or "know-how"[19] owned by it.[20]

## (2) Expenditure

**5.07**    In general, sums expended for the purposes of the company's business, otherwise than in the acquisition of fixed assets, may properly rank as a deduction in computing the company's trading surplus. Broadly speaking payments may be deducted if they represent the following.

### (a) *Staffing costs*

This category includes not only wages and directors' fees but also the cost of providing staff benefits and incentives.[21] Accordingly employers' pension fund

---

[13] What constitutes trading stock in any given case will obviously depend on the nature of the company's business, but as a general rule it can be said to conist of raw materials, finished products and work in progress.

[14] *Pontypridd and Rhondda Joint Water Board* v. *Ostime* [1946] A.C. 477, 489 *per* Viscount Simon. Note that F.A. 1980, s.42 specifically makes grants under the Industry Act 1972 (now Industrial Development Act 1982) revenue receipts for tax purposes. However, F.A. 1984, s.54 exempts regional development grants from tax and s.55 likewise exempts grants paid to assist industry in Northern Ireland.

[15] *British Commonwealth Newsfilm Agency Ltd.* v. *Mahany* (1963) 40 T.C. 550, H.L. See also *Moss Empires Ltd.* v. *I.R.C.* [1937] A.C. 785, H.L. and *I.R.C.* v. *Falkirk Ice Rink Co.* (1975) 51 T.C. 42.

[16] *I.R.C.* v. *Newcastle Breweries Ltd.* (1927) 12 T.C. 927.

[17] *Short Bros.* v. *I.R.C.* (1927) 12 T.C. 955, C.A.

[18] *London and Thames Haven Oil Co.* v. *Attwooll* (1967) 43 T.C. 491, C.A.

[19] See *Rolls-Royce Ltd.* v. *Jeffrey* (1962) 40 T.C. 443. For tax purposes I.C.T.A. 1970, s.386 now provides that all payments in return for know-how are trading receipts.

[20] Incidental payments received otherwise than in the course of the company's business apparently do not comprise business receipts, at least for tax purposes. See especially *Simpson* v. *John Reynolds & Co. Ltd.* [1974] S.T.C. 277 where a firm of insurance brokers had acted over a number of years for a company that came to be taken over by a large multi-national concern which then required the company's insurance business to be placed elsewhere. Subsequently the brokers received a payment from the company expressed to be in appreciation of services rendered. It was held by the Court of Appeal that this sum was in the nature of a gift and as such should not enter into the computation of the firm's profit for tax purposes.
Nevertheless this sum would clearly be an element in the "profit" calculation envisaged by the definition in *Re Spanish Prospecting Co.* (*supra* at § 5.05) and as such presumably be available for distribution or retention.

[21] *P.-E. Consulting Group Ltd.* v. *Heather* (1973) 49 T.C. 320, C.A.

contributions[22] and payments under approved stock option schemes[23] should be *Staffing Costs*
entered here. Equally statutory payments due under the National Insurance
Scheme also fall to be included here.

Additionally, amounts expended in reducing staffing costs, as for example in
the making of redundancy payments[24] or "golden handshakes"[25] would also be
included under this head.

### (b) *Overheads*

Expenditure within this category comprehends the costs of using the fixed
assets of the business. Where the company owns the premises in which it operates the costs of maintaining and repairing[26] (although not renewing or improv- *Overheads*
ing)[27] those premises may be deducted. Where the company's premises are
leased the rent[28] payable ranks as a deduction. In either case local authority
rates[29] are treated as deductible.

Costs of leasing or hiring[30] machinery and plant would also come within this
head, as would the costs of operating them. Accordingly, heating, lighting and
power charges should be entered here.

Premiums charged for insurance cover for company premises and other assets
and indeed for third party risks (including employees) would generally be
deductible here.[31]

### (c) *Production and administration costs*

Clearly the costs of acquiring the raw materials or component parts to be used
in any manufacturing process undertaken by the company will be deductible.
Equally any item of trading stock will be likewise treated. The law however *Production/*
draws a distinction between purchases of trading stock and the acquisition of *Operating*
assets bearing trading stock, the latter being treated as capital rather than *Costs*
revenue costs.[32]

---

[22] *Smith* v. *Incorporated Council of Law Reporting* (1929) 14 T.C. 349.
[23] F.A. 1978, s.60.
[24] I.C.T.A. 1970, ss.406 and 410.
[25] *Mitchell* v. *B.W. Noble Ltd.* [1927] 1 K.B. 729, C.A.
[26] *O'Grady* v. *Bullcroft Main Collieries* (1932) 17 T.C. 93, 107 *per* Rowlatt J. See also I.C.T.A. 1970,
s.130(*d*). Note *Rhodesia Railways* v. *Bechuanaland Protectorate I.T.A.* [1933] A.C. 388, P.C. for
distinction between maintenance/repairs and renewals.
[27] *Lurcott* v. *Wakeley* [1911] 1 K.B. 905; *Highland Railway* v. *Balderston* (1889) 2 T.C. 48; *L.C.C.* v.
*Edwards* (1909) 5 T.C. 387. Note the position of initial repairs undertaken immediately after purchase of an asset. Compare *Law Shipping Co.* v. *I.R.C.* 1924 S.C. 70 and *I.R.C.* v. *Granite City
SS. Co.* 1927 S.C. 705 with *Odeon Associated Theatres* v. *Jones* (1972) 48 T.C. 257, C.A.
[28] See I.C.T.A. 1970, s.130(*c*).
[29] *Wildbore* v. *Luker* (1951) 33 T.C. 46.
[30] See above at Chapter 3. Note for tax purposes only a commercial rent/hire-charge is deductible:
I.C.T.A. 1970, s.493.
[31] See Whiteman & Wheatcroft, *Income Tax* (2nd ed., 1976) at pp. 394–395.
[32] See *Alianza Co.* v. *Bell* [1906] A.C. 18, H.L. (mine purchased for extraction purposes) and *I.R.C.*
v. *Pilcher* (1949) 31 T.C. 314 (orchard purchased "including crop").

*Administration*    Administration costs not entered elsewhere would be brought in here.

### (d) *Marketing costs*

The costs of marketing a company's products or services are clearly deductible from the receipts produced by sales of such products or services. Thus the com-
*Marketing*    ponents of a marketing campaign, advertising,[33] business entertainment, gifts (and bribes) and other PR expenditure would be entered here. This is one area however where the tax legislation operates more restrictively than ordinary commercial accounting principles with the consequence that the cost of business entertainment[34] and gifts[35] may only be deducted for tax purposes if incurred in connection with export sales, the entertainment or gifts being supplied for or to "an overseas customer."[36]

### (e) *Interest*

Payments of interest on loans incurred for the purposes of the company's business rank as a deductible expense. In some cases a distinction is made between
*Interest*    interest on long-term debt used to finance the acquisition of fixed assets and other interest, with the former being treated separately from ordinary business expenditure. Clearly overdraft or other interest used to finance the acquisition of trading stock is appropriately dealt with under this head.

Nevertheless, while allowing the general deductibility of interest[37] as a business expense the tax system contains special provisions[38] applying to interest paid to non-residents. Such interest will only be allowed as a deduction for tax purposes to the extent that it does not exceed a reasonable commercial rate.

### (f) *Losses*

Losses occurring in the carrying on of the company's trade may generally be deducted in computing the company's trading profit. So where trading stock has
*Losses*    been destroyed by fire[39] or otherwise lost to the company the cost will be deduct-

---

[33] See *Morgan* v. *Tate and Lyle Ltd.* [1954] 35 T.C. 367, H.L. where even the expenses of an advertising campaign designed to prevent the nationalisation of the sugar refining industry were allowed.

[34] I.C.T.A. 1970, s.411. Furthermore, to be allowable the entertainment must be reasonable in all the circumstances.

[35] By s.411(7) small gifts (*e.g.* calendars or diaries) for advertising purposes are deductible.

[36] Defined as a non-resident trading overseas who might use the goods or services of the entertainer, or an agent for such non-resident trader or overseas government or public authority.

[37] It is sometimes the practice to include an item representing notional interest on capital. While this is consistent with accountancy principles it is not an allowable deduction for tax purposes. See I.C.T.A. 1970, s.130(*h*).

[38] I.C.T.A. 1970, s.130(*m*). Note also I.C.T.A. 1970, s.131 which provides that no deduction for *annual* interest may be claimed unless the person making the payments has deducted income tax at the basic rate and has accounted for the tax to the Revenue. Where however the interest is both payable and paid outside the United Kingdom under an obligation incurred exclusively for the company's trade it may be paid gross and still be deductible provided that the loan was taken out for a trade carried on outside the United Kingdom or, alternatively, that the interest is payable in foreign currency.

[39] Any insurance proceeds recovered will of course be entered as receipts. For tax purposes such losses are deductible only to the extent that they are not recoverable elsewhere: I.C.T.A. 1970, s.130(*k*).

ible. Equally where company property has been misappropriated by employees[40] the value of the property lost may be deducted. Bad debts are also recognised deductions,[41] as are losses resulting from fines[42] or damages[43] levied against the company in connection with its business activities, although these latter two items will not be allowed as deductions for tax purposes.[44] In the same way abortive expenditure, which normally is treated as an expense under ordinary accounting principles is not usually treated as an allowable deduction for tax purposes.[45]

"It has long been well settled that the effect of these provisions[46] as to deductions is that the balance of the profits and gains of a trade must be ascertained in accordance with the ordinary principles of commercial trading, by deducting from the gross receipts all expenditure properly deductible from them on these principles, save in so far as any amount so deducted falls within any of the statutory prohibitions contained in the relevant Rules, in which case it must be added back for the purpose of arriving at the balance of profits and gains assessable to tax."[47]

**5.08**

In computing a company's trading profit for tax purposes the right to deduct expenditure that might otherwise have been allowable has been removed in the following cases:

*Computation of Trading Profit for Tax Purposes: Statutory Disallowances*

(a) Expenditure not wholly and exclusively laid out for the purposes of the company's trade[48];

(b) Expenditure incurred for private purposes[49];

(c) Rent of dwelling-houses, etc. not used for the purposes of the company's trade[50];

(d) Surplus expenditure on the supply, repair or alteration of implements for the company's trade[51];

(e) Losses not connected with the company's trade[52];

(f) Capital withdrawn from or employed in the company's trade, not being interest[53];

---

[40] *A.T.A. Advertising Ltd.* v. *Bamford* (1972) 48 T.C. 359. The position would appear to be different in relation to massive defalcations by directors. But see Whiteman and Wheatcroft *op.cit.* at pp. 382–383.

[41] I.C.T.A. 1970, s.130(*i*).

[42] *I.R.C.* v. *Von Glehn & Co.* [1920] 2 K.B. 553; *I.R.C.* v. *E.C. Warnes & Co.* [1919] 2 K.B. 444.

[43] *Strong & Co.* v. *Woodifield* [1906] A.C. 448, H.L.

[44] See cases cited above in notes 42 and 43. Note also that losses incurred in ventures outside the scope of the company's business will equally be disallowed. See *Laver* v. *Wilkinson* [1944] 26 T.C. 105 in relation to I.C.T.A. 1970, s.130(*e*).

[45] Presumably because it could not be described as being "for the purpose of earning the profits." See *Strong & Co.* v. *Woodifield* [1906] A.C. 448, 453 *per* Lord Davey.

[46] *i.e.* the legislation governing the taxation of company profits.

[47] *Per* Jenkins L.J. in *Morgan* v. *Tate & Lyle Ltd.* (1954) 35 T.C. 367, 393, C.A.

[48] I.C.T.A. 1970, s.130(*a*). For the meaning of "wholly and exclusively" see judgment of Romer L.J. in *Bentley's Stokes & Lawless* v. *Beeson* (1952) 33 T.C. 491, 503, 504, C.A.

[49] *Ibid.* s.130(*b*).

[50] *Ibid.* s.130(*c*).

[51] *Ibid.* s.130(*d*).

[52] *Ibid.* s.130(*e*).

[53] *Ibid.* s.130(*f*).

(g) Capital employed in improvements to premises[54];

(h) Notional interest on capital expenditure[55];

(i) Debts, other than bad debts or estimation or doubtful debts[56];

(j) Average loss beyond actual loss[57];

(k) Sums recoverable under insurance or indemnity[58];

(l) Annuities or annual payments out of profits[59];

(m) Interest paid to non-residents over and above a commercial rate[60];

(n) Royalties or other sums paid for the user of a patent[61];

(o) Rents or other payments treated as patent royalties[62];

(p) Yearly interest paid to a partner[63];

(q) Notional rent of tied premises[64];

(r) Cost of trees on purchase of woodlands by company dealing in land[65];

(s) Contributions repaid under redundancy schemes[66];

(t) Business entertaining expenses[67];

(u) War risk expenditure[68];

(v) Payments for war injuries[69];

(w) Bondwashing transactions[70];

(x) Plant and machinery leased or rent in excess of commercial rent[71];

(xx) Rent payable under a sale and leaseback transaction in excess of a commercial rent[72];

(y) Annuities or annual payments[73];

(z) Deductions on account of diminution of capital or loss sustained in trade.[74]

**5.09**    By way of contrast certain sums are specifically allowed by statute as deductions in computing the profits of a company's trade. These are:

*Computation of Trading Profits for Tax Purposes: Statutory Allowances*

(a) Expenditure on abortive mining exploration[75];

(b) Non-capital expenditure on scientific research[76];

(c) (by implication) Expenditure wholly and exclusively laid out or expended for the purposes of the company's trade[77];

---

[54] *Ibid.* s.130(*g*).
[55] *Ibid.* s.130(*h*).
[56] *Ibid.* s.130(*i*).
[57] *Ibid.* s.130(*j*).
[58] *Ibid.* s.130(*k*).
[59] *Ibid.* s.130(*l*).
[60] *Ibid.* s.130(*m*).
[61] *Ibid.* s.130(*n*).
[62] *Ibid.* s.130(*o*).
[63] *Ibid.* s.131.
[64] *Ibid.* s.140.
[65] *Ibid.* s.142.
[66] *Ibid.* s.402.
[67] *Ibid.* s.411.
[68] *Ibid.* s.420.
[69] *Ibid.* s.421.
[70] *Ibid.* s.469.
[71] *Ibid.* s.493.
[72] *Ibid.* s.491 and F.A. 1972, s.80.
[73] *Ibid.* s.519(1)(*h*).
[74] *Ibid.* s.519(2).
[75] C.A.A. 1968, s.62.
[76] *Ibid.* s.90.
[77] I.C.T.A. 1970, s.130(*a*).

(d) (by implication) Actual expenditure on repairs of premises or on the supply, repair or alteration of implements used in the company's trade[78];

(e) (by implication) Debts proved to be bad and estimated loss on doubtful debts[79];

(f) Certain interest paid to non-residents[80];

(g) Expenses of obtaining patents[81];

(h) Payments for technical education[82];

(i) Allowance for lease premiums, etc.[83];

(j) Rents paid for tied premises[84];

(k) Rents for easements, etc. for radio relay services[85];

(l) Employer's contributions under certain pensions schemes[86];

(m) Payments by marketing boards to reserve funds[87];

(n) Contributions for rationalising industry[88];

(o) Contributions to statutory redundancy schemes[89];

(p) Redundancy payments made by employers[90];

(q) (by implication) Certain war risk premiums[91];

(r) (by implication) Commercial rent under a sale and leaseback transaction on premises[92];

(w) (implications) Commercial rent under a sale and leaseback transaction re plant and machinery[93];

(x) Employer's contributions to approved schemes[94];

(y) Income from trade carried on abroad[95];

 z) Payments under approved share option schemes[96];

(aa) Cost of incidental loan finance in relation to approved share option schemes[97];

(bb) Contributions to approved local enterprise[98] agencies.[99]

---

[78] *Ibid.* s.130(*d*).
[79] *Ibid.* s.130(*i*).
[80] *Ibid.* s.131.
[81] *Ibid.* s.132.
[82] *Ibid.* s.133.
[83] *Ibid.* s.134.
[84] *Ibid.* s.140.
[85] *Ibid.* s.157.
[86] *Ibid.* s.208.
[87] *Ibid.* s.348 (inserted by F.A. 1970, s.28).
[88] *Ibid.* s.406.
[89] *Ibid.* s.410.
[90] *Ibid.* s.412.
[91] *Ibid.* s.420.
[92] *Ibid.* s.491 and F.A. 1972, s.80.
[93] *Ibid.* s.493.
[94] F.A. 1974, s.21(3).
[95] *Ibid.* s.23(3).
[96] F.A. 1978, s.60.
[97] F.A. 1980, s.38.
[98] F.A. 1982, s.48.
[99] Note the comment of Whiteman and Wheatcroft (*op.cit* at p. 366) concerning the statutory allowances and disallowances: "The wording of I.C.T.A. 1970, in relation to computing profits is peculiar. It is expressly laid down that tax is to be charged without any deduction other than that allowed by statute and that "no other deduction shall be made [s.519(1)] than such as are here enumerated." Originally no deductions were enumerated at all, except by implication, and even now only a limited number of special cases have specific authorisation. . . . On the other hand the direction to charge tax "on the full amount of profits or gain" and the qualified extent of some of the specific prohibitions makes it clear that some deductions must be allowed: indeed, the basic conception of a profit of a trade is the surplus by which its receipts exceed the expenditure necessary to earn the receipts. The effect is that a deduction which is neither within the terms of an express statutory prohibition, nor such that an express allowances must be taken as the exclusive definition of its area is one to be made or not to be made according as it is or is not on the facts of the case a proper debit item . . . when computing the balance of profits."

### (3) Stock and work-in-progress

**5.10**

*Cash or Earnings Basis*

A company's trading profit or loss may, theoretically, be computed either on a cash or earnings basis. If a cash basis is adopted the profit or loss will be ascertained simply by deducting payments actually made from sums actually received during the relevant accounting period. However, since most businesses give and receive credit and carry stock from one period to the next, accounting on a cash basis will not normally be appropriate if a realistic picture of the company's trading position is required. The usual practice, therefore, is for companies to compute the profits of their businesses on an earnings basis. This involves the inclusion not only of those transactions actually settled[1] during the accounting period but also requires account to be taken of the business's stock and work in progress.

**5.11**

*Stock: Historic Cost Basis*

Account is taken of stock by crediting the company's trading account with a figure representing its value at the end of the accounting period. Naturally, this figure for "closing stock" will reappear as a debit in the accounts of the next period as "opening stock." Where the company's accounts are prepared on an historic cost basis the general rule is that items of stock carried forward from one accounting period to the next should be entered at their actual costs.[2] This general rule is subject to qualification, however, where it can be shown that the value of the stock has depreciated and so, at the relevant date, is less than its historic cost. In such a case the company may enter the stock at market value.[3] Accounting practice, therefore, provides companies with a useful discretion: they may enter stock which has risen in value at cost while, if they so wish, items

---

[1] In many cases the settlement of liabilities does not occur, or at least is not made in full, during the accounting period in which those transactions were incurred. In such cases the principle is that receipts should be matched with the period in which the services had been completely rendered or the goods supplied. As Viscount Simon L.C. explained in *I.R.C.* v. *Gardner, Mountain & D'Ambrumenil Ltd.* (1947) 29 T.C. 68, 93: " . . . services completely rendered or goods supplied which are not paid for till a subsequent year cannot generally be dealt with by treating the taxpayer's outlay as pure loss in the year in which it was incurred and bringing in the remuneration as pure profit in the subsequent year in which it was paid or due to be paid. In making the assessment . . . the net result of the transaction, setting expenses on the one side, and a figure for remuneration on the other side, ought to appear . . . in the same year's profit and loss account and that year will be the year when the service was rendered or the goods delivered. This may involve an estimate of what future remuneration will amount to . . . [which] could be corrected when the precise figure was known. . . . "
It ought to follow from this just as a payment can be related back to the period in which the service was performed or the goods supplied, so where a payment is received in advance it should be related forward so that it would only enter the accounts in the subsequent year in which the service was actually rendered or the goods supplied. It appears however that, at least for tax purposes, this is not permitted so that the sum involved will be treated as a receipt when actually received or due. See *Sun Insurance Co.* v. *Clark* [1912] A.C. 443, H.L.; *Elson* v. *Price's Tailors Ltd.* (1963) 40 T.C. 671, C.A. See generally Tiley *"Revenue Law"* (3rd ed., 1918), at pp. 249–257.
[2] *Steel Barrel Co. Ltd.* v. *Osborne (No. 1)* (1942) 24 T.C. 293, 307 *per* Lord Greene M.R.; see also *Julius Bendit Ltd.* v. *I.R.C.* (1945) 27 T.C. 44.
[3] "Under Scots Law [and, one might add, English law as well] the profits are the profits realised in the course of the year. What seems an exception is recognised when a trader purchases and still holds goods or stocks which have fallen in value. No loss has been realised. Loss may not occur. Nevertheless, at the close of the year he is permitted to treat these goods or stocks as at their market value." *Per* Lord Sands in *Whimster & Co.* v. *I.R.C.* (1925) 12 T.C. 813, 827. Approved by H.L. in *Duple Motor Bodies Ltd.* v. *Ostime* (1961) 39 T.C. 537.

that have depreciated may be brought in at market value.[4] As this practice is accepted for tax purposes[5] it provides companies with a degree of flexibility.

However, while a company is permitted to anticipate a loss in this way, for tax purposes at least, it is not permissible to anticipate a profit. In *Willingale* v. *International Commercial Bank Ltd.*[6] the bank held certain bills of exchange which it intended to retain until maturity. Its accounts included figures representing a proportion of the profit expected to be made by holding the bill until maturity and notionally attributable to the year in question. The House of Lords held that such proportions were not relevant in assessing the bank's profit for tax purposes since tax was chargeable on actual rather than anticipated profits.

Where stock has been purchased at different times and at different prices over an accounting period so that at the end of the period, with some stock used, a residue remains that cannot be matched with any particular purchase account-ancy practice has produced competing methods of arriving at a figure represent-ing the "cost" of this residue.

**5.12**

*"Cost" of Stock*

### (i) *First-in, first-out (FIFO)*

This method assumes that stock acquired first is used or sold first, and, as a consequence, treats the stock in hand at the accounting date as that most recently acquired, and therefore, in a period of rising prices, the most expensive. This technique has the advantage that the closing stock will be valued at the more recent prices and so at a figure close (or at least closer than would other-wise be the case) to the cost of replacement. It has, however, the disadvantage that as such closing stock appears on the credit side of the account it will serve to inflate the period's profits, thus giving rise to a potentially larger tax bill, but on a profit that has not actually been earned.[7]

### (ii) *Last-in, first-out (LIFO)*

While FIFO is clearly appropriate to perishable stock the opposite technique has been considered to be good accountancy practice for non-perishable stocks such as metals where, in theory, the latest deliveries are stacked on top of earlier deliveries and used first.[8] LIFO deems the most recently acquired, and therefore in an inflationary period the most expensive, stock to have been used first. This has the consequence of depressing the resultant profit figure and of ultimately producing a progressively more unreal figure for the stock, especially if the

---

[4] *I.R.C.* v. *Cock, Russell & Co. Ltd.* (1949) 29 T.C. 387. In measuring "market value" the Revenue in pactice accept any method of computation recognised as good accountancy practice so long as the method adopted does not violate the statutory provisions. Once a particular method has been adopted, that method should be followed in subsequent years, unless there is some good reason for the change. See further *Pearce* v. *Woodall Duckham Ltd.* [1978] S.T.C. 372.

[5] *B.S.C. Footwear Ltd.* v. *Ridgeway* [1972] A.C. 544, H.L.

[6] [1978] S.T.C. 75, H.L.

[7] Thus leading to the criticism that tax on company profits was being levied on "paper profits" rather than on real profits.

[8] See Whiteman and Wheatcroft, *op.cit.,* at pp. 446, 447.

physical condition, and so the saleable value, deteriorates. In *Minister for National Revenue* v. *Anaconda American Brass Ltd.*[9] the Privy Council held that a profit figure calculated on the basis of LIFO was unacceptable for tax purposes.

### (iii) *Average price*

A third method is in reality a compromise between the other two, effectively using the average price paid over the relevant period. This method is appropriate for purchases and sales in bulk.

For tax purposes FIFO is the only acceptable method unless it can be shown in a particular case that some other accounting assumption[10] more nearly approximates to the true[11] facts.

**5.13**

*Work-in-Progress*

Companies engaged in the provision of services will normally have little stock but a considerable amount of work-in-progress, some of which may be difficult to distinguish from debts due. For accounting purposes the work-in-progress of a company providing services is treated as being converted into a money credit when the bill is rendered.[12]

The same basic principle that the relevant entry in the accounts should be at cost applies to work-in-progress as it does to stock. In this case, however, there is the problem of arriving at a figure representing the cost. Clearly this should be obtained by some proper method of costing but different methods may apparently be equally appropriate and yet produce different results. In *Duple Motor Bodies Ltd.* v. *Ostime*[13] a motor body manufacturer sought to value work-in-progress by reference only to the cost of materials used together with that of the labour directly involved in the manufacture.[14] An alternative approach, favoured by the Revenue, was to include in addition a proportion of the overhead expenditure.[15] Accountants called as expert witnesses differed as to which method was the correct one. The House of Lords refused to decide the problem as a matter of law holding, in effect, that no general rule for costing work-in-progress for tax purposes could be laid down and that each case must be dealt with on its merits by the method best fitted to the circumstances of the particular business concerned.[16]

A further problem relating to work-in-progress concerns the right of a company to value such work-in-progress at market value rather than cost if this

---

[9] [1956] A.C. 85, P.C.

[10] In *Patrick* v. *Broadstone Mills Ltd.* (1953) 33 T.C. 44 another method—the base stock method—was also held to be inappropriate for tax purposes.

[11] The point is that although the law is guided by accountancy practice in ascertaining the cost of stock it does so on the basis that the results produced will not obviously conflict with the reality of the case. See further Whiteman and Wheatcroft, *op.cit.,* at p. 446.

[12] See Whiteman and Wheatcroft, *op.cit.,* at pp. 444, 445.

[13] (1961) 39 T.C. 537, H.L.

[14] Known as the "Direct Cost" Method.

[15] Known as the "On Cost" Method.

[16] The House of Lords held that in the circumstances, since the Revenue had failed to show that the company's method was incorrect, it should be used, the more especially as it had been used and accepted as correct by the Revenue over a long period of time.

should be lower. In the *Duple Motor Bodies* case there are dicta suggesting that such a right exists,[17] just as it does in the case of stock, but also dicta doubting[18] whether such a right is appropriate to work-in-progress. The question must therefore be regarded as open, although if such a right is found to exist this would raise the further problem as to the basis on which the figure representing market value should be arrived at.[19]

The effect of using for tax purposes a system of accounting that produced "paper profits" rather than real gains was that companies were becoming liable to pay tax on profits that had no existence in reality. This had the further effect of reducing the liquidity of many companies to a level at which they found it difficult to continue their business activities. As an ameliorative measure until such time as a system of inflation accounting won general acceptance (and the specific approval of the Revenue) a scheme was introduced to give relief in respect of profits obtained in whole or in part from stock appreciation.

**5.14**

*Stock Appreciation Relief*

*The 1976 Scheme*

In the form in which it was introduced the scheme made provision for claiming back relief[20] where stock value decreased in an accounting period or where the company ceased to carry on the business in respect of which the relief was claimed.[21] As such the scheme operated by deferring rather than eliminating tax liability, a feature which attracted considerable criticism. Another criticism was that, taking the form of an ordinary adjustment of taxable income, without taking account of the volume as well as the value of stock, the scheme produced a figure which was just as unreal a measure of profit as that produced by a straight application of the LIFO system. A further criticism has been that the scheme awarded excessive relief to expanding businesses and not enough to those who became more efficient by reducing wasteful stock levels.

The Finance Act 1981 recast the scheme measuring the relief given by reference to a new "All-Stocks Index."[22]

However, as one of the reforms included in the Finance Act 1984[23] as part of the overall design of reshaping the system of corporate taxation, stock relief was withdrawn in respect of accounting periods beginning after March 12, 1984.

The fact that a system of stock relief was felt to be necessary at all is perhaps a reflection on the limitations inherent in having to employ historic cost accounting methods in a period of inflation. Ideally, accepting inflation as an inevitable and continuing fact of business life, it became obvious to many people during the 1970s that what was urgently required was a system of inflation accounting that would express firms' paper profits in "real" terms. After a provisional state-

**5.15**

*Current Cost Accounting*

[17] *Per* Viscount Simonds (1961) 39 T.C. at pp. 567, 568.
[18] *Per* Lord Reid (1961) 39 T.C. at p. 573.
[19] Where work-in-progress consists of, for example, partially completed long-term construction contracts, it is now established accountancy practice to include in the valuation a measure of the profit expected to be made on completion. This practice would seem to fall foul of the rule against anticipated profits for tax purposes.
[20] F.A. 1976, Sched. 5, paras. 2 and 10.
[21] F. (No. 2) A. 1979, s.13.
[22] F.A. 1981, s.35 and Sched. 9.
[23] F.A. 1984, s.48.

ment[24] and comments thereon the Accounting Standards Committee in 1980 issued its Statement of Standard Accounting Practice[25] on "Current Cost Accounting" which was designed to fill this need in respect of companies with a Stock Exchange Listing and other large entities "whose annual financial statements are intended to give a true and fair view of the financial position and profit or loss."[26] And then, in the following year the Companies Act 1981[27] provided for such companies, if they so elected, to prepare their accounts on a current cost basis.

In so far as the current cost system affects stocks the present provisions are contained in the Companies Act 1985[28] which provides for stocks to be entered at their "current cost." In terms of S.S.A.P. 16[29] this means at their "value to the business," a term which is defined as net current replacement cost, or, if a permanent diminution to below net current replacement cost has been recognised, the recoverable amount.[30]

### (4) Current cost basis

**5.16**

*Current Cost Operating Profit*

Where current cost accounting techniques are employed[31] the concept corresponding to a trading profit is the "current cost operating profit." S.S.A.P. 16[32] directs that this is to be "derived by making the following main adjustments to the historical cost trading profit (before interest on net borrowing) to allow for the impact of price changes on the funds needed to maintain the net operating assets[33]:

(a) in relation to fixed assets, a depreciation adjustment[34] being the difference between the proportion of their value to the business consumed in the period and the depreciation calculated on the historic cost basis;
(b) in relation to working capital;
 (i) a cost of sales adjustment . . . ; and
(ii) an adjustment based on monetary working capital.[35]

---

[24] S.S.A.P. 7, May 1974 commented on upon adversely by the Sandilands Committee in its report "Inflation Accounting" Cmnd. 6225 (1975).

[25] S.S.A.P. 16.

[26] S.S.A.P. 16, Explanatory Note 1.

[27] Companies Act 1981, Sched. 1, paras. 29–34.; Now Companies Act 1985 Sched. 4, paras. 29–34.

[28] C.A. 1985 Sched. 4, para. 31(5).

[29] S.S.A.P. 16, para. 42.

[30] Defined as "the greater of the net realisable value of an asset and, where applicable, the amount recoverable from its further use—S.S.A.P. 16, para. 43.

[31] Where such techniques are employed the relevant account must be presented together with accounts compiled on an historical cost basis—S.S.A.P. 16, para. 47.

[32] *Ibid.* Para. 49.

[33] Defined as "the fixed assets (including trade investments) stock and monetary working capital . . . dealt with in an historical costs balance sheet—S.S.A.P. 16, para. 38.

[34] See further below at n. 51.

[35] S.S.A.P. 16, para. 44 provides: "Monetary Working Capital" is the aggregate of:
    (a) trade debits, prepayments and trade bills receivable, plus
    (b) stocks not subject to a cost of sales adjustment [see Explanatory Note 12], less
    (c) trade creditors, accruals and trade bills payable,
insofar as they arise from day-to-day operating activities of the business as distinct from transactions of a capital nature.
Bank balances or overdrafts may fluctuate with the volume of stock or the items in (a), (b) or (c)

The cost of sales adjustment allows for the impact of price changes when determining the charge against revenue for stock consumed during the period of account. It is the difference between the value to the business of stock consumed and the cost of stock charged on an historical cost basis. The resulting total charge thus represents the value to the business of stock consumed in earning the revenue of the period.[36]

*Cost of Sales Adjustment (COSA)*

The monetary working capital adjustment represents the amount of additional (or reduced) finance needed for monetary working capital as a result of changes in the input prices of goods and services used and financed by the business. Monetary working capital relates essentially to credit given and received by the business and can be seen as the quantum of funds additionally needed to support the giving of credit or the amount by which funds needed to support working capital are reduced when credit is received. However, monetary working capital is not confined to the giving and receiving of credit. Fluctuations in the volume of stock, debtors and creditors may lead to contrary fluctuations in cash or overdraft. S.S.A.P. 16 directs[37] that this element of cash or overdraft be included as monetary working capital if to do so would have a material effect on current cost operating profit. It further provides that cash floats required to support the operations of the business are to be included also.[38]

*Monetary Working Capital Adjustment (MWCA)*

It is to be noted that no account is taken of borrowing in the ascertainment of the current cost operating profit, (except insofar as interest figures in the calculation of the historical cost trading profit) the operating adjustments[39] making provision for the impact of price changes on all the net operating assets,[40] however financed.[41] Nevertheless provision is made elsewhere in the current cost profit and loss account by means of a "gearing adjustment."[42]

It should further be noted that profits arrived at according to current cost accounting techniques are not acceptable as a tax base for corporation tax purposes. A company's profits for tax purposes are computed by reference to historical cost or, where appropriate, market value.

*Investment income*

As a fund from which distributions or retentions may be made a company's current earnings may be supplemented by income produced by its investments. The form this investment income takes, that is whether it is received as interest or dividend, may have an effect on the company's distribution policy. The point is that dividends received will normally rank as franked investment income and so be available to frank distributions made by the company.[43]

**5.17**

above. That part of bank balances or overdrafts arising from such fluctuations should be included in monetary working capital together with any cash floats required to support day-to-day operations of the business, if to do so has a material effect on the current cost operating profit."
[36] See S.S.A.P. 16, Explanatory Note 10.
[37] *Ibid.* Para. 44.
[38] See S.S.A.P. 16, Explanatory Note 13.
[39] Depreciation Adjustment, Cost of Stock Adjustment, Monetary Working Capital Adjustment.
[40] Defined by S.S.A.P. 16, para. 38 as "the fixed assets (including trade investments), stock and monetary working capital . . . dealt with in an historical cost balance sheet."
[41] See S.S.A.P. 16, Explanatory Note 17.
[42] S.S.A.P. 16, paras. 50–51 and Explanatory Notes 16–21.
[43] See below at §§ 5.35–5.36.

**Capital profits**

**5.18**    Capital profits may accrue to a company from:

(i) the sale of fixed assets for more than their historic cost; or

(ii) the upward revaluation of fixed assets in the company's books; or

(iii) the sale or upward revaluation of investments held by the company.

Like current earnings and investment income, capital profits may have to be brought into account for corporation tax purposes and may supplement the fund from which distributions or retentions may be made.

# CHARGES AGAINST PROFITS

**5.19**    In arriving at the amount of a company's profit available for distribution or retention charges are normally made to take account of:

(1) Depreciation;

(2) Interest; and

(3) Taxation.

**Depreciation**

**5.20**    A charge for depreciation is made to permit the writing-off of the cost of a fixed asset over the period of its anticipated normal commercial life. In principle

*Method of Making Pro- vision for Depreciation*

a company may adopt whatever method of depreciating its assets it chooses and indeed complaints have on occasions been voiced about a lack of uniformity between companies in relation to their practices in charging depreciation.[44] In practice however, methods of charging depreciation came to achieve a degree of standardisation largely through the operation of the tax system on the basis of what was acceptable to the Revenue to qualify for available tax allowances.

In general terms it can be said that two such methods have been found to be acceptable. These are:

(i) *The straight-line method.* This is normally associated with the writing down of land and buildings. Using this method the company debits its trading account

*(i) Straight- Line Method*

each year with a fraction of the cost of the relevant asset and credits the same amount against the cost of the asset which will appear as a debit made in the company's accounting records when the asset was acquired. At the end of the writing-down period the value of the asset will appear in the company's books as nil. The fraction employed is the reciprocal of the number of years of the asset's expected or normal commercial life.

[44] See *The Economist,* April 30, 1932, p. 955. (P.E.). It seems that while most firms treated depreciation as a definite charge on the profit and loss account, the amount of such charge was often a matter of whim or judgment. If a company experienced poor trading results the depreciation provision was sometimes not made, or if it was made, was entered at a reduced level so that the fall in profits was obscured. At other times the depreciation provision was increased, having the effect of understating the extent of any improvement in profits, the primary object of this latter exercise being the reduction of tax payable on the amount of the company's profit. See further Thomas *op.cit.,* at p.84.

(ii) *The reducing balance method.* This is geneally accepted as appropriate for plant and machinery. Using this method the cost of the asset is written down by a standard percentage in each year of its expected or normal commercial life. Since the written-down value of the asset will be falling each year the amounts of depreciation permitted by this method will be greater in the earlier years of the asset's life than in the later years.

*(ii) Reducing Balance Method*

The tax allowances available in respect of depreciation are provided for in the Capital Allowances Act 1968 as amended by subsequent Finance Acts. The specific allowances are:

**5.21**

*Capital Allowances*

(a) *Initial or first-year allowances.* These permit the entire or a substantial proportion of the cost to be written off in the accounting period relative to the date on which the expenditure was incurred.

(b) *Writing-down allowances.* These permit the writing off of the balance of expenditure not absorbed by the initial or first-year allowance over the life of the asset.[45]

(c) *Balancing allowances.* These apply when the asset representing the qualifying expenditure is disposed of or otherwise ceases to qualify for the allowance that has been given. Balancing allowances have as their object the adjustment of the total allowances given in respect of the total qualifying expenditure[46] where the allowances already given have not fully matched the amount expended. Where the total amount of allowances given has exceeded the total qualifying expenditure the excess is recovered by means of a *balancing charge.*

Not all capital expenditure qualifies for an allowance and the allowances that are given vary according to the type of asset acquired. Consequent upon the changes made by the Finance Act 1984 the allowances currently available are as follows.

(1) *Industrial buildings and structures*

    (i) an initial allowance of a specified percentage (which differs according to the date on which it was incurred); and
    (ii) a writing-down allowance on the balance[47] at the rate of 4 per cent. per annum on a straight-line basis.

The Finance Act 1984[48] provided for the phasing out of the initial allowance leaving the writing-down allowance as the only allowance claimable and applicable to the total cost of the building or structure acquired.

---

[45] The writing-down allowance may be claimed for the accounting period relative to the date on which the expenditure was incurred and for each subsequent period until the expenditure has been written off, or the asset has been disposed of or otherwise ceases to qualify for the allowance.

[46] That is the original qualifying expenditure less any amount produced on a subsequent realisation. It should be emphasised that *all* the allowances operate on the basis of historical cost with the consequence that no further allowance can be made for inflation except insofar as the costs of replacement assets themselves qualify for allowances.

[47] Capital Allowances Act, 1968, s.2(1).

[48] F.A. 1984, s.58 and Sched. 12.

The scheme of the 1984 Act is for the initial allowance to be phased out by April 1, 1986. More specifically, capital expenditure incurred before this date which would hitherto have qualified for the full initial allowance will attract a reduced initial allowance as follows:

(i) expenditure incurred after March 13, 1984 but before April 1, 1985—50 per cent.;

(ii) expenditure incurred on or after April 1, 1985 but before April 1, 1986— 25 per cent.

No initial allowance is available in respect of expenditure incurred on or after April 1, 1986.[49]

(2) *Hotel buildings and extensions*

(i) an initial allowance of 20 per cent.[50]; and

(ii) a writing-down allowance on the balance at a rate of 4 per cent. on a straight-line basis.

The initial allowance is to cease on April 1, 1986 whereupon the only allowance available will be a simple 4 per cent. writing-down allowance.

(3) *Industrial and commercial[51] buildings in enterprise zones[52]*

(i) an initial allowance of 100 per cent. which may be disclaimed in whole or in part; and

(ii) a writing-down allowance on any balance at a rate of 25 per cent. on a straight-line basis.[53]

(4) *Machinery and plant[54]*

(i) a first-year allowance of a specified percentage (which differs according to the date on which it was incurred); and

---

[49] However, where qualifying expenditure is incurred during the period March 13, 1984—April 1, 1987 and consists of the payment of sums under a contract entered into on or before March 13, 1984 by the person incurring the expenditure then the full (pre-F.A. 1984) standard allowance of 75 per cent. will continue to be available in respect of it—F.A. 1984, Sched. 12, para. 1(2). Transitional relief is provided also in respect of certain capital expenditure incurred in connection with projects on development areas and Northern Ireland. In such cases the full pre-F.A. 1984 allowance of 75 per cent. will continue to apply to such expenditure—*ibid.* s.58(2)(a) and Sched. 12, para. 4.

[50] F.A. 1984, s.58(4)(a).

[51] Note that this allowance extends to all commercial buildings used for trading or professional purposes and therefore includes office accommodation.

[52] See further at Chapter 8, below.

[53] Balancing adjustments may arise if the building is sold within 25 years. Note that the special rates apply only during the first 10 years of a zone's life.

[54] Note that the writing-down allowance on machinery and plant operates by reference to a "pool" into which all machinery and plant used in a company's business are notionally placed, the allowance claimable being determined by reference to the value of the pool rather than to individual assets.

(ii) a writing-down allowance on the balance at a rate of 25 per cent. on a reducing balance basis.

In respect of expenditure incurred between April 1, 1985 and March 31, 1986 the first-year allowance is set at 50 per cent.; expenditure incurred thereafter does not attract first-year allowance.[55]

Special rules apply to machinery and plant acquired for lease or hire; these are considered separately in Chapter 3, above.

### (5) *Mines, oil wells and mineral deposits of a wasting nature*

The allowances available differ according to the activity involved. The activities in respect of which allowances may be claimed, and the allowances relative thereto are as follows.

(a) *Exploration and related activities outside the United Kingdom.* The allowances may be claimed in respect of expenditure incurred in searching for or discovering or testing deposits or winning access thereto and in acquiring mineral rights or the site of such rights outside the United Kingdom.[56] In respect of such activities the position is that:

(i) There is no initial allowance; but
(ii) A writing-down allowance[57] is available at a rate of 5 per cent. of expenditure incurred (less any other allowances granted) or, if greater, a fraction $\dfrac{A}{A + B}$ of the expenditure where:

$A$ = the output from the source during the basic period; and

$B$ = future estimated output from that source.
(iii) Balancing adjustments arise on the sale of assets and on such occasions when the source ceases to be worked.[58]

(b) *Construction works.* The allowance may be claimed in respect of works likely to be of little or no value where the deposits are worked out.[59] In respect of such activities the position is that:

(i) An initial allowance of 40 per cent. is available. In development areas and Northern Ireland the allowance is 100 per cent. claimable in whole or in part[60];
(ii) A writing-down allowance is available as in (1) above;
(iii) Balancing adjustments arise as in (1) above.

---

[55] F.A. 1984, Sched. 12, para. 2(1).
[56] Capital Allowances Act 1968, ss.51–54 and Sched. 5.
[57] *Ibid.* s.57.
[58] *Ibid.* ss.57, 58.
[59] *Ibid.* s.51(2).
[60] F.A. 1971, s.52.

(c) *Acquisition of mineral assets in the United Kingdom.*[61] In respect of such acquisitions the position is that[62]:

  (i) No initial allowance is given; but

  (ii) A writing-down allowance is available based on a fraction of the royalty value[63] of the output. The fraction varies according to the length of the period from the date of the first working of the source. If the period is:

      (A) less than 10 years the fraction is $\frac{1}{2}$;

      (B) from 10 to 20 years the fraction is $\frac{1}{4}$;

      (C) over 20 years the fraction is $\frac{1}{10}$.

## (6) *Dredging*[64]

The available allowances are:

  (i) an initial allowance of 15 per cent.; and

  (ii) a writing-down allowance at a rate of 4 per cent. on a straight line basis.

A balancing allowance may be available on the cessation of the trade; no balancing charge arises.

## (7) *Agricultural and forestry buildings and works*[65]

The available allowances are:

  (i) an initial allowance of 20 per cent. which is disclaimable; and

  (ii) a writing-down allowance at a rate of 10 per cent. on a straight line basis.

There are no balancing allowances or charges.

It is intended that these allowances be replaced as from April 1, 1986 by a simple 4 per cent. straight-line writing-down allowance.

## (8) *Scientific research*[66]

Expenditure attracts a first-year allowance of 100 per cent. Balancing charges and allowances may arise on the cessation of user of the asset acquired.

## (9) *Patents*

While no initial or first-year allowances are available, under the legislation currently in force[67] a writing-down allowance computed on a straight line basis over 17 years (the normal life of a patent) or such shorter period, if the patent is

---

[61] Note that the territorial sea of the U.K. is deemed to form part of the U.K. for corporation tax purposes: F.A. 1973, s.38.

[62] I.C.T.A. 1970, s.60.

[63] The amount of royalties hypothetically payable by a lessor under a lease ending in that year and providing for the payment of such royalties as might reasonably have been expected.

[64] Capital Allowances Act 1968, s.68.

[65] *Ibid.* s.68.

[66] *Ibid.* ss.90–94.

[67] I.C.T.A. 1970, s.385.

purchased for a lesser period, is available. This allowance is due to be replaced as from April 1, 1986 by a 25 per cent. reducing balance writing-down allowance.[68]

(10) *"Know-how"*

Again there are no initial or first-year allowances available. Under the legislation currently in force a writing-down allowance is available, computed on a straight-line basis over six years.[69] This allowance is due to be replaced as from April 1, 1986 by a 25 per cent. reducing balance writing-down allowance.[70]

(11) *Ships*[71]

Free depreciation is available in respect of ships.

While the purpose of making provision for depreciation is to accumulate funds for asset replacement the extent to which the amounts charged actually do fund the acquisition of replacement assets will, of course, vary as between industries and as between companies within the same industry. The point is that depreciation charges have been traditionally made on the basis of historical cost.[72] Given the continued presence of inflation within the economy, even the simplest operation of replacing one asset with another identical asset will produce a deficit since the replacement cost will necessarily exceed the amount set aside calculated on the basis of historical cost. Moreover, inflation is not the only factor affecting replacement cost. Technological advances tend to generate pressures of their own which often render inadequate ordinary historical cost depreciation provision. These pressures operate in two ways; first, the improvements in performance that are made possible are usually reflected in increased capital cost, either in relation to the replacement asset itself or in relation to ancillary equipment that has to be acquired in order that the system of which the asset is the centrepiece can produce the required improvements and secondly, in the fact that the rate of technological advance has produced situations where existing fixed assets become obsolete at a point much earlier than had been

**5.22**

*Historical Cost and Replacement Cost*

---

[68] Balancing adjustments may arise when the rights terminate or are disposed of: I.C.T.A. 1970, s.379.

[69] *Ibid.* s.385. Note that the six year period is a maximum.

[70] Balancing adjustments may arise on the cessation of the trade within six years.

[71] Capital Allowances Act, s.31. Balancing adjustments may arise as under the allowances for machinery and plant.

[72] Where accounts are prepared on a current cost basis, depreciation enters the calculation of the current cost operating profit by way of one of the operating adjustments to the historical cost trading profit. The depreciation adjustment is intended to allow for the impact of price changes when determining the charge to be placed against revenue for the part of the fixed assets consumed during the period. It is the difference between the value to the business of the part of the fixed assets consumed during the accounting period and the amount of depreciation charged on an historical cost basis. The resulting total depreciation charge thus represents the value to the business of the part of the fixed assets consumed in earning the revenue of the period. (S.S.A.P. 16, para. 49(a) and Explanatory Note 9).

planned for with the consequence that the need for replacement will arise before the full depreciation period has expired, thus creating a shortfall in the amount expected to have been "saved" by the provision being made.

The only answer to this problem is to make supplementary provision for asset replacement out of retained profits over and above that arising from the ordinary depreciation provision. Some companies create Special Asset Replacement Reserves to which the amounts covered by the ordinary and supplementary depreciation provisions are transferred. Others simply transfer the relevant amounts to general reserves.[73]

## Interest

**5.23**

*Treatment of Interest According to Accountancy Practice*

While interest may enter into the computation of a company's trading profit as an expense incurred in earning the receipts accruing in respect of its business activities, interest is also encountered in a company's accounts as a charge to be set against trading profits, once ascertained, or in some cases to be set against capital.

Accountancy practice sometimes differentiates between long-term loans and short or medium-term loans with the former being treated as a charge against profits rather than as an element in their composition. Alternatively, a distinction is sometimes made according to the underlying purpose of the loan and, in particular, whether it was incurred to finance fixed assets as opposed to working capital. Again, although comparatively infrequently in modern accounts, a distinction is sometimes drawn according to form; whether, for example, a loan is made by the issue of debentures or, perhaps, in the form of a bank overdraft.

The rules governing the form an structure of company accounts acknowledge these practices to some extent and make further distinctions of their own. Thus, the Companies Act requires[74] a company's profit and loss account to differentiate between bank loans and overdrafts and loan repayable within five years on the one hand and all other loans on the other.

*Charging Interest to Capital*

In certain circumstances it may be appropriate to charge interest to capital. For example, a company may wish to present a picture of profitability at a certain level to facilitate access to the capital market; interest charged to capital would avoid depressing profit levels. In *Hinds* v. *Buenos Ayres Grand National*

---

[73] Others, of course, make no provision at all, utilising any depreciation savings as part of general funds. See further Thomas: at pp. 282–284.

[74] See now Companies Act 1985, Sched. 4, para. 53(2) which draws distinctions between "the amount of the interest on or any similar charge in respect of (a) bank loans and overdrafts and loans made to the company (other than bank loans and overdrafts) which:

    (i) are repayable otherwise than by instalments and fall due for repayment before the end of the period of five years beginning with the day next following the end of the financial year; or

    (ii) are repayable by instalments the last of which falls due for repayment before the end of that period;

and (b) loans of any kind made to the company."

Para. 53(2) further provides that its provisions apply "to interest or charges on all loans whether made on the security of debentures or not."

*Tramways Co. Ltd.*[75] it was held that interest on debentures issued to raise capital for the construction of buildings, plant, track, etc., might be properly charged to capital, at least during the period of construction. Nevertheless, even if such a course is permitted by accountancy practice the consequences of adopting it should be carefully weighed. There is a rule of law that companies are bound by the book-keeping decisions. In *Chancery Lane Safe Deposit and Offices Co. Ltd. v. I.R.C.*[76] a company which had charged interest to capital was held bound by that decision for tax purposes, with the consequence that it was unable to deduct the interest payments either as trading expenses or as charges on income.[77]

In general, interest payable by a company is deductible for tax purposes. Where and how that deduction may be made will vary according to the category of interest, the class of lender, the nature of the payment and the nature of the paying company's operations.

**5.24**

*Tax Deductibility of Interest*

Interest may be deducted as a trading expense if it satisfies the following conditions:

(i) It is either "short interest" or "bank interest." "Short interest" is not defined in the corporation tax legislation but it would appear to be interest paid on a loan which represents a temporary facility which cannot last for more than 12 months. In determining whether or not the facility is to terminate within this period the contractual repayment date may not be decisive. The crucial point is whether the loan is intended by the parties to have some degree of permanence and to last for more than a year. "Bank interest" is self-explanatory.

An investment company cannot, generally speaking, deduct short interest as a trading expense, if only because it does not carry on a trade. Such a company should therefore avoid obligations involving the payment of short interest, except to a bank since bank interest may qualify as a charge on income even though it is short interest.[78]

(ii) It must have been wholly and exclusively laid out for the purposes of the company's business.

(iii) It must not have been charged to capital. As we have seen such interest will then be treated as capital for tax purposes. This does not however mean that it is entirely useless since capitalised interest is allowed as a deduction in computing the acquisition cost of the asset where liability in respect of chargeable gains is at issue.[79]

(iv) If paid to a non-resident, it must not be at more than a reasonable commercial rate of interest.[80] This may be of special importance where the overseas

**5.25**

*(i) As a trading Expense*

*(a) Short Interest*

*Bank Interest*

*(b) "Wholly and Exclusively"*

*(c) Must not be Charged to Capital*

---

[75] [1906] 2 Ch. 564. Such interest could also of course have been charged against profits or indeed as a trading expense. Note Companies Act 1985, Sched. 4, para. 20(3) which includes in the production cost of an asset "interest on capital borrowed to finance the production of hat asset, to the extent that it accrues in the period of production."

[76] [1966] A.C. 85, H.L. See also *Princes Investments Ltd. v. I.R.C.* [1967] 1 Ch. 953.

[77] Since F.A. 1981 interest charged to capital may rank for deduction as a charge on income, s.38.

[78] In practice it is sometimes possible for an investment company to have short interest allowed as a management expense.

[79] I.C.T.A. 1970, s.269.

[80] *Ibid.* s.130(*m*).

*(d) If Payable to a Non-Resident, must be Restricted to a Reasonable Commercial Rate*

borrowing has been effected in sterling rather than in foreign currency and at a higher rate of interest than would otherwise be charged in order to compensate the lender for any risk of loss arising from exchange rate fluctuations. The problem centres around a provision[81] of the Finance Act 1980 which disallows as a deduction sums "paid in consequence of or for obtaining protection against losses resulting from changes in the rate of exchange between different currencies." The provision deals with the deductibility of the incidental costs of taking loan finance and it is unclear whether this disallowance extends beyond the types of payment mentioned specifically therein to cover items, such as interest, deductible under other provisions. The view has been expressed[82] that interest and other items not specifically mentioned would be outside the scope of the provision but the matter remains to be settled.[83]

(v) It must not amount to a distribution. Given the general tax deductibility of interest payments, the lack of deductibility of company distributions and the fact that qualifying distributions[84] give rise to a liability to account for advance corporation tax (ACT) the incentive to attempt to disguise equity capital as a loan capital is obvious. To combat this the concept of distribution is defined in such a way that an effective disguise is difficult to achieve. Specifically, "interest" payments on various types of borrowing are treated as distributions. These are:

*(e) Must not amount to a Distribution*

(a) bonus redeemable securities[85];

(b) securities convertible into shares or securities issued after April 5, 1972 which carry any right to receive shares or securities in the company, unless the securities are quoted or are issued on comparable terms to such quoted securities[86];

(c) securities on which the interest or other consideration given is dependent upon the results of the company's business or is in excess of a reasonable commercial rate of return[87];

(d) securities held by a non-resident 75 per cent. associated company[88]; and

(e) securities linked with shares in the sense that both shares and securities have to be, or, to make financial sense, ought to be, held at the same time.[89]

---

[81] s.38.

[82] Malcolm Gammie in *Tax Strategy for Companies* (2nd ed., 1981) at p. 124.

[83] Note also the provisions of F.A. 1976, s.38, introduced as an anti-avoidance measure against artificial interest deduction schemes. Under s.38 interest may not be deducted if it is paid under a scheme or arrangement whose sole or main purpose is to obtain the benefit of an interest deduction for tax purposes. It is felt, however, that bona fide commercial transactions which includes the payment of extra interest to cover an exchange risk need not fall foul of this provision.

[84] See below at §§ 5.35 *et seq.*

[85] I.C.T.A. 1970, s.237.

[86] *Ibid.* s.233.

[87] *Ibid.* In this latter case only the interest over and above a reasonable commercial rate would be treated as a distribution. Note that with effect from March 9, 1982 (or April 1, 1983 in respect of loans made before March 9, 1982) interest paid on loans with categories (a)-(c) and (e) which is paid to a company within the change to corporation tax is no longer treated as a distribution unless the recipient would in any event be exempt from tax thereon: F.A. 1982, s.60.

[88] I.C.T.A. 1970, s.233.

[89] *Ibid.*

Interest may be deducted as a charge on income if it satisfies the following conditions:

(i) It is yearly interest.[90] Like "short" interest, yearly interest is not defined in the corporation tax legislation but it would appear that it means interest on a loan or other sum which is expressed to last 12 months[91] or longer. In ascertaining whether interest is yearly regard is to be had to the substance of the agreement. Thus interest payable under a mortgage, the terms of which stipulated for repayment of the principal at the end of six months was held[92] to be yearly interest, the reality being that both parties envisaged that the mortgage would not be repaid then, but was likely to last for longer than 12 months. By the same token a loan for three months was held not to carry yearly interest merely because the rate was expressed in annual terms.[93]

(ii) It is bank interest[94] of whatever kind. Since bank interest may also be deductible in computing a company's trading profit it follows that the company may make the deduction in the way most favourable to it.[95]

In many cases it will make little or no difference whether the deduction is made as a trading expense or as a charge on income. This will be the position where there are no other reliefs or allowances involved. Where the company's profitability is marginal, however, the deduction will usually be made as a trading expense since its application in this way would be likely to create a trading loss which could then be used to offset other income.

Where other reliefs and allowances are available the most advantageous point of deduction will often be determined by the rules governing the application of the relevant relief or allowance. For example, if a company has trading profits of £20,000, chargeable gains of the same amount, but has brought forward a trading loss of £20,000 it would seem to be to its advantage to deduct any bank interest as a charge rather than as an expense. The point here is that if the interest were deducted as an expense this would operate to reduce the trading profit and so restrict the relief that would be available for the loss brought forward. But if the interest is deducted as a charge the loss brought forward can be relieved against the trading income leaving the interest to be relieved against the chargeable gains.

*(ii) As a Charge on Income*

*(a) Yearly Interest*

*(b) Bank Interest*

**5.26**

---

[90] I.C.T.A. 1970, s.248 includes with yearly interest, annuities and certain other annual payments (*e.g.* patent rents, mining rents and royalties, etc.).

[91] See *Ward* v. *Anglo-American Oil Co.* (1934) 19 T.C. 94 where a loan for one year only was held to give rise to annual (*i.e.* yearly) interest.

[92] *Re Craven's Mortgage* ([1907] 2 Ch. 448. See also *Garston Overseers* v. *Carlisle* [1915] 3 K.B. 381.

[93] *Goslings and Sharpe* v. *Blake* (1889) 23 Q.B.D. 324; *Cairns* v. *MacDiarmid* [1982] S.T.C. 226. Equally, a loan of no fixed term (*e.g.* repayable on demand—*Corinthian Securities Ltd.* v. *Cato* (1969) 46 T.C. 93) will carry yearly interest albeit that that interest is payable quarterly or otherwise at intervals of less than a year: *Re Jane's Settlement* [1918] 2 Ch. 54.

[94] Interest payable in the U.K on an advance from a bona fide banking business, or discount house or member of the Stock Exchange: I.C.T.A. 1970, s.248(3).

[95] I.C.T.A. 1970 contains seemingly conflicting provisions governing bank interest, s.248(3) treating it as a change on income and therefore deductible from ascertained profits, while s.131 implies that it may be treated as a trading expense and therefore brought into account in ascertaining the trading profit. The consequence is that in practice the Revenue permit a company to deduct interest either as a charge or as an expense.

(c) *Valuable and Sufficient Consideration*
(iii) It must have been incurred for valuable and sufficient consideration, and be ultimately borne by the company.[96]
(iv) It must not rank as a distribution.[97]

(d) *F.A. 1981, s. 38*
(v) It ought not, prior to 1981, have been charged to capital. Now, however, Finance Act 1981, section 38 permits such interest to be deducted as a charge on income.

**5.27**
Where interest is paid to a non-resident special rules apply to restrict the deductibility of interest payments. Generally to be eligible for deduction the interest must come within one or other of the following categories:

(iii) *Interest Payable to Non-Residents*
(i) it must have been paid under deduction of tax[98]; or
(ii) the payment must have been covered by foreign income[99];
(iii) the payment is made outside the United Kingdom for overseas trading activities or, if payable in foreign currency, for any trading activity.[1]

**Taxation**

**5.28**
The prescriptions concerning the structure and form of company accounts require a company's profit and loss account to disclose the amount of tax payable for the period to which the account relates. The company's liability will be to corporation tax levied in respect of the company's taxable income profits and chargeable capital gains.

**5.29 Taxing company profits[2]**

Until the second world war the only permanent tax to which company profits were subjected was income tax, the standard rate of which fell to 4/– in the £ in

*Income Tax*
1924–1926 and which, throughout most of the 1930s was at 4/6d. The wartime excess profits duty had terminated in 1920–1921 and although a temporary corporation profits tax[3] was levied from 1920–1924, it was not until 1937 that any additional taxation of a permanent nature fell upon company profits. In 1937 a National Defence Contribution of 5 per cent.[4] was levied on company profits and it was from this levy that ultimately the modern corporation tax evolved.

Income tax continued as a charge[5] on corporate profits until 1965. In so far as

---

[96] I.C.T.A. 1970, s.248(3).
[97] See above at § 5.24.
[98] I.C.T.A. 1970, s.54. However, payment without deduction or with a restricted deduction will qualify if made under a double taxation agreement.
[99] I.C.T.A. 1970, s.131. The requirement is that the amount of foreign income arising in the company must equal or exceed the amount of the interest payment, even though the interest is not physically paid out of the foreign income or, indeed, is not charged to tax as being covered by other reliefs.
[1] I.C.T.A. 1920, s.131.
[2] See generally Bramwell, *Taxation of Companies* (3rd ed., 1985).
[3] At 5 per cent. during 1920–1923 and at 2½ per cent. for 1923–1924.
[4] And at 4 per cent. on the profits of unincorporated businesses.
[5] The standard rate rose to 5/6d in 1939, to 10/– in 1940 where it remained during the war. In the six years immediately preceding the introduction of corporation tax the standard rate stood at 7/9d.

profits were distributed to shareholders income tax operated as a withholding tax with the amount withheld being credited against the shareholder's income tax liability.

In 1939 a new tax, excess profits duty, was introduced, levied at 60 per cent. on the amount by which a company's profits exceeded the prescribed "standard profit." In 1940 the rate was increased to 100 per cent. at which level it remained until 1945.[6] All companies paid either excess profits duty or the National Defence Contribution, whichever was the larger. Excess profits duty was repealed in 1948. The National Defence Contribution became operative and from January 1947 became a permanent levy and was renamed "profits tax."[7]

Profits tax was chargeable by reference to profits earned and profits distributed by a company for each yearly accounting period. Until 1952 profits tax paid was deductible in computing the profits of the company for income tax purposes.

Profits tax was charged at a differential rate as between distributed and undistributed profits. Until 1952 the rates of charge were 25 per cent. on distributed profits and 10 per cent. on undistributed profits. With the abolition of deductibility for income tax these rates were reduced to $22\frac{1}{2}$ per cent. and $2\frac{1}{2}$ per cent. respectively. The purpose behind this discrimination in favour of retention of profits was to "discourage dividend increases which were seen as contributing to consumption expenditure and inciting wage claims, and to encourage companies to plough back more into the business."[8] However, the 1955 Royal Commission was sceptical as to this last point feeling that discrimination against distribution "does not encourage companies to plough back profits, so much as to retain them"[9] and that mere retention produced no economic advantage.[10] Accordingly in 1958 the differential charge was abolished and replaced by a charge at a single rate of 10 per cent. This rate was increased to $12\frac{1}{2}$ per cent. in 1960 and further increased to 15 per cent. in 1961.

*Profits tax*

The restructuring of the system of direct taxes in 1965 abolished the dual tax **5.30** charge on company profits and replaced it with a single tax. The new tax, corpor-

---

[6] It has been commented that while the duty "may have been a good short-term tax for revenue purposes, there is little doubt that by its very nature it encouraged extravagant and wasteful outlay" Thomas *op.cit.*, at p. 239 From 1941 20 per cent. of the Excess Profits Duty was treated as a reserve to be made available to industry for the post-war reconstruction. For several years after the war refunds were made.

[7] A temporary Excess Profits Levy was imposed during the Korean War rearmament boom.

[8] Thomas *op.cit.*, p. 230.

[9] Royal Commission on the *Taxation of Profits and Income* 1955 Cmnd. 9474, Majority Report at para. 536.

[10] *Ibid.* Minority Report at para. 103. "The artifical encouragement of the retention of profits by companies is not necessarily an advantage. Beyond a certain point it does not in itself stimulate the rate of capital formation—as is shown by the fact that in the last few years the net amounts retained by companies have greatly exceeded their financial requirements, both on account of capital expenditure and of investment in working capital. . . . The system of financing capital expenditure so largely out of the undistributed profits of companies does not ensure the best use of the community's savings. It makes it more difficult for fast expanding firms to raise capital in the capital market; it strengthens the monopolistic tendencies of the economy; and it encourages wasteful expenditure on behalf of those firms who have more money than they can use and who are prevented (by custom and tradition as well as by instruments of public control) from channelling these funds to their most profitable use."

*Corporation Tax: the Classical System*

ation tax, was in effect the uniform profits tax with its rate increased to 40 per cent. Thenceforth income tax was no longer chargeable on profits but was still levied on dividends in respect of which it operated as a withholding tax, companies acting as collecting agencies for the Revenue in deducting income tax at source and accounting for the tax so deducted. "Among the benefits accorded to the change were that it would divorce company and personal taxation, reduce tax avoidance and evasion, and lead to more company saving, permitting increased investment."[11] Savings were to be encouraged by reintroducing in a different form differential levels of taxation for retained and distributed profits. The new system operated on the premise that since retained profits would suffer only corporation tax they would escape the charge to income tax while they remained undistributed.

The 1965 reforms also instituted a comprehensive system of taxation for capital gains and the definition of profits for corporation tax purposes was so framed as to include such gains.

**5.31**

*Corporation Tax: the Imputation System*

The Finance Act 1972[12] introduced a further change in the system of taxing company profits, albeit retaining the single-tax structure. The object of the new system was to encourage distributions and, market conditions permitting, to raise new funds by equity issues rather than by fixed interest loans.[13] The new provisions came into operation in April 1973 and under them corporation tax was levied at a standard rate of 50 per cent. but deduction of tax from dividends ceased. Instead, when a company paid a dividend it was required to make a payment of advance corporation tax at a rate of 3/7ths of the distribution. This advance payment was then set against the corporation tax payable on the profits of the relevant accounting period. Resident shareholders to whom a distribution in respect of which advance corporation tax (ACT) had been payable were entitled to a tax credit to be set against their own tax liability in respect of the dividend.

In that way the "imputation system" was supposed to be neutral as between distributions and retentions of profits.

**5.32** **Corporation tax**

*Company Taxable Profits*

Corporation tax is charged[14] on the full amount of profits accruing to a company resident in the United Kingdom[15] during an accounting period.[16] Profits are defined as including both income and capital gains, but as specifically excluding distributions from other resident companies. Subject to this a company's

---

[11] Thomas, *op.cit.* at p. 231.

[12] F.A. 1972, Pt. V.

[13] One feature of the 1965 system had been (and still is) that interest on debt is an allowable deduction for corporation tax purposes. (See above at §§ 5.23–5.26). This led to a marked change in the relative proportions of debt and equity issued over the next few years.

[14] I.C.T.A. 1970, s.243.

[15] And on the profits of non-resident companies earned within the U.K. via a branch or agency.

[16] Although a company's profit is measured by reference to its accounting period corporation tax is levied for financial years which run from April 1, to March 31. Where an accounting period straddles a financial year the profits of that period are subject to apportionment.

income profits are computed in accordance with income tax principles[17] and the capital profits (or chargeable gains) in accordance with capital gains tax principles.[18]

Corporation tax is levied at a standard rate fixed annually in the Finance Act for that year. However since 1972 special rules have applied to reduce the effective rate of charge on chargeable gains and on the income of companies whose profits do not exceed specified limits.

(a) *Standard rate*

Prior to the Finance Act 1984 the standard rate of corporation tax had for many years remained at 52 per cent. However section 18 of that Act provided for the progressive reduction of that rate over the period covering the financial years 1983–1986 as follows:

| Financial Year | Rate of Tax |
| --- | --- |
| 1983 | 50 per cent. |
| 1984 | 45 per cent. |
| 1985 | 40 per cent. |
| 1986 | 35 per cent. |

(b) *Capital gains reduction*

From 1972 companies' chargeable gains suffered tax at an effective rate of 30 per cent. This was achieved by excluding from the charge to tax a fraction of the total chargeable gains while charging the full standard rate on the balance.[19] While the standard rate was 52 per cent. the fraction to be excluded was $\frac{11}{26}$ths.[20]

With the progressive reduction in the standard rate provided for by section 18 of the Finance Act 1984 the excluded fractions for the financial years 1983–1986 are as follows[21]:

| Financial Year | Standard Rate | Excluded Fraction |
| --- | --- | --- |
| 1983 | 50 per cent. | $\frac{2}{5}$ ths |
| 1984 | 45 per cent. | $\frac{1}{3}$ rd |
| 1985 | 40 per cent. | $\frac{1}{4}$ |
| 1986 | 35 per cent. | $\frac{1}{7}$ th |

[17] I.C.T.A. 1970, s.250.
[18] *Ibid.* s.265.
[19] F.A. 1972, s.93.
[20] F.A. 1974, s.10.
[21] F.A. 1984, s.18(2).

## (c) *Small companies rate*

*Small Companies Relief*

The small companies relief is available to those companies[22] whose profits[23] in an accounting period do not exceed specified limits. Where a company's profits do not exceed the lower limit (standing at £100,000) tax at a special lower rate—the "small companies rate" is applied to the company's income instead of tax at the full standard rate. For the financial years 1983–1986 the small companies rate has been fixed at 30 per cent.[24]

Where the lower limit is exceeded but the company's profits remain below the upper limit (standing at £500,000) the terms of the relief provide for an effective graduated increased in rate until the full standard rate is achieved.[25]

It will be apparent therefore that, where available, the utilisation of capital allowances and/or trading losses may obtain even greater savings then would otherwise be the case in that they may operate to effect a reduction in profits to within the limits at which the lower rates of tax will apply.

**5.34**

*Payment of Tax*

Satisfaction of a company's corporation tax liability is due nine months after the end of the accounting period to which it relates or one month after the issue of the Notice of Assessment, whichever is the latter.[26] In practice the average delay in settling corporation tax liability is about 18 months, thus providing the company with use of funds for that period.

---

[22] Although the purpose of the relief is supposed to be mitigation of the tax burden of small companies, in point of fact the relief is of general application to companies irrespective of their size and regardless of the amount of profits retained in previous years. However, restrictions (from F.A. 1972, s.95(4)) do apply where a company has one or more associated companies during the accounting priod in question. In such a case the upper and lower limits are divided by the total number of companies associated with each other.

[23] F.A. 1972, s.95(7) defines profits for the purposes of the relief as including income, the appropriate fraction of chargeable gains and franked investment income.

[24] F.A. 1984, s.20(1).

[25] F.A. 1972, s.95(2). This "marginal relief" operates by charging the company's taxable profits for the period at the full standard rate and then by reducing the liability so produced by an amount equal to the fraction:

$$X \times (m-P) \times \frac{I}{P}$$

where  I = the company's income
       P = profits as defined for the purposes of the relief; and
       X = fraction fixed annually by statute

F.A. 1984, s. 20(2) fixes the fraction for the financial years 1983–1986 as follows:

| Financial Year | Marginal Relief Fraction |
|---|---|
| 1983 | $\frac{1}{20}$ th |
| 1984 | $\frac{3}{80}$ ths |
| 1985 | $\frac{1}{40}$ th |
| 1986 | $\frac{1}{80}$ th |

The reduction declines as the profit approaches the upper limit so that the formula provides a smooth graduation in the effective rate of tax from 30 per cent. to the full standard rate for the relevant financial year.

[26] I.C.T.A. 1970, s.243(4).

The true extent of this advantage will however be affected by the operation of the rules governing the taxation of company distributions. These rules are founded on three main principles:

   (i) that a company, in paying a dividend to its shareholders, is required to account to the Revenue for advance corporation tax (ACT) in the amount of 3/7ths of the value of the distribution[27];

 (ii) that the recipient of the dividend in respect of which this ACT is paid is entitled to a tax credit in the amount of the ACT; and

(iii) that payments of ACT by a company in an accounting period may be set against the company's "mainstream" corporation tax liability (MCT) for that period.[28]

The extent of a company's liability to make payments of ACT will obviously be determined primarily by the amount of the qualifying distributions[29] it chooses to make. It will also be affected however by the amount of qualifying distributions it receives. The point is that dividends received by a company from another United Kingdom resident company will themselves have borne ACT and so carry with them a tax credit. Since a company can take credit for the tax imputed to it[30] the amount of tax credit received will reduce the ACT payable by the recipient company on its own distributions. That company will therefore pay ACT[31] only on the amount by which its dividends exceed the amount of the dividends it receives.[32]

The amount of corporation tax payable by a company on the date due for settlement of its liability will obviously be affected by the amount of ACT available for set-off. This availability is limited to two respects:

   (i) by the fact that ACT may be offset only against MCT which is defined[33] as a company's corporation tax liability excluding that attributable to the chargeable gains; and

---

[27] F.A. 1981, s.22.

[28] F.A. 1972, s.85.

[29] Primarily dividends. But see further below at §§ 5.50 *et seq.*

[30] F.A. 1972, s.89(1).

[31] It follows that the primary function of such distributions received (franked investment income) is to frank dividends paid by the recipient company for the accounting period in which they were received. If there is surplus franked investment income in any period I.C.T.A. 1970, s.177(2) provides that it may be used to offset trading losses. Alternatively s.248 permits it to be used to offset charges on income and to stimulate a tax repayment. This result is obtained by treating the surplus franked investment income as if it constituted profits chargeable to corporation tax but upon which tax, to the extent of the credit, has been paid (I.C.T.A. 1970, s.254). If, after this, a surplus still exists it may be carried forward to the next accounting period to frank dividends or offset trading losses, capital allowances or charges on income for that period. For lesser periods it may be used only to frank dividends.

[32] Where the paying and receiving companies are members of the same group I.C.T.A. 1970, s.256(1) permits the parties to elect to have the distribution treated as "group income" with the consequence that no liability to Act is incurred and no tax credit conferred. Where the election is made the income from the various group members is aggregated as are the losses and other reliefs and allowances, with corporation tax being levied on the groups profits thus resulting.

[33] F.A. 1972, s.85.

(ii) by rules restricting the amount of ACT that may be set against a company's MCT. Essentially these rules restrict the amount of ACT allowable to that which would have been payable in respect of a dividend of an amount which, together with the ACT payable thereon, is equal to the company's income profits for that period.[34]

As a consequence of these restrictions and of the fact that, because of the availability of capital allowances (and formerly of stock relief), a company's taxable profits may be substantially less than the accounting profits out of which the distribution is made, a situation may occur where a company incurs a heavy liability to ACT but is unable to offset the whole of the payments made,[35] and further, still has a liability to corporation tax to meet on the due date for settlement.

# DISTRIBUTIONS

**5.37**

*Limits on a Company's Ability to Distribute*

A company's memorandum or articles of association may contain specific provisions[36] defining or limiting what may be distributed by way of dividend. Subject to any such provision the rules governing a company's ability to make distributions are to be found in Part VIII of the Companies Act 1985.[37] These rules set out the basic requirement that a company may only make a distribution "out of profits available for the purpose."[38] Such profits are defined[39] as the company's "accumulated, realised profits so far as not previously utilised by distribution or capitalisation, less its accumulated, realised losses, so far as not previously written off in a reduction or reorganisation of capital duly made."

Questions as to whether a company has profits available for distribution are determined by reference to the company's accounts.[40]

**5.38**

*Revenue and Capital Profits*

The statutory rules make no distinction as between profits of a revenue or a capital nature. It follows therefore that profits of either type may be included in a distribution[41] by way of dividend provided that they fall within the scope of the definition of profits available for distribution.

---

[34] *Ibid.*

[35] Where the right of set-off is restricted and there occurs a balance of unrelieved ACT, this may be carried back over the two preceding accounting periods and set against the company's MCT for those periods, in effect serving to stimulate a repayment claim. If any balance remains after this it may be carried forward to the next accounting period and beyond until exhausted: F.A. 1972, s.85. In respect of accounting periods from April 1, 1984 the permissible carry back over two years has been extended to six: F.A. 1984, s.53.

[36] For example, a provision that dividends shall be paid "out of the profits arising from the business of the company."

[37] Formerly Pt. III of the Companies Act 1980, supplemented by ss.84–85 of the Companies Act 1981.

[38] Companies Act 1985, s.263(1).

[39] *Ibid.* s.263(2).

[40] *Ibid.* s.270.

[41] Except in the case of public investment companies: *ibid.* s.265. Distribution is defined by s.263(2) as "every discription of distribution of a company's assets to members of the company whether in cash or otherwise, except distribution made by way of:
    (a) an issue of shares as fully or partly paid bonus shares;

Profits available for distribution must be "realised profits"[42] which term would appear to comprehend profits resulting from some transaction,[43] in contrast to gains produced, for example, by a revaluation of current or fixed assets.[44]

The requirement that a company's profits available for distribution be its "accumulated" realised profits effectively means that losses incurred in earlier accounting periods must be made good before a distribution can be made in the current period.[45] It further means that, in a period in which it incurs a loss, a company may only use retained profits as a fund from which to pay dividends to the extent of the balance remaining after the current loss has been made good.[46]

In arriving at the amount of profits available for distribution the statutory rules require account to be taken of those accumulated realised profits which have been utilised by distribution or capitalisation.[47] Equally, accumulated realised losses are also to be brought into account except to the extent that they have been previously written off in a reduction or reorganisation of capital. It follows therefore that what is available to a company for distribution at any given time is:

    (b) the redemption of preference shares out of the proceeds of a fresh issue of shares made for the purpose of the redemption and the payment of any premium on their redemption out of the company's share premium account;

    (c) the reduction of the share capital by extinguishing or reducing the liability of any of the company's members on any of its shares in respect of share capital not paid up or by paying off paid up share capital; and

    (d) a distribution of assets to members of the company on its winding up."

It is apparent from this that cash dividends will be the principal type of distribution within the scope of Pt. VIII.

[42] Note s.275(2) which provides: "If, on the revaluation of a fixed asset, an unrealised profit is shown to have been made, and on or after the revaluation, a sum is written off or retained for depreciation of that asset over a period, then an amount equal to the amount by which that sum exceeds the sum which would have been so written off or retained for depreciation of that asset over that period, if that profit had not been made, shall be treated . . . as a realised profit made over that period." Note also s.275(1) which provides that any provision in the accounts of a company, other than a provision in respect of the diminution's value of a fixed asset, appearing on a revaluation of all the fixed assets of the company, is to be treated as a realised loss.

[43] See *Re Oxford Benefit Building and Investment Society* (1885) 35 Ch. D. 502, 510 *per* Kay J. Essentially the circumstances in which a profit or loss are regarded as realised are determined in accordance with normal accounting principles—see *Lee* v. *Neuchatel Asphalte Co.* (1889) 41 Ch. D. 1, 21 *per* Lindley L.J.

[44] This requirement effectively implements the recommendation of the Jenkins Committee (1962, Cmnd. 1749), para. 350 and affirms the decision of the Court of Session in *Westburn Sugar Refineries* v. *I.R.C.* 1960 S.L.T. 297. It overturns the decision of Buckley J. in *Dimbula Valley (Ceylon) Tea Co.* v. *Laurie* [1961] Ch. 353, thus assimilating English and Scots Law on the point of the basis of Scots law.

[45] This requirement likewise implements recommendations of the Jenkins Committee (*ibid.*) paras. 341 and 350, and again assimilates English and Scots Law on the point on the basis of the Scottish position *viz. Niddrie and Benber Coal Co.* v. *Hurll* (1891) 18 R. 805 and overturning the Court of Appeal decision in *Ammonia Soda Co.* v. *Chamberlain* [1918] 1 Ch. 266.

[46] Overturning *Re Hoare & Co. (No. 1)* [1904] 2 Ch. 298.

[47] According to C.A. 1985, s.280(2) the profits of a company are treated for the purposes of the distribution rules as having been capitalised if:

    (a) . . . they have been applied in wholly or partly paying up unissued shares in the company to be allotted to members of the company as fully or partly paid bonus shares; or

    (b) they have been transferred to the company's capital redemption fund."

    (i) the amount of its accumulated realised profits

    less

    (ii) the amount of:

        (a) its accumulated realised profits previously utilised by distribution or capitalisation; and

        (b) its accumulated realised losses

    plus

    (iii) those accumulated realised losses previously written off in a reduction or reorganisation.

**5.42**    Public companies are subject to a further restriction by virtue of s.264 of the 1985 Act. This permits public companies to make distributions only:

*Public Companies*

    (i) if at the time of the distribution the company's net assets[48] are not less than the aggregate of its called-up share capital[49] and its undistributable reserves[50]; and

    (ii) if, and to the extent that, the distribution does not reduce the amount of the company's net assets to less than the aggregate of its called-up share capital and its undistributable reserves.

It follows, therefore, that even if a public company has profits that would otherwise be available for distribution it may not distribute if the amount of its net assets is less than the aggregate of its called-up share capital and undistributable reserves. Where the company has net assets in excess of that aggregate it may distribute but only to the extent of that excess.

**5.43**    Investment companies,[51] being public companies, are subject to the restric-

---

[48] According to s.264(2)(*c*) a company's "net assets" are the aggregate of its liabilities.

[49] According to s.737(1) "called up share capital" means the aggregate of
    (i) so much of its share capital as equals the aggregate amount of the calls made on its shares (whether or not such calls have been paid);
    (ii) any share capital paid up without being called; and
    (iii) any share capital to be paid on a specified date under the articles, the terms of allotment of the relevant shares or any other arrangements for payment of these shares.

[50] For the purposes of s.264 a company's undistributable reserves comprise (s.264(3)):
    (i) its share premium account;
    (ii) its capital redemption reserve fund;
    (iii) the amount by which its accumulated, unrealised profits, so far as not utilised by capitalisation (other than capitalisation by the transfer of any of the company's profits to its capital redemption reserve fund—s.264(3)) exceed its accumulated unrealised losses so far as not previously written off in a reduction or reorganisation of capital duly made; and
    (iv) any other reserve which the company is prohibited from distributing by statute (other than the provisions of Part VIII of the 1985 Act) or by its memorandum or articles.

[51] An investment company is a public company (s.266(1)) in respect of which (s.266(2)):
    (i) the business of the company consists of investing its funds mainly in securities with the aim of spreading investment risk and giving the members of the company the benefits of the results of the management of its funds;
    (ii) none of the company's holdings in companies (other than companies which are for the time being investment companies) represents more than 15 per cent. by value of the investment company's investments;
    (iii) distribution of the company's capital profits is prohibited by its memorandum or articles; and
    (iv) the company has not retained (except in order to comply with Pt. VIII of the Act) in respect of any accounting reference period more than 15 per cent. of the income which it derives from securities.

tions contained in s.264 and as such may make a distribution if the amount of their net assets is at or above a level at which the requirements of that section can be satisfied. However, by virtue of s.265(1) an investment company may also[52] distribute at any time out of its accumulated, realised revenue profits so far as not previously utilised by distribution or capitalisation, less its accumulated revenue losses (whether realised or unrealised) so far as not previously written off in a reduction or reorganisation of capital. It may make a distribution under s.265(1):

*Investment Companies*

(i) if at that time the amount of its assets is at least equal to one and a half times the aggregate of its liabilities; and
(ii) if it satisfies the further restrictions imposed by s.266(2). These are:
    (a) that its shares are listed on a recognised stock exchange; and
    (b) that during the immediately preceding accounting reference period and the current accounting reference period up to the date of the distribution it has not distributed any of its capital profits or applied any unrealised profits or any capital profits (realised or unrealised) in paying up debentures or any amounts unpaid on any of its issued shares.
(iii) if it has given appropriate notice to the Register.[53]

It must be emphasised that distribution will be:

(a) the amount of the company's accumulated, realised revenue profits; less
(b) the amounts of its accumulated realised revenue profits previously utilised by distribution of capitalisation and its accumulated revenue losses (realised and unrealised); plus
(c) those accumulated revenue losses (realised and unrealised) previously written off in a reduction or reorganisation of capital.

Where profits are not available for distribution as not complying with the provisions of Part VIII of the Act they may be placed to reserve or used to pay up in full unissued shares to be allotted as fully paid bonus shares to members of the company who would be entitled to that sum if it were distributed by way of dividend.[54]

**5.44**

*Profits not Available for Distribution*

## DISTRIBUTION AND RETENTION

Where the requisite conditions are satisfied so as to render it legally permissible for a company to make a distribution questions then arise as to:

**5.45**

(i) how much should be distributed and how much retained; and
(ii) if a distribution is to be made, the form in which the distribution should be made.

[52] Investment companies therefore have the option of making distributions either in accordance with the provisions of s.264(1) or in accordance with the provisions of s.265(1).
[53] That is notice of its intention to carry on business as an investment company. The notice must be given (s.265(6)) either
    (i) before the period specified in s.265(5); or
    (ii) in the case of a recently incorporated company as soon as reasonably practicable after incorporation.
[54] Companies (Alteration of Table A etc.) Regulations 1984 (SI 1984 No. 1717) Reg. 110.

*Elements of a*
*Distribution*
*Policy*

Inevitably distribution policy will vary from company to company. Nevertheless, a number of factors would appear to be common to most companies and would have to be taken into account to some degree.

**5.46**

*(1) Profita-*
*bility*

Clearly, much will depend on the company's profitability. If a company has been consistently successful over a period of time it is obvious that, all other things being equal, the amount that can prudently be distributed at a given point will be higher than in the case of a company with low or negative profitability. Of significance in this respect will be the level of past profits, the proportion of those profits that has been distributed and the expected level of profits for the future. It may be assumed that, in the absence of external pressures,[55] companies will not increase distributions unless they have confidence that the new level can be maintained.

**5.47**

*(2) Financial*
*Requirements*
*of the Com-*
*pany's Busi-*
*ness*

Nevertheless, profitability will not be the sole factor. Of commensurate significance will be the company's financial requirements and the availability of funds to meet them. In determining distribution policy a company will have to give consideration to factors not reflected in profits,[56] such as capital expenditure plans, likely changes in production methods and efficiency, liquidity levels and new financing arrangements that may be or may become available. Essentially what is at issue here is the future operating capability of the company's business. If high levels of distribution are sought it may be necessary to procure additional finance to avoid an erosion of that operating capability.

**5.48**

*(3) Maintain-*
*ing Access to*
*Capital*
*Markets*

Connected with this last point is the extent to which the company, especially if it has a Stock Exchange listing, wishes to retain its position in the market place. There are several aspects to this, all of which work in favour of distribution rather than retention.

The first concerns the situation where a company foresees that it will have to come to the market for funds. Given the cost of fixed-interest loans the probability is that any new issue will have to be of equity, and this being so potential investors, especially institutional investors, are likely to be attracted or otherwise in part by level of income return they can expect on any investment. Accordingly companies expecting to come to the market may well seek to maintain the status of their shares by "dividend sweeteners."[57]

The second relates to trustee investment status, the point being that many private trusts and public bodies have their investment powers derived from the Trustee Investments Act 1961. Under the provisions of this Act[58] for the securities of any company to constitute an authorised investment that company must, *inter alia,* have paid a dividend on its ordinary shares for each of the preceding five years. It is not uncommon for companies to pay dividends solely for the purpose of retaining trustee status when other factors would indicate that it would be prudent to pass the dividend on the relevant occasion.

---

[55] Such as the prospect of having to resist a take-over bid currently or in the foreseeable future.

[56] See S.S.A.P. 16, Explanatory Notes 23 *et seq.* for the use of current cost accounting techniques in relation to these matters.

[57] Thomas *op.cit.* at p. 241.

[58] Sched. 1.

A further aspect of this element arises out of the possible vulnerability of a quoted company with large reserves to take-over bids. This matter is considered further in Chapter 7 below but for the present suffice it to note the tendency of quoted companies to be less inclined to hold large reserves of financial assets in periods of high take-over activity and to manifest this by raising their dividends partly in an attempt to reduce their vulnerability to bids inspired by asset-stripping motives and partly in an attempt to increase the attractiveness of their shares to investors generally.

An important influence on distribution levels since the last war has been the attempts by government to operate policies of dividend restraint.[59] In part these policies have been implemented via the tax system in the form of discrimination against distributed profits.[60] In addition, however, attempts at direct dividend control have been made at various times. Some of these have comprised "voluntary" compliance with government requests for "moral dividend limitation"[61] or "moderation and restraint," while others have been part of a "pay pause" or "wage restraint" package. In 1972 statutory controls were introduced[62] and put on an apparently permanent basis the following year. Under this system companies incorporated in the United Kingdom were forbidden from raising the amounts distributed by more than a specified percentage.

Inevitably these attempts at restraint provoked attempts by some companies to find ways round the controls. Thus in the 1940s during the period of voluntary "moral dividend limitation" companies sought to by-pass the constraints by issuing free bonus shares. In many cases this amounted to no more than a revival of the pre-war practice of paying a scrip bonus along with the dividend; and of course there were other cases where the scrip issues represented capitalisations of reserves. Nevertheless the scrip issues had the consequence that more shares came into existence in respect of which dividends became due. If companies merely maintained their previous percentage dividend payments the result was

**5.49**

(4) *Government Restrictions and Dividends*

*Avoiding Dividend Controls*

(a) *via Bonus Issues*

(b) *via Rights Issues*

---

[59] The main arguments in favour of restraint are economic in that:
    (i) restraint operates to increase corporate savings and thereby, hopefully, to encourage investment;
    (ii) restraint provides an incentive for wage restraint; and
    (iii) higher dividends may be sustained by higher prices, thereby adding to inflation.
  The main arguments against restraint are financial in that:
    (i) the control of dividends results in falling share prices which in turn increases the cost and difficulty of obtaining new capital from the market; and
    (ii) in an inflationary period with rising prices the real value of dividends subject to control declines leading to disenchantment with investment in industry.
[60] See above at §§ 5.28 *et seq.* Since the introduction of the imputation system by the Finance Act 1972 the tax system is designed to be neutral as between distributed and undistributed profits.
[61] During the period 1946–1949. See further Thomas, *op.cit.,* at pp. 238–245.
[62] Counter Inflation Act 1972. Under the 1972 Act no increase was permitted. From 1973 an increase of 5 per cent. was permitted on the level of the previous year, subsequently increased to $7\frac{1}{2}$ per cent. Interestingly a similar system was proposed in 1950. The White Paper "Control of Dividends" (Cmnd. 8318) proposed a limit on the gross amount of equity dividends by companies based on the average amount distributed or declared in respect of the two years to July 26, 1950. Companies which had paid no dividend in those two years were to be permitted distributions of up to 5 per cent. of their issued capital, with new companies being limited to 7 per cent. Distributions amounting to less than £10,000 were to be exempt from the controls. The scheme was overtaken by the general election of 1951 and consequent change of government.

that greater amounts were distributed.[63] And in 1975, during the period of statutory restraint, a variant of this device was introduced, this time employing rights issues as the instrument of avoidance. It has been estimated that issues under which the right to buy additional shares was available at a large discount had the effect of raising the shareholders dividend yield by more than 10 per cent.[64]

No system of dividend control, statutory or otherwise, has been in operation since 1979.

**5.50**

(5) *Taxation*

If the company does not have a Stock Exchange listing the taxation provisions relating to close companies may apply. Where this is the case it is generally preferable to distribute up to the appropriate level.

The close company provisions[65] apply to unlisted companies resident in the Uniged Kingdom[66] under the control[67] of five or fewer participators[68] or of any number of participators who are directors.[69] The incentive to distribute comes from what used to be known as the "shortfall"[70] rules. Essentially these can be expressed in three propositions.

(i) a close company is required to make distributions[71] up to "the required standard"[72];

---

[63] In 1949 a ban was introduced on such free bonus issues.

[64] From October 1975 Treasury consent was required for the making of rights issues. See further *Midland Bank Review,* February 1976, pp. 223 *et seq.*

[65] I.C.T.A. 1970, ss.282–303; F.A. 1972, Sched. 16; F.A. 1978, ss.35, 36 and Sched. 5; F.A. 1980, s.44. See generally Bramwell, Ivory and Brannan, *Taxation of Companies and Company Reconstructions* (3rd ed., 1985).

[66] They do not apply to Crown-controlled companies (s.282(1)(*c*)) or companies that are subsidiaries of non-close companies (s.282(4)).

[67] I.C.T.A. 1970, s.302(2) provides " . . . a person shall be taken to have control of a company if he exercises, or is able to exercise or is entitled to acquire control, whether direct or indirect over the companies affairs and in particular . . . if he possesses or is entitled to acquire

   (a) the greater part of the share capital or issued share capital of the company of of the voting power in the company; or

   (b) such part of the issues share capital of the company as would, if the whole of the income of the company were in fact distributed among the participators . . . entitle him to receive the greater part of the amount so distributed; or

   (c) such rights as would, in the event of the winding up of the company or in any other circumstances, entitle him to receive the greater part of the assets of the company which would then be available for distribution among the participators."

s.302(3) supplements this by providing that where two or more persons together satisfy any of these conditions they shall taken as having control. s.303(6) then enacts that a participator and his "associates" are to be treated as one person, "associate" being defined by s.303(3) as a relative or partner of the participator, or the trustees of any settlement created by the participator or any relative of his, or a person interested in any shares or obligations of the compaby subject to any trust or estate of which the participator and that person are both beneficiaries.

[68] A participator is a person who has or may obtain a share or interest in the capital or income of the company—I.C.T.A. 1970, s.303(1).

[69] I.C.T.A. 1970, s.282(1).

[70] Since F.A. 1972, "shortfall" has become the "excess of relevant income over distribution."

[71] A company's distributions for the period comprises: (F.A. 1972, Sched. 16, para. 10).

   (i) any dividends declared in respect of the period and paid during it or within a reasonable time (*i.e.* 18 months) after it; and

   (ii) all other distributions made in the period except dividends which are treated as distributions for a previous period under (1) above.

F.A. 1973, s.21(1) and Sched. 9, para. 3 provide that distributions do not include issues of bonus redeemable shares or bonus securities unless made to a non-close company.

[72] The required standard differs according to the nature of the company, the legislation distinguishing between trading companies which are members of a trading group on the one hand and invest-

(ii) if the level of its distribution does not reach this required standard the difference between the amount actually distributed and the required standard is deemed to have been distributed; and

(iii) this sum is then apportioned among the participators in proportion to their interests in the company.

Without further provision these principles would operate in such a way that it would always be advantageous to accept an apportionment rather than make a distribution since no liability for ACT would arise. Further provision[73] is made however in the form of a requirement that upon an apportionment the company becomes liable to make a payment of "notional ACT" as if the amount apportioned was a distribution. The notional ACT arising in this way may be set against any available franked investment income held by the company in the period and of course against the company's mainstream corporation tax up to the time of the apportionment. However, to the extent that the company is unable to offset this notional ACT elsewhere it becomes liable to account to the Revenue for the amount involved. Insofar as the company is concerned, therefore, it might just as well have distributed up to the required standard and if the amount distributed is required, say, as part of a projected expenditure programme, it can be taken back under a loan or in exchange for new shares.

From the standpoint of the participator an apportionment presents a two-fold disadvantage. In the first place the amount apportioned to him, grossed up to take account of the tax credit from the notional ACT, is treated as the highest part of his income and subjected to income tax accordingly.[74] Less immediately, the amount left in the company will increase the value of his shareholding and be subjected to capital gains tax when disposed of.

---

ment companies on the other. A "trading company" is defined (F.A. 1972, Sched. 16, para. 11) as a company which exists wholly or mainly for the purpose of carrying on a trade. A "member of a trading group" is defined (*ibid*) as a company which exists wholly or mainly for the purpose of co-ordinating the administration of a group of two or more trading companies each of which is under its control or a company which holds property used by other companies in the group for the purposes of their trades.

Insofar as such companies are concerned the required standard ("relevant income") is so much of its distributable income other than its trading income as can be distributed without prejudice to the company's business. (Distributable income does not include chargeable gains but does include franked investment income, group income and all other income less the amount of corporation tax payable in respect of it.)—F.A. 1972, Sched. 16, paras. 8 and 10, amended by F.A. 1980, s.44.

The rules governing investment companies distinguish between those companies which have trading or estate income (broadly, income from land) and those which do not. Investment companies having such income have as their required standard all their distributable investment income (defined as income other than trading or estate income—F.A. 1972, Sched. 16, para. 10(3)) plus so much of their trading or estate income as can be distributed without prejudice to the requirements of the company's business so far as concerned with the activities or assets giving rise to the trading or estate income—F.A. 1972, Sched. 16, para. 10(4). Investment companies with no trading or estate income have as their required standard the whole of their distributable investment income (*ibid.*).

It will be seen, then, that trading companies are at an advantage in that they will not suffer an apportionment on their trading income and *may* be able to justify retaining all other income on the ground that it is required for the purposes of the companies business (with regard to which see *MacTaggart Scott & Co.* v. *I.R.C.* (1973) 48 T.C. 708; *I.R.C.* v. *Thompson Bros. (London) Ltd.* (1974) 49 T.C. 110; *Wilson & Garden Ltd.* v. *I.R.C.* [1981] S.T.C. 301).

[73] F.A. 1972, Sched. 16, para. 7.

[74] *Ibid.* para. 5.

**5.51**

*Investment of Retained Profits*

Where profits are retained by a company they may be applied immediately for the purposes of the company's business. Alternatively, they may be invested until such time as they are needed for such purposes. It goes without saying that a major factor in the selection of such investments will be the level of return offered. Nevertheless, that level of return will be affected by the tax treatment afforded to the investment; indeed, if the company is subject to the close company rules the consequences may extend to the overall tax position of the company. From a tax standpoint, therefore, potential investments should be considered:

(i) in relation to their general tax consequences; and

(ii) in relation to their effect on the position of close companies.

**5.52**

*Tax Factors in Investment of Retained Profits*

Concerning the general tax consequences of investments:

(1) Where the investment is in land[75] the income return in the form of rent will be chargeable under Schedule A in the ordinary way. Equally, capital profits will constitute chargeable gains and so suffer corporation tax at the reduced effective rate.[76]

(2) Where the investment consists of British government securities the interest received will be chargeable under Schedule C in the ordinary way. In so far as capital gains or losses are concerned the rule is that such gains are exempt from tax provided that the disposal did not take place within twelve months of acquisition.[77-78] Certain losses incurred on disposals within this twelve-month period are not allowable.[79]

(3) Where the investment comprises loans, debentures or other interest bearing deposits the interest received is chargeable as "pure income"[80] in the ordinary way. However, the debt from which the interest arises will not give rise to any chargeable gain or allowable loss unless it constitutes a "debt on security."[81]

(4) Where the investment is in shares of a United Kingdom resident company the dividends arising are not chargeable to corporation tax[82] and may be used to frank the company's own distributions. Such shares generally constitute chargeable assets and will therefore give rise to a chargeable gain or allowable loss on disposal.

(5) Where the investment is in shares of a non-resident company the dividends

---

[75] In the United Kingdom.

[76] See above at para. 5.32.

[77-78] Capital Gains Tax Act (C.G.T.A.) 1979, s.67.

[79] Where a company disposes of gilt-edged stocks and sustains a loss, but acquires the same securities in the same capacity within one month (six months if the reacquisition took place otherwise than through a stock exchange) that loss is not allowable—C.G.T.A. 1979, s.70. Attempts to obtain corresponding benefits to those derived from these "bed and breakfast" transactions were made via "double banking," that is device whereby the same amount of securities is bought in and then the original holding disposed of one day later. C.G.T.A. 1979, s.70 nullifies this effect, however, at least insofar as the new holding is of the same issue of securities as the old. It would appear that the provisions may be avoided by acquiring different gilt-edged securities with similar, if not identical flat and/or redemption yields.

[80] See Whiteman and Wheatcroft, *op.cit.,* at Chapter 3.

[81] C.G.T.A. 1979, s.134. However a gain might arise if the loan was denominated in foreign currency which appreciated against sterling.

[82] F.A. 1972, s.88.

arising are chargeable to corporation tax,[83] subject to any double-taxation arrangements. Such shares generally constitute chargeable assets and will therefore give rise to a chargeable gain or allowable loss on disposal.

If a company is subject to the close company rules the manner in which retained profits are invested may be relevant to the status of the company as a trading company[84] and may have a significant effect on the calculation of any apportionment.[85] In particular: **5.53**

    (i) An investment yielding a capital gain will benefit not only from the effective lower rate of corporation tax[86] but additionally in that the gain will not be subject to apportionment;

    (ii) Investment in land will normally give rise to estate income[87] which may

---

[83] Under Case V. Secured loans would be chargeable under Case IV.

[84] On the basis that the income of the company may be increased and the proportion of investment income become such that the company's income could no longer be said to arise "wholly or mainly" from its trade so that its purpose as being "wholly or mainly" to carry on a trade would be called into question.

[85] The calculation of an apportionment is a complex matter and involves a number of steps: (F.A. 1972, Sched. 16).

    (i) The company's income is divided into four categories:
        (a) trading income (meaning primarily earned income. Where the trade is share-dealing dividends and similar incidental income are treated as trading income);
        (b) estate income (being income assessed under Schedules A, B or D which rises from the ownership or occupation of land);
        (c) investment income other than franked investment income;
        (d) franked investment income (exclusive of the element of tax credit) and group income.

    (ii) Changes on income and any other amounts deductible from total profits are deducted in stages, first, from investment income, then from estate income, then from trading income and finally from chargeable gains;

    (iii) Corporation tax is deducted from estate income and from investment income. While trading income is not subject to apportionment it will be relevant in relation to steps (v) and (vi) and should therefore have corporation tax deducted from it also;

    (iv) Franked investment income, net of the tax credit, should then be aggregated with the other investment income, leaving only two categories of apportionable income, namely estate income and investment income;

    (v) A special treatment is then given (para. 9(2)) to trading companies (but not companies in a trading group) for estate income. (Prior to 1980 trading income was subject to apportionment so that originally the abatement applied to trading and estate income. If such income were less than £25,000 it was ignored; if between £25,000 and £75,000 it was reduced by one half of the difference between £75,000 and the amount of such income. Now the apportionment of trading income no longer operates the figures of £25,000 and £75,000 are reduced in the proportion that the estate income bears to the total estate and trading income);

    (vi) The amount of investment income is also abated by the smaller of £3,000 or 10 per cent. of the total unabated estate and trading income. For companies which are neither trading companies nor members of a trading group £1,000 is substituted for £3,000 as the maximum abatement of investment income.

    (vii) The relevant income is 50 per cent. of the abated estate income plus 100 per cent. of the abated investment income.

    (viii) The excess is liable to be apportioned unless it is £1,000 or less or can be justified on the basis of business requirements. The £1,000 exemption does not apply to companies that are not trading companies or members of a trading group.

[86] See above at § 5.32.

[87] Income assessed under Schedules A, B or D which arises from the ownership or occupation of land.

benefit from abatement[88] and which will in any event attract a 50 per cent. reduction in the calculation of relevant income;

(iii) Interest may be excluded from distributable income[89] if it is covered by charges or other amounts capable of being off-set against total profits.

**5.54**

*Capitalisation of Retentions*

It frequently happens that companies making substantial retentions of profits will capitalise those retentions and make bonus issue to shareholders in respect of them. Such a practice has two apparent advantages for the company:

(i) it helps to keep actual capital and nominal capital in step; and

(ii) it will assist in maintaining the marketability of its shares. The point is that a company with a successful record and with a consistently high level of retention will find that its shares earn a high dividend and will be quoted above their nominal values, often to a high degree. Some investors display prejudice against "over-heavy" shares and it is generally accepted that shares with lower values enjoy a wider market. A bonus issue can reduce the nominal rate of dividend and thereby prevent the shares from becoming too heavy.

**5.55**

*Capitalisation: The Consequences*

An issue of bonus ordinary shares involves no distribution and as such no ACT consequences. However, if any bonus *redeemable* share capital or any security is issued by a company in respect of shares or securities of the company this is treated as a distribution, albeit a non-qualifying one.[90]

During the late 1960s/early 1970s some companies (especially investment trusts) on declaring a dividend gave shareholders the option of taking the dividend in cash or in the form of bonus shares. The advantage to the company was that the bonus shares issued did not rank as distributions and initially such an issue conferred an advantage on the shareholder as well in that the bonus shares received were not treated as income. Since 1975,[91] however, this latter advantage has ceased to apply with the shareholder being liable to tax at the higher rates on the basis of the equivalent cash dividend grossed up at the basic rate. This provision also applies where a class of shares gives a right to receive bonus shares and it seems that it catches "split level" investment trusts which provide for income shares to receive cash dividends and capital shares to receive bonus issues. In such cases the charge to tax wil be on the grossed-up market value of the bonus shares issued.

---

[88] See above at § 5.50 n. 67.

[89] Surplus franked investment income may also be excluded from distributable income if a claim is made under I.C.T.A. 1970, s.254 (losses and some capital allowances) is possible—s.255.

[90] I.C.T.A. 1970, s.233(2)(c) (substituted by F.A. 1972, Sched. 22, para. 2) non-qualifying distributions are distributions giving the recipient a potential claim on the profits of the company at a future date. They involve no liability for ACT on the part of the company and confer no tax credit on the recipient.

[91] F (No. 2) Act 1975, s.34 and Sched. 8.

# 6. Public Issue

The making of a public issue of securities is an important method of raising large amounts of long-term capital.[1] It is a form of financing however that is not available to all companies since it necessarily requires access to the securities markets. To secure such access a company must have complied or be in a position to comply with the provisions of the Companies Acts governing the issue of securities to the public[2] and to meet the requirements governing the admission of securities to the Stock Exchange Official List, the Unlisted Securities Market or an Over-the-Counter Market as the case may be.

**6.01**

In the United Kingdom a public issue may take one of a number of forms, namely—

**6.02**

## (a) Issue by prospectus

In a prospectus issue the company itself offers directly to the public a fixed number of shares at a specified price. The foundation of the issue is a prospectus[3] which has to be advertised and which includes an application form by means of which intending investors may subscribe. The issue is prepared and managed by an issuing house[4] acting as agent for the company. The issuing house also underwrites the issue for which it receives a fee or underwriting commission. In practice the underwriters will often arrange for the issue to be sub-underwritten with investing institutions such as pension funds and life assurance companies.

*Types of Public Issue*

## (b) Offer for sale

As in a prospectus issue securities made available for public subscription in an offer for sale are offered at a fixed price. With this method however the company issues the relevant securities en bloc to an issuing house (or stockbroker) at an agreed price. The securities are then resold by the issuing house or broker (acting in this situation as principal) to the public. The issuing house may sell the securities at the same price, in which case its remuneration will be in the form of

---

[1] In the eurobond markets it is quite common for public issues to be made of notes raising short or medium—term loan capital.

[2] In practice the largest subscribers to public issues are financial institutions. The Wilson Committee found (Appendix III, para. 3.327) that of listed U.K. company securities financial institutions held half of the ordinary shares, three-quarters of the preference shares and just over half of the loan capital. Of the institutions, the investing institutions (insurance companies, pension funds, investment trust companies and unit trusts) were by far the largest holders of such securities.

[3] See below at §§ 6.09 *et seq.*

[4] See below at §§ 6.27 *et seq.*

a fee, or the price may be fixed marginally higher, the differential being sufficient to cover the costs relating to the sale and to provide remuneration for the issuing house.

The basis of an offer for sale is also a prospectus which, as in the case of a prospectus issue, has to be advertised. A further similarity is that the offer will usually be sub-underwritten.

### (c) Issue by tender

An issue by tender differs from a prospectus issue or an offer for sale only in that the securities are not offered to the public at a fixed price. The prospectus in respect of such an issue will state only a minimum price, the public being invited to submit a tender specifying the price and the number of shares or amount of stock they would accept at this price. The total issue is allocated at the highest price which will clear the securities on offer.

### (d) Placing[5]

A placing resembles an offer for sale in that the securities are acquired first by an issuing house or broker. It differs however in that instead of being resold to the public the shares or stock are "placed" with clients (in practice, almost always institutions). Flotations on the Unlisted Securities Market are often made in this way, given the small size of some of the issues. For companies seeking a full Stock Exchange listing permission of the Stock Exchange Council is required.[6]

### (e) Rights issues[7]

A rights issue is the primary method[8] employed by a company to raise further capital from its existing shareholders by conferring on them a right to subscribe cash for further securities in the company in proportion to their existing holdings. Generally such issues are made at a discount to the ruling market price with the consequence that shareholders who do not wish to take up their rights may sell them in the market. Issues by companies with a Stock Exchange listing are normally underwritten by an issuing house (with sub-underwriting by the institutions).

---

[5] Placings are sometimes confused with "introductions," the latter being merely the name for the operation whereby securities already in issue but which lack a Stock Exchange listing or other market quotation are introduced to that market. While an introduction is a convenient method of creating a market in existing securities it is not a means whereby a company can raise new funds. Since no securities are offered to the public in an introduction no prospectus is required. Nevertheless, where a full listing is sought the Stock Exchange requires the placing of an advertisement in the prescribed form and for the directors of the company to accept responsibility for the accuracy of the information given. Admission of Securities to Listing, section 2, Chapter 3, para. 3.

[6] See further below at § 6.23.

[7] See further at § 2.70 above and at § 6.41, below.

[8] Placings are occasionally used if the amount to be raised is small and Stock Exchange permission is obtained.

Rights issues by public companies must be made by way of prospectus although the prospectus may be in an abridged form.[9]

## REQUIREMENTS OF THE COMPANIES ACTS

The Companies Acts lay down certain minimum requirements with which a company intending to make a public issue of securities must comply. These requirements:

**6.03**

(a) restrict the categories of company that may offer securities to the public; and

(b) provide for the disclosure of specified information about the company.

**Companies permitted to offer securities to the public**

Section 81 of the Companies Act 1985 effectively provides that only public companies may make issues of securities to the public by making it an offence[10] for a private company[11]:

**6.04**

*The Company Issuing*

(1) to offer to the public (whether for cash or otherwise) any shares in or debentures of the company;

(2) to allot, or agree to allot, (whether for cash or otherwise) any shares in or debentures of the company with a view to all or any of these shares or debentures being offered for sale to the public.[12]

*Securities Must be a Public Company*

A public company is defined[13] as a company limited by shares or limited by guarantee and having a share capital being a company the memorandum of which states that the company is to be a public company and in respect of which the registration requirements relating to public companies have been complied with.

It follows, therefore, that if a company wishing to raise capital through a public issue of securities is not a public company it must take steps to become one. This may be achieved by the passing of a special resolution altering its memorandum and articles of association and by re-registration as a public company.[14]

*Conversion of Private Company into Public Company*

The special resolution should:

**6.05**

(a) authorise steps to be taken to re-register the company as a public company; and, to that end,

(b) make such alterations to the ompany's memorandum as are necessary to

*(1) Special Resolution*

---

[9] C.A. 1985, s.56 (5)(*a*).

[10] A company committing an offence under C.A. 1985, s.81 and any officer of the company who is in default is liable on conviction on indictment to a fine and on summary conviction to a fine not exceeding the statutory maximum: s.81(2).

[11] Other than a company limited by guarantee and not having a share capital: s.81(1).

[12] However the prohibition in s.81 is not to affect the validity of any allotment or sale of shares or debentures or of any agreement to allot or sell shares or debentures: s.81(3).

[13] C.A. 1985, s.1(3).

[14] *Ibid.* s.43(2).

bring it into conformity with the statutory specifications[15] for memoranda of public companies; and

(c) make such alterations to the company's articles as are requisite in the circumstances.

**6.06**

*(2) Capital Requirements*

At the time the special resolution is passed the nominal value of the company's allotted share capital must not be less than the statutory authorised minimum,[16] currently fixed at £50,000,[17] and each of the shares allotted must be paid up at least as to one-quarter of the nominal value of that share and the whole of any premium on it.[18] However, where a company has allotted shares in pursuance of an employees' share scheme and those shares have not been so paid up they may be disregarded and treated as if they were not part of the allotted share capital of the company for the purpose of determining whether the company has met the statutory requirements[19] for a public company.[20]

Where shares are allotted[21] as fully or partly paid and payment for those shares and for any premium thereon takes a form other than cash or includes a non-cash element that non-cash element must have been subjected to an independent expert valuation[22] and a valuation report must have been made to the company during the six months immediately preceding the allotment. In cases where the consideration for an allotment consists of or includes an undertaking to do work or perform services, however, that undertaking must have been discharged by the date of the special resolution.[23] Any other undertaking comprising or forming part of the consideration must be discharged within five years of that date.[24]

**6.07**

*(3) Registration Requirements*

After the passing of the special resolution an application for re-registration may be made by the Registrar of Companies.[25] The application should be in the prescribed form and signed by a director or secretary of the company.[26] The application should be accompanied by the following documents, that is to say[27]:

(a) a printed copy of the memorandum and articles as altered in pursuance of the resolution;

---

[15] *Ibid.* ss.43(2)(*h*). The model form of memorandum for a public company is contained in the Companies (Alteration of Table A etc.) Regs 1984 (S.I. 1984 No. 1717), Table F.

[16] *Ibid.* s.45(2)(*a*).

[17] *Ibid.* s.118(1). The statutory authorised minimum may be altered from time to time by statutory instrument: *ibid.*

[18] *Ibid.* s.45(2)(*b*).

[19] *i.e.* those contained in C.A. 1985, ss.43–47.

[20] C.A. 1985, s.45(5)(*b*).

[21] This provison applies only to allotments made by the company between the "balance sheet date" and the passing of the special resolution (C.A. 1985, s.44(1)). The relevant balance sheet must have been prepared at a date not more than seven months before the application for re-registration as a public company—*ibid.* s.43(4).

[22] C.A. 1985, ss.44(1) and (2).

[23] *Ibid.* s.45(4)(*a*).

[24] *Ibid.* s.45(4)(*b*).

[25] *Ibid.* s.45(2)(*b*).

[26] *Ibid.*

[27] *Ibid.* s.43(3).

(b) a copy of a written statement by the auditors of the company that in their opinion the relevant balance sheet[28] shows that at the balance sheet date the amount of the company's net assets was not less than the aggregate of its called-up share capital and undistributable reserves[29];

(c) a copy of the relevant balance sheet, together with a copy of an unqualified report[30] by the company's auditors in relation to that balance sheet;

(d) a copy of any valuation report required in relation to non-cash consideration given in payment for shares allotted between the balance sheet date and the passing of the special resolution[31]; and

(e) a statutory declaration in the prescribed form by a director or secretary of the company that:

(1) the special resolution has been passed and the conditions governing the capital requirements of public companies satisfied; and that

(2) between the balance sheet date and the application of the company for re-registration, there has been no change in the financial position of the company that has resulted in the amount of the company's net assets becoming less than the aggregate of the called-up share capital and undistributable reserves.

The Registrar may accept the statutory declaration as sufficient evidence that the special resolution has been passed and the capital requirements satisfied.[32]

If the Registrar is satisfied that the company may be re-registered as a public company he is required to issue the company with a certificate of incorporation stating that the company is a public company.[33] Upon the issue of the certificate, the company shall by virtue of such issue become a public company and the alterations in the memorandum and articles set out in the special resolution will

*Re-Registration as a Public Company*

---

[28] *Ibid.* s.43(4).

[29] *Ibid.*

[30] s.46(2) and (3) provides that an unqualified report means, in relation to the balance sheet of a company:

    (a) if the balance sheet was prepared in respect of an accounting reference period of the company an auditors' report (made in pursuance of ss.236(2) and 262 which states without material qualification:

        (i) that in the opinion of the person making the report, the balance sheet has been properly prepared in accordance with the provisions of the Companies Acts; and

        (ii) that in the opinion of the person making the report, the balance sheet gives a true and fair view of the state of the company's affairs as at the balance sheet date; and

    (b) in any other case, a report stating without material qualification:

        (i) that in the opinion of the person making the report the balance sheet complies with the requirements of ss.228 and 238 (contents, form and signing of accounts); and

        (ii) that (except where the company has brought itself within one of the exemptions from the statutory requirements as to accounts) the balance sheet gives a true and fair view of the state of the company's affairs as at the balance sheet date.

A qualification is treated as being "not material" in relation to a balance sheet of the person making the report states in writing that the matter giving rise to the qualification is not material for determining (by reference to the balance sheet) whether at the balance sheet date the amount of the company's net assets was not less than the aggregate of its called-up share capital and undistributable reserves: s.46(5).

[31] *Ibid.* s.44(2)(*b*).

[32] *Ibid.* s.47(2). However where it appears to the Registrar that a court order has been made confirming a reduction in the company's capital which has the effect of bringing the nominal value of the company's allotted share capital below the authorised minimum the Registrar may not issue a certificate of re-registration: s.47(3).

[33] *Ibid.* s.47(1). The Registrar will retain the application and other documents delivered to him.

take effect accordingly.[34] A certificate of incorporation issued to a company is conclusive evidence that the requirements of the Companies Acts in respect of re-registration and of the matters precedent and incidental thereto have been complied with and that the company is a public company.[35]

### Disclosure

**6.08**    Where institutional or other finance is made available to a company in pursuance of a privately negotiated funding agreement the general rule is that in the absence of the provision to the contrary in the agreement it is the responsibility of the party providing the funds to satisfy himself that the company is a suitable object for its investment.[36] In the case of a public issue of securities statute places upon the company soliciting funds a duty to make disclosures about its affairs in the douments relating to the issue.

**6.09**    **Prospectuses**

Public issues of securities are made by reference to a "prospectus" which section 744 of the Companies Act 1985 defines as meaning, unless the context
*Companies*       otherwise requires, "any prospectus, notice, circular, advertisement or other
*Act 1985,*       invitation, offering to the public for subscription or purchase any shares or
*s.744*            debentures of the company." It is through the rules governing the form and content of prospectuses that the system of disclosure operates.

**6.10**    To qualify as a prospectus a document must offer securities to the public for *subscription* or *purchase*. In *Governments Stock and Other Securities Investment Company* v. *Christoper.*[37] Wynn-Parry J. had to consider whether a circular inviting an exchange of shares was a prospectus within the terms of section 744. The case arose out of the merger. between the Union Castle and Clan Lines which was to be effected by the creation of a new company, British and Commonwealth Shipping. Shares in Britain and Commonwealth were to be allotted to holders of Union Castle and Clan Line shares in return for their shares in those companies. It was held that the circular was not a prospectus since, *inter alia,* the exchange of shares proposed did not amount to an offer for the subscription or purchase of securities.

The invitation was said not to amount to an offer to subscribe for securities since this required the taking or agreeing to take shares for cash. In arriving at this conclusion the learned judge purported to follow *Arnison* v. *Smith.*[38] This decision, however, was disapproved by the Privy Council in *Akerhielm* v. *de Mare*[39] where it was held that a statement in a prospectus that share capital had been "subscribed" did not necessarily mean "subscribed for cash," its being sufficient for the shares in question to have been allotted in return for a consideration in money or money's worth (in this case patent rights and formation

---

[34] *Ibid.* s.47(4).
[35] *Ibid.* s.47(5).
[36] See above at §§ 1.21 *et seq.*
[37] [1956] 1 W.L.R. 237.
[38] (1889) 41 Ch.D. 348, *per* Kekewich J. and C.A.
[39] [1959] A.C. 789, P.C.

expenses). In *Broken Hill Proprietary Co. Ltd.* v. *Bell Resources Ltd*[40] Hampel J. sitting in the Supreme Court of Victoria, refused to follow *Christopher's* case holding that Wynn-Parry J.'s decision was not supported by the authorities relied on and was wrong. This case concerned an offer by Bell Resources to acquire shares in Broken Hill Proprietary in return for alternative considerations, both alternatives however including shares in Bell Resources. It was accepted that on this point the case was indistinguishable from *Christopher's* case. Hampel J. felt that a "close examination of the authorities on which His Lordship relied to conclude that the word 'subscription' in the definition of 'prospectus' means 'taking or agreeing to take shares for cash' shows in my view that they do not support such a conclusion. I can see no basis in law or in principle, having regard to the legislative scheme contained in the Companies [Acts], for limiting the definition in the way His Lordship did. There is no reason, in my view, why the provisions of the [Act] should be interpreted so as to deprive people who subscribe in shares in consideration for other shares of the protection of [s.58]. It is arguable that even greater protection is necessary in these circumstances."[41] It is suggested therefore that, on this point at least, *Christopher's* case may no longer be authoritative.

The ruling that the invitation in the circular did not amount to an offer for the purchase[42] of securities rested on the ground that the shares in British and Commonwealth Shipping were as yet unissued and as such could not be subject of an offer for purchase.[43] This ruling did not, however, cover situations where the securities had been issued, whether or not they had been taken up. Nevertheless if an exchange of such securities were to be regarded as *not* amounting to a purchase this would have the effect of restricting the form of consideration permissible to money. There is nothing in section 744 or elsewhere, it is suggested, to warrant such a construction.

Where the issue takes the form of an offer for sale the situation is covered by section 58 of the 1985 Act. This provides that where a company allots to agrees to allot any shares in or debentures of the company with a view to all or any of those shares or debentures being offered for sale to the public, any document by which the offer for sale to the public is made is for all purposes to be deemed to be a prospectus issued by the company and all enactments and rules of law as to the content of the prospectus, or otherwise relating thereto, are to apply and have effect accordingly as if the shares or debentures had been offered to the public for subscription, and as if the persons accepting the offer in respect of any

---

[40] (1984) 8 A.C.L.R. 609.

[41] *Ibid.* at p. 617. *Sed quaere.* While it can be argued that the statement of Kekewich J. (1889) 41 Ch.D. at p. 357) purporting to define "subscription" does not necessarily involve payment in cash, Wynn-Parry J. also relied on judgments in the Court of Appeal in *Chicago Railway Terminal Elevator Co.* v. *IRC* (1896) 75 L.T. 157 and *Brown* v. *IRC* (1900) 84 L.T. 71. Both cases concerned schemes of arrangement involving the exchange of bonds in one company for bonds in another company. In both cases the court had to decide, *inter alia*, whether such exchanges amounted to offers for subscription within the meaning of section 82(1)(*b*)(i), (ii) of the Stamp Act 1891, and in both cases the Court held that such exchanges did not. "The giving up of old bonds in exchange for new bonds is not subscribing to the new bonds." *Per* Smith M.R. in *Brown* v. *I.R.C.* (1900) 84 L.T. at p. 79.

[42] Following *Re V G M Holdings Ltd.* [1942] Ch. 23J C.A.

[43] [1956] 1 W.L.R. at p. 241.

269

shares or debentures were subscribers for those shares or debentures.[44] Further-more the provisions of section 64 as to the dating and registration of prospec-tuses[45] are to have effect as though the persons making the offer were persons named in the prospectus as directors of the company[46] and the rules as to con-tent contained in sections 56, 57 and 66[47] are to have effect with the addition of two further matters, namely:

(1) the net amount of the consideration received or to be received by the company in respect of the securities to which the offer relates; and

(2) the place and time at which the contract under which the said securities have been or are to be allotted may be inspected.[48]

**6.11**   The invitation offering shares for subscription or purchase must be made to "the public." In *Sleigh* v. *Glasgow and Transvaal Options*[49] the Court of Session held that a circular placed in the hands of 40 friends of the directors and intended to be shown by them to their friends was not an invitation to the public. And in *Sherwell* v. *Combined Incandescent Mantles Syndicate*[50] it was held that the printing of 1,000 copies of an offer document and the circulation of 200 of them by the directors and promoter amongst their friends was not such an invitation since the offer must be to any person who chose to take up the shares.

Section 59 of the Companies Act 1985 provides that any reference in the Act or in the articles of association of a company to "the public" is to be construed as including a reference to "any section of the public whether selected as members or debenture holders of the company concerned or as clients of the person issu-ing the prospectus or in any other manner." Section 60(1) then qualifies this pro-viding that section 59 "shall not be taken as requiring any offer or invitation to be treated as made to the public if it can properly be regarded, in all the circum-stances, as not being calculated to result, directly or indirectly, in the shares or debentures becoming available for subscription or purchase by persons other than those receiving the offer or invitation, or otherwise as being a domestic con-cern of the persons making and receiving it. . . . "[51]

---

[44] C.A. 1985, s.58(1) and (2). Under s.58(3) it is, unless the contrary is proved, evidence that an allotment of, or an agreement to allot, securities was made with a view to those securities being offered for sale to the public if it is show:
  (1) that an offer of any of the securities was made to the public within 6 months after the allot-ment or agreement to allot, or
  (2) that at the date when the offer was made the whole consideration for the securities had not been received by the company.

[45] See below at § 6.13.

[46] C.A. 1985, s.58(2).

[47] See below at §§ 6.14 *et seq.*

[48] C.A. 1985, s.58(4).

[49] (1904) 6 F. 420.

[50] (1907) 23 T.L.R. 482. However see *Re South of England Natural Gas Co.* [1911] 1 Ch. 573 where the distribution of 3,000 copies of an offer document to all members of certain gas companies was held to be an offer to the public.

[51] Section 60(1) continues " . . . and in particular a provision in the company's articles prohibiting invitations to the public to subscribe for shares or debentures shall not be taken as prohibiting the making to members or debebture holders of an invitation which can properly be regarded as afor-esaid." This provision is intended to safeguard the position of private companies by removing all doubt that, in such a company a pre-emptive offer of a new issue of securities to existing holders is not within s.59.

Where the form of issue is a placing it may be difficult to determine whether or not the issue can be properly regarded as being calculated to result directly or indirectly in the securities becoming available for subscription or purchase by persons other than those receiving the offer or invitation. It has been suggested[52] that where an issuing house places the whole or part of a new issue privately with a few institutional investors who have agreed to hold the securities as long-term investments the issue is not made to the public. The problem with this is that section 60(1) makes no mention of any timescale although alienation by the subscribers at some point must be taken as implicit. Another suggestion[53] is that a distinction can be drawn between public placings for which a securities market quotation is sought and purely private placings, a distinction of increasig significance in view of the preponderence of quotations on the Unlisted Securities Market obtained in respect of placings. The distinction however does not explain how purely private placings made in the expectation that a market quotation would be obtained after a period of time are to be accommodated within the terms of section 60(1). It may be that section 58(3) could be applied by analogy, this providing that it is evidence that an offer for sale of securities was made to the public if the offer was made to the public within six months after the allotment or agreement to allot or that at the date when the offer was made the whole consideration to be received by the company had not been so received.[54] *Sed quaere.*

*Placings*

A corresponding difficulty has been experienced in respect of rights issues. While section 59 is apparently in principle providing that such issues are to be regarded as being made to the public it is now clear that in certain circumstances rights issues may fall within the section 60 exclusion. Thus in *Governments Stock and other Securities Investment Company Ltd.* v. *Christopher*[55] an offer of shares was made to the shareholders of two companies on a rights basis. The terms of the offer were such that only those shareholders receiving it were entitled to accept and on acceptance received non-renounceable letters of allotment. It was held that since the only persons capable of accepting were the shareholders to whom the offer had been addressed[56] the offer came within the section 60 exclusion and so could not be regarded as having been made to the public. It seems clear, however, that had the letters of allotment been renounceable in favour of purchasers or other assignees the offer could be said to have been calculated to result in the shares becoming available for subscription or purchase by persons other han those receiving it and therefore outside section 60.

*Rights Issues*

Every prospectus issued by or on behalf of a company must be dated and that date, unless the conrary is proved, is to be taken as the date of the publication.[57]

**6.12**

---

[52] Palmer, at para. 21–17.
[53] Gore-Browne, at para. 10.4.
[54] See Gore-Browne, *op.cit.*
[55] [1956] 1 W.L.R. 237.
[56] *Ibid.* at p. 242 *per* Wynn-Parry J., "The test is not who received the circular but who can accept the offer."
[57] C.A. 1985, s.63.

On or before the date of publication a copy of the prospectus signed by every person named therein as a director (or proposed director) or by his agent authorised in writing must be delivered to the Register of Companies for registration.[58] The copy must be accompanied by a number of documents attached thereto or endorsed thereon. These are:

> (a) any consent to the issue of the prospectus required to be given by an expert[59]; and
>
> (b) in the case of a prospectus issued generally, that is to persons who are not existing members or debenture holders of the company[60]:
>
>> (i) a copy of, or memorandum of particulars of, all material contracts referred to in the prospectus[61]; and
>>
>> (ii) a statement signed by any persons who have made a report which is incorporated in the prospectus setting out any adjustments which they have made in that report.[62]

Until delivered to the Registrar the prospectus may not be issued[63] and when issued it must on its face bear a statement that it has been so delivered for registration and that statement must specify or refer to all documents which are required to be endorsed on or attached to the copy of the prospectus so delivered.[64]

### 6.13   Contents of prospectuses

*Companies*
*Act, 1985 s.56*
Section 56 of the Companies Act 1985 requires every prospectus issued by or on behalf of a company to contain all the matters specified in the Third Schedule[65] and renders void any condition purporting to compel an applicant for securities to waive compliance with the section or purporting to affect him with notice of any content, document or matter not specifically referred to in the prospectus.[66]

*Liability for*
*Non-Com-*
*pliance*
In view of the fundamental importance of section 56 it is perhaps surprising that the 1985 Act contains no provision[67] as to the consequences of failing to specify any of the matters required to be included in a prospectus. It seems clear, however, that some liability should result since section 66 purports to restrict such liability. Section 66 provides that in the event of non-compliance with or

---

[58] *Ibid.* s.64(1). In respect of every statement in the prospectus purported to be made by an expert, a consent by him to the issue of the prospectus with the statement included in the context and form in which it is included must be given: *ibid.* s.61.

[59] *Ibid.* ss.64(1)(*b*) and 61.

[60] *Ibid.* s.65(1).

[61] *Ibid.* s.65(2).

[62] *Ibid.* s.65(4).

[63] *Ibid.* s.64(1). If a prospectus is issued before delivery to the Registrar, or without the delivered copy having been endorsed or attached to the required documents, the company and every person knowingly a party to the issue will be liable to a fine of $\frac{1}{5}$ of the statutory maximum and, for continued contravention, to a daily default fine of $\frac{1}{50}$ of the statutory maximum from the date of issue to the date on which a copy is delivered for registration with the required documents endorsed thereon or attached thereto: *ibid.* s.64(5) and Sched. 24.

[64] *Ibid.* s.64(1).

[65] *Ibid.* s.56(1).

[66] *Ibid.* s.57.

[67] Except in respect of a contravention of s.56(2). This prohibits the issue of any application form unless in conjunction with a prospectus complying with s.56(1). Those contravening s.56(2) become liable to a fine: s.56(4).

contravention of any of the requirements of section 56 a director or other person responsible for the prospectus will not incur liability by reason of the non-compliance if he proves that:

(a) as regards any matter not disclosed he was not cogniscent thereof; or

(b) the non-compliance or contravention arose from an honest mistake of fact on his part; or

(c) the non-compliance or contravention was in respect of matters which in the opinion of the court dealing with the case were immaterial or was otherwise such as ought, in the opinion of the court, having regard to all the circumstances of the case, reasonably to be excused.[68]

It seems to be accepted that section 56 may form the basis of an action for damages against the directors and other persons responsible for the prospectus[69] although not an action for rescission[70] against the company, at least where the omission does not render the information included in the prospectus misleading.[71] The existence of a right to sue for damages rests on *dicta* of Swinfen-Eady J. in *Re South of England Natural Gas and Petroleum Co.*[72] and on the decision of the Court of Appeal in *Lynde* v. *Nash.*[73] This latter decision however was reversed by the House of Lords[74] on other grounds with the question of the right to damages being left open.[75] It follows, therefore, that the existence of such a right is not beyond question.

Part I of the Third Schedule to the Companies Act 1985[76] requires a company prospectus to specify the following matters: **6.14**

*Matters to be Specified in a Prospectus*

### (a) The company's business

Where the company has been carrying on a business the prospectus will invariably indicate the nature of that business. Paragraph 15 requires that the prospectus states the length of time the business has been carried on. In cases where the issue is being made to finance the acquisition of a business, and that business has

---

[68] According to Swinfen-Eady J. in *Re South of England Natural Gas and Petroleum Co.* [1911] 1 Ch. 573, 575 the effect of s.66(1) is "equivalent to saying that he [*i.e.* the director or other person responsible] is liable if he cannot prove" ignorance or mistake." In contrast, in s.66(2) the burden of proof of knowledge in the case of non-disclosure of the interest of a director in the promotion or property to be required falls on the plaintiff.

[69] See further below at § 6.28.

[70] In *Re Wimbledon Olympia* [1910] 1 Ch. 610 Neville J. felt that he could not "attribute to the legislature the intention that the mere fact of the omission of one of the facts required by this section to be stated should give the shareholders this right to get rid of their shares." Approved in respect of "unimportant matters" by Swinfen-Eady J. in the *South of England Gas* case [1911] 1 Ch. 573, 577.

[71] For a consideration of liability arising in respect of misleading statements see above at §§ 1.23 *et seq.* and below at §§ 6.17 *et seq.*

[72] [1911] 1 Ch. 573.

[73] [1928] 2 K.B. 93, C.A.

[74] *Sub nom. Nash* v. *Lynde* [1929] A.C. 158, H.L.

[75] Any person seeking damages under this possible right of action would, of course, have to show that he had suffered loss: *David* v. *Britannic Merthyr Coal Co.* [1909] 2 K.B. 146, C.A. at 157 *per* Fletcher Moulton L.J.

[76] Formerly Sched. 4 of C.A. 1948, as amended.

been carried on for less than three years, a corresponding disclosure must be made.

### (b) Share capital

If the prospectus invites the public to subscribe for shares in the company and the share capital of the company is divided into different classes of shares the prospectus must state the voting rights and the rights in respect of dividends and capital attached to the several classes of shares respectively.[77]

### (c) Founders, management or deferred shares

Paragraph 1(1)(a) of the Third Schedule requires the number of founders, management or deferred shares if any to be specified together with the extent of the interest of the holders of such shares in the property and profits of the company. To comply with paragraph 1(1)(a) the prospectus should contain details of the rights carried by such shares in respect of dividends and of assets in the event of winding up.[78]

### (d) The directors

Paragraph 1(1)(c) requires that the prospectus set out the names, addresses and descriptions of those persons who are directors of the company or who it is proposed should become directors. The requirement as to address is thought to refer to the residence of the person concerned rather than to his place of business.[79] The requirement as to description is usually satisfied by stating any qualifications held and by naming any other directorships held by the said person.

---

[77] C.A. 1985, Sched. 3, para. 14.

[78] C.A. 1985, does not actually define Founders or Management Shares, although they are in fact deferred shares in respect of which the holders do not become entitled to be paid a dividend until the preference and ordinary shareholders have been paid at a stipulated rate, the amount varying according to the terms on which the shares were issued. They thus carry an entitlement to the balance of a company's profits set aside for distribution with the consequence that where such profits are large the entitlement will be correspondingly large and will have a positive effect on the share price. The purpose in issuing such shares was to remunerate the promoters or founders of the company, or the underwriters of the share capital, by allotting to them such shares of a small nominal amount but carrying an entitlement to a substantial proportion of the net profits. The corollary of this, however, is that the existence of such shares diminishes the value of the company's ordinary shares since the right of ordinary shareholders to participate in large profits is restricted. The object of these provisions, therefore, is to inform potential subscribers as to the extent of such restrictions.
Sometimes, as an inducement to the public to subscribe for securities, the terms of issue would provide for one founder's or deferred share to be offered for every ordinary share taken. A similar motive lay behind the "dual capitalisation issues" which were popular in the 1920s and 1930s. Under the terms of these issues low denomination shares (of, say 1/–) where issued along with shares of high nominal values (of, say £1) but with each carrying the same entitlement as to dividends. See further on this matter Thomas, *op.cit.* at pp. 37–38.

[79] See *Story* v. *Rees* (1890) 24 Q.B.D. 748 where a requirement under a Rule of Court as to address was held to be satisfied by giving the residence of the person but that his place of business was insufficient.

*(e) Directors' qualifying shares*

Paragraph 1(1)(b) applies where the company's articles stipulate for a minimum shareholding as a qualification for any person to serve as a director. The nature and extent of this minimum shareholding must be specified, as must any provision in the articles relating to the remuneration of the directors.

As a matter of practice this requirement is usually met by reproducing verbatim any relevant provisions in the articles.

*(f) Securities issued otherwise than for cash*

Where shares or debentures have been issued or have been subject to an agreement for issue within the two preceding years as fully or partly paid up otherwise than in cash the prospectus must state the number and amount of such shares or debentures and the consideration involved. In the case of shares or debentures which are partly paid up the prospectus should also state the extent to which they are paid up.[80]

*(g) Options*

Where any person has or is entitled to be given an option to subscribe[81] for shares or debentures in the company the prospectus must state[82] the number, description and amount of the shares or debentures involved together with particulars as to:

(1) the period during which the option is exercisable;
(2) the price to be paid for the shares or debentures subscribed for under the option;
(3) the consideration, if any, given or to be given for the option or for the right to it; and
(4) the names and addresses of the persons to whom the option or the right to it was given or, if given to existing shareholders or debenture holders as such, the relevant shares or debentures.

*(h) Subscriptions and allotment*

The prospectus must state the time of the opening of the subscription lists[83] together with the amount payable on application and allotment on each share including the amount, if any, payable by way of a premium.[84] In the case of a second or subsequent offer of shares the prospectus must also state the amounts offered for subscription on each previous allotment made within the two preceding years, the amounts actually allotted, and the amounts, if any, paid on the

---

[80] C.A. 1985, Sched. 3, para. 5.
[81] Or to acquire from a person to whom they have been allotted or agreed to be allotted with a view to his offering them for sale: *ibid.* para. 4(3).
[82] *Ibid.* para. 4(2) and (3).
[83] *Ibid.* para. 3(1)(a).
[84] *Ibid.* para. 3(1)(b).

shares so allotted, including the amounts, if any, payable by way of premium.[85] Where it is intended that, even if the offer is not subscribed in full, the amount of the capital subscribed will be allotted in any event or on the satisfaction of specified conditions the prospectus must contain a statement to that effect and must set out the conditions, if any, to be satisfied.[86]

The prospectus must also state the minimum subscription for the issue, that is[87] the amount which in the opinion of the directors is the minimum amount which must be raised by the issue in order to provide for:

(1) the price of any property purchased or to be purchased out of the proceeds of the issue;
(2) any preliminary expenses payable by the company including underwriting commission;
(3) the repayment of moneys borrowed by the company in respect of any of the foregoing matters; and
(4) working capital.

Where provision for these matters is to be made otherwise than out of the proceeds of the issue, the amounts involved together with the sources from which they are to be provided (for example, from retention of past profits) must also be specified.[88]

There is no statutory provision as to what the minimum subscription shall be in the case of any issue. The matter is left entirely to the discretion of the directors. Where however the amounts specified in the prospectus in relation to the minimum subscription are the result of an unreasonable error of judgment causing them to be substantially at variance with the true figures this inaccuracy will constitute a material mis-statement which may give rise to an action for the rescission of the contract of allotment or for damages or indeed involve those responsible in criminal liability.[89]

The requirement to specify the minimum subscription for an issue or shares applies to all prospectuses relating to the issue of shares to the public.[90] Where the prospectus relates to the first such issue, however, it is provided that failure to attain the specified figure has the consequence that no allotment of shares may be made.[91]

### (i) Property

Paragraphs 6 to 8 of Schedule Three were aimed at a device which was at one time employed to procure a hidden profit for the promoters of a company out of the proceeds of issue. Essentially the device related to a property or business whose owners agreed to sell a nominee of the promoters who in turn procured the sale to the company at a profit which the promoters received and retained.

[85] *Ibid.* para. 3(2).
[86] C.A. 1985, s.84(1).
[87] C.A. Sched. 3, para. 2(*a*).
[88] *Ibid.* para. 2(*b*).
[89] See above at §§1.21 *et seq.* and below at §§6.18 *et seq.*
[90] Contrary to the view expressed in Palmer, op cit at para. 21–22.
[91] C.A. 1985 s.83(1).

Paragraph 6 now requires the disclosure of information in relation to "property purchased or acquired by the company or proposed so to be purchased or acquired which is to be paid for wholly or partly out of the proceeds of the issue offered for subscription by the prospectus." In addition, the disclosure requirements also apply to property the purchase or acquisition of which has not been completed at the date of the issue of the prospectus other than property as respects which the purchase money is not material or property the contract for the purchase or acquisition of which was entered into in the ordinary course of the company's business, the contract not being made in contemplation of the issue (nor the issue in consequence of the contract.)[92]

With respect to any property subject to paragraph 6 the prospectus must contain details of the following matters,[93] namely:

(1) the names and addresses of the vendors[94] (although where the vendors are a firm the members of the firm are not to be treated as separate vendors[95];

(2) the amount (if any) paid or payable as purchase money for any such property in cash, shares or debentures, specifying the amount (if any) payable for goodwill[96];

(3) the amount payable in cash, shares or debentures to the vendor, and where there is more than one separate vendor, or where the company is a sub-purchaser, the amount so payable to each vendor[97]; and

(4) any transaction relating to the property completed within the two preceding years in which any vendor of the property to the company or any person who is, or was at the time of the transaction, a promoter or director or proposed director of the company had any interest direct or indirect.[98]

Para. 9(3) extends the ambit of paragraph 6 to cover cases where property to be acquired by the company is to be taken on lease.[99]

## (j) Material contracts

Paragraph 11 requires the disclosure of the dates of, parties to and general nature of any material contracts entered into within the two years preceding the

---

[92] Sched. 3, para. 5.

[93] *Ibid.* paras. 7 and 8.

[94] By virtue of para. 9(2) the word "vendor" here includes, as well as the immediate vendor to the company, every person who has entered into a contract, absolute or conditional for the sale or purchase of any option of purchase of any property to be acquired by the company, where either the purchase money is not fully paid before the publication of the prospectus, or the purchase money is to be paid wholly or in part out of the proceeds of the issue, as the contract depends for its validity or fulfilment on the result of the issue.

[95] C.A. 1985, Sched. 3, para 9(4).

[96] *Ibid.* para. 8.

[97] *Ibid.* para. 7(*b*).

[98] *Ibid.* para. 7(*c*).

[99] By defining "vendor" to include "lessor" and the words "purchase money" to include the "consideration for the lease" and "sub-purchaser" to include a "sub-lessee." The comments of Gore-Browne (Appendix B–2) that "it is not clear whether the words "to be taken on lease" include the case of the company purchasing an "existing lease" and that, if not, such transactions would be outside the scope of the disclosure provisions seem misplaced. Such transactions would appear to fall within the ordinary scope of para. 6 without having to rely on para. 9(3) at all.

date of issue of the prospectus. Taken with the disclosure of details of property transactions provided for in paragraph 6 it is thought that the effect is to compel disclosure of all transactions of the type referred to in § 6.14(h) above.

A material contract is one which is "calculated to influence persons reading a company's prospectus in making up their mind whether or not they will apply for shares."[1]

Excluded from the scope of paragraph 11 are contracts entered into in the ordinary course of the business carried on or intended to be carried on by the company.

### (k) Benefits to promoters

Paragraph 10(1)(c) requires the disclosure of any amount or benefit paid or given within the two preceding years or intended to be paid or given to any promoter, and the consideration for the payment for the giving of the benefits.

### (l) Directors interests

Full particulars of the nature and extent of any interest a director may have in the promotion of the company, or in property proposed to be acquired by the company must be disclosed in the prospectus.[2] In addition the prospectus must contain a statement of all sums paid or agreed to be paid to him in cash or shares or otherwise by any person either to induce him to become, or to qualify him as a director, or otherwise for services rendered by him in connection with the promotion or formation of the company.

Where the interest of such a director derives from his being a partner in a firm the disclosure provisions apply to the firm so that the prospectus must give details of the firm's interest, together with statements as to sums paid or agreed to be paid to the firm for services rendered by the firm in connection with the company promotion or formation.

Paragraph 13(3), however, provides that these provisions are not to apply to a prospectus issued more than two years after the date on which the company is entitled to commence business.

### (m) Commission and preliminary expenses

Paragraph 10(1) requires the disclosure of any amounts paid within the two preceding years, or payable, as underwriting commission on shares and debentures, or, alternatively, the rate of such commission. In *Booth* v. *New Afrikander Gold Mining Co.*[3] it was held that where the underwriting agreement provides for the payment of a lump sum it is not sufficient, or indeed appropriate, for the prospectus to disclose the rate only. It is not necessary to disclose the amounts payable to sub-underwriters.[4]

---

[1] *Per* Coleridge L.C.J., Grove and Lindley J.J. in *Twycross* v. *Grant* (1877) 2 C.P.D. 485. See also *Sullivan* v. *Mitcalfe* (1880) 5 C.P.D. 455, *per* Baggallay L.J. at p. 465.
[2] C.A. 1985, Sched. 3, para. 13.
[3] [1903] 1 Ch. 195.
[4] *Booth* v. *New Afrikander Gold Mining Co., supra.*

By virtue of paragraph 10(1)(*b*) the prospectus must disclose the amount or estimated amount of preliminary expenses and the persons by whom any of these expenses have been paid or are payable. However, para. 10(2) provides that it will not affect a prospectus issued more than two years after the date on which the company is entitled to commence business.

Paragraph 10(1)(*b*), however, also concerns the expenses of issue so that the amount or estimated amount of such expenses and the persons by whom any of those expenses have been paid or are payable must be disclosed. It should be noted that paragraph 10(2) does *not* apply to the expenses of issue.

### (n) Auditors

Paragraph 12 requires the prospectus to state the names and addresses of the auditors (if any) of the company.

### (o) Offers for sale

Where the prospectus relates to an offer for sale of shares or debentures to the public section 58(4) of the Companies Act 1985 requires two additional matters to be disclosed, namely:

(1) the net amount of the consideration received or to be received by the company in respect of the shares or debentures to which the offer relates; and

(2) the place and time at which the contract under which the shares or debentures have been or are to be alloted may be inspected.[5]

Part II of the Third Schedule to the Companies Act 1985 requires a prospectus **6.15** to set out reports by the auditors of the company and, in certain circumstances, by accountants. In this latter case the accountants must be named in the prospectus.[6]

### (a) Auditor's reports

Paragraph 16(1) requires a prospectus to contain a report by the company's auditors dealing with the company's profits and losses, assets and liabilities and dividends.

(1) *Profits and losses*. The auditors' reports must deal with the profits and losses of the company for each of the five financial years[7] immediately preceding the issue of the prospectus.[8] If the company has subsidiaries the report may

---

[5] See above at §6.10.

[6] C.A. 1985, Sched. 3, para. 22(3).

[7] *Ibid.* para. 20 defines "financial year" for the purposes of Pt. II as meaning "the year in respect of which the accounts of the company, or of the business, as the case may be, are made up, and where by reason of any alteration of the date on which the financial year of the company or business terminates the accounts . . . have been made up for a period greater or less than a year that greater or less period shall . . . be deemed to be a financial year."

[8] *Ibid.* para. 16(2)(*a*). In the case of a company which has been carrying on business for less than five years para. 19 requires that the accounts should be made up for the relevant period of two, three or four years as the case may be.

either deal separately with the profits or losses of the various companies in the group or deal with them on a combined basis.[9] Alternatively, the report may deal with the profits or losses of the parent company separately while treating the profits and losses of the subsidiaries either on a combined or an individual basis.[10]

(2) *Assets and liabilities.* The report must deal with the assets and liabilities as at the last date to which the accounts of the company were made up.[11] As with profits and losses where the company has subsidiaries the report may deal with them on a combined or separate basis and, if the latter, the subsidiaries may be dealt with individually or together.[12]

(3) *Dividends.* The reports must detail the rate of dividends,[13] if any, paid by the company in respect of each of the five years[14] immediately preceding the issue of the prospectus giving the particulars of each class of shares on which such dividends were paid and particulars of the cases in which no dividends have been paid in respect of any class of shares in respect of any of these years.

If no accounts have been made up in respect of any part of the period of five years ending on a date three months before the issue of the prospectus the auditors' reports must contain a statement of that fact.[15]

### (b) Accountants' reports[16]

If the proceeds, or any part of the proceeds, of the issue are or is to be applied directly or indirectly in the purchase of a business paragraph 17 requires the prospectus to contain a report by accountants upon the profits and losses of the business in respect of each of the five financial years[17] immediately preceding the issue of the prospectus and upon the assets and liabilities of the business at the last date to which the accounts of the business were made up.

Where the proceeds, or any part of the proceeds, of the issue are or is to be applied directly or indirectly in any manner resulting in the acquisition by the company of shares in another company, and by reason of that acquisition or anything to be done in consequence thereof or in connection therewith, that other company will become a subsidiary of the company making the issue a corresponding report by accountants is required in relation to the profits and losses and assets and liabilities of the company to be taken over.[18] When this latter

---

[9] *Ibid.* para. 16(3)(*a*).
[10] *Ibid.*
[11] *Ibid.* para. 16(2)(*b*).
[12] *Ibid.* para. 16(3)(*b*).
[13] *Ibid.* para. 16(1)(*b*).
[14] See above at n.7.
[15] C.A. 1985, Sched. 3, para. 16(1).
[16] Any report by accountants required by Pt. II of the Sched. 3 must be made "by accountants qualified under this Act for appointment as auditors of a company . . . and shall not be made by an accountant who is an officer or servant or a partner of, or in the employment of any officer or servant, of the company, or of the company's subsidiary or holding company or of a subsidiary of the company's holding company": *ibid.* para. 22. "Officer" includes a proposed director but not an auditor. *ibid.*
[17] See above at n.7.
[18] C.A. 1985, Sched. 3, para. 18.

company has subsidiaries the reports may deal with the profits and losses and assets and liabilities either on a combined or a separate basis and, if the latter, the subsidiaries may be dealt with collectively or individually.[19] The accountants' report must indicate how the profits or losses of the company/group to be taken over would have concerned members of the company making the issue and what allowance would have fallen to be made, in relation to the assets and liabilities, for holders of other shares if the company had at all material times held the shares to be acquired.[20]

### (c) Adjustment to auditors' or accountants' reports

Where any report required to be included in a prospectus contains adjustments in relation to the figures for profit and loss or assets and liabilities, such adjustments having been considered necessary by the auditors of the report, a note of this fact must be incorporated therein.[21]

The disclosure requirements of Schedule Three need not be complied with in the following circumstances, namely: **6.16**

(a) where the issue is to existing holders of shares or debentures[22] whether the allotment letters are renounceable or non-renounceable[23];

(b) where application has been made to the Council of the Stock Exchange for admission of the securities to official listing and the Council has approved the listing particulars relative thereto[24];

(c) where the issue relates to shares or debentures which are in all respects uniform with shares or debentures previously issued and for the time being dealt in or listed on the Stock Exchange.[25]

### Defective information

Where a prospectus is substantively defective, its contents including false or misleading information or excluding material facts rendering the information given false or misleading,[26] civil and/or criminal liability may attach to the company or to its directors or other persons responsible for the prospectus. **6.17**

A prospectus is the foundation of the contract under which a company allots securities in return for the moneys subscribed by investors. The law of misrepresentation applies to such contracts of allotment as it applies to other contracts with the consequence that if it can be shown that the prospectus contains defec- **6.18**

*Civil Liability (1) Misrepresentation*

---

[19] *Ibid.* para. 18(3)(*b*).
[20] *Ibid.* para. 18(3)(*a*).
[21] *Ibid.* para. 21.
[22] Thereby covering rights and bonus issues insofar as such issues can be regarded as being made to the public and so requiring a prospectus.
[23] C.A. 1985, s.56(5)(*a*).
[24] Stock Exchange (Listing) Regulations 1984 (S.I. 1984 No. 716), reg. 7(1)(*b*).
[25] C.A. 1985, s.56(5)(*b*).
[26] In considering whether a prospectus is misleading the document must be read as a whole. See *Aaron's Reefs* v. *Twiss* [1896] A.C. 273, H.L; *R.* v. *Kylsant* [1932] 1 K.B. 442.

tive statements or omissions which are material and which can be shown to have induced subscriptions those aggrieved may:

(1) seek rescission of the contract whether the misrepresentation was fraudulent or not[27];

(2) affirm the contract and retain the securities allotted but sue for damages in respect of any loss suffered.

The principles governing such actions are in general the same as those applying to private funding agreements and as such reference should be made to the discussion at §§ 1.21 *et seq; ante*. However, a number of specific points arise in relation to their application to prospectuses.

### (a) Responsibility for prospectus contents

Where the securities to be subscribed for on the basis of the prospectus are to be admitted to official listing or to quotation on the unlisted securities market the directors of the company are made explicitly to accept responsibility for the accuracy of the information disclosed in the prospectus.[28]

### (b) Disclaimers

While theoretically it would be possible to insert disclaimers of responsibility (either a general disclaimer or a disclaimer confined to specified matters) into prospectuses[29] the practicalities of capital raising through the British securities markets (investors would simply not subscribe) ensure that such clauses are not encountered in public issues in this country.

### (c) Offers for sale

A problem may exist concerning the applicability of the Misrepresentation Act 1967[30] to issues effected by way of an offer for sale. The point is that while there is nothing in the Act to prevent its application to contracts for the allotment of shares its drafting raises doubts as to whether its possible effect on companies issuing prospectus was within the draftsman's contemplation.[31] More specifically, since the Act makes available a remedy only to those who are parties to a contract it may be asked whether such a remedy can be available to a subscriber where the issue is made by way of an offer for sale? And, furthermore, if it is not, what substantive justification can there be for its application to issues by prospectus and not to offers for sale?

Prima facie, since the relevant contract is between the issuing house and the investor, it should follow that an action founded on the Act would lie against the

---

[27] See above at §§1.21 *et seq.*

[28] See below at §6.43 (admission to official listing) and §6.85 (admission to quotation on the USM).

[29] In *Commercial Banking Co.* v. *Brown* (1972) 126 C.L.R. 336 the High Court of Australia held that such a disclaimer was effective to exclude liability in negligence although not in deceit.

[30] The Misrepresentation Act 1967 does not apply to Scotland.

[31] See Gore-Browne, *op. cit.* at § 11.5.

issuing house rather than against the company. It is possible, however, that section 58 of the Companies Act 1985 could be pressed into service to provide a remedy directly against the company.

Section 58 provides that where an allotment or agreement to allot is made with a view to shares or debentures being offered for sale to the public "any document by which the offer for sale to the public is made shall for all purposes be deemed to be a prospectus issued by the company." Furthermore, "all enactments and rules of law as to the contents of prospectuses and to liability in respect of statements in and omissions from prospectuses shall apply and have effect accordingly as if the shares and debentures had been offered to the public for subscription and as if the persons accepting the offer in respect of any shares or debentures were subscribers for those shares or debentures." From this it would appear as though the company is deemed to be the contracting party for the purposes of the 1967 Act. However, section 58 concludes with the qualification that it is "without prejudice to the liability, if any, of the persons by whom the offer is made, in respect of misstatements contained in the document or otherwise in respect thereof."

It is suggested that while section 58 may operate to provide a remedy directly against the company it does not exclude any right of action against the issuing house so that an aggrieved investor may proceed against either.

**6.19**

*(2) Companies Act 1985, s.67*

In addition to and independently of any remedies under the law of misrepresentation, section 67 of the Companies Act 1985 gives a right of action to those who suffer loss as a result of subscribing for securities on the faith of a defective prospectus. A prospectus is defective for the purposes of section 67 if an untrue statement is contained in it, or in any report or memorandum contained in the prospectus or incorporated by reference into it or issued with it.[32] An untrue statement includes a statement which is misleading in the form and context in which it appears.[33]

The right of action under section 67 is available against:

(1) the directors of the company;
(2) every person who has authorised hismelf to be named in the prospectus as a director or as having agreed to become a director either immediately or after an interval of time;
(3) the promoters of the company; and
(4) any other persons authorising the defective prospectus.[34]

A right of action under section 67 must be pursued with due diligence. In England and Wales a limitation period of six years applies. Where no fraud is shown

---

[32] C.A. 1985, s.71.

[33] *Ibid*. s.71(*a*).

[34] *Ibid*. s.67(1). Where the director or other person against whom a right of action under s.67 exists has died the action may be brought against his estate. In England, by virtue of the Law Reform (Miscellaneous Provisions) Act 1934, such an action may be brought against the estate if the proceedings were pending at the date of death, or the cause of acton arose not more than six months before his death and proceedings are commenced not later than six months after the grant of representation. In Scotland (where the 1934 Act does not apply) an action will lie against the estate subject to a five year period of negative prescription.

the period runs from the time when the securities were alloted to the plaintiff[35]; where fraud is shown the period begins to run from the time the fraud was, or might with reasonable diligence have been, discovered.[36] In Scotland the action must be brought within five years from the date the loss occurred.[37] If, however, the subscriber is not aware and could not with reasonable diligence have become aware that the loss had occurred at that time the period[38] will be extended and will be regarded as running from such time as the subscriber became or ought to have become aware of the loss.[39]

The burden of proof in any action under section 67 is one the defendant, the point being that once the requirements for liability have been established that liability can only be avoided if one of the statutory defences can be employed. In order to avail himself of one or other of these defences the defendant must show:

(a) that, having consented to become a director, he withdrew his consent before the issue of the prospectus and that it was issued without his authority or consent[40]; or

(b) that the prospectus was issued without his knowledge or consent and that on becoming aware of its issue he gave reasonable public notice forthwith that it had been issued without his knowledge or consent[41] and

(c) that after the issue of the prospectus and before the allotment thereunder he, on becoming aware of an untrue statement therein, withdrew his consent thereto and gave reasonable notice of such withdrawal and the reasons therefor[42]; or

(d)(i) that as regards every untrue statement not purporting to be made by the authority of an expert[43] or of a public official document or statement, he had reasonable ground to believe, and did up to the time of allotment of the securities believe, that the statement was true; and

(ii) that as regards every untrue statement purporting to be a statement made by an expert or contained in what purports to be a copy of or extract from a report or valuation of an expert, it fairly represented the statement, or

---

[35] Limitation Act 1980, s.9.

[36] *Gibbs* v. *Guild* (1882) 9 Q.B.D. 9, C.A.; *Thorn* v. *Head* [1895] A.C. 495, H.L.; *Bulli Coal Mining Co.* v. *Osborne* [1899] A.C. 351, P.C.; *Oelkers* v. *Ellis* [1914] 2 K.B. 139.

[37] Prescription and Limitation (Scotland) Act 1973, s.6.

[38] A period of prescription rather than limitation.

[39] Prescription and Limitation (Scotland) Act 1973, s.11.

[40] C.A. 1985, s.68(1)(*a*).

[41] *Ibid*. s.68(1)(*b*).

[42] *Ibid*. s.68(1)(*c*).

[43] "Expert" is defined (by s.62) as including engineer, valuer, accountant and any other person whose profession gives authority to a statement made by him.
A person who has given his consent to a statement in a prospectus may be liable as a person who authorised the prospectus (within s.67(1)(*d*)), but only in respect of an untrue statement purporting to be made by him as an expert (s.68(3)). The following defences are available to such a person (s.68(5)).
  (1) that, having given his consent to the issue of the prospectus, he withdrew it in writing before delivery of a copy of the prospectus for registration; or
  (2) that, after delivery of a copy of the prospectus for registration and before allotment thereunder, he, on becoming aware of the statement, withdrew his consent in writing and gave reasonable public notice of the withdrawal, and of the reason therefor; or
  (3) that he was competent to make the statement and that he had reasonable ground to believe, and did believe, that the statement was true.

was a correct and fair copy of or extract from the report or valuation, and that he had reasonable ground to believe and did up to the time of the issue of the prospectus believe that the person making the statement was competent to make it and had given consent[44] (which had not been withdrawn) before delivery of a copy for registration[45] or, to the defendant's knowledge, before allotment thereunder; and

(iii) that as regards every untrue statement purporting to be a statement made by an official person or contained in what purports to be a copy of or extract from a public official document, it was a correct and fair representation of the statement or copy of or extract from the document.[46]

Persons responsible for the contents of prospectuses may, in addition to any civil liability that may result, be guilty of one or more criminal offences should the prospectus contain any misleading or untrue statements.

**6.20**

*Criminal Liability* (1) *Companies Act 1985, s.70*

Section 70 of the Companies Act 1985 provides that where a prospectus contains an untrue statement any person who authorised the issue of the prospectus shall be guilty of an offence. A person is not to be deemed to have authorised the issue of a prospectus for the purposes of this provision by reason only of his having given the consent required by section 61 of the Act to the inclusion therein of a statement purporting to be made by him as an expert.

"Untrue statement" is defined to include statements contained in any report or memorandum appearing on the face of the prospectus, or incorporated by reference into it, or issued with it.[47] A statement is deemed to be untrue if it is misleading in the form an context in which it is included.[48] The word "statement," however, appears to refer only to statements of fact, for it is not defined so as to include forecasts or promises. Incorrect or misleading profit or production forecasts therefore would seem to be outside the ambit of section 70.

It is not necessary to show intent to secure a conviction under section 70. Once the elements of the offence have been established a conviction must follow unless the defendant can bring himself within one or other of the following defences, namely:

(1) that the statement was immaterial; or
(2) that he had reasonable ground to believe and did, up to the time of the issue of the prospectus, believe that the statement was true.[49]

---

[44] Required under s.61.

[45] Under s.61.

[46] *Ibid.* s.68(2)(*c*). Where a person is sued along with others but is able, either as a director or as an expert, to bring himself within one of the applicable statutory defences, then those others who may be liable under s.67 become liable to indemnify him in respect of all damages, costs and expenses to which he may become liable by reason of his name being inserted in the prospectus or in defending himself in any action or legal proceedings brought against him in respect of the prospectus: *ibid.* s.69.

[47] *Ibid.* s.71(*b*).

[48] *Ibid.* s.71(*a*).

[49] The penalties imposed under s.70 are:
   (1) on conviction on indictment, imprisonment for a term not exceeding two years, or a fine, or both; or
   (2) on summary conviction, imprisonment for a term not exceeding six months, or a fine not exceeding the statutory maximum, or both.

**6.21** Section 70 is specifically stated as applying to prospectuses. Other provisions, wider in application, may nevertheless be applied in respect of false or misleading statements contained in prospectuses or in documents incorporated therein.

Section 13(1) of the Prevention of Fraud (Investments) Act 1958 makes it an offence for any person, by any statement, promise or forecast which he knows to be, misleading, false or deceptive, or by any dishonest concealment of material facts, or by the reckless making (dishonestly or otherwise) of any statement promise or forecast which is misleading, false or deceptive to induce or to attempt to induce another person to enter into or to offer to enter into any agreement for, or with a view to, acquiring, disposing of, subscribing for or underwriting securities.[50] For the purposes of section 13(1) a statement is reckless if it is a rash statement to make and without a real basis of facts on which to support it.[51]

*(2) Prevention of Fraud (Investments) Act 1958, s. 13(1)*

Section 19 of the Theft Act 1968 makes it an offence for any officer or person purporting to act as an officer of a body corporate, with intent to deceive its members or creditors about its affairs, to publish or to concur in publishing a written document or account which to his knowledge is or may be misleading, false or deceptive in a material particular. Section 19[52] was introduced to replace the more narrowly drafted section 84 of the Larceny Act 1861. In *R.* v. *Kylsant*[53] a prospectus stated that the company had paid dividends in every year over the period 1921–1927. This statement was true so far as it went. It omitted, however, to indicate that the dividends had been paid out of reserves rather than out of current profits; indeed, the company had been trading at a loss during this period. It was held that his omission constituted an offence under section 84.

*(3) Theft Act 1968, s.19*

## OFFICIAL LISTING

**6.22** Responsibility for the admission of securities to official listing is vested in the Council of the Stock Exchange by reason first, of its constitutional position as the governing body of the Stock Exchange and, secondly, because of its position as the designated "Competent Authority"[54] for the purposes of the Admission,[55] Listing Particulars,[56] and Interim Reports[57] Directives which, following their implementation by the Stock Exchange (Listing) Regulations 1984[58] comprise the legislative background to the rules governing the admission of securities to official listing and their continued presence on the official list.

The Admissions Directive requires[59] that certain minimum conditions be satisfied before a security may be admitted to official listing. These conditions, however, do not comprise the definitive admissions code since the Council of the

---

[50] See above at §1.23.
[51] *R.* v. *Grunwald* [1963] 1 Q.B. 935.
[52] The Theft Act 1968 has no application in Scotland.
[53] [1932] 1 K.B. 442.
[54] Stock Exchange (Listing) Regulations 1984 (S.I. 1984 No. 716), reg. 4.
[55] Council Directive No. 79/279/EEC.
[56] Council Directive No. 80/390/EEC.
[57] Council Directive No. 82/121/EEC.
[58] S.I. 1984 No. 716, reg. 3.
[59] Arts. 3 and 4.

Stock Exchange is empowered to impose requirements that are more stringent that those of the Directive[60] or to impose additional obligations, provided that those more stringent conditions and additional obligations apply generally to all issuers or for individual classes of issuer.[61]

The Stock Exchange has stated[62] that in the exercise of its function in relation **6.23** to the market in listed securities[63] it sees its principal responsibility as being to investors and that its requirements governing the admission of securities to the official list are aimed at securing the confidence of investors by ensuring:

(a) that all applicants are of a certain minimum size, have a record of trading under their present management of adequate duration, and set out in the appropriate documents sufficient information about their history, prospects and financial condition to provide a reliable basis for the anticipated market valuation;

(b) that all marketings of securities are conducted on a fair and open basis, allowing the public access wherever possible; and

(c) that investors are treated with proper consideration at all times by company boards notwithstanding the possibility that the public may represent a minority.

### Minimum requirements for listing

The Admission Directive lays down two sets of conditions, the one applying to **6.24** the admission of company shares to listing and the other applying to debt securities.[64] The Rules of the Stock Exchange overlap to some extent but do not seek to differentiate between shares and debt securities, except in relation to the requirements as to the minimum value of the securities for which admission is sought.[65]

### Requirements relating to shares

The conditions laid down for the admission of a company's shares to official **6.25** listing are of two kinds, namely:

(i) those conditions relating to the company; and

(ii) those conditions relating to the shares for which admission is sought.

---

[60] Art. 5(1) and (2). It is also provided in specific conditions that the competent authority may permit derogations from the requirements of those conditions. Article 7 provides that any derogations must apply generally for all issuers where the circumstances justifying them are similar.

[61] The derogation provisions of Article 7 apply also to these more stringent conditions and additional obligations—Art. 5(3).

[62] Admission of Securities to Listing (hereafter ASL) Section 1, Chapter 1, para. 1.

[63] The general tenor of this policy statement (although not the part covering minimum size requirements) could apply equally well to the Stock Exchange's Unlisted Securities Market.

[64] Schedule A (shares) and Schedule B (debt securities).

[65] ASL, Section 1, Chapter 2, para. 3. See further at n.69, below.

*(a) Conditions relating to the company*

The Admission Directive sets out three conditions relating to the company seeking admission for its shares:

(1) *The legal position of the company.* The legal position of the company must be in conformity with the laws and regulations of the territory to which it is subject, as regards both its formation and its operation under its statutes.

This condition would appear to add little to the general law[66] save possibly that it would seem to make shares issued to raise funds for an *ultra vires* purpose inadmissible for listing.

(2) *Minimum size of the company.* The primary Admission Directive requirement is[67] that the foreseeable market capitalisation of the shares must be at least 1,000,000 European units of account.[68] However, companies unable to comply with this condition may still have their shares admitted to listing if they can satisfy the Council of the Stock Exchange that there will be an adequate market in the shares.[69]

This primary requirement has no application where admission is sought or a further block of shares of the same class as those already admitted.

(3) *Period of existence.* The requirement here is that the company must have published or filed its annual accounts for the three financial years preceding the application.[70] However, the Council of the Stock Exchange, as competent authority, is empowered to derogate from this condition where such derogation is considered desirable in the interests of the company or of investors and where it is satisfied that investors have the necessary information available to be able to arrive at an informed judgment on the company and the shares for which admission is sought.

The Rules of the Stock Exchange require that the company should have a record of trading,[71] the Council having given notice that it will not be prepared to consider applications from companies whose assets consist wholly or substantially of cash or short-dated securities.

*(b) Conditions relating to the shares*

The Admission Directive lays down four main[72] conditions relating to the shares for which admission is sought.

[66] See above at §§6.04 *et seq.*
[67] Sched. A,I.2.
[68] The equivalent in sterling of 1m. European units of account on the date of adoption of the Directive (May 22, 1984). 1 European unit of account approx. £0.50 sterling.
[69] Under the Stock Exchange rules (ASL, Section 1, Chapter 2, para. 3) the minimum market capitalisation that the Council would normally be prepared to consider is £700,000 in the case of shares and £200,000 in the case of debt securities. In exceptional cases, however, the Council may admit securities to a lower value if it is satisfied as to marketability.
[70] Sched. A,I.3.
[71] ASL, Section 1, Chapter 1, para. 1 Note also *ibid.* para. 5. which also requires that the company have filed accounts in accordance with the rules of the national law applicable to it for 5 years prior to the listing.
[72] Sched. A II. Further conditions are laid down (II.6 and 7) relating to admission of shares of foreign companies. (See also ASL, section 8.)

(1) *Negotiability.*[73] The primary rule is that the shares must be freely nego-tiable. This effectively renders the shares of companies whose articles of associ-ation impose restrictions on transferability inadmissible. While competent authorities are empowered to derogate from this condition in the case of shares which may be acquired only subject to approval (and then only if the use of the approval clause does not disturb the market) the practice of the Stock Exchange has long been to refuse admission in such cases.[74]

It is provided that the competent authority may treat shares which are not fully paid up as being freely negotiable if arrangements have been made to ensure that the negotiability of such shares is not restricted and that dealing is made open and proper by providing the public with all appropriate information. This provision would appear to cover allotment letters issued, for example, in relation to a take-over, provided that such allotment letters were freely transfer-able.[75]

(2) *Distribution.* The primary rule is that a sufficient number of shares must be distributed to the public.[76] The requirement of the Stock Exchange was that the applicant company should be prepared to see at least 25 per cent. of its issued equity capital, or securities convertible into equity capital, in the hands of the public[77] albeit that the Council was prepared to countenance a smaller percent-age in the case of very large issues.[78] This practice has been in substance incor-porated into the Admission Directive condition.

(3) *Shares of the same class.* An application for admission must cover all shares of the same class already issued.[79] However, in the case of a new public issue of shares of the same class as those already offically listed, the company is required, where the new shares are not automatically admitted, to apply for their admission to the same listing, either not more than a year after their issue or when they become freely negotiable.[80]

(4) *Public issue preceding admission.* Where public issue precedes admission, the first listing may be made only after the end of the period during which sub-scription applications may be submitted.[81]

## Requirements relating to debt securities    **6.26**

The conditions relating to the admission of a company's debt securities to official listing are divided into three categories.

---

[73] Ibid. II.2.
[74] ASL, Section 1, Chapter 2, para. 4.
[75] See *Governments Stock and Other Securities Investments Trust* v. *Christopher* [1956] 1 W.L.R. 237. See above at § 6.11.
[76] Sched. A, II.4.
[77] Defined as persons who are not associated with directors or major shareholders.
[78] ASL, Section 1, Chapter 2, para. 8.
[79] Sched. A, II.5; ASL, Section 1, Chapter 2, para. 9.
[80] Sched. C, 1.
[81] Sched. A, II.3.

### (a) Conditions relating to the company

The Directive lays down only one such condition and this replicates the condition as to the legal position of the company imposed in relation to the admission of a company's shares to listing.[82]

### (b) Conditions relating to the debt securities

The Directive imposes conditions corresponding to those imposed in relation to shares and in particular the conditions governing negotiability[83] and public issue preceding admission.[84] The condition covering shares of the same class is adapted to apply to all debt securities ranking *pari passu*[85] so that relevant applications for admission must cover all such securities.

### (c) Other conditions

In this category the Directive includes conditions dealing with the minimum amount of loan permissible if the securities are to be admitted—200,000 European units of account[86]—and with debt securities carrying conversion rights. It is provided[87] that convertible or exchangeable debentures and debentures with warrants may be admitted to official listing only if the related shares are also officially listed or are quoted on another regulated, regularly operating, open market or are so admitted simultaneously.[88]

In the United Kingdom context this provision has the effect that convertible securities may be admitted to official listing if the shares into which they may be converted are listed or are the subject of a simultaneous application for listing or are quoted on the unlisted securities market, that being a "regulated, regularly operating, recognised open market." *Quaere* whether any of the over-the-counter markets would be so regarded.

### Participants in the issue procedure

**6.27**            It is customary (although not explicitly required by the rules of the Stock Exchange) for the flotation of a company on the Stock Exchange to be handled

*Role of Sponsor to the Issue*      by an issuing house or by a sponsoring broker. Notwithstanding the fact that it is the directors of the company who assume responsibility for the accuracy of the information set to on the prospectus (as they are required to make clear in a

---

[82] Sched. B, Part A, I.
[83] *Ibid*. II. 2.
[84] *Ibid*. II. 3.
[85] *Ibid*. II. 4.
[86] *Ibid*. III.1. See above at §619, n.39.
[87] *Ibid*. III.2.; ASL, Section 1, Chapter 2, para. 18.
[88] However, convertible, *etc.*, securities may be admitted to official listing if the Council of the Stock Exchange, as the competent authority, is satisfied that holders have at their disposal all the information necessary to form an opinion concerning the value of the shares to which the debt securities relate—Stock Exchange (Listing) Regulations 1984 Sched. 2, para. 5.

statement at the head of the prospectus[89]) the Council of the Stock Exchange attaches particular responsibility to the role of the sponsors in preparing the company for its flotation. That role effectively involves undertaking the responsibility for preparing the company, planning the flotation and preparing the prospectus. The sponsor advises on the appointment of other professional advisers and co-ordinates their activities, on the choice of market and on the method, timing and pricing of the issue.

In so far as the Stock Exchange is concerned it sees the role of sponsors as including a general responsibility to the market for the fairness of the impression given by the prospectus.[90]

Reputable sponsors exercise a high degree of care in deciding whether to lend their name to flotation since they have an obvious interest in being associated with successful issues and well-managed companies likely to perform well in the future and maintain investors' confidence. Accordingly, in assessing a company's suitability for flotation, sponsors will go beyond the minimum requirements referred to in § 6.25 above and satisfy themselves as to:

(1) *The company's profit record.* A good profit record is essential for a successful issue, investors being concerned to see that the company has progressively increased its profits over a period.

(2) *Risk.* Investors are naturally concerned with the level of risk attached to any stake they may take in a company. Sponsors will accordingly need to be convinced that the company's range of products and/or services, the geographical location of its operations, its spread of customers and sources of supply are such that a reasonable diversification of risk is achieved. Furthermore there must be confidence that there will be a continuing and increasing demand for the company's products/services, a judgment that will involve an assessment of the industry or sector in which the company operates and of the potential effects of competition and technological changes.

(3) *The company's management.* The company should have sufficient breadth and depth of management talent to ensure that it not only conducts its business efficiently at the time of issue but has the capacity to succeed in the future. Over-dependence on a single individual is often seen as a disadvantage in this context.

(4) *Balance sheet and financing.* It is essential that the company should be seen to have a strong balance sheet. Furthermore, since the prospectus is required to contain an assurance as to the adequacy of the company's working capital,[91] sponsors should be satisfied that the financial resources of the company and the facilities available to it are adequate.

In relation to their responsibilities to the market sponsors are expressly[92] expected to satisfy themselves:

---

[89] See below at §6.43. Note also the requirements of the Listing Particulars Directive (Council Directive No. 80/390/EEC) Sched. A, Chapter 1. See further below at §6.43.
[90] ASL, Section 1, Chapter 1, para. 5.
[91] See below at §6.52.
[92] ASL, Section 1, Chapter 1, para. 4.

> (a) that the directors of the company can be expected to prepare and publish all information necessary for an informed market to take place in the company's securities;
>
> (b) that the directors appreciate the nature of the responsibilities they will be undertaking as directors of a listed company; and
>
> (c) that the directors can be expected to honour their obligations both in relation to shareholders and to creditors.

Such responsibilities include those formerly set out in the Listing Agreement,[93] those imposed by the City Code on Takeovers and Mergers and those arising from the statement by the Council for the Securities Industry relating to insider dealing when taken together with the provisions of the Company Securities (Insider Dealing) Act 1985[94] on the same subject.

**6.28**

*Role of the Brokers to the Issue*

The primary role of the brokers to the issue (whether or not they are acting as sponsors to the issue) is to present the company to the Stock Exchange, to the market and to the investing public at large. The brokers are likely to be involved in arrangements for the sub-underwriting of the issue or for placing the securities issued where appropriate.

The rules of the Stock Exchange also require the brokers to the issue to be responsible for handling all matters relating to the application for listing and to act as a channel of communication between the company and the Stock Exchange after flotation. Specifically in relation to the application for listing the brokers are required[95] to submit documents in support of an application for listing to the Quotations Department of the Stock Exchange at the earliest opportunity so that comments raised by the Department may be dealt with.

**6.29**

*Other Advisers*

The other advisers to the flotation (normally solicitors and accountants[96]) are chosen by the company taking into account the recommendations of the sponsor. Together with a committee of the board, the issuing house, the brokers, the reporting accountants and the company's auditors, the solicitors to the issue and the solicitors to the company[97] make up the flotation team.

## Preparing for flotation

**6.30**

The first major step (and in many respects the single most important one) in the flotation procedure is the commissioning of an investigation into the com-

---

[93] See below at § 6.68. (The obligations formerly contained in the Listing Agreement are now set out in Section 5 of ASL.)

[94] Replacing C.A. 1980, ss.68–73.

[95] ASL, Section 1, Chapter 1, para. 4.

[96] Other participants in the flotation will be the company's registrars, receiving bankers, security printers, property valuers and where appropriate financial public relations consultants.

[97] In the usual case the solicitors to the issue are primarily concerned with the prospectus and the documents ancillary to it while the solicitors to the company are concerned with the interests of the directors and existing shareholders and with the domestic documents (*e.g.* new articles of association) needed for the company's prospective status as a listed company. Occasionally where the issue takes the form of a placing one firm of solicitors may discharge both sets of tasks.

pany's affairs by the reporting accounts. The results of this investigation are submitted in a report—the "long form" report—addressed to the directors of the company and to the sponsors of the issue. This report will examine all aspects of the company and will include sections on the history of the company's business(es), its share capital and structure, the company's present activities and production processes, its branches and subsidiaries, its management and organisation, its accounting, reporting systems and internal controls, its trading record, its current trading position and prospects, its fixed assets, its current financial position and requirements consequent thereupon and its taxation position.

Much of the information contained in this report will find its may into the listing particulars and the financial sections will form the basis of the accountants' report—the "short form" report—which appears as a separate section the in the listing particulars.[98] At a later stage this financial information will be updated to enable the accountants to report on the company's cash-flow, on the adequacy of the company's working capital and on the profit forecast. In relation to working capital the prospectus rules require the inclusion of a statement by the directors as to its adequacy[99] and the Stock Exchange insistes upon a letter from the sponsors stating that they believe that the statement by the directors has been made after due and careful enquiry.[1]

**6.31**

*Recommendations for
Changes to be
made Prior to
Flotation*

To a great extent the remaining stages in the flotation procedure follow naturally from the long form report. In particular the report may bring to light various matters to which attention may need to be given at an early stage in order to bring the company's circumstances within Stock Exchange requirements and to make them more acceptable to potential investors. Such matters often include the following:

(1) *Board structure and membership.* It is often the case that a private company will have developed with a very small board of directors, frequently drawn from within the family or families of the original proprietors. A common recommendation is that the breadth (and depth) of experience and expertise be increased with the appointment of additional directors. Further, the question of succession may have been raised, with a recommendation that appointments be made to ensure that when the time comes the board contains those willing and able to assume control of the company's affairs.

(2) *Service agreements.* It is usual for the salary and pensions rights of directors and key employees to be placed on a more formal basis than hitherto in preparation for the issue. The normal practice is for directors (and others) to enter into service agreements with the company the details of which will be disclosed in the prospectus.[2] Service agreements are considered to have the effect of giving some form of assurance to investors about the stability of management and succession.

---

[98] See below at §§6.53 *et. seq.*
[99] See below at §6.52.
[1] ASL, Section 2, Chapter 1, para. 5.15.
[2] See below at §6.58. It is not open to the company after flotation to arrange exceptional remuneration for director—shareholders in a particularly good year.

(3) *Employee's shares.* It is not uncommon for companies to wish to provide certain key employees with an opportunity to acquire shares before flotation. In addition it is common for all employees to be offered preferential application forms to ensure that they are allocated shares at the issue price. Such forms are usually restricted to 10 per cent. of the shares to be marketed.[3]

(4) *Capital structure.* Sponsors prefer companies coming to the market to have a relatively simple capital structure since such a structure facilitates evaluations of a company by potential investors. Where there are minority interests in subsidiaries it is thought to be preferable for them to be acquired before the flotation. Likewise, if the business is split between several companies, all owned directly by the vendors the report will normally recommend their amalgamation into a group.

(5) *Status of the company.* If the company is a private company it will need to be re-registered as a public company.[4]

(6) *Articles of association.* The Stock Exchange requires that the company's articles of association or other corresponding documents conform with the provisions set out in Chapter 1 of Section 9 of the Admissions of Securities to Listing. Where necessary a certified copy of a resolution of the board of directors undertaking to comply with the appropriate provisions must be lodged with the Department.[5]

The relevant provisions are as follows:

*(a) As regards transfer and registration*

(1) That transfers and other documents relating to or affecting the title to any shares shall be registered without payment of any fee.

(2) That fully-paid shares shall be free from any restriction on the right of transfer and shall also be free from all liens.[6]

(3) That where power is taken to limit the number of shareholders in a joint account, such limit shall not prevent the registration of a maximum of four persons.

(4) That the closing of the registers shall be discretionary.

*(b) As regards definitive certificates*

(1) That all certificates for capital shall be under the common seal, which shall only be affixed with the authority of the directors.

(2) That a new certificate issued to replace one that has been worn out, lost or destroyed shall be issued without charge and that where the holder has sold part of his holding, he shall be entitled to a certificate for the balance without charge.

---

[3] ASL, Section 1, Chapter 3, para. 1.2.
[4] See above at §§6.03–6.07.
[5] Admission of Securities to Listing, Chapter 1 of Section 9.
[6] In exceptional circumstances approved by the Quotations Committee a company may take power to disapprove the transfer of shares provided that such powers do not disturb the market—ASL, Section 1, Chapter 2, para. 4.

(3) Where power is taken to issue share warrants to bearer, that no new share warrant shall be issued to replace one that has been lost, unless the company is satisfied beyond reasonable doubt that the original has been destroyed.

### (c) As regards dividends

(1) That any amount paid up in advance of calls on any share may carry interest but will not entitle the holder of the share to participate in respect of such amount in any dividend.

(2) Where power is taken to forfeit unclaimed dividends, that power will not be exercised until 12 years or more after the date of the declaration of the dividend.

### (d) As regards directors

(1) That, subject to such exceptions specified in the articles of association as the Committee may approve, a director will not vote on any contract or arrangement or any other proposal in which he has a material interest.

(2) That any person appointed by the directors to fill a casual vacancy on or as an addition to the board will hold office only until the next following annual general meeting of the company, and will then be eligible for re-election.

(3) That, where not otherwise provided by law, the company in general meeting will have power by ordinary resolution to remove any director (including a managing or other executive director, but without prejudice to any claim for damages under any contract) before the expiration of his period of office.

(4) That the minimum length of the period during which notice to the company of the intention to propose a person for election as a director, and during which notice to the company by such person of his willingness to be elected may be given, will be at least 7 days.

(5) That the latest date for lodgment of the notices referred to in paragraph 4 above will be not more than 7 days prior to the date of the meeting appointed for such election.

(6) That where power is taken to delegate the powers of directors to a committee, which includes co-opted persons not being directors, the number of such co-opted persons will be less than one half of the total number of the committee and no resolution of the committee shall be effective unless a majority of the members of the committee present at the meeting are directors.

### (e) As regards accounts

That a printed copy of the directors' report, accompanied by the balance sheet (including every document required by law to be annexed thereto) and profit and loss account or income and expenditure account, shall, at least 21 days previous to the general meeting, be delivered or sent by post to the registered address of every member, provided such address is within the United Kingdom.

*(f) As regards rights*

(1) That adequate voting rights are in appropriate circumstances secured to preference shareholders.

(2) That a quorum for a separate class meeting (other than an adjourned meeting) to consider a variation of the rights of any class of shares shall be the holders of at least one-third of the issued shares of the class.

*(g) As regards companies to be included in the "investment trusts" section of the Official List*

That all moneys realised on the sale or other realisation of any capital assets in excess of book value and all other moneys in the nature of accretion to capital shall be treated as profits available for dividend.

*(h) As regards notices*

(1) That where power is taken to give notice by advertisement such advertisement shall be inserted in at least one national daily newspaper.

(2) That where it is provided that notices will be given only to those members whose registered addresses are within theUnited Kingdom, any member, whose registered address is not within the United Kingdom, may name an address within the United Kingdom which, for the purpose of notices, shall be considered as his address.

*(i) As regards redeemable shares*

That, where power is reserved to purchase for redemption a redeemable share:

(a) purchases will be limited to a maximum price which, in the case of purchases through the market or by tender, will not exceed the average of the middle market quotations taken from the Stock Exchange Official List for the 10 business days before the purchase is made or, in the case of a purchase through the market, at market price, provided that it is not more than 5 per cent. above such average; and

(b) if purchases are by tender, tenders will be available to all shareholders alike.

*(j) As regards capital structure*

That the structure of the share capital of the company be stated and where the capital consists of more than one class of share it must also be stated how the various classes shall rank for any distribution by way of dividend or otherwise.

*(k) As regards non-voting or restricted voting shares*

(1) That, where the capital of the company includes shares which do not carry

voting rights, the words "non-voting" must appear in the designation of such shares.

(2) That, where the equity capital includes shares with different voting rights, the designation of each class of shares, other than those with the most favourable voting rights, must include the words "restricted voting" or "limited voting."

*(l) As regards proxies*

(1) That where provision is made in the articles as to the form of proxy this must be so worded as not to preclude the use of the two-way form.

(2) That a corporation may execute a form of proxy under the hand of a duly authorised officer.

One of the principal functions of the issuing house, in conjunction with the brokers, is to arrange for the issues to be underwritten to ensure that the company succeeds in raising the amount required in the event of under subscription. On the case of a prospectus issue the sponsors will undertake that if the whole or a certain proportion of the capital is not applied for by the public they will themselves apply or find responsible persons to apply for the balance or a certain proportion of the balance of the capital.[7] Where the issue takes the form of a placing the agreement between the issuing house and the company for the placing of the relevant securities is in effect an underwriting agreement, although it differs from other such contracts in that, in the event of breach, the remedy of the company is in damages only,[8] whereas in other cases the company can place the underwriter on the register of members[9] and proceed to enforce the allotment accordingly.

**6.32**

*Underwriting Arrangements*

An underwriting letter is usually sent by the sponsor of the issue to a number of financial institutions inviting them to participate in the underwriting for a stipulated commission,[10] acceptance to be signified by a specified time.[11] The letter will be accompanied by a final proof print of the prospectus[12] (subject to last-minute amendment) and will be dispatched a few days before it is intended to advertise the issue. The agreement will become binding when the underwriting letter is accepted and the acceptance communicated to the sponsors. [13]

Where, as in the most usual case of a flotation the Stock Exchange, the issue takes the form of an offer for sale the underwriting arrangements centre on a subscription agreement to which the issuing house, the company and its directors

---

[7] See *Re Licensed Victuallers Mutual Trading Association* (1889) 42 Ch.D.1,C.A. In such cases the consideration to the underwriter is the payment of a commission to be received by them whether or not they are called upon to take up any shares.

[8] *Gorrissen's Case* (1873) 8 Ch. App. 507.

[9] Or debenture holders, as appropriate.

[10] Normally $1\frac{1}{4}$ per cent.

[11] See *Hindley's Case* [1896] 2 Ch. 121, C.A.

[12] Where the underwriting letter contains a provision that it is to hold good notwithstanding any variation in the prospectus, the underwriter will not be bound if the changes are such as practically to constitute a different venture—*Warner International Co.* v. *Kilburn Brown & Co.* [1914] W.N. 61.

[13] *Re Consort Deep Level Gold Mines, ex p. Stark* [1897] 1 Ch. 575.

are parties.[14] This agreement provides for the subscription of the securities to which the issue relates by the issuing house and for their subsequent offer for sale by that institution. The agreement will incorporate warranties by the directors as to the accuracy of statements made in the prospectus, including a confirmation that no facts have been omitted therefrom which render any statement made therein misleading. Additional warranties will be given by the directors in respect of:

(1) returns filed with or delivered to the Registrar of Companies;
(2) the balance sheet and profit and loss account for the immediately preceding financial year;
(3) disclosure of unusual, long-term or abnormal contracts;
(4) disclosure of litigation to which the company is or may become a party; and
(5) the taxation liabilities of the company.

The agreement will also include a provision for the company to bear all the costs of the issue including a fee to the issuing house. Annexed to the text of the agreement will be final proof prints of the prospectus and of the allotment documents.[15] (including the application form).

In the normal course the issuing house will make arrangements, in conjunction with the brokers to the issue, for its commitment under this agreement to be underwritten.

An underwriting contract, if under seal, attracts a fixed duty of 50p.[16]

Where an issue is only partly underwritten prior approval must be obtained from the Stock Exchange authorities, the granting of such approval depending on the proportion of the total issue that is underwritten.[17]

**6.33**

*Pricing*

It is normally possible for the sponsor, at the beginning of the flotation to give a general idea as to how the issue should be priced and such an indication is obviously necessary for the company to decide whether or not a public issue is the most appropriate method of raising the finance required.

A more informed estimate will be possible after receipt of the long form report and this estimate, subject to amendment to take into account the subsequent trading performance of the company, changes (if any) in investment attitudes in the sector in which the company operates, and, inevitably, the prevailing sentiment in the markets, will form the basis on which the issue is priced.

Ideally the price chosen should be pitched at a level sufficient to ensure that all the securities being marketed will be taken up and, if possible, to produce a small premium in initial dealings.[18] In recent years the difficulties in assessing the varous factors have led to an increase in the popularity of issues by tender.

---

[14] Where the issue includes shares already held by existing shareholders the agreement with the issuing house will be for subscription and purchase. In such cases the existing shareholders involved will be parties to the agreement.

[15] Renounceable and Split Letters of Acceptance, Letters of Regret.

[16] If under hand no stamp duty is payable—Finance Act 1970, Sched. 7.

[17] ASL, Section 1, Chapter 3, para. 1.2.

[18] The difficulties inherent in this process were fully exposed in some of the early privatisation issues, eg Britoil, Amersham International.

Even here however a minimum price must be arrived at. In relation to such issues the Quotations Department will require to be satisfied as to the procedure for determining the price and basis of allotment.[19]

Of the factors that go towards determining the issue price and subsequently the success or otherwise of the flotation perhaps the most important is the extent to which the company compares favourably with similar companies whose shares are listed. Points of comparison will be the company's price-to-earnings ratio, its dividend yield (which will depend to some extent on dividend policy), its dividend cover and its asset cover.

The Bank of England, with the object of maintaining an orderly new issue market,[20] exercises control over the flow, and therefore the timing, of issues where the amount of money to be raised is £3,000,000 or more. Where an issue falls within the ambit of this control the sponsoring broker should apply to the Government Broker for a date on which the terms and size of the issue may be made public. The rules of the Stock Exchange emphasise the responsibility of sponsors for ensuring that no publicity is given to an issue prior to this date or "Impact Day" as it is referred to.[21]

**6.34**

*Timing*

Subject to this requirement the timing of an issue is entirely a matter for the company and its advisers. A number of considerations figure in the determination of a suitable Impact Day.

(1) *The business cycle.* It is generally thought to be inadvisable to float a company at or near the peak of the growth cycle, the point being that although this can work to maximise the "take" from an issue the downturn in the cycle which will follow may lead to depressed profits and a poor share price performance.

(2) *Holiday periods.* Sponsors normally seek to avoid bringing a company to the market during or near holiday periods such as July and August, Christmas, New Year and Easter.

(3) *The company's financial year.* Since the Stock Exchange requires[22] that the latest financial accounting period reported on prior to flotation must have ended not more than six months before the date of the prospectus, it follows that a company's accounting dates will to some extent influence the timing of an issue.[23]

(4) *Seasonal businesses.* For companies whose businesses are seasonal, it is obviously of importance that flotation be arranged on the basis of figures achieved at the end of the season.[24]

---

[19] ASL Section 1 Chapter 3 para. 1.2.

[20] Control of Borrowing Order 1958 Art. 8(2). ASL Section 1 Chapter 2 para. 11.

[21] ASL Section 1 Chapter 2 para. 11.

[22] *Ibid.* Section 4, para. 6.

[23] It is of course possible to arrange for an interim audit to meet the Stock Exchange requirement but this has the disadvantage of adding to the costs of the issue.

[24] In addition it may be sensible, from the point of view of the burden imposed on management, to prepare for flotation during a period of relatively low activity if this is possible.

(5) *Profit forecasts*. While the Stock Exchange does not require specific fore-casts as to future profits[25] such a forecast can influence the pricing and attractive-ness of an issue and is thus often desirable.[26] Profit forecasts inevitably become more reliable as the company's accounting year progresses, a factor which would suggest that the flotation should take place in the latter part of the company's accounting period. However, such timing would have the consequence in most cases that an interim audit would be necessary in order to comply with the six-months rule as to accountants' reports.[27]

### Listing Particulars and the prospectus

**6.35** The requirements of the Stock Exchange as to the form and content of pro-spectuses overlap with those of the Companies Acts[28] but in many respects go further and are generally more demanding. The position has been[29] that a com-pany seeking a full listing for its securities would need to comply with both statu-tory and Stock Exchange rules since, in the ordinary course,[30] compliance with the latter did not confer exemption from the former.

The Stock Exchange (Listing) Regulations 1984[31] have removed the need for such a company to comply with the Companies Acts requirements as to form and content. The 1984 Regulations implement and give effect to the Council Direct-ive on Listing Particulars.[32] This Directive makes the admission of securities to official listing conditional upon the publication of listing particulars[33] approved by the Council of the Stock Exchange as competent authority[34] and containing all the information required by the Directive to be included therein.[35]

The 1984 Regulations provide[36] that where an application is made to the Council of the Stock Exchange for the admission of a security to official listing and the Council has approved the listing particulars relating thereto then:

(a) a form of application for any of those securities, if issued with a document which sets out the approved listing particulars or indicates where they can be obtained or inspected, need not have with it the prospectus otherwise required by the Companies Acts;

(b) in relation to an offer of those securities for subscription or purchase made by means of such a document those provisions of the Companies

---

[25] As opposed to a statement of trading prospects.

[26] If a forecast is made the assumptions on which it is based must be set out in the prospectus and reported on by the reporting accountants and the sponsor.

[27] *Supra*. at §6.27, n.92.

[28] See above at §§6.14–6.16.

[29] Prior to January 1, 1985.

[30] Exemption could be given under s.39, Companies Act 1948 where the Stock Exchange was pre-pared to certify that compliance with the statutory rules would cause hardship or inconvenience. s.39 was repealed by the Stock Exchange (Listing) Regulations 1984, reg. 7(4).

[31] S.I. 1984 No. 716.

[32] Council Directive No. 80/390/EEC.

[33] *Ibid*. Art. 3.

[34] *Ibid*. Art. 18(2).

[35] *Ibid*. Art. 18(3).

[36] reg. 7(1).

Act otherwise applicable with respect to prospectuses[37] and their contents will not apply; and

(c) if the approved listing particulars have been published as required and an offer of any of the securities for subscription or purchase is made by means of a document which does not set out the published listing particulars but indicates where they can be obtained or inspected, the validity of the offer, or of any transaction entered into by reference to it, may not be impugned on the grounds of absence of notice, or of insufficient notice of any matter comprised in the particulars.[38]

Prima facie, the adoption of the Listing Particulars Directive would seem to acknowledge acceptance of the Continental idea that the admission of securities to listing is a separate operation from offering the securities for subscription or sale to the public by way of a prospecus issue, an offer for sale or a placing, even though the two operations may take place at the same time or within a short time of each other. According to this idea the respective functions of a prospectus and a set of listing particulars are somewhat different.[39] Whereas a prospectus is a contractual document on the basis of which an investor subscribes for securities allotted to him by the issuer or purchases securities which the issuer has allotted to an intermediary[40] so that they may be sold to the investing public either directly [41] or indirectly[42] via institutions or dealers, a set of listing particulars is merely an "information sheet,"[43] its function being simply to provide information for all potential investors who may wish to purchase securities for which a Stock Exchange listing is given, or, more specifically, "to enable investors and their investment advisers to make an informed assessment of the assets and liabilities, financial position, profits and losses, and the prospects of the issuer and of the rights attaching to such securities.[44]

**6.36**

*Prospectuses and Listing Particulars*

In the United Kingdom these two functions have traditionally been combined in one document so that British practice is for listing particulars to operate both as a statement of information relating to the securities to be issued and, should an investor wish to subscribe, the document embodying the terms of the subscription contract.[45]

The Listing Particulars Directive requires[46] that listing particulars be published either:

**6.37**

---

[37] Or with respect to the consequences attending the issue of a prospectus or the inclusion of any statement in, or the omission of anything from, a prospectus shall not apply—reg. 7(1)(*b*).
[38] For liabilities attaching to non-compliance with the requirements of the Directive and the defences see below at §6.40.
[39] Pennington (1983) *The Company Lawyer*) 151–152.
[40] An issuing house or sponsoring broker—see above at §6.23.
[41] By an offer for sale.
[42] Through a placing.
[43] Listing Particulars Directive (LPD), Art. 3.
[44] LPD, Art. 4(1).
[45] The Council of the Stock Exchange (ASL Definitions) defines listing particulars merely as "the document of the type required by the directives to be published as a condition of admission of securities to listing."
[46] LPD, Art. 20.

(a) by insertion in one or more newspapers circulated throughout the United Kingdom, or widely circulated therein; or

(b) in the form of a brochure to be made available free of charge to the public at the offices of the Stock Exchange (and any other Stock Exchange where the securities are to be admitted to official listing), at the registered office of the issuer and, where appropriate, at the registered offices of any financial organisations retained to act as the issuer's paying agents.

These basic statutory requirements have been amplified by the Stock Exchange to take account of British practice. Thus, in the case of securities offered generally to the public for cash other than by a placing, listing particulars must be published in two national daily newspapers except that where the issuer has a strong regional connection publication in one national daily newsper and in a daily newspaper circulating in the region will suffice.[47]

In the case of a placing of securities (other than euroccurrency securities) by a new applicant a formal notice must be published in two national daily newspapers[48] In the case of a eurocurrency placing this requirement is relaxed to the extent that publication of the formal notice in one national daily newspaper will suffice.[49]

Where a formal notice is required it must contain at least the following information, namely[50]:

(1) the name and country of incorporation of the issuer;

(2) the amount and title of the securities for which listing is sought;

(3) the name and country of incorporation of any guarantor of the principal of or interest on such securities;

(4) in the case of a placing, that a proportion (to be stated) of the securities has been offered to the market and may be available to the public;

(5) that, in the case of a class of securities new to listing, details are contained in the new issue cards circulated by the statistical services[51];

(6) the addresses where copies of the listing particulars (in the form of a brochure) are available to the public for 14 days from the date of the formal notice, which must include the addresses of the registered office of the issuer, any paying agents of the issuer in the United Kingdom and the Company Announcements Office. In the case of the Company Announcements Office the formal notice must state that copies of the listing particulars will be available to the public there only for the two business days following the publication of the formal notice; and

(7) the date of the publication of the notice.

---

[47] ASL, Section 2, Chapter 3, para. 1. Note however that in cases where (because of the small size of the issue) a placing would have been permissible, publication in one national daily newspaper and a formal notice in another such newspaper will suffice: *ibid*.

[48] ASL, Section 2, Chapter 3, para. 2. No publication is required for placings by an issuer already listed in respect of any securities howsoever issued unless the security is of a class new to listing; in this event a formal notice in one newspaper is required: *ibid*.

[49] ASL, Section 2, Chapter 3, para. 4.

[50] *Ibid*. para. 6.

[51] The statistical services maintained by Extel Statistical Services Ltd.

In addition, either the complete listing particulars or a notice stating where the listing particulars have been published and where they may be obtained by the public must be inserted in The Stock Exchange Weekly Intelligence.[52]

On or before the date of their publication, a copy of the listing particulars must be delivered to the Registrar of Companies in England and Wales or in Scotland, as the case may be.[53]

**6.38**

*(2) Registration*

It is a requirement that any document which is published as, or containing, listing particulars must state, on its face, that a copy of those particulars has been delivered for registration.[54] If any such document is published without a copy of the relevant particulars having been duly delivered, the issuer and every person who is knowingly a party to the publication is guilty of an offence under the Stock Exchange (Listing) Regulations 1984.[55]

The Listing Particulars Directive requires that the listing particulars contain the information which, according to the particular nature of the issuer and of the securities for which admission to official listing is sought, is necessary to enable an informed investment decision regarding them to be made.[56] More particularly, the listing particulars are to contain, "in as easily analysible and comprehensible a form as possible,"[57] information on specified matters. The Directive, however, does provide for some flexibility in that the Council of the Stock Exchange, as the competent authority, is empowered to authorise the omission of certain information from listing particulars which would otherwise be required if it considers that:

**6.39**

*(3) Contents-General Requirements*

(a) such information is of minor importance only and is not such as will influence assessment of the assets and liabilities, financial position, profits and losses and prospects of the issuer; or

(b) disclosure of such information would be contrary to the public interest or seriously detrimental to the issuer, provided that, in the latter case, such omission would not be likely to mislead the public with regard to facts and circumstances, knowledge of which is essential for the assessment of the securities in question.[58]

Furthermore, where certain items[59] "appear inappropriate to the issuer's

---

[52] LPD, Art. 4(2) and Stock Exchange (Listing) Regulations 1984, reg. 6 and Sched. 2, para. 8. Note that in all cases where listing particulars have been published in a newspaper they must be accompanied by a statement that the listing particulars are available at the addresses specified in item 6 in the text: ASL, Section 2, Chapter 3, para. 5.

[53] Stock Exchange (Listing) Regulations 1984, reg. 7(5).

[54] *Ibid*. reg. 7(6).

[55] *Ibid*. reg. 7(7). Any person convicted of this offence will be liable, on summary conviction, to a fine not exceeding $\frac{1}{5}$ of the statutory maximum, or £2,000, whichever is the less, or on conviction after continued contravention, to a default fine not exceeding $\frac{1}{50}$ of the statutory maximum, or £100, whichever is the less: *ibid*.

[56] LPD, Art. 4(1).

[57] *Ibid*. Art. 5(1).

[58] *Ibid*. Art. 7.

[59] *Ibid*. Art. 5(3).

sphere of activity,"[60] listing particulars giving equivalent information are to be drawn up by adapting those items to the circumstances of the issuer.

**6.40**

*Failure to Comply with Formal Requirements*

As with the prospectus requirements of the Companies Acts the Listing Particulars Directive does not specify what liability is to attach to those responsible for publishing particulars which contravene or fail to comply with the relevant requirements as to form and subject-matter. The Stock Exchange (Listing) Regulations 1984[61] follow section 38(4) of the Companies Act 1948 (now section 66(1) and (2) of the Companies Act 1985) in providing that such persons will not incur any liability by reason of non-compliance with or contravention of the requirements if:

(a) as regards any matter not disclosed the party responsible proves that he was not cogniscant thereof; or

(b) he proves that the non-compliance or contravention arose from an honest mistake of fact on his part; or

(c) the non-compliance or contravention was in respect of matters which in the opinion of the court dealing with the case were immaterial or was otherwise such as ought, in the opinion of the court, having regard to all the circumstances of the case, reasonably to be excused.[62]

No transaction will be void or voidable by reason only of the fact that it was entered into in contravention of, or not in conformity with, the specified requirements.[63] It would appear therefore that, as with section 38(4), infringement of the requirements will, at most, give rise to an action for damages for breach of statutory duty. If it is sought to rescind the contract of allotment or sale an investor will have to show that the listing particulars contain a material misrepresentation.[64]

**6.41**

*Responsibility for Listing Particulars*

The Council of the Stock Exchange requires that the directors of the applicant company accept responsibility for the accuracy of the information contained in the listing particulars. This acceptance should take the form of a declaration as follows[65]:

"The Directors of the Company, whose names appear on page . . . are the persons responsible for the information contained in this document. To the best of the knowledge and belief of the Directors (who have taken all reasonable care to ensure that such is the case) the information contained in this document is in accordance with the facts and does not omit anything likely to affect the import of such information. The Directors accept responsibility accordingly."

[60] Or inappropriate to its legal form: *ibid.*
[61] reg. 5(2).
[62] See further at §6.13 above for a consideration of liability under C.A. 1948, s.38(4) (now C.A. 1985, s.66(1) and (2)).
[63] Stock Exchange (Listing) Regulations 1984, reg. 8(2). Note that reg. 8(1) expressly envisages the possibility of liability in damages.
[64] See above at §6.18.
[65] ASL, Section 3, Chapter 2, Part 1, para. 1.7.

In cases where the directors of the issuer are responsible for part of the listing particulars, the directors of another company being responsible for the remainder, the declaration should be appropriately adapted. Such a situation would be likely to arise where the securities of the issuing company are guaranteed or secured by a second company; equally, where the issue is of convertible debt securities and the issuer of the securities is not the issuer of the shares into which they are convertible, a declaration by the directors of both companies accepting responsibility for the accuracy of those parts of the listing particulars relating to their respective companies should be made.[66]

The information required to be disclosed in listing particulars is specified in **6.42** the Schedules to the Listing Particulars Directive, each Schedule setting out the items demanded in respect of different categories of security. Schedule A applies where a listing is sought for shares and Schedule B[67] where the listing sought is in respect of debt securities. The particular requirements of these Schedules are incorporated into the Stock Exchange's Requirements for the Admission of Securities to Listing.[68] However the matters specified in the Schedules are minimum requirements rather than comprising a definitive prescription.[69] Accordingly it is open to the Council of the Stock Exchange in its regulations to demand disclosure of matters not mentioned in the Schedules and to require declarations from the directors beyond what may otherwise be required.[70] Over and above such requirements which are intended to be of general application the Stock Exchange demands disclosure of additional matters where the issuer is a property company,[71] a company substantially involved in mineral exploration or exploitation,[72] or is an investment trust or investment company.[73]

The Schedules provide for a "Layout" to be adopted for listing particulars relating to each of the categories of security. Those layouts group the items of information required under various "headings." These headings are:

(1) Information concerning those responsible for the listing particulars and the auditing of the company's accounts;

(2) Information concerning the securities in respect of which the application for admission is being made;

(3) General information about the issuer and its capital;

---

[66] *Ibid.*

[67] The Listing Particulars Directive contains a third Schedule, Schedule C, appertaining to Certificates in respect of Shares. The Council of the Stock Exchange has stated (ASL, Section 1, Chapter 1, para. 13) that it does not grant listing to certificates representing shares. However, the Official List does contain quotations in respect of certain depositary receipts. These apparently have been included for convenience only and are not to be taken as indicating that such receipts (as opposed to the underlying securities) are admitted to listing: *ibid.*

[68] ASL, Section 3, Chapter 2.

[69] LPD, Art. 5(1).

[70] As, for example, in the requirement that in the case of a statement or report attributed to an expert, the listing particulars contain a statement that such expert has given and has not withdrawn his written consent to the issue of the listing particulars, with the statement included in the form and context in which it is included: ASL, Section 3, Chapter 1, Part 1, para. 1.8.

[71] ASL, Section 10, Chapter 1.

[72] *Ibid.* Chapter 2.

[73] *Ibid.* Chapter 3.

(4) Information concerning the issuer's activities;

(5) Information concerning the issuer's assets and liabilities, financial position, and profits and losses;

(6) Information concerning administration, management and supervision;

(7) Information concerning the recent developments and prospects of the issuer.

However, the Council of the Stock Exchange has stated that, subject to the overriding requirement that information contained in the listing particulars be set out in a form that can be understood and analysed easily,[74] it need not follow the same layout or order as that set out in the relevant Schedule.

**6.43    Information concerning those responsible for the Listing Particulars, etc.**

Under this heading listing particulars must disclose:

(a) The names and functions of the natural persons and the name(s) and registered office(s) of any legal persons responsible for the particulars. As has been mentioned[75] the Stock Exchange requires the directors of the issuing company to accept this responsibility.

Where different persons or bodies have been responsible for different parts of the document the persons and the parts for which they are responsible should be respectively named and identified. This requirement is of especial importance where an expert opinion or report has been incorporated into the particulars, or where valuations of assets have been prepared. In such cases the Stock Exchange requires information about the qualifications and experience of such persons.[76]

(b) The names, addresses and qualifications of the official auditors who have audited the company's annual accounts for the preceding three financial years.[77]

(c) The names and addresses of the issuer's bankers, brokers and solicitors and of the solicitors to the issue.[78]

**6.44    Information concerning the securities**

The listing particulars must contain a statement announcing that application has been made to the Council of the Stock Exchange for the securities to be admitted to the Official List.[79] Where admission to other stock exchanges is being sought or will at some future time be sought the particulars should indicate the stock exchanges in question.[80] Likewise, if securities of the same class are already listed on some other stock exchange,[81] or, if not listed, are dealt in one or more other markets which are subject to regulation, are in regular operation

---

[74] ASL, Section 3, Chapter 1, para. 1.3.

[75] At §6.41 above.

[76] ASL, Section 4, para. 13.

[77] LPD, Sched. A, para. 1.3.; ASL, Section 3, Chapter 2, Part 1, para. 1.9.

[78] ASL, Section 3, Chapter 2, Part 1, para. 1.10.

[79] LPD, Sched. A, para. 2.1; ASL, Section 3, Chapter 2, Part 2, para. 2.1. Note that this statement should indicate whether or not all the securities have been sold or are available in whole or in part to the public in conjunction with the application: ASL, *Ibid.*

[80] LPD, Sched A, para. 2.2.6; Sched B, para. 2.3.0.; ASL, *ibid.* para. 2.2.

[81] LPD, Sched A, para. 2.4.3; Sched B, para. 2.3.3.; ASL, *ibid.* para. 2.3.

and are recognised and open[82] an indication of these other exchanges or markets should be given.

## (1) Shares                                                                                6.45

Where the application for admission relates to shares in the issuer information must be disclosed on the following matters:

### (a) Constitution

The listing particulars must indicate the legal mechanisms (*i.e.* the resolutions, authorisations and approvals) by virtue of which the shares have been or will be created and/or issued, the nature of the issue and the amount thereof, together with a statement as to the number of shares which have been or will be created and/or issued, if such number has been determined.[83]

### (b) Rights attaching to the securities

The particulars should contain a "concise description" of the rights and privileges attaching to the shares, and in particular the extent of the voting rights, entitlement to share in profits and any entitlement to participate in any surplus in the event of liquidation.[84]

The listing particulars should state the date on which entitlement to dividends arises.[85] Where such dividend entitlement is subject to time limits the date on which the entitlement lapses should also be mentioned together with an indication of the party in whose favour the lapse provision operates.[86] Where paying agents have been appointed to handle the payment of dividends the financial institutions so acting must be identified.[87]

If there is more than one class of share the listing particulars should set out the rights of each class as regards dividend, capital, redemption and the creation or issue of further shares ranking in priororiity to or *pari passu* with each class other than the lowest ranking equity.[88] A statement comprising a summary of any consents necessary for the variation of such class rights should also be included.[89]

Details of the arrangements applicable to transfers of shares should be set out.[90]

---

[82] LPD, Sched A, para. 2.4.4; Sched B, para. 2.3.4.; ASL, *ibid*. para. 2.4.
[83] LPD, Sched A, para. 2.2.0; ASL, *ibid*. para. 2.5.
[84] LPD, Sched. A, para. 2.2.2.; ASL, *ibid*. para. 2.9.
[85] LPD, Sched. A, para. 2.2.5.; ASL, *ibid*. para. 2.15.
[86] LPD, Sched. A, para. 2.2.2. Note that the English text refers to the party "in whose favour the entitlement operates." Since this apparently refers to dividend entitlement the provision would appear to be meaningless as it stands.
[87] LPD, Sched. A, para. 2.2.7.; ASL, *ibid*. para. 2.16; Note that this extends to registrars.
[88] LPD, Sched. A, para. 2.2.2.; ASL, *ibid*. para. 2.9.
[89] LPD, Sched. A, para. 3.2.4.; ASL, *ibid*. para. 2.10.
[90] LPD, Sched. A, para. 2.2.4.; ASL, *ibid*. para. 2.14.

## (c) Admission matters

Obviously the listing particulars must set out the terms on which the issue is being made. Accordingly the particulars must include a description of the issue specifying[91]:

(1) the number of shares involved;
(2) the exact designation or class of shares;
(3) the nominal or par value of each share;
(4) the details of any coupons attached (where appropriate); and
(5) the price.[92]

If known, the dates on which the listing will take place and dealings will begin should be given[93] and if shares of the same class are already listed on one or more stock exchanges those exchanges should be indicated.[94]

If, simultaneously or almost simultaneously with the creation of shares[95] for which the listing is being sought, shares of the same class are subscribed for or

---

[91] LPD, Sched. A, para. 2.4.; ASL *ibid*. para. 2.21.
[92] In the case of a tender offer the minimum office price should be given.
[93] LPD, Sched A, para. 2.4.2.
[94] *Ibid*. para. 2.4.3.
[95] Where the shares for which the listing is being sought were issued or placed within the 12 months preceding admission the listing particulars should include the following information (*ibid*. para. 2.3):

> 2.3.0. Indication of the exercise of the right of pre-emption of shareholders or of the restriction or withdrawal of such right.
>   Indication, where applicable, of the reasons for restriction or withdrawal of such right; in such cases, justification of the issue price, where an issue is for cash; indication of the beneficiares if the restriction or withdrawal of the right of pre-emption is intended to benefit specific persons.
> 2.3.1. The total amount of the public or private issue or placing and the number of shares offered, where applicable, by category.
> 2.3.2. If the public or private issue or placing were or are being made simultaneously on the markets of two or more States and if a tranche has been or is being reserved for certain of these, indication of any such tranche.
> 2.3.3. The issue price or the offer or placing price, stating the nominal value or, in its absence, the accounting par value or the amount to be capitalized; the issue premium and the amount of any expenses specifically charged to the subscriber or purchaser.
>   The methods of payment of the price, particularly as regards the paying-up of shares which are not fully paid.
> 2.3.4. The procedure for the exercise of any right of pre-emption; the negotiability of subscription rights; the treatment of subscription rights not exercised.
> 2.3.5. Period of the opening of the issue or offer of shares, and names of the financial organizations responsible for receiving the public's subscriptions.
> 2.3.6. Methods of and time limits for delivery of the shares, possible creation or provisional certificates.
> 2.3.7. Names, addresses and descriptions of the natural or legal persons underwriting or guaranteeing the issue for the issuer. Where not all of the issue is underwritten or guaranteed, a statement of the portion not covered.
> 2.3.8. Indication or estimate of the overall amount and/or of the amount per share of the charges relating to the issue operation, stating the total remuneration of the financial intermediaries, including the underwriting commission or margin, guarantee commission, placing commission or selling agent's commission.
> 2.3.9. Net proceeds accruing to the issuer from the issue an intended application of such proceeds, e.g., to finance the investment programme or to strengthen the issuer's financial position.

placed privately or if shares of other classes are created for public or private placing, the listing particulars should give details of the nature of such operations and of the number and characteristics of the shares to which they relate.[96]

If, during the current or immediately preceding financial years, there have been:

(a) any public takeover offers by third parties in respect of the issuer's shares; or

(b) any public takeover offers by the issuer in respect of other company's shares,

the listing particulars should indicate what has occurred and set out the price or exchange terms attaching to such offers and the outcome thereof.[97]

### (2) Debt securities

In relation to debt securities the Listing Particulars Directive requires dis-  **6.46** closure of the following matters:

*(a) Legal matters*

As with shares listing particulars in respect of debt securities must indicate the resolutions, authorisations and approvals by virtue of which the securities have been or will be created and/or issued, together with a statement as to the amount or number of the securities in question.[98]

With debt securities, however, the principal legal matters to be disclosed relate to the conditions of the loan and the position with regard to enforcement. The particulars must set out:

(1) the nominal amount of the loan[99];
(2) the issue and redemption prices[1];
(3) the nominal interest rate (if several rates are provided for an indication should be given of the conditions for changes in the rate)[2];
(4) the currency of the loan (if there is a currency option the details of this option should be given)[3];
(5) the relevant dates and time limits in relation to the loan and specifically[4]—:
    (a) the period of the loan and any interim due dates,
    (b) the date from which interest becomes payable and the due dates for interest;

---

[96] *Ibid.* para. 2.5.
[97] *Ibid.* para. 2.4.5.
[98] LPD, Sched. B, para. 2.2.0.
[99] *Ibid.* para. 2.1.0. If the amount of the loan is not fixed the particulars should contain a statement to this effect.
[1] *Ibid.* para. 2.1.1. Except in the case of continuous issues.
[2] *Ibid.* para. 2.1.1. Except in the case of continuous issues.
[3] *Ibid.* para. 2.1.6. If the loan is denominated in units of account the contractual status of these should be given.
[4] *Ibid.* para. 2.1.7.

    (c)  the time limit on the validity of claims to interest and repayment of principal; and

    (d)  the procedures and time limits for delivery of the debt securities.[5]

(6)  an indication of the yield together with a statement as to the method by reference to which that yield is calculated.[6]

Where any other benefits or advantages attach or may attach to the securities the particulars should specify the procedures for the allocation of such benefits together with the method for their calculation.[7]

It is required that the particulars specify what arrangements have been made in relation to the amortisation of the loan.[8] Thus, where a sinking fund is to be set up, mention, together with relevant details, should be included under this head.

The listing particulars should indicate whether the debt securities are regis-tered or bearer,[9] and if the former whether there are any restrictions on transfer-ability.[10] They should also give information concerning the present and possible future ranking of the securities; specifically, the particulars should mention any provision under which the loan in relation to which the securities have been issued is subordinated to other debts of the issuer already contracted or to be contracted.[11] The nature and scope of the guarantees, sureties and commitments given in relation to the payment of interest and the repayment of the principal should also be spelled out.[12]

As has been mentioned[13] the practice is for debt securities to be issued via trustees for the stockholders. The listing particulars should state who the trus-tees are to be and where their head office is situated. They should set out the main terms of the trusteeship and in particular the conditions under which the trustees might be replaced.[14]

Where appropriate, the listing particulars should indicate the legislation[15] under which the debt securities have been created and in any event should state the courts competent in the event of litigation.[16]

---

[5] And, where appropriate, creation of provisional certificates.

[6] LPD, Sched. B, para. 2.1.8. Except in the case of continuous issues. Note that the particulars should also mention any tax on the income from the debt securities withheld at source and indicate whether the issuer assumes responsibility for the withholding of tax at source: *ibid.* para. 2.1.3.

[7] *Ibid.* para. 2.1.2. Where the distribution of interest or any other benefit involves the use of a pay-ing agent details of such agent should be given: *ibid.* para. 2.1.5.

[8] *Ibid.* para. 2.1.4. These details should include repayment procedures.

[9] *Ibid.* para. 2.2.5.

[10] *Ibid.* para. 2.2.6.

[11] *Ibid.* para. 2.2.3.

[12] *Ibid.* para. 2.2.1. Indication should also be given of the places where the public may have access to the texts of the contracts relating to these guarantees, sureties and commitments.

[13] See above at §§2.63: *et seq.*

[14] LPD, Sched. B, para. 2.2.2. Indication should also be given as to where the public may have access to the contracts relating to the trusteeship.

[15] For example, debt securities issued by undertakings recently privatised or other statutory com-panies.

[16] LPD, Sched. B, para. 2.2.4.

*(b) Admission matters*

Clearly the listing ˙particulars must specify the stock exchanges where admission to listing is being sought.[17] If the issue is being made simultaneously on markets in more than one EEC state and if a tranche has been or is being reserved for certain of these, an indication of the tranche should be given.[18] Where debt securities of the same class are already listed on one more stock exchanges, an indication of these exchanges should be given.[19]

Where the issue of the debt securities coincides with admission or took place within the three months preceding such admission the listing particulars should set out:

(1) the method of payment of the issue or offer price[20];
(2) the period of the opening of the issue or offer and any possibilities of early closure[21];
(3) the financial organisations responsible for receiving the public's subscriptions[22]
(4) the negotiability of subscription rights and the treatment of such rights as are not exercised[23];
(5) the procedure for the exercise of any right of pre-emption[24];
(6) an indication of the net proceeds of the loan[25] and a statement as to the purpose of the issue and intended application of the proceeds.[26]

In almost every case the issue will have been underwritten. The listing particulars should state the names, addresses and descriptions of those who are underwriting or guaranteeing the issue. It is not entirely clear as to the extent of this obligation; in particular does the obligation relate only to primary underwriting (in which case, mention of the issuing house managing the issue and of its having underwritten the issue should be sufficient) or does it extend to sub-underwriting arrangements? One would expect the former to be the case if only because in specifications as detailed as those laid down in the Listing Particulars Directive, had the obligation been intended to extend to sub-underwriting arrangements a specific provision would have been included (*sed quaere*).

**Incorporation statement** **6.47**

All listing particulars are required[27] to set out the full name of the company, the address of its registered office and, if different, its head office[28] and principal

---

[17] *Ibid*. para. 2.3.0.
[18] *Ibid*. para. 2.3.2.
[19] *Ibid*. para. 2.3.3. If debt securities of the same class have not yet been admitted to listing but are dealt in on one or more other markets which are subject to regulation, are in regular operation and are recognised and open an indication of such markets should be given: *ibid*. para. 2.3.4.
[20] *Ibid*. para. 2.4.1.
[21] *Ibid*. para. 2.4.2. This does not apply in the case of continuous issues.
[22] *Ibid*. para. 2.4.3.
[23] *Ibid*. para. 2.4.0.
[24] *Ibid*.
[25] *Ibid*. para. 2.4.5. Except in the case of continuous debt security issues.
[26] *Ibid*. para. 2.4.6.
[27] LPD, Scheds. A and B, paras. 3.1.0.
[28] ASL, Section 3, Chapter 2, Part 1, para. 1.1.

administrative establishment. The date of incorporation of the company[29] and the authority under which the company was incorporated[30] must also be stated. Normally this requirement will be met by specifying the relevant Companies Act or Acts, although where the company is a charter company details of the charter should be given.[31] The incorporation statement should also mention the place of incorporation; if this is outside the United Kingdom the address of the company's head office and principal place of business (if any) in the United Kingdom should be given.[32]

The particulars should provide an indication of the issuer's objects, with reference being made to the clauses of the memorandum of association in which they are described.[33] Mention should also be made of the entry number in the Register of Companies relating to the issuer.[34]

**6.48  Capital statement**

Companies are required to state their authorised share capital, the amount issued, or agreed to be issued, the amount paid up and the description and nominal value of the shares, broken down where appropriate according to the extent to which they have been paid up.[35]

The Regulations of the Stock Exchange[36] also require companies to give details of their loan capital outstanding or created but unissued, and of all mortgages or charges. If no such loan capital exists the listing particulars should contain a statement to that effect.[37]

Details should be given of the amount of any convertible debt securities, exchangeable debt securities or debt securities with warrants, with an indication of the conditions governing and the procedures for conversion, exchange or subscription.[38] Where there is authorised but unissued share capital or an undertaking to increase the capital of the company, *inter alia* in connection with convertible loans issued or subscription options granted, the listing particulars should give an indication of[39]:

(1) the amount of such authorised capital or capital increase and, where appropriate, the duration of the authorisation;

(2) the categories of persons having preferential subscription rights for such additional portions of capital; and

(3) the terms and arrangements for the share issue corresponding to such portions.

---

[29] LPD, Scheds. A and B paras. 3.1.1.

[30] LPD, Scheds. A and B, paras. 3.1.2.

[31] Likewise where the company was incorporated under authority of a private or special Act of Parliament details of the Act should be given.

[32] ASL, Section 3, Chapter 2, Part 1, para. 1.3.

[33] LPD, Scheds. A and B, paras. 3.1.3. Indication should be given of where the documents referred to in the listing particulars may be inspected: *ibid*. paras. 3.1.5.

[34] *Ibid*. paras. 3.1.4.

[35] *Ibid*. paras. 3.2.0.

[36] ASL, Section 3, Chapter 2, Part 5, paras. 5.16.

[37] *Ibid*.

[38] LPD, Sched. A, para. 3.2.3.; Sched. B, para. 3.2.1.

[39] LPD, Sched. A, para. 3.2.1.

Where the memorandum or articles of association of the company impose conditions governing changes in the company's capital and in the rights attached to the various classes of shares those conditions should be set out in the listing particulars where they are more stringent than those required under the ordinary law.[40] In cases where such changes have occurred during the three years preceding the publication of the listing particulars the operations resulting in the changes should be summarised.[41]

The Listing Particulars Directive lays down[42] a number of requirements which must be met in relation to the disclosure of those having control of, or substantial stakes in the capital of the company. The requirements differ, however, according to whether the securities for which listing is being sought are shares or debt securities. Where the issue is of either shares or debt securities, if the issuer is a member of a group of companies the particulars should provide a description of the group and of the issuer's position within it.[43] Two further requirements, however, apply in respect of share issues, namely:

(a) as far as they are known to the issuer, an indication should be given of the natural or legal persons who, directly or indirectly, severally or jointly, exercise or could exercise control over the issuer, and details of the proportion of the voting capital held by such persons should be disclosed[44]; and

(b) insofar as they are known to the issuer, an indication should be given of the shareholders who, directly or indirectly, hold a proportion of the issuer's capital in excess of five per cent.[45]

Likewise, the listing particulars are required to disclose any shares held by the issuer, directly or indirectly, in itself. Specifically, the requirement is for the disclosure of the number, book value and nominal value[46] of any of its own shares which the issuer or another company in which it has a direct or indirect holding of more than 50 per cent. has acquired and is holding.[47]

### The company's business activities                                      **6.49**

The Regulations of the Stock Exchange have for many years required companies coming to the market for the first time to describe the general nature of the businesses which they or their groups carry on.[48] This requirement has been

---

[40] *Ibid.* para. 3.2.4.
[41] *Ibid.* para. 3.2.5.
[42] LPD, Sched. A, paras. 3.2.6.–3.2.9.; Sched. B, paras. 3.2.2.–3.2.3.
[43] LPD, Sched. A, para. 3.2.8.; Sched. B paras. 3.2.2.
[44] LPD, Sched. A, para. 3.2.6. Joint control means control exercised by more than one company or by more than one person having concluded an agreement which may lead to their adopting a common policy in respect of the issuer: *ibid.*
[45] *Ibid.* para. 3.2.7.
[46] Or, in the absence of a nominal value, the accounting par value.
[47] LPD, Sched A, para. 3.2.9.; Sched. B, para. 3.2.3. This item is only required to be disclosed if it does not appear as a separate item on the balance sheet.
[48] See now ASL, Section 3, Chapter 2, Part 4. Where a company or group carries on two or more activities which are material the listing particulars should provide information as to the relative importance of each such activity having regard to the profits/losses, assets employed or any other factors: *ibid.* para. 4.4.

made more specific by the Listing Particulars Directive which demands the disclosure of information in relation to three areas.

### (a) Activities, products, etc.

Listing particulars are required to include information giving a description of the issuer's principal activities and stating the main categories of products sold and/or services performed.[49] Where the company has developed significant new products or embarked upon new activities or areas of activity of significance these should be indicated.

A breakdown of net turnover during the last three financial years should be included, such breakdown being made by categories of activity and into geographical markets insofar as these categories and markets differ substantially from one another. This breakdown should take into account the manner in which the sale of products and the provision of services falling within the company's ordinary activities are organised.[50] Furthermore the information given should state the location and size of the company's principal establishments[51] and contain a summary or relevant details about real estate owned.[52]

### (b) Research and development, etc.

Listing particulars are required to contain information concerning policy on the research and development of new products and processes over the past three financial years, where significant.[53] In addition summary information should be included indicating the extent to which the issuer is dependant, if at all, on patents or licences, industrial, commercial, or financial contracts or new manufacturing processes where such factors are of fundamental importance to the issuer's business or profitability.[54]

### (c) Investment policy

Listing particulars must provide a description, with figures, of the main investments made by the company in other undertakings over the past three financial years and the months already elapsed of the current financial year.[55] In this context "investments" include interests such as shares and debt securities. Information should also be given concerning the company's present direct investment and future investment plans. In relation to present direct investment the details provided should indicate the distribution of such investment geographically (home and abroad).[56] With regard to future investment the particulars should

---

[49] LPD, Sched. A, para. 4.1.0.; Sched. B, para. 4.1.0.
[50] *Ibid.* paras. 4.1.1.
[51] Any establishment which accounts for more than 10 per cent. of turnover or production is to be regarded as a principal establishment: *ibid.* paras. 4.1.2.
[52] *Ibid.* paras. 4.1.1.
[53] LPD, Sched. A, para. 4.3; ASL, Section 3, Chapter 2, Part 4, para. 4.9. Note that this information is not required in relation to an issue of debt securities.
[54] LPD, Scheds. A and B, paras. 4.2.; ASL, *ibid.* para. 4.8.
[55] LPD, Sched. A, para. 4.7.0.; Sched. B, para. 4.4.0.
[56] LPD, Sched. A, para. 4.7.1.; Sched. B, para. 4.4.1.

give information concerning the company's principal future investments with the exception of those comprising interests to be acquired in other undertakings on which its management bodies have already made firm commitments.[57]

### (d) Working capital statement

Stock Exchange regulations require that all listing particulars contain a statement by the directors that in their opinion the company's working capital is sufficient for its needs or, if it is not, a statement as to how it is proposed to acquire such additional amount as may be thought to be necessary.[58]

### (e) Recent developments and prospects

General information concerning the trend of the company's business since the end of the financial year to which the last published accounts relate should be included. In particular the most recent trends in production, sales and stock, costs and selling prices and the state of the order book should be disclosed.[59] In addition, the listing particulars should contain information on the issuer's prospects for at least the current financial year.[60]

### (f) Claims against the company

Whether the listing sought is for shares or debt securities the listing particulars relative thereto must disclose information on any legal or arbitration proceedings which may have or which in the recent past have had a significant effect on the issuer's financial position.[61] Stock Exchange requirements are slightly broader and more precise than those of the Listing Particulars Directive demanding a statement on any legal or arbitration proceedings pending or threatened against the company or any member of the group to which it belongs which may have or which have had during the previous 12 months a significant effect on the financial position of the company or group, as the case may be.[62]

In relation to any potential liability to capital transfer tax the company should either have obtained an indemnity from the persons involved or, alternatively, the listing particulars should contain a statement to the effect that no material liability is likely to fall upon the company or any of its subsidiaries.[63] Likewise any necessary income tax or shortfall clearances should have been obtained. In the absence of such clearances the listing particulars should include a statement that appropriate indemnities have been given.[64]

---

[57] LPD, Sched. A, para. 4.7.2.; Sched. B, para. 4.4.2.
[58] ASL, Section 3, Chapter 2, Part 2, para. 2.19.
[59] LPD, Scheds. A and B, paras. 7.1.
[60] *Ibid.* paras. 7.2.
[61] LPD, Sched. A, para. 4.4.; Sched. B, para. 4.3.; ASL, Section 3, Chapter 2, Part 3, para. 3.15.
[62] ASL, Section 3, Chapter 2, Part 2, para. 3.15.
[63] *Ibid.* para. 3.14.
[64] *Ibid.* para. 3.13. Note that the Stock Exchange may require such indemnities to be supported by continuing guarantees: *ibid.*

*(g) Other matters*

Where a listing is being sought for shares[65] the listing particulars should contain information on two other matters relating to the company's activities, namely:

(1) any interruptions in the company's business which may have or which in the recent past (the last 12 months) have had a significant effect on the issuer's financial position[66]; and

(2) average numbers employed and changes in such numbers over the past three financial years, if such changes are material, with, if possible, a breakdown of persons employed by main categories of activity.[67]

**6.50** In addition to the information indicated in § 6.49, which is required whatever the nature of the company's activities, listing particulars issued where a listing is sought for securities of companies whose business activities cause them to be classified as property companies, mineral companies or investment trusts must include information on a number of other matters.

*(a) Property companies*

The property company rules are intended to apply to those companies whose activities comprise property investment and/or property development. In such cases the valuation of the company's property assets will be the single most important element in the information available to potential investors when deciding whether or not to subscribe for the securities on offer. Accordingly the Stock Exchange requires that the valuation observe certain standards and that the valuation report should as a minimum contain specified information.

The valuer employed to prepare the valuation and report must, unless otherwise approved by the Quotations Committee, be an external valuer and have appropriate professional qualifications.[68] The listing particulars should give the name and address of the valuer and specify his professional qualifications.[69] It should also state the date on which the valuation was made.

The valuation report to be included in the listing particulars must indicate the basis on which the valuation has been made. In particular, it must state whether the valuation is based on open market value, or, if necessary, depreciated replacement cost subject to adequate profitability. Where the valuation is in respect of land currently being developed or with development potential the report should state:

---

[65] There is no corresponding requirement for debt securities.

[66] LPD, Sched. A, para. 4.5.; ASL, Section 3, Chapter 2, Part 4, para. 4.10.

[67] LPD, Sched. A, para. 4.6.; ASL, *ibid.* para, 4.11.

[68] ASL, Section 10, Chapter 1, para. 3. The valuer should not be either a director or an employee of the company or any of its subsidiaries or in partnership with or employed by such a director or employee. A partnership or company may not act as valuer if any of its partners or directors would be so disqualified. Where the company maintains a qualified surveyor's department the Quotations Committee may consider waiving the necessity for an external valuation.

[69] *Ibid.* para. 2.

(1) whether planning consent has been obtained and, if so, the date and whether there are any conditions attached to such consent;

(2) the date when the development is expected to be completed and any estimate of letting or occupation dates;

(3) the estimated total cost of carrying out the development including the cost of financial carrying charges, letting commissions, etc., or, (where the development has already been carried out) the estimated cost of completing the development similarly;

(4) the estimated capital value of the property in the open market in its present condition; and

(5) the estimated capital value after development has been completed and after completion and letting of the property.[70]

The valuation report should contain information in respect of each property[71] and should, in particular, state—[72]:

(a) the address;

(b) a brief description (*e.g.* land or buildings, approximate area, etc.);

(c) existing use;

(d) tenure;

(e) terms of tenants' leases or underleases (including repairing obligations);

(f) estimated current and (where different) future net annual rental income[73];

(g) approximate age of the buildings;

(h) present capital value in existing state;

(i) terms of any intra-group leasing arrangement affecting the property; and

(j) any other matters which materially affect the value.

In cases in which directors or promoters have been interested in any acquisition or disposal of any of the properties during the two years preceding the valuation there must be disclosed, either in the valuation report or elsewhere in the listing particulars, details of such interests together with—

(i) the nature of the interest in question;

(ii) the dates of the transactions; and

(iii) the prices paid or received, or other terms on which the transactions were effected.[74]

---

[70] *Ibid.* para. 5.

[71] If the properties held are too numerous to enable all such particulars to be given without undue length, applicants should consult the Quotations Department. In some cases suitable condensed details may be acceptable. In other cases it may be acceptable to have a detailed valuation report available for inspection and a summarised valuation report included in the listing particulars: *ibid.* para. 4.

[72] *Ibid.* para. 4.

[73] *Ibid.* para. 6. Current net annual rental means the current net annual income (ignoring any special receipts or deductions) arising from the property before tax on profits and any allowance for interest on capital or loans but after making deductions for superior rents (but not for any amortisation) and all disbursements including the expenses of managing the property and appropriate annual allowances to maintain it in a condition to continue to command its rent.
Where rentals are mentioned in a valuation report it should be stated whether they are based on present-day rental values or, if not, the basis adopted: *ibid.*

[74] *Ibid.* para. 7.

The valuation report should conclude with a summary in which the number of properties and their aggregate current value should be split to show the separate totals for the freehold and leasehold properties.[75]

### (b) Mineral companies

Mineral companies are those companies whose activities (whether directly or through a subsidiary company) include exploration for or production of natural resources consisting of substances such as metal ores, mineral concentrates, industrial minerals, mineral oils, natural gases, or solid fuels, mining, extraction of hydrocarbons, quarrying or similar activities.[76]

It is a Stock Exchange requirement that companies whose activities include or are to include exploration for natural resources to a material degree have available to them the technical adivce of persons possessing appropriate experience of the type of exploration activity undertaken or proposed to be undertaken.[77] The listing particulars relative to securities issued by such companies must set out the full name, address, professional qualifications and relevant experience of such persons. Where the listing particulars contain statements by such persons as to the existence of natural resources such statements must be substantiated by the professional adviser in question from his own knowledge and supported by details of drilling results, analyses or other evidence.[78]

In the case of a new applicant for listing, in addition to the above, listing particulars must contain the following information, namely[79]:

(1) a statement of the interests of each promoter or technical adviser in the share capital of the company together with the amounts of the holdings in question;

(2) the general nature of the business of the company or group, distinguishing between different activities which are material having regard to the profits/ losses, assets employed or any other factor affecting the importance of each activity; if the activities of the company or group take place to a material extent outside the United Kingdom, a statement of the geographical location of the activities;

(3) the nature and extent of the company's right of exploration and exploitation and a description of the properties to which such rights attach, giving particulars of the duration and other principal terms of the concessions;

---

[75] *Ibid.* para. 8.

[76] ASL, Section 10, Chapter 2, para. 1. Note that an application for listing from a company whose current activities consist solely of exploration will not normally be considered unless the company is able to establish:
  (1) the existence of adequate economically exploitable reserves of natural resources, which must be substantiated by the opinion of an expert, in a defined area over which the company has exploration and exploitation rights;
  (2) an estimate of the capital cost of bringing the company into a productive position; and
  (3) an estimate of the time and working capital required to bring the company into a position to earn revenue: *ibid.*

[77] *Ibid.*para. 2.

[78] *Ibid.* para. 3. If important evidence which must remain confidential for legal or other valid reasons has to be excluded from the listing particulars or from the technical adviser's report incorporated therein the company must allow an independent consultant, mutually approved, to verify to the Quotations Department in confidence the importance of such evidence: *ibid.*

[79] *Ibid.* para. 5.

(4) in the case of a proposed exploration for natural resources, a general description of the areas to be studied and the exploration techniques to be used and technical staff to be employed should be given; a statement as to the company's rights, if any, over such areas and of the rights obtainable under existing legislation must be included;

(5) in the case of proposed exploitation of mineral bodies, the nature and extent of the company's rights and a description of the properties to which such rights attach, giving particulars of the duration and other principal terms of the concessions or other rights; an estimate of the proved exploitable reserves (including as precise a description of the nature and quality as the evidence allows) should be given together with a statement as to the economic conditions for working them;

(6) a report by the technical adviser to the company with respect to the estimated reserves and the evidence on which the evidence is based; the report, made up to a date not more than six months prior to the publication of the listing particulars, must be dated and should include adequate information on the following:

(a) the number of holes drilled and their distribution;
(b) a statement describing very briefly the geological characteristics of the occurrence, the type of deposit, its dimensions and the grade of mineral; for fluid and/or gaseous deposits the porosity and permeability characteristics of the reservoirs, the thickness of the net pay, the pressure of the fluid or gas within it and the recovery mechanism planned;
(c) an estimate of the proven reserves and the anticipated mining recovery and dilution factors of recovery factors with respect to oil and gas factors in place on a field by field basis together with the expected period of working;
(d) when the concession includes probable or possible reserves relevant to the long-term future of the company this should be stated with a note as to the type of evidence available;
(e) the nature of any geophysical and geographical evidence used in making reserve estimates and the name of the organisation that did the work;
(f) a statement on production policy; and
(g) an indication of the progress of actual working;

(7) a statement setting out additional information where it is necessary for a proper appraisal of any special factors affecting the exploration business of the company[80];

(8) in addition to the statement as to the sufficiency of working capital which is required to be given by the directors:

(a) an estimate of the requirements of the company for funds for at least two years following publication of the listing particulars;
(b) where the company already has income or expects to receive income dur-

[80] For example, difficulties of access to or recovery of minerals on properties where the company has exploitation rights, or special economic, environmental, political or other circumstances surrounding their exploitation which may affect the commercial viability of the project.

ing the period covered by this statement, particulars of the estimated cash flow for at least the two years following publication of the listing particulars; and

(c) an estimate of the further finance required to enable the company to exploit its proved reserves and commence recoveries on a commercial scale, together with an estimate of the time needed to achieve this;

(9) full particulars of the nature and extent of the interest direct or indirect, if any, of every director, technical adviser or promoter named in the listing particulars in the promotion of, or in the assets which have been within the past two years acquired or disposed of by or leased to the company or any of its subsidiaries including:

(a) the consideration passing to and from the company and its subsidiaries, and

(b) short particulars of all transactions relating to any such assets which have taken place

or an appropriate negative statement.

Where the company seeking funds already has a listing[81] and its activities include to a material extent exploration for natural resources the listing particulars need contain only the following additional items of information beyond those required under the general rules, namely[82]:

(a) a description of the deposits, an estimate of economically exploitable reserves and the expected period of working;

(b) an indication of the periods and main terms of concessions and the economic conditions for working them; and

(c) indications of the progress of actual working.

Where the information has been influenced by exceptional factors that fact must be mentioned.

*(c) Investment trusts and investment companies*

In addition to the matters to be disclosed about the business of an investment trust or company under the general rules the Stock Exchange requires that listing particulars include[83]:

(1) a list of all investments with a value of greater than five per cent. of the fund, and at least the ten largest investments stating:

---

[81] Where a listed company proposes to explore for natural resources either as an extension to or change from its existing activities a circular must be sent to shareholders where the proposal involves a transaction which might reasonably be expected to result in either the diversion of 25 per cent. or more of the net assets of the company to the exploration of natural resources or the contribution from such exploration of 25 per cent. or more to the pre-tax trading results of the company. (Any such transaction should be conditional on approval by the shareholders in general meeting.): ASL, Section 10, Chapter 2, para. 4.

[82] ASL, Section 10, Chapter 2, para. 6. Note that these items are not required where the issue is of debt securities (not being convertible debt securities) or in a rights issue.

[83] ASL, Section 10, Chapter 3, para. 5.

(a) a brief description of the business;

(b) proportion of the share capital owned;

(c) cost;

(d) directors' valuation;

(e) dividends received during the year (including any abnormal dividends);

(f) dividend cover or underlying earnings;

(g) any extraordinary items; and

(h) net assets attributable to investment.

(2) an analysis of any provision for diminution in value of investments, naming the investments against which provision has been made and stating for each investment:

(a) cost;

(b) provision made;

(c) book value; and

(d) reason for the provision.

### Assets and liabilities, profits and losses and financial position

Financial information in respect of companies coming to the market for the **6.51** first time has, under Stock Exchange Regulations governing the admission of securities to listing, been contained in a report[84] by the company's auditors dealing with various matters specified in the regulations.

The Listing Particulars Directive lays down a number of requirements to be met in relation to the form and content of the information which should be included in listing particulars. In general terms these requirements are less stringent than those of the Stock Exchange but, in some respects, provide for the inclusion of statistical information which would not otherwise be present in a prospectus.

The auditors' report should deal with the following matters: **6.52**

(a) *Profits and losses.* These are to be in respect of the five completed years immediately preceding the issue of the listing particulars, or, if the company has been in existence for less than five years, in respect of each of the completed financial years since incorporation. The report as to profits and losses should, where relevant, be on a consolidated basis and should disclose separately the following items:

(1) turnover or other operating income or revenue with an indication of how turnover is calculated;

(2) cost of sales, showing separately by way of notes:

(a) amortisation, depreciation and obsolescence of fixed assets, etc.; and

(b) leasing and hire charges;

---

[84] ASL, Section 4.

(3) investment and other income;

(4) interest payable;

(5) exceptional items;

(6) share of profits or losses of associated companies;

(7) profit before taxation and extraordinary items;

(8) taxation of profits (United Kingdom, overseas and share of associated companies) indicating basis;,

(9) minority interests;

(f) *The company's interest capitalisation statement.* This is to be in respect of each of the periods reported upon the amount of interest capitalised by the company or group with an indication of the amount and treatment of any related tax relief.

(g) *The accounting policies.* The policies followed in dealing with those items which are judged to be material in determining the profits/losses and net assets reported upon are to be set out.

(h) *Any other matters which appear to be relevant.* The report should be prepared in historical cost terms as to these matters but, in order to comply with S.S.A.P. 16, it should also include current cost profit and loss information for the latest two years together with the latest balance sheet prepared on a current cost basis.

**6.53**    In the case of listed companies seeking to raise capital for the acquisition of unlisted companies or businesses an accountants' report is required dealing with the profits/losses and assets and liabilities of the target company or business together with any other matter which may appear to be relevant having regard to the purpose of the report.[85]

**6.54**    In producing their report the auditors may make such adjustments as may seem to them appropriate for the purposes of the listing particulars.[86] Any adjustments should be made in a written statement which should set out for each of the years reported upon each adjustment made in respect of any of the items mentioned in § 6.52 above so as to demonstrate the reconciliation between the figure appearing in the audited accounts and the corresponding figure in the report.

Ideally the report should be unqualified. Where, however, a report is made subject to qualification the matters to which the qualification relates should be specified along with the reasons for the qualification and the quantification of its effect.[87]

**6.55**    The Listing Particulars Directive requires that listing particulars include the following:

---

[85] See further at §§7.36 *et seq*, below.
[86] ASL, Section 4, para. 4.
[87] *Ibid*. para. 8.

*(a) Accounts of the issuing company*

These should include[88]:

(1) the last three balance sheets and profit and loss accounts drawn up by the company set out as a comparative table;
(2) the notes on the annual accounts for the last financial year;
(3) the profit/loss per share for the last financial year;
(4) the amount of dividend per share for the last three financial years.

*(b) Consolidated accounts*

In the case of a group of companies the Listing Particulars Directive[89] permits the accounts for the group to be presented in consolidated form. In such a case the consolidated annual accounts must disclose[90]:

(1) the principles on which the consolidated accounts have been prepared;
(2) the names and registered offices of the undertakings included in the consolidation, where the information is important for the purpose of assessing the assets and liabilities, the financial position and the profits and losses of the issuer;
(3) for each of these undertakings:
    (i) the total proportion of third party interests, if annual accounts are consolidated globally; and
    (ii) the proportion of the consolidation calculated on the basis of interests, if consolidation has been effected on a *pro rata* basis.

Where the issuer includes only consolidated accounts in the listing particulars, those particulars must indicate also:

(4) the consolidated profit or loss per share per financial year for the last three financial years.[91]

*(c) Interim statements*

Where more than nine months have elapsed since the end of the financial year to which the last published own and/or consolidated annual accounts, relate, an

---

[88] LPD, Sched. A, para. 5.1.; Sched. B, para. 5.1.
[89] LPD, Sched. A, para. 5.1.5.; Sched. B, para. 5.1.1.
[90] LPD, Sched. A, para. 5.4.; Sched. B, para. 5.3.
[91] LPD, Sched. A, para. 5.1.2.; Sched. B, para. 5.1.2., each of which provides:

The profit or loss per share of the issuing company, for the financial year, arising out of the company's ordinary activities, after tax, for the last three financial years, where the company includes its own annual accounts in the listing particulars.

Where the issuer includes only consolidated annual accounts in the listing particulars, it shall indicate the consolidated profit or loss per share, for the last three financial years. This information shall appear in addition to that provided in accordance with the preceding sub-paragraph where the issuer also includes its own annual accounts in the listing particulars.

If in the course of the abovementioned period of three financial years the number of shares in the issuing company has changed as a result, for example, of an increase or decrease in capital or the rearrangement or splitting of shares, the profit or loss per share referred to in the first and second paragraph above shall be adjusted to make them comparable; in that event the adjustment formulae used shall be disclosed.

interim statement covering at least the first six months must be included in the listing particulars or appended to them. If such an interim statement is unaudited that fact must be stated.[92]

Any significant change which has occurred since the end of the last financial year or the preparation of the interim financial statement must be described in a note inserted in the listing particulars or appended thereto.[93]

*(d) Investments*

Where the issuing company holds a substantial proportion of the capital of another undertaking or undertakings and such holdings are likely to have a significant effect on the assessment of its assets and liabilities, financial position or profits and losses details of those undertakings must be included in the listing particulars.[94]

[92] LPD, Sched. A, para. 5.1.4.; Sched. B, para. 5.1.2.

[93] Where the issuer prepares consolidated accounts, the Stock Exchange, as competent authority, must decide whether the interim financial statement to be submitted must be consolidated or not: *ibid.*

[94] LPD, Sched. A, para. 5.2.; Sched. B, para. 5.2., the provisions of which read as follows:

> The items of information listed below must be given in any event for every undertaking in which the issuer has a direct or indirect participating interest, if the book value of that participating interest represents at least 10 per cent of the capital and reserves or accounts for at least 10 per cent of the net profit or loss of the issuer or, in the case of a group, if the book value of that paticipating interest represents at least 10 per cent of the consolidated net assets or accounts for at least 10 per cent of the consolidated net profit or loss of the group.
>
> The items of information listed below need not be given provided that the issuer proves that its holding is of a purely provisional nature.
>
> Similarly, the information required under points (e) and (f) may be omitted where the undertaking in which a participating interest is held does not publish its annual accounts.
>
> Pending subsequent coordination of provisions relating to consolidated annual accounts, the Member States may authorize the competent authorities to permit the omission of the information prescribed in points (d) to (j) if the annual accounts of the undertakings in which the participating interests are held are consolidated into the group annual accounts or if the value attributable to the interest under the equity method is disclosed in the annual accounts, provided that, in the opinion of the competent authorities, the omission of that information is not likely to mislead the public with regard to the facts and circumstances, knowledge of which is essential for the assessment of the security in question.
>
> The information provided for under points (g) and (j) may be omitted if, in the opinion of the competent authorities, such omission does not mislead investors.
>
> (a) Name and registered office of the undertaking.
> (b) Field of activity.
> (c) Proportion of capital held.
> (d) Issued capital.
> (e) Reserves.
> (f) Profit or loss arising out of ordinary activities, after tax, for the last financial year.
> (g) Value at which the issuer obliged to publish listing particulars shows shares held in its accounts.
> (h) Amount still to be paid up on shares held.
> (i) Amount of dividends received in the course of the last financial year in respect of shares held.
> (j) Amount of the debts owed to and by the issuer with regard to the undertaking.

Note that items (g) and (j) in the above are not required in listing particulars published in respect of debt securities. Likewise Sched. A, para. 5.3 has no counterpart in Sched. B. Para. 5.3. provides:

> Individual details relating to the undertakings not referred to in heading 5.2 in which the

*(e) Borrowings*

Where a listing is sought for debt securities The Listing Particulars Directive requires that the prospectus give an indication as at the most recent date possible (which must be stated) of the following items, if material[95]:

(1) the total amount of any loan capital outstanding, distinguishing between loans guaranteed (by the provision of security or otherwise, by the issuer or by third parties) and loans not guaranteed;

(2) the total amount of all other borrowings and indebtedness in the nature of borrowing, distinguishing between guaranteed and unguaranteed borrowings and debts; and

(3) the total amount of any contingent liabilities.

In cases where the company does not have any such loan capital, borrowings and indebtedness and contingent liabilities the prospectus should contain an appropriate negative statement.[96]

However, while the obligations described above are limited to listing particulars published in respect of debt securities, a similar requirement is imposed by the Stock Exchange regulations governing the admission of securities to listing in respect of all securities for which a listing is sought. Under these regulations all companies seeking a listing for their securities (whether or not any part of their capital is already listed) must give particulars in relation to the company and its subsidiaries of borrowings or indebtedness in the nature of borrowing, including bank overdrafts and liabilities under acceptances (other than normal trade bills) or acceptance credits, mortgages, charges, hire purchase commitments, guarantees or other contingent material liabilities.[97]

*(f) Profit forecasts*

Where the financial information provided includes a profit forecast Stock Exchange regulations require[98] that the principal assumptions, including commercial assumptions, upon which that forecast is based be stated. The accounting bases and calculations for the forecast must be examined and reported on by the auditors of the company and any reporting accountants joined with the auditors in their report (which must be set out in the body of the prospectus).

In addition, the issuing house or, in the absence of an issuing house, the sponsoring broker must report whether or not they have satisfied themselves that the forecast has been arrived at after careful inquiry, which report must likewise be set out in the body of the prospectus.

---

issuer holds at least 10 per cent of the capital. These details may be omitted when they are of negligible importance for the purpose of the objective set in Article 4 of this Directive:

    (a) name and registered office ofthe undertaking;

    (b) proportion of capital held.

[95] LPD, Sched. B, para. 5.1.4.

[96] *Ibid.* As a general rule, no account should be taken of liabilities between undertakings within the same group, a statement to that effect being made if necessary.

[97] ASL, Section 3, Chapter 2, Part 5, para. 5.16.

[98] *Ibid.* Section 3, Chapter 2, Part 7, para. 7.2.

## Management, administration, supervision and related matters

**6.56**     The Listing Particulars Directive requires[99] the disclosure of information concerning members of the administrative, management and supervisory bodies of the company, together with information concerning its founders in cases where the listing being sought is in respect of securities of a company which has been in existence for less than five years. The particular information specified in the Directive is also required by the more stringent provisions of the Stock Exchange regulations governing the admission of securities to listing. These regulations impose obligations to disclose information as follows:

### (a) Directors

All prospectuses to which the Stock Exchange requirements apply must state the full name, address and description of every director and, if required by the Quotations Committee, particulars of:

(1) any former Christian names or surnames;
(2) his nationality, if not British; and
(3) his nationality of origin if his present nationality is not his nationality of origin.[1]

A prospectus should also state the interests of each director in the share capital of the company, distinguishing beneficial and non-beneficial interests. Where *Directors Inter* a director does not have an interest in the company the prospectus should con-*ests* (i) *in the* tain a statement to that effect.[2]
*Company*

Details of directors' existing or proposed service contracts with the company or any subsidiary must be disclosed[3] as must the aggregate emoluments of the (ii) *Emolu-* directors during the last completed financial period together with an estimate of *ments* the amount payable to the directors, including proposed directors, for the current financial periods under the arrangements in force at the date of the listing particulars.[4]

The prospectus must set out full details of any contract or arrangement subsisting at the date of its publication in which a director of the company is mater-(iii) *Material* ially interested and which is significant in relation to the business of the company *Contracts* and its subsidiaries, taken as a whole, or an appropriate negative statement.[5] Full particulars are also required of the nature and extent of the interest, if any, direct or indirect of every director in the promotion of, or in any assets which have been within the two years preceding the publication of the prospectus, acquired or disposed of by or leased to, the company or any of its subsidiaries, or are proposed to be acquired, disposed of by or leased to the company or any of its subsidiaries including the consideration passing to or from the company or any of its subsidiaries and short particulars of all transactions relating to any such

---

[99] LPD, Sched. A, paras. 6.1–6.3.; Sched. B, para. 6.1.
[1] ASL, Section 3, Chapter 2, Part 6, para. 6.1.
[2] *Ibid*. para. 6.6.
[3] ASL, Section 3, Chapter 2, Part 6, para. 6.5.
[4] *Ibid*. para. 6.3.
[5] *Ibid*. paras. 6.5. and 6.6.

assets which have taken place within the two years immediately preceding the publication of the prospectus. If no such interest exists then the prospectus should contain an appropriate negative statement.[6]

*(b) Promoters' and other interests*

A prospectus must state the name of any promoter[7] of the company and set out the amount of cash or securities paid or benefit given within the two years immediately preceding the publication of the prospectus or proposed to be paid or given to any promoter and the consideration for such payment or benefit.[8]  *Promoters*

Where the company has entered into a material contract or contracts within the two years immediately preceding the publication of the prospectus the date of and parties to all such contracts must be disclosed together with a summary of the principal contents of each contract, including particulars of any consideration passing to or from the company or any subsidiary.[9] This rule does not apply to contracts entered into in the ordinary course of business.

**Expenses**

Listing particulars should give details of any preliminary expenses incurred or proposed to be incurred and should state by whom such expenses are payable.[10] The amount or estimated amount of the expenses of the issue and of the application for listing should also be given in so far as they are not included in the statement of preliminary expenses. Again, details of who is to make the payment should be given.[11]  **6.57**

Companies coming to the market for the first time should also set out particulars of any commissions, discounts, brokerages or other special terms granted within the two years immediately preceding the publication of the prospectus where such were granted in connection with the issue or sale of any capital of the company or of any of its subsidiaries.[12]

**Exhibition of documents**

The listing particulars should contain a statement that for a specified period, being not less than 14 days, at a named place within the City of London[13] the following documents or copies thereof may be inspected[14]:  **6.58**

---

[6] *Ibid.*
[7] ASL, Section 3, Chapter 2, Part 2, para. 2.20.
[8] *Ibid.*
[9] ASL, Section 3, Chapter 2, Part 3, para. 3.16 This requirement does not apply if such contracts have been on view in the last two years, in which event it will be sufficient to refer to them as being on view. In cases where it is contended that contracts cannot be offered for inspection without disclosing to trade competitors important information, the disclosure of which might be detrimental to the interests of any of the parties, application may be made to the Quotation Committee to dispense with the offering of such documents for inspection: *ibid.*
[10] ASL, Section 3, Chapter 2, Part 2, para. 2.18.
[11] *Ibid.*
[12] *Ibid.*
[13] ASL, Section 3, Chapter 2, Part 3, para. 3.17.
[14] *Ibid.*

(1) the memorandum and articles of association of the company;
(2) the trust deed (where relevant);
(3) each contract required to be disclosed, or in the case of a contract not reduced to writing, a memorandum giving full particulars thereof;
(4) all reports, letters or other documents, balance sheets, valuations and statements by experts[15] any parts of which are extracted or referred to in the prospectus;
(5) written statements signed by the auditors or accountants setting out the adjustments made by them in arriving at the figures shown in their reports and giving their reasons therefor; and
(6) the audited accounts of the company and its subsidiaries for each of the two financial years preceding the publication of the prospectus together wth all notes, certificates or information required by the Stock Exchange (Listing) Regulations 1984.

**6.59**     The general rules as to the contents of listing particulars are modified in a few special cases. Those applicable to companies whose securities are already listed and which relate to issues made for the purpose of raising additional capital are considered below at §§ 6.71–6.76. The modifications in such cases are in the nature of relaxations of some requirements. In the cases considered below (with one exception) the modifications require the furnishing of additional information.

*(a) Convertible securities*

Where the application for admission to listing relates to convertible debt securities, exchangeable debt securities or debt securities with warrants, the listing particulars must include[16]:

(1) information concerning the nature of the shares offered by way of conversion, exchange or subscription, and the rights attaching thereto;
(2) the conditions of and procedures for conversion, exchange or subscription and details of the situations in which they may be amended;
(3) the information stipulated in Schedule A as to:
    (i) the official auditors of the issuer;
    (ii) the issuer and its capital;
    (iii) the issuer's activities;
    (iv) the issuer's assets and liabilities, profits and losses and financial position;
    (v) the issuer' administration, management and supervision; and
    (vi) the recent development and prospects of the issuer;

---

[15] Where the prospectus includes a statement purporting to be made by an expert it should state that the expert has given and has not withdrawn his written consent to the issue of the prospectus with the statement included in the form and context in which it appears—ASL, Section 3, Chapter 2, Part 1, para. 1.8.
[16] LPD, Art. 14.

(4) the information stipulated for in Schedule B as to the loan and the admission of the relative debt securities to listing.

Where the issuer of the convertible, etc., debt securities is not the issuer of the shares the listing particulars must include the items mentioned in categories (1) and (2) above and, in respect of the issuer of the debt securities, the items mentioned in category (4) above, and, in respect of the issuer of the shares, the items mentioned in category (3) above.

*(b) Guaranteed debt securities*

Where admission to listing is sought for debt securities guaranteed by a company or other legal person the listing particulars must include[17]:

(1) with respect to the issuer, the information required by Schedule B;
(2) with respect to the guarantor, the information stipulated in Schedule B as to:
    (i) the official auditors of the guarantor;
    (ii) the guarantor and its capital;,
    (iii) the guarantor's activities;
    (iv) the guarantor's assets and liabilities, profits and losses and financial position;
    (v) the guarantor's administration, management and supervision;
    (vi) the recent development and prospects of the guarantor.

Where there is more than one guarantor the information specified is required in respect of each one.[18] The contract of guarantee must be made available for inspection by the public at the offices of the issuer and at the offices of those financial organisations retained to act as paying agents.[19]

*(c) Debt securities with a narrow and specialised market*

Where the appliction for admission to listing relates to debt securities nearly all of which, because of their nature, are normally bought and traded in by a limited number of investors who are particularly knowledgeable in investment matters, the Stock Exchange, as competent authority, may allow the omission from the listing particulars of certain information provided for in Schedule B or allow its inclusion in summary form, provided that such information is not material from the point of view of the investors concerned.[20]

**Completion meeting**

It is the practice for a meeting of the company's board to be convened prior to **6.60** submission of the formal application for listing to the Stock Exchange authorities

---

[17] *Ibid*. Art. 13(1).
[18] *Ibid*. Art. 13(3). The Stock Exchange, as competent authority, may allow abridgement of this information with a view to achieving greater comprehensibility of the listing particulars.
[19] *Ibid*. Art. 13(4). Copies of the contract must be provided to any person concerned on request.
[20] *Ibid*. Art. 10.

in order to give formal authorisation to the implementation of such arrangements as are necessary in connection with the issue.

At this meeting it will be reported that resolutions considered at an extraordinary general meeting for the alteration of the company's memorandum so as to conform with the requirements of the Companies (Alteration of Table A etc.) Regulations 1984,[21] the alteration of the company's articles so as to compny with the requirements of the Stock Exchange[22] and for any reconstruction of capital were passed. The board will then proceed to:

(a) approve and complete the subscription (and purchase, where appropriate) agreements[23];

(b) authorise the secretary to issue renounceable allotment letters;

(c) appoint the registrars;

(d) appoint receiving bankers and approve the giving of necessary authorisations concerning the handling of applications;

(e) confirm the accuracy of the stated profit forecast and accept responsibility for the contents of the listing particulars;

(f) approve the listing particulars and associated documents[24];

(g) approve and date any shareholders' indemnities in respect of taxation liabilities of the company;

(h) authorise the completion of Stock Exchange forms;

(i) authorise the advertising in relation to the issue;

(j) authorise any two directors to act on behalf of the company in connection with the issue; and

(k) instruct the company's solicitors to deliver to the Registrar of Companies immediately:

(1) a signed print of the resolutions passed at the extraordinary general meeting;

(2) a print of the new articles of association;

(3) a print of the new memorandum of association;

(4) a notice of increase of capital;

(5) a statement of increase of capital duly stamped;

(6) a signed print of the prospectus and accompanying document and in due course to deliver a return of allotments.

### Application

**6.61**     Application for listing should be made at the earliest possible date via the brokers to the issue and should be in the prescribed form.[25] The procedures applicable in respect of applications differ to some extent according to whether

---

[21] Formerly C.A. 1980, Sched. I, Part I.

[22] See above at §6.31.

[23] Or, in the case of a placing, the placing agreement.

[24] The Form of Application, Accountants' Reports, Accountants' Consent Letters, Statement of Adjustments, Letter of Acceptance, Receiving Bankers' Consent Letter, Valuers' and other Experts' Consent Letters.

[25] See Appendix for a specimen form.

the issue is to be made through a public offer (whether an offer for subscription made by or on behalf of the issuer or an offer for sale made by an issuing house or issuing broker) or a placing.

*(a) Public offers*

Comparatively few special requirements apply to public offers with those demanded relating to three matters.[26]

(1) *Preferential treatment on allocation or allotment.* Any such preferential treatment must be approved by the Quotations Committee prior to the publication of the listing particulars. Such treatment must not reduce by more than 10 per cent. the minimum amount required to be made available to the public and may be given only to shareholders or present and past employees.

(2) *Underwriting arrangements.* Prior approval must be obtained for any part underwritten firm. This must be strictly limited, the amount permitted depending upon the proportion of the total amount of the security offered it represents.

(3) *Tender offers.* The Quotations Committee requires to be satisfied as to the procedure for determining the price and basis of allotment.

*(b) Placings*

Concessionary rules apply to three types of placing subject to the prior approval of the Quotations Committee. The Stock Exchange demands that such approval be sought at an early date, albeit that approval in principle is not to be taken as implying that listing will ultimately be granted. The purpose of this requirement is to determine the extent of the market's participation in an attempt to ensure adequate marketability for the security. The concessionary rules apply to:

(1) placings (other than eurocurrency placings) having an equity element by an issuing house or broker to their clients, with a proportion being made available to the public through the market[27];
(2) as in (1) above save that the placing is of fixed or floating rate income securities having no equity element; and
(3) eurocurrency placings.

(1) *Equity placings.* In the case of securities having an equity element approval in principle will not be given if the expected market value of the securities placed exceeds a prescribed maximum amount fixed from time to time by the Quotations Committee. Currently the maximum amount allowable in respect of

---

[26] ASL, Section 1, Chapter 3, para. 1.2.
[27] Where the issuer is a new applicant.

equity shares is £3,000,000 in money value at the placing price in the case of a new applicant and £5,000,000 in the case of a listed company.[28]

A company may raise up to £5,000,000 by an issue of other securities having an equity element (not being equity shares) subject to the observance of limits as to dilution of the underlying equity upon a full conversion or exercise of the sub-scription rights.[29]

Issues of securities having an equity element (not being equity shares) in excess of £5,000,000 will, however, be permitted subject to three conditions, namely:

   (a) that the conversion or subscription rights cannot be exercised for at least three years from the date of issue;

   (b) that the conversion price or subscription rights represent a premium over the middle market quotation of the underlying equity capital at the time of issue; and

   (c) full conversion or exercise of the subscription rights relating to the amount of the placing will not result, at the time of the issue, in an increase in the underlying equity capital of more than 10 per cent.[30]

Where the placing is of securities having equity element (not being equity shares) 10 per cent. of the amount placed must be offered to the market and a further 10 per cent. must be at the call of the market until noon on the day after the listing particulars or formal notice appear in the press, or, if that is not a business day, on the first business day thereafter.[31]

In general the marketing arrangements for the placing of securities having an equity element (whether or not they are equity shares) must provide that of the amount placed not less than 25 per cent. is offered to the market. Where a placing of less than 25 per cent. of the equity capital of a new applicant is permitted such an amount will be required to be offered to the market as the Committee considers necessary to ensure adequate marketability of the security.[32] In the case of securities only partly convertible or exchangeable into equity capital at least 30 per cent. of the issued amount must be placed.[33]

When applying for placing permission the sponsoring broker must supply the following information to the Quotations Committee, namely[34]:

---

[28] In relation to such companies there is a further limitation in that the shares to be placed must not increase the underlying equity in any period of 12 months by more than the following:

| Money Value | Increase in Equity |
|---|---|
| up to £1,500,000 | no limit |
| up to £3,000,000 | 20% |
| up to £5,000,000 | 10% |

[29] On the same terms as in n.28, above.

[30] ASL, Section 1, Chapter 3, para. 2.3.

[31] *Ibid*. paras. 2.3. and 2.7.

[32] *Ibid*. para. 2.5. In this context references to the "market" should be taken to apply to firms recog-nised as jobbers by the Stock Exchange: *ibid*. para. 2.11.

[33] *Ibid*. para. 2.5.

[34] *Ibid*.

 (i) the nature of the company's business;
 (ii) its profit record before taxation for the past five years or since inception, whichever is the less;
(iii) whether any profit is to be forecast for the next year;
(iv) whether any dividend is expected to be paid;
 (v) the profits cover;
(vi) the expected placing price and yield at that price; and
(vii) the total amount of capital in issue or to be issued.

(2) *Placings of securities having no equity element.* In the case of placings (other than euro-currency placings) of fixed or floating rate income securities having no equity element the application for approval in principle must state the total amount of the securities to be issued and the proportion to be placed. At least 30 per cent. of the issued amount must be placed. For placings of up to and including £3,000,000 the marketing arrangements must provide that of the amount placed not less than 20 per cent. is offered to the market. For placings in excess of £3,000,000 but less than £15,000,000, 10 per cent. of the amount placed must be offered to the market and a further 10 per cent. must be at the call of the market until noon on the day after the listing particulars or formal notice appears in the press, or, if that is not a business day, on the first business day thereafter.[35]

So far as the placing is in respect of debt securities a discount of $\frac{1}{2}$ per cent. of the nominal value of the securities should be allowed to be market on the nominal value of the first or only tranche and $\frac{1}{4}$ per cent. on any second tranche. Corresponding discounts of 1 per cent. and $\frac{1}{4}$ per cent of nominal value should be allowed in placings of preference capital.

(3) *Eurocurrency placings.* Eurocurrency placings are normally undertaken pursuant to an arrangement[36] under which underwriting and selling groups receive commission on a uniform price basis. It is a Stock Exchange requirement that in such placings the market should be included in the selling group. While the Stock Exchange is willing to permit such arrangements to apply in the case of eurocurrency securities it is not normally prepared to extend these facilities to other securities. For these purposes, where the eurobonds or other debt securities, whether or not convertible, are denominated solely in sterling, the Quotations Committee, when considering whether to grant placing permission in principle, will have regard to the life of the securities on the basis of their policy from time to time in force.[37]

In the case of eurocurrency securities not having an equity element the market must be offered not less than 1 per cent. of the amount placed, subject to a minimum of U.S. $300,000.[38]

For eurocurrency placings of securities having an equity element the Committee's general policy is to require an amount not exceeding 5 per cent. of the mount placed to be offered to the market. In considering what the market's par-

[35] *Ibid.* para. 2.7.
[36] See further at §§2.73–2.75, above.
[37] ASL, Section 1, Chapter 3, para. 2.9.
[38] *Ibid.* para. 2.10.

ticipation should be in individual issues the Committee will have regard to whether the convertibility is into:

(a) a foreign security listed on another stock exchange;

(b) a foreign security listed on the Stock Exchange; or

(c) a domestic company's shares.

In deciding the extent of the market's participation the Committee will consider the nature of any trading operations the applicant has in the united Kingdom. In the case of an applicant having limited trading operations here and seeking a placing for a foreign currency security convertible into a security not listed on the Stock Exchange the market should be offered 1 per cent. of the issue. In the two remaining cases companies would be expected to offer a greater proportion up to a maximum of 5 per cent. to the market.[39]

**6.62**     Applicants must submit for initial approval, at least 14 days prior to publication or posting of the particulars of the issue, the following documents, namely[40]:

(1) four proof prints of the listing particulars, circular, formal notices or other appropriate document intended for publication by the issuer or on its behalf;

(2) four copies of any application form to purchase or subscribe securities;

(3) four copies of any temporary documents of title proposed to be issued[41];

(4) four copies of the definitive certificate or other definitive document of title proposed to be issued[42];

(5) two copies of the memorandum and articles of association or equivalent documents[43];

(6) in the case of a new applicant, a statement, duly signed by an authorised officer, of the name of any promoter in respect of any member of the group including (where relevant) any director, the amount of any cash, securities or benefits paid, issued or given within the two years immediately preceding the date of intended publication, or proposed to be paid, issued or given to any promoter and the consideration for such payment, issue or benefit;

(7) in the case of listed companies, two copies of all special resolutions or resolutions increasing the capital or providing for the issue of securities to be listed;

(8) in the case of debt securities, two copies of the proposed trust deed or other document securing or constituting the securities[44]; and

(9) two copies of any statement of adjustments relating to the accountants' reports.

---

[39] *Ibid.*

[40] ASL, Section 2, Chapter 1, para. 2.

[41] Which must be in the prescribed form. See ASL, Section 9, Chapter 3.

[42] Which must be in the prescribed form. See ASL, Section 9, Chapter 4.

[43] Which should observe the prescribed requirements. See ASL Section 9, Chapter 1 (reproduced in Appendix).

[44] Which should observe the prescribed requirements. See ASL, Section 9, Chapter 2 (reproduced in Appendix).

A formal declaration relating to any other business activities must be submitted by each director and proposed director at least 14 days prior to intended publication of the listing particulars.[45]

In the event of any amendment being made to any of the above documents after submission a corresponding number of further copies must be submitted for approval, these copies to be marked in red to indicate amendments made to conform with points raised by the Department and in blue or black to indicate other amendments.[46]

The rules governing advertising and publicity for flotations and other public issues require that, unless the Committee otherwise directs, the listing particulars must be published in two national daily newspapers.[47] In the case of a placing listing particulars must be published in one national daily newspaper with a formal notice to be published in a second such newspaper.[48]

Where application is made for listing by a company whose business and shareholding has strong regional connections part of the advertising may be inserted in newspapers circulating within that region.[49]

*Advertising and Publicity*

**6.63**

An important part of the application procedure is devoted to ensuring that the Quotations Committee has in its hands all the necessary information and documentation to enable it to reach a decision after a formal hearing. In order to ensure that the Committee has available to it all that it needs the relevant documents these must be lodged with the Quotations Department at least two business days prior to the hearing.[50]

**6.64**

As soon as practicable after the hearing details of the results of the issue should be lodged with the Department.[51] As soon as practicable there should also be lodged a declaration by a duly authorised officer of the company announcing the results of the issue and confirming that all requirements of statute and of the Stock Exchange have been met in relation to the issue.[52]

**Flotation timetable**

The critical date in any flotation is "impact day," that is to say when the issue is announced and thereby makes its effective "impact" on the market. In the case of a prospectus issue or an offer for sale impact day is also the day when the underwriting agreement is signed and the sub-underwriting arranged. As has been mentioned[53] the choice of impact day is, in capital-raising operations involving £3,000,000 or more, subject to approval by the Bank of England,

**6.65**

---

[45] ASL, Section 2, Chapter 1, para. 3.
[46] *Ibid.* para. 4.
[47] ASL. Section 2, Chapter 3, para. 1.
[48] *Ibid.* para. 2.
[49] *Ibid.* para. 1.
[50] The documents required to be lodged are set out in paras. 5 and 6 of Section 1, Chapter 2, of ASL. The list is set out in the Appendix.
[51] ASL, Section 1, Chapter 2, para. 7 (reproduced in Appendix).
[52] *Ibid.* para. 8. The declaration must be in the prescribed form.
[53] At § 6.34, above.

application being made via the Government Broker at least two months in advance. In practice impact day is usually a Thursday.

On the last practicable day before impact day a flotation meeting is held at which the sponsors in conjunction with the solicitors to the issue take the directors of the company through the listing particulars so that all can be satisfied that it may go forward for printing and publication.

In the case of an offer for sale or prospectus issue the flotation timetable thenceforward is usually as follows:

*(1) Prospectus Issues/Offers for Sale*

| | | |
|---|---|---|
| (1) | Prospectus signed | Impact Day (ID) |
| | Underwriting agreement signed and sub-underwriting begins | |
| (2) | Press conferences, publicity briefings, etc. | ID or ID + 1 |
| (3) | Prospectus advertised in the press and available to the public | ID + 4 |
| (4) | Listing granted by the Stock Exchange | ID + 6 |
| (5) | Subscription lists open and close | ID + 7 |
| (6) | Basis of allotment announced | ID + 8 |
| (7) | Allotment letters dispatched/proceeds of issue paid to the company | ID + 11/12 |
| (8) | Dealings begin | ID + 12/13 |

*(2) Placings*

In the case of a placing dealings normally begin within a week of the placing agreement being executed. It is a requirement however that no dealings may take place before listing is granted.[54] Payment of the proceeds of issue is made prior to the commencement of dealings.

**Continuing obligations**

**6.66**    Prior to January 1, 1985 it was a condition of admission to listing that companies coming to the market for the first time enter into a formal Listing Agreement with the Stock Exchange under which the company undertook to observe certain practices in relation to its status as a listed company. The principal object of the Listing Agreement was to require the company to procure the immediate release of information which might reasonably be expected to have a material effect on market activity in and prices of listed securities. It had the effect of establishing arrangements under which the company would inform its members and the market and, where appropriate, consult shareholders on matters of significance.

On January 1, 1985 the Stock Exchange (Listing) Regulations 1984[55] came into general operation and brought into force with them the Admission[56] and Interim Reports[57] Directives each of which imposed on a statutory basis certain

---

[54] ASL, Section 1, Chapter 2, para. 2.6.
[55] S.I. 1984 No. 716.
[56] E.E.C. Council Directive No. 79/279/EEC.
[57] E.E.C. Council Directive No. 82/121/EEC.

continuing obligations to be observed by listed companies. In view of the changed circumstances the Council of the Stock Exchange felt that it would no longer be necessary to require these continuing obligations to be embodied in a formal agreement; any obligations over and above those imposed by the Directives could be imposed as conditions of admission to listing.[58]

The continuing obligations to which a listed company is subject relate to the following matters, namely: **6.67**

(1) Communication of relevant information;
(2) Treatment of Share/Stockholders;
(3) Annual Accounts;
(4) Interim Reports; and
(5) Obligations incumbent upon directors of listed companies.

Article 13 of the Admission Directive imposes an obligation to provide the Stock Exchange with all the information which it (*i.e.* the Stock Exchange) considers appropriate in order to protect investors or to ensure the smooth operation of the market.[59] Furthermore, a company may be required to publish information in such form and within such time limits as the Stock Exchange might deem appropriate. In the event of a company's failing to comply with such a requirement the Council of the Stock Exchange is itself empowered to publish the information, having given the company a hearing on the matter.[60] **6.68**

More specifically, notification of the following matters is required by the Stock Exchange, namely:

(a) any major new developments in its sphere of activity which are not public knowledge and which: *Communication of Relevant Information*
    (1) in the case of a company having listed shares in issue may, by virtue of their effect on its assets/liabilities or financial position or on the general course of its business, lead to substantial movements in the price of its shares; or
    (2) in the case of a company having listed debt securities in issue may significantly affect its ability to meet its commitments.[61]

(b) the date fixed for any board meeting at which the declaration or recommendation or payment of a dividend on listed shares is expected to be decided, or at which any announcement of the profits/losses in respect of any year, half-year, or other period is to be approved for publication[62];
(c) (after board approval) any decision to pay or make any dividend or other distribution on listed securities or to pass any dividend or interest payment on such securities[63];

---

[58] ASL. Section 5, Chapter 2.
[59] Admission Directive, Art. 13(1); ASL, Section 5, Chapter 2, para. 1.
[60] *Ibid*. Art 13(2).
[61] ASL, Section 5, Chapter 2, para. 5.
[62] *Ibid*. para. 6.
[63] *Ibid*. para. 7.

(d) (after board approval) any preliminary announcement of profits/losses for any year, half-year or other period[64];

(e) in the case of a company having debt securities in issue, any new issues of debt securities and, in particular, any guarantee or security in respect thereof[65];

(f) (after board approval) any proposed change in capital structure, including that of the company's listed debt securities[66];

(g) (after board approval) any drawing or redemption of listed securities[67];

(h) any change in the rights attaching to any class of listed securities (including any change in the rate of interest carried by a debt security) and any change in the rights attaching to any shares into which any listed debt securities are convertible or exchangeable[68];

(i) the basis of any allotment of securities offered generally to the public for cash, other than by a placing, and of open offers to shareholders[69];

(j) details of certain acquisitions or realisations of assets[70];

(k) any information required to be disclosed to the Stock Exchange under the provisions of the City Code on Take-overs and the Mergers for the time being in force[71];

(l) in the case of a United Kingdom company,[72] any information notified to the company under Part VI of the Companies Act 1985[73];

(m) any purchases by the company, or the group of which the company is part, of its listed securities[74];

(n) any board decision to change the general character or nature of the business of the company or of the group of which the company is a part[75];

(o) any change in the status of the company for taxation purposes under the statutory provisions relating to close companies or to approved investment trusts.[76]

In addition, a company whose securities are also listed on other stock exchanges must ensure that equivalent information is made available to the market at the Stock Exchange and each of the other stock exchanges.[77]

---

[64] *Ibid.* para. 8.

[65] *Ibid.* para. 9.

[66] *Ibid.* para. 10.

[67] *Ibid.* para. 11.

[68] *Ibid.* para. 12; Admission Directive, Sched. C, para. 5(*b*); Sched. D, paras. 4(*b*) and (*d*).

[69] *Ibid.* para. 13. The Quotations Department should also be notified of any extension of time granted for the currency of temporary documents of title.

[70] *Ibid.* para. 14. See further at §7.61 below.

[71] *Ibid.* para. 15.

[72] Foreign companies are subject to different requirements. See ASL, Section 5, Chapter 2, paras. 21–23.

[73] ASL, Section 5, Chapter 2, para 16. This provision relates to the disclosure of directors' interests in the company.

[74] *Ibid.* para. 17.

[75] *Ibid.* para. 18.

[76] *Ibid.* para. 19.

[77] *Ibid.* para. 3; Admission Directive Sched. C, paras. 6(*a*) and (*b*); Sched. D, paras 5(*a*) and (*b*).

The company must ensure that equal treatment is accorded to all shareholders who are in the same position.[78] Likewise, holders of debt securities ranking *pari passu* must be given equal treatment in respect of all the rights attaching to those debt securities.[79] In particular the company must: **6.69**

*Treatment of Share/Stock-Holders*

    (a) inform share/stockholders of the holding of any meetings and enable them to exercise their right to vote[80];

    (b) publish notices or distribute circulars[81] concerning the allocation and payment of dividends or interest in respect of such securities, the issue of new securities (including arrangments for the allotment, subscription, renunciation, conversion or exchange of such securities) and repayment of securities[82]; and

    (c) appoint a registrar and/or, where appropriate, a paying agent in the United Kingdom unless the company itself performs these functions.[83]

Unless its shareholders in general meeting otherwise permit, a company must offer any securities having an equity element to be issued for cash to its existing equity shareholders in proportion to their existing holdings and, where appropriate, to holders of other securities of the company having an equity element entitled to be offered them. Only to the extent that the securities are not taken up by such persons may the company issue them to others or otherwise than in proportion as mentioned.[84]

Where the company has subsidiaries it must obtain the consent of its shareholders in general meeting before any major subsidiary makes any issue of securities having an equity element for cash so as materially to dilute the per-

---

[78] *Ibid.* para. 4(*a*); Admission Directive, Sched. C para. 2(*a*).

[79] *Ibid.* para. 4(*b*); Admission Directive, Sched. D para. 1(*a*).

[80] *Ibid.* para. 36; Admission Directive, Sched. C, para. 2(*b*) and Sched. D, para. 1(*b*). Note that the company must send proxy forms, with provision for two-way voting on all resolutions intended to be proposed, with the notice convening a meeting of holders of listed securities to all persons entitled to vote at the meeting. ASL, Section 5, Chapter 2, para. 37.

[81] Whenever shareholders are sent a notice of a meeting which includes any business, other than routine business at an annual general meeting, an explanatory circular must accompany the notice or, if the business is to be considered at or on the same day as an annual general meeting, an explanation must be incorporated in the directors' report. An explanatory circular must also accompany any notice of meeting sent to holders of listed debt securities: *ibid.* para. 32.

    Where an increase in authorised capital is proposed, the directors must state in the explanatory circular or other document accompanying the notice of meeting whether they have any present intention of issuing any part of that capital: *ibid.* para. 33.

    Where an increase of authorised capital is proposed and 10 per cent or more of the voting capital will remain unissued, the explanatory circular or other document accompanying the notice of meeting must state that no issue will be made which would effectively alter the control of the company without prior approval of the company in general meeting: *ibid.* para. 34.

    In the event of a circular being issued to the holders of any particular class of security, the company must issue a copy or summary of such circular to the holders of all other listed securities unless the contents of such circular are irrelevant to such other holders: *ibid.* para. 39.

    The company must forward to the Company Announcements Office six copies of all circulars, notices, reports, announcements or other documents at the same time as they are issued and four copies of all resolutions passed by the company other than resolutions concerning routine business at an annual general meeting: *ibid.* para. 35.

[82] *Ibid.* para. 36.

[83] *Ibid.*

[84] *Ibid.* para. 38(*a*). Note that unlike the provisions of s.89 of C.A. 1985 this provision may not be disapplied. However, it need not be complied with in respect of fractional entitlements.

centage equity interest of the company and its shareholders in such subsidiary.[85]

The Admission Directive requires[86] a listed company to make available to the public, as soon as possible, its most recent annual accounts and its last annual report. If the company prepares both annual own and annual consolidated accounts it must make both available. However, the Council of the Stock Exchange, as competent authority, may authorise the company to make available to the public either one or other set of annual accounts, provided that the accounts not made available do not contain any significant additional information.[87]

The Stock Exchange requires that the annual report and accounts be issued within six months of the end of the period to which they relate. If the company has subsidiaries the accounts must be in consolidated form. If the relevant annual accounts do not give a true and fair view of the state of affairs and profit/loss of the company of group, more detailed and/or additional information must be provided.[88]

The company must include in its annual report and accounts the following matters namely[89]:

(a) in the case of domestic companies, a statement by the directors as to the reasons for any significant departure from applicable standard accounting practices;

(b) an explanation in the event of trading results shown by the accounts for the period under review differing materially from any published forecast made by the company;

(c) a geographical analysis of both net turnover and contribution to trading results of those trading operations carried on by the company or group outside the United Kingdom and the Republic of Ireland;

(d) the name of the principal country in which each subsidiary operates;

(e) the following particulars regarding each company (not being a subsidiary) in which the group interest in the equity capital amounts to 20 per cent. or more, namely:

    (1) the principal country of operation;

    (2) particulars of its issued capital and debt securities; and

    (3) the percentage of each class of debt securities attributable to the company's interest (direct or indirect).

(f) a statement as at the end of the financial year showing as regards bank loans and overdrafts and other borrowings of the company or group the aggregate amounts repayable:

    (1) in one year or less, or on demand;

---

[85] *Ibid.* para. 38(*b*). A subsidiary representing 25 per cent. or more of the consolidated net assets or pre-tax trading profits of the group is to be regarded as a major subsidiary; however if such subsidiary is itself listed para. 38(*b*) does not apply since the subsidiary will be bound by para. 38(*a*).
[86] Sched. C, para. 4(*a*); Sched. D, para. 3(*a*).
[87] Sched. C, para. 4(*b*); Sched. D, para. 3(*b*).
[88] ASL, Section 5, Chapter 2, para. 20.
[89] *Ibid.* para. 21.

(2) between one and two years;

(3) between two and five years; and

(4) in five years or more.

(g) in respect of the financial year, a statement of the amount of interest capitalised by the company or group during the year, with an indication of the amount and treatment of any related tax relief;

(h) in the case of a United Kingdom company a statement as at the end of the financial year, showing the interests of each director in the capital of any member of the group appearing in the register maintained under the provisions of the Companies Act 1985, together with any options in respect of such capital, distinguishing between beneficial and non-beneficial interests. Such statement should include by way of note any change in those interests or options occurring between the end of the financial year and a date not more than one month prior to the date of the notice of meeting or, if there has been no such change, disclosure of that fact;

(i) in the case of a United Kingdom company, a statement showing particulars as at a date not more than one month prior to the date of the notice of meeting, of an interest of any person, other than a director, in any substantial part of the share capital appearing in the register maintained under the provisions of section 211 of the Companies Act 1985 and the amount of the interest in question or, if there is no such interest, a statement of that fact;

(j) in the case of a United Kingdom company, a statement showing whether, so far as the directors are aware, the company is a close company for taxation purposes and whether there has been any change in that respect since the end of the financial year;

(k) particulars of any contract of significance[90] subsisting during or at the end of the financial year in which a director is or was materially interested, or, if there has been no such contract, a statement of that fact;

(l) particulars of any contract of significance between the company, or one of its subsidiaries, and a corporate substantial shareholder. Where a company has subsidiaries, comparison will be made with the purchases, sales, payments, receipts or net assets of the group on a consolidated basis;

(m) particulars of any contract for the provision of services to the company or any of its subsidiaries by a corporate substantial shareholder. Exceptionally such a contract need not be disclosed, if it is a contract for the provision of services which it is the principal business of the shareholder to provide and it is not a contract of significance;

(n) particulars of any arrangement under which a director has waived or agreed to waive any emoluments;

---

[90] A contract of significance is one which represents in amount or value a sum equal to 1 per cent. or more of:

    (i) in the case of a capital transaction or a transaction of which the principal purpose is the granting of credit, the net assets of the company or

    (ii) in other cases, the total purchases, sales, payments or receipts, as the case may be, of the company: *ibid.* para. 21.9.

(o) particulars of any arrangement under which a shareholder has waived or agreed to waive any dividends;

(p) in the case of a United Kingdom company, particulars of any shareholders' authority for the purchase by the company of its own shares existing at the end of the year and, in the case of such purchases made otherwise than through the market or by tender or partial offer to all shareholders, particulars of the names of the sellers of all such shares purchased, by the company during the year. In the case of such purchases, or options or contracts to make such purchases, entered into since the end of the year covered by the report, equivalent information to that required under Part II of Schedule 7 to the Companies Act 1985 should be given.

(q) in the case of an investment trust:

(1) a statement confirming, in the case of a United Kingdom company, that the Inland Revenue has approved the company as an investment trust for the purpose of section 359 of the Income and Corporation Taxes Act 1970, specifying the last accounting period in respect of which such approval has been given (or, in the case of a newly listed company, a statement that it has announced that it will direct its affairs to enable it to seek approval) and also that the company has subsequently directed its affairs so as to enable it to continue to be approved;

(2) a broad geographical analysis based on country of incorporation of the companies whose securities are held in the portfolio;

(3) an analysis of the portfolio by broad industrial or commercial sectors;

(4) a list of the largest investments by market value, such value being stated in the case of each such investment;

(5) an analysis of the portfolio between equity capital, securities having an equity element and fixed income securities;

(6) an analysis of income between dividends, interest and other forms of income, distinguishing, where significant, between underwriting income and the results of dealing by subsidiaries;

(7) an analysis, where material to an appreciation of the investment trust's financial position, of realised and unrealised profits/losses as between listed and unlisted investments; and

(8) the name of the group or company which manages the investments, together with an indication of the terms and duration of their appointment and the basis of their remuneration.

(r) in the case of an investment company:

(1) a list of all investments with a value greater than 5 per cent. of the company's assets, at at least the 10 largest investments stating, with comparative figures where relevant:

(i) a brief discription of the business,

(ii) proportion of the share capital owned,

(iii) cost,

(iv) directors' valuation,

     (v) dividends received during the year (indicating any abnormal dividends),

     (vi) dividend cover or underlying earnings,

     (vii) any extraordinary items, and

     (viii) net assets attributable to the investment;

  (2) an analysis of any provision for diminution in the value of investments, naming the investments against which provision has been made and stating for each investment:

     (i) cost,

     (ii) provision made, and

     (iii) book value;

  (3) an analysis of realised and unrealised surpluses, stating separately profits and losses as between listed and unlisted investments.

The Interim Reports Directive imposes obligations on listed companies concerning the preparation and publication of interim reports.   **6.71**

Article 5 of the Directive requires that a listed company's half-yearly report shall consist of figures and an explanatory statement relating to the company's activities and profits/losses during the relevant six-months period. The figures should be in table form and must state at least the following[91]:   *Half-Yearly Reports*

(1) net turnover;

(2) profit or loss before taxation and extraordinary items;

(3) taxation on profits[92];

(4) minority interests;

(5) profit or loss attributable to sharcholders, before extraordinary items;

(6) extraordinary items (net of taxation);

(7) profit or loss attributable to shareholders;

(8) rates of dividend(s) paid and proposed and amount absorbed thereby; and

(9) earnings per share expressed as pence per share;

Against each figure there should be shown the figure for the corresponding period in the preceding financial year.

The explanatory statement must include any significant information enabling investors to make an informed assessment of the trend of the company's activities and profits/losses together with an indication of any special factor or factors which have influenced those activities and profits/losses during the period in question, and to enable a comparison to be made with the corresponding period of the preceding financial year. The statement must also, insofar as is possible, refer to the company's future development in the current financial year.[93]

Where a company publishes consolidated accounts it may publish its half-yearly report in either consolidated or unconsolidated form. However, should the Council of the Stock Exchange, as competent authority, consider that the

---

[91] ASL, Section 5, Chapter 2, para. 25(*b*).

[92] U.K. taxation and, if material, overseas and share of associated companies to be shown separately.

[93] Interim Reports Directive, Art. 5(6).

form not adopted would have contained additional material information, it may require the company to publish such information.[94]

In those cases where the accounting information has been audited by the official auditor of the company's accounts, that auditor's report and any qualifications he may have must be reproduced in full.[95]

**6.72** The Stock Exchange requires that listed companies keep it informed as to the composition of its board; any change in the directorate must be notified immediately.[96]

*Directors* Copies of all directors' service contracts of more than one year's duration[97] or, where any such contract is not reduced to writing, a memorandum of the terms thereof, must be made available at the for inspection[98] at the registered office or transfer office during usual business hours on any weekday (Saturdays and public holidays excluded) from the date of the notice convening the annual general meeting until the date of the meeting and made available for inspection at the place of the meeting for at least 15 minutes prior to the meeting and at the meeting.[99]

The company must adopt rules governing dealings by directors in the listed securities of the company in terms no less exacting than those of the Model Code issued by the Stock Exchange.[1]

### Raising additional capital

**6.73** The public issue process may be used by a listed company to raise additional capital either:

(1) through rights issue; or
(2) through an issue to the public at large.

In practice an issue to the public at large is only available as a means of raising additional capital through fixed interest securities, whether debt securities or preference shares. Where the securities to be issued comprise or include equity the issue must be by way of rights.[2] Thus if the additional funds are to be raised by the issue of equity capital, capital having an element of equity or being convertible into equity, or share options or warrants to subscribe equity capital *and* the issue is for cash then it must take this form.[3]

---

[94] *Ibid*. Art. 6.
[95] *Ibid*. Art. 8.
[96] ASL, Section 5, Chapter 2, para. 42.
[97] The company must state in the directors' report the period unexpired of any service contract of any director proposed for re-election at the forthcoming A.G.M. where the service contract falls within ASL, Section 5, Chapter 2, para. 43(*a*). If there is no such service contract the report should contain an appropriate negative statement: *ibid*. para. 43(*c*).
[98] The company must state in a note to the notice convening the A.G.M. the place and time at which copies of all such service contracts will be available for inspection or, if so, that there are no such contracts: *ibid*. para. 43(*b*).
[99] *Ibid*. para. 43(*a*).
[1] *Ibid*. para. 45. The Model Code is set out in the Appendix.
[2] See above at §§2.100 *et seq*.
[3] ASL, Section 5, Chapter 2, para. 38(*a*).

Whichever of the two forms is used the issue procedure is substantially the same as that considered above at §§ 6.22–6.72, but with amendments to take into account the fact that the company already has listed status and as such need not be subjected to the same levels of disclosure as are demanded of a company coming to the market for the first time.[4]

Where the additional capital is to be raised by a further issue of shares and the **6.74** issue is of such a size as to require an increase in the amount of authorised share capital the consent of the shareholders must be obtained at an extraordinary general meeting. In any case where it is proposed to increase a company's authorised share capital the directors must state in an explanatory circular or other document accompanying the notice of meeting whether they have any present intention of issuing any part thereof. In the event that 10 per cent. of the voting capital will remain unissued[5] the directors must undertake that no issue will be made which would effectively change the control of the company without the prior approval of the company in general meeting.[6]

Once the arrangements for the issue are sufficiently well advanced the com **6.75** pany must notify the Quotations Department pursuant to the continuing obligations accepted by it on admission to listing.[7] An announcement will be made in the press and this will be followed by a circular to shareholders giving the same information. This circular will have to comply with the listing particulars requirements of Section 3 of the Stock Exchange rules for the Admission of Securities to Listing which take account of the requirements of the Listing Particulars Directive.

The requirements imposed correspond to (and are indeed based on) the requirements to be met in the case of a flotation. However a number of special rules apply to rights and certain other issues as follows:

*(a) Rights issues*

Offers of securities by way of rights are normally required to be conveyed by renounceable letter of allotment or other negotiable document.[8] This document must show:

(1) the *pro rata* entitlement, the last day on which transfers were accepted for participation in the issue, how the securities rank for dividend or interest, the nature of the document of title and the proposed date of issue, and how fractions (if any) are to be treated[9];

---

[4] See Articles 8 (relating to shares and convertible, etc., securities) and 9 (relating to debt securities).
[5] Disregarding shares received for issue against the exercise of existing conversion rights and options.
[6] ASL, Section 5, Chapter 2, para. 34.
[7] See above at §§6.68 *et seq.*
[8] ASL, Section 1, Chapter 3, para. 4.2.
[9] ASL, Section 3, Chapter 2, para. 2.23.

(2) how securities not taken up will be dealt with and the time, not being less than 21 days, in which the offer may be accepted[10];

(3) the information required to be included in listing particulars is substantially reduced, its being regarded as unnecessary to repeat information already published. However details as to the purpose of the issue must be made together with specified items as to the company's present state and condition.[11] Where the securities in question will not be identical with securities of the company already listed the listing particulars must provide details of the rights attaching to the securities as regards dividends/interest, capital, voting, redemption and (except as regards the lowest ranking equity) as to the right of the company to create and issue further securities ranking in priority to or *pari passu* with them. Where consents are necessary for a variation of such rights the listing particulars must contain a summary of such consents.[12] Where the securities in question are debt securities to which conversion rights attach (whether into shares or debt securities) the listing particulars should give details of the rights attaching to the new securities. Where the issue is to be made as a replacement for old debt securities the listing particulars should state the material differences between the new and old securities.[13]

*(b) Issues to finance the acquisition of another company or business*[14]

Where the issue is being made to finance the acquisition of another company or business the Stock Exchange requirements relating to the Accountants' Reports[15] are modified so that a report on the company or business to be acquired must be included therein.[16]

## QUOTATION ON THE UNLISTED SECURITIES MARKET

**6.76**  Given that both the official listed market and the unlisted securities market are operated and administered by the Stock Exchange it is not surprising that the procedures for obtaining access to the latter are modelled on those governing the admission to full listing. There are however a number of differences reflecting

---

[10] *Ibid.* In general securities not taken up must be sold for the benefit of the holders entitled unless arrangements to the contrary have been specifically approved by the shareholders in general meeting. However before any alternative method is adopted (*e.g.* the use of excess application forms) the Quotations Department must be consulted. Where the amount to which a holder would be entitled is small the securities may be sold for the benefit of the company. If no premium exists on the expiry of the subscription period the securities may be allotted to underwriters—ASL, Section 1, Chapter 3, para. 4.3.
However, the Quotations Committee may be prepared to permit such unsubscribed-for securities to be the subject of a placing. See ASL, Section 1, Chapter 3, para. 2.8.
[11] The items to be included are detailed in ASL, Section 3, Chapter 1, para. 3.
[12] *Ibid.* paras. 3.1 and 3.2.
[13] *Ibid.* para. 3.3.
[14] See further at §§7.36 *et seq.* below.
[15] ASL, Section 4, para. 1.
[16] ASL, Section 6.

the differences between the two markets. Furthermore the position of the Council of the Stock Exchange differs also, with the statutory functions and jurisdiction delegated to it as the appointed competent authority for the purposes of the Admission, Listing Particulars and Interim Reports Directives having no application in relation to the unlisted securities market.[17] The obligations assumed by companies in connection with the quotation of their securities on this market[18] are primarily contractual in nature deriving from the agreement in pursuance of which access is obtained. In relation to such companies the legislative background against which the agreement operates is the Companies Act 1985 rather than that Stock Exchange (Listing) Regulations 1984 and the Council Directives incorporated therein.

**Public issues on the USM**

The rules governing admission to the USM envisage the marketing of securities by two main methods, namely: **6.77**

  (i) placings; and
  (ii) offers for sale.[19]

Of the two, placing in the primary method with the bulk of USM flotations being made in this way.[20] The monetary limit for a marketing by this method is at present £3,000,000 in terms of the issue or sale price of the shares being placed, provided that the total market capitalisation of the company will not exceed £15,000,000. The admission requirements stipulate that, in the ordinary course, at least 25 per cent. of the amount placed must be available to the public in that the securities in question must be offered to the jobbers in the market to make them available to the clients of brokers other than the sponsoring broker.[21]

Where the £3,000,000 limit is exceeded the issue must be effected by way of an offer for sale and may be so effected in the case of issues below this figure if desired.[22]

**Participants in a USM flotation** **6.78**

As in the case of a full listing the flotation team must include a broker since someone who is a member of the Stock Exchange is required to act as a channel of communication between the Council of the Stock Exchange and the company. Many flotations however are handled by an issuing house in the same way as if the application were for a full listing. In other cases the issue is managed by the

---

[17] However if and when the proposed Directive on Prospectuses is adopted and implemented this will affect companies coming to the USM.

[18] Hereafter referred to in the text as the USM.

[19] Whether at a fixed price or by tender.

[20] Where the purpose of the quotation is merely to achieve marketability for the securities in question rather than to raise capital access to the USM can be obtained by way of an introduction. In such a case companies need not present an accountant's report.—The Stock Exchange: *Unlisted Securities Market* (hereafter referred to as SE:USM) Introduction, para. D.

[21] *Ibid.* Introduction para. E.

[22] *Ibid.*

broker acting as sponsor or by a firm of Licensed Securities Dealers. As in a full listing the flotation team will include solicitors and accountants.

**6.79 Admission requirements**

The principal admission requirements correspond to those applicable to a full listing in that they relate to the company's trading record and its willingness to accept that a minimum proportion of its equity capital or securities convertible into equity capital should be in the hands of the public.[23]

*(a) Trading record*

The basic rule is that the company must normally have been trading for at least three years. However, and exceptionally, companies having a shorter trading record, or indeed no record at all may be admissible. Where the company does not have a record of trading at all admission would only be granted if it could show that the funds were required to finance a project or product and that the project or product had been fully researched and costed, and where the expected time-scale before it began to yield income was not unduly protracted.[24]

Where trading results are available they would be expected to support the market capitalisation.[25]

*(b) Minimum size*

Unlike the position with regard to a full listing there are no minimum size restrictions on entry to the USM. The Stock Exchange advises, however, that a very small company would be unlikely to find a public flotation practicable.[26]

As mentioned above, placings are the normal method of flotation and these are subject to an overall limit of £3,000,000 in the case of equity shares or securities convertible into equity, provided that the total market capitalisation is not expected to exceed £15,000,000.[27]

*(c) Spread of share ownership*

The Stock Exchange imposes two requirements as to the spread of share ownership in a company coming to the USM in an attempt to secure a wider spread of shares to the public. "Public" in this context means shareholders other than directors, their related interests, and, in certain circumstances, other substantial shareholders, especially those with board representation.[28] The requirements are:

---

[23] See above at §6.25.
[24] SE:USM, Introduction, para. A.
[25] *Ibid*. Terms and Conditions for Entry, para. 1.
[26] *Ibid*. Introduction, para. A.
[27] *Ibid*. Terms and Conditions of Entry, para. 3. Note that this limit may be varied from time to time at the discretion of the Quotations Committee: *ibid*.
[28] *Ibid*. Introduction, para. B.

(1) that a minimum of 10 per cent. of the equity capital must normally be in public hands when dealings begin[29]; and

(2) in the case of a placing, not less than 25 per cent. of the capital placed should be offered to the jobbers in the market.

*(d) Prospectus/listing particulars*

The prospectus or particulars card containing the requisite information must be published and advertised in accordance with Stock Exchange requirements.[30]

The date to which the latest audited figures referred to in the prospectus or particulars card are made up should not precede the date of publication of such doments by more than nine months.[31]

**Preparation for flotation** 6.80

While there is no technical requirement for one to be obtained, at least where the flotation is being managed by an issuing house, it is usual for the procedure leading up to the flotation to be centred on the obtaining of a Long Form Report on the company after the model of that used for a full listing.[32] On the basis of the recommendations in this report any necessary changes in the company's articles, its capital structure and management can be put in hand.

It will be recalled in that in relation to an application for full listing the Stock Exchange insisted upon a letter from the issue's sponsors stating that they believed that the working capital statement by the directors had been made after due and careful inquiry. No such statement is necessary in the case of a USM application although in practice most sponsors would require such a statement.

Where the issue is to be made by way of an offer for sale the sponsors will arrange for it to be underwritten so that the flotation will be certain to raise the funds required. The position described above[33] in relation to the underwriting arrangements for a full listing apply here also.

**The flotation prospectus**

One of the attractions of a USM flotation is that the prospectus requirements 6.81 are less stringent that those demanded in respect of listing particulars published in connection with an application for full listing. Companies seeking a USM quotation for their securities must, of course, ensure that the document they prepare meets the requirements of the Third Schedule to the Companies Act 1985.[34]

---

[29] *Ibid.* Terms and Conditions for Entry, para. 5.

[30] A copy of the prospectus or particulars card containing at least the minimum information demanded must be inserted in the Extel Unlisted Companies Service: *ibid.* Terms and Conditions of Entry, para. 7.

[31] *Ibid.* Terms and Conditions of Entry, para. 2.

[32] See above at §6.30.

[33] At §6.32.

[34] See above at §§6.14–6.15.

**6.82** While the disclosure requirements of USM prospectuses are less demanding than those for a full listing they nevertheless bear a strong resemblance, unsurprisingly in view of the fact that the prospectus requirements for a full listing served as a model.

The Stock Exchange requires that a prospectus published in connection with an application for a USM quotation should contain the following matters, namely[35]:

(1) The full name of the company.

(2) A statement by the directors accepting responsibility for the contents of the prospectus in the same form as that used in a listing particulars issued in relation to an application for full listing.[36]

(3) A statement as follows:

> "Application has been made to the Council of the Stock Exchange for the grant of permission to deal in the Company's [state the securities] in the Unlisted Securities Market. It is emphasised that no application has been made for these securities to be admitted to listing."

(4) (a) The authorised share capital, the amount issued or to be issued, the amount paid up and the description and nominal value of the shares.

(b) A statement that (apart, where applicable, from issues or proposed issues specified in the prospectus) no material issue of shares (other than to shareholders *pro rata* to existing holdings) will be made within one year without prior approval of the company in general meeting.

(c) In a case where 10 per cent. or more of the voting capital (unclassified shares being regarded as voting capital) will remain unissued (disregarding unissued shares reserved for issue against exercise of subsisting conversion rights or options) a statement that no issue will be made which would effectively alter the control of the company or nature of its business without prior approval of the company in general meeting.

(5) In relation to the company and its subsidiaries:

(a) Particulars of the loan capital (including term loans) outstanding or created but unissued, and of all mortgages or charges, or an appropriate negative statement; and

(b) Particulars (as at the latest date reasonably practicable) of other borrowings or indebtedness in the nature of borrowing,[37] including bank overdrafts and liabilities under acceptances (other than normal trade bills) or acceptance credits, hire purchase committments, or guarantees or other contingent liabilities, or, if there are no such liabilities, a statement to that effect.

Inter-company liabilities within a group should normally be disregarded, a statement to that effect being made, where necessary.

(6) The full name, address and description of every director and, if required by the Committee, particulars of:

---

[35] SE:USM, Section C. Note that the requirements stated in the text are those generally regarded as applicable to an industrial company. The Quotations Committee may require additional or alternative information for companies engaged in other enterprises.

[36] See above at §6.41.

[37] See above at §§2.10 *et seq.*

(a) any former forenames or surnames,

(b) his nationality, if not British, and

(c) his nationality of origin if his present nationality is not his nationality of origin.

(7) The full name and professional qualifications (if any) of the secretary and the situation of the registered office and transfer office (if different).

(8) The names and addresses of the bankers, brokers solicitors, registrars and trustees (if any).

(9) The name, address and professional qualifications of the auditors.

(10) The date and country of incorporation and the authority under which the company was incorporated. In the case of a company not incorporated in the United Kingdom, the addresses of the head office and principal place of business (if any) in the United Kingdom.

(11) If the application is in respect of shares:

(a) The voting rights of shareholders.

(b) if there is more than one class, the rights of each class as regards dividend, capital, redemption, and the creation or issue of further shares ranking in priority to or *pari passu* with each class other than the lowest ranking equity; and

(c) A summary of the consents necessary for the variation of such rights.

(12) The provisions or a sufficient summary of the provisions of the articles of association, by-laws or other corresponding document with regard to:

(a) Any power enabling a director to vote on a proposal, arrangement, or contract in which he is materially interested.

(b) Any power enabling the directors, in the absence of an independent quorum, to vote remuneration (including pension or other benefits) to themselves or any members of their body.

(c) Borrowing powers exercisable by the directors and how such borrowing powers can be varied; and

(d) Retirement or non-retirement of directors under an age limit.

(13) Where the application relates to loan capital, the rights conferred upon the holders thereof, and particulars of the security (if any) therefor.

(14) The general nature of the business of the company or group and, in cases where the company or group carries on two or more activities which are material, having regard to profits or losses, assets employed or any other factor, information as to the relative importance of each such activity. If the company or group trades outside the United Kingdom a statement showing a geographical analysis of its trading operations.

(15) (a) In regard to:

(i) every company whose results are, or are proposed to be, dealt with in the consolidated accounts, and

(ii) other investments which are material in relation to the company, particulars of the name, date, country of incorporation, whether public or private, general nature of business, issued capital and the proportion thereof held or about to be held.

(b) In regard to the company and every subsidiary or company about to become a subsidiary, particulars of the situation, area an tenure (including in the case of leaseholds the rent and unexpired term) of the factories and main buildings, the principal products and number of employees.

(16) A statement showing the sales, turnover figures or gross trading income during the preceding three financial years containing a reasonable breakdown between the more important trading activities. In the case of a group, internal sales should be excluded.

(17) (a) A statement as to the financial and trading prospects of the company or group, together with any material information which may be relevant thereto, including all special trade factors or risks (if any) which are not mentioned elsewhere in the document and which are unlikely to be known or anticipated by the general public, and which could materially affect the profits.

(b) Where a profit forecast appears in the document the principal assumptions, including commercial assumptions, upon which the directors have based their profit forecast, must be stated. The accounting bases and calculations for the forecast must be examined and reported on by the auditors to the company, and any reporting accountants joined with the auditors in their report, and such report must be set out. The issuing house, or, in the absence of an issuing house, the sponsoring broker, must report in addition whether they have satisfied themselves that the forecast has been stated by the directors after due and careful enquiry, and such report must be set out.

(c) Where the application relates to fixed income securities, particulars of the profits cover for dividend/interest, and of the net tangible asset cover.

(d) A statement as to any waiver of future dividends.

(18) A statement by the directors that in their opinion the working capital available is sufficient or, if not, how it is proposed to provide the additional working capital thought by the directors to be necessary.

(19) Where the securities to which the application relates were issued for cash within the two years preceding the publication of the document or will be issued for cash, a statement or an estimate of the net proceeds of the issue and a statement as to how such proceeds were or are to be applied.

(20) (a) A statement of financial statistics in the form of a table covering the profits and losses of the company or if the company has subsidiaries the group, for the latest five financial years, or such lesser period since incorporation. The table should include at least the following information:

(i) Turnover or other operating income or revenue.
(ii) Depreciation and amortisation.
(iii) Investment and other income.
(iv) Interest payable and (shown separately) leasing or hire charges.
(v) Exceptional items.
(vi) Share of profits or losses of associated companies.
(vii) Profits/losses before taxation and extraordinary items.
(viii) Taxation (United Kingdom, overseas and share of associated companies).

(ix) Minority interests.

(x) Amount absorbed by preferential dividends.

(xi) .Profits/losses attributable to equity shareholders before extraordinary items.

(xii) Extraordinary items (and related tax), and

(xiii) Profit attributable to equity shareholders.

(b) A statement of financial statistics in the form of a table covering the assets and liabilities of the company or, if the company has subsidiaries, the group at the end of each of the accounting periods covered in (a) above.

(c) The rate of dividend and the amount absorbed thereby for each class of shares during each of the financial periods covered by (a) above.

(d) A note of the principal accounting policies in operation at the date of the latest balance sheet, together with anotice of any significant changes in policies during the period covered by (a) above, with an indication of the effect of any such changes.

(e) Such notes as are necessary for a reasonable understanding of the figures given under (a) and (b) above. Movements on reserves not reflected in the profit attributable to equity shareholders should be described and quantified.

(f) A statement that the annual accounts for the last three years contained no qualification in the audit reports, or, where that was not the case, the nature of such qualifications, together with such explanations by the directors as appear relevant. (Any qualifications casting doubt on the accuracy of the figures provided for any of the three years may render the company inadmissible to the USM.)

(g) Particulars of any material changes in the trading or financial position of the company, or group, since the date to which the last accounts have been made up, or an appropriate negative statement.

(21) Comparable information to that required in 20 above should be provided in respect of any business, or interest in the company or group, which has been acquired or agreed to be acquired after the date to which the latest financial statistics dealt with in 20(b) above are made up.[38]

(22) Particulars of any capital of the company or of any of its subsidiaries which has within the two years immediately preceding the publication of the document been issued or is proposed to be issued fully or partly paid up otherwise than in cash and the consideration for which the same has been or is to be issued, or an appropriate negative statement.

(23) Particulars of any capital of the company or of any of its subsidiaries which has within the two years immediately preceding the publication of the document been issued or proposed to be issued for cash, the price and terms upon which the same has been or is to be issued and (if not already fully paid) the dates when any instalments are payable with the amount of all calls or instalments in arrear, on an appropriate negative statement.

(24) Particulars of any capital of the company or of any of its subsidiaries

---

[38] The Quotations Department should be consulted about the requirements in the case of any acquisition of 50 per cent. or less of a company.

which is under option, or agreed conditionally or unconditionally to be put under option, with the price and duration of the option and consideration for which the option was or will be granted, and the name of the grantee, or an appropriate negative statement.

Provided that where options have been granted or agreed to be granted to all the members or debenture holders or to any class thereof or to employees under a share option scheme, it shall be sufficient, so far as the names are concerned, to record that fact without giving the names of the grantees.

(25) (a) Particulars of any preliminary expenses incurred or proposed to be incurred and by whom the same are payable.

(b) The amount or estimated amount of the expenses of the issue and of the application for grant of permission to deal in the USM so far as the same are not included in the statement of preliminary expenses, and by whom the same are payable.

(26) Particulars of any commissions, discounts, brokerages or other special terms granted within the two years immediately preceding the publication of the document in connection with the issue or sale of any capital of the company or any of its subsidiaries, on an appropriate negative statement.

(27) A statement showing:

(a) any alterations in the share capital of the company within the two years preceding the publication of the document, or an appropriate negative statement;

(b) the interests of each director in the share capital of the company appearing in the register maintained under the provisions of the Companies Act 1985 (or which would be required so to appear if the company were subject to the provisions of that Act) distinguishing between beneficial and non-beneficial interests, or an appropriate negative statement;

(c) particulars of any interest, other than that of a director, in any substantial part of the share capital of the company and the amount of the interest in question, or an appropriate negative statement.

(28) (a) Details of directors' existing or proposed service contracts with the company or any subsidiary, excluding contracts, expiring, or determinable by the employing company without payment of compensation (other than statutory compensation) within one year, or an appropriate negative statement.

(b) The aggregate emoluments of the directors during the last completed financial period together with an estimate of the amount payable to the directors, including proposed directors, for the current financial period under the arrangements in force at the date of the document.

(29) (a) Full particulars of the nature and extent of the interest, direct or indirect, if any, of every director in the promotion of, or in any assets which have been, within the two years preceding the publication of the document, acquired or disposed of by or leased to the company or any of its subsidiaries, or are proposed to be acquired, disposed of by or leased to the company or any of its subsidiaries, including:

(i) the consideration passing to or from the company or any of its subsidiaries, and

(ii) short particulars of all transactions relating to any such assets which have taken place within the two years immediately preceding the publication of the document;

or an appropriate negative statement.

(b) Full particulars of any contract or arrangement subsisting at the date of the document in which a director of the company is materially interested and which is significant in relation to the busines of the company and its subsidiaries, taken as a whole, or an appropriate negative statement.

(30) A statement that the company or any of its subsidiaries has or has not (as the case may be) any litigation or claims of material importance pending or threatened against it.

(31) (a) The name of any promoter. (If the promoter is a company, the Committee may require a statement of its issued share capital; the amount paid up thereon; the date of its incorporation; the names of its directors, bankers and auditors; and such other particulars as the Committee think necessary in connection therewith.)

(b) The amount of any cash or securities paid or benefit given within the two years immediately preceding the publication of the document, or proposed to be paid or given to any promoter, and the consideration for such payment or benefit.

(32) Where the document contains a statement purporting to be made by an expert, a statement that the expert has given and has not withdrawn his written consent to the issue of the document with the statement included in the form and context in which it is included.

(33) When relevant, in the absence of a statement that income tax, surtax and shortfall clearances as appropriate have been obtained, a statement that appropriate indemnities have been given.[39]

(34) When relevant, in the absence of a statement that estate duty and capital transfer tax indemnities have been given, a statement that the directors have been advised that no material liability for estate duty or capital transfer tax would be likely to fall upon the company or any subsidiary.[40]

(35) The dates of and parties to all material contracts (not being contracts entered into in the ordinary course of business) entered into within the two years immediately preceding the publication of the document, together with a summary of the principal contents of each contract including particulars of any consideration passing to or from the company or any subsidiary.

(36) A statement that for a period (being not less than 14 days) at a named place in the City of London (or such other centre as the Committee may determine) the following documents where applicable (or copies thereof) may be inspected:

---

[39] The Committee may require such indemnities to be supported by continuing guarantees.
[40] See n.39 above.

    (i)  the memorandum and articles of association;

    (ii)  the trust deed;

    (iii)  each contract disclosed pursuant to paragraph 28(a) and 35, or, in the case of a contract not reduced to writing, a memorandum giving full particulars thereof;

    (iv)  all reports, letters or other documents, balance sheets, valuations and statements by any expert reproduced or referred to in the document;

    (v)  written consents of experts; and

    (vi)  the audited accounts of the company and its subsidiaries for each of the three financial years preceding the publication of the document together with all notes, certificates or information required by the Companies Acts.

### Completion meeting

**6.83**    As in the case of an application for a full listing it is the practice for a meeting of the company's board to be convened prior to submission of the formal application for admission to quotation on the USM in order that formal authorisation may be given to the implementation of such arrangements as are necessary in connection with the operation. Reference should be made to § 6.60 above for the details of the business to be transacted at this meeting.

### Application

**6.84**    As in other aspects of the admission procedure that concerned with the formal application to the Stock Exchange for admission to quotation on the USM is derived from and modelled on that appertaining in respect of a full listing. [41]

    Thus, in the same way as applicants for full listing are encouraged to make their preliminary application at the earliest possible date, so also are applicants for the USM; and, in the same way, such applications should be made on the prescribed form [42]

**6.85**    Applicants are required to submit for approval at least 14 days prior to publication [43]:

    (1) Four proof prints of the prospectus or particulars card;

    (2) Four proof prints of any temporary document of title proposed to be issued;

    (3) Two proof prints of the definitive certificate or other definitive documents of title proposed to be issued;

    (4) Two proof prints or copies of the memorandum and articles of association or other corresponding document; and

---

[41] See above at §§6.61 *et seq.*

[42] Adapted from that used in an application for full listing—see at §6.61.

[43] SE:USM Section A, para. 2.

(5) In the case of loan capital two proof prints or copies of the trust deed or other document securing or constituting the loan capital.

The following documents must be lodged at least two days prior to the hearing **6.86** of the application by the Quotations Committe, namely[44]:

(1) The formal application on the prescribed forms (issued by the Department), one signed by the broker appointed by the company and supported by two firms of jobbers who are prepared to register as dealers in the security,[45] the second signed by the company, together with payment of the first annual charge.[46]

(2) Four copies of the prospectus or particulars card conforming with the requirments for the contents of such documents, one copy of which must be dated and signed by every person who is named therein as a director or proposed director or by his agent authorised in writing[47];

(3) A copy of every newspaper in which the "box" advertisement[48] (and any of the advertisements in connection with the application) appeared;

(4) A certified copy of the certificate of incorporation;

(5) A certified copy of the certificate (if any) entitling the company to commence business;

(6) A copy of the memorandum and articles of association or other corresponding document;

(7) A copy of the trust deed or other document securing or constituting the loan capital;

(8) The General Undertaking in the form available from the Department;

(9) A certified copy of—

(a) the resolution(s) of the board authorising the issue of all new securities to be traded and subsequently allotting the same, and

(b) the resolution(s) of the board approving and authorising the issue of the prospectus or particulars card;

(10) In the case of a placing, a copy of the placing letter and a marketing statement by the broker in the form available from the Department;

(11) A certified copy of every letter, report, balance sheet, valuation, contract, resolution or other document reproduced or referred to in the prospectus or particulars card;

(12) A certified copy of the written consent of any expert to whom reference is made in the prospectus or particulars card;

(13) Two copies of any notice of meeting referred to in the prospectus or particulars card and of any temporary document of title;

(14) A specimen of the definitive certificate or other definitive document of title;

---

[44] *Ibid.* para. 4.

[45] The support of jobbers is not required where application is made for the sponsoring broker to act as matching broker; such application must be made on the form available in the Department.

[46] Of £1,000. SE:USM Terms and Conditions of Entry, para. 8.

[47] Where any document is signed by an agent a certified copy of the authorisation is required.

[48] See below at §6.87.

(15) A declaration in the form supplied by the Department as to filing of documents and other matters;

(16) Where any scrip is to be issued by any person other than the company whose scrip it is, a certified copy of the resolution or other document evidencing the authority to issue the scrip;

(17) Where the vendor of a security being marketed has not paid in full for that security at the date of the marketing:

(a) a certified copy of an irrevocable authority given by the vendor to the bankers to the marketing authorising the bankers to discharge the obligation of the vendor to pay for the security as laid down in the contract; and

(b) a certified copy of the banker's acknowledgement of this authority and an agreement to act on it; and

(18) A declaration by each director in conformity with the Rules and Regulations of the Stock Exchange.

**6.87**     The issue must be publicised by the insertion of a "box" advertisement in a leading daily newspaper at least two days before the hearing of the application by the Quotations Committee. This advertisement should state the authorised and issued share capital together with the price at which any such shares are currently being issued or placed.[49]

The advertisement is required to contain as a rubric the following statement:

> "Application has been made for grant of permission to deal in the Unlisted Securities Market on The Stock Exchange in the undermentioned securities. It is emphasised that no application has been made for these securities to be admitted to listing."

The advertisement must state the addresses at which the particulars of the company may be obtained.

The particulars must be available through the Extel Unlisted Securities Market Service on the day the advertisement appears in the press.

**Listing Agreement/General Undertaking**

**6.88**     Just as companies seeking a full listing for their securities were required to enter into a Listing Agreement with the Stock Exchange so also those seeking access to the USM are required to provide a "General Undertaking" as to the future conduct of the company, its directors and officers, as to the regular release of financial and trading information, the preparation of interim and annual reports and accounts and disclosure of price-sensitive information and significant share dealings. Following the model of the Listing Agreement procedure companies are required to adopt the terms of the General Undertaking as a resolution of the board.

---

[49] SE:USM Section A, para. 3.

The form of the General Undertaking is as follows:                    **6.89**

## THE UNLISTED SECURITIES MARKET GENERAL UNDERTAKING

.................................................................. (NAME OF COMPANY)
The following is an extract from the minutes of a meeting of the board of directors held the ........................................................................ day of ....................................19...........

In compliance with the requirements of the Council of The Stock Exchange, it was resolved that the company agrees to comply with the provisions set out below (each such provision in which reference is made to a note to be read and construed in accordance with and subject to the related notes appearing in the document "The Stock Exchange Unlisted Securities Market.")

1. Generally and apart from compliance with all specific requirements which follow, to keep The Stock Exchange informed by means of notifications to the Quotations Department ("the Department") of any information necessary to enable the shareholders and the public to appraise the position of the company and to avoid the establishment of a false market in its securities.

2. To notify the Department in advance of the date fixed for any board meeting at which the declaration or recommendation or payment of a dividend is expected to be determined upon, or at which any announcement of the profits or losses in respect of any financial period or part thereof is to be approved for publication.

3. To notify the Department immediately after approval by or on behalf of the Board:—

   (a) any decision to pay or make any dividend or other distribution or to pass any dividend or interest payment;
   (b) a preliminary announcement of profits or losses for any year, half-year or other period;
   (c) any proposed change in capital structure;
   (d) short particulars of any drawing or redemption of securities.

4. To notify to the Press the basis of allotment of securities in prospectus and other offers, and, if applicable, in respect of excess applications, such notice to appear not later than the morning of the business day next after the allotment letters or other relevant documents of title are posted.

5. To notify the Department immediately after the relevant event of:—

   (a) particulars of acquisitions or realisations of assets as from time to time required[50];

---

[50] Reference should be made to the following tests in order to classify transactions entered into by the company:
    (1) the value of the assets acquired or disposed of, compared with the assets of the acquiring or disposing company;
    (2) net profits (after deducting all charges except taxation and excluding extraordinary items) attributable to the assets acquired or disposed of, compared with the profits of the acquiring or disposing company;

(b) any information required to be disclosed to The Stock Exchange under the provisions of The City Code on Take-overs and Mergers for the time being in force;

(c) any information known to the company which would be notifiable under the provisions of [Part IV of the Companies Act 1985] if the company were subject to such provisions;

(d) any change in the directorate[51];

(e) any purchase by the company, or the group of which the company is part, of its redeemable securities;

(f) any board decision to change the general character or nature of the business of the company or of the group;

(g) particulars of dealings by directors in any of the securities of the company traded in the Unlisted Securities Market.

6. To forward to the Department (through the company's brokers) four copies of proofs, for approval, of all circulars to holders of the company's securities, documents relating to take-overs, mergers, offers, notices of meeting and forms of proxy.

7. To forward to the Department six copies of:—

(a) all circulars, notices, reports, announcements or other documents at the same time as they are issued;

(b) all resolutions passed by the company other than resolutions concerning routine business at an annual general meeting.

8. To issue annual reports and accounts within the six months following the date of the end of the financial period to which they relate.

9. To prepare a half-yearly or interim report which must be sent to the holders of securities or inserted as a paid advertisement in one leading daily newspaper not later than six months from the date of the notice convening the annual general meeting of the company.

(3) the aggregate value of the consideration given or received, compared with the assets of the acquiring or disposing company;

(4) equity capital issued by the company as consideration for the acquisition compared with the equity capital already in issue.

Notification to the Department is required when any of the above tests amounts to 5 per cent. or more. The notification should be in the form of an announcement including details of the assets acquired or disposed of, how the consideration was satisfied, the value of the assets, and the profits attributable to those assets.

If one of the above tests amounts to 25 per cent. or more, the transaction is considered to be sufficiently material to call not only for an announcement but for a circular to be sent to shareholders. For the contents of such circulars see SE:USM, Section D.

Circulars are required irrespective of whether the consideration was in cash or securities.

The Department must be consulted in advance where the relative tests amount to 100 per cent. or more, or where a change of control might result.

Transactions which involve, or involve an associate of, a director, substantial shareholders, or past substantial shareholders of the company (or any other company being its subsidiary, holding company or a subsidiary of its holding company) should be subject to prior approval of the company in general meeting and the issue of an explanatory circular. Where it is proposed to enter into such a transaction the Department must be consulted as soon as possible, and prior to any contract being entered into.

[51] A new director may be required to submit a declaration to the Stock Exchange on the form available through the company's brokers.

10. To circulate with the annual report of the directors:—

(a) a statement by the directors as to the reasons for any significant departure from standard accounting practices;

(b) an explanation in the event of trading results shown by the accounts for the period under review differing materially from any published forecast made by the company;

(c) a geographical analysis of turnover and of contribution to trading results of those trading operations carried on by the company (or group) outside the United Kingdom;

(d) the name of the principal country in which each subsidiary operates;

(e) the following particulars regarding each company (not being a subsidiary) in which the group interest in the equity capital amounts to 20 per cent. or more:—

    (i) the principal country of operaion;

    (ii) particulars of its issued share and loan capital and, except where the group's interest therein is dealt with in the consolidated balance sheet as an associated company, the total amount of its reserves;

    (iii) the percentage of each class of loan capital attributable to the company's interest (direct or indirect);

(f) a statement as at the end of the financial year showing as regards (a) bank loans and overdrafts and (b) other borrowings of the company (or group) the aggregate amounts repayable:

    (i) in one year or less, or on demand;

    (ii) between one and two years;

    (iii) between two and five years; and

    (iv) in five years or more.

(g) in respect of the financial year, a statement of the amount of interest capitalised by the company (or group) during the year, with an indication of the amount and treatment of any related tax relief;

(h) a statement as at the end of the financial year showing the interests of each director in the share capital of the company and subsidiary companies appearing in a register maintained under the provisions of the Companies Act [1985] (or which would be required so to appear if the company were subject to the provisions of that Act), distinguishing between beneficial and non-beneficial interests; such statement should include by way of note any change in those interests occurring between the end of the financial year and a date not more than one month prior to the date of the notice of meeting or, if there has been no such change, disclosure of that fact;

(i) a statement showing particulars as at a date not more than one month prior to the date of the notice of meeting of an interest of any person, other than a director, in 5 per cent. or more of the share capital of the company and the amount of the interest in question or, if there is no such interest, a statement of that fact so far as known to the company;

(j) a statement showing whether or not, so far as the directors are aware, the company is a close company for taxation purposes and whether there has been any change in that respect since the end of the financial year;

(k) particulars of any arrangement under which a director has waived or agreed to waive any emoluments;

(l) particulars of any arrangement under which a shareholder has waived or agreed to waive any dividends.

11. To state in a note to the notice convening the annual general meeting the place and time at which copies or, as the case may be, memoranda of all service contracts will be available for inspection or, if there are no such contracts, to state that fact.

12. To send with the notice convening a meeting of holders of securities to all persons entitled to vote thereat proxy forms with provisions for two-way voting on all resolutions intended to be proposed.

13. In the absence of special Stock Exchange dispensation, to obtain the consent of the company in general meeting prior to:—

(i) the company issuing for cash:—
  (a) equity capital (including capital having an equity element),
  (b) securities convertible into any such capital, or
  (c) warrants or options to subscribe for any such capital or convertible securities:

  otherwise than to the equity shareholders of the company in proportion to their existing holdings and where appropriate, holders of other equity securities of the company entitled thereto; or

(ii) any major subsidiary of the company making any issue for cash so as materially to dilute the percentage equity interest of the company and its shareholders in such subsidiary.

14. In the event of a circular being issued to the holders of any particular class of security, to issue a copy or summary of such circular to the holders of all other securities, whether listed or traded in the Unlisted Securities Market, unless the contents of such circular are irrelevant to such other holders.

15. To certify transfers against certificates or temporary documents and to return them on the day of receipt or, should that not be a business day, on the first business day folowing their receipt and to split and return renounceable documents within the same period.

16. To register transfers and other documents without payment of any fee.

17. To issue, without charge, certificates within:—

(a) one month of the date of expiration of any right of renunciation;
(b) 14 days of the lodgement of transfers.

18. To arrange for designated accounts if requested by holders of securities.

19. To pay an annual fee to The Stock Exchange at the rate fixed from time to time.

20. To adopt rules governing dealings by directors in the securities of the company, whether listed or traded in the Unlisted Securities Market, in terms no less

exacting than those of the Model Code issued by the Council of The Stock Exchange.''

### Raising additional capital

Companies with securities quoted on the USM may raise additional capital **6.90** through the market either:

    (a) by way of rights; or
    (b) through a general public issue.

Where the securities to be issued are equity shares or securities containing an element of equity the issue must in general be by way of rights in order to comply with the pre-emption right provisions of the Companies Act 1985.[52]

In general the procedure for raising additional capital on the USM follows that **6.91** applicable in respect of such operations on the full listed market and reference should accordingly be made to §§ 6.73–6.75, above.

The rules governing the USM however do make special provision in relation to the application procedure and the prospectus rules.

### (a) The application procedure[53]

As in the case of a full listing where application is made for the quotation of further securities on the USM the standard procedure applicable on first admission is abbreviated. Thus it is provided that the standard procedure[54] is to apply save that:

    (1) a preliminary application will only be necessary where it is desired to place any further securities of a class already traded, or where a new class of security is concerned;
    (2) copies of all resolutions increasing the share capital or authorising the issue of the securities to be dealt it must be submitted; and
    (3) an advertisement will be necessary only where a new class of security is the subject of the application.

### (b) Prospectuses[55]

In general, but with modifications and exceptions appropriate to the circumstances, prospectuses and circulars issued by a company already having securities traded in the USM should contain the information required as standard in

---

[52] See above at §§2.100 *et seq.*
[53] SE:USM, Section B.
[54] See above at §6.84–6.87.
[55] SE:USM, Section D. The rules are stated as applying to the contents of a ''Prospectus, Circular Letter or Other Document to Shareholders issued by Companies some part of whose capital is already traded'' in the USM.

ordinary USM issues.[56] However these standard requirements are modified in that:

(a) it will not be necessary to repeat information carried in an Erxtel Services Card which remains correct at the time of the prospectus or circular provided that a copy of the card is sent with that document; and

(b) in the case of an application for grant of permission to deal in securities offered by way of rights to holders of a security already traded in the USM the provisional allotment letter, letter of rights or other documents of offer must show:

(1) as a heading, the date the offer expires and that the document is of value and negotiable and that in all cases of doubt, or if prior to receipt the addressee has sold (other than ex rights) all or part of his registered holding of the existing securities, a stockbroker, bank manager, solicitor, accountant or other professional adviser should be consulted immediately; and state that permission to deal in the USM has been granted;.

(2) how securities not taken up will be dealt with, and the time, being not less than 21 days, in which the offer may be accepted; and

(3) the *pro rata* entitlement, the last date on which transfers were accepted for registration for participation in the issue, how the securities rank for dividend and interest, the nature of the document of title and proposed date of issue, and how fractions (if any) are to be treated.

### Transition from USM to full listing

**6.92**    When the USM was established in its present form it was envisaged that some companies would obtain a USM quotation as a first step to securing a full listing at some future time. In order to facilitate such transitions provision was made for the procedure applicable when companies with a USM quotation sought a full listing to be simplified so that applications for admission to listing from such companies could be made on the basis of the information previously disclosed but suitably updated.[57]

**6.93**    While it will frequently be the case that the decision to seek a full listing will be made on the recommendation or advice of an issuing house the simplified procedure makes it more likely that the transition application will, in the ordinary course, be handled by the company's brokers alone.

The application should, of course, be made through the company's brokers who will act as its channel of communication with the Stock Exchange authorities.

---

[56] See above at §6.82.

[57] The updating will usually take the form of an auditor's report. Such a report may not be required where a full report was provided at the time of entry to the USM. Where a full report was not provided at that time one will almost always be required when a full listing is sought. The Department should be consulted in each case.

The normal listing requirements as to length of trading record and market **6.94** capitalisation will apply. Likewise the the requirement that the proportion of equity capital in public hands be at least 25 per cent. must be complied with so that, if necessary, the company should be prepared to increase the existing proportion of such capital that is so held.

The following documents must be lodged at least 48 hours before the hearing **6.95** of the application by the Quotations Committee, namely

(1) the formal application on the forms issued by the Department together with payment of the appropriate charge for listing[58];
(2) the listing agreement;
(3) four copies of the particulars cards,[59] one of which must be dated and signed by every person who is named terein as a director or proposed director of the company or by his agent authorised in writing. Where the signature is that of an agent a copy of the agent's authority to act must also be submitted;
(4) the resolution of the board approving and authorising the issue of the prospectus or particulars card.

A "box" advertisement must be inserted in two leading daily newspapers. **6.96**

## FLOTATION ON THE OVER-THE-COUNTER MARKETS

An essential difference between flotation on an Over-the-Counter (OTC) mar- **6.97** ket and one on the USM or Stock Exchange is that responsibility for marketing the issue is undertaken by the market-maker rather than by an intermediary such as an issuing house or broker and it is the market-maker who will advise the company on whether a public flotation is the best way of satisfying its requirements.[60]

*Difference between OTC and USM Flotation*

Like a sponsor to a Stock Exchange or USM flotation the market-maker will **6.98** carry out a preliminary investigation of the company involving a detailed analysis of the company, the management and the future prospects, and of the industry in which it operates. This investigation, like the accountants' "long-form" report, forms the basis of the investment report on the basis of which the company's securities are marketed.

*Preliminaries*

---

[58] The normal initial listing fees will be payable, together with the first annual fee according to the scale for listed companies.
[59] A particulars card, a copy of which must be submitted in proof form to the Department, must be inserted in the Extel Statistical Services.
[60] Indeed the market-maker frequently takes a stake in the company, either directly through a subscription for some of the securities marketed or through the acquisition of warrants to subscribe for securities within a specified period.

### Investment reports

**6.99**    Virtually all OTC flotations take the form of placings. The investment report, like a prospectus, is prepared to provide potential investors and especially institutional investors with the information necessary to enable them to take a decision as to whether or not to take a stake in the company. The investment report centres on an assessment of the company's future earning power and involves the further development of the analysis of the company and its industry carried out in the preliminary investigation. The report normally contains a profit forecast and includes historical figures taken from the company's audited accounts.

The investment report is supported by warranties from the company's directors as to the accuracy of the information contained in it and, since in any flotation the market-makers act as agents of the company, any liability arising from negligent or fraudulent mis-statement will fall on the company and its directors unless it can be shown that the market-makers in preparing the report have themselves been independently negligent.

*Investment Report a Prospectus?*    The investment report is not constructed primarily to satisfy the requirements of the Companies Acts as to the form and content of prospectuses. Indeed in many cases the narrowness of the market and long-term nature of the investments may be sufficient to justify the view that such issues are not to "the public" at all, despite the quotation.[61]

Where, however, it is anticipated that the shares on offer will be fairly widely held and that they may be actively traded the statutory prospectus requirements must be complied with and the investment report will be framed so to do by including auditors' reports on the historical figures and on the profit forecast and by the giving of indemnities by existing shareholders in favour of the company in relation to potential liabilities of the company for capital transfer tax and income tax.

### OTC undertakings

**6.100**    All companies seeking a quotation on an OTC will be required to sign an undertaking intended to ensure an effective market in their securities committing them to disseminate relevant and timely price-sanctions information to all shareholders and to the market-makers. The undertakings differ in detail but are all based on or are similar to the Stock Exchange Listing Agreement and USM General Undertaking.

The General Undertaking required by Granville & Company Limited, originators of the OTC market concept in the United Kingdom, is in the following terms.

---

[61] See above at §6.11. When a company's securities are first brought to an OTC market an initial block of 10–15 per cent. of the ordinary share capital is made available to investors.

# OTC MARKET—GENERAL UNDERTAKING

## PLC

In compliance with the requirements of Granville & Co. Limited (hereinafter called "Granville") and in consideration of Granville agreeing to make a market in some or all of the classes and categories of the company's securities IT WAS RESOLVED that the company undertake to comply with the obligations set out below together with any amendments or additions which may be introduced by Granville from time to time, or as interpreted by Granville in consultation with the company where necessary, that is to say, to:—

1. Notify Granville promptly of the date fixed for any Board meeting at which a declaration or recommendation of a dividend will be considered, at which an announcement of profits or losses for any fiancial period (or any part of such a period) will be approved for publication or at which it is proposed that a decision regarding a change in the capital structure of the Company will be taken.

2. Notify Granville immediately after the relevant Board meeting has been held of:—

(a) all dividends and/or other distributions recommended or declared and of any decision to pass a dividend or interest payment;

(b) any preliminary profit announcements for the year, half-year or other period;

(c) particulars of any proposed change in the capital structure of the Company, including the issue or redemption of securities or the purchase by the Company of its own shares.

3. Give Granville immediately full particulars of:—

(a) any transaction by the Company or any of its subsidiaries falling within paragraphs 13 or 14 below;

(b) any proposed change in the general nature of the business either of the Company or of the Company and its subsidiaries taken as a whole;

(c) any event of which the Directors arc aware as a result of which any person become or ceases to be "a substantial shareholder" under paragraph 14(c) below or as a result of which there is any change in the interest of a substantial shareholder in the equity share capital of the Company;

(d) any matter of which the Company is notified by a director under section [324] or section [328] of the Companies Act [1985] (duty of directors to notify the company of acquisition etc. of securities of the Company);

(e) the appointment of any director of the Company or the ceasing of any such director to hold office;

(f) any allotment of any securities of the Company (pursuant to a prospectus or otherwise) or of excess applications, or any agreement by the Company (including any conditional agreement) to make such an allotment;

(g) any change in the status of the Company under the close company provisions of the Income and Corporation Taxes Act 1970 of which the directors become aware;

(h) any other information necessary to enable shareholders or debenture or loan stock holders to appraise the position of the Company or to avoid a false market in its securities being established.

4. Comply with the City Code on Take-overs and Mergers and all rulings and interpretations made by the Panel on Take-overs and Mergers and to keep Granville informed of any discussions with the Panel on Take-overs and Mergers.

5. Forward to Granville:—

(a) proofs for approval of all circulars, notices of meetings other than notices of annual general meetings when containing notice of routine business only, reports, announcements or other documents (other than statutory accounts) proposed to be sent to holders of securities of the Company;

(b) all circulars, notices, reports, announcements or other documents at the same time as they are sent to holders of any securities of the Company; and

(c) all resolutions passed by any holders of securities of the Company (or any class of them) other than those concerning routine business at an annual general meeting.

6. (1) Use its best endeavours to procure that its annual report and accounts are issued within the six months following the date of the end of the financial period to which they relate.

(2) In the event that no annual report and accounts are issued within the period specified in (1) above, provide Granville with a full explanation for the delay and to take such action as Granville may reasonably consider to be appropriate in the circumstances.

7. Circularise a half-yearly interim report to holders of securities not later than six months from the date of the notice convening the latest annual general meeting.

8. Send with the notice convening a meeting of holders of securities to all persons entitled to vote thereat proxy forms with provision for two-way voting on all resolutions intended to be proposed.

9. (1) Include in the annual report of the Directors:—

(a) an explanation, where applicable, as to why the trading results shown by the accounts for the period under review differ materially from any published forecast made either by the Company or by Granville with the prior approval of the Company;

(b) a statement as to the reasons for adopting an alternative basis of accounting in any case where the auditors have stated that the accounts are not drawn up in accordance with standard accounting practices approved by the accounting bodies;

(c) a broad geographical analysis of turn-over by way of figures and percentages (not necessarily given country by country) and an appropriate statement regarding trading results of those trading operations carried on by the Company or any of its subsidiaries outside the United Kingdom where, for a proper appraisal of the business of the Company and its subsidiaries, shareholders should be aware of significant contributions derived from activities carried out in any one territory;

(d) the name of the principal country (outside the United Kingdom) in which each subsidiary has a presence;

(e) a statement showing any changes, between the end of the financial period under review and a date not more than one month prior to the date of the notice of annual general meeting, in the interests of Directors of the Company in shares in or debentures or the Company or any of its subsidiaries or, if there has been no such change, an appropriate negative statement;

(f) a statement showing particulars so far as the Directors are aware as at a date not more than one month prior to the date of the notice of the annual general meeting of any interests of any person other than a Director of the Company in 5 per cent. or more of the share capital of the Company or any part thereof or, where appropriate, an appropriate negative statement;

(g) a statement showing whether or not, so far as the Directors are aware, the close company provisions of the Income and Corporation Taxes Act 1970 apply to the Company and whether there has been any change in that respect since the end of the financial year;

(h) the following particulars regarding each company (not being a subsidiary) in which the interest of the company and its subsidiaries in the equity capital amounts to 10 per cent. or more.

(i) the principle companies of operation;

(ii) particulars of its issued share and loan capital and except where the interest of the country and its subsidiaries therein is dealt with in the consolidating balance sheet as an associated company, the total amount of its reserve; and

(iii) the percentage of each class of loan capital distributable to the company's interest (direct or indirect);

(i) A statement as at the end of the financial year showing as regards bank loans and overdrafts and other borrowings of the company and/or its subsidiaries the aggregate amounts repayable

(i) in one year or less or on demand;

(ii) between one and five years;

(iii) in five years or more;

(j) particulars of any other matters which should be disclosed in order to avoid a false market in any of the securities of the Company being established, other than matters the disclosure of which will, in the opinion of the Directors of the Company, be harmful to the business of the Company or of any of its subsidiaries.

(2) Ensure that there is inserted as a note to the audited accounts of the Company full particulars of any contract or arrangement subsisting during or at the end of the financial year:—

(a) which represents or represented "a transaction with a director" under paragraph 14(a) below; or

(b) in which a Director of the Company or any of his associates is or was interested (otherwise than through a Company in which they control less than 10 per cent. of the voting power) and which represents in amount or value more than 1 per cent. of the total purchases, sales, payments or receipts, as the case may be, of the Company and its subsidiaries or, in the case of a capital transaction, of the net tangible assets of the Company and its subsidiaries and for this purpose two or more associated transactions shall be taken together.

10. (1) Require that any service contract granted by the Company or any of its subsidiaries to any Director or proposed Director of the Company is previously approved by the Company in General Meeting, unless such contract expires or is determinable by the employing company without compensation (other than statutory) within three years of the date of commencement of employment under such contract;

(2) make all service contracts of any Director with the Company or any of its subsidiaries, unless they expire or are determinable by the employing company without compensation within one year of the date of commencement of employment thereunder, available during usual business hours on any weekday (Saturdays and Public Holidays excepted) for inspection at the registered office or transfer office of the Company from the date of the notice convening the Annual General Meeting until the date of the meeting and at the place of the meeting for at least 30 minutes before the meeting and during it and, where any such contract is not reduced to writing, a memorandum of the terms thereof;

(3) state in the notice convening the Annual General Meeting that copies of such service contracts, and, if applicable, copies of memoranda embodying the terms of such contracts, will be available for inspection or, in the event that there are no such contracts, state that fact.

11. (1) Certify transfers against certificates or temporary documents and return them on the date of receipt or, if that is not a business day, on the first business day following receipt, and split and return renounceable documents within the same period;

(2) Register transfers and other documents without payment of any fee;

(3) Issue, without charge, certificates within:—

 (i) one month of the date of the expiration of any right of renunciation;

 (ii) fourteen days of the lodgment of transfers;

(4) Where warrants to bearer have been issued or are available for issue:—

 (i) issue certificates in exchange for warrants (or vice versa) within fourteen days of the deposit of the warrants (or certificates);

 (ii) certify transfers against the deposit of warrants.

(5) Where warrants to bearer or securities which are convertible into ordinary share capital are in existence

 (i) to maintain sufficient authorised but unissued share capital;

 (ii) to retain from shareholders in general meetings the relevant allotment powers and this application of pre-emption rights; so as to be able to implement at all times the exercise of such warrants or the conversion of such securities as the case may be.

12. Obtain the consent of the Company in general meeting (save under circumstances which have been agreed by Granville to be exceptional or immaterial) prior to

    (i) the company issuing for cash

    (ii) any major subsidiary of the company making any such issue so as either

        (a) to reduce the equity interest of the company in such subsidiary below 50 per cent.; or

        (b) materially to dilute the percentage equity interest of the company and its shareholders in such subsidiary.

    For this purpose a major subsidiary is a subsidiary representing 25 per cent. or more of the consolidated net assets or pre-tax trading profits of the company and its subsidiaries as shown in their latest audited consolidated accounts; or

  (iii) seeking a quotation for or arranging for dealing in or trading of its shares on any other market

        (a) equity capital or capital having an equity element;

        (b) securities convertible into equity capital;

        (c) warrants or options to subscribe for equity capital;

otherwise than to the equity shareholders of the Company and, where appropriate, holders of other securities entitled to equity shares in the Company, in either case in proportion to their holdings.

13. (1) Issue to shareholders in the Company a circular in terms approved by Granville giving full details of any "15 per cent. transaction."

For this purpose a "15 per cent. transaction" is a transaction for which the Company or any of its subsidiaries is a party, or if Granville shall so determine, two or more such transactions which have taken place since the publication of the last accounts, where—

    (i) the aggregate value of the consideration involved amounts to 15 per cent. or more of the value of the net assets of the Company (excluding goodwill and other intangibles and after deducting liabilities including loan capital and amounts set aside for future taxation) as shown in the latest audited consolidated accounts of the company and its subsidiaries, adjusted to take account of such subsequent acquisitions or disposals as Granville considered necessary; or

    (ii) the profits attributable to the assets involved for the period of twelve months ending on the date of the relevant transaction or, in the case of a series of transactions, on the last of them, computed after deducting all charges except taxation and excluding extraordinary items, amounts to 15 per cent. or more of the aggregate profits of the Company in respect of that period computed on the same basis; or

  (iii) the equity capital issued by the Company as consideration amounts to 15 per cent. or more of the equity capital of the Company in issue at the time of the relevant transaction or, in the case of a series of transactions, the last of them.

For the purpose of paragraph 1(i) the value of any acquisition or dispersal of equity share capital is to be assessed by reference to the book value of the net asset (excluding goodwill and other intangibles and after deducting loan capital and amounts set aside for future taxation) represented by such share capital. In any acquisition or disposal of assets other than equity share capital, the value of such assets shall be assessed by reference to the consideration. Where the consideration is in the form of equity share capital, Granville may determine the value of the consideration by reference either to the market value of such share capital or the book value of the net assets represented by such share capital as defined above.

(2) Notify Granville as soon as possible after agreement in principle has been reached as to the terms of any 25 per cent. transaction, and thereinafter, accept with the consent of Granville, which may be given or withheld in Granville's absolute discretion and which will only be given in circumstances which Granville considers exceptional, only to enter into a 25 per cent. transaction if that transaction had received or is conditional on approval of the company in general meeting. For this purpose a "25 per cent. transaction" shall have the same meaning attributed to a 15 per cent. transaction in 13(1) above, but with the figure 25 substituted for the figure 15.

14. Only enter into a "transaction with a Director or substantial shareholder" with the prior approval of the Company in general meeting (at which the Director and substantial shareholder concerned shall not vote). For this purpose—

  (a) (a) "a transaction with a director or a substantial shareholder" is any transaction whereby the Company or any of its subsidiaries would—
    (i) (section [330] of the Companies Act [1985] make a loan to a director, a substantial shareholder or an associate of either, or enter into any guarantee or provide security in connection with such a loan or provide any kind of financial assistance to a director, a substantial shareholder or an associate of either, unless the sole purpose of such arrangement would be to provide a director with funds, not exceeding at any time £5,000, to meet expenditure incurred or to be incurred by him for the purposes of the company making the arrangement or for the purpose of enabling him properly to perform his duties as an officer of such company;
    (ii) acquire or dispose of assets from or to a director, a substantial shareholder or an associate of either unless the true value of the assets involved amounts to less than 1 per cent. of the net assets of the Company (excluding goodwill and other intangibles and after deducting liabilities including loan capital and amounts set aside for future taxation) taken at the date of the transaction, when, with the agreement of Granville, the transaction may be disclosed in full in the next annual report and accounts and not placed before the Company in general meeting for prior approval.
        Any reference in paragraph 14 to "interest" means an interest as defined by either or both of [section 208 and Pt. I of Schedule 13 to the Companies Act 1985]
    (iii) take an interest in a company, whether existing or about to be formed, any part of the equity share capital of which has within the previous two years been, or is or may be, acquired, whether by

subscription or otherwise, by a director, a substantial shareholder or an associate of either;

(b) "director" is any person who is or was within the preceding 12 months a director of the Company or any of its subsidiaries or any person in accordance with whose instructions the Company or any of its subsidiaries is accustomed to act;

(c) "substantial shareholder" is any person who, is or was within the preceding 12 months, in either case so far as the Directors are aware, interested in 5 per cent. or more of the issued share capital of the Company (or any class thereof) which carries rights to vote in all circumstances at general meetings of the Company;

(d) "associate" means:—

    (i) in relation to an individual: (I) that individual's spouse and any children under the age of 18 (hereinafter referred to as that individual's "family") (II) the trustees (as such) of any trust in which that individual or any member of his family is interested beneficially or is a discretionary object (III) any company in which that individual and/or any member(s) of his family is/are or, following exercise of rights to subscribe or acquire securities, could become interested either directly or indirectly in 5 per cent. or more of the share capital of that company having full voting rights;

    (ii) in relation to a company: any holding company or subsidiary or fellow subsidiary of that company or one in the issued share capital of which it and/or such other companies taken together are directly or indirectly interested to the extent of 30 per cent. or more and any other company those profits are consolidated in the accounts of any such company.

15. Endeavour to procure that, except with the prior written approval of Granville in circumstances which Granville considers to be exceptional—

(a) a Restricted Person, that is to say,

    (i) any person who is a director of the Company or any of its subsidiaries; and

    (ii) any associate of any such person;

will only purchase or sell securities of the Company:—

    (aa) in the period from the date of the preliminary announcement of the results for the full year till two months after the annual general meeting of the Company; and

    (bb) in the period from the publication of the interim results of the Company to the date one month after such publication or the end of the current financial year of the Company whichever is the later; and

(b) a Restricted Person who has information which the public has not and which would, if known, materially affect the value of any securities of the Company will not buy or sell any such securities unless and until such information becomes public, and any Restricted Person who believes he may have such information will consult with the Chairman of the Company or (if he is the Chairman) the other directors before purchasing or selling securities of the Company;

(c) a Restricted Person will not in any period of twelve months buy or sell any securities of the Company which have an aggregate current market value of more than £5,000 before discussing his proposed dealing with the Chairman of the Company or if he is Chairman of the Company, with the other directors;

(d) any Restricted Person who purcases securities of the Company will hold them for not less than twelve months, provided that for the avoidance of doubt this restriction shall not apply to securities of the company subscribed for by a restricted person pursuant to any share option scheme of the Company.

Provided that:—

(aa) sub-paragraphs (a) and (b) above shall not apply to any purchase or sale of securities of the Company which is effected by Granville on behalf of a Restricted Person pursuant to an authority which:—

(i) is irrevocable for a period during which the purchase or sale takes place;

(ii) specifies the terms on which the sale and purchase can be effected; and

(iii) was given by the Restricted Person either on or before the date of this Deed or at a time when he could have purchased or sold such securities under sub-paragraphs (a) or (b).

(bb) sub-paragraph (a) shall not apply to any purchase or sale of securities of the Company which is effected between Restricted Persons provided that neither party involved is a Restricted Person who has information of the nature specified in sub-paragraph (b) above.

16. Procure that, if a circular is issued to the holders of any one class of security, a copy or summary of that circular is issued to the holders of any other securities unless the contents of the circular are irrelevant to such other holders.

17. Procedure that no person is appointed a director of the Company unless he has undertaken with Granville to comply and do his utmost to ensure compliance with the terms of this general undertaking.

18. Keep all shareholders informed of the existence of The Granville Over-The-Counter Market and attempt to ensure that all sales and purchases (except between associates) of the Company's securities in which such a market is made are effected through such market.

---

I hereby certify that the above is a true and correct extract from the minutes of the board.

# 7. Asset Realisation, Merger and Take-Over

Companies, like individuals, may raise funds to meet existing or future commit- **7.01**
ments by disposing of assets. Such a course may be forced upon a company by
circumstances giving rise to capital needs which it cannot, or cannot conveniently, meet from reserves or from increased borrowing. Alternatively, a
company may, following a review of its activities, choose to dispose of a part of
its business as being incompatible with its long-term strategy. In some cases the
view may be taken that the best interests of the company or group as a whole
would be served by the divestment of one or more subsidiary companies. In
others such partial divestment may be insufficient or inappropriate, the company's capital requirements being such that they could best be met by a merger
with or a take-over by another company or group possessing or with access to the
resources necessary to satisfy those requirements.

Such an assessment is often made at the stage in a company's development
when institutional funding alone becomes insufficient to satisfy its needs. At this
point merger or take-over is seen as an alternative to a public issue and may be
considered the more attractive option where access to the required funding can
be guaranteed, where independence is not regarded by the company's principal
shareholders as an overriding consideration and where other and collateral
advantages would result.[1]

A merger or take-over[2] may be regarded as an appropriate financing mechan- **7.02**
ism in its own right where the objective of one or both parties is or includes
(apart from the procurement of new investment):

    (a) the achievement of economies of scale;
    (b) the advantageous acquisition of assets;
    (c) the advantageous acquisition of greater earnings capacity;
    (d) the procurement of tax advantages; or

---

[1] For example, a company may need funds to finance new investment to update its product-line and
equipment because its current return on capital is too low, because its markets are static or declining or because its products are obsolete or about to become so as a result of technological
advance. In such a case a merger may bring with it the collateral advantages of savings in development costs (as a result, possibly, of economies of scale) or the buying of time and/or reputation
which may be needed to compete effectively with others in the same field. Alternatively, a company's very success may present it with problems which could be better overcome in concert with
others than alone. This would seem to be the case where a company lacks the financial resources
to provide effective protection for its patents against infringement by larger concerns or where it is
unable fully to exploit an advantage gained through lack of cash or productive capacity or through
inadequate market coverage.
[2] See generally on the law of take-overs and mergers Weinberg and Blank, *Take-overs and Mergers*
(4th ed., 1979). See also Palmer (Chaps. 79–81) and Gore-Browne (Chaps. 29 and 30).

(e) the obtaining of a Stock Exchange listing.[3]

**7.03**

*Economies of Scale*

In many cases a merger is undertaken primarily to achieve savings by making economies of scale. It is usual for a merger effected for this reason to be followed by:

(1) rationalisation of research and development projects and personnel;

(2) centralisation of services, thereby achieving lower management expenses and accounting costs;

(3) the implementation of a central buying policy so as to achieve greater discounts from bulk buying;

(4) centralisation of the marketing operation of the merged concerns; and

(5) a reduction of stock and work-in-progress to release working capital.

**7.04**

*Acquisition of Assets*

A company may, through a take-over or merger, acquire assets for use in its business more cheaply and conveniently than by other means. For example, if new premises are urgently required the acquisition of a company with such premises may be cheaper in both the shorter and longer term than either putting up a new building or making a single purchase.

Quite independently of such considerations, however, the acquisition of a company may be justified in purely financial terms because of the assets that thereby become available to the acquirer. At its simplest, a merger may bring together assets which are already or will become surplus to the business requirements of the new combine. Such assets will, in many cases, be capable of being disposed of for cash thereby raising or releasing capital for other purposes.

Some companies, of course, are attractive to others simply because they are asset-rich. Where the value of a company's assets exceeds by a substantial margin the value of its shares it is generally considered to be ripe for take-over, the acquisition of such a company serving to add to the asset base of the acquirer and thereby increase its borrowing capacity. Often, however, the motive for the acquisition of such companies is "asset-stripping," the victim company's assets being sold off to produce a quick and easy profit over the acquisition cost of the shares.

**7.05**

The acquisition of a company with a lower price-to-earnings ratio than that of the acquiring company will usually result in an increase in the earnings per share

---

[3] Take-overs and mergers may, of course, be entered into for reasons other than purely financial: *e.g.*

(a) for family or fiscal reasons—shareholders may wish to have their assets in the form of quoted rather than the unquoted securities of a private close company;

(b) to acquire management with special technical or other skills and experience in other fields, or to acquire a young, successful and dynamic management. However, this would seem to be a valid reason only if the new management is to be used at the correct level of responsibility and motivation to make it worthwhile for them to stay. Alternatively where there exists an efficient and capable management which is under-employed it can be turned to advantage by the acquisition of businesses which can be "turned round" and made profitable;

(c) the company may wish to integrate backwards by acquiring a source of supply, or forward by taking over a customer. These operations can ensure either a source of raw materials or components, or deny markets to competition.

of the latter and therefore an improvement in that company's income cover for its borrowing.[4] However, such an improvement is unlikely to be immediate and where what is acquired is a company that is not trading profitably there will inevitably be a delay while it is brought to profitability and its pre-acquisition profit forecasts attained.

*Acquisition of Greater Earnings Capacity*

In certain circumstances it is possible for a company to obtain the benefit of accumulated trading losses incurred by another company by acquiring that company. Prior to 1969 the possibilities for obtaining such benefits were much wider than they are today. The current position is governed by section 483 of the Income and Corporation Taxes Act 1970[5] which disallows the carrying forward of unrelieved trading losses incurred before a substantial change of ownership of the company's shares where:

**7.06**

*Procurement of Tax Advantages*

(a) that change in ownership is followed by a major change[6] in the nature or conduct of the company's trade within a period of three years; or
(b) the activities of the trade have become small or negligible and the change of ownership is followed by a considerable revival of the trade.

These provisions are not without difficulty for companies making acquisitions. In the first place condition (a) would appear to inhibit attempts to improve an acquired company's profitability (at least within the three year period) since action towards that end might be regarded as changing the conduct of that company's trade. In addition there is the point that condition (b) applies without limit of time. Accordingly it would seem possible that a substantial revival of trade, even if achieved over a long period of time, would potentially fall within the ambit of the provision and thereby cause the loss to be disallowed.

It sometimes occurs that an unquoted company can acquire a Stock Exchange listing[7] by carrying out a reverse take-over of a listed company. Such a transaction takes the form of a take-over by the listed company of the unlisted concern but in such a way that a majority shareholding (and therefore control) of the listed company becomes vested in the proprietors of the unlisted company.

**7.07**

*Obtaining a Stock Exchange Listing*

Reverse take-overs are subject to Stock Exchange regulation[8] in that the Council of the Stock Exchange will normally require that the transaction be subject to the approval of the shareholders of the listed company and that the listing of that company's securities be temporarily suspended. This suspension will normally operate from the time when the acquisition is announced until all relevant information is made available.[9]

---

[4] At least where the consideration for the acquisition comprised shares in the acquiring company.
[5] Re-enacting F.A. 1969, s.30.
[6] A "major change in the nature or conduct of a trade" includes a major change in the property dealt in, services or facilities provided or in customers or markets: I.C.T.A. 1970, s.483(3).
[7] Or quotation on the USM by the acquisition of a company with such a quotation.
[8] Admission of Securities to Listing—Section 6, Chapter 1, para. 7.
[9] This must include an Accountant's Report on the business or unlisted company or companies involved and a *pro forma* balance sheet of the group as reorganised. These must be included in an advertised statement or (in exceptional cases) in a new issue card in the statistical services to which

# FORMS OF AMALGAMATION

## Amalgamation under the Companies Acts

**7.08**     The Companies Act 1985 makes provision for companies to effect a merger of their undertakings by way of:

  (a)  a scheme of arrangement under sections 425–427; or
  (b)  a liquidation and reconstruction under section 582.

## 7.09   Schemes of arrangement

Section 425 provides that where any compromise or arrangement[10] is proposed between a company and its creditors or any class of them, or between a company and its members of any class of them, the court may on the application[11] of the company, or any creditor or member of the company, or the liquidator, order a meeting of the creditors or class of creditors, or of the members or class of members, as the case may be, to be called. If a majority in number representing three fourths in value of the creditors or class of creditors, or members or class of members, present either in person or by proxy, agree to the compromise or arrangement and it is also sanctioned by the court, it will be binding on all the creditors or the class of creditors, or on the members or class of members, as the case may be, and on the liquidator and the contributories of the company.

**7.10**     Where a meeting is convened under this provision there must be sent with every notice summoning the meeting which is sent to a creditor or member a

*Procedure under s.425*  statement explaining the effect of the scheme. This statement must include particulars[12] of any material interests of the directors of the company whether as directors or as members or as creditors of the company or otherwise and must explain the effect of the scheme on such interests insofar as that effect is different from the scheme's effect on the like interests of other persons.[13] In cases where the scheme affects debenture holders a corresponding statement as to the scheme's effect on the material interests of the trustees of any deed securing the issue of the debentures[14] must also be provided.

---

attention is drawn by a box advertisement in the Press. In certain circumstances the Council may require the Accountant's Report to cover the accounts of the listed company as well.

The Council will not normally grant listing following a suspension until after the publication of accounts showing a record of operation covering a sufficient period of time. Where the company making the reverse take-over operates a business of such a nature that it is not possible to publish such a past record the suspension will remain in operation until after the expiration of the necessary period. (Admission of Securities to Listing—Section 6, Chapter 1, para. 7).

[10] "Arrangement" is defined by s.425(5) to include a reorganisation of the share capital by the consolidation of shares of different classes or by the division of shares into different classes or by both of these methods.

[11] *Ex parte*, by originating summons under R.S.C., Ord. 102, s.2(1).

[12] As to what amounts to sufficient disclosure of the interests of directors see: *Rankin & Blackmore, Petitioners* 1950 S.C. 218; *Peter Scott & Co., Petitioners* 1950 S.C. 507; *Coltness Iron Co., Petitioners* 1951 S.L.T. 344; *City Property Investment Trust Corporation Ltd., Petitioners* 1951 S.L.T. 371.

[13] C.A. 1985, s.426.

[14] See *Second Scottish Investment Trust Corporation, Petitioners* 1962 S.L.T. 392.

Where the notice summoning the meeting is given by advertisement that advertisement is required to include the statement as to directors' interests or alternatively, to give notification of the place at which and the manner in which creditors or members entitled to attend the meeting may obtain copies thereof.

The usual practice is for explanatory circulars to be sent out to members and/ or creditors of the company setting out all information reasonably necessary to enable the recipients to determine how to vote.[15] In *Re National Bank Ltd.*[16] objections were made to a scheme of arrangement on the ground, *inter alia*, that the information provided failed to disclose the assets and profitability of the bank. It was held that nothing in what is now section 426 operated to force the disclosure of information concerning the bank's accounts. Such non-disclosure was (at that time[17]) not regarded as improper since banking companies were allowed to withhold such information from their published accounts. The primary requirement of the information provided was that it should be fair and adequate to enable an intelligent judgment as to the scheme to be made.[18] In this case Plowman J. was satisfied from other evidence of the scheme's objective fairness and felt that further disclosure of information might have damaged the bank's prospects and thereby injured the interests of the shareholders both before and after the scheme.

A draft of the proposed circular should be exhibited to the affidavit in support of the summons[19] for an order to convene the relevant meeting or meetings. If the requisite majorities are obtained the company or companies may then apply by petition to the court for its sanction of the scheme.

The power of the courts to sanction a scheme of arrangement is discretionary **7.11** and in determining whether approval should be given in any particular case the court is concerned to see:

(a) that the resolutions have been passed by the requisite statutory majority; and

(b) whether the proposal is such that an intelligent and honest man, as a member of the class concerned and acting in respect of his interests might reasonably approve.[20]

In *Re San Francisco Brewery Co.*[21] the court rejected a scheme which pro-

---

[15] Such persons are, by s.426(3), entitled to a copy of the statement free of charge.

[16] [1966] 1 W.L.R. 819.

[17] Since 1969 the clearing banks have agreed that their annual accounts should be prepared in accordance with the requirements of the Companies Acts as to companies in general and that they would cease to take advantage of the exemptions available to them (under C.A. 1948, Sched. 8; Part III, para. 23 and C.A. 1967, Sched. 2). See now Banking Companies (Accounts) Regulations 1970: S.I. 1970 No. 317.

[18] *Re Dorman Long & Co.* [1934] Ch. 635; *Re Imperial Chemical Industries Ltd.* [1936] Ch. 587, 615, C.A.; affd. [1937] A.C. 707, H.L.

[19] Such an application is made by originating summons and a copy of the proposed statement should form part of the evidence in support of the summons.

[20] *Re Alabama, New Orleans, Texas and Pacific Junction Rly. Co.* [1891] 1 Ch. 213, C.A.; *Re English, Scottish & Australian Chartered Bank* [1893] 3 Ch. 385, C.A.; *Re Dorman Long & Co., supra*; See also *Carruth* v. *Imperial Chemical Industries* [1937] A.C. 707, H.L.; *Re National Bank, supra*; and *Re Holder's Investment Trust Ltd.* [1971] 1 W.L.R. 583.

[21] [1909] Unreported, C.A.

vided for shares already fully paid to be treated as being subject to a new liability of 15p per share. On the other hand in *Re Guardian Assurance Co.*[22] the court approved a scheme requiring each shareholder to hand over a portion of his fully paid shares to form a consideration for the purchase of another undertaking.

**7.12**

*Orders under s.427*

Where an application is made to the court under section 425 for the sanctioning of a compromise or arrangement and it is shown to the court that the compromise or arrangement has been prepared for the purposes of or in connection with a scheme for the reconstruction of any company or companies, or for the amalgamation of two or more companies, and that under the scheme the whole or any part of the undertaking of any company concerned in the scheme is to be transferred to another company the court may, either by the order sanctioning the arrangement or compromise or by any subsequent order,[23] make provision for all or any of the following matters,[24] namely:

(1) the transfer to the transferee company of the whole or any part of the undertaking and of the property[25] or liabilities[26] of the transfer company;

(2) the allotting or appropriation by the transferee company of any shares, debentures, policies or other like interests in that company which, under the compromise or arrangement, are to be allotted or appropriated by that company to or for any person;

(3) the continuation by or against any transferee company of any legal proceedings pending by or against the transferor company;

(4) the dissolution without winding up, of any transferor company;

(5) the provision to be made for any persons who, within such time and in such manner as the court directs, dissent from the compromise or arrangement; and

(6) such incidental, consequential and supplementary matters as are necess-

---

[22] [1917] 1 Ch. 431, C.A.

[23] The proper procedure is:

(1) to obtain an order under s.425 sanctioning the scheme; and then (2) to make an application in chambers under s.427 (in accordance with R.S.C., Ord. 102, s.7(2)(*b*)) to which the transferee company should be a party—see Practice Note [1939] W.N. 121.

An order made under s.425 is of no effect until an office copy thereof has been delivered to the Registered Companies for registration. After an order has been made a copy of it must be annexed to every copy of the memorandum issued after the order has been made. In the case of a company not having a memorandum a copy of the order must be annexed to every copy of the instrument comprising or defining the constitution of the company after the order is made: s.425(3).

Where an order is made under s.427 every company in relation to which the order has been made must cause an office copy thereof to be delivered to the Registrar for registration within seven days after the making of the order. Default in compliance with these requirements renders the company and every officer of the company who is in default liable to a fine: s.427(5).

[24] C.A. 1985, s.427(3).

[25] "Property" includes property, rights and powers of every description—*ibid.* s.427(6). However it does not include:

(1) the right to carry forward losses and capital allowances for the purposes—*United Steel Companies* v. *Cullington* [1940] A.C. 812, H.L.

(2) the rights of the transferor company under contracts of service with its employer—*Nokes* v. *Doncaster Amalgamated Collieries* [1940] A.C. 1014, H.L.

[26] "Liabilities" includes duties: C.A. 1985, s.427(6). But not a duty to serve under or contract of personal service—*Nokes* v. *Doncaster Amalgamated Collieries, supra.*

ary to secure that the reconstruction or amalgamation will be fully and effectively carried out.

The effect of an order is to make the arrangement binding on all share or debenture holders to which it relates, overriding any dissent. Accordingly, a scheme of arrangement under which the requisite majority of debenture holders agreed to forgo their security and accept preference shares in the new company in exchange for their debentures in the original company was held, upon being sanctioned by the court, to be binding on the minority opposed to be exchange.[27] Furthermore a scheme, once sanctioned by the court, cannot be varied or departed from with the mere acquiescence of the shareholders and creditors but requires the approval of court.[28]

Where an order provides for the transfer of property that property is, by virtue of the order, transferred to and becomes vested in the transferee company.[29] Similarly an order providing for the transfer of liabilities will have the effect of transferring those liabilities so that they become vested in the transferee company.[30] Where an order relates to property over which there exists a charge the order will, if it so directs, transfer the property free from the charge. Such an order will be made where one of the terms of the arrangement or compromise is that the charge shall cease to have effect.[31]

## Liquidation and reconstruction 7.13

Unlike schemes of arrangement which may but do not inevitably involve the winding up of the transferor company a merger effected by way of a reconstruction under section 582 of the Companies Act 1985 inevitably does involve such a winding up.[32]

The procedure for effecting a merger under section 582 involves three steps:

(a) the making of the merger agreement pursuant to which the reconstruction is to be effected;
(b) the passing of the special resolutions by the company or companies to be wound up; and

---

[27] *Re Empire Mining Co. Ltd.* (1890) 44 Ch.D. 402; *Re Alabama, New Orleans, Texas Rly. Co.* [1891] 1 Ch. 213, C.A.: *Follitt* v. *Eddystone Granite Quarries* [1892] 3 Ch. 75, 85.
[28] *Devi* v. *People's Bank* [1938] 4 All E.R. 337, P.C.
[29] C.A. 1985, s.427.
[30] *Ibid.* s.427(4).
[31] *Ibid.*
[32] C.A. 1985, s.582 is in fact primarily concerned with the powers of a liquidator to accept assets as consideration for the sale of the company's property. Sections 582(1) and (2) provide:
(1) The following applies where a company is proposed to be, or is being, wound up altogether voluntarily, and the whole or part of its business or property is proposed to be transferred or sold to another company ("the tranferee company"), whether or not this latter is a company within the meaning of this Act.
(2) The liquidator of the company to be, or being, wound up ("the tansferor company") may, with the sanction of a special resolution of that company, conferring either a general authority on himself or an authority in respect of any particular arrangement, receive, in compensation or part compensation for the transfer or sale, shares, policies or other like interests in the transferee company for distribution among the members of the transferor company.

(c) the implementation of the scheme by the liquidator(s) of such company or companies.

**7.14**     The statutory procedure presupposes an agreement between the parties as to the principle of a merger and as to the terms on which such merger is to take effect. Such agreement may be on the basis that one company agrees to transfer its assets and undertaking to another or that both or all of the merging companies agree to transfer their assets and undertakings to a new company formed especially for the purpose.

**7.15**     The second stage in the procedure under section 582 is for the company (or companies) in question to pass special resolutions[33]:

*(2) Special Resolutions*

(a) for the voluntary winding up of its (or their) affairs; and then

(b) to authorise the liquidator to carry out the arrangements and to receive in return for the transfer of assets and undertaking(s) shares and/or other securities in the transferee company for distribution among its (or their) members.

Express notice of each resolution must be given to the shareholders. Such notice must specify that a sale is intended under section 582[34] and must make disclosure of any special advantage obtained by the directors from the reconstruction.[35]

**7.16**     The third stage is the implementation by the liquidator(s) of the transferor company (or companies) of the agreement by way of a sale to the transferee company of the assets and undertaking(s) of the transferor company (or companies). Any sale or arrangement pursuant to section 582 is binding on all members of a transferor company.[36] However, dissentient members of such companies[37] are given the right to express in writing their dissent to the liquidator and to require that their interests be purchased at a price to be determined by agreement or arbitration.[38] If a liquidator elects to purchase the interest of such a member the purchase money must be paid before the company is dissolved and be raised by the liquidator in such manner as may be determined by special resolution.[39]

*(3) Implementation of Scheme by Liquidator*

---

[33] Where a draft agreement for sale is prepared the special resolution may refer to and approve it and thereupon no further scheme of reconstruction is necessary. It is usual however to incorporate into the resolution the power to implement the agreement with or without modification.

[34] *Imperial Bank of China* v. *Bank of Hindustan* (1868) 6 Eq. 91; *Re Irrigation Co. of France, ex p. Fox* (1871) 6 Ch. App. 176, 193.

[35] *Kaye* v. *Croydon Tramways* [1898] 1 Ch. 358, C.A.; *Tiessen* v. *Henderson* [1899] 1 Ch. 861; *Clarkson* v. *Davies* [1923] A.C. 100, P.C.

[36] C.A. 1985, s.582(4).

[37] See further Palmer at § 80.07 *et seq.*

[38] C.A. 1985, s.582(5) and (8). Note that the notice must state in terms both alternatives for the liquidator to choose from in order to be valid: see *Re Demarara Rubber Co.* [1913] 1 Ch. 331; *Re Union Bank of Kingston-upon-Hull* (1880) 13 Ch.D. 808.

[39] *Ibid.* s.582(7).

It is often the case that the terms of a scheme or arrangement stipulate for a **7.17**
time limit within which a member of a transferor company must take his interest
in the transferee company. Such a time limit may be fixed specifically or be *Time Limits*
defined by reference to "a reasonable time."[40] Where such a time-limit provision is present it is usually accompanied by a further clause providing for the
eventuality of shares in the transferee company not being taken up by those
entitled to them.[41] Such a clause however, while obviously useful, would appear
not to be strictly necessary since the court, having jurisdiction under section 427
in respect of section 582 schemes, may make any necessary order to deal with
such a case.

### Amalgamation by acquisition of shares

In cases of an agreed merger an alternative and in many respects simpler **7.18**
method of achieving the same commercial result as that obtainable under the
procedures provided for in sections 425–427 or section 582 of the Companies Act
1985 is for the transaction to take the form of a take-over. Indeed it is more common for mergers to be effected by this method than by using the statutory
forms.[42]

The essential elements of a take-over are:

(i) that one company (the offeror company) makes an offer to the shareholders of another company (the offeree company) for their shares; *Elements of a*
*Take-over*
(ii) that a sufficient proportion of the offeree company's shareholders accept
the offer to give the offeror company control;
whereupon, following a transfer of those shares,
(iii) the offeree company becomes a subsidiary of the offeror.

Where, of course, the wishes of the offeror company for an amalgamation are
not reciprocated by the offeree company such a transaction becomes in substance as well as in form a take-over.

The principles and rules applicable to take-overs of independent companies **7.19**
apply equally to acquisitions of subsidiary companies or businesses of other concerns. Accordingly, where a company wishes to raise capital through the sale of
a part of its undertaking held through a subsidiary company the transaction is
likewise essentially one of a sale and purchase of shares.[43]

---

[40] Such time stipulations will be valid provided that the period involved is reasonable: *Weston* v. *New Guston Co.* (1889) 62 L.T. 275; *Zuccani* v. *Nacupai Gold Mining Co.* (1889) 61 L.T. 176; *Postle-thwaite* v. *Port Philip & Colonial Gold Mining Co.* (1889) 43 Ch.D. 452.
[41] *Burdett-Coutts* v. *True Blue (Hannan's) Gold Mine* [1898] 2 Ch. 616; *Nicholl* v. *Eberhardt Co.* (1889) 59 L.J. Ch. 103; *Liquidator of Melville Coal Co.* v. *Clark* (1904) 6 F. 913.
[42] See the Gower Report: *Review of Investor Protection* (Cmnd. 9125, January 1984) at p. 134.
[43] While the disposal of a business and its assets *per se* is common enough in practice it is often
thought to be preferable for the business to have been incorporated and for the company resulting
from that incorporation to be sold. This is in part because the transactions involved are simpler (a
single transfer of shares rather than possibly multiple transfers of goodwill and individual assets)
and in part because the tax position of vendor and purchaser are more clear-cut with there being
no question of forfeiting any accumulated relief for past losses or, so far as applicable, capital
allowances.

## SALES AND ACQUISITIONS BY PRIVATE TREATY

**7.20**

*Preliminaries*

Transactions within this category will in practice tend to comprise sales of small family companies or divestments of subsidiaries by their parent concerns. Such transactions will normally be arranged through the mediacy of a merchant bank and/or broker, in part to avoid any possible (albeit unlikely) contravention of section 14 of the Prevention of Fraud (Investments) Act 1958,[44] but primarily to identify companies with a potential acquisition interest and to make initial approaches to such companies without disclosing the identity of the vendor (or of the company to be sold) until interest in principle has been expressed.[45]

*Acquisition Report*

After the formal expression of interest by the prospective purchaser and the agreement in principle by the vendor(s) to sell to such purchaser the next stage is often (and almost always in the case of a sale of a family company) the preparation of a full acquisition report by accountants on behalf of the purchaser.[46] This report fulfils a comparable function to that of the reporting accountants' long form report in a company's preparations for a flotation.[47]

The acquisition report will normally deal with the following matters:

(1) the history and business of the company to be acquired;
(2) its corporate structure;
(3) management and personnel;
(4) operations and systems;
(5) taxation and indemnities;
(6) accounting policies;
(7) turnover and profits;
(8) assets and liabilities;
(9) source and application of funds;
(10) borrowing facilities;
(11) insurance;
(12) future prospects[48]; and
(13) summary and conclusions.

**7.21**

In some cases the sale and purchase of a company may have consequences affecting other commitments and obligations of the vendor or purchaser which

---

[44] s.14 makes it an offence for an unauthorised person to distribute a document which is a circular containing an invitation to dispose of or to acquire securities without the consent of the Department of Trade and Industry or unless the document is sent by a member of the Stock Exchange or of a recognised association of dealers in securities or by a licensed or exempted dealer in securities. See further at § 7.36 below.
Note also that s.13 of the 1958 Act makes it an offence, punishable by a term of imprisonment not exceeding 7 years, for any person to induce or to attempt to induce another to enter into an agreement for the acquisition or disposal of securities by making any statement, promise or forecast which he knows to be misleading, false or deceptive or by any dishonest concealment of material facts, or by the reckless making of any statement, promise or forecast which is misleading, false or deceptive. Note further that s.13 is not confined to written statements.
[45] It will obviously be of the utmost importance to the vendor that his position is not undermined by the premature disclosure of the information the company is up for sale.
[46] The report is usually prepared by the purchaser's auditors.
[47] See above at §§ 6.30–6.31.
[48] Including an assessment of the impact of any government legislation in so far as it affects the company being acquired.

render it necessary or desirable for some consent or approval to be obtained for the transaction.

*Consents and Approvals for Sale/ Acquisition*

The principal consents and approvals likely to be required in practice are as follows:

### (a) Loan agreements

It is not uncommon for loan agreements to contain provisions stipulating that the loan will become payable in the event of a change of control of the company. Accordingly the purchaser of a company which has loan finance on these terms must (assuming it wishes this facility to be retained) take steps to inform the lender of the proposed sale and obtain an undertaking that this term of the agreement will not be enforced.

Equally, and especially where the company to be sold is a subsidiary of the vendor, where the vendor has entered into loan agreements it is usual for these agreements to contain provisions restricting the alienation of any substantial part of the vendor's undertaking or assets. In such cases the lenders or trustees for loan/debenture stock holders will normally be required to give their consent.[49]

### (b) Articles of association

In some instances the articles of association of the purchasing company may require that the approval of the shareholders be obtained for the acquisition. Such approval will most commonly be required where the consideration for the acquisition involves the issue of shares in the acquiring company and where that issue requires an increase in that company's capital. Such an increase (and with it approval for the purchase) may of course be obtained by the passing of an ordinary resolution.

Provisions are sometimes encountered in the articles of private companies conferring pre-emption rights on existing shareholders in respect of any new shares issued by the company. In such cases the consents of these shareholders would have to be formally obtained before any new shares could be issued.[50]

### (c) Sale to an overseas company

While the requirement under the Exchange Control Act 1947 that permission be obtained for the acquisition of shares in a company incorporated and carrying on business in the United Kingdom by a non-resident company or undertaking is no longer operative Treasury permission may still be required under section 482 of the Income and Corporation Taxes Act 1970 for the transfer by a United Kingdom resident holding company of a subsidiary to a non-resident purchaser where the transaction will result in a substantial change in the character or extent of the trade or business of the vendor.

---

[49] Likewise trust deeds in respect of convertible loan stock may contain terms restricting the issue of further share capital.

[50] Especially shareholders not involved in the management of the company.

Section 482 provides, *inter alia*, that it is unlawful, without the consent of the Treasury, for a body corporate resident in the United Kingdom to cease to be so resident, or for the trade or business or any part of the trade or business of a body corporate so resident to be transferred from that body corporate to a person not so resident. If, therefore, the sale relates to one subsidiary among many Treasury consent will not be required since the residence of the subsidiary will not change as a result of the transaction. If, however, the purchaser is non-resident and the shares in the subsidiary that are sold from part of the undertaking of a resident company vendor it may be that the sale will involve part of the vendor's trade or business to a non-resident and as such come within the scope of the consent requirement. Under section 482(9), where the functions of a body corporate consist wholly or mainly of the holding of investments or other property (as will be the case where the organisation of a business is in group form with ultimate control vested in a single holding company) the holding of the investments or property will be deemed to be a business carried on by the body corporate. Accordingly therefore the transfer of a subsidiary by the holding company would seem to amount to a transfer of part of the trade or business. However, section 482(9) provides that a mere transfer of assets by a body corporate not resulting in a "substantial change in the character or extent of the trade or business" of such a body corporate will not be treated as a transfer of a part of the trade or business for the purposes of section 482. It follows therefore that for consent to be required the transfer of a subsidiary by a United Kingdom resident company to a non-resident purchaser the sale must bring about such a substantial change.

Consent[51] is not required if the transaction is a sale and

    (1)  the sale is for full consideration paid in cash;

    (2)  the consideration for the sale does not exceed £50,000;

    (3)  the purchaser is not a body corporate over which persons ordinarily resident in the United Kingdom have control;

    (4)  the purchaser has no interest in the business of the vendor and the vendor has no interest in the business of the purchaser; and

    (5)  the sale is not associated with any other operation, transaction or arrangements whereby the business (or the part of the business which is sold) or any interest in that business (or part of a business) may revert to the vendor or any partner who has an interest in the business of the vendor.

## 7.22  Sales and acquisitions by private treaty—the sale agreement

In principle there is nothing to prevent the contract for the sale of the shares in the company from being in simple form, as follows:

---

[51] Certain general consents have been issued by the Treasury which consents also prescribe the mode of application under s.482.

WHEREAS

*Simple Form of Sale Agreement*

(1) XYZ Ltd./plc is a private/public company incorporated on . . . with limited liability under the Companies Acts 1948–81 and has an authorised share capital of £ . . . divided into . . . ordinary shares of . . . each all of which have been issued and are fully paid.

[(2) XYZ Ltd./plc is a wholly owned subsidiary[52] of the vendor.]

NOW IT IS HEREBY AGREED AND DECLARED

as follows:

1. The vendor(s) shall sell and the purchaser shall purchase free from all liens charges or incumbrances and together with all rights now or hereafter attaching thereto all the said shares in XYZ Ltd./plc.

2. The total consideration payable by the purchaser for the said shares shall be £ . . . payable in cash.

3. Completion of the sale and purchase of the said shares shall take place on . . . when

    (a) the vendor(s) shall deliver to the purchaser forms of transfer in respect of the said shares duly executed by the vendor(s) in favour of the purchaser or its nominees together with the share certificates relating thereto; and

    (b) the purchaser shall pay to the vendor(s) the consideration stated in para. 2 above.

AS WITNESS etc.

In practice this simple form of agreement would be expanded to take account of:

    (i) cases where the consideration was otherwise than in cash;

    (ii) the possible requirement of the purchaser that a capitalisation issue be made by the company prior to completion;

    (iii) any conditions to which completion is subject;

    (iv) warranties given in respect of the sale; and

    (v) indemnities given in respect of the sale.

## The sale agreement—the consideration

**7.23**

Where the transaction is a sale by a parent company of one of its subsidiaries in order to raise additional funds it will normally be a requirement that the consideration be in cash. Nevertheless, such a vendor may be prepared to accept shares as consideration if the purchaser is a listed[53] company since the shares would be readily marketable and available either as security for further borrowing or for subsequent sale for cash at an appropriate time.

Even where the vendor's requirement is for cash on completion or in the immediate period thereafter a consideration in the form of shares may be acceptable if arrangements can be made for them to be placed. If the entire allotment is to be disposed of, or if a specified number of shares only are to be sold, the prac-

*Vendor Placings*

---

[52] If there are any minority shareholdings the recitals and sale and purchase clause should state the number of shares held by the vendor and as such subject to the agreement.

[53] Or, possibly, one whose shares are quoted on the USM.

tice is for the placing to be arranged by the purchaser[54] on the vendor's behalf without specific provision being made in the sale agreement. However, where the vendor's stipulation is that the shares issued by the purchaser and allotted to it realise a specified sum it is usual for the agreement to contain an express term to the effect that "the number of shares alloted to the vendor shall be sufficient to realise the cash sum equal to the full amount of the consideration by a placing of consideration shares at the highest price reasonably obtainable for them at completion."

The implementation of such a term would proceed through the mediacy of an agreed broker whose functions would be to certify the number of consideration shares required to realise the stipulated sum and to purchase or to procure the purchase of these shares "against receipt of duly renounced allotment letters covering the consideration shares in such form as we shall request and split as we shall direct."

The broker's obligation to place and the vendor's obligation to sell the shares in the purchasing company are invariably made conditional upon:

(a) the passing at a general meeting of the purchaser of a resolution to increase its authorised share capital by the required amount; and

(b) the Council of the Stock Exchange's having admitted the consideration shares to the Official List[55] (or USM, as the case may be).

**7.24**    If the sale and purchase can be carried through on a "shares for shares" basis possible tax advantages may accrue the vendor(s) or purchaser in respect of liability to capital gains tax, stamp duty and capital duty.

*Consideration in Form of Shares—Tax Advantages*

*(a) Capital gains tax*

A shares for shares (or, indeed, any other type of security) transaction would have the advantage for the vendor that no immediate liability would result, any capital gain accruing on the disposal being "rolled-over."[56]

*(b) Stamp duty*

Under the provisions of the Stamp Act 1891[57] stamp duty is chargeable on transfers of registered shares and is payable by the purchaser. The current rate of charge is 1 per cent.[58] of the consideration.[59] However, where the consideration for the transfer consists of shares the transaction may be eligible for relief under the provisions of section 55 of the Finance Act 1927 (as amended). Section 55 provides:

(1) If in connection with a scheme for the reconstruction of any company or companies or the amalgamation of any companies it is shown to the satis-

---

[54] Via brokers

[55] These conditions will be incorporated into the agreement as Completion Conditions.

[56] C.G.T.A. 1979, s.87.

[57] s.55.

[58] F.A. 1984, s.109.

[59] Or, if higher, the market value of the securities transferred.

faction of the Commissioners of Inland Revenue that there exist the fol- *Finance Act 1927, s.55*
lowing conditions, that is to say—

(*a*) that a company with limited liability is to be registered, or that since the commencement of this Act a company has been incorporated by letters patent or Act of Parliament, or the nominal share capital of a company has been increased;

(*b*) that the company (in this section referred to as "the transferee company") is to be registered or has been incorporated or has increased its capital with a view to the acquisition either of the undertaking of, or of not less than ninety per cent. of the issued share capital of, any particular existing company;

(*c*) that the consideration for the acquisition (except such part thereof as consists in the transfer to or discharge by the transferee company of liabilities of the existing company) consists as to not less than ninety per cent. thereof—

(i) where an undertaking is to be acquired, in the issue of shares in the transferee company to the existing company or to holders of shares in the existing company;

or

(ii) where shares are to be acquired, in the issue of shares in the transferee company to the holders of shares in the existing company in exchange for the shares held by them in the existing company:

then, subject to the provisions of this section,—

(*A*) . . . [60]

(*B*) Stamp duty under the heading "Conveyance or Transfer on Sale" in the First Schedule to the Stamp Act 1891, shall not be chargeable on any instrument made for the purposes of or in connection with the transfer of the undertaking or shares [or on any instrument made for the purposes of or in connection with the assignment to the transferee company of any debts, secured or unsecured, of the existing company][61] nor shall any such duty be chargeable under section twelve of the Finance Act 1895, on a copy of any Act of Parliament, or on any instrument vesting, or relating to the vesting of, the undertaking or shares in the transferee company:

Provided that—

(*a*) no such instrument shall be deemed to be duly stamped unless either it is stamped with the duty to which it would but for this section be liable or it has in accordance with the provisions of section twelve of the Stamp Act 1891, been stamped with a particular stamp denoting either that it is not chargeable with any duty or that it is duly stamped; and

---

[60] Repealed by F.A. 1973, s.59(7) and Sched. 22, Pt. V.
[61] Inserted by F.A. 1928, s.31.

(b) in the case of an instrument made for the purposes of or in connection with a transfer to a company within the meaning of the Companies (Consolidation) Act 1908, the provisions of paragraph (B) of this subsection shall not apply unless the instrument is either—

    (i) executed within a period of twelve months from the date of the registration of the transferee company or the date of the resolution for the increase of the nominal share capital of the transferee company, as the case may be; or

   (ii) made for the purpose of effecting a conveyance or transfer in pursuance of an agreement which has been filed, or particulars of which have been filed, with the registrar of companies within the said period of twelve months [; and

(c) the foregoing provision with respect to the release and assignment of debts of the existing company shall not, except in the case of debts due to banks or to trade creditors, apply to debts which were incurred less than two years before the proper time for making a claim for exemption under this section.][61]

(2) For the purposes of a claim for exemption under paragraph (B) of subsection (1) of this section, a company which has, in connection with a scheme of reconstruction or amalgamation, issued any unissued share capital shall be treated as if it had increased its nominal share capital.

(3) A company shall not be deemed to be a particular existing company within the meaning of this section unless it is provided by the memorandum of association of, or the letters patent or Act incorporating, the transferee company that one of the objects for which the company is established is the acquisition of the undertaking of, or shares in, the existing company, or unless it appears from the resolution, Act or other authority for the increase of the capital of the transferee company that the increase is authorised for the purpose of acquiring the undertaking of, or shares in, the existing company.

(4) . . . [62]

(5) Where a claim is made for exemption under this section, the Commissioners of Inland Revenue may require the delivery to them of a statutory declaration in such form as they may direct, made in England by a solicitor of the Supreme Court or in Scotland by an enrolled law agent, and of such further evidence, if any, as the Commissioners may reasonably require.

(6) If—

    (a) where any claim for exemption from duty under this section has been allowed, it is subsequently found that any declaration or other evidence furnished in support of the claim was untrue in any material particular, or that the conditions specified in subsection (1) of this section are not fulfilled in the reconstruction or amalgamation as actually carried out; or

[62] See above at n. 60.

(*b*) where shares in the transferee company have been issued to the existing company in consideration of the acquisition, the existing company within a period of two years from the date, as the case may be, of the registration or incorporation, or of the authority for the increase of the capital, of the transferee company ceases, otherwise than in consequence of reconstruction, amalgamation or liquidation, to be the beneficial owner of the shares are issued to it; or

(*c*) where any such exemption has been allowed in connection with the acquisition by the transferee company of shares in another company, the transferee company within a period of two years from the date of its registration or incorporation or of the authority for the increase of its capital, as the case may be, ceases, otherwise than in consequence of reconstruction, amalgamation or liquidation, to be the beneficial owner of the shares so acquired;

the exemption shall be deemed not to have been allowed, and an amount equal to the duty remitted shall become payable forthwith, and shall be recoverable from the transferee company as a debt due to His Majesty, together with interest thereon at the rate of five per cent. per annum in the case of duty remitted under paragraph (A) of subsection (1) of this section from the date of the registration or incorporation of the transferee company or the increase of its capital, as the case may be, and in the case of duty remitted under paragraph (B) of the said subsection from the date on which it would have become chargeable if this Act had not passed.

(7) If in the case of any scheme of reconstruction or amalgamation the Commissioners of Inland Revenue are satisfied that at the proper time for making a claim for exemption from duty under subsection (1) of this section there were in existence all the necessary conditions for such exemption other than the condition that not less than ninety per cent. of the issued share capital of the existing company would be acquired by the transferee company, the Commissioners may, if it is proved to their satisfaction that not less than ninety per cent. of the issued capital of the existing company has under the scheme been acquired within a period of six months from the earlier of the two following dates, that is to say—

(*a*) the last day of the period of one months after the first allotment of shares made for the purposes of the acquisition; or

(*b*) the date on which an invitation was issued to the shareholders of the existing company to accept shares in the transferee company;

and on production of the instruments on which the duty paid has been impressed, direct repayment to be made of such an amount of duty as would have been remitted if the said condition had been originally fulfilled.

(8) In this section, unless the context otherwise requires—
References to the undertaking of an existing company include references to a part of the undertaking of an existing company.
The expression "shares" includes stock.

Section 55 "is designed to secure exemption from stamp duties . . . where, as a result of the amalgamation of the businesses of more than one company, the businesses remain in substance owned by the same persons.[63]

Such a result may be achieved in two classes of case. In the first class of case the result may be achieved by a transaction whereunder the business of one of the companies is acquired by the other company ('the transferee company') in return for an issue of shares in the transferee company to the transferor company or to its shareholders. If, as will normally be the case, the shares in the transferee company so issued are of a value equal to the value of the business transferred, the shareholders of the two companies will after the transaction have an interest in the two businesses which have become one having a value corresponding to the value of their former interests in the separate businesses. And if it is then shown that the transferee company was to be registered or had been incorporated or had increased its capital with a view to the acquisition it acquired, and the transaction is not otherwise complicated, relief from stamp duty which would otherwise be payable will to the extent specified in the section be accorded. . . .

A similar result will be achieved in the second class of case, where the transferee company acquires the shares of the existing company in exchange for shares in the transferee company issued to the shareholders of the existing company. Again, if the value of the shares so issued corresponds to the value of the shares transferred, the shareholders of the two companies[64] will after the transaction have, through their holding in the transferee company, an interest in the two businesses equivalent to their former interests in the separate businesses."[65]

For the relief to apply there must be a scheme for the reconstruction or amalgamation of companies. The terminology used here is clearly that of sections 425–427 and section 582 of the Companies Act 1985. Nevertheless it seems clear that the relief extends beyond arrangements effected under those provisions and applies to merger and acquisitions by takeover. However, such arrangements must amount either to a "reconstruction" or to an "amalgamation." "In ordinary speech the word 'reconstruction' is . . . used to describe the refashioning of any object in such a way as to leave the basic character of the object unchanged. In relation to companies, the word 'reconstruction' has a fairly precise meaning which corresponds, so far as the subject matter allows, to its meaning in ordinary speech. It denotes the transfer of the undertaking or part of the undertaking of an existing company to a new company with substantially the same persons as members as were members of the old company."[66] It will be noted that this definition refers to the transfer of an undertaking of a company rather than a transfer of shares in that company. It would seem therefore that if relief is to be obtained in respect of a transaction comprising a transfer of shares the arrangement would have to come within the definition of "amalgamation." Although the term has no statutory definition "the essence of an amalgamation . . . is that

---

[63] See *Brotex Cellulose Fibres Ltd.* v. *I.R.C.* [1933] 1 K.B. 158 *per* Rowlatt J. at p. 171.
[64] In this context "company" means a company having a share capital and registered in either England or Scotland. Both purchaser and subject company should satisfy this requirement: see *Nestle & Co.* v. *I.R.C.* [1953] Ch. 395.
[65] *Per* Stamp L.J. in *Crane Fruehauf* v. *I.R.C.* [1975] 1 All E.R. 429 at p. 435.
[66] *Per* Pennycuick J. in *Brooklands Selangor Holdings* v. *I.R.C.* [1970] 1 W.L.R. 429 at p. 444. See also *Baytrust Holdings* v. *I.R.C.* [1971] 1 W.L.R. 1333.

after the relevant transactions have taken place the businesses or property shall remain in substantially the same hands as they were before those transactions took place."[67] In *I.R.C.* v. *Ufitec Group Ltd.*[68] it was argued that "amalgamation" meant simply the acquisition by one company of the requisite shareholding of another for valuable consideration. That contention was rejected, it being held that the result of the transaction(s) must be to leave the businesses or property in substantially the same hands and in substantially the same proportions as before.

The scheme, even if it does qualify as an amalgamation, must involve the acquisition of at least 90 per cent. of the issued share capital of the company to be taken over (the "target")[69] and at least 90 per cent. of the consideration for the acquisition must be shares[70] in the purchaser issued *and* allotted[71] *pro rata* among the shareholders of the target company.

The consideration shares must be issued to the holders themselves and not merely to nominees.[72] This raises the question of how the relief is affected where the holders, or some of them, have already agreed to dispose of the shares coming to them so that in substance they hold only as nominees for the purchaser of those shares. The matter is further complicated in cases where the vendors are accepting the shares as consideration with the intention of converting them into cash (as in a vendor placing) in the immediate future. These matters fell for consideration by the Court of Appeal in *Crane Fruehauf* v. *I.R.C.*[73] where it was held that because it was a term of the offer by the purchaser in that case that the shareholders in the target agreed to sell their consideration shares for cash to a stipulated third party the cash formed part of the consideration. On this basis the cash element amounted to more than the permitted 10 per cent. so that the relief was not available. However, it was accepted by Russell L.J. that had the sale been effected as a result of an independent bargain the result would have been different.[74] On the other hand, Stamp L.J. was of the opinion that even in such a case the consideration shares must be issued to holders beneficially rather than as nominees so that where the allotment is subject to a vendor placing or otherwise subject to an agreement for their disposal the conditions for the granting of the relief would not have been met.[75]

---

[67] *Per* May J. in *I.R.C.* v. *Ufitec Group Ltd.* [1977] 3 All E.R. 924.

[68] [1977] 3 All E.R. 924.

[69] This apparently means 90 per cent. of the nominal share capital, even though the shares may be of different classes. *Quaere* the position where the purchaser already holds more than 10 per cent., the point being that the acquisition in that case must of necessity be of less than 90 per cent. It would appear that mere acquisition of the remainder would not be sufficient: *Lever Bros.* v. *I.R.C.* [1938] 2 K.B. 518, C.A.

[70] This requirement is strict so that an element of cash or loan stock in the consideration may result in the relief being withheld. Where there is an element of other (*i.e.* not shares) consideration care must be taken to ensure that the consideration shares do represent at least 90 per cent. of the total consideration.

[71] The consideration shares must be *issued* to shareholders of the target company. Note that allotment alone is insufficient. Shares allotted to such shareholders should not therefore be renounced by the vendors before issue (*i.e.* before entry onto the register of the purchaser.)

[72] *Murex* v. *I.R.C.* [1933] 1 K.B. 173.

[73] [1975] 1 All E.R. 429, C.A.

[74] *Ibid.* at p. 433.

[75] *Ibid.* at p. 436.

Where the purchaser has to increase its capital in order to effect the acquisition the relevant resolution providing for this increase should expressly state that the share capital is being increased "with a view to the acquisition" of the target company.[76]

The relief will be lost if the purchaser disposes of the shares in the target company within a period of two years; however, this period of two years begins to run not from the date of completion of the acquisition but rather from the date of the registration or incorporation of the purchaser, or of the authority for the increase in its capital, as the case may be.

### (c) Capital duty

A corresponding, if not exactly coterminous, relief to that given by section 55 of the Finance Act 1927 in respect of stamp duty is made available by paragraph 10 of Schedule 19 to the Finance Act 1973 in respect of capital duty. But for this relief an acquirer of shares in a merger would be liable to pay duty in respect of the issue of the consideration shares. Duty is charged[77] at a rate of 1 per cent. on the value of the shares acquired.

Paragraph 10 provides:

*Finance Act 1973, Sched. 19, Para. 10*

10. (1) A chargeable transaction shall be an exempt transaction for the purposes of section 47 of this Act if it is shown to the satisfaction of the Commissioners—

    (*a*) that, by virtue of the transaction, a capital company which is in the process of being formed or which is already in existence—

        (i) has acquired share capital of another capital company to the extent that, after the transaction, not less than 75 per cent. of the issued share capital of that other company is beneficially owned by the first company, or

        (ii) has acquired the whole or any part of the undertaking of another capital company, and

    (*b*) that the conditions specified in sub-paragraph (2) below are fulfilled in relation to the transaction;

and in this paragraph the first company mentioned in paragraph (*a*) above is referred to as "the acquiring company" and the other company mentioned in sub-paragraph (i) or (ii) of that paragraph is referred to as "the acquired company."

(2) The conditions referred to in sub-paragraph (1) above are—

---

[76] It should be noted that while failure to observe this requirement will be fatal in a claim for relief under s.55, it will not be fatal in respect of the corresponding claim for relief from capital duty.

[77] Capital duty is charged under the Finance Act 1973 if a "capital company" is involved in a "chargeable transaction," and if at the time or as a result of the transaction either:

    (a) the place of effective management of the company is in Great Britain, or

    (b) the registered office of the company is in Great Britain but the place of its effective management is outside the EEC.

A capital company is a company incorporated with limited liability according to the law of any part of the United Kingdom; chargeable transactions include an increase in the capital of a company by the contribution of assets of any kind: F.A. 1973, Sched. 19, para. 1.

(*a*) that the place of effective management or the registered office of the acquired company is in a member State; and

(*b*) that so much, if any, of the consideration (taking no account of such part thereof as consists of the assumption or discharge by the acquiring company of liabilities of the acquired company) for the acquisition referred to in that sub-paragraph as does not consist—

(i) where shares are to the acquired, of the issue of shares in the acquiring company to the holders of shares in the acquired company in exchange for the shares held by them in the acquired company,

(ii) where the whole or any part of the undertaking is to be acquired, of the issue of shares in the acquiring company to the acquired company or to holders of shares in the acquired company,

consists wholly of a payment in cash which does not exceed 10 per cent. of the nominal value of the shares which make up the balance of the consideration.

(3) If, at any time within the period of five years beginning with the occurrence of a chargeable transaction which is an exempt transaction falling within paragraph (*a*)(i) of sub-paragraph (1) above, the acquiring company—

(*a*) ceases to retain at least 75 per cent. of the issued share capital of the acquired company, or

(*b*) disposes of any of the shares in the acquired company which it held immediately after the occurrence of the chargeable transaction,

duty shall then become chargeable, and shall be payable in accordance with sub-paragraph (4) below; but for the purpose of determining whether paragraph (*a*) or paragraph (*b*) above applies, any disposal of shares shall be disregarded if it is effected—

(i) by a transfer forming part of a chargeable transaction which is itself an exempt transaction by virtue of any provision of sub-paragraph (1) above, or

(ii) in the course of the winding-up of the acquiring company.

(4) If sub-paragraph (3) above applies, then, within one month of the date on which the holding of share capital referred to in paragraph (*a*) of that sub-paragraph first falls below 75 per cent. or, as the case may be, the date of the first disposal of any of the shares referred to in paragraph (*b*) of that sub-paragraph (in this paragraph referred to as "the date of charge"), there shall be paid to the Commissioners duty corresponding to the stamp duty which would have been charged under subsection (5) of section 47 of this Act on the relevant document if the chargeable transaction had not been an exempt transaction.

(5) If sub-paragraph (4) above applies, subsection (7) of section 47 of this Act shall apply—

(*a*) as if the chargeable transaction had never been an exempt transaction; and

(*b*) as if for the reference in that subsection to the date of the transaction there were substituted a reference to the date of charge;

and, in addition, interest on the duty payable under that sub-paragraph at
the rate of 5 per cent. per annum from the date when the chargeable
transaction occurred to the date of charge shall be a debt due to Her Majesty from the acquiring company.

[(6) This paragraph applies also where the acquired company is a corporation
or body of persons which is not a capital company for the purposes of this
Schedule but which is treated as such in another member State; and paragraph 3(1) above shall apply for the interpretation of this sub-paragraph
as it applies for the interpretation of paragraph 1 above.][78]

It will be noted that the relevant percentage for the purposes of the capital
duty relief is 75 per cent. as opposed to the 90 per cent. required for the stamp
duty relief under section 55 of the 1927 Act. Furthermore, it is only necessary
that the requisite 75 per cent. be owned[79] rather than, as in the case of section
55, be acquired as a result of the amalgamation or reconstruction. Accordingly
the problems associated with existing shareholdings in the target company[80] that
are present in relation to the section 55 relief are noticeably absent. However,
the exemption will be lost if the acquiring company ceases to retain at least 75
per cent. of the issued share capital of the target company within five years[81] or
disposes of any shares in that company which it held immediately after the occurrence of the chargeable transaction.[82] For this purpose any disposal of shares is
disregarded if it is effected in the course of a transaction which is itself exempt or
in the course of the winding up of the acquiring company.

There being no provision in paragraph 10 corresponding to that contained in
section 55(7) of the 1927 Act, if the allotment of the consideration shares is made
before the requisite 75 per cent. of the target company's share capital has been
acquired no relief will be granted.[83]

In relation to the paragraph 10 relief where the consideration is not comprised
wholly of shares the balance must take the form of cash. It follows from this that
should the terms of the sale agreement stipulate for such portion of the consider-

---

[78] Added by F.A. 1976, s.128.

[79] Owned here means "beneficially owned": para. 10(1)(*a*). For an analysis of the meaning of beneficial ownership in this context see further Sergeant and Sims: *Stamp Duties* (7th ed., 1977) at p.
502.

[80] See above at n. 69.

[81] As opposed to two years in the case of the s.55 relief.

[82] It follows therefore that if the exempted transaction involved the acquisition of 100 per cent. of the
shares in the target company the disposal of 1 share at any time within five years thereafter will
cause the relief to be lost. However if 75 per cent. is acquired in one exempt transaction, and
further shares are subsequently acquired in a further exempt transaction, a disposal of shares up to
the number acquired in that second exempt transaction will result in the loss of that second
exemption, while any further disposals will result in the loss of both exemptions.

[83] While this should not create problems for an acquisition by private treaty it can be the source of
difficulty where, as in the case of a public bid, the target company's share capital is acquired over a
period.

ation as does not consist of shares to be in the form of loan stock the relief will be lost.[84]

Where the consideration comprises or includes shares the sale agreement will   **7.25**
normally seek to ensure equality of rights with shares already issued and to provide an adequate basis on which the shares can be valued.[85] The relevant clauses would be drafted along the following lines:

> "(1) The total consideration for the shares shall be . . . which amount shall be satisfied by the allotment to the vendor of . . . ordinary shares in the capital of the purchaser credited as fully paid (hereafter referred to as 'the consideration shares').
>
> (2) The consideration shares shall rank *pari passu* in all respects with the existing ordinary shares of . . . each in the capital of the purchaser and so far as regards any dividend declared as paid by reference to any recent date falling on or after the date of the regulation thereof in the register of members of the purchaser shall rank as if they had been issued (fully paid) on and from the commencement of the period in respect of which such dividend is paid.
>
> (3) For the purpose of para. (1) above the value of each of the consideration shares shall be the sum equal to the average of the middle market quotations on the Stock Exchange (ascertained by reference to the Stock Exchange Official Daily List) of an ordinary share of . . . in the capital of the purchaser on the last day on which the Stock Exchange is open for business in each of the . . . weeks last preceding completion.
>
> (4) The purchaser reserves the right to satisfy all or part of the consideration for the ordinary shares in cash."[86]

### The sale agreement—capitalisation issue                                     7.26

Where the circumstances are such that section 55 of the Finance Act 1927 cannot be used to provide exemption from stamp duty it may be possible to achieve an effective exemption by resorting to a device commonly known as the "Preftrick." The device relies on the circumstance that while share transfers giving effect to a contract of sale or exchange are prima facie liable to stamp duty as conveyances on sale securities acquired as a result of the renunciation of a renounceable allotment letter may escape the charge.[87]

The preftrick and its variants operate by the adoption of measures to render

---

[84] Note that the cash element is not to exceed 10 per cent. of the nominal value of the shares making up the balance of the consideration. This is not the same as saying that 90 per cent. of the total consideration must be in the form of shares.

[85] Where the purchasing company has a Stock Exchange listing or USM quotation the Revenue practice is to assess the value of the target company's shares (and therefore the value of the contribution to assets for the purpose of the capital duty relief) by reference to the market price of the consideration shares. However, *quaere* the position where the consideration is stated as a stipulated sum to be satisfied by the allotment of consideration shares?

[86] This clause is included because clause (3) might have the effect of obliging the purchaser to issue shares at a discount contrary to C.A. 1985, s.100.

[87] F.A. 1963, s.65.

the existing shares of the target company worthless by the creation of a class of share (usually preference shares) carrying superior entitlements in respect of dividends and capital to the existing ordinary shares. The rights to these newly created shares are transferred to existing shares by means of letters of allotment which may be renounced within a period of six months from the date of issue. Since the new shares usually represent a capitalisation of reserves they are made as a bonus issue, thereby avoiding any capital duty charge on the company. The acquisition of the company by the purchaser is then completed by sale or exchange of the valuable (non-stampable) allotment letters and the by now worthless (but stampable) shares.

The potential of this device as an instrument of stamp duty saving depends on the extent to which there are reserves available for capitalisation. If there are no available reserves and it is impossible to create any[88] the device may be adapted for use through a rights issue if the target company is a public[89] company, with the new shares being allotted to the vendor(s) and renounced, nil paid, in favour of the purchaser. While the letter of allotment must be filed with the Registrar of Companies as a prospectus it is not subject to the formal requirements of the Third Schedule to the Companies Act 1985.[90]

It is important that the terms of the sale agreement make clear that the contract embodied therein is not a contract for the sale of the existing shares "cum" the bonus or rights issue. Were this to be the case the whole of the consideration could still be regarded as being referable to such shares rather than merely the part apportioned to them.[91] It is usual to achieve this result by providing that the shares are to be sold and purchased together with all rights "now or hereafter attaching thereto, except the rights to receive the allotments [in respect of the bonus or rights issue]."[92]

**7.27**        The preftrick and its variants were developed before the decisions of the House of Lords in *Ramsay* v. *I.R.C.*,[93] *I.R.C.* v. *Burmah Oil Co. Ltd.*,[94] and *Furniss* v. *Dawson*.[95] The view of the Revenue appears to be that the principle emerging from these cases, that steps having no commercial purpose in their own right which are inserted into a composite transaction will be rendered

---

[88] For example by a revaluation of the company's fixed assets. See above at §§ 5.39 *et seq.*

[89] Although not, it would seem, if the company is a private company. Since a rights issue made by way of renounceable allotment letters apparently constitutes an offer of shares to the public, (see above at § 6.11), the more so since the object of the exercise in these cases is that the new shares become available for purchase by persons other than the vendor(s) it would be in breach of the articles of association of a private company.

[90] C.A. 1985, s.56(5).

[91] Such apportionment be fair and reasonable. If the registered shares are transferred at a figure which is less than their market value stamp duty may fall to be levied under F.(1909–10)A. 1910, s.74 on the basis that the transaction is a voluntary disposition with duty being charged on the market value of the shares transferred as at the date of the instrument: Stamp Act 1891, s.6. In practice a value slightly in excess of their market value is placed on the shares in order to avoid argument and adjudication.

[92] Some agreements seek to make the transaction conditional upon the capital reorganisation. *Quaere*, however, whether this would be acceptable to a purchaser who would be bound.

[93] [1982] A.C. 300, H.L.

[94] [1982] S.T.C. 30, H.L.

[95] [1984] 2 W.L.R. 226, H.L.

ineffective if the only purpose of the exercise was the avoidance of tax, is applicable to stamp duty and to the preftrick in particular.[96] If this view were to be tested and upheld by the courts the consequence would be that its application identified the sale of ordinary shares as the means by which the disposal of the company was effected, so that the sale of the renounceable letters of allotment should be disregarded and duty charged on the total sale consideration.

It has been suggested[97] that if the operation of the scheme were varied so that the ordinary shares were not sold, application of the anti-avoidance rules would be made more difficult, the point being that in applying the principle the Revenue, instead of excising a step and thus exposing a transaction (the sale of the ordinary shares) to the duty it would have borne but for the artificial act, would be seeking to tax a specifically exempted document (the renounceable letter of allotment).[98]

The essence of the preftrick is to transfer the value from one set of securities **7.28** to another set of securities issued by the same company. Prima facie such operations would seem liable to fall within the ambit of the "value-shifting" provisions of the Capital Gains Tax Act 1979. Two provisions of this Act would appear relevant to a preftrick operation:

(a) Section 25(2) provides that where a person having control of a company exercises his control so that value passes out of shares in the company owned by him or a person with whom he is connected, or out of rights over the company exercisable by him or by a person with whom he is connected, and passes into other shares in or rights over the company, that shall be a disposal of the shares or rights out of which the value passes by whom they were owned or exercisable. Historically, this provision[99] has been directed at transactions whereby value passes out of shares held by one shareholder and into shares held by other shareholders; in the operation of the preftrick, of course, the intention is that the value passes into new securities held by the same shareholder. Nevertheless, the terms of section 25(2) contain no expressed limitation precluding its application to preftrick cases. If it applies, section 25(2) would appear to bring about a deemed disposal of the shares and/or rights at market value.[1] This in turn could prevent deferment of tax on share-for-share exchanges and could, in the case of a part disposal, result in a continuing shareholder who controls the company incurring a chargeable gain.

(b) Section 26 is aimed at value-shifting arrangements which operate to reduce to a material extent the value of an asset prior to its sale.[2] However, for section 26 to apply there must be some "asset" whose value has been materially reduced. Since section 78 (which applies to reorganisations of share capital) treats the new shares in the hands of the vendor as the same asset for capital gains tax purposes as the original shares and since the holding(s) of the vendor(s)

---

[96] See Revenue Consultative Document *"The Scope for Reforming Stamp Duties."*
[97] See (1984) New L.J. 756.
[98] The Revenue have indicated that provisions will be introduced in the Finance Act 1985 to extend the scope of statutory exemption to cover the situations in which the preftrick is currently used.
[99] Formerly F.A. 1965, Sched. 7, para. 15(2).
[1] C.G.T.A. 1979, s.25(1).
[2] The section applies to schemes or arrangements made before or after the disposal.

is/are worth exactly the same both before and after the reorganisation effected through the preftrick the precondition necessary to bring the section into operation (a material reduction in the value of such holding(s)) would seem not to be present.

**7.29**     The arrangements inherent in the operation of a preftrick scheme involving, as many of them do, the making of bonus issues of shares, would appear to fall within the ambit of the provisions of the Finance (No. 2) Act 1975[3] governing the taxation of stock dividends. However the Revenue appear to operate this piece of legislation as if it is not applicable to those bonus issues in which a company capitalises reserves and issues the bonus shares to all shareholders in proportion to their existing holdings.[4]

**7.30**     Although in normal circumstances adverse tax consequences to the vendor(s) do not result from a disposition effected through a preftrick arrangement, given the uncertainties that have been indicated above it is common practice to extract an indemnity from the purchaser.[5]

**7.31     Completion conditions**

In addition to the payment of the purchase price and delivery of the share certificates by the vendor(s) the main agreement will usually seek to deal with the practicalities of transferring control of the company to the purchaser. Specific terms will deal with the replacement of directors, and, where appropriate, the company secretary, the revocation of all authorities to the company's bankers and providing new authorities to such persons as the purchaser may nominate to operate the same, the resignation of the auditor of the company, and the delivery up to the purchaser of the statutory and other books of the company (duly written up to date), its certificate of registration and common seal, the title deeds in respect of its properties and other ancillary documents relating to the transaction.

**7.32     Warranties**

All sale agreements will incorporate warranties by the vendor as to the accuracy of information given and representations and forecasts made. The specific items are normally set out in a schedule to the agreement. Frequently a specific term is included in the agreement providing that each item is to be regarded as separate from and independent of other items and is to be construed accordingly.

In many cases a "disclosure letter" is annexed to the agreement. Such a letter

---

[3] F.(No. 2)A. 1975, s.34.
[4] Likewise the bonus issue is not treated as a distribution by the company (unless there has been a previous repayment of share capital: I.C.T.A. 1970, s.234). However if there occurs any subsequent repayment of the bonus shares the amount so repaid may be treated as a distribution: I.C.T.A. 1970, s.235.
[5] See below at § 7.33.

contains elaborations of or qualifications to individual warranties. The sale agreement will normally stipulate that the warranties given and set out therein are subject to the matters contained in the disclosure letter.

While the precise terms of warranties given will vary from agreement to agreement according to the requirements of the parties most agreements will seek to include warranties as to the following matters:

(a) *The constitution of the company.* Share capital, memorandum and articles, company resolutions, returns, charges, liens, incumbrances or options over or in respect of shares.

(b) *Accounts.* The preparation of accounts, provision for liabilities, valuation and accounting policies, books.

(c) *The business of the company.* The nature of the company's business, its financial position, distributions, loan repayments, debts owing to the company, stock, licences, permits, authorities, insurance, litigation, material contracts to which the company is a party.

(d) *Staffing.* The directors of the company,[6] particulars of its employees, service contracts, pensions, industrial disputes.

(e) *Taxation.* Tax provision made, returns, payment, PAYE, payments under deduction, group income and relief (where applicable), surrender of advance corporation tax, shortfall clearances, claims by or against the company, gifts, loans to participators, distributions, tax losses and carry forward, national insurance, value added tax, capital duty, development land tax, tax status of pension scheme.

(f) *Properties.* Title, restrictions and other matters affecting properties owned by the company or in which the company has an interest.

**Indemnities**                                                                                   **7.33**

The sale agreement will normally include provisions whereby each party will indemnify the other against specified losses. The indemnities most commonly given relate to tax liabilities although on occasion purchasers demand protection against the consequences of particular matters disclosed to them[7] and insist on an indemnity provision to cover this.

*(a) Indemnities given by the vendor[8]*

These almost invariably relate to the taxation of the company to the time of completion. Usually such indemnities are both general and specific. The general indemnity is framed so as to apply to any claim made against the company resulting from or by reference to income profits or gains earned, accrued or received

---

[6] It is common practice to set out details of each director (including details of other directorships held by him) in a schedule to the agreement.
[7] Thereby nullifying the effect of any warranties given.
[8] They are often given in a separate deed executed at the time of completion.

on or before the date of completion or any event on or before the date of completion whether alone or in conjunction with other circumstances and whether or not the tax in question was chargeable against or attributable to any other firm or company. The specific indemnities relate to claims arising under specific statutory provisions in their application to the period up to completion. It is usual for the indemnity provision to cover all reasonable costs and expenses properly payable by the purchaser or the company in connection with any claim.

The indemnities given by the vendor normally seek to exclude claims:

(a) to the extent that provision or reserve has been made for them in the accounts, or if such provision is insufficient, where that insufficiency is due only to an increase in rates of taxation made after the date of the agreement;

(b) for which the company is or may become primarily liable as a result of transactions in the ordinary course of its business after the balance sheet date; and

(c) which would not have arisen but for a voluntary act or transaction which could reasonably have been avoided having been carried out by the purchaser or the company after the date of completion otherwise than in the ordinary course of business and which the purchaser was aware could give rise to such a claim.

*(b) Indemnities given by the purchaser*

The indemnities given by the purchaser relate to claims for taxation arising out of the implementation of any stamp duty avoidance scheme[9] and in relation to any voluntary acts carried out by the purchaser after completion otherwise than in the ordinary course of business.[10]

**7.34   Management "buy-outs"**

The sale of a company to its management (and, sometimes, to its employees) has in recent years been regarded with increasing favour both by governments[11] and by investing institutions, the idea being that, given a significant stake in the company for which they work, the commitment and enthusiasm of management can have a marked effect on the company's performance in terms of greater efficiency and productivity and, on the basis of that, in terms of greater profitability.

From the point of view of the investing institutions management buy-outs represent a generally safer investment than providing funds for some completely new venture since management will already possess an intimate knowledge of

---

[9] See above at §§ 7.26 *et seq.*

[10] This latter indemnity is particularly useful to cover possible liability under Pt. XII of I.C.T.A. 1970 (transactions in securities).

[11] In the form of the shares "buy-back" provisions of the Companies Act 1981 (now ss. 159–181 C.A. 1985) (see above at § 5.75) which provides a means of allowing control to pass to management on the acquisition of a minority shareholding with the company buying out the interests of the major proprietors.

the company's business and its markets and should therefore be able to expand the business and take advantage of profitable opportunities without some of the risks inherent in a completely new venture. In these circumstances financial institutions will generally be prepared to fund a significant part of the purchase price while leaving control with the managers thereby providing management with the opportunity to build up a successful business with a relatively small initial capital contribution, and by taking advantage of the gearing effect which an institutional shareholder can bring, with the prospect of a substantial capital profit in due course.

Management buy-outs tend to occur in three situations, namely: **7.35**

(a) where a company or group hives off one or more of its activities as no longer falling within the mainstream of its business as defined by its corporate plan;

(b) where family shareholders in a private company wish to realise their investment and no natural management succession exists within the family; and

(c) where an attempt is made to resurrect a profitable business which is in the hands of a receiver.

While management buy-outs are, by definition a means of permitting the acquisition of control of a company by its managers they do not directly operate to provide funds for the company itself, although it is not uncommon for a buy-out package to be arranged which provides access to loan or other facilities for the company over a specified period. Even in situation (a) above, while the disposal will clearly produce funds for the disposing company or group it will not as such provide any funds for the company or business that is being sold off.

The essence of a management buy-out transaction is that it is a combination of two separate transactions, the first being a sale of the share capital of the company to its managers (usually coupled with a loan to the managers in order to provide the necessary funds) and a subscription for loan and share capital by the investing institutions). Often the sale agreement will contain covenants restricting:

(1) the activities of the company so that they do not compete with the business of the disponer;

(2) the dissemination and use of confidential information acquired by the purchasers concerning the disponer and its business activities; and sometimes

(3) the circumstances in which management shares may be disposed of and the possible disponees.

## TAKE-OVER PROCEDURES

Where a take-over or merger cannot be effected by private treaty (and in almost **7.36** every case where a public company is to be acquired this will be so) the transaction will be effected by a formal offer and subsequent acceptance involving the disclosure of information about the parties and in support of their contentions that the bid be accepted or rejected.

In many respects the interests which the law should seek to protect are the same as those requiring protection when a company is floated on one of the securities markets. It might be expected therefore that the provisions of the Companies Acts applicable to public issues of securities would also apply to take-overs and mergers involving public companies. The reality, however, is that the present prospectus provisions of the Companies Act 1985 have no application whatever to take-overs. This is because, it will be recalled,[12] those provisions relate only to public issues for cash. Hence, while an offer to sell may be a prospectus, an offer to buy cannot be; nor can an offer to exchange shares for shares or other property.[13] The result is that the Companies Acts do not seek to prescribe the information to be disclosed in the case of a bid; indeed their sole function is to facilitate the acquisition of the remaining shares when 90 per cent. acceptances have been received.[14]

Nevertheless, a takeover offer document is a circular relating to investments within the meaning of section 14 of the Prevention of Fraud (Investments) Act 1958. This provision makes it an offence for an unauthorised person to distribute a document which is a circular containing any invitation to dispose of or to acquire securities unless either the consent of the Department of Trade and Industry has been obtained authorising such distribution or the document is sent by a member of the Stock Exchange or of a recognised association of dealers in securities or by a licensed or exempted dealer in securities.[15]

Section 14 was not drafted with take-over offer documents in mind. Hence in 1960 the Board of Trade (as the Department of Trade and Industry then was) promulgated the Licensed Dealers (Conduct of Business) Rules[16] imposing requirements applicable to all offers to buy or sell securities[17] and additional requirements relating to take-over offers and to the circulars relating to them.[18] These Rules, however, were binding only on licensed dealers and in practice most take-overs were managed by a merchant bank as an exempt dealer. While exempt dealers were "expected"[19] to comply with the Rules in principle there was no sanction in cases where they did not.

In 1959 a City working party published *Notes on Amalgamation of British Businesses,* which in 1968 led to the *City Code on Take-overs and Mergers,* and the Panel which administers it. Under its aegis and, more recently, that of the Council for the Securities Industry, the Code[20] has been expanded and refined

---

[12] See above at § 6.10. See also Gower Report (Cmnd. 9125) at para. 9.09.
[13] This view is based upon a continued acceptance of *Christopher's Case* [1956] 1 W.L.R. 237. But see now *Broken Hill Proprietary Co. Ltd.* v. *Bell Resources Ltd.* (1984) 8 A.C.L.R. 609.
[14] And to seek to prevent undisclosed payments to directors for loss of office: C.A. 1985, ss.314–316; also to recognise the opportunities for the misuse of price-sensitive information when a take-over is in progress or is about to be launched: Company Securities (Insider Dealing) Act 1985, s.2.
[15] See above at n. 44.
[16] S.I. 1960 No. 1216 replacing earlier Rules of 1939. The 1960 Rules have themselves been replaced by the Licensed Dealers (Conduct of Business) Rules 1983 (S.I. 1983 No. 585).
[17] First Sched., Pt. I and Second Sched.
[18] First Sched. Pt. II and Third Sched.
[19] See Gower Report *op. cit.* at § 9.10.
[20] Now in its 5th edition (1981) subsequently amended.

and constitutes a comprehensive set of rules governing take-over procedures and their requirements. Companies with a Stock Exchange listing are required to comply with its provisions under the terms of the continuing obligations entered into as a condition of admission to listing.[21] Such companies are also subject to further requirements imposed by the Regulations of the Stock Exchange.[21a]

The flexibility and sophistication of the City Code and of the Stock Exchange requirements in practice rendered the 1960 Rules largely obsolete. These tended to be ignored except when a bidder applied to the Department for permission to enable him to circulate directly.[22] However, the Panel regarded the Code and its own functions as applicable only to public companies listed or unlisted. When, as a result of the new definitions of public and private companies in the Companies Act 1980, most unlisted public companies re-registered as private companies, a sizeable gap in the system of regulation of take-overs appeared. In order to deal with this the Department issued a General Permission under the terms of section 14(2) of the 1958 Act regarding take-overs of those private companies whose securities have not within the previous ten years (that is from June 1, 1983) been available on any sort of regular market or the subject of a public issue.[23] The General Permission specifies the information that will have to be disclosed if bidders are to take advantage of it. In addition the Code has been amended to make it applicable, so far as possible, to those companies not covered by the General Permission. In any cases not covered by either the General Permission or the Code licensed dealers are required and exempted dealers expected to observe the general requirements laid down in the new Licensed Dealers (Conduct of Business) Rules 1983[24] while others will need to obtain an ad hoc permission from the Department if they wish to distribute take-over circulars.[25]

### Take-overs and mergers between listed companies

The standard procedures that have developed in relation to take-overs and **7.37** mergers where only listed companies are involved cover four phases, namely:

    (a)  activities prior to the making of a formal offer;
    (b)  the making of a formal offer;
    (c)  acceptance; and
    (d)  completion of the take-over.

### Activities prior to the making of a formal offer         7.38

One of the more striking contrasts in the practices relating to take-over and merger transactions between unlisted and listed companies is that concerning initial approaches. Whereas in transactions involving unlisted companies initial

---

[21] ASL Section 5, Chapter 2, para. 15.
[21a] ASL, Section 6.
[22] And even then the Department sought to secure observance of the provisions of the Code in addition to the requirements of the Rules. See further Cmnd. 9125 at para. 9.11.
[23] General Permission No. 3 dated April 20, 1983, coming into force on June 1, 1983.
[24] S.I. 1983 No. 585.
[25] See generally Cmnd. 9125 at paras. 9.09–9.24.

soundings and approaches are almost invariably made through intermediaries who take care not to disclose the identity of their principals, in so far as listed companies are concerned the City Code requires[26] that the identity of principals be declared at the outset.

If an offer is to be made that offer should be made in the first instance either to the Board of the offeree company or to its advisors.[27] Once a bona fide offer has been communicated to the Board of an offeree company or, after the Board of such a company has reason to believe that a bona fide offer might be imminent, that Board is placed under an obligation not to take any action in relation to the affairs of the company which could effectively result in any bona fide offer being frustrated or in the shareholders of the offeree company being denied an opportunity to assess the offer on its merits without the approval in general meeting of its shareholders.[28]

**7.39**      One of the primary functions of City Code regulation is to ensure that adequate information is made available to those who need it.[29] "Shareholders shall have in their possession sufficient evidence, facts and opinions upon which an adequate judgment and decision can be reached and shall have sufficient time to make an assessment and decision. No relevant information shall be withheld from them."[30]

*Announcement of Approach/ Offer*      To this end, when any firm intention to make an offer is notified to a board from a serious source, the board must (irrespective of whether it views the offer favourably or otherwise) publicise it by press notice without delay.[31] Joint statements by the boards of both companies are generally felt to be desirable whenever possible and are recommended[32] provided that agreement thereon does not lead to undue delay.

Problems may arise as to whether in any given situation there has been a "firm intention to make an offer" from a "serious source," especially where there is some doubt as to whether the offeror company is or will be in a position to implement the offer in full.[33] Certainly it is recognised that where approaches have been made which may or may not lead to an offer the board of the (possible) offeree company may be in difficulties as to precisely what its obligations are with regard to press statements. There is the rule that absolute secrecy should be observed before any announcement is made,[34] and there are obvious dangers in announcing prematurely an approach which may not lead to an offer. By way of guidance the Panel has indicated[35] that an announcement that talks

---

[26] Rule 2.
[27] Rule 1.
[28] General Principle 4.
[29] And available to them equally. General Principle 10 provides that during "the course of a take-over or merger transaction, or when such is in contemplation, neither the offeror, the offeree company nor any of their respective advisers shall furnish information to some shareholders which is not made available to all shareholders."
[30] General Principle 3.
[31] Rule 5(1).
[32] Rule 5(3).
[33] Rule 3.
[34] Rule 7.
[35] Rule 5(1).

are taking place together, where appropriate, with a request to the Stock Exchange[36] to grant a temporary halt in dealings will normally be expected where:

(1) negotiations have reached a point at which a company is reasonably confident that an offer will be made for its shares; or

(2) negotiations or discussions are about to be extended to embrace more than a small group of people, as, for example, where more than a very restricted number of shareholders are to be consulted, perhaps with a view to their irrevocably undertaking to accept the offer.

However, the obligation to make announcements lies no less with the potential offeror than with the offeree company. This is especially so where the offeree company is the subject of rumour and speculation and it is clear beyond reasonable doubt that it is the offerer's actions (whether through inadequate security, purchasing of offeree company shares or otherwise) which have directly contributed to this situation. Nevertheless, it is recognised[37] that there are limitations to the extent to which it is practicable or fair to expect a potential offeror to assume responsibility for movements in the share price of the offeree company before any approach has been made and possibly before the tactical situation allows it to make any meaningful statement.

When a firm intention to make an offer is announced the identity of the offeror and the terms of the offer must be disclosed[38] including all conditions[39] to which the offer is subject.[40] Promptly after the first announcement of the offer or possible offer a copy of the press notice or a circular setting out the contents of the notice should be sent by the offeree company to its shareholders.[41]

**7.40**

*Disclosure of Offer Terms*

Where appropriate the announcement should mention the possibility of the takeover or merger's being referred to the Monopolies and Mergers Commission.[42]

The Offer Document should normally be posted within 28 days of the announcement of a firm intention to make an offer.[43] At the same time, or as soon as practicable thereafter, the board of the offeree company should circulate its views on the offer.

**7.41**

---

[36] A potential offeror should not attempt to prevent an offeree company from making an announcement or from requesting the Stock Exchange to grant a temporary halt in dealings at any time the offeree company considers appropriate—Rule 5(4).

[37] Rule 5(3).

[38] The offeror must also disclose any existing holding in the offeree company:
    (a) which it owns or over which it has control; or
    (b) which is owned or controlled by any person acting in concert with it; or
    (c) in respect of which it has received an irrevocable undertaking to accept the offer—Rule 8(1).

[39] Where there has been an announcement of a firm intention to make an offer (as opposed to an announcement that talks are taking place which may lead to an offer) the offer cannot be withdrawn without the consent of the Panel unless the posting of the offer was expressed as being subject to the fulfilment of a specific condition and this condition has not been met in Rule 10(2).

[40] Rule 8(1) and (2).

[41] Rule 6.

[42] Rule 9(1). See further below at § 7.67.

[43] Rule 10(1).

*Issue of Offer Document*

Any information, including particulars of shareholders, given to a preferred suitor should, on request, be furnished equally and as promptly to a less welcome but bona fide potential offeror.[44]

In cases where a "shut-out" bid[45] is made special arrangements apply. In the first place such bids come within the general requirement that the Offer Document must disclose any arrangements between the offeror and the directors of the offeree company.[46] In addition, however, the success of such a bid places the offeror under an obligation to make an offer either in cash or accompanied by a cash alternative for the remaining shares[47] at not less than the highest price paid by the offeror for the shares acquired by it in the preceding twelve months.[48]

**7.42    The making of a formal offer**

The formal offer for the shares in the offeree company is made by the dispatch of the "Offer Document" to the shareholders in that company.[49] The contents of such Offer Documents are subject to detailed regulations deriving from the Rules of the Stock Exchange[50] and from the City Code. The latter, however, lays down the general principle as to the standard of information required to be included by providing[51] that such documents should be prepared with the same standard of care as would be demanded of a prospectus within the meaning of the Companies Act 1985. Furthermore such document or circular issued or each advertisement addressed to or directed at shareholders must state that each director of the offeror (and/or where appropriate the offeree) company has taken reasonable care[52] to ensure both that the facts stated and opinions expressed therein are fair and accurate and, when appropriate, that no material facts have been omitted. The document must state that each director accepts responsibility accordingly.[53]

**7.43**    Like any other document forming the basis of a contract the Offer Document issued in respect of a take-over must specify the terms on which the transaction is to proceed and in particular the nature and amount of the consideration.

Where the consideration is wholly or partly in the form of securities the Offer

---

[44] Rule 12. However this applies only to specific information given to a potential bidder for the purpose of deciding whether or not to make a bid: Panel statement on *Scottish Investments Ltd.* [1975] J.B.L. 303.

[45] A bid under which acceptances of the terms by the directors of the offeree company would give the offeror sufficient shares to render the bid successful.

[46] Rule 13(1)(*a*).

[47] Of the relevant class.

[48] Rule 11 (incorporating Rule 34).

[49] Listed companies are required by ASL, Section 5, Chapter 2, para. 31, to submit to the Quotations Department of the Stock Exchange proofs of all documents to be issued in connection with take-overs.

[50] ASL, Section 6, Chapter 1.

[51] General Principle 12.

[52] Either by taking part himself in supervising the preparations of the document or advertisement, or by delegating that task to persons reasonably believed by him to be competent to carry it out and by disclosing to such persons any relevant facts known to him and any relevant opinions held by him: Rule 14(1), see also Practice Note 4.

[53] Rule 14(1).

Document must state precisely the terms of issue of these securities, whether they may be transferred cum or ex any dividend or interest payment, how such securities will rank for dividends or interest and how they will rank in respect of a capital redemption.[54] The Offer Document must give particulars of the first dividend or interest payment in which the new securities will participate and a statement indicating the effect of acceptance on the capital and income position of the offeree company's shareholders. If the new securities are not to be identical in all respects with an existing listed security, full particulars of the rights attaching thereto and whether application for listing has been or will be made to The Stock Exchange must be stated.[55] The Offer Document must also state when and how the documents of title to any such exchange securities will be issued.[56]

*Consideration for Offer*

In cases where the offer is for cash or where it includes an element of cash the Offer Document must specify the total consideration offered and the period within which and the method by which any cash element will be paid.[57] Furthermore, it must include a statement by an appropriate party (normally the offeror's banker or possibly its independent financial advisor) confirming that resources are available to the offer or sufficient to enable a full acceptance of the offer to be satisfied.[58]

In some take-overs, and more especially where the take-over mechanism is being employed to implement an agreed merger, the companies involved have shareholding links with each other. The Offer Document and the documents issued by the board of the offeree company to their shareholders indicating their response to the offer are required to disclose these links. Thus the Offer Document is required to state[59]:

**7.44**

*Disclosure of Cross Shareholding*

(a) the shareholdings of the offeror in the offeree company;

(b) the shareholdings in the offeror[60] and in the offeree company in which directors of the offeror are interested;

(c) the shareholdings in the offeror[60] and in the offeree company which any person acting in concert with the offeror owns or controls[61]; and

(d) the shareholdings in the offeror[60] and in the offcree company owned or controlled by any persons who, prior to the posting of the Offer Document have irrevocably committed themselves to accept the offer together with the names of such persons.[62]

Likewise the Response Document, whether recommending acceptance or rejection of the offer, must contain statements as to[63]:

---

[54] ASL, Section 6, Chapter 2, para. 3(*b*).
[55] *Ibid.* para. 3(*f*)(iii).
[56] *Ibid.* para. 3(*b*).
[57] *Ibid.*
[58] City Code Rule 18. See also Practice Note No. 17 (Rules 18 and 3A(5)).
[59] *Ibid.* Rule 17(1).
[60] In the case of a securities exchange offer only.
[61] With the names of such persons acting in concert.
[62] See further Practice Note No. 9.
[63] City Code Rule 17(2).

(a) the shareholdings of the offeree company in the offeror;
(b) the shareholdings in the offeree company and in the offeror in which directors of the offeree company are interested;
(c) the shareholdings in the offeree company owned or controlled by the independent advisor to the offeree company, or by funds whose investments are managed by the advisor on a discretionary basis, if those shareholdings in the offeree company amount in total to 10 per cent. or more of the offeree company's equity share capital,[64] and
(d) whether the directors of the offeree company intend, in respect of their own beneficial shareholdings[65] to accept or reject the offer.

**7.45**   The Offer Document must state the nature and particulars of the business of the offeror company[66] and, as a matter of practice, will usually seek to justify the take-over in terms of the requirements of that business.[67] In this connection the offer document will normally be expected to set out[68]:

*Statement of Offeror's Intentions Re Offeree Company*

(a) the offeror's intention with regard to the business of the offeree company;
(b) its intentions regarding any major changes to be introduced in that business, including any redeployment of the fixed assets of the offeree company;
(c) the long-term justification for the proposed offer[69]; and
(d) its intentions with regard to the continued employment of the employees of the offeree company and its subsidiaries. Where it is proposed to shed staff or terminate the contracts of directors the Offer Document should disclose any payment proposed for loss of office.[70]

**7.46**   Where consideration for the offer is wholly or partly in the form of securities in the offeror company shareholders in the offeree company clearly have an interest in obtaining adequate information about the affairs of the offeror to be able to make an informed judgment as to the advantages or otherwise of accepting the offer. In particular such shareholders will require to have access to information as to:

*Financial Information*

(a) the quoted prices of the relevant securities in the respective companies;
(b) the performance of each company;

---

[64] The funds need not be named.
[65] *Quaere* whether such disclosure is necessary (or desirable) in respect of shareholdings held by directors as trustees.
[66] ASL, Section 6, Chapter 2, para. 3(*f*)(i).
[67] See above at §§ 7.01–7.07.
[68] City Code Rule 15(2).
[69] See below at § 7.46.
[70] ASL, Section 6, Chapter 2, para. 3(*c*)(i). Note that no offer may be made conditional on such payment.
Note also that Response Documents must contain particulars of all service contracts of any directors or proposed directors with the offeree company or any of its subsidiaries (unless expiring, or determinable by the employing company without compensation within 12 months); if there are none, this fact should be stated. If such contracts have been entered into or have been amended within six months of the date of the document, the particulars of the contracts amended or replaced should be given; if there have been no new contracts or amendments, this should be stated: City Code, Rule 19(1). See also Practice Note No. 10.

   (c) the current financial position of each company; and

   (d) future prospects.

### (a) Quoted prices

The Stock Exchange requires[71] that the Offer Document contain the middle-market quotations (if any) of the relevant securities so that shareholders in the offeree company can make a comparison. In the case of listed securities these quotations should be taken from the Stock Exchange Official List. The quotations to be specified in the Offer Document are:

   (1) the latest available middle market quotations prior to the date of the offer;

   (2) at least six middle market quotations during the period of six months immediately preceding the date of the offer so as to give a fair view of fluctuations in the price of the securities during that period (the statement should give the respective dates of the quotations); and

   (3) where the offer has been the subject of a preliminary public announcement in newspapers or by other means, the latest middle market quotation immediately prior to that public announcement.

### (b) Performance

The Stock Exchange requires[72] that the Offer Document contains in respect of both offeror and offeree companies their turnover, net profits before tax and the rate per cent. of dividends paid and the total amount absorbed thereby for each of the past five financial years.

### (c) Current financial position

The Stock Exchange requires[73] that the Offer Document contains a statement in respect of both offeror and offeree companies giving their assets and liabilities as shown in their last published audited accounts. When valuations of assets are given these should be supported by the opinion of a named independent valuer and the basis of valuation should be clearly stated. The document should also state that the valuer has given and has not withdrawn his consent to the publication of his name therein.[74]

In the case of offers relating to substantial acquisitions[75] the Offer Document

---

[71] ASL, *ibid.* para. 3(*d*).

[72] *Ibid.* para. 3(*f*)(ii).

[73] *Ibid.*

[74] City Code Rule 16(3). See also Practice Note No. 8.

[75] ASL, Section 6, Chapter 1, para. 3. Substantial acquisitions are defined as those falling with Class 1 of Chapter 1 of section 6. A Class 1 transaction is one where the relative figures amount to 15 per cent. or more in respect of:
   (i) the value of the assets acquired or disposed of, compared with the assets of the acquiring or disposing company;
   (ii) net profits (after deducting all charges except taxation and excluding extraordinary items) attributable to the assets acquired or disposed of, compared with those of the acquiring or disposing company;

should also set out details of group borrowing and other indebtedness at the latest date reasonably practicable.[76]

### (d) Future prospects

The Offer Document is required to give particulars of the financial and trading prospects of the offeror company.[77] The City Code lays down guidelines for dealing with profit forecasts and emphasises that such forecasts are the sole responsibility of the directors of the offeror company and that their compilation should be undertaken with the greatest possible care.[78]

When profit forecasts appear in any document addressed to shareholders in connection with an offer, the assumptions, including commercial assumptions, upon which the forecasts have been based must be set out.[79]

The accounting policies and calculations for the forecasts must be examined and reported on by the auditors or consultant accountants. Where the Document mentions a financial advisor that advisor must also report on the forecasts and his report must be included therein. The Document must contain a statement by those making reports that they have given and have not withdrawn their consent to publication.[80]

Wherever profit forecasts appear in relation to a period in which trading has already commenced any previously published profit figures which are available in respect of any expired portion of that trading period together with comparable figures for the preceding year must be stated.[81]

**7.47**     If the Offer Document or any circular issued in connection therewith includes expressly or by implication a recommendation or an opinion by a financial

*Recommend-ation by Experts*

advisor or other expert in favour of acceptance of the offer the Document may be required to include a statement that the expert has given and not withdrawn his written consent to the issue of the Document and to the inclusion therein of his recommendation in the form and context in which it is included.[82]

**7.48  Acceptance**

The Offer Document must set out the procedure to be followed by share-

*Procedure for Acceptance*

holders of the offeree company who wish to accept the offer. It is the almost invariable practice that take-over offers are made conditional upon acceptance

---

(iii)  the aggregate value of the consideration given or received, compared with the assets of the acquiring or disposing company.

(iv)  equity capital issued by the company or consideration for an acquisition, compared with the equity capital previously in issue.

ASL, Section 6, Chapter 1, para. 3.

[76] *Ibid.*

[77] *Ibid.*

[78] Rule 16(2)(*e*): See further Practice Notes 6 and 7.

[79] Rule 16(2)(*b*).

[80] Rule 16(2)(*c*).

[81] Rule 16(2)(*d*).

[82] ASL, Section 6, Chapter 2, para. 4. Note that this provision applies equally to recommendations, etc., contained in a Response Document or circulars issued in connection therewith.

being received in respect of more than 50 per cent. of the voting shares.[83] Once this has been achieved the offer is declared unconditional as to acceptance, the offeror thereby undertaking to fulfil each contract of purchase ratified by acceptances received thereafter within a stipulated time.

The City Code contains detailed provisions as to:

(a) the time conditions that may be imposed;
(b) the circumstances in which an offer may be declared unconditional; and
(c) how long this undertaking to receive acceptances is to remain open.

The Stock Exchange requires[84] that the Offer Document give particulars of all documents required to be lodged for valid acceptance.

The City Code requires[85] that no offer, which, if accepted in full, would result **7.49** in the offeror holding shares carrying over 50 per cent. of the voting rights of the offeree company, be made unless it is a condition of such offer that the offer will not become or be declared unconditional as to acceptance unless the offeror has acquired or agreed to acquire (either pursuant to the offer or otherwise) shares carrying over 50 per cent. of the votes attributable to the equity share capital.

An offer must initially be open for at least 21 days after its posting.[86] In cases of contested take-over bids (and especially those involving two or more offeror companies bidding against each other for the same offeree) it is not uncommon *Revision of* for an initial offer to be revised in the light of ensuing events. Where a revision *Offer* occurs the revised offer must be kept open for at least 14 days from the date of posting written notification of the revision to shareholders.[86]

If an offer is revised all shareholders who accepted the original offer must receive the revised consideration.[86]

Where an offer is extended the announcement of the extension must state the new expiry date.[87]

An acceptor must be given the right to withdraw his acceptance in any case **7.50** after the expiry of 21 days from the first closing date of the initial offer in circumstances where the offer has not by such date become or been declared uncon- *Withdrawal of* ditional as to acceptances. This entitlement to withdraw is to remain exercisable *Acceptance* until such time as the offer becomes or is declared unconditional as to acceptance.[88]

---

[83] Where a company has more than one class of equity share capital, a comparable offer must be made for each class. An offer for non-voting equity capital should not be made conditional on any particular level of acceptance in respect of that class unless the offer for the voting capital is also conditional on the success of the offer for the non-voting equity capital: City Code, Rule 21(3). Classes of non-equity capital need not be the subject of an offer: *ibid.* Rule 21(2). However where an offer is made for equity share capital and the offeree company has convertible securities outstanding the offeror must make appropriate arrangements to ensure that the interests of the holders of the stock are safeguarded and in particular that the existence of the conversion option over a period of time is adequately recognised. Taking this into account the offeror should make an appropriate offer or proposal to the stockholders: *ibid.* Rule 29(1).
[84] ASL, Section 6, Chapter 2, para. 3(*e*).
[85] Rule 21(1).
[86] Rule 22(1).
[87] Rule 22(3). See further at § 7.50 below.
[88] Rule 22(1).

**7.51**

*Offer Declared*
*Unconditional*

An offer for equity share capital may only be declared unconditional as to acceptances where the offeror has acquired or agreed to acquire shares carrying more than 50 per cent. of the voting rights of the offeree company.[89] Subject to this, no offer (whether revised or not) may become or be declared unconditional as to acceptance after 3.30 pm on the sixtieth day after the date of the offer is initially posted nor of being kept open after the expiry of such period unless it has previously so become or been declared unconditional.[90]

No offer may be revised after the forty-sixth day.

**7.52**       Except with the consent of the Panel all conditions to the offer must be fulfilled or the offer must lapse within 21 days of the first closing date or of the date the offer becomes or is declared unconditional as to acceptances, whichever is the later.[91]

**7.53**       Where an offer provides for alternative forms of consideration neither the offer nor any alternative may close for acceptances at a time when the offer is capable of being declared unconditional. Exceptions to this rule however operate where either[92]:

(1) 14 days have elapsed since the first expiry date on which the offer was capable of being declared unconditional; or

(2) the offeror agrees or has given 14 days notice in writing to the shareholders of the offeree company in the prescribed form[93] that the offer will not be open for acceptances beyond a stated expiry date.

**7.54**       After an offer has become or is declared unconditional as to acceptances, the offer must remain open for acceptance for not less than 14 days after the date on which it would otherwise have expired[94] except for the case where the offer becomes or is declared unconditional on or before an expiry date and the offeror gives or has given at least 14 days written notice to the shareholders of the offeree company that the offer will not remain open beyond that date.[95]

If, once an offer is unconditional as to acceptances,[96] it is stated that the offer

---

[89] Rule 21(2).

[90] Rule 22(2). Note however that an offer may be extended beyond that period of 60 days with the permission of the Panel, which permission will normally be granted only if a competing offer has been announced.

[91] Rule 22(4).

[92] Rule 23(2).

[93] Is in accordance with Rule 23(1). See § 7.54.

[94] Rule 23(1).

[95] No such notice may be given from the time when a competing offer has been announced until the resultant competitive situation has ended: *ibid.*

[96] By 9.30 am at the latest on the dealing day next following the day on which an offer is due to expire, or becomes or is declared unconditional as to acceptances, or is revised or extended the offeror shall announce and simultaneously inform the Stock Exchange of the position and he shall also state the total number of shares (as near as practicable):
   (a) for which acceptance of the offer have been received;
   (b) held before the offer period;
   (c) acquired or agreed to be acquired during the offer period; and should specify the percentage of the relevant classes of share capital represented by these figures: Rule 24. See also Practice Note No. 17 and Rule 25.

will remain open until further notice, 14 days notice should be given before it is closed.[97]

### Completion of the transaction 7.55

In some cases a successful bidder will be satisfied with whatever majority holding is obtained and the degree of control afforded thereby. In other cases it may be desired to buy out remaining shareholders so as to achieve a total shareholding. Section 428 of the Companies Act 1985 provides for a procedure whereby, if certain conditions are satisfied, the offeror company may exercise compulsory acquisition powers in relation to outstanding shares in the offeree company.[98]
Section 428 provides:

(1) This section applies where a scheme or contract involving the transfer of shares or any class of shares in a company ("the transferor company") to another company, whether or not a company as defined in section 735(1) ("the transferee company") has, within 4 months after the making of the offer in that behalf by the transferee company, been approved by the holders of not less than nine-tenths in value of the shares whose transfer is involved (other than shares already held at the date of the offer by, or by a nominee for, the transferee company or its subsidiary).

(2) In those circumstances, the transferee company may, at any time within 2 months after the expiration of the 4 months mentioned above, give notice in the prescribed manner to any dissenting shareholder that it desires to acquire his shares.

(4) If such a notice is given, the transferee company is then (unless on an application made by the dissenting shareholder within one month from the date on which the notice was given, the court thinks fit to order otherwise) entitled and bound to acquire those shares on the terms on which, under the scheme or contract, the shares of the approving shareholders are to be transferred to the transferee company.

This power to "mop up" outstanding shareholdings comes into being: **7.56**

(a) when acceptances have been received from a required number of shareholders in the transferee company; and

(b) when these acceptances have been received within the stipulated time.

### (a) The requisite number of shares

The power under section 428 will not come into being unless acceptances have been received from the holders of at least 90 per cent. of the relevant shares. By relevant shares is meant shares of the class to which the offer relates. An offer may, for example, relate to more than one class of shares and acceptances may

*90 per cent. Acceptance*

---

[97] Rule 23(3).
[98] Where an offer is made for more than one class of shares, separate offers must be made for each class: Rule 28.

have been received amounting to more than 90 per cent. of the aggregate of the shares involved but distributed between the classes in such a way that acceptances for one or more classes of shares have not attained the 90 per cent. level. In such a case the position will differ according to whether the offers can be considered a single composite offer or whether the offers for each class of shares are considered to be separate. In the former case section 428 can be invoked in relation to all the outstanding shares of whatever class; in the latter case the power will only come into being in relation to the class or classes where a 90 per cent. or higher acceptance level has been achieved. It should be noted that the City Code requires[99] that where an offer is made for more than one class of shares, separate offers must be made for each class. Accordingly therefore insofar as take-overs by listed companies of other listed companies are concerned a 90 per cent. acceptance for each class is necessary for the power to come into being in relation to each class.

*Calculation of 90 per cent.*

In calculating whether in a given case the requisite 90 per cent. level has been achieved any shares held by the transferee company are to be ignored.[1] Where the transferee company already holds more than 10 per cent. of the class of shares for which the offer is made at the time the offer is made the power of compulsory acquisition will not come into being unless[2]:

(1) the offer is made to the holders of all the shares other than those held by the transferee company; and

(2) the assenting shareholders not only hold 90 per cent. of the shares involved but are also not less than three-fourths in number of the holders of those shares.[3]

In *Re Simo Securities Trust Ltd.*[4] the case involved the extent to which convertible loan stock, which, at the option of the stockholder, could be converted into shares of the transferor company affected the 90 per cent. calculation where the offer of the transferee company extended to the shares issued on conversion. It was held that the shares of stockholders who had exercised their option to convert were to be included in the calculation but that those shares in relation to which conversion rights might at some future time be decided should not be included.

### (b) Time limits for acceptance

Acceptances in respect of the requisite number of shares must have been received within four months after the making of the offer.[5] In practice the terms of an offer will normally require that acceptances be received within a shorter period and within the limits specified in the City Code.[6]

---

[99] Rule 28. Furthermore the offeror must state that, if it intends to resort to the powers given in s.428, that section will be used only in respect of each class separately.

[1] s.428(1).

[2] s.428(5).

[3] See Palmer at para. 81–10 for examples.

[4] [1971] 1 W.L.R. 1455.

[5] s.428.

[6] See above at § 7.54.

Where, as a result of opposition to the bid from the transferor company or the emergence of a competing bid, the offer is revised and the revised offer is ultimately accepted it is unclear as to whether the four-month period is to run from the date of the original offer or the date of the revised offer. The better view would appear to be that the latter date is the preferable one since it was this latter offer whose terms resulted in acceptance rather than the original one.[7]

It should be noted that the power given under section 428 is permissive other than mandatory; "it is entirely a matter for the transferee company whether or not it exercises its powers of compulsory acquisition. . . . It does not have to do so."[8] What it does have to do, however, within one month of the transfer giving it the requisite 90 per cent. shareholding, is to give a notice to dissenting shareholders[9] in the prescribed manner[10] of this fact and informing the dissenting shareholder of his right under section 429 to require the transferee company to acquire his shareholding.[11]

**7.57**

*Nature of Power Under s.209(1)*

Where the power of compulsory acquisition has come into being the transferee company may, after the expiration of the four-month period for acceptances, within two months give notice to any shareholder who has not accepted the offer that it desires to acquire his shares.[12] Where the time for acceptance of the offer has been extended the time for giving notice is to be calculated by reference to the date when the offer was originally made rather than from the date of any extension.[13]

**7.58**

*Procedure for Compulsory Acquisition*

---

[7] But not where the original offer is merely extended: *Nusson* v. *Howard Glasgow Associates* 1961 S.L.T. 87.

[8] *Per* Brightman J. in *Re Carlton Holdings Ltd.* [1971] 1 W.L.R. 918, 925.

[9] The expression "dissenting shareholder" includes a shareholder who has not assented to the scheme or contract and any shareholder who has failed to transfer his shares to the transferee company in accordance with the scheme or contract: s.428(3).

[10] On Department of Trade Form 100 A.

[11] See further at § 7.58 below. Section 429 provides:

    (1) This section applies where, in pursuance of such a scheme or contract as is mentioned in section 428(1), shares in a company are transferred to another company or its nominee, and those shares (together with any other shares in the first-mentioned company held by, or by a nominee for, the transferee company or its subsidiary at the date of the transfer) comprise or include nine-tenths in value of the shares in the first-mentioned company or of any class of those shares.

    (2) The transferee company shall within one month from the date of the transfer (unless on a previous transfer in pursuance of the scheme or contract it has already complied with this requirement), give notice of that fact in the prescribed manner to the holders of the remaining shares or of the remaining shares of that class (as the case may be) who have not assented to the scheme or contract.

    (3) Any such holder may, within 3 months from the giving of that notice to him, himself give notice (in the prescribed form) requiring the transferee company to acquire the shares in question.

    (4) If a shareholder gives notice under subsection (3) with respect to any shares, the transferee company is then entitled and bound to acquire those shares on the terms on which under the scheme or contract the shares of the approving shareholders were transferred to it, or on such other terms as may be agreed or as the court on the application of either the transferee company or the shareholder thinks fit to order.

[12] Section 428(2).

[13] *Musson* v. *Howard Glasgow Associates Ltd.* 1961 SLT 87. But note this was a case where the substantive terms of the offer remained unaltered. For the position re a revised offer see § 7.56, above.

The notice must be in the prescribed form, that is on Department of Trade Form 428.[14]

The compulsory acquisition of the shareholdings of dissentient shareholders must be on the same terms and conditions as those accepted by the approving shareholders. "The policy of the Act is . . . quite clearly that a dissenting shareholder is not to be penalised as a result of his dissent. [It] is that he shall receive no less favourable treatment than an approving shareholder."[15] In *Re Carlton Holdings Ltd.*[16] an offer was made consisting of shares in the transferee company, or, alternatively in the form of cash to be paid by bankers acting on behalf of the transferee company. This cash alternative was, however, subject to a time limit. It was held that a dissenting shareholder, on whom a notice under the predecessor of section 428(2) had been served, could insist on the transferee company's making or procuring a comparable cash offer to him in circumstances where (as here) it had been impossible for him to opt for the cash alternative in time.

Under the strict terms of section 428(2) the notice may be served on some only, and not all, of these shareholders who have not accepted the offer. In such a case however these shareholders not receiving a section 428 notice may require the company to acquire their shares under section 429. Such dissenting shareholders may within three months of the issue to them of notice that the transferee company has acquired 90 per cent. or more of the shares in the transferor company to which the offer related serve a notice on the company[17] requiring it to acquire their shares either upon the same terms as those in the offer, or upon terms agreed between the company and the shareholder concerned, or, ultimately, upon such terms as the court[18] may order.[19]

**7.59**

The operation of a notice under section 428 is subject to the right of any dissenting shareholder served with such a notice to apply to the court[20] seeking a declaration that the company is not entitled to acquire the shares of the applicant upon the terms of the scheme, notwithstanding the scheme's acceptance by the requisite number of shareholders, on the ground that those terms are unfair. If the application is to succeed it must be shown that the scheme is obviously and conspicuously unfair,[21] the test of fairness being judged by reference to its application to the offerees as a whole rather than to individual applicants. In making its assessment the court will attach considerable weight to the fact that the vast majority of shareholders have accepted the offer.[22]

---

[14] See the Companies (Forms) Regulations 1985 (S.I. 1985 No. 854), repealing S.I. 1979 No. 1547 for Forms 428, 429(2) and 429(3).

[15] *Per* Brightman J. in *Re Carlton Holdings Ltd.* [1971] 1 W.L.R. 918, 925.

[16] [1971] 1 W.L.R. 918.

[17] In the prescribed form is on Department of Trade Form 100B.

[18] In a court having jurisdiction to wind up the transferor company's application in the High Court is by summons under R.S.C. 1965, Ord. 102, r. 2.

[19] Section 429(4).

[20] See n. 18 above. See also *Re Samuel Heap & Son Ltd.* [1965] 1 W.L.R. 1458, C.A.

[21] *Per* Vaisey J. in *Re Evertite Locknuts* [1945] Ch. 220, 224; *Re Press Caps* [1949] Ch. 434, C.A.; *Nidditch* v. *Calico Printers Association Ltd.* 1961 S.L.T. 282; *Re Grierson, Oldham & Adams Ltd.* [1967] 1 W.L.R. 385.

[22] *Re Hoare & Co.* (1933) 150 L.T. 374; *Re Sussex Brick Co. Ltd.* [1961] Ch. 289 and cases cited in n. 21, *supra*.

If the court refuses the application the position with regard to the applicant's shareholding is as it would have been had no application been made, namely that the transferee company becomes, upon the expiration of one month from the notice, entitled and bound to acquire the shares of those persons served with a notice.[23] Should therefore the company wish to withdraw, it may be faced with an action for specific performance at the instance of the shareholder.[24]

*Ad valorem* stamp duty is payable on the transfer as on the transfers of the shares of consenting shareholders of the transferor company.[25]

It will be noted that the compulsory acquisition procedure under section 428 **7.60** does not involve sanction of the scheme by the court, accept insofar as this arises in dealing with the application of a dissenting shareholder referred to in § 7.59 *s.429 and s.425* above, unlike the position of schemes under section 425 which may likewise become binding on dissenting shareholders. In *Re Hellenic and General Trust Ltd.*[26] it was said that the smaller majority required for expropriation under the predecessor of section 425 (75 per cent.) was not inappropriate given the additional requirement of the court's consent to the scheme.

### Bids for and acquisitions of unlisted companies

It has been mentioned[27] that the City Code applies to all public companies and **7.61** to those companies now registered as private companies whose securities had been dealt in on a regular market within the period of ten years prior to June 1, 1983. Accordingly, those provisions of the Code considered above at §§ 7.37–7.54 apply equally to such unlisted companies as they apply to transactions between listed companies only. Likewise the provisions of section 428 of the Companies Act 1985 conferring on an offeror company the right to acquire compulsorily the outstanding share capital of the offeree company under certain conditions[28] apply to unlisted companies also. Certain transactions involving the acquisition by a listed company of another business, company or companies, all or some of which are not listed are subject to Stock Exchange regulation. These transactions are:

(1) "very substantial acquisitions"[29];
(2) reverse take-overs.[30]

---

[23] Section 428(4).
[24] For procedure re transfer see s.430.
[25] *Ridge Nominees Ltd.* v. *I.R.C.* [1962] Ch. 376, C.A.
[26] [1976] 1 W.L.R. 123.
[27] See above at § 7.36.
[28] See above at §§ 7.55–7.60.
[29] A transaction in which the relevant figures amount to 100 per cent. or more in respect of:
    (i) the value of the assets acquired compared with the assets of the acquiring company;
    (ii) the net profits (after deducting all charges except taxation and excluding extraordinary items) attributable to the assets acquired compared with those of the acquiring company;
    (iii) the aggregate value of the consideration given compared with the assets of the acquiring company;
    (iv) equity capital issued by the company as consideration for an acquisition compared with the equity capital previously in issue: ASL, Section 6, Chapter 1, para. 2 adopting the criteria set out in para. 3.1.
[30] Transactions which would result in change in control through the introduction of a majority holder or group of holders: *ibid.* para. 2.

In such cases the Council of the Stock Exchange normally requires that the transaction be subject to the approval[31] of the shareholders of the listed company and that the listing of that company's securities be suspended until such approval has been given and all relevant information made available. For these purposes the information made available must include an accountant's report on the business or unlisted company or companies to be acquired, and a *pro forma* balance sheet of the group as reorganised. In certain circumstances the Council may require the accountant's report to cover the accounts of the purchasing or listed company as well as the companies to be acquired.

Cases may arise in which the accountants reporting in respect of acquisitions are unable to report without qualification on the profits and net assets of the companies or businesses acquired, whether because of the absence of adequate records relative to stock-in-trade, work-in-progress or other assets and liabilities. In such cases the Council may require that the approval of shareholders be sought for the acquisition.[32]

**7.62**    Where the offeror company is a listed company and the consideration for the acquisition consists of or includes securities (whether in the offeror company or otherwise) for which a listing is to be sought the offeror company must publish listing particulars in respect of such securities in accordance with the terms of the Listing Particulars Directive.[33] Without prejudice to this requirement to publish listing particulars there must be made available for inspection by the public at the offices of the issuer of the securities[34] documents describing the terms of the transaction in consequence of which the securities are being issued, together with, where appropriate, any opening balance sheet[35] if the issuer has not yet prepared its annual accounts.[36]

---

[31] Para. 7 requires that any acquisition where any comparison on the basis of the tests set out in n. 29(i)–(iv) shows a figure of 25 per cent. or more should be made conditional on approval by the company in general meeting. In relation to this, for the purpose of comparing the acquiring company with the company to be acquired an additional test is imposed based on the respective "gross" capitals of each party.
"Gross" capital for this purpose is calculated by aggregating:
  (a)  For the acquiring company:
       its equity share capital at its market value immediately prior to the announcement, its preference capital and loan stock (also at market value if listed), all other liabilities (other than current liabilities) including for this purpose minority interests and deferred taxation, and any excess of current liabilities over current assets.
  (b)  For the company being acquired:
       a similar aggregation to that stated above is required save that the value of the consideration payable is to be taken instead of the equity share capital at market value.
In (a) above the aggregation should be made on the basis that 100 per cent. of the equity share capital is to be acquired whether or not such is the case.
[32] *Ibid.* para. 8.2.
[33] Council Directive No. 80/390/EEC. Note that this requirement applies equally to transactions between listed companies only.
[34] And at the offices of any financial organisations retained to act as the issuer's paying agents.
[35] Whether or not *pro forma*.
[36] LPD, Art. 15(1). The Council of the Stock Exchange, as the competent authority, may dispense with this requirement where the relevant transaction (defined in Art. 15(1) as "a merger involving the acquisition of another company or the formation of a new company, the division of a company, the transfer of all or part an undertaking's assets and liabilities, a take-over offer) took place more than two years previously.

# TRANSACTIONS INVOLVING UNLISTED COMPANIES

Where the offer is for all of the equity or preference share capital or all the debentures (other than shares or debentures held by or on behalf of the offeror) of a private company whose securities are not and have not within the ten years preceding the offer been[37]:

**7.63**

*Companies to which General Permission 3 Applies*

(a) listed or quoted on a stock exchange (whether in Great Britain or elsewhere);

(b) securities in respect of which information has, with the agreement or approval of any officer of the company, been published for the purpose of facilitating deals in those securities, indicating the prices at which persons have dealt or were willing to deal in those securities other than with persons who were at the time the information was published existing members of a relevant class;

(c) subject to a marketing arrangement which accorded the company the facilities referred to in section 163(2)(*b*) of the Companies Act 1985[38]; or

(d) the subject of an offer (whether in Great Britain or elsewhere) in relation to which a copy of a prospectus was delivered to the Registrar of Companies in accordance with section 64 of the Companies Act 1985.

and complies with certain conditions it falls within the ambit of General Permission 3[39] issued by the Department of Trade and Industry authorising the distribution of documents (in this case, the offer document) containing stipulated information.

To come within the authorisation the terms of the offer must have been recommended by all the directors of the offeree company[40] and the consideration for the acquisition must be cash or securities in the offeror company or both.[41]

**7.64**

*Requirements for a Valid Offer*

In the case of an offer for equity share capital where at the date of the offer shares carrying 50 per cent. or less of the voting rights[42] are held by or on behalf of the offeror, the offer must be conditional upon sufficient shares being acquired or being agreed to be acquired by the offeror pursuant to or during the offer to result in shares carrying more than 50 per cent. of the voting rights being held by him or on his behalf.[43]

Where the offer relates to non-equity share capital or debentures and where at the date of the offer shares carrying 50 per cent. or less of the voting rights attributable to the equity share capital are held by or on behalf of the offeror,

---

[37] General Permission 3 (issued under s.14(2) of the Prevention of Fraud (Investments) Act 1958), para. 5.

[38] Facilities for dealings to take place on a stock exchange without prior permission for individual transactions from the stock exchange authorities and without limit as to time during which those facilities are available: in Britain such facilities are available on the USM.

[39] General Permission 3, para. 4.

[40] *Ibid.* para. 3(*a*).

[41] *Ibid.* para. 3(*f*).

[42] *Ibid.* para. 3(*c*). Voting rights here refers to the "voting rights then exerciseable in general meetings of the offeree company" and "the voting rights attributable to equity share capital."

[43] *Ibid.*

the offer must include or be accompanied by an offer made by the offeror for the rest of the equity share capital.[44]

The offer (except insofar as it may be totally withdrawn and every person released from any obligation incurred thereunder) must remain open for acceptance by every offeree for at least 21 days from the date on which it was made.[45] Furthermore, it must not be the case that the acquisition of the securities to which the offer relates is conditional upon the offerees approving or consenting to any payment being made or given to any director or former director of the offeree company in connection with, or in compensation or consideration for, his ceasing to be a director, or loss of an office held in conjunction with any directorship or, in the case of a former director, loss of any office which he held in conjunction with his former directorship and which he continued to hold after ceasing to be a director.[46]

Copies of the following documents must be made available for public inspection free of charge during normal office hours at a place named in the offer document.[47] The relevant documents are:

(1) the memorandum and articles of association of the offeree company and, if the offeror is a corporation, the memorandum and articles of association of the offeror or, if it has no memorandum and articles of association, any other instrument constituting or defining the constitution of the offeror, and, if such instrument is not written in the English language, a certified translation thereof;

(2) audited accounts of the offeree company and, if the offeror is a corporation which is required to deliver accounts to the Registrar of Companies under the Companies Act 1985, of the offeror in respect of the last accounting reference periods for which the period required for laying and delivering accounts under the said Act has passed and, if accounts have been delivered to the Registrar of Companies in respect of a later accounting reference period, copies of those accounts;

(3) all contracts of service entered into for a period of more than a year between the offeree company and any of its directors and, if the offeror is a corporation, the offeror and any of its directors;

(4) any report, letter, valuation or other document any part of which is exhibited or referred to in the offer document;

(5) if the offer document contains any statement purporting to be made by an expert, that expert's written consent to the inclusion of that statement;

(6) all material contracts (if any) of the offeree and the offeror (not being contracts entered into in the ordinary course of business) entered into during the two years immediately preceding the date of the offer.

**7.65**      The offer document must, to come within the authorisation,[48]:

[44] *Ibid.* para. 3(*b*).
[45] *Ibid.* para. 3(*d*).
[46] *Ibid.* para. 3(*e*).
[47] *Ibid.* para. 3(*g*).
[48] *Ibid.* Sched.

(a) identify the offeror and, if the offer is being made on behalf of another person, identify that other person;

(b) contain a statement of the fact that the terms of the offer are recommended by all the directors of the offeree company;

(c) contain prominently the following words:

> "If you are in any doubt about this offer you should consult a stockbroker, licensed dealer, bank manager, solicitor or other professional adviser" or other words to a like effect;

(e) contain the following information:

  (i) particulars of all securities in the offeree company held by or on behalf of the offeror or each of them if there is more than one or, if none are so held, an appropriate negative statement;

 (ii) a statement as to whether or not the offer is conditional upon acceptances in respect of a minimum number of shares being received and, if so, that fact and the number;

(iii) where the offer is so conditional the date which is the latest date on which it can become unconditional;

(iv) if the offer is, or has become, unconditional the fact that it will remain open until further notice and that at least 14 days' notice will be given before it is closed;.

 (v) if applicable, a statement as to whether or not, if circumstances arise in which an offeror company is able compulsorily to acquire the shares of any dissenting minority in accordance with the provisions of section 428 of the Companies Act 1985, that offeror company intends so to acquire those shares;

(vi) if securities are to be acquired for cash, that period within which payment will be made and the method of payment;

(vii) if the consideration or part of the consideration for the securities to be acquired is securities in an offeror company ("the offeror company");

    (aa) the nature and particulars of the offeror company's business, its financial and trading prospects and its place of incorporation;

    (bb) in respect of both the offeror company and the offeree company, their turnover, net profit before tax, and the rate per cent. of dividends paid adjusted as appropriate to take account of relevant changes over the period and the total amount absorbed thereby for the five years immediately preceding the date of the offer[49];

    (cc) particulars of the first dividend in which any such securities will participate and of the rights attaching to them (including, in the case of debentures, rights as to interest) and of any restrictions on their transfer;

*Contents of Offer Document*

---

[49] Where an offeror or offeree company was incorporated during the 5 years immediately preceding the date of the offer or has passed a resolution in accordance with s.252(2) of the Companies Act 1985 this information need be included only to the period since its incorporation or since it last ceased to be exempt from the obligation to appoint auditors, as the case may be.

(dd)  an indication of the effect of acceptance on the capital and income position of the holders of securities in the offeree company; and

(ee)  particulars of all material contracts (not being contracts entered into in the ordinary course of business) entered into by each of the offeree company and the offeror company;

(viii)  particulars of the terms on which securities in the offeree company acquired in pursuance of the offer will be transferred and of any restrictions on their transfer;

(ix)  whether or not it is proposed in connection with the offer that any payment or other benefit be made or given to any director or former director of the offeree company in connection with or in compensation or consideration for his ceasing to be a director or loss of any office held in conjunction with a directorship or, in the case of a former director, loss of any office which he held in conjunction with his former directorship and which he continued to hold after ceasing to be a director and if so, particulars of each such benefit;

(x)  whether or not there exists any agreement or arrangement between the offeror or any person with whom the offeror has an agreement of the type described in section 204 of the Companies Act 1985 and any directors or shareholders of the offeree company or any persons who have been such directors or shareholders in the 12 months immediately preceding the date of the offer having any connection with or dependence on the offer and particulars of each such agreement or arrangement;

(xi)  whether or not there has been, within the knowledge of the offeror, any material change in the financial position or prospects of the offeree company since the end of the accounting reference period to which the accounts which accompany the offer document relate and, if there has, particulars of any such change;

(xii)  whether or not there is any agreement or arrangement whereby any securities acquired by the offeror will or may be transferred to any other person together with the names of the parties to each such agreement or arrangement and particulars of all securities in the offeree company held by such persons, or any appropriate negative statement;

(xiii)  particulars of any dealings in the securities of the offeree company or the offeror during the period of 12 months immediately preceding the date of the offer by every person who was a director of either of them during that period or, if there have been no such dealings, an appropriate negative statement;

(xiv)  in the case of any offeror which is a corporation and is required to deliver accounts to the registrar of companies under the Companies Act 1985, particulars of the assets and liabilities as shown in its audited accounts in respect of the latest accounting reference period for which the period allowed for laying and delivering accounts under the Companies Act 1985 has passed or, if accounts in respect of a later accounting reference period have been delivered to the registrar of companies under that Act, as shown in those accounts and not the earlier accounts;

(xv) when valuations of assets are given in connection with an offer, the basis upon which the value of the assets has been arrived at and the names of the persons who valued them or particulars of their qualifications for doing so; and

(xvi) if any profit forecast is given in connection with the offer, a statement of the assumption on which such forecast was based;

(f) it is accompanied by:

(i) the audited accounts of the offeree company in respect of the latest accounting reference period for which the period allowed for laying and delivering accounts by section 242 of the Companies Act 1985 has passed, or, if accounts in respect of a later accounting reference period have been delivered to the registrar of companies in accordance with that section, those accounts and not the earlier ones; *Accompanying Documents*

(ii) a letter advising the directors of the offeree company on the financial implications of the offer from a competent person who has no substantial interest in it or the offeror and is independent of them setting out the advice that person has given in relation to the offer;

(iii) a statement by the directors of the offeree company, acting as a board, stating—

(aa) whether or not there has been any material change in the financial position or prospects of the offeree company since the end of the accounting reference period to which the accounts which accompany the offer document relate of which they are aware and, if there has, particulars of any such change;

(bb) any interests, in percentage terms, which any of them have in the securities of the offeree company or any offeror which is a corporation being interests which, in the case of interests in the offeree company, are required to be inscribed in the register kept by the company under section 325 of the Companies Act 1985 or, in the case of an offeror, would be required to be so inscribed were the director a director of the offeror and, if any offeror is not a company within the meaning of the Companies Act 1985, were the offeror such a company;

(cc) any material interest which any director has in any contract entered into by the offeror and in any contract entered into by any member of any group of which the offeror is a member;

(iv) a statement as to whether or not each director intends to accept the offer in respect of his own beneficial holdings in the offeree company;

(v) a statement by the directors of any offeror company securities in which are the consideration or part of the consideration for the offer that the information in relation to that corporation and those securities contained in the offer document is correct;

(vi) if the offeror is making the offer on behalf of another person, a statement by the offeror as to whether or not he has taken any steps to ascertain whether that person will be in a position to implement the offer if it is accepted and, if so, what steps and the offeror's opinion as to whether the person will be in such a position; and

(vii) a statement that each of the directors of the offeree company the offeror or, if the offeror is a corporation, each of its directors has taken reasonable care to ensure that the facts stated and the opinions expressed in the offer document and the documents which accompany it are fair and accurate in so far as they relate to their respective corporations and themselves and that no material fact has been omitted and that each of them accepts responsibility accordingly.

**7.66**    Where the preconditions for the application of the City Code and the General Permission are not met and it is desired to distribute offer documents or other circulars in connection with a proposed take-over or merger the position differs according to whether the offeror is utilising the services of a licensed dealer, an exempt dealer or is seeking to effect the transaction without the assistance of members of either of these groups.

In cases where the transaction is being managed by a licensed dealer the requirements of the Licensed Dealers (Conduct of Business) Rules 1983[50] must be observed. Insofar as these relate to written offers it is provided[51]:

**9.**—(1) A licensed dealer shall not, subject to paragraph (2), make a written offer to any person (other than a section 14(5) person)[52] to acquire or dispose of any investment, unless—

*Circulars Within the Licensed Dealers (Conduct of Business) Rules 1983*

(a) subject to sub-paragraph (b), the offer document discloses sufficient information about the investment to provide a person such as the person or persons to whom the offer is addressed with an adequate and reasonable basis for deciding whether or not, or on what terms, to accept the offer (having regard to all the circumstances including the nature of the offer and the other information likely to be available to such a person or to a professional financial adviser whom such a person might reasonably be expected to consult); and

(b) where any of that information is not available for disclosure, but is information which a professional financial adviser might be expected to regard as essential in determining whether or not, or on what terms, to advise that the offer be accepted, the offer document discloses that fact and gives an indication of the nature of the information concerned; and

(c) the offer document contains prominently the words "If you are in any doubt about this offer you should consult a stockbroker, licensed dealer, bank manager, solicitor or other professional adviser" or other words to a like effect.

Provided that a licensed dealer shall not be taken to have committed a breach of this rule if he can establish that he took all reasonable care to ensure that the offer document satisfied its requirements.

---

[50] S.I. 1983 No. 585.
[51] *Ibid.* Rule 9.
[52] A s.14(5) person is a person whose business involves the acquisition and disposal, or the holding, of securities whether as principal or agent.

(2) Paragraph (1) shall not apply to a newspaper announcement or the circulation of a copy of a newspaper announcement relating solely to a tender offer to acquire shares which are subject to a marketing arrangement on a recognised stock exchange, provided that that announcement states—

(*a*) the name of the buyer;

(*b*) the name of any dealer, broker or other agent acting for the buyer;

(*c*) the name of the corporation in which shares are sought;

(*d*) the maximum number of shares or proportion of relevant share capital offered for;

(*e*) that, if tenders are received totalling less than 1 per cent. (or such higher percentage as may be specified) of the relevant share capital of the corporation, the tender offer shall be void;

(*f*) that, subject to (*e*), a shareholder's tender will be irrevocable;

(*g*) the fixed or maximum price offered;

(*h*) the holding of shares and of any rights to shares, as at the date of the offer, of the buyer and any person with whom the buyer has entered in any agreement or arrangement to which section 204 of the Companies Act 1985 applies, distinguishing between shares and rights over shares and specifying the nature of any rights concerned and giving the relevant number of shares in each case; and

(*i*) the closing day and time for tender and arrangements for delivery and settlement.

(3) For the purposes of this rule—

(*a*) information shall be taken to be available for disclosure unless—

(i) it is not known to or reasonably ascertainable by the licensed dealer; or

(ii) the licensed dealer makes the offer on behalf of one of his clients and the information is subject to an obligation of confidence owed to some other person; and

(*b*) shares are subject to a marketing arrangement on a recognised stock exchange if either—

(i) they are listed on that stock exchange; or

(ii) the corporation has been accorded facilities for dealings in those shares to take place on that stock exchange without prior permission for individual transactions from the authority governing that stock exchange and without limit as to the time during which those facilities are to be available.[53]

While exempt dealers are not bound by the Rules they are by convention "expected"[54] to observe them, albeit that no legal sanctions are available to compel observance.

In cases where an offeror wishes to circularise shareholders of the offeree

---

[53] See also Rules 10 and 11 as to the conduct of licensed dealers in take-over situations.
[54] See Gower Report *op. cit.* at paras. 9.10 and 9.11.

company without the mediacy of any other party it will be required to apply to The Department of Trade and Industry for permission on an ad hoc basis.

## TAKE-OVERS, MERGERS AND COMPETITION LAW

**7.67**   Some mergers and take-overs may fall within the provisions of the Fair Trading Act 1973[55] under which the Secretary of State may refer[56] to the Monopolies and *Fair Trading* Mergers Commission any merger or take-over if it appears to him that it is or *Act 1973* might be the fact that two or more enterprises, of which one at least is carried on in the United Kingdom by or under the control of a body corporate incorporated in the United Kingdom, have ceased to be distinct enterprises and that either[57]:

(a) the result of the merger or take-over would be to create or increase a monopoly[58] in the supply of any goods or services in the United Kingdom or any part of it; or

(b) that the value of the assets taken over exceeds £5 million.[59]

If a merger reference is made and if the Commission finds that the merger or take-over operates or may be expected to operate against the public interest the Secretary of State may, if he so chooses, block the proposed arrangement or, if the arrangement has already been implemented, make orders for it to be unscrambled.[60]

---

[55] Pts. IV–VII.

[56] The Secretary of State may make a reference in 2 situations:
   (a) under s.64, which empowers him to make a reference within 6 months after the date of the merger or the date of its becoming public; and
   (b) under s.75, which empowers him to make a merger reference in advance where it appears to him that it is or might be the fact that arrangements are in progress or in contemplation which, if carried into effect would result in the creation of a merger qualifying for investigation.

[57] Fair Trading Act 1973, s.64.

[58] For the purposes of the legislation a monopoly in market terms exists where the merger operates to create or add to a market share of one quarter or more. Further, the definition of what is a market and what constitutes the commodity or service to which the market share relates are in the determination of the Secretary of State: see s.64(2) and (3).

[59] In practice most mergers and take-overs that qualify for reference do so on this ground. Note s.65 which provides that the assets taken over are the assets employed in or appropriated to the business of the company that is being acquired and that their value is the value at which they stand in the books of the relevant business less any relevant provisions for depreciation, renewals or diminution in value. Note also s.67(3) which provides that account is also to be taken of assets of the company being acquired which, on the change in control are dealt with in the same way as assets appropriated for that company.

[60] Fair Trading Act 1973, s.73 and Sched. 8, Pts. I and II.

# 8. Finance from Government Sources

Twenty-five years ago a survey of the sources of finance available to corporate **8.01**
enterprise in the United Kingdom would have been concerned with government
primarily as a source of funds for the public corporations,[1] with only a modest
role to play in the financing of private sector activities.[2] Such a survey would
have noted that from time to time specific appropriations would be made to
assist with the funding of particular projects considered to be of national importance and, further, that financial aid was available to certain industries under a
number of statutes[3]; it would have mentioned a few agencies that then existed
which had been established on government initiative or which operated with
government participation[4]; and it would have mentioned the financial assistance
that could be made indirectly available to exporters through schemes administered by the Export Credits Guarantee Department. Certainly until the 1960s
government assistance to industry tended to be given piecemeal rather than on
the basis of programmes that were of general application.

The beginning of the change can be perceived with the passing of the Local
Employment Acts of 1960 and 1963, permitting financial assistance to be given
to schemes for the generation of employment-creating activities in areas of high
unemployment, and the Science and Technology Act 1965, which enabled financial support to be given to projects involving technological innovation. The
Industrial Development Act 1966, which provided for the payment of mandatory grants in respect of qualifying investment in the manufacturing and extrac-
tive industries, and the Industrial Expansion Act 1968, which made provision,
*inter alia*, for investment schemes, represent an increase in the scale of government involvement with the private sector.

The growing realisation of the extent and accelerating pace of the nation's
industrial decline resulted in the passing in 1972 of the Industry Act and the
Local Employment Act which two enactments brought into being a legislative
framework within which numerous schemes to assist industry were set up.
Although in 1982 these Acts were in large measure repealed their substance was
re-enacted and consolidated in a new Industrial Development Act which, in its

---

[1] See above at §§ 2.105 *et seq.*
[2] The Wilson Committee (Main Report) noted—at para. 532—that "companies have an equivocal
attitude towards using this source of finance. On the one hand they may object in principle to the
idea of relying on government assistance for any significant part of their financing arrangements.
On the other hand they are prepared to make use of such assistance when it is considered to be
available on advantageous terms."
[3] See generally Ganz, *Government and Industry* (1977).
[4] As, for example the National Research Development Corporation (now merged with the National
Enterprise Board to form the British Technology Group) which operated as a source of venture
capital, concentrating mainly on financing the research and development efforts of small companies.

amended form,[5] now constitutes, together with the Science and Technology Act 1965, the legal foundation on which the major part of government financial aid to industry rests.

**8.02**    The primary source of funds or other assistance is the Exchequer although the administration of particular programmes is usually vested in the Department of Trade and Industry and/or the appropriate sub-departments in the Scottish, Welsh and Northern Ireland Offices or in one or other of a number of statutory agencies set up to promote, *inter alia*, industrial development in the regions.[6]

Membership of the European Economic Community provides British companies and public corporations with access to Community funds and institutions either directly or through the Department or one of the agencies referred to above. The Community's Budget includes allocations to a number of funds such as the Social Fund and the Regional Development Fund which seek to promote EEC objectives by financing suitable projects. A substantial proportion of aid made available to industry by the Department or the agencies originates from these allocations. Additionally finance may be available from specific Community institutions such as the European Investment Bank.

Over the last decade local authorities have become increasingly concerned to promote (or preserve) economic activity within their areas and have adopted a wide range of measures designed to encourage investment and employment. In addition to specifically locally inspired measures[7] some authorities seek to establish programmes in conjunction with central government and/or EEC agencies to put together packages of incentives tailored to meet the needs of companies considering siting projects in the area for which the authority is responsible.

**8.03**    The range and scope of the facilities available to companies and public corporations from public funds is now such that eligibility for benefit has become an important element in the corporate planning exercises of most undertakings. In considering the nature and types of assistance available it is convenient to consider also the bodies responsible for their administration and operation. On this basis finance from public sources can be seen to involve:

(1) assistance from the Department of Trade and Industry[8]; which divides naturally into:
   (i) assistance available on a nationwide basis, irrespective of geographical considerations; and
   (ii) assistance to promote economic development in the regions;
(2) assistance from the statutory agencies; and
(3) EEC and other assistance not covered under (1) and (2).

---

[5] By the Co-operative Development Agency and Industrial Development Act 1984.
[6] A notable exception is the British Technology Group which has a primarily national but also a regional role.
[7] Such as the establishment of economic development corporations and enterprise boards.
[8] Or other relevant central government departments.

## DTI ASSISTANCE: NATIONWIDE AID PROVISION

Facilities provided by the Department[8] on a national, as distinct from a regional   **8.04**
basis fall into four groups, namely:

   (i)　those providing support for innovation[9];
  (ii)　those providing selective assistance;
 (iii)　those providing export services; and
 (iv)　those promoting energy conservation.

### Support for Innovation

Under the terms of section 5(1) of the Science and Technology Act 1965 the   **8.05**
Department,[10] with the consent of the Treasury, is empowered to provide funds
for the carrying on or support of scientific research[11] or the dissemination of the
results of scientific research, and for the furtherance of the practical applications
of the results of scientific research.

Under the authority of this provision the Department makes available a range
of facilities intended to encourage industry to undertake research and development with the aim of improving the technology base of British industry and of
helping companies to get new or significantly improved products and processes
onto the market more quickly. This assistance operates on two levels:

  (a)　through a general facility for providing assistance to any manufacturing
     company undertaking research and development; and
  (b)　within this general facility through special arrangements announced from
     time to time to encourage the application of important new technologies.

### The general facility　　　　　　　　　　　　　　　　　　　　　　　　8.06

To qualify for support the applicant company must satisfy the Department[12]
on a number of matters:

  (a)　that it has the technical, financial and managerial resources to undertake　　*Eligibility for*
     the project;　　　　　　　　　　　　　　　　　　　　　　　　　　*Assistance*

---

[9] Note also the facilities provided by the British Technology Group. See below at § 8.111 *et seq.*
[10] Originally together with the Ministry of Technology (now subsumed under the jurisdiction of the
   DTI).
[11] Defined by s.6(1) as "research and development in any of the sciences . . . or in technology."
[12] The Department is advised on the balance and direction of its support for Research and Development by five Research Requirements Boards. Each Board deals with a broad sector of industry
   and technology, is chaired by a senior industrialist and contains strong industrial representation.
   The five are:

    (1) Textiles and other manufacturers requirements board;
    (2) Electronics and avionics requirements board;
    (3) Materials, chemicals and vehicles requirements board;
    (4) Mechanical and electrical engineering requirements board; and
    (5) Metrology and Standards requirements board.

   In addition, the Boards also examine some individual applications especially in relation to projects on a large scale or involving special features.

(b) that government assistance is essential to ensure that the project goes ahead at all or in the form or on the timescale proposed;

(c) that the project falls within the recognised expenditure limits: normally not more than £6,000,000 or less than £25,000[13];

(d) that the company makes its required contributions to the project's costs. This contribution is set at two-thirds, or, in the case of a shared cost project, one half;

(e) for projects involving the design, development and launch of a new product or process that the company has the ability and intention to exploit commercially the results of the project; and

(f) for longer term projects that they satisfy an identified industrial need related to competitiveness, added value, energy saving, improved environment or safety, or better or new standards.

Where the Department is satisfied that these requirements have been met and that the project should be supported assistance may be given from the design stage, through development to the launch of the products or processes. However, support cannot be given retrospectively. It follows therefore that only work done after the approval of the application can be assisted.

**8.07**   Assistance may be provided in one of three ways.

(a) *Grants*

*Forms of Assistance*   The standard form of assistance is by way of a grant towards eligible project costs. The normal level of grant is 25 per cent., although in respect of applications received prior to May 31, 1984 and expenditure incurred and claimed by May 31, 1987 the grant level is $33\frac{1}{3}$ per cent. Technically, these grant levels represent maxima within which the Department may exercise a discretion and certainly for longer projects grants will be individually negotiated within this limit. However for projects not falling within this category the Department has publicised the maximum limit as its standard terms.

(b) *Share-cost contracts*

Shared-cost contracts in relation to product and process developments tend to be offered only in exceptional circumstances, although they are more common for longer term research and development projects. Under such contracts the Department contributes 50 per cent. of eligible costs, although the level of assistance may be greater where the project offers considerable national benefits. This contribution is recovered by a levy on sales.

(c) *Pre-production order*

The essence of this form of assistance is that the Department will purchase up to four pre-production models embodying new techniques or principles and lend

---

[13] Applications in relation to projects costs of less than £25,000 may be considered from small companies.

them to potential users for a trial period so that the user can satisfy itself that the equipment meets its requirements before deciding whether to purchase. If at the end of the trial[14] the user does not purchase the equipment the manufacturer is required to buy the equipment back from the Department at an agreed price.

Projects receiving assistance under this general facility are not eligible for assistance under other government schemes unless that assistance is non-selective, as in the case of regional development grants. Any aid of this kind will be deducted from eligible costs of the project before an offer of assistance is made. **8.08**

### Special facilities **8.09**

Within the general facility offered by the Support for Innovation programme special arrangements are announced from time to time to encourage the application of important new technologies. One or more of the main forms of support provided are available to companies carrying out research and development projects in these areas. In addition, support may be extended to feasibility studies and to activities to improve the awareness of the potential of the technology. Some special facilities have complementary arrangements[15] to support capital investment.

*Areas where Special Facilities Provided*

The more important of these special facilities that have been in operation over the past few years have been:

*Biotechnology in industry* (BIOTECH). For the promotion of the application of biotechnology in industry for firms in or closely associated with the manufacturing sector.

*Computer-aided Design/Computer-aide Manufacture* (CADCAM). For the promotion of the application of computer-aided design and manufacturing techniques, primarily in the mechanical and electrical engineering industries.

*Computer-aided Design, Manufacture and Test* (CADMAT). To encourage the adoption of computer-aided design, manufacture and test techniques in the electronics industry.

*Computer-aided Design and Test Equipment* (CADTES). To support the Cadcam and Cadmat schemes by providing assistance for the purchase of capital equipment in the fields of computer-aided design, computer-aided manufacture and computer-aided tests.[16]

*Flexible Manufacturing Systems* (FMS). For the application of flexible manufacturing techniques for computer-controllable batch production.

*Fibre Optics and Opto-electronics Scheme* (FOS). For the advancement of projects involving the design, development and launching of a new or signifi-

---

[14] The trial period is normally one year.
[15] Under the National Selective Assistance programmes. See below at § 8.20.
[16] This programme is designed to increase the use of computer-aided engineering by assisting first-time users.

cantly improved product or process in relation to optical fibres, opto-electronics, optical sensors and instruments for such activities.[17]

*Micro Electronics Application Project* (MAP). To encourage the wider application of micro-electronics in products in products and production processes in manufacturing industry.

*Micro-electronics Industry Support Programme* (MISP). To further:

(a)  research and development of products and processes;
(b)  investment in plant and buildings; and
(c)  product launch and marketing capability.

*Industrial Robots* (ROBOTICS). To promote the industrial application and manufacture of robotic devices.

*Software Products Scheme* (SPS). To encourage the development and marketing of innovative software products.

*Telecoms Products Scheme* (TPS). To provide grants for capital equipment and product development in the telecommunications field.[18]

*Innovation-linked Investment Scheme* (IIS). To help to "pull-through" new products and processes to the market when development work had already been supported by the Department, or where such work would have been eligible for support.

### National selective assistance

**8.10**

*Purposes for Which Aid may be Given Under s. 8*

Selective financial assistance on a nationwide (as opposed to a regional) basis may be available to companies under the provisions of section 8 of the Industrial Development Act 1982. Like regional selective assistance, aid under section 8 is entirely discretionary with the Department of Trade and Industry having laid down comparatively few guidelines.

Under the terms of section 8 the Secretary of State, with the consent of the Treasury, may provide financial assistance in order[19]:

(a)  to promote the development or modernisation of an industry;
(b)  to promote the efficiency of an industry;
(c)  to create, expand or sustain productive capacity in an industry, or in undertakings in an industry;
(d)  to promote the reconstruction, reorganisation or conversion of an industry or of undertakings in an industry;
(e)  to encourage the growth of, or the proper distribution of undertakings in, an industry; and
(f)  to encourage arrangements for ensuring that any contraction of an industry proceeds in an orderly way.

---

[17] In addition, assistance is also given to work on the application of such products or processes.
[18] This scheme is aimed particularly at small and medium-sized companies and applies only to equipment designed to be attached to public telecommunications networks.
[19] I.D.A. 1982, s.8(1) (incorporating s.7(2)).

Before financial assistance may be provided under section 8 the Secretary of
State must be of the opinion[20]:

(a) that the financial assistance is likely to benefit the economy of the United
Kingdom or of any part or area of the United Kingdom; and

(b) that it is in the national interest that the financial assistance should be provided on the scale, and in the form and manner, proposed; and

(c) that the financial assistance cannot, or cannot appropriately, be so provided otherwise than by the Secretary of State.

It should be noted that these requirements are cumulative rather than alternative with the consequence that any application for section 8 assistance must be
capable of satisfying the Department in respect of each of the three heads before
that application can be entertained.

Two further points can be made in relation to these requirements. The first is
that, although applications are to be judged by reference to "the national interest," the Act nowhere defines or even indicates what factors are relevant in
ascertaining what the national interest is. Perhaps this is inevitable given that
changing economic, social and political conditions will produce different percep-
tions and priorities. Nevertheless, in relation to the predecessor of section 8[21]
the Department described "the national interest" as being "the benefit to the
economy as a whole of a particular development, whether it contributes to
employment, efficiency, profitability, productivity, ability to export, ability to
substitute for imports, ability to provide greater social benefits to the community
involved, not only in the industry but in the surrounding regions and in the
country as a whole."[22]

The second point is that section 8 envisages the Department as financier of last
resort, providing support which the private sector has been unable or unwilling
to provide on commercial grounds.

The Department may provide assistance under section 8[23] "on any terms and
conditions and by any description of investment or lending or guarantee or by
making grants,[24] subject only to the provisions:

(1) that no money may be used under section 8 for the acquisition or assistance of banks or insurance companies[25];

(2) that assistance shall not be provided in the form of an investment by
acquisition of loan or share capital in any company unless the Secretary of

---

[20] *Ibid.*
[21] Industry Act 1972, s.8.
[22] H.C. 617–I (1974–75) Q.57. See generally Ganz *op.cit* at pp. 24–32.
[23] As also in the case of Regional Selective Assistance. See further at §§ 8.38 *et seq.*
[24] I.D.A. 1982, s.8(2) incorporating s.7(3). In addition to the general descriptions contained in the
text aid may be given in particular by:
    (a) investment by acquisition of loan or share capital in any company;
    (b) investment by the acquisition of any undertaking or of any assets;
    (c) a loan, whether secured or unsecured, and whether or not carrying interest or interest at a
       commercial rate; or
    (d) any form of insurance or guarantee to meet any contingency and in particular to meet
       default on payment of a loan, or of interest on a loan, or non-fulfilment of a contract.
[25] I.D.A. 1982, s.8(2).

State is satisfied that it cannot or cannot appropriately be given in any other way[26];

(3) that the Secretary of State shall not, in providing assistance, acquire any shares or stock in a company without the consent of that company.[27]

**8.13**

*Assistance under Industry Act 1972*

In operating section 8 of the Industry Act 1972 the Department listed three broad categories of cases in which assistance might be appropriate. The first of these, where the market mechanism does not provide support for projects which merit support on commercial grounds, has been incorporated into section 8 of the 1982 Act. The second, that of giving temporary help to a declining industry or company in difficulties to put it back on its feet[28] has not. Indeed, the literature put out by the Department publicising what may be available under section 8 makes no mention of rescues. Nevertheless it is undoubted that should it be considered appropriate a company or industry rescue could still be effected under the provisions of the section. Furthermore, the previously operating restraint that expenditure in excess of £5,000,000 needed an affirmative resolution in the House of Commons is absent from the 1982 Act.[29] Equally, the third category of case, that of providing assistance leading to wider economic or social benefits such as balance of payments considerations receives no statutory mention in the new Act. However it would likewise appear that the new provisions do not inhibit the provision of such assistance in appropriate circumstances.

**8.14**

Apart from rescue cases the current operation of section 8 is directed towards the provision of assistance for "investment and restructuring." This, of course, is not new. Under the authority of the 1972 Act a scheme[30] was set up to modernise the woollen industry, by means of capital grants for re-equipment and rebuilding together with loans and interest-relief grants for more comprehensive restructuring plus further grants for the elimination of uneconomic capacity. Similar schemes in connection with the machine tools and ferrous foundary industries made available loans at concessionary rates towards the development of new machine tools and grants towards expenditure on new equipment and plants and towards new buildings and extensions.[31]

Within the parameters of section 8 assistance for capital investment is made available either:

(a) for major capital projects by manufacturing and some service industries; or

---

[26] *Ibid.* s.8(3).

[27] *Ibid.*

[28] Or to help a planned contraction.

[29] The only financial limits now imposed by statute are the global limits set out in I.D.A. 1982, ss.8(4)–(11) and 9. These sections are set out in Annex A to this Chapter.

[30] The Wool Textile Industries Scheme. See Ganz *op. cit.* at pp. 25/26 and references cited there.

[31] Further schemes set up under s.8 of the 1972 Act include those for the paper and book industries and for the textile and printing machinery makers—see *Trade and Industry* 1976, June 19 and August 20, 1976.

Additionally, there exists the Offshore Supplies Interest Relief Grant Scheme set up under s.10 of the 1972 Act, making available credit to finance contracts for providing British goods and services in the construction of oil platforms. Assistance under s.8 has also been provided to two offshore projects for the conversion of ships for use in connection with the North Sea exploitation.

(b) under special schemes set up to assist a particular industrial sector or to achieve a particular industrial objective.

**General capital projects**

Under the administrative guidelines within which the Department administers **8.15** selective national assistance projects for which aid is sought should normally involve new investment of at least £500,000 including working capital and ancil- *Eligible Project* lary costs directly associated with the project. Not all project costs are con- *Costs* sidered as being eligible for assistance. In the ordinary course where a project is to be assisted the principle eligible project costs are those for new fixed capital investment in buildings, plant and machinery. Other project costs which may, depending on the circumstances, be eligible include working capital, pre-production or development costs, market development expenditure, licensing arrangements and relevant training costs.

For a project to be considered for section 8 assistance it must meet a number **8.16** of requirements. Even if it does meet these requirements, however, there is no guarantee that aid will be forthcoming. It must be emphasised that the assistance *Criteria* is selective and that the discretion resting with the Secretary of State is sufficient *Against which* to prevent assistance in any given case.[32] *Applications for Assistance* The criteria against which applications are judged are as follows: *are Considered*

(a) *Viability*

Projects must be shown to be commercially viable before applications in respect of them will be entertained. Even where other requirements are to a greater or lesser degree met an inability to demonstrate a project's commercial viability will eliminate any chance of assistance.

(b) *Mobility*

Projects must be shown to be internationally mobile; that is, there must be a genuine choice of international location for the projects. It might be noted at this point that assistance under section 8 is one of the primary instruments for inducing foreign concerns to direct investment into the United Kingdom.

(c) *Additionality*

In the context of section 8 the fundamental requirement of additionality that attaches to both national and regional selective assistance has the effect of making it necessary for the applicant company to demonstrate:

(1) that the project will lead to substantial improvements in performance, usually through increased productivity, although other improvements in,

---

[32] See Ganz *op. cit.* at pp. 204 *et seq.* on the exercise of discretion under the Industry Act 1972.

for example, the quality or reliability of the company's products can be considered[33]; or

(2) that the project will lead to the introduction of new products by the plant or company[34];

and in either case

(3) that the project will produce a substantial net contribution to United Kingdom output or introduce a significant degree of innovation to the United Kingdom. Insofar as a net contribution to output is concerned, this may arise from additional exports, or import substitution, or from the meeting of an increased (or new) domestic demand.

(d) *Necessity*

As with selective assistance under section 7, aid will only be considered for projects which would not go ahead at all or on the basis proposed (in relation to their timing, scale or nature) without it. In practice, time means that, as a result of the assistance there must be a genuine and significant enhancement of the project as for example:

(1) by a substantial acceleration; or
(2) by a substantial increase in the scale of the project; or
(3) through other additional features such as a desirable extension of product range.

The element of necessity is reflected in the amount of any assistance granted, the point being that the amount of assistance which may be provided will be the minimum necessary to achieve this enhancement.

**8.17**       Companies wishing to apply for section 8 assistance should initially provide the following details:

*Applications
for Assistance
under s.8*

(a) a brief summary of the company's activities and copies of accounts for the previous three years;
(b) an outline of the project, indicating its purpose and rationale, its intended location, what products and/or manufacturing processes are involved, its industrial significance, the markets involved and the project's relationship with the existing activities of the company;
(c) a summary of project costs, broken down into plant, buildings, working capital and other elements with details as to how the project is to be financed; and
(d) an indication of how the matters referred to in § 8.16 above are to be met.

**8.18**       In order to establish what impact the provision of assistance would have on the project the Department will arrange for an appraisal of the project to be under-

---

[33] In determining the most appropriate measure of improvement regard will be had to the nature of the project and the industry. It will normally be expected that the resulting productivity of assisted projects will be significantly better than the average for the industry.
[34] In this case it will be necessary to demonstrate that appropriate up-to-date and efficient manufacturing methods will be used.

taken. This may be effected by the Department's Industrial Development Unit (which administers the provision of aid under section 8) or, and especially if the project is large, by referring the application to the Industrial Development Advisory Board.[35] Although the Department is under no statutory obligation to follow recommendations made by the Board where it does not do so it is required (through the Secretary of State) to lay a statement on the matter before the House of Commons should the Board so request.[36]

*Project Appraisal*

An appraisal will take account of the company's existing investment commitments and programme, its investment criteria, the capital availability of the company and of any group of which it is a part.

The amount and terms of project assistance under section 8 are matters for individual negotiations between the Department and the company concerned undertaken on the basis that what assistance is provided will be the minimum necessary for the project to proceed. The normal form of assistance is that of grant, payment of which is usually made in instalments linked to defrayals of fixed capital expenditure on the project and the achievement of its forecast objectives.

**8.19**

*Payment*

Grant payable to a company under section 8 is treated as a trading receipt for tax purposes.[37]

**Special schemes**

**8.20**

Although the Department imposes no restriction as to the size of companies from which it is prepared to entertain applications for assistance with general capital projects the normal minimum cost requirement has the consequence that such assistance is not normally available to small companies. However, where a particular industrial sector or overall industrial objective has been identified for assistance under a special section 8 scheme smaller companies with eligible projects will also be considered for assistance. Some of these schemes support capital investment alone, while others include research and development as well, overlapping with the Support for Innovation programme.

Among the more important special schemes operating in recent years under the auspices of section 8 have been the following:

*Small engineering firms investment schemes* (SEFIS). The object of these schemes has been to provide assistance towards the purchase of certain types of technologically advanced capital equipment. An initial scheme was launched in March 1982 (SEFIS 1) and was considered so successful that even with additional funds it had to be closed after two months because the funds allocated to it had been exhausted. In the 1983 Budget £100,000,000 was allocated to its successor SEFIS 2.

*Support for innovation.* Certain of the schemes in the Support for Innovation programme[38] qualify for section 8 assistance.

[35] I.D.A. 1982, s.10(1).
[36] *Ibid.* s.10(4). See further Ganz *op. cit.* at pp. 28 *et seq.*
[37] F.A. 1980, s.42.
[38] See above at §§ 8.05–8.09.

*Loan guarantee scheme for small businesses.*[39] The Small Business Loan Guarantee Scheme was introduced in 1981 to assist small businesses in obtaining loan finance from the private sector. The scheme was directed at those propositions which were "on the margin" in the sense that banks and other lending institutions would be reluctant to supply finance under the ordinary canons of lending. The scheme is operated by the Department in conjunction with participating financial institutions which include the clearing banks, accepting houses, issuing houses and other lending institutions.

### Export services

**8.21**        Assistance with export finance or with ancillary matters concerned with the promotion of British exports may be available:

(1) via the Export Credits Guarantee Department; and
(2) from the British Overseas Trade Board.

**8.22**    **The Export Credits Guarantee Department (ECGD)**

The Export Credits Guarantee Department is a government department (within the Department of Trade and Industry) whose primary function is to assist exporters of British goods and services by providing insurance against the risks of not being paid.[40] As an additional function ECGD also provides guarantees of 100 per cent. repayment to banks providing finance to insured exporters. It is by way of this facility that ECGD operates indirectly as a source of finance.

       ECGD operates under the authority of the Exports Guarantees and Overseas Investment Act 1978. This Act confers certain powers and duties on the Sec-
*Powers of*    retary of State but provides[41] that all such powers and duties[42] "shall be exer-
*ECGD*      cised and performed through the Export Credits Guarantee Department."

       The powers conferred on the Secretary of State and exercisable by ECGD are in relation to:

---

[39] The essence of the scheme is that the government will guarantee repayment of 80 per cent. of the principal of medium-term loans (but not overdrafts) made by participating lenders to eligible small businesses provided that the loan is made for business purposes only. The guarantee covers amounts lent up to a maximum of £75,000 with the loan being repayable over periods of between two and seven years. The loan is required to be secured (where the company has assets capable of being used as security, although the absence of such assets does not automatically disqualify an applicant from taking advantage of the scheme) and companies should be prepared to pledge all available assets used or available for use in the business as security for guaranteed loans.
In making its appraisal of a proposal the lending institution will (as a matter of practice) require sight of the company's business plans, projected bugets and cash-flow forecasts over the first two or three years of the loan period. The Department operates the scheme on a selective basis so that even if an application is forwarded from the lending institution concerned it does not follow that the guarantee will be automatically forthcoming, albeit that the Department's power to refuse appears to be used sparingly.
In consideration of this guarantee provision the Department charges a premium on the amount borrowed. The premium is at a rate of three per cent. per annum of the amount of the loan and is payable quarterly.
[40] Whether through the default of the purchaser or from other causes (for example restrictions on the transfer of currency).
[41] s.12(1).
[42] With the exception of the power to make certain orders.

(a) *Export guarantees*

Section 1 provides that for the purpose of encouraging trade with other countries the Secretary of State may, after consultation with the Export Guarantees Advisory Council[43] and with the consent of the Treasury, provide guarantees to or for the benefit of persons carrying on business in the United Kingdom in connection with the export, manufacture, treatment or distribution of goods, the rendering of services or any other matter which appears conducive to the purpose of encouraging trade with other countries.

Guarantees given under section 1 may be subject to such terms and conditions as may be arrived at in accordance with the arrangements made for the giving of the guarantee.[44]

(b) *Guarantees and other arrangements in the national interest*

Additional to the power under section 1 to provide export guarantees is that under section 2, where, again with the consent of the Treasury, the Secretary of State may:

(1) give such guarantees to or for the benefit of persons carrying on business in the United Kingdom as appear to him to be expedient in the national interest; and/or

(2) facilitate, where it appears expedient to do so in the national interest, the payment of sums payable under contracts with persons carrying on business in the United Kingdom.

The powers under section 2 may be exercised only:

(a) for the purpose of encouraging trade with other countries; or

(b) for the purpose of rendering economic assistance to countries outside the United Kingdom.

It should be noted that, as in other contexts in which it is used, the "national interest" is not defined.

Again facilities provided under this section may be on such terms as may be agreed between ECGD and the recipient.

(c) *Loans and interest grants*

Section 3 of the 1978 Act confers powers, subject to Treasury consent, to make:

(a) loans to any persons in connection with their provision of financial facilities in respect of export contracts, provided that such persons are resident and carrying on business in the United Kingdom; and

(b) grants to any persons for the purpose of supplementing any interest received or receivable by them as consideration for their provision of such

---

[43] s.12(2).
[44] s.1(3).

facilities. Interest grants may be payable to persons carrying on business or other activities outside the United Kingdom in respect of interest paid or payable under export contracts.

Loans or grants made under the authority of section 3 may be on such terms and conditions as the Secretary of State may determine.

### (d) *Securities*

Section 4 gives the Secretary of State power to acquire, hold or dispose of any securities which have been the subject of guarantees under the Act.

### (e) *Payments to exporters in respect of cost increases*

Power under section 5 is given (for the purposes of encouraging trade with other countries and subject to Treasury consent) to make payments to persons carrying on business in the United Kingdom who have entered into export contracts being payments related to increases in the cost of labour, materials or such other matters as may be agreed.[45]

Payments under this provision may be made subject to such terms and conditions as the Secretary of State may think fit.

### (f) *Overseas investment*

Section 11 of the Act confers power on the Secretary of State (with the consent of the Treasury) to make arrangements for meeting non-commercial risks attached to investment overseas. The power is widely drawn permitting the making of agreements to indemnify British companies against agreed categories of loss arising from war, expropriation, currency restrictions or other such risks as appear to the Secretary of State not to be commercial risks.

## 8.23   ECGD finance

*Insurance Cover as a Source of Finance*

Although ECGD does not directly provide finance for export credit it has nevertheless over the years become increasingly important in facilitating lending by the banks. The point is that ECGD insurance policies are generally acceptable as collateral security for bank advances. Under an ECGD credit policy[46] an exporting company is assured that if its customer should fail to make payment for goods or services the Department will do so.

---

[45] Under s.5(4) this power, unless expressly extended by order, ceased to be operable after March 26, 1979.

[46] ECGD provides the following insurance guarantees:

    (1) *A Comprehensive Short-term Guarantee* which provides exporters of consumer and similar goods sold on credit terms of up to 180 days with insurance against non-payment. Cover is on a whole turnover basis: exporters are normally expected to offer all their overseas business for insurance.

    (2) *A Comprehensive Extended Terms Guarantee* provides holders of the comprehensive short-term guarantee with insurance against non-payment for goods such as machinery normally sold on credit terms of between 180 days and 5 years.

    (3) A *Comprehensive External Trade Guarantee* protects U.K. merchants and confirming

Under the normal policy an exporter is insured:

(1) for 90 per cent. of his loss if it has occurred because of the default or insolvency of his purchaser; or

(2) for 95 per cent. if it is due to "country" risks such as exchange difficulties or export or import licence restrictions.

Where an ECGD 100 per cent guarantee has been obtained the banks will make funds available to exporters at special (*i.e.* lower) export rates.

## (1) Assignment of policy 8.24

It is often the case that the very fact that an exporting company has an ECGD policy insuring against the main risks that might result in non-payment is sufficient for a bank to safeguard its own position as direct supplier of the company's export finance. Where more security is required, however, the company can provide this by assigning to its bank payments due under the policy. Such assignments may be of the company's rights:

(1) under all transactions covered by the policy; or

(2) for all transactions in a specified market; or

(3) for all transactions with a named purchaser; or

(4) for individual bills.

In each of these cases ECGD is prepared to give the bank formal acknowledgement of such arrangements and make payment accordingly should a claim under the policy fall due.

Although assignment of an ECGD policy is an accepted method for obtaining export finance it must be emphasised that assignment arrangements do not provide more than a collateral security. Whether bank finance will be made available in any given case will depend on other factors such as whether the policy conditions are being observed and the competence and reputation of the exporting company.

## (2) Comprehensive bank guarantees[47] 8.25

While an assignment of an ECGD policy will generally be sufficient to enable an exporting company to arrange its financing, especially over the short term, for

houses trading in goods despatched from one overseas country to another against the risks of non-payment. The goods must be sold on credit terms of not more than 180 days.

(4) *A Services Guarantee* provides insurance against non-payment for firms carrying out service contracts overseas (*e.g.* consultancies) Cover can be given either on a whole turnover basis under a comprehensive services guarantee or case by case under a specific services guarantee.

(5) *A Specific Guarantee* provides insurance against non-payment on a case by case basis for capital goods exports unsuited to cover under a comprehensive guarantee.

(6) *Consortium Insurance* covers U.K. consortium members contracting for major overseas projects against some of the risks arising from contractual responsibilities., Contracts must be worth at least £20 million for insolvency of fellow members; £50 million for other contingent risks.

(7) *The Overseas Investment Insurance Scheme* provides cover for both capital and interest on new U.K. private overseas investment against the risk of war, expropriation and restrictions on remittances for periods of 3–15 years.

[47] External merchanting trade does not qualify under this scheme.

longer term lending a bank may be prepared to provide funds only against hard security. To meet such cases ECGD has developed a range of direct guarantees to banks. Since the practice is for banks to offer favourable interest rates for funds secured by these guarantees[48] companies often prefer this method of financing where available.

ECGD comprehensive guarantees to banks are operated under a two-part scheme.

(a) *Banker's guarantee (bills or notes)*

The first part of the scheme applies to exporters who:

(1) have a Comprehensive Policy[49]; and
(2) are transacting business by means of bills of exchange or promissory notes on credit terms of less than two years.

In such cases an ECGD guarantee direct to the financing bank may be obtained in consideration of a premium[50] payable by the exporter. The guarantee provides a Government-backed security to the bank which will then provide finance from the date of shipment on presentation of the bills or notes at a maximum interest rate of five-eighths per cent. above base rate.

On issue of the guarantee to the bank, and on renewal annually thereafter, a revolving credit is established for the amount the exporters may have outstanding at any one time, the credit limit being determined on the level of the company's business during the preceding 12 months plus a margin for increased trade. An exporting company is thus able to finance bills or notes in respect of business transacted up to the credit limit. This facility, however, only applies:

(1) where the business transacted complies with the conditions of the Comprehensive Policy; and
(2) provided the purchaser is not in default under any contract with the purchaser.

The guarantee to the bank covers 100 per cent. of the principal amount of the bill or note as well as interest due to the bank on outstanding amounts. Furthermore ECGD undertakes to pay unconditionally three months after the due date if the purchaser fails to pay an accepted bill or note or if the exporter fails to pay interest due to the bank. In addition in the case of an unaccepted bill ECGD undertakes to pay unconditionally one month after demand if the exporter fails to reimburse the bank.

Because of the extent of cover given by the guarantee and its unconditional nature the exporter is required to sign an agreement at the outset giving ECGD recourse in the event of payment being made to the bank in advance or in excess of the amount due to the exporter under his credit insurance policy.

---

[48] The guarantee applies to financing confined to business covered by the guarantee.
[49] See above at n. 46.
[50] The premium is payable on commencement of cover and on renewal annually by the exporter at a flat rate of 25p per £100 of the agreed revolving limit. For business with associate companies overseas the premium is 50p per £100.

(b) *Banker's guarantee (open account)*[51]

This part of the scheme covers the application of direct guarantees to banks to direct exports on CAD terms or an open accounts providing for up to six months credit.

Under this part of the scheme, the bank advances money to the exporter under ECGD's guarantee. These advances will be for 100 per cent. of the net invoice amount of insured exports, within a borrowing limit specified by ECGD. The exporter warrants that the goods have been exported and that the transaction is insured with ECGD, and produces a copy invoice showing the terms of payment and acceptable evidence of export. Against each advance the exporter gives the bank a promissory note with an appropriate repayment date, namely the last day of the month in which payment by the buyer is due. (In determining the month of repayment where terms are CAD or where credit runs from arrival of the goods, up to one month will be allowed for shipping or taking up the goods.) The charges made by banks for handling notes are settled by negotiation between the exporter and his bank, but advances whose due dates of repayment fall within the same calendar month may normally be covered by a single promissory note. Should the exporter fail to honour his note, ECGD pays the bank and in turn takes recourse to the exporter.

As with the bill guarantee, a limit[52] for the finance to be guaranteed is agreed by ECGD. To borrow against the guarantee the exporter provides evidence of shipment and warranty that the transaction is insured with ECGD, and in addition a copy invoice showing the terms of repayment of his loan (his obligation to repay his bank thus not being dependent on his receiving payment from his buyer on the due date.

British banks have agreed to finance lending against these guarantees at up to five-eighths per cent. over base rate; there is also a charge for each promissory note handled, although any number of transactions for which payment falls due in the same month can be covered by one note. ECGD's annual premium is 50p per £100 of the agreed borrowing limit for business with all buyers.

Should the exporter not honour his promissory note after six months overdue ECGD pays his bank and recovers the amount from him. As with the Comprehensive Bill Guarantee, ECGD needs to determine the recourseworthiness of the exporter.

### (3) Specific bank guarantees 8.26

Specific guarantees to banks are appropriate where an exporter is negotiating a contract on credit terms of two years or more and is to be covered by a Specific Policy or a Supplemental Extended Terms Guarantee to his Comprehensive

---

[51] This differs from other bank guarantee schemes because, in the absence of buyer's bills or notes, the bank has recourse to the exporter in respect of the fnance it provides. The exporter's obligation to honour his promissory note to the bank is independent of the actual date on which he may receive payment from the buyer. ECGD's guarantee to the bank is a guarantee that the exporter will repay the sums borrowed. ECGD must therefore be satisfied that the exporter can meet this commitment before giving its guaratee.

[52] Exporters pay a premium of 50p per £100 annually on the amount of the borrowing limit agreed.

Policy.[53] Under this facility an exporter may supplement such insurance cover with a specific ECGD guarantee to his bank.

These guarantees promise unconditional payment to the bank of 100 per cent. of any bill or note against which payment has not been received three months after the due date of payment. The bank will finance the credit in such cases, without recourse to the exporter, at a fixed rate of interest in line with the guidelines for officially supported export credit.

The bank guarantee is usually operative when the goods have been shipped or accepted, the works have been completed or the services have been satisfactorily performed. The exporter's standard credit insurance policy is endorsed so as to recognise that payment in respect of insured losses may be paid direct to the financing bank under the bank guarantee. A separate recourse agreement between ECGD and the exporter is made for each contract to safeguard ECGD in the event of its paying under the bank guarantee amounts which would not have been paid under the exporter's own policy.

In suitable cases, where exporters are frequent users of the Specific Bank Guarantee, ECGD may be able to issue a Comprehensive Extended Terms Bank Guarantee for those contracts covered under an exporter's Supplemental Extended Terms Guarantee. Cover under this bank guarantee is on similar lines to that given under the Comprehensive Bill Guarantee to banks, and provides the same financial assistance to the exporter, but does away with the need for a separate guarantee for each contract, so reducing paperwork for both the exporter and ECGD.

In 1978 ECGD introduced the "foreign currency specific bank guarantee." This applies to one-off contracts with credit terms of two years or more normally worth in excess of £1 million. It enables exporters to opt for supplier credit financing in U.S. dollars or Deutschmarks if this method is more in line with their normal business arrangements, or if they are trading with countries which traditionally prefer supplier credit. Before the introduction of this new guarantee exporters financing major one-off contracts of this kind had been restricted to sterling or to buyer credit financing. As with buyer credit foreign currency guarantees ECGD undertakes to continue funding the loan if the lending bank is unable to continue raising sufficient funds on the Euromarket.[54]

A premium for the guarantee to the bank is payable and ranges from 40p to a maximum of 60p per £100 according to the length of credit.

---

[53] See above at n. 46.

[54] In addition to the facilities described in §§ 8.24–8.26 which all relate to sales by the supplier on deferred payments terms ECGD also offers facilities for the purchaser to be financed direct by a British bank to enable him to pay on cash terms. These are:

*A buyer credit* which is an ECGD guaranteed loan by a bank in the U.K. direct to an overseas buyer or bank. The loan finances up to 85 per cent. of the contract value of a capital goods export or overseas project. The minimum eligible contract value is £1 million; and

*A line of credit* which is a loan on buyer credit terms under which a number of contracts for capital goods can be financed. In some cases contract with values as low as £20,000 are eligible.

## The British Overseas Trade Board (BOTB)    **8.27**

The British Overseas Trade Board was established administratively in January 1972 to provide information, help and advice to exporters. Its specific responsibilities are:

(1) to advise the Government on strategy for overseas trade;
(2) to direct and develop the Government's export promotion services on behalf of the Secretary of State;
(3) to encourage and support industry and commerce in overseas trade with the aid of appropriate governmental and non-governmental organisations at home and overseas; and
(4) to contribute to the exchange of views between Government and industry and commerce in the field of overseas trade and to search for solutions to problems.

The Board seeks to discharge its responsibilities by gathering, storing and disseminating overseas market information and by providing help and advice to individual firms, by organising collective trade promotions and by assisting in the stimulation of export promotion publicity.

In so far as it can be regarded as a source of funds BOTB provides financial assistance:

(1) towards exhibiting at overseas trade fairs;
(2) for market research abroad;
(3) towards the funding of overhead costs in breaking into new overseas markets; and
(4) towards the cost of visiting overseas markets.

### Energy conservation

A measure of financial assistance is available in certain circumstances to companies to enable them to become more energy-efficient. These programmes have included the following.    **8.28**

*The energy survey scheme*

This scheme is designed to encourage industrial, commercial and public sector organisations to employ consultants to assist them to reduce their energy consumption and costs.

*The energy conservation demonstration project*

The Department of Trade and Industry, acting under section 5 of the Science and Technology Act 1965, instituted this scheme to encourage the more widespread adoption of energy conservation technologies by demonstrating their technical and economic effectiveness in working situations.

While assistance is selective, eligibility for aid extends to demonstration projects of energy conservation relating to all aspects of energy use.

*The coal firing scheme*

Under this scheme assistance was available in the form of capital grants for replacement or conversion of oil or gas-fuelled industrial equipment with coal-fired equipment.

## DTI ASSISTANCE: REGIONAL AID

**8.29** The idea underlying the regional aid policies of successive governments is to make available to "assisted areas"[55] a level of financial assistance not available in other parts of the country with the object of encouraging businesses to move to or to expand or modernise existing facilities in those areas.

Under the legislation applicable to mainland Britain assisted areas may be either "intermediate areas" or "development areas,"[56] with the latter attracting the broadest range of incentives. As from November 29, 1984 those parts of mainland Britain with assisted area status are as follows:

### Development areas

**England**
*North-west*
Liverpool
Widnes & Runcorn
Wigan & St Helens
Wirral & Chester[1]
Workington

*North-east*
Bishop Auckland[2]
Hartlepool
Middlesbrough
Newcastle-upon-Tyne
South Tyneside
Stockton-on-Tees
Sunderland

*Yorkshire & Humberside*
Huddersfield
Rotherham &
   Mexborough
Scunthorpe
Whitby[2]

*East Midlands*
Corby

*South-west*
Falmouth
Helston
Newquay
Penzance & St Ives
Redruth·& Camborne

**Scotland**
Arbroath
Bathgate
Cumnock & Sanquhar
Dumbarton
Dundee
Glasgow
Greenock
Irvine
Kilmarnock
Lanarkshire

**Wales**
Aberdare
Cardigan
Ebbw Vale &
   Abergavenny
Flint & Rhyl
Holyhead
Lampeter & Aberaeron
Merthyr & Rhymney
Neath & Port Talbot
Pontypridd & Rhondda
South Pembrokeshire
Wrexham

[1] Chester NWA previously a non-assisted area.
[2] Previously an intermediate area.

[55] Industrial Development Act 1982, s.1.
[56] *Ibid.* as amended by the Co-operative Development Agency and Industrial Development Act 1984, s.4.

## Intermediate areas

**England**

*North-west*
Accrington &
  Rossendale[3]
Blackburn[4]
Bolton & Bury[4]
Part of Manchester[4]
Oldham[4]
Rochdale

*North-east*
Darlington
Durham
Morpeth & Ashington

*Yorkshire & Humberside*
Barnsley
Bradford
Doncaster
Grimsby
Hull
Sheffield[4]

*West Midlands*[4]
Birmingham
Coventry & Hinckley
Dudley & Sandwell
Kidderminster
Telford & Bridgnorth
Walsall
Wolverhampton

*East Midlands*
Gainsborough

*South-west*
Bodmin & Liskeard
Bude
Cinderford & Ross on
  Wye
Plymouth

**Scotland**
Ayr
Alloa
Badenoch
Campbeltown
Dunfermline
Dunoon & Bute
Falkirk
Forres
Girvan
Invergordon & Dingwell
Kirkcaldy
Lochaber
Newton Stewart
Skye & Wester Ross
Stewartry
Stranraer
Sutherland
Western Isles
Wick

**Wales**
Bangor & Caernarfon
  (DA)
Bridgend (SDA)
Cardiff (DA)
Fishguard (DA)
Haverfordwest (DA)
Llanelli (DA)
Newport (DA)
Pontypool & Cwmbran
  (DA)
Porthmadoc & Ffestiniog
  (DA)
Pwllheli (DA)
Swansea (DA/IA)

[3] Accrington previously a non-assisted area.
  Rossendale a development area.
[4] Previously a non-assisted area.

Northern Ireland has its own system of investment incentives outside the framework of the 1982 Act. These are considered separately at § 8.129–8.132, below.

The instruments through which regional aid policy is implemented are: **8.30**

(1) Regional Development Grants;
(2) Selective Financial Assistance;
(3) Government Contract Preferences; and
(4) Government Factory Provision.

In addition, assisted areas attract a number of facilities from European Community Funds.[57]

[57] In addition, that is, to the proportion of the funds administered by the DTI and the statutory agencies (see below at §§ 8.56 *et seq.*) that derive from EEC sources.

**Regional Development Grants**

**8.31**   Regional Development Grants (RDGs) were introduced by the Investment
and Building Grants Act 1971.[58] The relevant provisions of that Act were carried forward as Part I of the Industry Act 1972 and subsequently re-enacted as
Part II of the Industrial Development Act 1982. The provisions of Part II of the
1982 Act were themselves repealed by the Co-operative Development Agency
and Industrial Development Act 1984[59] which substituted a new Part II containing provisions setting out the framework within which the RDG system will now
operate.

**8.32**   Although often described as "mandatory" or "automatic," according to the
terms of the legislation governing their provision RDGs have always been, and
indeed continue to be, discretionary in that the particular statutory stipulations
empower, rather than require, the Secretary of State to make a grant[60] available. The current legislation provides that the Secretary of State may make a
grant to a person in respect of the carrying out of a project of investment in the
productive capacity or productive processes of an undertaking in a development
area.[61] However, a project is not to be eligible for grant unless or except to the
extent that the Secretary of State approves it for grant,[62] further emphasising the
discretionary nature of the RDG.

The exercise of a discretion of this nature was considered by the House of
Lords in *British Oxygen Co.* v. *Minister of Technology.*[63] In this case the Ministry had published guidance stating, *inter alia*, that no grant would be payable in
respect of bulk expenditure on items below a specified unit cost. The company
sought a declaration that the Minister could not decline to make a grant to it (its
expenditure being within the terms of the exclusion) on the ground that a refusal
to consider such expenditure for grant amounted to an abrogation of discretion
rather than its exercise. The House of Lords held that the Minister was within his
rights: the grants were clearly discretionary under the terms of the statute[64] and
the Ministry was under no duty to make grants to any applicant even though that
applicant might be prima facie eligible. Lord Reid drew a distinction between
refusing to hear a case (the company's contention) and adopting a policy: "What
a Ministry or authority must not do is to refuse to listen at all. But a Ministry or
large authority may have to deal already with a multitude of similar applications
and then they will almost certainly have evolved a policy so precise that it could
be called a rule. There can be no objection to that, provided that the authority is
always willing to listen to anyone with something new to say."[65]

[58] To replace investment grants payable under the Industrial Development Act 1966.
[59] s.5 and Sched. 1.
[60] See Ganz *op.cit.* at pp. 35–45.
[61] I.D.A. 1982, s.2(1).
[62] *Ibid.* s.2(4).
[63] [1970] 3 W.L.R. 488, H.L.
[64] The Industrial Development Act 1966. Note that RDGs were, albeit with certain differences,
modelled on investment grants and the nature of the discretion gven to the Minister was virtually
identical. See Ganz, *supra*.
[65] [1970] 3 W.L.R. 488 at p. 495. Lord Reid went on to say that there were only two general grounds
on which the exercise of such a discretion could be impeached, namely bad faith and unreasonab-
leness; if either or both of these elements were present there could be no genuine exercise of the
discretion.

Over the period since RDGs were introduced guidance has been issued on how the power to make an RDG will be exercised in particular cases. In this way "rules" have been laid down as to who or what will or will not qualify for grant and in what circumstances. In the sense that adherence to these "rules" is automatic then eligibility for and approval of a grant will also be automatic in the case of a company and a project within the stated categories of eligibility. However these categories are susceptible to change from time to time to meet what are conceived to be appropriate cases and circumstances and the making of such changes, provided the terms of the Act and of the Regulations made thereunder[66] are not infringed, is not appealable. "Entitlement" to an RDG remains a matter for the exercise of a ministerial discretion rather than a matter of legal right.

Eligibility for grant depends upon "the carrying out of a project of investment **8.33** in the productive capacity or productive processes of an undertaking" in a development area.[67] Productive capacity and productive processes are defined[68] as including respectively both the capacity to produce and the process of producing goods and the capacity to provide and the process of providing services.[69]
Grant is payable in respect of capital expenditure[70]:

(1) on the provision of assets[71]; and
(2) in respect of the provision[72] of jobs[73] comprised in a project.

---

[66] The Co-operative Development Agency and Industrial Development Act (Commencement) Order 1984 (S.I. 1984 No. 1845); The Assisted Areas Order 1984 (S.I. 1984 No. 1844); The Regional Development Grant (Prescribed Percentage, Amount and Limit) Order 1984 (S.I. 1984 No. 1843); and The Regional Development Grant (Qualifying Activities) Order 1984 (S.I. 1984 No. 1846).

[67] I.D.A. 1982, s.2(1).

[68] *Ibid.* s.2(2).

[69] It is a feature of the 1984 reforms that RDGs are now available to companies providing services. Under the previous scheme they were available only to companies in the manufacturing sector.

[70] "Expenditure" is defined (by s.2(7)) in relation to an asset provided by being manufactured, constructed or devised by any person as including "such sum as appears to the Secretary of State to be properly attributable to its provision by that person in that manner, and the sum so attributed shall be treated as having been paid at such time as the Secretary of State may direct."
"Capital Expenditure" is not directly defined in the new Part II save that in s.4(5)(a) "the approved amount of capital expenditure" is defined as "the amount determined by the Secretary of State under section 3(4) above—see § 8.34 below—in approving the project for grant subject, as respects a project the whole or any part of which, at the date of approval, is to be carried out, to any adjustment falling to be made at that time. . . . ."
Under the original 1982 provisions "expenditure of a capital nature" was defined (by the then s.6(2)) as including the capital element in expenditure consisting of instalments under a hire-purchase agreement or otherwise consisting of instalments of, or payments towards, the purchase price of, or cost of providing, the asset in question." There is no comparable specification under the new provisions although the definition of expenditure above is sufficiently wide to permit a continuation of this rule.

[71] "Asset" is defined (by s.2(7)) as meaning "machinery, plant, buildings or works or any part respectively thereof."

[72] "Provision" or "Provide" are defined (s.2(7)) as:
    (a) in relation to jobs, including provision by way of maintaining or safeguarding jobs;
    (b) in relation to machinery or plant, meaning the provision of unused machinery or plant; and
    (c) in relation to a building, including provision by the adaptation of an existing one, or by the purchase of a new one, that is to say one not previously occupied, or, if previously occupied then only by the purchaser, and only as part of arrangements made in contemplation of purchase.

[73] "Jobs" means full-time jobs (s.2(7)).

The investment involved may be in a new or in an existing undertaking[74] and the assets or jobs may be provided in more than one development area.[75] Nevertheless, a project is not eligible for grant without official approval,[76] albeit that that approval may be given where the project has been wholly or partly carried out as well as where the project is to be carried out.[77]

**8.34**    It is provided that the Secretary of State may approve a project for grant if, in his opinion, the project satisfies[78] a number of conditions. These are[79]:

(a) that its purposes are to create new or expand existing productive capacity or to effect a change in the product or in the process of producing it;

(b) that the activities to which it relates are "qualifying activities"; and

(c) that the assets or jobs to be provided are to be, in the case of assets, situated or used or, in the case of jobs, carried out in a development area.

If these conditions cannot be wholly met in that not all of the activities are qualifying activities or not all of the assets are to be situated or used in a development area or not all of the jobs involved are to be carried out in a development area, provided that most of the activities or assets or jobs relating to the project do satisfy the conditions the project may still be eligible for grant. In such cases the Secretary of State may approve so much of the project as, in his opinion, satisfies[80] the conditions.[81] By way of a relaxation of the specifications for approval the Secretary of State is empowered[82] to treat as qualifying activities[83] those activities which are not and to give his approval accordingly.[84]

**8.35**    The basis on which the amount of grant payable is to be determined is[85]:

---

[74] I.D.A. 1982, s.2(2). "Undertaking" is defined (by s.2(7), as including an undertaking carried on otherwise than for profit.
[75] *Ibid.* s.2(3).
[76] *Ibid.* s.2(4).
[77] *Ibid.*
[78] Or, as the case may be, satisfied those conditions on the qualifying date. For grant to be payable the conditions must be satisfied *on the qualifying date.* This is the date at which (s.3(3)):
  (a) in the case of a project the whole of which, at the date of the application for approval, is to be carried out, the date of the receipt of the application;
  (b) in the case of a project which has been wholly carried out at the date of the application for approval, the date when the first asset or job was provided under the project or, if earlier, the date when expenditure was first defrayed on the provision of any asset comprised in the project;
  (c) in the case of a project which has been partly carried out at the date of the application for approval, the date when the first asset or job was provided under the project or, if earlier, the date when expenditure was first defrayed on the provision of any asset comprised in the project.
[79] I.D.A. 1982, s.3.(1).
[80] Or, as the case may be, satisfied the said conditions.
[81] I.D.A. 1982, s.3(2).
[82] *Ibid.*
[83] *Ibid.*, s.5(1) defines "qualifying activities" as "such activities as are specified by order of the Secretary of State made with the consent of the Treasury." The relevant Order is the Regional Development Grant (Qualifying Activities) Order 1984 (S.I. 1984 No. 1846). See Appendix B. to this Chapter.
[84] *Ibid.*, s.3(2).
[85] *Ibid.* s.3(4).

(a) the amount of capital expenditure on assets to be provided by the project[86]; and/or

(b) the number of jobs to be provided by the project.[87]

However, it is the Secretary of State who is charged with making the determination as to what in any case is the amount of capital expenditure or the number of jobs involved.[88] In making this determination the Secretary of State may direct that his approval will extend to such additional assets or jobs as he indicates in his direction.[89]

In any particular case the amount of grant payable in respect of an approved **8.36** project is to be:

(a) in the case of a project which is eligible for grant in respect of both capital expenditure on assets and jobs provided, the higher of:

    (i) the amount which represents the prescribed percentage of the approved amount of capital expenditure[90] reduced, where the prescribed limit for capital expenditure is applicable, by such amount as is required to be deducted to give effect to that limit; and

    (ii) the amount produced by multiplying the approved number of jobs[91] by the prescribed amount.

(b) in the case of a project which is eligible for grant only in respect of capital expenditure, the amount which represents the prescribed percentage of the approved amount of capital expenditure reduced, where a prescribed limit for capital expenditure is applicable, by such amount as is required to be reduced to give effect to that limit;

(c) in the case of a project which is eligible for grant only in respect of jobs provided, the amount produced by multiplying the approved number of jobs by the prescribed amount.[92]

In applying these rules the prescribed percentage for capital expenditure on the provision of assets is 15 per cent.,[93] the prescribed amount for jobs provided is £3,000[94] and the prescribed limit on the amount of grant payable in respect of capital expenditure on the provision of assets is[95]:

---

[86] In making a determination as to the amount of capital expenditure the Secretary of State may take account of the provision of assets of some classes or descriptions but not others: *ibid.* s.3(5)(*a*).

[87] In making a determination as to the number of jobs the Secretary of State may take account of the provision of jobs in one way but not in another, aggregate jobs which are less than full-time and make such other allowance for the effects of the project on employment in any development area or in any part of Northern Ireland as he considers appropriate: *ibid.* s.3(5)(*b*).

[88] *Ibid.* s.3(4).

[89] *Ibid.* s.3(6).

[90] The "approved amount of capital expenditure" is the amount determined by the Secretary of State in approving a project for grant subject, as respects a project the whole or any part of which, at the date of approval is to be carried out, to any adjustment falling to be made at that time: *ibid.* s.4(5)(*a*).

[91] The "approved number of jobs" is the number determined by the Secretary of State in approving the project for grant subject, as respects a project the whole or any part of which, at the date of approval, is to be carried out, to any adjustment falling to be made at that time: *ibid.* s.4(5)(*b*).

[92] *Ibid.* s.4(1).

[93] The Regional Development Grant (Prescribed Percentage, Amount and Limit) Order 1984 (S.I. 1984 No. 1843) Art. 3.

[94] *Ibid.* Art. 4.   [95] *Ibid.* Art. 5.

(1) in the case of a large undertaking[96]:
> (i) where the project in question provides jobs, £10.000 multiplied by the approved number of jobs;
> (ii) where the project in question does not provide jobs, £500;

(2) in the case of any other undertaking:
> (i) where the project in question provides jobs, the larger of £75,000 and £10,000 multiplied by the approved number of jobs;
> (ii) where the project in question does not provide jobs, £75,000.

The time for payment of grant is at the discretion of the Secretary of State.[97] However grant in respect of capital expenditure on the provision of an asset may be paid at any time after the time when the asset is provided or the expenditure is defrayed.[98] Grant in respect of any job may be paid at any time after the time when the job is provided.[99]

**8.37** The award of a grant may be made subject to conditions and in particular subject to a condition for repayment of all or any part of the grant in the event of non-compliance with some other condition subject to which the grant was made.[1]

Conditions may be imposed either when the project is approved for grant or when payment is made.[2]

Under the provisions of Schedule 1 to the Act failure to notify the Department of an event specified in the conditions may constitute a criminal offence.

### Selective financial assistance

**8.38** Selective financial assistance for industry in assisted areas was introduced by section 7 of the Industry Act 1972. During the decade that followed details of the

---

[96] A large undertaking is an undertaking which at the qualifying date for the project in question employed, employs or will employ more than 200 employees each normally required to work 30 or more hours per week—("full time" employees): *ibid.* Art. 5(2).

For the purposes of determining whether an undertaking is or is not a large undertaking: (*ibid.* Art. 6)
> (a) any two employees who are not full-time employees but are normally required to work 15 or more hours per week are to be counted as one full-time employee for the purpose of determining the number of full-time employees; and
> (b) the employees of an undertaking are to include the employees of any associated undertaking

An "associated undertaking": (*ibid.* Art. 7)
> (a) in relation to any undertaking which is carried on by one or more companies, includes all other undertakings carried on by companies which are members of the same group of companies; and
> (b) in relation to any undertaking which is carried on under the direct or indirect control of one or more persons (including companies which are not members of the same group of companies) includes them and any other undertaking carried on under their direct or indirect control.

[97] I.D.A. 1982, s.4(3).
[98] It is a term of any approval for grant of a project which includes the provision of assets that the amount of capital expenditure approved by the Secretary of State is to be subject to revision as the project is carried out: *ibid.* s.3(7).
[99] *Ibid.* s.4(4).
[1] *Ibid.* s.6(1) and (2).
[2] *Ibid.* s.6(1).

scheme were changed[3] insofar as they concerned the terms on which assistance might be given and the form the assistance could take. The relevant provisions are now contained in section 7 of the Industrial Development Act 1982.

Section 7 empowers the Secretary of State, with the consent of the Treasury, **8.39** to provide financial assistance to undertakings wholly or mainly within the assisted areas. The assistance is discretionary although the nature of the discretion and the circumstances of its exercise have produced a regime markedly different from that applying to regional development grants. In the case of regional development grants the assistance was "non-selective" in the sense that if a project fell within the detailed criteria governing the exercise of the discretion a grant would automatically follow. Practice (in pursuance of Departmental policy) rendered the discretion under section 2 essentially a negative one.

In contrast, to obtain assistance under section 7 an applicant company must satisfy the Department not only that its project comes within the terms on which assistance might be given, but also that assistance should be given in the particular case. While statements as to Departmental policy have to some extent "fleshed out" the broad principles set out in the section these statements are much more in the nature of guidelines indicating what is not acceptable rather than being the kind of formalised and structured rules of practice through which the system of regional development grant operates. Under section 7 the discretion is very much a positive one; that, after all, is what "selectivity" is about.[4]

Section 7(1) provides that assistance may be provided for specified purposes **8.40** where the Secretary of State is of the opinion that the assistance is likely to provide, maintain or safeguard employment in any part of the assisted areas. The purposes for which assistance may be provided are set out in section 7(2). They are:

(1) to promote the development or modernisation of an industry;
(2) to promote the efficency of an industry;
(3) to create, expand or sustain productive capacity in an industry, or in undertakings in an industry;
(4) to promote the reconstruction, reorganisation or conversion of an industry or of undertakings in an industry;
(5) to encourage the growth of, or the proper distribution of undertakings in an industry;
(6) to encourage arrangements for ensuring that any contraction of an industry proceeds in an orderly way.

Financial assistance under section 7 may be provided "on any terms or con- **8.41** ditions and by any description of investment or lending or guarantee or by making grants."[5] Four methods of aid provision are specifically mentioned, however. These are:

---

[3] By the Industry Acts of 1975, 1979 and 1980.
[4] See generally Ganz *op.cit.*
[5] I.D.A. 1982, s.7(3).

(1) investment by acquisition[6] of loan or share capital in any company[7];

(2) investment by the acquisition of any undertaking or of any assets;

(3) a loan, whether secured or unsecured, and whether or not carrying interest or interest at a commecial rate;

(4) any form of insurance or guarantee to meet any contingency, and in particular to meet default on payment of a loan or of interest on a loan or non-fulfilment of a contract.

During the 1970s the principal instruments for dispensing aid under section 7 were loans at concessionary rates[8] and interest relief grants, which were given as an alternative to concessionary rate loans and were available in respect of funds obtained from commercial sources. The advantage of this form of assistance was felt to be that it permitted a company to seek funds from private sources and produced the same quantum of benefit as a concessionary loan but placed less strain on public expenditure and also avoided the full vetting procedure applied to safeguard public money which would come into operation when a loan was provided.[9]

It has been estimated[10] that at one point over 70 per cent. of regional selective assistance under section 7 was provided by way of interest relief grants.

**8.42**      At the present time regional selective assistance may be provided under one or more of four schemes. These are:

### (a) *Project grants*

Assistance may be given in the form of a grant towards the fixed and working capital costs of projects in the mining, manufacturing and construction industries. Projects qualifying for assistance fall into two broad categories:

*Category A.* This relates to new projects and expansions which create additional employment. In such cases account is taken of the amount of new employment to be provided in determining an application.

*Category B.* This relates to projects which do not provide extra jobs but which maintain or safeguard employment. Modernisation programmes or rationalisation schemes would fall within this category. In such cases the implications of maintaining and/or safeguarding the employment involved are taken into account in assessing an application.

The amount and terms of any assistance provided are negotiated individually as the minimum necessary to bring about the benefits associated with the proj-

---

[6] Including an acquisition effected by the Secretary of State through another company, being a company formed for the purpose of giving financial assistance under Pt. III of the 1982 Act or Pt. II of the Industry Act 1972.

[7] However, assistance is not to be given in this form unless:
    (i) the Secretary of State is satisfied that it cannot, or cannot appropriately, be given in any other way; and
    (ii) the company consents to the acquisition of its shares or stock—I.D.A. 1982, s.7(4).

[8] Towards normal capital (including working capital) requirements.

[9] See Sharp, *The Industry Act 1975* at pp. 24 *et seq.*

[10] See Ganz *op.cit.* at pp. 22 *et seq.*

ect. It follows that other public sector finance[11] procured in relation to the project such as regional development grants, grants towards training costs, mortgage or amortisation finance[12] will be taken into account in determining the amount of grant payable.

Payments of grants are made in instalments related to expenditure on the project and progress towards its stated objectives.

(b) *Office and service industries scheme*

Special grants are available to "non-manufacturing" activities of all industries[13] and to service industries falling within Orders XXII to XXVI of the 1968 Standard Industrial Classification.[14] The purpose of the grants is to encourage growth in employment in these industries through projects that would not otherwise go ahead in the assisted areas. Activities which may qualify for assistance include new projects, expansion *in situ* of existing operations or moves to assisted areas. However, projects must normally have a genuine choice of location between the assisted areas and the rest of Great Britain. Projects serving primarily local needs, such as retail shops, garages, high-street banking services, etc., do not qualify under this scheme.

Assistance may take three forms, namely:

(1) Job Creation Grants;
(2) Employee Removal Grants; and
(3) Feasibility Grants.

(c) *In-plant training scheme*

This scheme applies to manufacturing projects providing a minimum of 25 new jobs in Development Areas in cases where the training element is an essential part of the project. Normal replacement training to acquire or improve basic skills is not eligible for assistance.

Assistance takes the form of a grant which covers 40 per cent. of eligible costs[15] and attracts a matching contribution from the European Social Fund. It is thus possible to receive assistance amounting to 80 per cent. of eligible costs.

Payment of the grant is by instalments throughout the training programme.

The grant payable under this scheme may be provided in addition to a Project Grant or a grant under the Office and Service Industries Scheme.

(d) *Exchange risk guarantee scheme*

Companies in assisted areas may be able to obtain fixed-interest loans from the European Investment Bank for investment projects creating or safeguarding

---

[11] Finance from certain public sector bodies such as the British Technology Group, the Scottish and Welsh Development Agencies count as private sector finance for this purpose.

[12] From local authorities or new town development corporations or in respect of the purchase of government factories.

[13] *e.g.* offices, research and development units and training centres.

[14] Orders XXII–XXVI are set out in Annex C to this Chapter.

[15] Defined as the basic costs of trainees and instructors plus the net cost of materials consumed.

jobs, or from the European Coal and Steel Community for investment projects providing new job opportunities for ex coal and steel workers. Such loans are usually made in foreign currency with the interest and capital repayments also to be made in foreign currency. The essence of the Exchange Risk Guarantee Scheme is that it covers private sector borrowers against the risk of exchange losses on these loans. Under the scheme borrowers take on only a fixed sterling liability while being able to take advantage of lower foreign currency interest rates. The government takes the exchange risk in return for an annual premium, usually of the order of 1 per cent.

**8.43**     Over and above the statutory requirement that the project should have a beneficial effect on employment within the assisted area the Department has issued guidelines setting out criteria which applicants for assistance under any of the section 7 schemes must meet. These are:

(a) *Viability*

Projects should have good prospects of achieving viability without further government assistance.

(b) *Additionality*

The Secretary of State must be satisfied that the project will not go ahead at all or on the basis proposed without assistance. More specifically, the provision of assistance must lead to a significant change in the nature or scale of the project, or a significant advance in its timing, or to a desirable change in its location. The amount of assistance offered is the minimum necessary to achieve additional benefits provided by the projects and will take account of other finance from the public sector, such as regional development grants.

(c) *Contribution to economy*

Projects should strengthen the regional and national economy, for example, by improving efficiency or by introducing new technology or products and thereby provide more productive and more secure jobs in the assisted area.

(d) *Finance*

The applicant company should provide the greater part of the finance required for the project from its own funds or from other private sector sources.[16] For this purpose loans from the EEC and money provided on commercial terms by public sector bodies such as the British Technology Group and Scottish and Welsh Development Agencies count as private sector finance.

---

[16] In general, selective assistance is normally directed to those projects where a contribution of around 10 per cent. of the project costs will bring the risks within the limits allowed for in a company's general investment criteria.

(e) *Timing*

Assistance will not normally be given for projects which have already begun.

Application for assistance should be made on Form RSA/A and submitted to **8.44**
the Department of Trade and Industry. The Department will require the following information which should be sent with the completed application form, or,
insofar as it is not immediately available, as soon as possible thereafter.

(a) *Information about the company*

What is required here is a summary of the company's activities and two copies
of each of the last three years' audited accounts. Where detailed accounts are
not included in the audited accounts this information for the past three years
should also be provided. The Department may require sight of later accounts
during the course of their investigation.

(b) *Information about the project*

An outline of the project indicating its purpose and rationale is what is
required here. Special features such as location, product, manufacturing process, industrial significance, markets involved and the project's relationship with
the existing activities of the company should also be emphasised.

(c) *Estimates of future performance*

What are required under this head are estimates of cash flow, and forward
trading estimates commencing at the date of the last audited balance sheet and
continuing for three of the company's financial years after the year in which capital expenditure on the project is expected to start. The forecasts should be in the
form of summarised manufacturing, trading and profit and loss accounts.[17]

(d) *Statement of capital costs*

An itemised statement of capital costs to be incurred during the first three
years indicating the year in which each item of cost is likely to arise.

(e) *Information about project finance*

Essentially what is required here is evidence that private sector capital is committed to the project. For example, an undertaking from the company's bankers
confirming the loan or overdraft facilities should be submitted.

---

[17] This information can be provided in the form set out in the pro formas provided by the Department.

(f) *An indication as to the amount of assistance required*

**8.45**

*Form of
Assistance
Provided*

The amount of assistance to be provided under section 7 and the terms on which it will be made available will be the subject of negotiation between the company and the Department. It should be emphasised however that what assistance is provided will be forthcoming on the basis that it is the minimum necessary to bring about the additional benefits associated with the project.

Assistance will normally be provided in the form of a grant, payable in instalments related to expenditure on the project and the achievement of its forecast objectives.[18]

## Government factory provision

**8.46**

*Factory
Provision*

In the assisted areas the Department of Trade and Industry through the English Industrial Estates Corporation and the Scottish and Welsh Development Agencies operates a factory building programme and provides new and existing factories for sale or rent.[19] Factories may be provided for projects creating additional employment or for rehousing an operation already in business in the general area of the factory where existing premises may be unsuitable.

Depending on the estate, industrial premises may be available, from very small workshop units of 50 square metres up to large detached units of 2,300 square meters. On some estates even larger units may be provided.

All factories are built to as near a state of completion as possible and are designed to suit the widest possible range of manufacturing activities. If the necessary resources are available factories may be built to companies' own specifications. Large factories and others with unusual features, however, are built only for sale on completion.

Where space permits extensions may also be built for existing tenants.

**8.47**     Premises may be acquired under the factories provision scheme as follows:

(a) *Under a lease or tenancy agreement*

*Terms of
Provision*

The terms of any such lease or tenancy agreement will conform to normal commercial practice and rent will be charged at the normal commercial rate having regard to the type of factory offered. Each lease or tenancy agreement contains a rent review clause permitting reviews every three or seven years.

Where the lease is for a long period it is possible to provide for "rent-free" periods to be available.

(b) *Disposal of long lease*

Where estate management considerations permit premises may be disposed of on long leases of 99 or 125 years. These leases may be purchased for a capital sum together with an appropriate ground rent. In some cases it is possible for the

---

[18] Only in exceptional circumstances will other forms of assistance be considered.
[19] Under the provisions of the English Industrial Estates Corporation Act 1981, s.3, Scottish Development Agency Act 1975, s.2(2); and the Welsh Development Agency Act 1975, s.1(3).

purchase price of the lease to be spread over a period of 24 years at a fixed rate of interest.

(c) *Disposal of the freehold*

On some sites it may be possible to acquire the freehold of the premises, the more especially so in the case of premises which are large or have unusual features. As with purchases of long leases it may be possible to spread payment of the purchase price over a period up to 24 years at a fixed rate of interest.

The provision of government factories is to a limited extent connected with the making available of selective financial assistance (either regional or national), the point being that any assistance or rent-free period available will be taken into account when considering the respective applications. Where companies intend to apply for selective financial assistance they should submit their applications to the Department before commiting themselves to an agreement to occupy premises.

**8.48**

*Factory Provision and Selective Financial Assistance*

**Government contract preferences**

The government, acting in furtherance of administrative policy rather than under the authority of a specific statutory provision, operates two contract preference schemes open to firms in development areas and Northern Ireland. The respective schemes are:

**8.49**

*The general contract preference scheme*

Under the scheme preferential opportunities are provided for approved manufacturers to secure orders from government purchasing departments, nationalised industries and certain other public bodies. Under this scheme orders are allocated to manufacturers if, taking account of price, quality, delivery date an other considerations, their tenders are broadly as attractive as tenders received from undertakings outside the development area.

(b) *The special contract preference scheme*

This scheme is operated by government purchasing departments and the Post Office. Under its terms, if a firm has been unsuccessful with its first tender, it will be given an opportunity to requote for 25 per cent. of the order at a price which will not increase the total cost.

**EEC funds and regional aid provision**

Loan finance on favourable terms may be available to companies in assisted areas from two EEC institutions, the European Investment Bank (EIB) and the European Coal and Steel Community (ECSC). Provided that the borrowing company can furnish security loans from these institutions are treated as private

**8.50**

sector funding for the purposes of regional selective assistance with the consequence that loan finance from these sources may be additional to that obtained under section 7 of the Industrial Development Act 1982.

**8.51**

*EIB Loans*
*(1) Terms*

EIB loans are available to companies engaged in manufacturing, the service industries and tourism for up to 50 per cent. of the fixed capital costs[20] of investment projects in assisted areas. The loans are normally for terms of seven to ten years at fixed interest rates and are usually taken in a cocktail of foreign currencies.[21] Capital repayments begin two years after the drawing of the loan and are made in half-yearly instalments of capital and interest.

Exchange risk cover may be available in respect of those projects qualifying for assistance under section 7.[22]

**8.52**

*(2) Guarantees*

An EIB loan in excess of £4,250,000 must be negotiated directly between the borrowing company and the EIB. Loans from this figure down to a minimum of £15,000 are processed by central government departments[23] as agents for the EIB where the company is engaged in manufacturing or in the service industries.[24] Under the agency agreement the department concerned is required to give the EIB a guarantee of repayment. A counter-guarantee is normally sought from the company's bankers or, where appropriate, from the company's parent organisation. If an acceptable counter-guarantee is not available the Department will consider taking other security and make an annual charge for the guarantee of one per cent. of the outstanding balance of the loan.

*(3) Agency*
*Agreements*

Agency arrangements have also been made with the Midland Bank, the Clydesdale Bank and the Scottish and Welsh Development Agencies. These arrangements are intended to help finance small scale industrial and tourism ventures creating or safeguarding employment and will allow for sub-loans of between £15,000 and £100,000 in foreign currencies at interest rates lower than those available for comparable sterling funds. As with loans arranged through the agency of central government, exchange risk cover may be available.

**8.53**

*ESCS Loans*

ESCS loans are available for projects creating or safeguarding employment for coal or steel workers. The loans are of two types, namely:

(1) Direct loans, for investment projects in the coal and steel industries; and
(2) Conversion Loans, for investment projects which lead to the resettlement or redeployment of redundant coal and steel works.

ESCS loans may be obtained for up to 50 per cent. of the fixed capital costs[25] of the relevant investment project. Loans are normally for eight years at fixed

---

[20] Loans are not available for working capital requirements.
[21] Single currency loans may be arranged if required.
[22] See above at § 8.42.
[23] Department of Trade and Industry, Scottish Economic Planning Department, Welsh Industry Department and the Northern Ireland Department of Commerce.
[24] For tourism projects the relevant agents are the English, Scottish and Welsh Tourist Boards, as appropriate.
[25] But not working capital costs.

interest rates with capital repayments phased over the last four years of the loan. The loan will be in foreign currency and exchange risk cover may be available.[26]

Direct loans are available to companies in the private sector of the coal and steel industries and, of course, to the public corporations. These loans are provided for rationalisation and/or modernisation projects intended to safeguard employment in coal and steel areas.

Conversion loans are available to any manufacturing business which will create jobs in an area affected by the closure or rundown of local coal or steel industries subject to the following conditions, namely that:

(1) a minimum of two new jobs must be created; and
(2) in offering new jobs created by the project priority must be given to redundant coal and steel workers.

However, the loans are limited to businesses with up to 50 employees.
Conversion loans may attract a 3 per cent. interest rebate annually during the first five years of the loan, depending on the number of jobs provided for ex coal and steel workers.


## ASSISTANCE FROM GOVERNMENT AGENCIES


In addition to (or in some cases as an alternative to) aid provided by central government departments companies may be eligible for financial assistance under programmes operated by various agencies set up by government but, within the parameters of government policy, working independently of central government. Some of these agencies have a purely regional jurisdiction being charged with promoting industrial development and related activities in a given area; others operate without geographical restrictions but for the furtherance of a specific area of activity; yet others operate under restrictions as to geography and as to area of activity. Of these bodies the most important from the standpoint of provision of finance for companies are:

(i) The Development Agencies;
(ii) The Development Boards;
(iii) The Council for Small Industries in Rural Areas;
(iv) The British Technology Group; and
(v) The English Industrial Estates Corporation.


### The Development Agencies

Following upon the two general elections of 1974 the incoming government embarked upon a substantial legislative programme designed to provide the

---

[26] See above at §§ 8.51–8.52 for facilities associated with these loans.

statutory framework within which its policies for the regeneration of British industry[27] could be implemented. An important part of this programme was the establishment of independent agencies, financed by government funds, to foster and promote industrial and commercial development in the regions for which they were given responsibility. The Scottish and Welsh Development Agency Acts of 1975[28] established agencies for Scotland and Wales respectively. Subsequently a Development Agency was established for Northern Ireland although in 1982 its functions were merged with those of the Northern Ireland Department of Commerce which now operates through a new "unified" arm, the Industrial Development Board for Northern Ireland. The activities of the Board in relation to company finance are considered below at §§ 8.129 *et seq.*

**8.58**    Although the terms of the two Acts are not identical the purposes for which the agencies were established and the statutory functions they are bound to discharge are virtually the same, as are the powers vested in them for the discharge of those functions.

The purposes for which the agencies were established are, within the region concerned[29]:

*Purposes for
which Agencies
may Discharge
Statutory
Functions*

(a)  furthering economic development[30] and, in that connection the provision, maintenance and safeguarding of employment;

(b)  the promotion of industrial efficiency and international competitiveness; and

(c)  furthering the improvement of the environment.

**8.59**    The functions to be discharged by the agencies in furthering their statutory functions are[31]:

*Statutory
functions of
Agencies*

(a)  providing or assisting in the provision of finance to persons carrying on or intending to carry on industrial undertakings[32];

(b)  carrying on, or establishing and carrying on, whether by themselves or jointly with any other person, industrial undertakings[33];

(c)  otherwise promoting or assisting the establishment, growth, modernisation or development of industry or any undertaking in an industry[34];

(d)  providing or adopting sites and providing, adopting, modernising or reconstructing premises for industrial undertakings, or assisting any other person to do any of those things, and providing or assisting in the provision of related services or facilities[35];

---

[27] See further the White Paper, *The Regeneration of British Industry* (1975) Cmnd. 5710.
[28] Scottish Development Agency Act 1975 (S.D.A.) and Welsh Development Agency Act 1975 (W.D.A.).
[29] S.D.A., s.2(1); W.D.A., s.1(2).
[30] *Ibid.* as amended by Industry Act 1980, ss.1(2) and (3).
[31] S.D.A., s.2(2); W.D.A., s.1(3).
[32] *Ibid.* s.2(2)(*a*); *ibid.* s.1(3)(*b*).
[33] *Ibid.* s.2(2)(*h*); *ibid.* s.1(3)(*c*). These functions may only be exercised through a company or (additionally in Scotland) a partnership firm.
[34] *Ibid.* s.2(2)(*a*); *ibid.* s.1(3)(*d*); in both cases as amended by Industry Act 1980, ss.1(2) and (3).
[35] *Ibid.* s.2(2)(*d*). The corresponding provisions in WDA are slightly different, s.1(3)(*f*) empowering the agency "to provide sites, premises, services and facilities for industrial undertakings."

(e) managing or assisting in the management of sites and premises for industrial undertakings[36];

(f) undertaking or assisting the undertaking of the development, redevelopment and improvement of the environment[37];

(g) bringing derelict land into use or improving its appearance[38];

(h) promoting the private ownership of interests in industrial undertakings by the disposal of securities and other property held by the agency or any of their subsidiaries[39]; and

(i) such other functions as may be conferred under the terms of the relevant Act.[40]

Furthermore the agencies are empowered[41] to do anything, whether in the region concerned or elsewhere, which is calculated to facilitate the discharge of their functions or is incidental or conducive to their discharge.[42]

Clearly, viewing the agencies as a source of direct finance, the exercise of powers in discharge of the functions of providing finance and of carrying on, or establishing and carrying on, industrial undertakings are of prime importance. In relation to these functions the agencies are specifically empowered[43]:

*Specific Powers in Relation to Providing Finance*

(1) to acquire, hold and dispose of securities;

(2) to form bodies corporate;

(3) to form partnerships with other persons;

(4) to make loans; and

(5) to guarantee obligations (whether arising out of loans or otherwise) incurred by other persons.

Additionally, the agencies are empowered to make grants although only with

---

[36] S.D.A., s.2(2)(*e*); W.D.A., s.1(3)(*g*).

[37] *Ibid.* s.2(2)(*g*); *ibid.* s.1(3)(*i*).

[38] *Ibid.* s.2(2)(*h*); *ibid.* s.1(3)(*h*).

[39] *Ibid.* s.2(2)(*j*); *ibid.* s.1(3)(*j*) added by Industry Act 1980, s.1(2) and (3).

[40] S.D.A., s.2(2)(*i*).

[41] S.D.A., s.2(3); W.D.A., s.1(6).

[42] In particular, but without prejudice to the general enabling powers contained in S.D.A., s.2(3) and W.D.A., s.1(6), the agencies are given (by S.D.A., s.2(4) and W.D.A., s.1(7)):

    (a) to acquire, hold and dispose of securities;

    (b) to form bodies corporate;

    (c) to form partnerships with other persons;

    (d) to make loans;

    (e) to guarantee obligations (arising out of loans or otherwise) incurred by other persons;

    (f) to make grants;

    (g) to act as agent for other persons;

    (h) to acquire and dispose of premises, plant, machinery and equipment and other property;

    (i) to manage land, to develop land or to carry out works on land, and to maintain or assist in the maintenance of any such works;

    (j) to make land, premises, plant, machinery and equipment and other property available for use by other persons;

    (k) to reclaim land from the sea;.

    (l) to provide or assist in the provision of advisory or other services or facilities or any person or undertaking; and

   (m) to promote or assist in the promotion of publicity relating to the functions of the agency.

[43] S.D.A., s.2(6); W.D.A., s.1(8).

the consent of the Secretary of State either specifically or in accordance with a general authority given by him.[44]

Within these broad statutory parameters each agency has developed its own programmes for providing financial assistance to companies.

### 8.60 Scottish Development Agency finance

*SDA Finance (1) Small Business Schemes*

The SDA offers financial assistance to businesses, especially small businesses, by way of loans, equity participation, acquisition of preference shares or a combination of these. Projects eligible for such assistance are those which will improve the economy and:

(1) maintain or increase job opportunities; or
(2) make, or have potential to make, a contribution to exports—either directly or by reducing the need for imports; or
(3) hold promise of significant further developments.

Projects in urban areas of high unemployment, rural areas suffering from depopulation and areas affected by coal and steel plant closure are given special priority for financial assistance.

Any investment or loan will be considered by the Agency in the light of other sources of finance that might be available. Thus any other institutional participation, any relevant bank finance and the proprietor's own capital contribution would be taken into account.

**8.61**

*Types of Finance*

Assistance involving equity participation or the taking up of preference shares is negotiated with the company concerned according to the needs and merits of the case. Assistance by way of loan finance only, however, may be provided under "off the peg" schemes, the terms of which may differ according to the location of the project, the employment factor and the amount of finance applied for. Such loans are primarily designed to provide capital to assist the development of manufacturing and service industries.

**8.62**

*Loans— General terms*

*and Conditions*

Loans under these schemes are made in respect of building, the purchase of equipment and working capital. The normal repayment periods allowed are:

(a) Building Loans—up to a maximum of twenty years;
(b) Equipment Loans—up to a maximum of five years; and
(c) Working Capital Loans—up to a maximum of five years.

*Repayment*

Loans may be repayable either monthly, quarterly or half-yearly.[45] By special arrangement low interest[46] loans made in coal and steel plant closure areas are required to be repaid in monthly instalments over eight years.

In certain circumstances a moratorium on capital or interest, or both, for

---

[44] *Ibid.* s.2(7); *ibid.* s.1(9).
[45] The SDA recommend that smaller businesses opt for the more frequent repayment intervals in order to minimise the effect on the company's cash flow.
[46] See above at § 8.55.

periods of up to two years may be considered in order to assist the business in its early stages.

The SDA policy with regard to interest rates imposed is that a differential is operated as between businesses in large towns and cities and those in rural areas. Companies operating in large towns and cities can expect to be required to pay interest at rates not less than those paid by commercial firms of the highest standing. Companies operating in rural areas can expect a rate lower by up to 0.875 per cent.[47] on a corresponding loan for an urban project. If the project has significant job-creation prospects a further reduction of up to 3 per cent. is possible.

*Interest*

Loans granted in coal and steel closure areas under ECSC schemes or from the EIB may be obtained via the SDA. Details of those are given above at §§ 8.50–8.55.

It is the SDA's policy to provide loans on security where this is possible and appropriate, the nature and extent of the security taken depending on the merits of each case. Where loan finance is to be provided to a company the directors may be required to give personal guarantees, jointly and severally, in addition to the security provided by the company.

*Security*

A further standard condition of an SDA loan is that the company is required to submit annual audited accounts together with periodic management accounts during the repayment period. Furthermore the borrower is required to submit to visits by members of the Agency's Advisory Staff during this period.

*Submission of
Accounts
Inspection*

The SDA require applications for loans to be accompanied by:

**8.63**

(1) a description of the project for which finance is required;
(2) any estimates and plans made in relation to the projects;
(3) information as to the basis and assumptions on which these estimates and plans have been made; and
(4) in the case of existing businesses:
    (a) audited balance sheets and profit and loss accounts for at least the two previous years' trading; and
    (b) cash and profit forecasts for at least the first twelve months trading after advancement of the loan.
(5) in the case of new businesses, cash and profit forecasts as in 4(b) above.

*Loan
Application
Requirements*

A report on the project by the Agency's Development Officer and Advisory Accountant will be prepared following upon receipt of the application together

**8.64**

---

[47] At the time of writing the rates were as follows:
    (1) *Urban loans* (whether (Building, Equipment or Working Capital)
    Up to 5 years—12.875 per cent.
    Over 5 years but not over 10 years—13.25 per cent.
    Over 10 years but not over 15 years—13.50 per cent.
    Over 15 years but not over 20 years—13.00 per cent.
    (2) *Rural Area Loans* (whether Building, Equipment or Working Capital)
    Up to 5 years—12 per cent.
    Over 5 years but not over 20 years—$12\frac{1}{2}$ per cent.

*Appraisal* with all the required information. In making an appraisal the Agency is concerned to ensure that the proposed enterprise is founded upon a sound economic basis, that repayment is feasible within the relevant period and that the applicant company can meet the residual costs in excess of the requested investment.

If the application is rejected the Agency is not obliged to give reasons for its decision.

**8.65** Where the Agency is prepared to provide finance the type of assistance offered will be at the discretion of the Agency, the size and nature of the offer *Offers of* being determined by the size and total financing of the project. The offer of a *Assistance* loan will remain open for the duration of the period stated in the letter of offer subject to the completion of legal arrangements. Offers may be withdrawn if not taken up by the company within the stated period, unless the reason for the delay is accepted by the Agency.

**8.66** Loans made do not normally exceed 80 per cent. of the eligible costs of the project. However, subject to satisfactory repayments on primary loans the SDA *Amount of* is prepared to consider further requests for additional projects.
*Loans* Loans for small business projects are normally limited to amount to a maximum of £150,000. Larger sums may however be negotiated with the Agency's Investment Division.

**8.67** The SDA's Loan Schemes for Small Businesses are of three types namely:

*Loan Schemes* (a) Building Loans;
*for Small* (b) Equipment Loans; and
*Businesses* (c) Working Capital Loans.

**8.68 Building loans**

Under the Building Loans Scheme the SDA is prepared to consider applications for loans towards the cost of:

*Eligible Project*
*Costs* (1) the purchase of new sites;
(2) the erection of new premises or the improvement or extension of buildings on land already held by the applicant company;
(3) the purchase of existing buildings with a view to the adaptation or conversion; or
(4) the improvement and modernisation of existing accommodation.[48]

In addition to these items the costs of site preparation, of installation of services and of solicitors', architects' and other professional fees are regarded as eligible costs of the project.

**8.69** Building loans are normally granted which impose obligations on the borrower with regard to the following matters:

[48] Including the provision of fire precautions.

(a) *Plans*

Any plans should be prepared (normally by a registered architect) and submitted to the Agency for approval along with the application. When planning permission and/or other local authority approval is required this must be obtained before the loan can be paid over.

(b) *Insurance*

Where the buildings are to form all or part of the security for the loan they are required to be adequately insured by the borrower against the risk of loss or damage by fire, storm, impact and explosion. The policy must be in the name of the borrower and endorsed in favour of the Agency as heritable creditors.

Responsibility for paying the premium on the policy rests with the borrower and the premium receipts must be produced for the Agency's inspection immediately after they fall due and have been paid.

(c) *Repairs*

The borrower is required to keep the premises in good repair to the satisfaction of the Agency during the whole of the loan repayment period.

(d) *Change in use of premises*

Change of use of the premises constitutes a "determining event" with the consequence that if at any time during the loan repayment period there occurs a change of use of the premises, the Agency may, at its discretion, call in the balance of the loan still outstanding together with any interest thereon.

Where the Agency has undertaken to make finance available by way of a **8.70** Building Loan, payment of the loan will normally be made by instalments as the work proceeds, with the final payment being made when the building is completed.

Where the loan is for purchase of an existing property the whole loan will be paid on completion of the conveyancing formalities.

**Equipment loans** **8.71**

Equipment loans are available towards the cost of purchasing equipment necessary for the carrying on or expansion of the company's business. Loans will only be made in respect of equipment approved on technical grounds by the Agency.

Applications must contain full details of the equipment, its costs, together with the supplier's quotation. No order should be placed until the loan application has been approved.

Once the order has been placed there must be no alteration in the make or type of equipment from that detailed in the application except where (and even here only with the Agency's agreement) such a change becomes necessary or desirable because of prolonged delivery or some other good reason.

Failure to observe this condition will invalidate the loan.

**8.72**    **Working capital loans**[49]

The Agency may provide companies with loans towards its working capital requirements where such are related to the expansion, development or reorganisation of its business.

Working Capital Loans may be paid in a lump sum or by instalments according to the company's requirements.

**8.73**

*SDA Finance*
*(2) Investments*
*over £50,000*

SDA assistance in excess of £50,000 tends to be tailor-made funding being provided in what is considered to be the form most suitable for the individual project. The principal criterion for investment is that of commercial viability.

The policy of the Agency is to provide assistance both to established businesses and to new ventures, in the latter case the Agency being particularly interested in innovative high technology areas of activity.[50]

**8.74**

*Application*
*and Appraisal*

Project appraisal is undertaken by the investment unit staff of the Agency. In general an application for SDA financial assistance should contain (where possible)[51]:

(1) three years audited accounts;
(2) cash flow projections for the following two years (the first year on a monthly basis with the second on a quarterly basis);
(3) projected trading accounts and balance sheets; and
(4) a statement of the rationale and assumptions behind the business ideas and projections.

**8.75**      The SDA frequently provides finance in conjunction with the clearing banks and other financial institutions as part of an overall financial package.

**8.76**

*SDA Finance*
*(3) "Products"*

The SDA also enters into commitments to assist in the economic development of localities within its area. In particular it has entered into "Proper Agreements" with local and regional authorities providing for funds to be made available to stimulate economic activity and making available co-ordinating staff with special responsibilities for the development of these areas.

Additionally the Agency is active in the development of the Clydebank Enterprise Zone. Apart from the provision of finance in any of the ways detailed

---

[49] The Agency may acquire shares in any kind of company pursuing an activity consistent with the SDA's general purposes. Working capital may therefore also be provided as ordinary or preference shares.

[50] Especially in the fields of health care and electronics.

[51] New ventures will clearly have difficulty in supplying information as to past performances. In these cases the SDA's appraisal will be on the basis of the company's business plan and projections.

above and in the provision of factories on terms allowing for up to two years without payment of rent, the Agency in partnership with the Bank of Scotland, has set up the Clydebank Enterprise Fund Ltd., a company created to provide low interest loans to help fund business projects within Clydebank District and the Enterprise Zone.

*(4) Clydebank Enterprise Trust Ltd.*

The intention is that the Fund's resources be channelled into the widest range of business projects including retail, commercial, professional and industrial concerns and, although primarily directed towards new ventures it nevertheless is prepared to consider applications from established businesses for finance to assist with new projects.

Applicants will need to show that sufficient funding is not available from normal commercial sources and must be prepared to bank with the Bank of Scotland.

The Fund will make loans of up to £25,000 normally unsecured for periods of up to ten years at an interest rate of up to five per cent. per annum. Loans are repayable in equal quarterly instalments with the interest rate reviewable after five years. If necessary the Fund will be prepared to consider moratoria on the repayment of capital for up to two years.

### Welsh Development Agency finance

**8.77**

The WDA operates a factory building and letting/selling programme at numerous locations throughout Wales on a similar basis to that initiated by the Department of Trade and Industry and operated by the English Industrial Estates Corporation in England.[52] It also provides grants for the conversion of redundant farm and other buildings in rural areas into workshops suitable for industrial use. Its primary role, however, is as a source of finance for businesses situated in or relocating to Wales.[53]

Finance may be available from the WDA.

---

[52] See above at § 8.46 and below at §§ 8.123 *et seq.*

[53] WDA grants are available towards the cost of converting redundant buildings in rural areas of Clwyd, Gwynedd, Dyfed and Gwent for approved business use.

Grants will usually cover 35 per cent. of the actual costs of conversion work together with the costs of professional fees. At least £1,000 will require to be spent before projects will qualify for grants; maximum eligible expenditure will normally be £50,000. Projects with total costs exceeding £50,000 will be considered on their merits. Approved projects may in addition qualify for regional development grants and capital allowances.

Eligible projects are not confined to those intended to be accepted by the applicants but may also include conversion undertaken where the finished building is to be leased to others. In considering applications the WDA has regard to the existing supply of business premises in the areas concerned. The grant is discretionary and the Agency's decision in any case is final.

Any application for grant must be made and approved before works commence. Applications should be accompanied by drawings and costings. Building regulations and planning consents must be obtained before grant can be paid.

The WDA will undertake an appraisal of the project to ensure that the extent and nature of the works represent value for money. Claims for reimbursement of expenses must be supported by receipts and/or other evidence of costs actually incurred. In the event of the actual costs proving to be lower than estimates submitted at the time of application the WDA may reduce its contribution *pro rata*.

Grant is paid only in respect of works completed to the satisfaction of the Agency.

Applicants are required to ensure that the premises are reasonably maintained and adequately

(a) *A development capital.* This is normally provided by the Agency direct in various forms ranging from loans at commercial or, in some cases, reduced rates of interest, to ordinary shares.

(b) *As venture capital.* This is normally provided through the Agency's subsidiary, Hafren Investment Finance Ltd, and usually takes the form of a package of subscriptions for ordinary and preferences shares.

(c) *As start-up or development capital.* This category deals with those cases where the Agency uses its facility to arrange ECSC and EIB loans.[54]

**8.78**  **(1) Development capital**

Development capital may be provided by the WDA in the form of ordinary shares, preference shares, secured or unsecured loans or in a combination of these. WDA has given the following examples of what it describes as typical investments illustrating the kinds of packages they have put together or in which they have participated.

**Company A.** Relatively new company in new technology with high risk project and large market potential—£50,000 share capital and no reserves.
Agency investment: £100,000 cumulative redeemable convertible Preference shares.
Term: five years; Coupon: 10 per cent. gross;
Redemption—if not converted: par + 10 per cent.
Agency conversion option at any time for five years of that proportion of Preference shares to give 30 per cent. Ordinary shareholding in the company. Principal shareholder buy-back option—exercisable in event of Agency conversion until the end of the 7th year—to re-purchase Ordinary shares at a price determined by the higher of:
(a) par
(b) 30 per cent. of the net assets of the company
(c) 30 per cent. of the average of the previous two years' profits times 8, i.e. at a P/E of 8.
NOTE: The P/E ratio chosen will be substantially less than the average P/E in that sector of industry in which the company operates, thus giving the major shareholder the opportunity of making a substantial capital gain at the time of repurchase of the Agency's Ordinary shares and subsequent re-sale to a third party.

insured for a period of five years after payment of a grant. If, during that period, the premises are sold or the use is charged the W.D.A. is entitled to reclaim a proportion of the grant on a sliding scale as follows:

| Months | Repayments |
|--------|------------|
| 0–12 | 100 per cent. |
| 13–24 | 80 per cent. |
| 25–36 | 60 per cent. |
| 37–48 | 40 per cent. |
| 49–60 | 20 per cent. |
| 61 plus | Nil |

[54] See above at § 8.50 *et seq.*

**Company B.** Management buy-out of profitable operation which is being sold as a result of a group rationalisation. The ex-managers need £200,000 to purchase fixed assets and a further £100,000 for working capital.
Sources of funds: Agency: £150,000;
Managers: £50,000; 'Parent company'
loan: £50,000; Bank overdraft: £50,000.
Agency investment:
£100,000—eight-year European Investment Bank
loan at 13 per cent.
£20,000—Ordinary shares
£30,000—cumulative redeemable participating convertible Preference shares; term—seven years; dividend—8 per cent. gross with a participation. element of 1 per cent. of sales; redemption—at par + 10 per cent.

**Company C.** Relatively new company in rural Wales with fair growth potential but little security and limited reserves. The existing shareholders have already invested £10,000 in the business and have guaranteed a bank overdraft of £5,000.
Agency Investment:
£15,000 five-year subsidised rural loan at 12 per cent.
£10,000 cumulative redeemable participating. Preference shares redeemable five to seven years at par + 10 per cent., the dividend being the higher of 8 per cent. or one-fifteenth of pre-tax profits.

**Company D.** A new company involved with high technology but no track record.
Sources of funds: Agency: £70,000;
Directors: £30,000 equity;
Bank overdraft: £40,000; Government selective assistance: £30,000.
Agency investment:
£30,000—eight-year European Coal and Steel Community loan at an interest rate of 10 per cent. for the first five years, then 13 per cent.
£40,000 cumulative redeemable participating convertible Preference shares; the dividend the higher of 10 per cent. or one-tenth of pre-tax profits; the shares redeemable between years five and seven at par + 10 per cent. At the Agency's option £10,000 will be convertible to 25 per cent. of the company's equity.

While the WDA's idea of the most appropriate funding package will vary as **8.79** between companies it has provided indications as to the forms in which funds will be made available.

(a) *Equity investments*

As a matter of policy the Agency is prepared to invest in the equity of companies undertaking projects in manufacturing, hotels/tourism, major distribution operations and some service activities. The Agency does not, however, invest in the media, retailing, building and construction, agriculture, forestry, sea-fishing or service firms meeting a purely local need.
In general terms the Agency will seek an equity stake where the total funds

required by the company exceed £100,000 although it is prepared to consider an equity investment for funding as low as £25,000.[55] There is an upper limit of £1,000,000 although for investments of more than £500,000 the Agency invariably seeks to involve a merchant bank or finance house in a joint venture.

It is the Agency's policy not to seek to hold more than 30 per cent. of the equity of any company, but its stake will normally be at least 20 per cent. The usual arrangement entered into with companies is for the Agency to sell back to shareholding (either to other shareholders or to the company under the provisions of the Companies Act 1985)[56] after five to ten years on a formula linked to profits. Such formula would, of course, be incorporated in the funding agreement.

### (b) *Preference shares*

The policy of the WDA is to use preference shares as a way of supporting new and rapidly growing companies which have not yet acquired a sufficiently strong balance sheet to support either the costs or the security necessary to obtain further borrowers and/or where an existing shareholder is not prepared to see his percentage equity stake reduced by the introduction of a new ordinary shareholder.

The terms on which the Agency is prepared to take a preference shareholding in a company involve five principal matters.

(a) *Coupon.* The Agency's policy is to fix the coupon at a level approximately 5 per cent. less than the company would expect to pay on funds borrowed from a clearing bank.

(b) *Profits and dividends.* Under the general law dividends on preference shares are payable only out of profits. If, therefore, the company has no profits for any given accounting period and no reserves which can be employed no preference dividends can be paid. To preserve the Agency's yield on its investment it normally insists that the preference shares it takes be cumulative so that dividend payments which cannot be paid in any year become payable in later years, as profits permit, or at redemption.

Furthermore, as the Agency's policy is to link its shareholding directly to company performances, it provides for a participation in the company's profits over and above the coupon rate. This additional dividend is payable either as a share of pre-tax profits cashed or, alternatively, as a percentage of sales achieved.[57]

(c) *Redemption.* Preference shares are normally held by the Agency for five to seven years. The cost of redemption is usually fixed either as a percentage of the net assets of the company or a multiple of annual profits at the date of redemption. With a view to encouraging the growth of companies the Agency is normally prepared to agree a fixed price for redemption, relying for its return on the

---

[55] Funding below £100,000 is normally provided (especially for high-technology projects) by Hafren Investment Finance Ltd.
[56] ss.171 *et seq.*
[57] The Agency favours a small royalty on sales (usually less than 1 per cent.) when investing in new and expanding companies.

participation element of the package. The standard redemption term of a preference share hold by the Agency is fixed at par plus 10 per cent.

(d) *Conversion.* In certain cases, and especially where new technology is involved, the Agency will seek to negotiate a conversion option into not more than 30 per cent. of the ordinary shares of the company. In such cases the Agency will also agree to a "buy-back" option with the principal shareholders. The price to be paid to repurchase the ordinary shares will be the higher of 30 per cent. of the net assets of the company or a multiple of the annual profits earned to date.[58]

(e) *Board Representation.* It is the Agency's practice to reserve the right to nominate a non-executive director to the company's board. However in the ordinary course no nomination will be made unless the company is clearly "in need of guidance."

(c) *Loans*

The WDA will provide loans of between £10,000 and £500,000 to companies in manufacturing and some service industries towards the purchase of buildings, equipment and, in appropriate cases, to provide working capital for expanding businesses or businesses seeking to modernise or become more efficient.

WDA loans are normally for terms of between five to ten years with interest being paid at a fixed rate at current commercial rates. Interest is paid on the amount of capital outstanding. Where security is available the Agency usually seeks a first charge over the fixed assets of the business.

In addition to the finance generally available loans are available from the **8.80** WDA for small businesses in rural locations which create new jobs. The underlying idea is similar to that on which the SDA loan schemes are based albeit that the details differ.

WDA Small Business Loans of up to £50,000 may be provided for the purchase of buildings and equipment but on occasions also towards the working capital requirements of expanding businesses. The Loans Scheme is open to companies in manufacturing and some service industries employing fewer than 20 people. Agriculture, horticulture and retail trades do not qualify. As a basic requirement and a guideline to the amounts that may be borrowed the WDA policy is to lend £7,000 for each new job created.

Loans are at fixed rates of interest approximately 3 per cent. below current commercial lending rates, with monthly repayments of interest and capital.

As with its ordinary commercial loans the WDA usually seeks a first charge over the company's fixed assets by way of security.

The loans are medium to long term[59] and are not limited to new projects but are also available for projects already begun.[60]

---

[58] The formula will take no account of expected profits.
[59] 5–20 years, depending on the project.
[60] Or indeed for new businesses.

**8.81**    **(2) Venture capital**[61]

Venture capital is provided by the WDA through its subsidiary Hafren Investment Finance Ltd. Like its parent, Hafren makes investments in companies by way of ordinary shares, preference shares and (in appropriate circumstances) by way of loans or in a combination of these. Investment by Hafren is subject to lower financial limits of £10,000 and a maximum of £100,000.

Hafren's policy is to invest in risk ventures with high growth potential, and especially in projects involving new technology. It is prepared to consider venture projects which find risk capital difficult to obtain from traditional services.

**8.82**     Hafren's investment packages are tailored to suit the needs of individual applicants. Nevertheless the overall package and its component parts will normally be subject to a number of conditions.

(a) *General terms*

(1) Hafren reserves the right to nominate a non-executive director to the board of a client company to assist with the development of the company's business; and
(2) Legal costs of documentation are to be borne by the client company.

(b) *Terms attaching to investment via ordinary shares*

(1) Hafren will subscribe for ordinary shares in a company at current market value up to a maximum holding of 30 per cent.; and
(2) Equity investments are subject to "buy-out" provisions permitting shareholders, or the company itself, to reacquire Hafren's shares on terms agreed prior to the provisions of funds.

(c) *Terms attaching to investment via preference shares*

Preference shares are a favoured vehicle for financial assistance by the WDA, and through it, by Hafren. The standard terms attaching to preference share investments by Hafren are:

(1) the shares will carry a gross coupon of $7\frac{1}{2}$ per cent. gross over seven years;
(2) dividends will be cumulative;
(3) the shares will carry in addition a participation in profits to the extent that they will enjoy the same dividend payments as those declared on ordinary shares should they be higher than the fixed coupon rate;
(4) the shares will be redeemable at the company's option at any time between the seventh and tenth year after issue on a predetermined formula based on either the net asset value of the company or its profit performance;

---

[61] No arrangement fee is charged for Hafren investments.

(5) in the event of an offer for the whole or part of the company's ordinary share capital Hafren will have the option to convert its preference shares into ordinary shares on specified terms; and

(6) if, at the end of the tenth year, the company is unable to comply with the agreed redemption terms, Hafren will have the option to convert a proportion of its preference shares into a maximum holding of 30 per cent. of the equity of the company and to raise the coupon on the remainder to a normal commercial rate.

### (d) *Unsecured loans*

Venture capital provided in the form of loans will be unsecured but will be subject to the following conditions:

(1) Loans will be for a term of five years;

(2) Interest will be at Clearing Bank base rates plus two per cent.;

(3) Capital repayments will be deferred for the first two years; and

(4) In parallel with the loan Hafren will seek to purchase at current market value share warrants entitling it to subscribe for the company's ordinary share capital, up to a maximum holding of 30 per cent. at any time after three years. Hafren will, however, undertake not to exercise this right on receipt of repayments made in accordance with a predetermined formula.

Applications for financial assistance from Hafren should contain: **8.83**

(1) a brief history of the company together with a description of the business or businesses it carries on;

(2) a full description of the project for which the funds are required including

    (a) details of how the funds will be spent;

    (b) details of the key personnel involved;

(3) an assessment of the market it is proposed to enter;

(4) anticipated benefits from the project;

(5) details of other service of finance approached by the company together with information on the result of those approaches;

(6) amounts of funds requested and information as to the forms in which those funds can be taken on board;

(7) the company's latest management accounts;

(8) its latest audited account;

(9) cash flow and profit and loss forecasts for the next three years;

(10) projected balance sheets; and

(11) any other information that might be considered helpful in an appraisal of the project.

Following receipt of an application an appraisal of the project will be made **8.84** and, subject to adequate information having been provided, an investment decision will be taken. Applicant companies have 14 days in which to decide whether or not to accept any offer that might be forthcoming.

**8.85    (3) Start-up capital and/or development capital**

Funds may be available for start-up and/or for expansion under:

(a)  the rural areas loan scheme; and
(b)  the ESCS and EIB facilities;

both of which have been discussed above.

**The Development Boards**

**8.86**    The object underlying the establishment of Development Boards was to arrest the decline of sparsely populated rural areas and to promote economic development there. The first of the two Boards to be set up, the Highlands and Islands Development Board, was established "for the purpose of assisting the people of the Highlands and Islands to improve their economic and social conditions and of enabling the Highlands and Islands to play a more effective part in the economic and social development of the nation."[62]

In 1976,[63] as part of the then government's general strategy for the regeneration of industry, a corresponding Board with similar powers was established with responsibility for providing support and undertaking schemes for the economic development of rural Wales.

The powers of the Boards overlap with the functions and powers of the Scottish and Welsh Development Agencies respectively. In practice this overlap is reconciled by the Development Boards undertaking the smaller developments within their more limited geographical areas.

**8.87    Highlands and Islands Development Board**

For the purpose of implementing its broad statutory remit the Board is given the following powers,[64] namely:

(1)  to acquire, hold and manage land;
(2)  to erect buildings and carry out other operations on land, to provide equipment and services in connection therewith and to hold, manage, maintain, let, hire or otherwise dispose of the same;
(3)  to acquire plant and equipment for leasing to developers;
(4)  to conduct in its own right either directly or indirectly any business or undertaking; and
(5)  to provide advisory and other services on a range of topics, to engage in publicity and to undertake such ancillary activities as may be necessary for economic and social development.

**8.88**    In the exercise of its powers the Board's activities fall into four broad categories:

---

[62] Highlands and Islands Development (Scotland) Act 1965, s.1.
[63] Development of Rural Wales Act 1976.
[64] Highlands and Islands Development (Scotland) Act 1965, ss.8 and 9 as amended by Highlands and Islands Development (Scotland) Act 1968, ss.1 and 2.

(a) assisting private business with finance (primarily capital funding) and advice;

(b) providing factories and other buildings such as hotels and tourist information centres;

(c) initiating other development schemes designed to assist particular sectors or areas; and

(d) undertaking policy liaison and advocacy with other public bodies, undertaking or commissioning research and formulating proposals on strategic issues affecting the HIDB area.

Although projects carried out by the Board itself are increasing in importance, the Board's main area of activity is in the provision of financial assistance to businesses carrying out developments in its area.[65] Assistance from the Board is entirely discretionary. Nevertheless it is the Board's policy to make financial assistance available, wherever possible, to any person or body carrying on or proposing to carry on any industrial, commercial or other undertaking or any activity which, in the opinion of the Board, will contribute to the economic or social development of the Highlands and Islands. However, priority is given to projects on locations which are particularly remote, which have above-average unemployment and which are otherwise socially and economically disadvantaged.

## (1) General principles of HIDB financing 8.89

Given the discretionary nature of HIDB financial assistance each case is dealt with on its merits. In considering applications, however, the Board evaluates them against the following criteria:

(a) the likely contribution the project will make to the economic and social development of the HIDB area;

(b) the estimated additional employment that should result;

(c) the potential financial viability of the project and its ability to service its commitments;

(d) whether the project is to be located wholly or partly within the HIDB area and the remoteness of the location within that area;

(e) the security offered;

(f) any distinctive features of the project which make it of especial significance to the HIDB area;

(g) whether the estimated project cost is appropriate to the needs of the development;

(h) whether the appropriate private sector finance can be raised;

(i) whether the forecast trading results appear to be reasonably attainable; and

(j) whether all necessary statutory and other consents for the development have been obtained.

---

[65] The Board is financed by a grant in aid through the Scottish Economic Planning Department.

The Board will only provide financial assistance for projects of genuine development and not merely the continuation of a previous activity or the replacement of existing finance. As with other forms of selective assistance, that provided by the Board may only be given if it can be shown that the project would not go ahead without it or would not go ahead in the same way or on the same scale or timescale.

Subject to the above requirements the Board has indicated that the following types of outlay are eligible for consideration for assistance, namely expenditure on:

(1) the erection of new buildings (eligible costs include architects ad surveyors fees);
(2) the extension, alteration or improvement of existing buildings (including services and fire precaution work);
(3) site preparation, access roads, residuary sidings and airstrips;
(4) the construction of piers and other seaward works;
(5) land improvement schemes (fencing, drainage, etc.);
(6) the purchase of plant and equipment (whether new or secondhand);
(7) the purchase of furniture and fittings (again whether new or secondhand);
(8) the purchase of fishing, cargo and pleasure craft (new or secondhand);
(9) the purchase of specialised vehicles (new or secondhand);
(10) working capital[66];
(11) removal expenses (provided that the developer is moving to the HIDB area from a non-development area of the U.K.);
(12) training costs; and
(13) start-up costs generally.

On the other hand the following types of expenditure are not normally eligible for specific assistance, although such expenditure is taken into account by the Board in its appraisal of the overall cost of the project and its proposed financing. The categories of such excluded expenditure are:

(1) the purchase of land and legal costs;
(2) the purchase of existing buildings;
(3) the purchase of motor vehicles.

The policy of the Board is against providing assistance for the acquisition of property. However, in exceptional cases it is prepared to consider assistance for the provision of housing for staff of the business where other housing is not available.

**8.91**

*Amount of
HIDB
Assistance*
HIDB assistance is provided to supplement investment in a project by individual companies and financial institutions. Where assistance is made available this can be up to 50 per cent. of the project costs, with the balance being raised by the company either from its own resources or from external commercial sources. Where other government assistance is available (for example, regional develop-

---

[66] Including livestock in the case of farms.

ment grants) companies are expected to utilise this and the amount of assistance provided by the Board will be reduced accordingly.

Very exceptionally, the proportion of public sector finance can be increased to a maximum of 70 per cent. Such level of assistance, however, is only provided in cases of extreme economic or social need.

Over and above these percentage restrictions projects involving assistance of over £250,000 require the consent of the Secretary of State[67] in addition to Board appraisal. Furthermore HIDB assistance is subject to a ceiling of £400,000 in the total amount of assistance it can provide for any single project.

### (2) Normal assistance                                                **8.92**

The normal forms of financial assistance available from the Board are:

(a) Loans;
(b) Share and Stock Participation;           *Forms of*
(c) Interest Relief Grants; and              *HIDB*
(d) Removal Grants.                          *Assistance*

### (a) *Loans*

Loans, normally made at concessionary rates, constitute the commonest form   **8.93**
of financial assistance provided by the Board. HIDB loans fall into three categories:

(1) *Building Loans,* which are normally given for a period of up to 20 years[68];
(2) *Plant and Equipment Loans,* which normally extend over a period of up to 10 years; and
(3) *Working Capital Loans,* the maximum period of which is 10 years.

The rate of interest charged on all three categories of loan is normally three per cent. below the prevailing commercial rate at the date of approval. This rate is fixed for the duration of the loan and is applied to the reducing balance as capital repayments are made. Depending on individual circumstances an initial interest-free period of up to three years can be allowed.

Repayments are normally required annually although should it be deemed appropriate quarterly or monthly repayments may be stipulated. In addition a "capital holiday" of up to three years can be arranged before the first repayment will fall due.

### (b) *Share and stock participation*

As an alternative to loan financing HIDB can itself promote or join in the pro-   **8.94**
motion of new companies, subscribing for ordinary or preference shares. Equally the Board is prepared to subscribe for shares in existing companies and, in appropriate circumstances acquire warrants to convert loans into shares.

---

[67] Via the Scottish Economic Planning Department.
[68] In exceptional cases the term may be extended to 20 years.

An HIDB shareholding will not normally exceed one third of the issued share capital.

The total financial involvement of the Board is subject to the same limitations as other forms of assistance.

(c) *Interest relief grants*

**8.95**    In some cases, as an alternative to offering a loan itself the Board may provide an Interest Relief Grant to reduce the cost to the company of borrowing from commercial or other non-public sources. The grant is intended to compensate for the difference between the amount of interest payable and the amount which would have been payable had loan finance been provided by the Board at its concessionary rates.[69]

Normally a grant is made equivalent to interest at three per cent. for four years.

Interest relief grants are paid retrospectively, usually on a quarterly or annual basis.

(d) *Removal Grants*

**8.96**    Removal Grants are available towards the expenses incurred in moving a business from a non-development area of the United Kingdom to the HIDB area. The rate of grant payable is restricted to 80 per cent. of such eligible expenditure as the Board considers to have been reasonably incurred.

Eligible expenditure includes:

(1) travel and accommodation during preliminary visits to the HIDB area;
(2) removing plant and machinery (including dismantling and re-installation);
(3) removing necessary stocks, including raw materials, partly completed and finished goods, spare parts, loose tools, etc.;
(4) voluntary retention payments to enable labour to be kept on at the old workplace prior to moving to prevent work breakdown;
(5) employers' net statutory redundancy payments made by the firm to workers discharged because of the move.

**8.97    (3) Special Assistance**

HIDB Special Assistance may be provided:

(a) by way of a special grant given in additional to its normal assistance[70]; or
(b) as relief or emergency assistance.

---

[69] This method of assistance involves the concept of the "Notional Loan," which is the amount the Board could, in theory, have provided had it been asked and chosen to do so. The amount of the grant is intended to be the difference between the commercial interest payable on this amount and that which would have been payable had the Notional Loan been a reality.

[70] Subject, of course, to the overall financial limits on individual projects.

(a) *Special Grants*

HIDB Special Grants may be provided for general purposes or towards build-   **8.98**
ing costs, in all cases being completely discretionary both as to whether or not it
should be made and, if so, as to the rate and/or amount of the award.

Projects being considered for Special Grant assistance must meet three basic
requirements, namely:

(1) that the project is not likely to succeed on the basis of normal assistance
alone;

(2) that the project demonstrates reasonable prospects of viability with the
special assistance prepared; and

(3) that the project is essential to the proper development of the area.

In addition the Board has regard to the following circumstances in assessing an
application for special assistance, namely:

(1) what distinctive features are possessed by the project and the extent to
which they demonstrate good grounds for additional assistance[71] and

(2) whether the project is of special significance or has a high potential for
generating ancillary enterprises in the HIDB area.

Special Grant assistance may be made towards building costs which are not   **8.99**
eligible for regional development grant, DAFS grant or assistance from any
other public body. The maximum rate of this grant is 35 per cent. of the eligible
building costs (including architects' and surveyors' fees) subject to the overriding
requirement that the grant cannot normally exceed 20 per cent. of the total project cost.

Special Grant assistance towards building costs is not treated as a revenue
receipt for tax purposes. Instead it is brought into account in calculating any
capital allowances available in respect of the buildings, being deductible[72] from
the cost of the building.

(b) *Relief or emergency assistance*

The Board may provide relief or emergency assistance to existing projects   **8.100**
(whether or not they have been in receipt of Normal Assistance) which are in
financial difficulties in order to preserve employment and to prevent redundan-
cies. In determining whether or not to provide such assistance the criteria against
which the case is judged are broadly similar to those applied to new developments and expansion proposals, considered above at § 8.89.

(4) *Building and plant leasing*

In addition to the direct provision of financial aid HIDB is also a source of   **8.101**

---

[71] For example, exceptional need to train workers to new skills or the high cost of equipping due to
the remoteness of the site.
[72] Unlike regional development grants.

indirect finance to companies in that, in appropriate cases it can provide on lease:

(a) *Advance or purpose built factories and workshops.* The Board's standard lease is for a term not exceeding 20 years, with the tenant responsible for the full costs of repairs and insurance. Rents are set by the District Valuer, but as a general rule at levels below commercial rates and less than rents for equivalent premises in other parts of the country. In appropriate cases rent-free periods of up to two years can be provided for.

(b) *Equipment and plant.* The Board sometimes enters into leasing arrangements for plant and equipment. Depending on the life of the items concerned the leasing agreement is normally for five to seven years and provides for repayment by equal instalments of capital and interest with the agreement conferring on the lessee an option to purchase the relevant item for a nominal sum at the expiry of the agreement.

**8.102   The Development Board for Rural Wales**

The Development Board for Rural Wales was established under the provisions of the Development of Rural Wales Act 1976. Its general function is[73]

*Functions and Duties of DBRW*

"to prepare, concert, promote, support and undertake measures for the economic and social development of the area for which it is responsible."[74]

In pursuance of this general function the Board is charged with, *inter alia*, the following duties, namely[75]:

(a) to keep under review all matters relating to the economical and social development of the area for which it is responsible;

(b) to prepare and submit to the Secretary of State for his approval proposals (whether of a general or specific nature) for the economic and social development of the area or any part of it; and

(c) to concert, promote, support or undertake measures to implement any proposal so approved.

**8.103**   For the purpose of enabling it to carry out its statutory function and to discharge the statutory duties pursuant thereto the Board is given the following powers, namely power[76]:

*Powers of DBRW*

(a) to acquire, hold, manage, develop and dispose[77] of land or other property;

(b) to carry out building and other operations;

(c) to provide services for land or other property;

(d) to provide finance[78]

---

[73] Development of Rural Wales Act 1976, s.1(5).
[74] *Ibid.* "and in particular for the development of any area of a new town or new town situated within the area for which it is responsible."
[75] *Ibid.* s.3(1)(*a*)-(*c*).
[76] *Ibid.* s.4.
[77] With the consent of the Secretary of State: Development of Rural Wales Act, s.4(6).
[78] With the consent of the Secretary of State and approval of the Treasury: *ibid.*, s.4(7).

> (i) for the taking by any local authority or statutory undertaker of such measures as the Board considers will contribute to the economic or social development of the area for which it is responsible; or
>
> (ii) for such activities of other persons as the Board considers will contribute to the social development of that area;

(e) as agent of the Welsh Development Agency to provide finance for persons carrying on or intending to carry on industrial undertakings in that area;

(f) as agent of the Welsh Development Agency, to provide services (other than finance) for any undertaking or business which is or is intended to be carried on in that area;.

(g) to carry on or acquire any undertaking or business[79];

(h) to do anything which is likely to facilitate the discharge of the Board's functions or is incidental or conducive to their discharge.

In relation to the Board's powers to provide finance these may be exercised by way of grant, loan, the giving of guarantees or any combination of these.[80] The provision of finance by the Board may be made subject to conditions and in particular as to conditions for repayment of the whole or any part of a grant in any circumstances.[81]

**DBRW finance—Mid-Wales Development**          **8.104**

The Board provides financial assistance to companies operating within or relocating to the area for which it is responsible through a programme known as Mid-Wales Development. Under this programme assistance is available for projects that create or maintain jobs in manufacturing and in certain service industries (including mining and construction) and in certain cases for agriculture, fishing and fish farming, tourism and forestry.

The programme comprises two elements, namely:

(a) facilities available generally throughout the DBRW area; and

(b) facilities which vary according to the location, within the DBRW area, of the project.

**Mid-Wales Development—facilities generally available throughout the DBRW**          **8.105**
**area**

This group of facilities are essentially those offered under section 4(1)(*e*) and (*f*) of the 1976 Act whereby the Board acts as agent for the Welsh Development Agency in relation to the provision of finance and/or services. These facilities include the provision of—

---

[79] With the consent of the Secretary of State: *ibid.* s.4(6).
[80] *Ibid.* s.4(4).
[81] *Ibid.* s.4(5).

   (a) Low Interest Loans;
   (b) Guaranteed Loans;
   (c) Medium and Long-Term Loans;
   (d) Development Capital through equity or preference share participation;
   (e) Venture Capital (through Hafren Investment Finance Ltd.); and
   (f) Factories at Low Rentals, including where appropriate rent-free periods.

The terms and conditions on which these facilities are made available correspond with those imposed by the WDA and are discussed above at §§ 8.78–8.85.

**8.106**    **Mid-Wales Development—facility packages varying according to location within the DBRW area**

The Mid-Wales Development programme provides for three packages, differing according to the location of the project, each of which offers a selection of types of financial assistance.

The various elements from which these packages are constructed are as follows.

(a) *Mid Wales Development Grant*

This is a grant available direct from the Board having as its object the creation or maintenance of employment in the DBRW Area. It is available primarily to companies in manufacturing, mining and construction, although in certain cases the Board will consider projects relating to agriculture, forestry, fishing and fish farming, and business.

To qualify for grant a project must satisfy a number of conditions. These are that:

   (1) the project must be viable;
   (2) it must involve expenditure on fixed assets;
   (3) the greater part of finance for the project should come from the private sector;
   (4) the project will not go ahead or will not go ahead on the scale or in the timescale proposed without the grant; and
   (5) the project, if in manufacturing, will create new jobs or safeguard existing jobs in the medium term, or, if not in manufacturing, will create new permanent employment.

Where a project is approved for grant the amount payable will be subject to individual negotiation with the company concerned but will almost always be influenced by the number of jobs created or preserved. The payment of any grant awarded is generally in instalments related to the expenditure on the project and the achievement of its forecast objectives.

In cases where grant is payable this will not in general affect a company's eligibility for loan assistance in one of the forms mentioned in § 8.105 above. However such loan assistance as may be forthcoming in these cases will not normally be at the subsidised rate unless it can be demonstrated that additional finance is still required to enable the project to go ahead.

(b) *Regional Development Grants*

These are available in the Development Areas of the DBRW Area, are non-selective and provide assistance towards the costs of building and equipment and plant in eligible premises. Regional development grants are considered above at § 8.31 *et seq.*

(c) *Regional Selective Grants*

These are grants payable under section 7 of the Industrial Development Act 1982 towards the costs of projects creating or maintaining employment. Grants under section 7 are considered above at §§ 8.38 *et seq.*

(d) *Wage Subsidy Grants*

These are grants available to small firms in the form of a subsidy of 30 per cent. of the basic pay for 26 weeks in respect of new jobs created.

(e) *Office and Service Industry Grants*

These are grants payable under section 7 of the Industrial Development Act 1982 towards selected office and service businesses. Grants under this scheme are considered above at § 8.42 It should be emphasised that the two elements of the Mid-Wales Development Programme are cumulative rather than alternative. Companies, therefore, may qualify for aid under the facilities mentioned in § 8.105 in addition to what is available under their appropriate package.

**The Council for Small Industries in Rural Areas**

The Council for Small Industries in Rural Areas (CoSIRA) is the main agent **8.107** of the Development Commission, a body established in 1909[82] with the primary objective of helping the rural parts of England to support viable on prosperous *CoSIRA* communities and thus of improving the general quality of life, especially in areas where the population is declining or which are in other ways disadvantaged.

CoSIRA was set up in 1968 from the three separate bodies existing at that time—the Rural Industries Bureau, the Rural Industries Loan Fund and the Rural Industries Organisers[83]—as a company limited by guarantee. Its objects are to promote economic development in accordance with the policies of the Development Commission, by whom it is financed. Within the parameters of its broad objectives CoSIRA is charged with improving the prosperity of small businesses in the countryside by providing a local service of advice, backed up by technical and management services, training facilities and assistance, financial services and, in certain cases, finance itself.

---

[82] Under the Development and Road Improvement Fund Act 1909.
[83] Employed by the county Rural Community Councils.

**8.108**      CoSIRA's main efforts and resources are directed towards rural regeneration
and development and in pursuing these ends concentrates[84] its attention on busi-

*Eligibility for*     nesses which provide an important service to their local communities and those
*CoSIRA*       which intend to provide additional and/or diversified employment or need help
*Assistance*     to protect the jobs of existing employees.

CoSIRA facilities are normally available to firms employing up to 20 skilled
workers (with no formal limit on the unskilled) operating in the countryside or in
country towns with a population of up to 10,000 (exceptionally up to 15,000)
people. The Council's facilities are intended primarily for manufacturing and
service industries[85] with agriculture, horticulture and the professions being
expressly excluded.

**8.109**      Finance from CoSIRA is normally in the form of loans, albeit that the amount
of funds is limited. A maximum of £15,000 per borrower may be available with
assistance not normally exceeding 50 per cent. of a given project cost in Priority
Areas[86] or $33\frac{1}{3}$ per cent. in Non-Priority Areas.

Expenditure qualifying for assistance includes:

(1) the acquisition of buildings;
(2) building repairs and alterations;
(3) the construction of new buildings; and
(4) the purchase of plant and equipment.

Repayment periods vary according to the type and amount of expenditure.[87]

Rates of interest on CoSIRA loans are specified by the Treasury but may be
reduced by 3 per cent. if the project for which the loan is sought is directly
attributable to the creation of jobs. The interest rate is fixed for the full term of
the loan and there is no penalty for early repayment of the loan.[88]

**8.110**      Grants of 35 per cent. are available in priority areas for CoSIRA towards the
cost of actual expenditure to convert redundant buildings to workshops.[89]

**The British Technology Group**

**8.111**      The British Technology Group is a company established in 1982 to bring
together the operations and investments of two public corporations, the

---

[84] CoSIRA has stated 3 priorities, namely:
    (1) Businesses in Special Investment (Development) Areas and those within the surrounding
       area;
    (2) Businesses in the most needy other rural areas as identified by CoSIRA's local committees;
       and
    (3) Beyond this, responding to requests from eligible businesses in all rural areas.
[85] Including small tourism enterprises, *e.g.* small hotels, guest houses, bed and breakfast establishments, motels and holiday chalets.
[86] See above at n. 84.
[87] Building loans have terms of up to 20 years; plant and equipment loans have terms of up to 5
years.
[88] Where a project is funded jointly by the National Westminster Bank and CoSIRA under the Nat
West/CoSIRA joint lending scheme Nat West have agreed to provide the businesses concerned
loans at preferential rates of interest and a reduced arrangement fee.
[89] Latest date for application under this scheme is May 31, 1985.

National Research Development Corporation and the National Enterprise *BTG*
Board, to promote the development of technology throughout British industry.
BTG is financed via its two parent corporations and operates to discharge their
statutory functions and under their statutory powers.

## The National Research Development Council

NRDC was established by the Development of Inventions Act 1948. This Act **8.112**
was replaced by the Development of Inventions Act 1967 which presently constitutes the governing legislation for the activities of the Council. Section 2 of this *NRDC*
Act stipulates that the NRDC shall have the following functions, that is to say:

"(1)(a) securing, where the public interest so requires, the development or
exploitation of inventions resulting from public research,[90] and of any other
invention as to which it appears to the Corporation that it is not being devel- *Functions*
oped or exploited or sufficiently developed or exploited;
(b) acquiring, holding, disposing of and granting rights (whether gratui-
tously or for consideration) in connection with inventions resulting from
public research and, where the public interest so requires, in connection
with inventions resulting from other sources;
(c) promoting and assisting, where the public interest so requires, research
for satisfying specific practical requirements brought to the knowledge of
the Corporation where they are of the opinion that the research is likely to
lead to an invention; and
(d) assisting, where the public interest so requires, the continuation of
research where it appears to the Corporation that the research has resulted
in any discovery such that the continuation of the research may lead to *and*
inventions of practical importance."

In discharging its duties under the Act, NRDC is empowered "to carry on any
activity" which appears to it "to be requisite, advantageous or convenient" and
in particular the Corporation may carry on or promote or facilitate the carrying *Powers*
on by other persons of any business.[91] Where, however, the exercise of its
powers involved the Corporation in:

(1) any project for the making of goods[92];
(2) the construction of works or the provision of services[92];
(3) the setting up of a company or other organisation[92];

---

[90] Public research means "research carried out by a government department or other public body or
any other research in respect of which financial assistance is provided out of public funds: 1967
Act, s.2(5).
[91] Development of Inventions Act 1967, s.2(2). The Act goes on to provide:
"(3) The activities which may be carried on by the Corporation under the last foregoing subsection shall include promoting and assisting research where in the opinion of the Corporation the results of the research are likely to further the development or exploitation of
inventions to which the Corporation's functions extend or to enhance the value of such inventions.
(4) The Corporation shall, except where it appears to them that special circumstances otherwise require, exercise their function of securing the exploitation of any invention by entrust-
ing the exploitation thereof, on terms appearing to the Corporation to be appropriate, to
persons engaged in the industry concerned."
[92] Act of 1967, s.4(1).

(4) the acquisition of or of any interest in any undertaking[93];

(5) the provision of financial assistance for any person undertaking the development or exploitation of any invention[93]; and

(6) the exercise by the Corporation of the functions conferred on them by section 2(1)(*c*) and (*d*) of the Act the consent of the Secretary of State is required.

**8.113**    **The National Enterprise Board**

*NEB*

The National Enterprise Board was set up by Part I of the Industry Act 1975 to secure where necessary large-scale sustained investment to offset the pull of market forces[94] with its guiding financial objective being to secure an adequate return "on that part of the nation's capital for which it is responsible.[95] The change of government in 1979 brought with it a change in attitude to the appropriate role of the Board and in the Industry Act 1980 its powers and functions were severely curtailed. Those powers and functions are set out in section 2 of the 1975 Act, as amended, which provides:

"(1) The purposes for which the Board may exercise their functions are:

*Purposes*

(a) the development or assistance of the economy of the United Kingdom or any part of the United Kingdom;

(b) the promotion in any part of the United Kingdom of industrial efficiency and international competitiveness; and

(c) the provision, maintenance or safeguarding of productive employment in any part of the United Kingdom.

(2) The function of the Board shall be:

*Functions*

(a) establishing, maintaining or developing, or promoting or assisting the establishment, maintenance or development of any industrial undertaking;

(b) promoting or assisting the development of any industry or undertaking in an industry;

[(c) and (d) repealed by the 1980 Act.]

(e) taking over publicly owned securities and other publicly owned property and holding and managing property when taken over;

(f) promoting the private ownership of interests in industrial undertakings by the disposal of securities and other property held by the Board and their subsidiaries.

*And Powers*

(3) The Board may do anything, whether in the United Kingdom or elsewhere, which is calculated to facilitate the discharge of the functions [of the Board] or is incidental or conducive to their discharge.

(4) In particular, but not so as to derogate from the of subsection (3) above, the Board shall have power:

(a) to acquire, hold and dispose of securities;

---

[93] *Ibid.*
[94] White Paper, *The Regeneration of British Industry* (1974) Cmnd. 5710, para. 23.
[95] *Ibid.* para. 25.

(b) to form bodies corporate;

(c) to form partnerships with other persons;

(d) to make loans;

(e) to guarantee obligations (arising out of loans or otherwise) incurred by other persons;

(f) to acquire and dispose of land, premises, plant machinery and equipment and other property;

(g) to make land, premises, plant, machinery and equipment and other property available for use by other persons; and

(h) to provide services in relation to finance, management, administration or organisation of industry."

## (1) General activities of BTG

8.114

The primary thrust of the new grouping is towards the promotion of innovative technology in British industry and the development of new industries in the assisted areas of England.[96] The resources of the group have been directed towards the provision of assistance in four ways:

(i) by investment in technical innovation;

(ii) in promoting and developing public sector technology;

(iii) in providing finance for small companies; and

(iv) by facilitating investment in the assisted areas.

## (2) Investment in technical innovation

8.115

Through NRDC the Group offers joint venture finance, equity and loan finance on venture capital terms,[97] recirculating loans[98] and lease finance for large capital assets. Under a joint venture agreement NRDC will contribute an agreed proportion—normally 50 per cent.—of the project costs and will expect to recover its investment by means of a percentage levy on sales of the resulting product. This form of finance can be extended to include not only development costs but also project introduction costs such as manufacturing equipment, working capital and marketing.

*Finance for Technical Innovation*

*NRDC*

Eligibility for NRDC assistance extends to projects from all sectors of industry including products, processes and computer software. There is no restriction on the size of companies and those companies which have applied for and received grants under Department of Industry Schemes may apply to NRDC for additional finance.

8.116

*Eligibility for NRDC Aid*

The primary criterion of NRDC support is that the proposed project be based on a new invention or contains a new technical innovation. Support is not con-

---

[96] See above at § 8.29.

[97] Normally applicable where a new company is set up for the specific purpose of exploiting an invention or new technology.

[98] A form of working capital loan.

fined to entirely novel projects; evolutionary improvements which are significant in their industry may also qualify.

The standard Department of Industry requirement of "additionality" is not a criterion for NRDC assistance.

**8.117    (3) Public Sector Technology**

BTG is the primary channel for developing and exploiting technology derived from United Kingdom public sector sources, *i.e.* universities, polytechnics, research councils, government research establishments and other public bodies. BTG will take responsibility for protecting and licensing inventions from these sources, provide funds for development that may be required, seek licensees and negotiate licence agreements. In the case of universities, polytechnics and certain other sources, BTG will share the resulting licence income with the institution concerned or the individual researcher.

These activities account for a considerable part of BTG's efforts and proven successes. BTG has a current portfolio of 1,700 United Kingdom patents and patent applications, 600 licensees in the United Kingdom and overseas, and 350 revenue-earning inventions.

**8.118    (4) Small companies finance**

About half of the companies in which BTG has invested are small businesses, and many are start-up situations. The Small Companies Division of BTG currently offers two straightforward schemes for financing small companies with growth potential:

    (a) Oakwood Loan Finance Ltd. which provides loans up to £50,000 for technology-based companies and also more traditional businesses.

    (b) The Small Company Innovation Fund (SCIF) which specialises in providing finance where the business as a whole is innovative.

(a) *Oakwood Loan Finance Ltd.*

Oakwood was established as a wholly-owned subsidiary of the National Enterprise Board in March 1981 to finance small businesses in England.

Through the Oakwood scheme, BTG offers standarised five-year loans of up to £50,000 to limited companies which, probably because their success has produced high growth rates, may be unable to provide the security normally required by traditional sources of finance.

Assistance is designed to aid small companies achieve a profitable growth and to alleviate some of the restraints on expansion during the early years. To this end the quarterly capital repayments on Oakwood loans start at the beginning of the fourth year of the loan period.

The interest on the loans is paid quarterly, net of deduction of tax, throughout the period of the loan, at a rate, fixed for each year, of 2 per cent. over the clearing banks' base rate.

In parallel with each loan Oakwood usually seeks to purchase, at current market value, a warrant entitling it to subscribe for equity in the business at a future date.

The terms are fixed in advance at no more than 20 per cent., but the proprietor of the company will have the right to prevent Oakwood subscribing for these shares should he wish to do so. Oakwood undertakes not to exercise its subscription rights on receipt of a payment made at a predetermined time.

Such a payment will only fall due at the end of the loan period, and the lump sum payment will be related to your company's profits. Oakwood loans are totally unsecured with the consequence that these warrants enable it to participate in the successes as well as the risks of the company's business.

(b) *Small Companies Investment Fund*

SCIF was established by the National Research Development Corporation in September 1980 to provide finance for small companies throughout the United Kingdom where the business as a whole is innovative.

Whereas the Oakwood scheme offers a standardised approach based on loans, SCIF provides individually designed packages which may incorporate more than one form of finance. Most packages will involve equity, recognising that such finance is often most appropriate for small businesses in the early years of growth. In all cases SCIF would only want to take a minority stake in the company.

The flexibility of this scheme allows us to assist existing firms or start-ups, and SCIF is often able to provide a substantial proportion of forecast requirements. SCIF would, however, normally expect existing shareholders to make, or have made, an appropriate financial commitment alongside its investment.

**(5) Finance for regional enterprise** **8.119**

Within the English assisted areas, BTG has a wider investment role. In addition to supporting the development of companies involved in technical innovation, it will support companies in the more traditional industries. BTG's aim is to stimulate economic activity in these areas by investing equity and loan finance in new and established companies which have soundly based growth potential or can improve their efficiency by modernisation or rationalisation.

BTG has local offices in the assisted areas which are staffed to handle investment proposals, and has established Regional Boards which are familiar with the needs of their areas and have delegated authority to approve investments.

BTG's principal method of promoting enterprise in the regions is the provision of long-term investment funds, by way of share capital or loans. The criteria for investment are deliberately widely set, but in general BTG regards itself as a particularly suitable source of finance for: **8.120**

*Eligibility*

(1) New ventures in the assisted areas with potential for long-term growth, especially those seeking to develop areas of advanced technology;

(2) Medium-sized companies with major modernisation or expansion projects, particularly where these will lead to an improvement in efficiency or competitiveness;

(3) Rationalisation projects where a strong partner takes the lead or can be introduced;

(4) Companies (inside or outside the assisted areas) requiring a financial partner to assist in setting up a new self-contained .venture in an Assisted Area; and

(5) Established companies with good long-term prospects which require temporary financial support to help them through a difficult period.

**8.121**

*Form of BTG
Finance*

BTG investment packages are individually tailored to suit the needs of the applicant company and can include equity capital, preference capital or loans or, where appropriate, a mixture of the three.

BTG's role is that of a catalyst, enabling projects to go ahead which might otherwise fail for lack of support. BTG therefore seeks to withdraw from an investment when the purpose for which the investment was made has been fulfilled. Where appropriate, the terms and route by which BTG will dispose of its interest will be agreed at the outset of the project.

BTG does not give grants or subsidised funds. It provides finance only on normal commercial terms. BTG aims wherever practicable to make investments in conjunction with private sector sources of investment finance, applying the same criteria to determine the commercial viability of the venture in question. However, BTG recognises that in some cases it may be appropriate to take a long-term view of prospects, although it will always seek a return commensurate with the risks involved.

BTG Keeps in close contact with Government agencies, financial institutions[99] and other sources of finance, making sure that all possible contributors to a financial package are taken into account.

**8.122**

*Protecting
BTG's
Investment*

When making an investment, appropriate monitoring arrangements will be agreed and local staff will seek to establish a good working relationship with management. BTG attaches considerable importance to the monitoring of investments but does not wish to become involved in the day-to-day management of the business.

In most cases BTG will reserve the right to appoint one or sometimes two non-executive directors to the Board of the company.

---

[99] BTG's general regional role under the Regional Enterprise Boards has been augmented by a series of initiatives to meet specific needs within the assisted areas:

(1) *Anglo-American Venture Fund Ltd.,* set up by BTG in association with a Californian venture capitalist, can provide venture capital for electronics-related businesses with high growth potential located or to be located in the Assisted Areas.

(2) *Western Enterprise Fund Ltd.,* set up by BTG in association with Dartington & Co. (part of Dartington Trust), specialises in investment propositions concerning Devon and Cornwall.

(3) *Merseyside Enterprise Fund Ltd.,* set up by BTG in association with Sapling Enterprise Ltd. and local agencies, concentrates on investment opportunities in smaller businesses arising in this special development area, taking account of the region's special problems.

**The English Industrial Estates Corporation**

The English Industrial Estates Corporation operates a factory building pro-     **8.123**
gramme in England and provides new and existing factories for sale or rent.[1]
Details of the facilities offered by the Corporation are considered above at §§
8.46 *et seq.*

The statutory functions of the Corporation are set out in the English Corporation Act 1981 as follows:

> "2.—(1) The Corporation may, in accordance with directions given [by the
> Secretary of State[2]]—
>> (a) provide, facilitate the provision of, and manage sites and premises in
>> England for occupation by industrial or commercial undertakings;
>> (b) provide, and facilitate the provision of, means of access, services and
>> other facilities required in connection with sites and premises in Eng-
>> land occupied or to be occupied by such undertakings; and
>> (c) dispose for any purpose of land and other property held by the Cor-
>> poration.
>
> (2) Subject to directions given [by the Secretary of State] below, the Cor-
> poration may do anything, whether in England or elsewhere, which is calcu-
> lated to facilitate or is conducive or incidental to the discharge of its
> functions, and in particular, without prejudice to the generality of the pre-
> ceding provisions of this subsection may:
>> (a) act alone or with other persons, either in partnership or otherwise;
>> (b) acquire land, plant, machinery and equipment and other property;
>> (c) form, or acquire interests in, bodies corporate; and
>> (d) make loans and guarantee obligations (arising out of loans or other-
>> wise) incurred by other persons."[3]

## ASSISTANCE FROM THE EEC

A significant proportion of the funds dispensed as a assistance under pro-     **8.124**
grammes administered by the Department of Trade and Industry and by the
Development Agencies derive ultimately from the EEC and in particular
through Community Regional Grants originating from the European Regional
Development Fund. Assistance from this source takes two forms, namely:

(a) "Quota aid," which comprises the greater part of Community Regional
Aid and is provided as a fixed amount of "quota" to each member state,
and
(b) "Non-quota aid," which makes up the balance and may be applied to

---

[1] EIE also builds and manages small factories and workshops in rural areas on behalf of the Development Commission.
[2] English Industrial Estates Corporation Act 1981, s.2(4).
[3] EIE also has power to provide or assist in the provision of advisory services in relation to the
building of factories or in the development or arrangement of industrial estates outside Great
Britain as well as in England and Wales: *ibid.* s.2(6).

projects in any country as dictated by the specific regional problems affecting the Community.

**Quota aid**

**8.125** The British government utilises the funds allocated to it under the quota to help finance projects in the private or public sectors of the economy which encourage development in the assisted areas. In particular a part of the funds received from this source are used towards the payment of regional development grants.[4]

Besides regional development grants quota aid to the United Kingdom[5] is used to support projects in two main areas, namely:

(1) Industrial, Tourist and Service Activities; and
(2) Infrastructure Development.

**8.126 Aid for industrial, tourist or service activities**

The European Regional Development Fund may contribute 20 per cent. of the investment costs of such activities. In some cases the Fund contribution may exceed 20 per cent. but may not exceed have the aid granted by the national government.

To qualify for assistance under this head a project must be in receipt of a regional grant from the British government. This requirement has the consequence that to qualify for a Community Regional Grant a project must be sited within an assisted area and must fit into the framework of the United Kingdom Regional Development Programme.

Projects eligible for assistance include roads, telecommunications, gas, electricity, water supply and the construction of advance factories. Assistance may also be provided for tourist infrastructure projects if these are likely to attract visitors to the region in question.

**8.127 Infrastructure development**

For infrastructure projects the Fund may contribute between 10 and 30 per cent. of expenditure incurred by public authorities on investment in infrastruc-

---

[4] See above at §§ 8.31 *et seq.*
[5] Only the government may submit applications to the Commission. The Commission decides with representatives of the Member States which of the eligible projects will receive aid from the annual quotas. Private individuals and organisations and public authorities may not apply directly to the Commission for Fund assistance.
*Private organisations* (including companies) may however receive regional aid from the Department of Trade and Industry. The Department then selects industrial, tourist and service projects which are eligible for Fund support, and forwards them to the Commission.
*Public authorities* should submit possible infrastructure projects to the regional office of the Department of the Environment, or its equivalent in Scotland, Wales and Northern Ireland. The Department will offer advice and guidance, and it will then select projects which are eligible for Fund support and forward them to the Commission. Money is not available for all eligible projects.

ture projects.[6] In Britain the practice is for the amount of Fund assistance to be passed on to the authority concerned, thereby reducing the amount it has to borrow and in consequence its interest charges.[7]

### Non-quota aid

"Non-quota" aid is used to finance, along with aid provided by national authorities, specific regional development programmes designed to help overcome problems caused by the Community's structure, or by decisions taken in other areas. Among the measures receiving assistance from this source in recent years have been the provision of funds for small and medium-sized enterprises in steel closure and shipbuilding areas. **8.128**

The non-quota portion of Community Regional Aid is currently limited to 5 per cent. of the Fund's total aid.[8]

## NORTHERN IRELAND "PROGRAMMES OF ASSISTANCE"

Although Northern Ireland is an integral part of the United Kingdom its peculiar problems have caused many schemes to be devised for assistance to industry either in or relocating to the province which have no application to mainland **8.129**

---

[6] Depending on the size of the expenditure. In special cases the grant may amount to as much as 40 per cent.

[7] ERDF regulations allow aid from the Fund to take the form of interest relief (3 percentage points) on loans granted by the European Investment Bank. In practice the British government has decided not to make this option available in the U.K.

[8] Other instruments of EEC assistance include:

*(1) Employment and Training Grants*
These are non-repayable grants from the European Social Fund for certain employment, training, retraining, resettlement and job-creation schemes. They may be payable to public bodies (including nationalised industries) and private sector undertakings (including companies and voluntary organisations)
Grants are payable only in respect of "eligible costs" which, in general, means the costs of preparing and operating the schemes, and in any event are only available in respect of such schemes as will affect a group of people or type of operation within one of the Fund's areas of operation, such as:
Schemes within assisted areas ex-agricultural workers, women aged 25 and over, unemployed young people, textile and clothing workers, disabled people, groups of undertakings, migrant workers and Technical Progress

*(2) Agriculture Grants*
The European Agriculture Guidance and Guarantee Fund (EAGGF) supports a number of schemes aimed at improving agricultural productivity. These schemes fall into 2 categories, namely:
    (a) schemes for the processing and marketing of agricultural and fish products; and
    (b) schemes to assist inshore fishing projects.
From time to time the Government negotiates special schemes with EAGGF for infrastructure and agricultural development in certain difficult areas. Currently schemes have been negotiated for the Western Isles of Scotland and parts of Northern Ireland.

*(3) Finance for Energy*
Financial support for projects conforming with the EEC's objective ensuring adequate supplies of energy for its future development are available under a number of schemes *e.g.* Hydrocarbon Sector Support Scheme, Euratom Loan Schemes.

Britain and for many of the facilities available in mainland Britain to be adapted to meet the special conditions prevailing in Ulster.

Until September 1, 1982 government assistance to industry in Northern Ireland was administered through the Northern Ireland Department of Commerce, the Northern Ireland Development Agency[9] and the Local Enterprise Development Unit.[10] Following a review of Development institutions in the province the Departments of Commerce and Manpower Services were merged to form a new Department of Economic Development. Within the umbrella of this new department there has been established a new unified "arm" bringing together the powers, functions and responsibilities for industrial development and assistance previously held by the Department of Commerce and the Northern Ireland Development Agency. This new arm is the Industrial Development Board for Northern Ireland.[11]

**8.130**      The Industrial Development Board operates two alternative "Programmes of Assistance." The First Programme comprises a range of "off the peg" incentives and cash grants which are automatically given to companies establishing factories in Northern Ireland.[12] These incentives and grants are of two kinds:

(1) capital grants[13] towards factory construction costs and towards the cost of new plant and equipment[14]; and

(2) cash grants towards labour training,[15] and for key workers.

In addition, where the project relates to manufacturing industry a derating of the industrial premises used amounting to 75 per cent. is claimable.

The Second Programme is intended to apply to projects that are considered to be particularly attractive in terms of the number of new jobs created, especially if these jobs are located in areas of high unemployment, or because of their contribution to the structure of the economy, as for example, by introducing the manufacture of new projects into the province. Assistance under this Second Programme is on a selective basis with approved projects attracting a package that is tailor-made for the company and project concerned. Assistance under the Second Programme attracts all the benefits available under Head 2 of the First Programme[16] together with a number of special benefits that are either not available at all, or else are improvements upon corresponding benefits, under the First Programme. These are:

---

[9] Which provided development capital.

[10] Which dealt with small firms employing less than 50 people.

[11] The Local Enterprise Development Unit continues to have responsibility for providing assistance to small companies in Northern Ireland.

[12] Assistance under this Programme is non-selective.

[13] Under Pt. IV of the Industrial Development (Northern Ireland) Order 1982, Arts. 7 and 8. (These correspond to regional development grants on the mainland.)

[14] These, like regional development grants on the mainland, qualify for the Capital Allowance transitional relief under Pt. II of Sched. 12 to F.A. 1984.

[15] Made under the Employment and Training Act (N.I.) 1950 or the Employment Subsidy Act 1978 (U.K.).

[16] And the industrial derating of 75 per cent.

(a) Factory Construction Grants and Machinery and Equipment Grants at higher rate[17];
(b) Government Factory Provision (as an alternative to building a factory with cost grant assistance[18];
(c) Cash grants towards working capital requirements[19]; and
(d) Interest Relief Grants.[20]

Assistance may also be available for projects in the service industries sector **8.131** provided:

(1) that the siting of the project involves a genuine choice of location within the United Kingdom; and
(2) it holds prospects of net additional employment in Northern Ireland.[21] All forms of assistance available to the manufacturing sector under the Industrial Development Acts (N.I.) 1966 and 1971[22] may be available for suitable service sector projects.

Prior to the reorganisation of industrial development institutions in 1982 the **8.132** Northern Ireland Development Agency was empowered[23] to assist existing undertakings and to stimulate new investment by making loans or providing loan guarantees and, where appropriate, by taking an equity stake in companies. These powers are now exercised by the Industrial Development Board on behalf of the Department of Economic Development.[24]

## LOCAL DEVELOPMENT INITIATIVES

Within the framework of central government-inspired national and regional **8.133** development policies local authorities have traditionally sought to maintain the prosperity of the areas for which they are responsibile by attracting new industries. Most authorities have officials whose function is to promote industrial

---

[17] Of 40–50 per cent. (as compared with 30 per cent. under the First Programme).

[18] Under the scheme factories can be acquired on lease (usually for a term of 21 years) at a low rental. In some cases the rental agreement may provide for a rent-free period of up to 5 years.
The factory provision scheme also permits the purchase of government-built factories in some cases, especially where the unit has been purpose-built. The purchase may be on a negotiated repayment basis with the amount to be repaid being subject to a reduction of 45 per cent. of the cost.

[19] These grants are individually negotiated in relation to the overall capital requirements of the project and take account of the employment provided and of the project's location within Northern Ireland. This form of assistance is designed to ensure that new projects benefit from a substantial inflow of revenue during the build-up period.

[20] These grants are available to reduce the commercial costs of borrowing from non-government sources. They can apply for a period of up to 7 years.

[21] Under s.7 of the Industrial Development Act (U.K.) 1982. This represents an application of the OSIS scheme to Northern Ireland.

[22] *i.e.* the special benefits under heads (a)-(d) in § 8.130 above.

[23] Northern Ireland Development Agency Act 1980.

[24] A system of cash grants (of between 40–50 per cent.) is available under the Science and Technology Act 1967 towards basic research, related design work, the making and testing of prototypes and final design and production drawing, subject to a ceiling of £250,000 on any single R and D project.

investment within the locality by the publicising of the incentives that are available under national and regional aid programmes and by the construction of packages of incentives to suit the needs of individual companies. In some areas local authorities have set up enterprise boards or economic development corporations to implement economic initiatives.

In addition to the activities of local government authorities the last five years have seen attempts by central government to stimulate economic activity at local level through the establishment on an experimental basis of special "zones," each administered by its own zone authority, in which some of the restrictions that would otherwise affect business activities are relaxed. These special zones are of two kinds, namely:

(a) Enterprise Zones, which are characterised by the removal of certain tax burdens and by a streamlining of the planning and administrative regimes; and

(b) Free Zones, where the object was to provide cash flow advantages for manufacturing or processing activities by the postponement of the requirement for immediate payment of customs duties or V.A.T.[25]

### Local authority initiatives

**8.134**     Apart from incentives derived from central government or EEC funds a primary inducement offered by local authorities to attract new companies to their areas is a "rates holiday" under which the authority undertakes not to levy rates on the premises occupied by those companies for a stipulated period. Such an undertaking is almost invariably incorporated in a more wide-ranging agreement with the company covering all aspects of the assistance to be provided to the company. In general, the terms and conditions attached to the provision of particular items of aid will vary as between authorities but will normally be linked directly to the creation of additional employment.

**8.135**     Section 137 of the Local Government Act 1972[26] provides local authorities with the power to assist industrial or commercial undertakings by way of loans, grants or guarantees. The provisions are framed in general terms permitting local authorities to spend up to a 2p rate on such items.

More specifically, the Local Government (Miscellaneous Provisions) Act 1982[27] extended the powers of local authorities to grant loans at commercial rates of interest for the purchase or leasing of land, for the carrying out of work on land or for the erection of buildings thereon. In each case the authority is empowered to lend up to 90 per cent. of the mortgageable value of the property.

**8.136**     **Inner urban aid schemes**

Companies may be in a position to benefit from schemes under the Inner Urban Aid Act 1978 under which an area that has been designated as appropri-

---

[25] Originally referred to as "Free Ports."
[26] As clarified by the Local Government (Miscellaneous Provisions) Act 1982.
[27] s.43. The original powers derive from the Local Authorities (Land) Act 1963.

ate for assistance may qualify for various forms of aid for the purpose of bringing about its rehabilitation. Assistance under the Act is discretionary and its terms vary as between authorities. However, insofar as it is likely to be of use to companies it falls into four broad groups, namely:

(a) Loans for the acquisition of land or the carrying out of building works thereon in order to effect improvements;

(b) Loans or grants (or both) towards the cost of setting up co-operative enterprises;

(c) Loans and/or grants for the improvement or conversion of industrial and commercial buildings; and

(d) Special Inner City Partnership Area Assistance.

Certain areas in large conurbations have been designated as Inner City Part- **8.137** nership Areas and as such qualify for special assistance in addition to the aid otherwise available under urban aid schemes. This additional aid is of two kinds.

(a) *Land acquisition assistance*

Assistance under this head comprises loans towards the cost of site preparation and grants towards rent or interest payable on loans incurred for the purpose of land or the financing of works thereon. It should be noted, however, that grants for loan interest are available only to small firms employing less than 50 people.

(b) *Urban development grants*[28]

This form of assistance was payable under a scheme originally intended to operate for 1983/84 but subsequently extended. The object of the scheme was to induce significant private sector investment into rundown urban areas.

The areas designated as Inner City Partnership Areas at present are Liverpool, Manchester/Salford, Newcastle/Gateshead, Inner Birmingham and parts of Inner London.

# SPECIAL ZONES

## (1) Enterprise Zones

Enterprise Zones were established by the Local Government, Planning and **8.138** Land Act 1980[29] and represented the implementation of an experiment to ascer-

---

[28] Urban Development Grants are payable to local authorities rather than to companies. The system is that a local authority will approve a project for assistance in a project area and award financial support. Where this condition has been met grant may be payable to the extent of 75 per cent. of the expenditure incurred by the local authority in assisting the project but subject to the principle that the amount of grant payable is to be the minimum necessary to enable the project to proceed.

[29] s.179 and Sched. 32.

tain the extent to which industrial and commercial activity could be encouraged by the removal of certain tax burdens and by the relaxation or acceleration of the application of various statutory or administrative controls or procedures.

More specifically, the advantages to companies who choose to set up operations in an Enterprise Zone are:

(1) exemption or relief from certain taxes and levies;
(2) a greatly simplified planning regime; and
(3) an improved administrative service from government.

**8.139 Fiscal benefits**

The fiscal benefits to companies in Enterprise Zones relate to capital allowances and rates.

(a) *Capital allowances*[30]

The system of capital allowances applicable to enterprise zones was provided by section 74 of the Finance Act 1980. This permits companies to claim an initial allowance of 100 per cent. in respect of capital expenditure on the construction, extension or improvement of industrial and commercial buildings. This initial allowance may be disclaimed in whole or in part with the amount disclaimed becoming eligible for an annual writing-down allowance at a rate of 25 per cent. On a sale of the building within 25 years of its first having been brought into use a balancing charge or allowance may arise under the ordinary rules.

The allowances apply to expenditure incurred within the designation period[31] and to expenditure incurred after that period has come to an end under a contract entered into during that period.

The provisions of the Finance Act 1984[32] providing for the phasing out of Initial Allowances have no application to expenditure in enterprise zones.[33]

(b) *Rates*[34]

Industrial and commercial properties (including retail shops) situated within Enterprise Zones are exempted from local authority rates.[35] For properties having a mixed business and domestic use the rateable value is apportioned with the exemption attaching only to the part used for business purposes.[36]

---

[30] See above at § 5.21.
[31] 10 years from the time of designation of land as being or being included in an Enterprise Zone. The 10-year period was intended to be the length of the experiment in the case of each zone.
[32] s.58 and Sched. 12.
[33] *Ibid.* s.58(4).
[34] F.A. 1980, s.110(1) also granted exemption from development land tax. However with the removal of DLT as from the 1985 Budget this exemption is no longer relevant.
[35] Local government, Planning and Land Act 1980, Sched. 32, Pt. IV (England and Wales) and Pt. V (Scotland).
[36] *Ibid.* para. 28 (England and Wales).

**Relaxation of planning requirements and procedures**                    **8.140**

Much criticism had been levelled at local planning authorities in relation to the delays and difficulties put in the path of companies seeking to embark on projects of industrial or commercial development. In order to test the validity of this complaint planning controls in Enterprise Zones have been relaxed in two ways.

In the first place zone authorities have been required to prepare a "scheme" setting out the type of development desired by the authority and, in consequence, for which planning permission will be deemed to have been granted without individual applications having to be made.[37] Schemes are to contain certain development conditions with a limited number of matters being reserved to the authority.[38] Any development proposal not conforming to the conditions of the scheme will require individual planning permission in the ordinary way.[39] In cases where individual application are needed special administrative arrangements are operated to ensure that these are determined expeditiously.

The second relaxation is in relation to the requirement under the general law that applications for planning permission for industrial development outside the assisted areas be supported by an Industrial Development Certificate. Applications in respect of industrial development within an enterprise zone are exempted from this requirement.[40]

**Improved administrative service from Government and Government agencies**   **8.141**

The criticisms of delay and "red tape" that had been levelled at planning authorities were also made about local authorities generally and in some cases in relation to central government and nationalised industry activities. A primary feature of administration in Enterprise Zones has been the efforts made to ensure that administrative matters are handled as quickly as possible and with as few burdens as possible being placed on businesses. This policy has been applied in the following ways.

(a) *Residual planning applications, etc.*

Most Enterprise Zone Authorities have set themselves the target of determining any residual planning applications and building regulation approvals within 14 days wherever possible.

(b) *Local Authority responsibilities*

Queries concerning land availability and release, highways, access and public transports are to be dealt with by local authorities as a matter of priority.

---

[37] *Ibid.* Pt. III.
[38] *Ibid.* para. 17.
[39] *Ibid.*
[40] Town and Country Planning (Industrial Development Certificates) (Prescribed Classes of Buildings) Regulations 1981 (S.I. 1981 No. 867).

(c) *Public utilities*

The suppliers of gas, electricity, water and sewerage facilities, and telecommunications services have also made special arrangements for customers in enterprise zones.

(d) *Government requests for statistical information*

These are reduced in relation to Enterprise Zone businesses.

(e) *Customs facilities*

Applications from firms within enterprise zones for "inward processing relief"[41] and general and private warehouses are processed as a matter of priority, and the criteria that apply to decisions on private customs warehouses are relaxed.

(f) *Industrial training: information and levy*

The Industrial Training Act 1982[42] confers powers on Industrial Training Boards to impose a levy on employers and to require information from them on specified matters. Section 16 of this Act, however, exempts establishments in Enterprise Zones from these obligations.

**(2) Free Zones**

**8.142**    A further experiment based on the relaxation of fiscal and administrative controls was proposed in the 1983 budget. Implementing legislation was contained in the Finance Act 1984[43] which provided for the establishment of "Free Zones." Unlike the idea underlying the foundation of Enterprise Zones the purpose of the 1984 legislation is not to confer any tariff or tax exemptions but rather to secure a cash-flow advantage for manufacturing or processing concerns operating within the zone by dispensing with the requirement for immediate payment of customs duties or V.A.T. that would otherwise apply in respect of goods or materials coming into the zone.[44]

The ability to carry on trading activity in a Free Zone is dependent on permission from the Commissioners of Customs and Excise. Authorisation may be granted on such conditions as the Commissioners consider appropriate.[45] At the time of writing six areas have been designated as Free Zones, the areas in question being at Belfast, Birmingham, Cardiff, Liverpool, Prestwick and Southampton.

[41] Inward Processing Relief is an arrangement which allows goods to be imported for processing and subsequent export outside the EEC without payment of customs charges.
[42] ss. 6 (provision of information) and 11 (levy).
[43] s. 8 and Sched. 4 (inserting a new Pt. VIIIA into the Customs and Excise Management Act 1979).
[44] Customs and Excise Management Act 1979 s.100C.
[45] *Ibid.* s.100E.

# Annex A

**ss. 8(4)–(11) and 9 of the Industrial Development Act 1982.**

(4) The aggregate of—

(a) the sums paid by the Secretary of State under this section or section 8 of the Industry Act 1972, other than sums paid in respect of foreign currency guarantees, and

(b) the liabilities of the Secretary of State under any guarantees given by him under this section or that section, (exclusive of any liability in respect of interest on a principle sum so guaranteed and of any liability under a foreign currency guarantee),

less any sum received by the Secretary of State by way of repayment of loans under this section or that section, or repayment of principal sums under this section or that section (other than a foreign currency guarantee), shall not at any time exceed the limit specified in subsection (5) below.

(5) The said limit shall be £1,900 million, but the Secretary of State may, on not more than four occasions, by order made with the consent of the Treasury increase or further increase that limit by a sum specified in the order, being a sum not exceeding £200 million.

(6) Subject to section 9 below, the aggregate of—

(a) the liabilities of the Secretary of State under foreign currency guarantees (exclusive of any liability in respect of interest on a principal sum guaranteed by him under this section or section 8 of the Industry Act 1972), and

(b) any sums paid by the Secretary of State in respect of foreign currency guarantees,

less any sums received by the Secretary of State by way of repayment of principal sums paid to meet foreign currency guarantees, shall not at any time exceed the limit specified in subsection (7) below.

(7) The said limit shall be 1,000 million special drawing rights, but the Secretary of State may, on not more than four occasions, by order made with the consent of the Treasury increase or further increase that limit by an amount specified in the order, being an amount not exceeding 500 million special drawing rights.

(8) Subject to subsection (9) below, the sums which the Secretary of State pays or undertakes to pay by way of financial assistance under this section in respect of any one project, excluding sums paid or to be paid in respect of foreign currency guarantees, shall not suceed £10 million, except so far as any excess over the said sum of £10 million has been authorised by a resolution of the Commons House of Parliament.

(9) Subsection (8) above shall not apply where the Secretary of State is satis-

fied that the payment or undertaking is urgently needed at a time when it is impracticable to obtain the approval of the Commons House of Parliament; and in that case the Secretary of State shall lay a statement concerning the financial assistance before each House of Parliament.

(10) An order under subsection (5) or (7) above shall be contained in a statutory instrument; and such an order shall not be made unless a draft of the order has been approved by a resolution of the Commons House of Parliament.

(11) In this section—

"foreign currency" means any currency other than sterling, including special drawing rights;

"foreign currency guarantee' means a guarantee given under this section or section 8 of the Industry Act 1972 by the Secretary of State under which his liability is measured in a foreign currency, whether or not it is to be discharged in a foreign currency, and for this purpose—

    (a) a liability measured in sterling but expressed to be subject to a limit in a foreign currency shall be taken to be measured in foreign currency, and

    (b) a liability measured in foreign currency but expressed to be subject to a limit in sterling shall be taken to be measured in sterling;

"guarantee" includes any form of insurance.

Limit on foreign currency liabilities: supplementary provisions

9. (1) The amount to be taken into account under section 8(6) above at any time in respect of a liability of the Secretary of State shall, if the amount of the liability is not expressed in special drawing rights, be the equivalent at that time in special drawing rights of the amount of the liability.

(2) The equivalent in special drawing rights of the amount of a liability shall be determined by the Secretary of State—

    (a) by reference to the day on which the guarantee is given, and

    (b) by reference to the last day of each quarter at the end of which the guarantee remains in force,

and shall be so determined having regard to what appears to him to be the appropriate rate of exchange.

(3) A determination under subsection (2)(a) above shall take effect as from the day reference to which it is made and (unless it ceases to be required at an earlier date) shall remain in force until the end of the quarter in which the guarantee is given.

(4) A determination made by reference to the last day of the quarter under subsection (2)(b) above shall take effect as from the end of that quarter and (unless it ceases to be required at an earlier date) shall remain in force throughout the next succeeding quarter.

(5) The amount to be taken into account under section 8(6) above in respect of a sum paid or received by the Secretary of State otherwise than in special drawing rights shall be an amount determined by him, by reference to the day of payment or receipt and having regard to what appears to him to be the appropriate rate of exchange, as being the equivalent in special drawing rights of that sum.

(6) The limit imposed by section 8(6) above may be exceeded if the excess is attributable only to, or to a combination of—

(a) a quarterly revaluation;

(b) the Secretary of State's liability under a guarantee given in pursuance of a previous undertaking of his, so far as the amount to be taken into account for the purposes of the limit in respect of the liability exceeds what it would have been if determined by reference to the day on which the undertaking was given;

(c) a payment made by the Secretary of State under a guarantee, so far as the amount to be taken into account for the purposes of the limit in respect of the payments exceeds what it would have been if determined by reference to the day on which the guarantee was given.

(7) In this section—

"guarantee" has the same meaning as in section 8 above;

"quarter" means a quarter ending with 31st March, 30th June, 30th September or 31st December in any year;

"quarterly revaluation" means a determination made, or (in relation to any time in the quarter current at the commencement of this Act) having effect as if made, under subsection (2)(b) above.


# Annex B

*Qualifying Activities*

3. The qualifying activities defined in section 5(1)(a) of the 1982 Act shall for the purposes of section 3 of that Act be the activities specified in the Schedule to this Order.

4. In this Order, "the SIC" (by reference to which some qualifying activities are specified) means the 1980 revision of the 1979 edition of the publication entitled "Standard Industrial Classification", "the SIC indexes" means the 1980 revision of the indexes to the SIC, an "Division" means a Division of the SIC.

5. For the purposes of this Order, the SIC and the SIC indexes have effect without regard to any other purpose (whether statutory or not) for which they are or may be applied.

| | |
|---|---|
| DIVISION 1 | ENERGY AND WATER SUPPLY INDUSTRIES |
| Activity 1115 | Manufacture of solid fuels. |
| Activity 1200 | Coke ovens. |
| Activity 1300 (part) | Extraction of mineral oil and natural gas (operation of land terminals for stabilization, separation and storage, and the activity of retorting of oil shale only). |
| Activity 1401 | Mineral oil refining. |

| | |
|---|---|
| DIVISION 1 | ENERGY AND WATER SUPPLY INDUSTRIES |
| Activity 1402 | Other treatment of petroleum products (excluding petro-chemicals manufacture). |
| Activity 1520 | Nuclear fuel production (excluding disposal of nuclear waste). |

DIVISION 2    EXTRACTION OF MINERALS AND ORES OTHER THAN FUELS: MANUFACTURE OF METALS, MINERAL PRODUCTS AND CHEMICALS

All of Division 2 except Class 21 (extraction and preparation of metalliferous ores) and Class 23 (extraction of minerals not elsewhere specified).

DIVISION 3    METAL GOODS, ENGINEERING AND VEHICLES INDUSTRIES

All of Division 3 except Activity 3480 (electrical equipment installation).

DIVISION 4    OTHER MANUFACTURING INDUSTRIES

All of Division 4.

DIVISION 7    TRANSPORT AND COMMUNICATION

Activity 7700/2 (part) Freight brokers and other agents facilitating freight transport, not including porterage or messenger services.

DIVISION 8    BANKING, FINANCE, INSURANCE, BUSINESS SERVICES AND LEASING

| | |
|---|---|
| Activity 8150/1 (part) | Institutions specialising in the granting of credit (export finance companies not licensed under the Banking Act 1979(a) only). |
| Activity 8370/2 | Technical services not elsewhere specified. |
| Activity 8380 (part) | Advertising (excluding bill posting agencies and window dressers). |
| Activity 8394 | Computer services. |
| Activity 8395/1, 2 | Management consultants and market research and public relations consultants. |

2. In addition to the activities specified in paragraph 1 above, and subject to paragraph 16 below, the activities specified in paragraphs 3 to 15 below shall be qualifying activities.

3. The activity of processing coal mined or extracted from deep coal mines and opencast coal workings and mined or extracted metalliferous ores where that processing activity (such as crushing or grinding) can be identified separately from the activity of mining or extraction, together with activities (such as cleaning, washing or grading) which are ancillary and subsequent to that processing activity.

4. The processing of scrap and waste materials.

5. Scientific research relating to any other qualifying activity and whether or not also within SIC Activity 9400 to the extent specified in paragraph 1 above.

6. The repair or maintenance of any machinery or plant save for that falling

within either SIC Class 67 (repair of consumer goods and vehicles) or Activity 9812 (dry cleaning and allied services).

7. The repair or maintenance of premises used wholly or mainly for qualifying activities, including, for the purposes of this paragraph, this activity.

8. The training of staff for work in any other qualifying activity.

9.—(1) Central services provided from a single location by an undertaking (the principal activities of which are carried out at more than one place) exclusively to itself in respect of a principal activity of that undertaking which is carried out on an international, national or regional basis.

(2) Without prejudice to the generality of sub-paragraph (1) above, central services include those relating to management and planning of the undertaking's operations, accounting, audit and records, personnel, computer services, data and word processing, typing, internal telecommunications, marketing, market research and advertising, but do not include distribution, transport of goods or persons or the production or distribution of energy for heating or other purposes.

(3) For the purpose of sub-paragraph (1) above, "undertaking" has the same meaning as in section 2(7) of the 1982 Act.

10—(1) The provisions of a service which consists of the conveyance of messages by means of a telecommunication system together with the provision of an additional service by means of that telecommunication system other than—

(*a*) switching incidental to that conveyance; or

(*b*) a directory information service.

(2) In sub-paragraph (1) above—

"directory information service" means a service as described in section 4(3) of the Telecommunications Act 1984(a);
"messages" means anything falling within paragraphs (*a*) to (*d*) of section 4(1) of that Act;
"telecommunication system" means a system as defined in the said section 4(1).

11. The provision of a cable programme service as defined in section 2(1) of the Cable and Broadcasting Act 1984(b) if that service is also a licensable service as defined in section 2(2) of that Act.

12. Refurbishment of manufactured goods for resale or exchange.

13. The provision of goods or services by mail order, whether or not as part of a mixed retail business.

14. The provision of venture capital to industry by specialist institutions which do not take deposits.

15. The issuing of credit cards and the provision of credit card services where these activities are the sole or principal activities of the provider at the location at which they are carried on.

16. For the purpose of determining whether an activity is a qualifying activity the following ancillary or associated activities shall not be regarded as part of that activity:—

(*a*) haulage;

(*b*) distribution;

(*c*) storage;

(*d*) production and distribution of energy and heating;

but office work, including accountancy, audit, advertising and market research, where it is ancillary to or associated with any other activity, shall be regarded as part of that activity.

# Annex C

## Order XII—Transport and Communication

  701  Railways
  702  Road Passenger Transport
  703  Road Haulage Contracting For General Hire or Reward
  704  Other Road Haulage
  705  Sea Transport
  706  Port and Inland Water Transport
  707  Air Transport
  708  Postal Services and Telecommunications
  709  Miscellaneous Transport Services and Storage

## Order XXIII—Distributive Trades

  810  Wholesale Distribution of Food and Drink
  811  Wholesale Distribution of Petroleum Products
  812  Other Wholesale Distribution
  820  Retail Distribution of Food and Drink
  821  Other Retail Distribution
  831  Dealing in Coal, Oil, Builders' Materials, Grain & Agricultural Supplies
  832  Dealing in Other Industrial Materials and Machinery

## Order XXIV—Insurance, Banking, Finance and Business Services

  860  Insurance
  861  Banking and Bill-discounting
  862  Other Financial Institutions
  863  Property Owning and Managing etc.
  864  Advertising and Market Research
  865  Other Business Services
  866  Central Offices not allocable elsewhere

## Order XXV—Professional and Scientific Services

871   Accountancy Services
872   Educational Services
873   Legal Services
874   Medical and Dental Services
875   Religious Organisations
876   Research and Development Services
879   Other Professional and Scientific Services

## Order XXVI—Miscellaneous Services

881   Cinemas, Theatres, Radio, etc.
882   Sport and Other Recreations
883   Betting and Gambling
884   Restaurants, Cafes, Snack Bars
886   Public Houses
887   Clubs
888   Catering Contractors
889   Hairdressing and Manicure
891   Private Domestic Service
892   Laundries
893   Dry Cleaning, Job Dyeing, Carpet Beating etc.
894   Motor Repairers, Distributors, Garages and Filling Stations
895   Repairers of Boots and Shoes
899   Other Services

# Appendix

## SECTION 1

## CHAPTER 2

### The 48 Hour Rule

5. The following documents must be lodged with the Department at least 2 business days prior to the hearing of the application by the Committee ("the 48 hour rule"):—

5.1 an application for admission to listing, in the form set out in Schedule 1 to this Section, signed by a duly authorised officer;

5.2 an application by the sponsoring broker in the form issued by the Department and (where relevant) a letter requesting deferred settlement, both signed by a partner or director of the broker and normally, except in the case of rights or capitalisation issues, supported by two firms of jobbers who are prepared to register as dealers in the security;

5.3 payment of the appropriate charge for listing and (where relevant) the annual charge;

5.4 four copies of the listing particulars or circular satisfying all requirements for the content of such documents, one of which (in the case of a new applicant or an application in respect of a class of securities no part of which is already listed) must be dated and signed by every director or proposed director of the company or by his agent or attorney authorised in writing.

5.5 where any document referred to in 5.4 above is signed by an agent or attorney, a certified copy of his authority;

5.6 a certified copy of each card circulated in the statistical services and of each newspaper containing the listing particulars or any formal notice or other notice submitted for approval under paragraph 2.1 above;

5.7 in the case of a new applicant;—

    (*a*) a copy of the certificate of incorporation or equivalent document;

    (*b*) a copy of the memorandum and articles of association or equivalent documents (if shareholders' approval to any necessary alteration cannot be obtained before the hearing of the application for listing, an undertaking to amend these documents at the earliest possible opportunity may be accepted);

    (*c*) the annual report and accounts for each of the five completed financial years of the company or group and of any guarantor or its group preceding the publication of the listing particulars or in respect of each of the years since incorporation if less; and

(*d*) any interim audited accounts made up since the date to which the last annual report and accounts were made up and referred to in the listing particulars;

5.8 a copy of the executed trust deed and any supplemental trust deeds or other documents securing or constituting debt securities together with a letter from the trustee's solicitors, confirming that the executed trust deed or other documents accord in every respect with the last proof submitted for approval by the Department or, in the case of euro-currency securities, a copy of the fiscal agency agreement or equivalent document. If the deed, agreement or other document cannot be executed prior to the hearing, the executed document together with the trustee's solicitors' letter must be lodged with the Department as soon as possible after execution;

5.9 a certified copy of the resolutions of the board giving the necessary authority for the issue and allotment of all securities for which listing is sought and authorising the making of the application for listing in the form set out in Schedule 1 to this Section and publication of the documents referred to in paragraph 2.1 above together with any resolution of the shareholders relating to the issue;

5.10 in the case of a placing, a copy of the brokers letter offering the securities and a marketing statement, in the form set out in Schedule 2 to this Section signed by the sponsoring broker;

5.11 three copies of any temporary document of title, and of any definitive document of title, marked, where appropriate in either case, to show the holder's entitlement to dividends or interest;

5.12 a certified copy of every letter, report, statement of adjustments, valuation, contract, resolution and other document referred to in the listing particulars or other document referred to in paragraph 2.1 above;

5.13 three copies of any notice of meeting referred to in the listing particulars or other document referred to in paragraph 2.1 above, and of any excess share application forms;

5.14 where the vendor of a security offered for sale has not paid in full for that security at the date of the offer, certified copies of an irrevocable authority given by the vendor to the receiving bank to discharge the outstanding debt, and of the bank's acknowledgement;

5.15 a letter from the issuing house or sponsoring broker, confirming that they are satisfied that the statement as to the sufficiency of working capital has been made by the directors after due and careful enquiry and that persons or institutions providing finance have stated in writing that such facilities exist;

5.16 a certified copy of any agreement to acquire any assets, business or share(s) in consideration for which the securities the subject of the application are being issued;

5.17 an undertaking given by the issuing house, or sponsoring broker, to split letters of acceptance, and to have such splits certified by an official of the company's registrars, to issue all letters of acceptance simultaneously, numbered serially, and, in the event of it being impossible to issue letters of regret at the same time, to insert in the press a notice to that effect, so that the notice will appear on the morning after the letters of acceptance have been posted;

5.18 a letter, signed by a duly authorised officer of the company, confirming that holders of securities represented by allotment letters which do not comply with the requirements of Chapter 3 of Section 9 are aware that, in the event of wishing to deal in such securities, they must first obtain registration and deal subject to stamp duty, transfers being certified against the register; and

5.19 if the securities are bearer securities other than debt securities issued only in the United Kingdom and the issuer is incorporated in a member state other than the United Kingdom, a certificate given by a suitable independent party as to compliance with the standards laid down in that other member state as referred to in Chapter 4 of Section 9. This will not be required if the documents of title comply in all respects with the requirements of Chapter 4.

**Other Documents Which May be Required**

6. The following documents may also be required to be lodged at the same time as the documents listed in paragraph 5 above:—

6.1 in the case of a new applicant, in respect of which any company or firm is a promoter, a statutory declaration as to the identity of those who control or are interested in the profits or assets of such company or firm;

6.2 in the case of a listed company, a copy of the memorandum and articles of association or equivalent documents and certified copies of all subsequent resolutions amending them; and

6.3 in the case of a new applicant with corporate shareholders holding over 5 per cent. of the issued capital, a declaration by a duly authorised officer of that corporate shareholder, giving details *inter alia* of its registered office, directors, shareholders and objects.

**Documents to be Lodged after Hearing of Application**

7. As soon as practicable after the hearing of the application by the Committee, the following documents must be lodged with the Department:—

7.1 in the case of an offer of securities to the public or an open offer, a copy of a national daily newspaper containing an announcement of the basis of allotment of the securities;

7.2 in the case of an offer for sale by tender, a copy of a national daily newspaper containing an announcement of the striking price;

7.3 in the case of a placing of securities having an equity element, a list setting out the names and addresses of all placees;

7.4 where securities are offered with a cash alternative, a statement of the total amount of securities issued;

7.5 in the case of a rights issue:—

    (*a*) an announcement of the issue price and of the basis of allocation;

    (*b*) an announcement that shares not taken up by the holders entitled to them have been sold together with the date of sale and price per share and/or the aggregate number or amount of securities issued pursuant to any excess applications accepted; and

    (*c*) a copy of a national daily newspaper containing an announcement of the basis of any acceptance of excess applications;

7.6 in the case of a rights or capitalisation issue, a statement of the amount of fractional entitlements and how distributed;

7.7 in the case of securities issued as consideration for shares in a listed company which are acquired pursuant to Section 209(1) of the Companies Act 1948, a certified copy of the notice given under that subsection;

7.8 where the listing particulars or other documents referred to in paragraph 2.1 above provide for a capital reduction, scheme of arrangement or similar proposal, requiring the approval of the court, a certified copy of the court order and of any certificate of registration issued by the Registrar of Companies;

7.9 a statement of the price at which the securities admitted to listing opened, together with payment of any consequential increase in the charges mentioned in paragraph 5.3 above; and

7.10 a declaration from the security printers responsible for production of bearer documents of title in accordance with paragraph 2.11 of Chapter 4 of Section 9.

## MODEL CODE FOR SECURITIES

## TRANSACTIONS BY DIRECTORS

## OF LISTED COMPANIES

The Committee regards it as highly desirable that directors of listed companies should hold securities in their own companies. Directors wishing to buy or sell such securities must first have regard to the statutory provisions in Part V of the Companies Act 1980 [now Company Securities (Insider Dealings) Act 1985] on insider dealing. It is regarded as axiomatic that directors of listed companies will not deal in their companies securities when prohibited from doing so by those statutory provisions. The statutory provisions are not confined to directors of listed companies but concern themselves more widely with individuals "connected with a company."

The Committee believes that special considerations apply to directors of listed companies. There are occasions where, even though not expressly prohibited by the statutory provisions, it would be undesirable for a director to buy or sell his company's securities.

These occasions are:—

(*i*) where a director is himself unaware of a price sensitive matter under discussion (perhaps because it has not yet been made known to the board) which is likely ultimately to call for an exceptional announcement and where for his own protection he should be told not to deal; and

(*ii*) the periods prior to the regular announcements of results and dividends.

The purpose of the model code remains primarily to give guidance on these two occasions so as to enable companies to establish an agreed procedure which would provide general protection against misinformed criticism both for the company and for the individual directors, given that, under the statutory provision, a director might otherwise be free to deal. The Committee sees the model code (including the basic principles set out below) as setting a minimum standard of good practice against which companies should measure their own company codes. The model code should therefore be seen as setting guidelines rather than rigid rules to be followed in every detail.

Two further aspects should be mentioned:—

(*i*) compliance with the model code is not a defence in law and it may therefore be necessary to be satisfied that a proposed dealing would not be in contravention of the statutory provisions. It should not, for example, be assumed that compliance with the procedure set out in basic principle 4 (to establish the time at which an intended acquisition by a company should be deemed price sensitive information) or that dealing under the extenuating circumstances indicated in rule 3.1 (where a pressing financial commitment has to be met) would necessarily preclude contravention of the statutory provisions. Basic principle 4 and rule 3.1 are intended as guidance for the chairman (or whoever is nominated to receive notification of dealing intentions) as to circumstances where exceptions to the model code may be considered, always assuming that no breach of the statutory provisions would result; and

(*iii*) the statutory provisions do not specifically relate to other interests of a director, nor to the position of spouses or infant children. In this respect the model code has broader application than the statutory provisions.

### The basic principles

1. Directors should not deal in their companies' securities on considerations of a short-term nature.

2. Directors will always be thought to be in possession of more information than can at any particular time be published. Accordingly they must accept that they cannot at all times feel free to deal in their companies' securities, even when the statutory provisions would not prohibit them from doing so.

3. Notwithstanding this general constraint there must be periods in the year when directors are in principle (but subject to the statutory provisions) to be regarded as free to deal in their companies' securities. The following model rules have been formulated on the basis that:—

(*i*) dealings should not normally take place for a minimum period prior to the announcement of regularly recurring information, particularly profits, dividends and other distributions, whether or not the information is price-sensitive (this period being defined in rule 3.1); and

(*ii*) dealings should not take place prior to the announcement of matters of an exceptional nature involving unpublished price-sensitive information in relation to the market price of the securities of the company (or where relevant any other listed company).

4. For the purposes of the model code, the grant to a director of an option to subscribe or purchase his company's securities is to be regarded as a dealing by him, if the price at which such option may be exercised is fixed at the time of such grant. If, however, an option is granted to a director on terms whereby the price at which such option may be exercised is to be fixed at the time of exercise, the dealing is to be regarded as taking place at the time of exercise.

5. Matters of an exceptional nature cause particular difficulty. A director who has knowledge of the exceptional matter in question will normally be prohibited from dealing by the statutory provisions but even if he is not so prohibited he should nevertheless not deal in the circumstances outlined below. Similarly, a director who has no such knowledge should be advised, when he notifies his intention to deal under rule 2.1 that it would be inappropriate for him to deal where the same circumstances apply. Those circumstances are where:—

(*i*) the matter in question constitutes unpublished price-sensitive information in relation to the company's securities, and

(*ii*) the proposed dealing would take place after the time when the likelihood of an announcement ultimately being necessary has become a reasonable probability.

An exhaustive definition of price-sensitive information is not possible. Nevertheless it should be assumed for this purpose that the matters referred to in paragraph 10 and paragraphs 14 to 19 inclusive of Chapter 2 of this Section are to be so regarded.

6. In principle, a director should seek to secure that all dealings in which he is or is deemed to be interested should be conducted in accordance with the provisions of the model code. Rule 4.1 sets this out as a general proposition. Nevertheless it is recognised that a director's duty in this respect will depend on the particular circumstances. A director who is sole trustee, for example, should follow the same procedure as for any dealings on his own account and should deal only if he would be personally allowed to deal under the code, even if he is excepted from the general prohibitions imposed by the statutory provisions by virtue of the special defences relating to trustees granted by such provisions. Where a director has co-trustees who are not themselves directors of the com-

pany, he may not be able to ensure that the procedure applicable to his personal dealings is followed in respect of dealings on behalf of the trust. The director/trustee has to avoid acting in breach of trust and at the same time to refrain from divulging or abusing confidential information, and it may not therefore always be practicable to expect that trustees will refrain from dealing at a time when one of their number is not personally free to deal.

On the other hand if a director, whether or not himself a trustee, has, as settlor or otherwise, an important influence over the decision of the trustees, the procedure applicable to his personal dealings ought to be followed and the trustees should not deal when he personally is not free to deal. Again, the remoteness of some interests may be such as to make the imposition of any duty under rule 4.1 impracticable or inappropriate. Rule 4.2 and 4.3 indicate certain precautions which should be taken.

It is an over-riding principle that under no circumstances should a director deal where prohibited from doing so by the statutory provisions or make any unauthorised disclosure of any confidential information, whether to co-trustees or any other person, or make any use of such information for the advantage of himself or others, even those to whom he owes a fiduciary duty.

7. When a director places investment funds under professional management, even where discretion is given, the managers should nonetheless be made subject to the same restrictions and procedures as the director himself in respect of proposed dealings in the company's securities.

### The following model rules should be used as guidelines for companies in formulating their own codes:

1.1 A director should not deal in any of the securities of the company at any time when he is in possession of unpublished price-sensitive information in relation to those securities.

1.2 The same restrictions should apply to dealings by a director in the securities of any other listed company when by virtue of his position as a director of his own company, he is in possession of unpublished price-sensitive information in relation to those securities.

### At other times, a director WHO IS NOT PROHIBITED FROM DOING SO BY [THE COMPANY SECURITIES (INSIDER DEALINGS) ACT 1985] can feel free to deal subject to the provisions of the rules which follow:

2.1 A director should not deal in any securities of his own company without first notifying the chairman (or other director(s) appointed for the specific purpose), and receiving acknowledgement. In his own case the chairman should first notify the board at a board meeting, or alternatively notify the other director(s) appointed for the purpose and receive acknowledgement.

2.2 The procedure established within the company should, as a minimum, provide for there to be a written record maintained by the company that the appropriate notification was given and acknowledged, and for the director concerned to have written confirmation to that effect.

3.1 During the periods of two months immediately preceding the preliminary announcement of the company's annual results and of the announcement of the half-yearly results together with dividends and distributions to be paid or passed, a director should not purchase any securities of the company nor should he deal in securities in the circumstances set out in basic principle 4 above; nor should he sell any such securities unless the circumstances are exceptional, for example, where a pressing financial commitment has to be met. In any event he must comply with the procedure in rule 2 above.

3.2 Companies producing quarterly results should consult the Department on the formulation of modified dealing procedures appropriate to their case.

4.1 The restrictions on dealings by a director contained in this code should be regarded as equally applicable to any dealings by the director's spouse or by or on behalf of any infant child and any other dealings in which for the purposes of the Companies Act [1985] he is or is to be treated as interested. It is the duty of the director, therefore, to seek to avoid any such dealing at a time when he himself is not free to deal.

4.2 Any director of the company who acts as trustee of a trust should ensure that his co-trustees are aware of the identity of any company of which he is a director so as to enable them to anticipate possible difficulties. A director having funds under management should likewise advise the investment manager.

4.3 Any director who is a beneficiary, but not a trustee, of a trust which deals in securities of the company should endeavour to ensure that the trustees notify him after they have dealt in such securities on behalf of the trust, in order that he in turn may notify the company. For this purpose he should ensure that the trustees are aware of the companies of which he is a director.

5. A list of directors' dealings in the securities of the company since the date of the previous list should be circulated to members of the board with the board papers; alternatively the register maintained in accordance with Section [325] of the Companies Act [1985] should be made available for inspection at every meeting of the board.

6. The directors of a company should as a board and individually endeavour to ensure that any employee of the company or director or employee of a subsidiary company who, because of his office or employment in the company or a subsidiary, is likely to be in possession of unpublished price-sensitive information in relation to the securities of any listed company, deals in those securities in accordance with this model code.

7. References in this code to "securities" have the meanings ascribed thereto by Section [12 of the Company Securities (Insider Dealings) Act 1985].

## SECTION 9

## CONSTITUTION AND DOCUMENTS OF TITLE

## CHAPTER 1

## ARTICLES OF ASSOCIATION

The articles of association or equivalent document must conform with the following provisions and, where necessary, a certified copy of a resolution of the board of directors undertaking to comply with the appropriate provisions must be lodged with the Department.

### 1. As regards transfer and registration

1.1 That transfers and other documents relating to or affecting the title to any shares will be registered without payment of any fee.

1.2 That fully-paid shares be free from any restriction on the right of transfer (except when permitted as mentioned in paragraph 4 of Chapter 2 of Section 1) and from all lien.

1.3 That where power is taken to limit the number of shareholders in a joint account, such limit will not prevent the registration of a maximum of four persons.

1.4 That the closing of the registers will be discretionary.

### 2. As regards definitive certificates

2.1 That all certificates for capital will be under the common seal, which may only be affixed with the authority of the directors.

2.2 That a new certificate issued to replace one that has been worn out, lost or destroyed will be issued without charge (other than exceptional out of pocket expenses) and that where the holder has sold part of his holding, he will be entitled to a certificate for the balance without charge.

2.3 Where power is taken to issue share warrants to bearer, that no new share warrant will be issued to replace one that has been lost, unless the company is satisfied beyond reasonable doubt that the original has been destroyed.

### 3. As regards dividends

3.1 That any amount paid up in advance of calls on any share may carry interest but will not entitle the holder of the share to participate in respect of such amount in any dividend.

3.2 Where power is taken to forfeit unclaimed dividends, that power will not be exercised until 12 years or more after the date of the declaration of the dividend.

## 4. As regards directors

4.1 That, subject to such exceptions specified in the articles of association as the Committee may approve, a director will not vote on any contract or arrangement or any other proposal in which he has a material interest.

4.2 That any person appointed by the directors to fill a casual vacancy on or as an addition to the board will hold office only until the next following annual general meeting of the company, and will then be eligible for re-election.

4.3 That, where not otherwise provided by law, the company in general meeting will have power by ordinary resolution to remove any director (including a managing or other executive director, but without prejudice to any claim for damages under any contract) before the expiration of his period of office.

4.4 That the minimum length of the period during which notice to the company of the intention to propose a person for election as a director, and during which notice to the company by such person of his willingness to be elected may be given, will be at least 7 days.

4.5 That the latest date for lodgment of the notices referred to in 4.4 above will be not more than 7 days prior to the date of the meeting appointed for such election.

4.6 That where power is taken to delegate the powers of directors to a committee, which includes co-opted persons not being directors, the number of such co-opted persons will be less than one half of the total number of the committee and no resolution of the committee shall be effective unless a majority of the members of the committee present at the meeting are directors.

## 5. As regards accounts

That a printed copy of the directors' report, accompanied by the balance sheet (including every document required by law to be annexed thereto) and profit and loss account or income and expenditure account, will, at least 21 days previous to the general meeting, be delivered or sent by post to the registered address of every member provided such address is in the United Kingdom (but see 8.2 below).

## 6. As regards rights

6.1 That adequate voting rights will, in appropriate circumstances, be secured to preference shareholders.

6.2 That a quorum for a separate class meeting (other than an adjourned meeting) to consider a variation of the rights of any class of shares will be the holders of at least one-third of the issued shares of the class.

## 7. As regards companies to be included in the "Investment Trusts" section of the Official List

That all moneys realised on the sale or other realisation of any capital assets in excess of book value and all other moneys in the nature of accretion to capital will not be treated as profits available for dividend.

## 8. As regards notices

8.1 That where power is taken to give notice by advertisement such advertisement will be inserted in at least one national daily newspaper.

8.2 That where it is provided that notices will be given only to those members whose registered addresses are within the United Kingdom, any member, whose registered address is not within the United Kingdom, may name an address within the United Kingdom which, for the purpose of notices, will be considered as his address.

## 9. As regards redeemable shares

That, where power is reserved to purchase for redemption a redeemable share:—

- (*a*) purchases will be limited to a maximum price which, in the case of purchases through the market or by tender, will not exceed the average of the middle market quotations taken from The Stock Exchange Official List for the 10 business days before the purchase is made or in the case of a purchase through the market, at the market price, provided that it is not more than 5 per cent. above such average; and
- (*b*) if purchases are by tender, tenders will be available to all shareholders alike.

## 10. As regards capital structure

That the structure of the share capital of the company will be stated and where the capital consists of more than one class of share it must also be stated how the various classes will rank for any distribution by way of dividend or otherwise.

## 11. As regards non-voting or restricted voting shares

11.1 That, where the capital of the company includes shares which do not carry voting rights, the words "non-voting" will appear in the designation of such shares.

11.2 That, where the equity capital includes shares with different voting rights, the designation of each class of shares, other than those with the most favourable voting rights, will include the words "restricted voting" or "limited voting."

## 12. As regards proxies

12.1 That where provision is made in the articles as to the form of proxy this will be so worded as not to preclude the use of the two-way form.

12.2 That a corporation may execute a form of proxy under the hand of a duly authorised officer.

## 13. As regards conversion rights

That no purchase by the company of its own shares will take place unless it has been sanctioned by an extraordinary resolution passed at a separate class meeting of the holders of the convertible securities.

## 14. As regards votes of members

That, where provision is made in the articles to disfranchise members in cases where there is default in supplying information in compliance with a notice served under Section [212] of the Companies Act [1985], disfranchisement will not take effect earlier than 28 days after the service of the notice.

## 15. As regards untraceable members

15.1 That where power is taken to cease sending dividend warrants by post, if such warrants have been returned undelivered or left uncashed, it will not be exercised until such warrants have been so returned or so left uncashed on two consecutive occasions.

15.2 That where power is taken to sell the shares of a member who is untraceable it will not be exercised unless:—

(*a*) during a period of 12 years at least 3 dividends in respect of the shares in question have become payable and no dividend during that period has been claimed; and

(*b*) on expiry of the 12 years the company gives notice by advertisement in 2 national daily newspapers of its intention to sell the shares and notifies the Department of such intention.

## SECTION 9

## CHAPTER 2

## TRUST DEEDS OR OTHER DOCUMENTS SECURING OR CONSTITUTING DEBT SECURITIES

Unless otherwise agreed by the Committee, there must be a trustee or trustees. One of the trustees or the sole trustee must be a trust corporation which must have no interest in or relation to the company which might conflict with the position of trustee.

In the event of the office of trustee becoming vacant a new trustee appointed under any statutory or other power must prior to appointment be approved by an extraordinary resolution of the holders of the relevant class of debt securities unless such holders have a general power to remove any trustee and appoint another trustee in his place.

Trust deeds or other corresponding documents must contain provisions to the following effect.

## 1. As regards redemption

1.1 That, where power is reserved to purchase a security:—

(*a*) purchases will be limited to a maximum price which, in the case of purchases through the market or by tender, will not exceed the average of the middle market quotations taken from The Stock Exchange Official List for the 10 business days before the purchase is made or in the case of a purchase through the market, at the market price, provided that it is not more than 5 per cent. above such average; and

(*b*) if purchases are by tender, tenders will be available to all holders alike.

1.2 That where the outstanding amount of a security subject to redemption by drawings is not less than £2,000,000 the lots into which the issue is to be divided for the purposes of any drawing if required, may, be of not more than £1,000 but otherwise will be of not more than £100.

1.3 That where a security is repayable on a particular date the year of redemption will be indicated by inclusion in the title of the security; that where a security may be repaid within a fixed period that period will be indicated in the title by the inclusion of the first and last years of the period, and where a security will be irredeemable that security will be described as such.

## 2. As regards conversion rights

2.1 That during the existence of conversion rights:—

(*a*) unless provision is made for appropriate adjustment of the conversion rights, the company will be precluded (subject to specified exceptions referred to in the terms of issue which have been approved by the Committee) from effecting any reduction of capital involving repayment of capital or reduction of uncalled liability;

(*b*) the creation or issue of any new class of equity capital will be prohibited or restricted within specified limits referred to in the terms of issue;

(*c*) no capitalisation of profits or reserves will be effected except in shares of the appropriate class and in the case of such an issue the conversion rights will be appropriately adjusted;

(*d*) if the company makes or gives to its shareholders any offer or right in relation to shares or debt securities of the company or any other company then unless provision is made for appropriate adjustment of the conversion rights, the company will at the same time make or give to the holders of the convertible securities the like offer or right on the basis appropriate having regard to their conversion rights;

(e) in the event of voluntary liquidation except for the purpose of reconstruction or amalgamation on terms previously approved by the trustees, or by an extraordinary resolution of the holders, the holders of the convertible securities will for a limited period have rights equivalent to conversion;

(f) the company will maintain at all times sufficient unissued capital to cover all outstanding conversion rights;

(g) where provision is made enabling the company at its option to repay or convert the security, if a specified proportion of the security has been converted, such right will apply to the whole of the security outstanding and will only be exercisable if notice of intention of such exercise is given within one month after the expiry of those conversion rights which were at the holder's option;

(h) all necessary allotments of shares consequent upon a conversion will be effected not later than 14 days after the last date for lodging notices of conversion; and

(i) no purchase by the company of its own shares will take place unless it has been sanctioned by an extraordinary resolution passed at a separate class meeting of the holders of the convertible securities.

2.2 That holders will be given not less than 4 nor more than 8 weeks notice in writing prior to the end of each conversion period reminding them of the conversion right then arising or current and stating the relative basis of conversion (after taking into account any required adjustments).

2.3 That the designation of the security will include the word "convertible," until the expiration of conversion rights, whereupon that word will cease to form part of the designation.

## 3. As regards meetings and voting rights

3.1 That not less than 21 days notice will be given of a meeting for the purpose of passing an extraordinary resolution.

3.2 That a meeting of holders of the securities will be called on a requisition in writing signed by holders of at least one-tenth of the nominal amount for the time being outstanding.

3.3 That the quorum for a meeting (other than an adjourned meeting) for the purpose of passing an extraordinary resolution will be the holders of a clear majority of the outstanding securities.

3.4 That the necessary majority for passing an extraordinary resolution will be not less than three-fourths of the persons voting thereat on a show of hands and if a poll is demanded then not less than three-fourths of the votes given on such a poll.

3.5 That on a poll, each holder of securities will be entitled to at least one vote in respect of each of those amounts held by him which represents the lowest denomination in which such securities can be transferred.

3.6 That a proxy need not be a holder of the securities.

## 4. As regards transfer

4.1 That transfers and other documents relating to or affecting the title to any securities will be registered without payment of any fee.

4.2 That the closing of the registers will be discretionary.

## 5. As regards definitive certificates

5.1 That a new certificate issued to replace one that has been worn out, lost or destroyed will be issued without charge and that where a holder has sold part of his holding, he will be entitled to a certificate for the balance without charge.

5.2 That on any partial repayment of the amount due on the security, a note of such payment will, unless a new document is issued, be enfaced on the document.

## 6. As regards security

6.1 In the case of securities which constitute an unsecured liability, that they will be entitled "Unsecured."

6.2 That the designation of securities will not include the word "Mortgage" unless they are secured to a substantial extent by a specific mortgage or charge.

## 7. As regards unclaimed interest

Where power is taken to forfeit unclaimed interest, that power will not be exercised until 12 years or more after the due date of payment of the interest.

## SECTION 2—SCHEDULE 1

This form, suitably adapted for an issuer which is not a public limited company must be lodged duly completed at least TWO BUSINESS DAYS prior to the hearing of the application by the Committee.

## APPLICATION FOR ADMISSION OF SECURITIES TO LISTING

..................... 19..........

*To*: The Secretary,
      Quotations Department,
      The Stock Exchange

We................................[Public Limited Company]*
hereby apply for the undermentioned securities to be admitted to the Official List of The Stock Exchange subject to the requirements from time to time of the Council of The Stock Exchange, and published in "Admission of Securities to Listing".

### SHARE CAPITAL

| Authorised | | | Issued (and paid up) inclusive of present issue |
|---|---|---|---|
| ........................ | in | ............................. | ......................... |
| ........................ | in | ............................. | ......................... |
| ........................ | in | ............................. | ......................... |
| ........................ | in | ............................. | ......................... |
| £ _____ | | | £ _____ |

Amounts and descriptions of securities for which application is now made (include distinctive numbers if any)

...................................................................................................

...................................................................................................

...................................................................................................

The securities for which application is now made
(*a*) are/are not †identical in all respects and

...................................................................................................

...................................................................................................

* NOTE—Insert name of issuer of securities.
† NOTE—See †Note at end of schedule.

(b) are/are not †identical in all respects with an existing class of security

..................................................................................

..................................................................................

(c) either have been in the previous six months, or will be the subject of an application for listing in another member state of the European Economic Community.

stating when .................................................................

and on what stock exchange(s) .........................................

(*Delete as appropriate*)

We declare that

(1) all the conditions listed in Chapter 2 of Section 1 of "Admission of Securities to Listing", insofar as applicable and required to be fulfilled prior to application, have been fulfilled in relation to the company and the securities for the admission of which application is now made, and

(2) all information required to be included in the listing particulars has been included therein, or, if the final version has not yet been submitted (or approved), will be included therein before it is so submitted.

Details of renounceable document (where applicable):

(a) Type of document ......................................... (which must comply with Chapter 3 of Section 9 of Admission of Securities to Listing).

(b) Proposed date of issue .............................................

(c) Last day for splitting:

(i) nil paid .........................................................

(ii) partly paid ...................................................

(iii) fully paid ...................................................

(d) Last day for renunciation .........................................

† NOTE.—"Identical" means in this context:—
(1) The securities are of the same nominal value with the same amount called up or paid up.
(2) They are entitled to dividend/interest at the same rate and for the same period, so that at the next ensuing distribution the dividend/interest payable per unit will amount to exactly the same sum (gross and net).
(3) They carry the same rights as to unrestricted transfer, attendance and voting at meetings and are *pari passu* in all other respects.
If the securities are not identical, but will so become in the future, a statement as to when they will become identical must be added to (a) or (b) above and definitive certificates issued before that date must be enfaced with a note to this effect.

Definitive certificates (in respect of the class of security/securities for which listing is sought) have already been issued for ..........................
.................................................................................. stock/shares
and will be ready on .................. for ..........................stock/shares.

We undertake to lodge with you the required declaration in due course.


*Signed* .................................................
                          *Director or Secretary*
                          *or other duly authorised officer*
                          *for and on behalf of*


                          .............................................
                          *public limited company.*

## SECTION 2—SCHEDULE 3

# DECLARATION
(The following is a suggested form of declaration which may be amended to meet individual cases)

I, ....................................................................................................................
a director/the secretary† of .......................................................................
[Public Limited Company] ("the company"), declare as follows:—

1. that all documents required by the Companies Acts or The Stock Exchange (Listing) Regulations 1984 to be filed with the Registrar of Companies in connection with the issue/offer/placing/introduction† on .....................
19.......... of the following securities of the company, namely
..............................................................................................................
(insert particulars), have been duly filed and that to the best of my knowledge, information and belief, compliance has been made with all other legal requirements in connection with such issue/offer/placing/introduction†;

2. that all conditions listed in Chapter 2 of Section 1 of "Admission of Securities to Listing" entitled "Basic conditions to be fulfilled by an applicant" have (insofar as applicable) been fulfilled in relation to the company and the securities of the company referred to in paragraph 1 above;

3. that ............... shares of .................................... (number and class) £.............. debenture stock .................................... debentures/notes† have been subscribed/purchased† for cash and fully allotted/transferred to the subscribers/purchasers† (and that the said shares have been converted into £.............. stock);

4. that all money due to the company in respect of the issue/offer has been received by it;

5. that .............. shares of ................................................................ £.......... debenture stock ...................................... debentures/notes† have been issued credited as fully paid by way of conversion/exchange/consideration† for property acquired/other consideration not being cash† and have been duly allotted/transferred† to the persons entitled thereto (and that the said shares have been converted into £.......... stock);

6. that the definitive documents of title have been delivered/are ready to be delivered;

† Please delete as appropriate.

7. that completion has taken place of the purchase by the company of all property shown in the listing particulars or circular to members dated ....................19.......... to have been purchased or agreed to be purchased by it and the purchase consideration for all such property has been duly satisfied;

8. that the trust deed relating to the said debenture stock or notes has been completed and executed and a copy has been lodged with the Quotations Department of The Stock Exchange and that particulars thereof, if so required by law, have been delivered to the Registrar of Companies;

9. that all the shares/debentures/debenture stock/notes† of each class referred to above are in all respects identical*;

10. that no alterations have been made to the listing particulars approved for publication by The Stock Exchange other than in relation to the pricing of the issue or take-over offer, number of securities, figures depending on the information, and correction of errors; and

11. that there are no other facts bearing on the company's application for listing of such securities which, in my opinion, should be disclosed to The Stock Exchange.

Signed

........................... Director/Secretary†
or other duly authorised officer
for and on behalf of

......................................
public limited company.

...................... Date

* NOTE.—"Identical" means in this context:—
   (1) The securities are of the same nominal value with the same amount called up or paid up.
   (2) They are entitled to dividend/interest at the same rate and for the same period, so that at the next ensuing distribution, the dividend/interest payable per unit will amount to exactly the same sum (gross and net).
   (3) They carry the same rights as to unrestricted transfer, attendance and voting at meetings and are *pari passu* in all other respects.
† Please delete as appropriate.

## SECTION 2—SCHEDULE 4

# THE STOCK EXCHANGE

# DECLARATION WITH REGARD TO DIRECTORS

**NOTES:**

(1) Please answer all questions, and if a question is answerable in the negative, please answer "No". Do not leave any section blank.

(2) If insufficient space is provided for completion of any paragraph, additional information may be entered on a separate sheet of paper duly signed and attached.

(3) In this form, the term "company" includes any company or corporation wherever incorporated.

---

1. State:—

    (a) Present surname and any former surname(s) ...................................................

    (b) Present forename(s) and any former forename(s) ...................................................

    (c) Date of birth ...................................................

    (d) Residential address ...................................................

    ...................................................

    (e) Nationality and former nationality, if any ...................................................

    (f) Professional qualifications, if any ...................................................

2. Are you a director of any other companies?

If so, state the names of such companies, nature of business where this is not indicated in title and date of commencement of each directorship.

Note:
Where a relevant company has securities listed on The Stock Exchange, the name of any subsidiary company of which you are also a director need not be stated.

---

3. Have you at any time been adjudged bankrupt either in the United Kingdom or elsewhere?

   If so, state the Court by which you were adjudged bankrupt and, if discharged, the date and conditions on which you were granted your discharge.

4. Have you at any time been a party to a deed of arrangement or made any other form of composition with your creditors? If so, give particulars.

5. Are there any unsatisfied judgements outstanding against you? If so, give particulars.

6. Has any company been put into liquidation (otherwise than by a members' voluntary winding up when the company was solvent) or had a receiver appointed during the period when you were (or within the preceding six months had been) one of its directors?

   "Director" includes a person in accordance with whose directions or instructions the company's directors are or were accustomed to act.

   If so, in each case state the name, nature of business, date of commencement of winding-up or receivership and the amount involved together with an indication of the outcome of current position.

7. Have you at any time been convicted in the United Kingdom or elsewhere of any offence involving fraud or dishonesty, or in the United Kingdom of any offence (whether or not involving fraud or dishonesty) under the Companies Acts, the Bankruptcy Acts, the Prevention of Fraud (Investments)

Acts, the Protection of Depositors Act, 1963, or any Act relating to taxation?

If so, state the Court by which you were convicted, the date of conviction and full particulars of the offence and the penalty imposed.

8. Have you, in connection with the formation or management of any body corporate, partnership or unincorporated institution been adjudged by a Court in the United Kingdom or elsewhere civilly liable for any fraud, misfeasance or other misconduct by you towards such a body or company or towards any members thereof? If so, give full particulars.

9. Have you, in the United Kingdom or elsewhere, been refused to be admitted to membership of any professional body or been censured or disciplined by any such body to which you belong or belonged or have you held a practising certificate subject to conditions? If so, give full particulars.

I ................................ of (Company) ..............................................
declare that the answers to all the above questions are true and I hereby give my authority to the Secretary to the Council of The Stock Exchange, or to any person authorised by him to disclose any of the foregoing particulars given by me to such Members of The Stock Exchange and, with the approval of the Chairman or a Deputy Chairman of The Stock Exchange, to such other persons as the said Secretary in his absolute discretion may think fit.

Signature ......................................................

Dated........................................ 19.......

# Index

*[References in this index are to paragraph numbers.]*